BOOKS IN
THE WILLARD J. GRAHAM SERIES IN ACCOUNTING

CONSULTING EDITOR ROBERT N. ANTHONY *Harvard University*

ANDERSON, SCHMIDT, & MCCOSH *Practical Controllership* 3d ed.
ANTHONY *Management Accounting: Text and Cases* 4th ed.
ANTHONY *Management Accounting Principles* rev. ed.
ANTHONY, DEARDEN, & VANCIL *Management Control Systems: Text, Cases, and Readings* rev. ed.
BARR & GRINAKER *Short Audit Case* rev. ed.
FREMGEN *Accounting for Managerial Analysis* rev. ed.
GORDON & SHILLINGLAW *Accounting: A Management Approach* 4th ed.
GRIFFIN, WILLIAMS, & LARSON *Advanced Accounting* rev. ed.
GRINAKER & BARR *Audit Practice Case*
GRINAKER & BARR *Auditing: The Examination of Financial Statements*
HAWKINS *Corporate Financial Reporting: Text and Cases*
HENDRIKSEN *Accounting Theory* rev. ed.
HOLMES, MAYNARD, EDWARDS, & MEIER *Elementary Accounting* 3d ed.
HOLMES & OVERMYER *Auditing: Principles and Procedure* 7th ed.
HOLMES & OVERMYER *Basic Auditing Principles* 4th ed.
KENNEDY & MCMULLEN *Financial Statements: Form, Analysis, and Interpretation* 6th ed.
LADD *Contemporary Corporate Accounting and the Public*
MAURIELLO *The Irwin Federal Income Tax Course: A Comprehensive Text*
MEIGS, LARSEN, & MEIGS *Principles of Auditing* 5th ed.
MIKESELL & HAY *Governmental Accounting* 4th ed.
MOORE & STETTLER *Accounting Systems for Management Control*
MURPHY *Advanced Public Accounting Practice*
MURPHY *Auditing and Theory: A CPA Review*
NEILSON *Interactive Computerized Accounting Problems Set*
NEUNER *Cost Accounting: Principles and Practice* 8th ed.
NICHOLS *Programmed Cost Accounting: A Participative Approach*
NIELSEN *Cases in Auditing*
O'NEIL, FARWELL, & BOYD *Quantitative Controls for Business: An Introduction*
PATON *Corporate Profits*
PYLE & WHITE *Fundamental Accounting Principles* 6th ed.
SALMONSON, HERMANSON, & EDWARDS *A Survey of Basic Accounting*
SCHAFER *Elements of Income Tax—Individual*
SCHRADER, MALCOLM, & WILLINGHAM *Financial Accounting: An Input/Output Approach*
SHILLINGLAW *Cost Accounting: Analysis and Control* 3d ed.
SPILLER *Financial Accounting: Basic Concepts* rev. ed.
STAUBUS *Activity Costing and Input-Output Accounting*
VATTER *Accounting Measurements for Financial Reports*
WELSCH, ZLATKOVICH, & WHITE *Intermediate Accounting* 3d ed.
WILLIAMS & GRIFFIN *Management Information: A Quantitative Accent*

Fundamental
accounting
principles

Sixth edition

Fundamental accounting principles

WILLIAM W. PYLE
College of Business Administration
University of Hawaii

JOHN ARCH WHITE
Emeritus, Graduate School of Business
University of Texas

 1972

Richard D. Irwin, Inc.
Homewood, Illinois 60430

IRWIN-DORSEY LIMITED,
Georgetown, Ontario L7G 4B3

IRWIN-DORSEY INTERNATIONAL,
London, England WC2H 9NJ

Sixth Edition

First Printing, January, 1972
Second Printing, July, 1972
Third Printing, September, 1972
Fourth Printing, July, 1973

Library of Congress Catalog Card No. 78–162057

Printed in the United States of America

LEARNING SYSTEMS COMPANY —
a division of Richard D. Irwin, Inc. — has developed a
PROGRAMMED LEARNING AID
to accompany texts in this subject area.
Copies can be purchased through your bookstore
or by writing PLAIDS,
1818 Ridge Road, Homewood, Illinois 60430.

■ The Sixth Edition of *Fundamental Accounting Principles,* as previous editions, is designed for use in the first accounting course at the college level. It describes how accounting data are accumulated and gives an understanding of the concepts necessary to use such data effectively. A key objective of the text is to maintain a balance between financial and managerial materials and thus meet the needs of students who will make accountancy a career, as well as students who will use accounting as a tool in other fields of specialization or in their personal affairs.

A new edition always offers an opportunity to reorganize, to rewrite, to condense, to expand, and to add new materials. In this edition many chapter sections were completely rewritten, several chapters were combined, and both chapters and topics were shifted to improve instructional efficiency. The condensation of purely procedural matters was continued to make room for the expansion of such important topics as internal control, accounting for plant and equipment, and capital budgeting. Also, additional new materials explaining accounting concepts and the uses and limitations of accounting data have been included.

Since the needs of students differ, the assignment flexibility of previous editions was maintained. A minimum of time may still be devoted to Chapters 6 and 9, and almost any chapter beyond the fifth may be omitted, quickly covered, or taught out of sequence without detriment to an understanding of the materials that follow.

Again, an extensive set of supplementary materials has been prepared. Available to students are the Workbook of Study Guides, Practice Sets 1 and 2, Working Papers, and Check Figures. To aid the instructor, comprehensive Solutions Manuals for the text, Achievement Tests, and Practice Sets, plus professionally manufactured transparencies are again free to adopters.

To present the usefulness of the computer in the accounting area, the Revised Edition of *Accounting with the Computer: A Practice Case and Simulation* by Professor Joseph Wilkinson of Arizona State University has been developed and keyed to the text. Professor Wilkinson's case builds on the material covered in Chapter 14, "Accounting Systems: Manual, Mechanical, and Electronic." A detailed Instructor's Manual, that assumes no expertise in the computer area, is available for adopters of the case.

Among the many users of the previous edition who offered valuable suggestions for its improvement, those to whom the authors owe a special debt of gratitude are Professors David Arant and Robert G. Wrenn, Los Angeles Harbor College; Phyllis A. Barker, Indiana State University; Floyd A. Beams, Rosalind A. Newell, and W. E. Seago of Virginia Polytechnic Institute and State University; Al A. Evans, Drury College; W. Baker Flowers, The University of Alabama; Robert E. Hansen and R. Bruce Kincaid, University of Toledo; John K. Harris, The University of Nebraska; Virginia Huntington and Calvert Krueger, Arizona State University; Philip S. Malafsky, Orange County Community College; George Murphy, Mt. Wachusett Community College; Earl P. Purkhaiser, Mount San Antonio College; Joseph E. Rhile, Lake-Sumter Junior College; and Charles E. Thompson, El Camino College.

January, 1972

WILLIAM W. PYLE
JOHN ARCH WHITE

Contents

Chapter 1

Accounting, an introduction to its concepts

■ Accounting is the art of identifying, measuring, recording, and communicating financial information about an economic unit.

If the unit is a business, the information is used by its management in answering questions and making such decisions as: What are the resources of the business? What debts does it owe? Does it have earnings? Are expenses too large in relation to sales? Is too little or too much merchandise being kept? Are amounts owed by customers being collected rapidly? Will the business be able to meet its own debts as they mature? Should the plant be expanded? Should a new product be introduced? Should selling prices be increased?

Beyond the foregoing, grantors of credit such as banks, wholesale houses, and manufacturers use accounting information in answering such additional questions as: Are the customer's earning prospects good? What is his debt-paying ability? Has he paid his debts promptly in the past? Should he be granted additional credit?

Likewise, governmental units use accounting information in regulating businesses and collecting taxes; labor unions use it in negotiating working conditions and wage agreements; and investors make wide use of accounting data in investment decisions.

Why study accounting

■ Information for use in answering questions like those in the foregoing section is conveyed in accounting reports. If a business owner, manager, banker, lawyer, engineer, or other person is to use these reports effectively, he must have some understanding of how their data were gathered and the figures put together. He must appreciate the limitations of the data and the extent to which portions are based on estimates rather than precise measurements, and he must understand accounting terms and concepts. Needless to say, these understandings are gained in a study of accounting.

Another reason to study accounting is to make it one's lifework — to become a professional accountant. The work can be very interesting and highly rewarding.

Accountancy as a profession

■ Over the past half century accountancy as a profession has attained a stature comparable with that of law or medicine. All states license *certified public accountants* or CPAs just as they license doctors and lawyers, and for the same reason — to help ensure a high standard of professional service. Only individuals who have passed a rigorous examination of their accounting and related knowledge, met other requirements, and have received a license may designate themselves as certified public accountants.

The requirements for the CPA certificate or license vary with the states. In general an applicant must be a citizen of unquestioned moral character and at least a high school graduate; many states require that he be a college graduate with a major in accounting. He must have passed a rigorous three-day examination in accounting theory, accounting practice, auditing, and business law; and he must have had from one to five years' experience in the office of a certified public accountant or an acceptable equivalent. Some states permit an applicant to substitute collegiate level accounting education for one or more years of the experience requirement. The three-day examination is uniform in all states, although some states require an additional examination in, for example, economics. The examination is prepared by the American Institute of Certified Public Accountants and is given in all states on the same days twice each year. The American Institute of Certified Public Accountants is the accounting profession's equivalent of the American Medical Association or the American Bar Association.

Although all states license certified public accountants, many states do not restrict the practice of public accounting to such license holders. In some states, those in which the law does not expressly prohibit it, any person may designate himself a public accountant or PA and practice public accounting. In others, both CPAs and PAs are licensed and the practice of public accounting is limited to such license holders. Commonly, states licensing PAs have granted such licenses to people who were practicing public accounting at the time laws providing for such licenses became effective and now grant such licenses only to applicants who have passed one or more sections of the certified public accounting examination and have met other requirements.

The work of an accountant

■ Accountants are commonly employed in one or the other of three main fields: (1) in public accounting, (2) in private accounting, or (3) in government.

Public accounting

A public accountant is one who offers his professional services and those of his employees to the public for a fee, in much the same manner as a lawyer or a consulting engineer.

AUDITING. The principal service offered by a public accountant is auditing. Banks commonly require an audit of the accounting records of a company applying for a sizable loan, and usually the audit must be made by a certified public accountant. Also, companies whose securities are offered for sale on a major stock exchange must have such an audit before the securities may be sold, and thereafter additional audits must be made periodically if their sale is to continue.

The purpose of an audit is to enable the accountant making it to express the independent professional opinion that he believes the audited company's financial reports fairly reflect its financial position and operating results. Banks, investors, and others rely on information in a company's financial reports in making loans, granting credit, and in buying and selling securities; and they rely on the independent certified public accountant's opinion that the reports fairly reflect the company's position.

In making an audit, a certified public accountant carefully examines the audited company's financial reports and the accounting records from which they were prepared, making such tests and checks of their information as he deems necessary in order that he may risk his professional reputation on the accuracy of the opinion he expresses.

MANAGEMENT ADVISORY SERVICES. In addition to auditing, accountants commonly offer management advisory services.

An accountant gains from an audit an intimate knowledge of the audited company's accounting procedures and its financial position, and thus is in an excellent position to offer constructive suggestions for improving the procedures and strengthening the position. Clients expect these suggestions as a useful audit by-product, and they also commonly engage certified public accountants to conduct additional investigations for the purpose of determining ways in which their operations may be improved. Such investigations and the suggestions growing from them are known as management advisory services.

Management advisory services include the design, installation, and improvement of a client's general accounting system and any system he may have for determining and controlling manufacturing and distributing costs. They also include the application of punched cards, electronics, and other modern machine methods to these systems, plus advice in financial planning, budgeting, forecasting, inventory control—in fact, in all phases of record keeping and related matters.

TAX SERVICES. In this day of increasing complexity in income and other tax laws and continued high rates, few important business decisions are made without consideration being given to their tax effect. A certified public accountant, through his training and experience, is well qualified to render important service in this area. The service includes not only the preparation and filing of tax returns but also advice as to how transactions may be completed so as to incur the smallest tax.

Private accounting

When an accountant is employed by a single enterprise, he is said to be in private accounting. A small business may employ only one accountant or it may depend upon the services of a public accountant and employ none. A large business, on the other hand, may have more than a hundred employees in its accounting department, working under the supervision of a chief accounting officer, commonly called the *controller,* who is often a CPA. The title, controller, results from the fact that one of the chief uses of accounting data is to control the operations of a business.

The one accountant of the small business and the accounting department of a large concern do a variety of work, including general accounting, cost accounting, budgeting, and internal auditing.

GENERAL ACCOUNTING. Although it is hard to draw a line of demarcation, general accounting has to do primarily with recording transactions and preparing financial and other reports for the use of management, owners, creditors, and governmental agencies. The private accountant may design or help the public accountant design the system used in recording the transactions, and he will supervise the clerical or data processing staff in recording the transactions and preparing the reports.

COST ACCOUNTING. The phase of accounting that has to do with collecting, determining, and controlling costs, particularly costs of producing a given product or service, is called cost accounting. Since a knowledge of costs and controlling costs are vital to good management, a large company may have a number of accountants engaged in this activity.

BUDGETING. Planning business activities before they occur is called budgeting. The objective of budgeting is to provide management with an intelligent plan for future operations, and after the plan has been put into effect, to provide summaries and reports comparing actual accomplishments with the plan. Many large companies have within their accounting departments a number of people who devote all their time to this phase of accounting.

INTERNAL AUDITING. In addition to an annual audit by a firm of certified public accountants, some companies maintain a staff of internal auditors who constantly check the records prepared and maintained in each department or company branch. It is the responsibility of these internal auditors to make sure that established accounting procedures and management directives are being followed throughout the company.

Governmental accounting

Furnishing governmental services is a vast and complicated operation in which accounting is just as indispensable as in business. Elected and appointed officials must rely on data accumulated by means of accounting if they are to complete effectively their administrative duties. Accountants are responsible for the accumulation of these data. Accountants also check and audit the millions of income, payroll, and sales tax returns that accompany the tax payments upon which governmental units depend. And finally, federal and state agencies, such as the Interstate Commerce Commission, Securities and Exchange Commission, Federal Power Commission, Federal Communication Commission, and so on, use accountants in many capacities in their regulation of business.

Accounting and book-keeping

■ Many people confuse accounting and bookkeeping and look upon them as one and the same — in effect they identify the whole with one of its parts. Actually, bookkeeping is only part of accounting, the record-making part. To keep books is to record transactions, and a bookkeeper is one who records transactions. The work is often routine and primarily clerical in nature. The work of an accountant goes far beyond this, as a rereading of the previous section will show.

Accounting statements

■ Accounting statements are the end product of the accounting process, but a good place to begin the study of accounting. They are used to convey to management and interested outsiders a concise picture of the profitability and financial position of a business. The two most important are the income statement and the balance sheet.

The income statement

A company's income statement (see Illustration 1–1) is perhaps more important than its balance sheet, since it shows whether or not the business achieved or failed to achieve its primary objective — earning a "profit" or net income. A net income is earned when revenues exceed expenses, and an income statement is prepared by listing the revenues earned during a period, listing the expenses incurred in earning the revenues, and subtracting the expenses from the revenues.

Revenues are inflows of cash or other properties received in exchange for goods or for services rendered. Rents, dividends, and interest earned are also revenues. Coast Realty of Illustration 1–1 had revenue inflows from services which totaled $19,650.

Expenses are goods and services consumed in operating a business or other economic unit. Coast Realty consumed the services of its employees (salaries expense), the services of a telephone company, and so on.

Illustration
1-1

Coast Realty
Income Statement for Year Ended December 31, 19—

Revenues:

Commissions earned	$18,450	
Property management fees	1,200	
Total revenues		$19,650

Operating expenses:

Salaries expense	$ 3,600	
Rent expense	1,800	
Utilities expense	315	
Telephone expense	260	
Advertising expense	1,310	
Total expenses		7,285
Net Income		$12,365

The heading of an income statement tells the name of the business for which it is prepared and the time period covered by the statement. Both bits of information are important, but the time covered is extremely significant, since the items on the statement must be interpreted in connection with a period of time. For example, the item "Commissions earned, $18,450" on the income statement of Illustration 1–1 has little significance until it is known that the amount represents one year's commissions and not the commissions of a week or a month.

The balance sheet

The purpose of a balance sheet is to show the financial position of a business on a particular date, and it is often called a *position statement.* Financial position is shown by listing the *assets* of the business, its *liabilities* or debts, and the *equity of the owner or owners.* The name of the business and the date are given in the balance sheet heading, and it is understood that the item amounts shown are as of the close of business on that day.

Before a business manager, investor, or other person can make effective judgments based on balance sheet information, he must gain several concepts and understandings; therefore, assume that on August 3, Gary Ball began a new business, called World Travel Agency, by investing $18,000 of his personal savings. He then completed these additional transactions:

Aug. 3 Paid $15,000 of the agency's cash for a small office building and the land on which it rests (cost of the building, $10,000, and cost of the land, $5,000).

3 Purchased from Office Equipment Company *on credit* (purchased with a promise to pay at a later date) office equipment costing $2,000.

A balance sheet reflecting the effects of these transactions and showing the financial position of World Travel Agency after their completion appears in Illustration 1–2.

World Travel Agency
Balance Sheet, August 3, 19 —

ASSETS		LIABILITIES	
Cash	$ 3,000	Accounts payable	$ 2,000
Office equipment	2,000		
Building	10,000	OWNER EQUITY	
Land	5,000		
		Gary Ball, capital	18,000
Total Assets	$20,000	Total Equities	$20,000

Illustration
1–2

The assets of a business are, in general, the properties or economic resources owned by the business. They include cash, amounts owed to the business by customers for goods and services sold to them on credit (called *accounts receivable*), merchandise held for sale by the business, supplies, equipment, buildings, and land. Assets may also include such intangible rights as those granted by a patent or copyright.

The liabilities of a business are its debts and include amounts owed to creditors for goods and services bought on credit (called *accounts payable*), salaries and wages owed employees, taxes payable, notes payable, and mortgages payable.

Liabilities are sometimes called *equities*. An equity is a right, claim, or interest; and a liability represents a claim or right to be paid. Law recognizes this right; and if a business fails to pay its creditors, law gives the creditors the right to force the sale of the assets of the business to secure money to meet creditor claims. Furthermore, if the assets are sold, the creditors are paid first, with any remainder going to the business owner. Obviously, then, by law creditor claims take precedence over those of a business owner.

Owner equity is the interest of the owner or owners of a business in the assets of the business. When a business is owned by one man, his equity is shown on the balance sheet of the business by listing his name, followed by the word *capital,* and then the amount of the equity. The use of the word, capital, comes from the idea that the owner has furnished the business with resources or "capital" equal to his equity.

Since creditor claims take precedence over those of an owner, owner equity in a business is always a residual amount. Creditors recognize this; and when they examine the balance sheet of a business, they are always interested in the share of its assets furnished by creditors and the share furnished by its owner or owners. The creditors' interest results from knowing that if the business must be liquidated and its assets sold, any shrinkage in converting the assets into cash can be as great as the equity of the owner or owners before the creditors will lose.

In examining the Illustration 1-2 balance sheet, bear in mind that the $18,000 equity of Gary Ball in this business may not be all the assets he owns. In addition to his equity in the new business he may own a farm, a home, and many personal assets. However, these are not included on the balance sheet of the business because if the personal property, affairs, and transactions of an owner are intermingled with those of his business, the records and statements of the business are misleading and fail their intended purpose, which is to show the financial position and operating results of the business.

The idea discussed in the previous paragraph is known in accounting as the *business entity concept*. Under this concept it is assumed that a business is an entity that is separate and distinct from the person or persons who own it, and the business is treated as though it owns the business assets and in turn owes both the creditors and its owner or owners the amounts of their claims. Also, under this concept the re- sources and activities of the business are kept separate from those of its owner or owners.

In addition to the business entity concept, an accounting principle called the *cost principle* should be borne in mind when reading a balance sheet. Under this principle all transactions are recorded at cost and the goods and services purchased appear on the statements at cost. For example, if a business pays $50,000 for land to be used in carrying on its operations, the purchase should be recorded at $50,000. It makes no difference if the owner and several competent outside appraisers thought the land "worth" at least $60,000; it cost $50,000 and should appear on the balance sheet at that amount. Furthermore, if five years later, due to booming real estate prices, the land's fair market value has doubled, this makes no difference either. The land cost $50,000 and should continue to appear on the balance sheet at $50,000 even though its estimated market value is twice that.

In the previous paragraph it is said that the land cost $50,000. What is cost or what is included in the cost of an asset? The answer is that in principle the cost of an asset includes all expenditures and charges in- curred in getting the asset into its existing location and condition. More is said about this later.

Why are assets and services recorded at cost? The answer is that ac- counting must be factual and costs are factual. When costs are used, a buyer and a seller, each trying to strike the best bargain for himself, establish the costs; and these "bargained costs" are normally a fair measure of the goods and services acquired. If amounts other than costs were used, for example, amounts based on estimates, judgments, and appraisals, accounting records would lose much of their usefulness.

Also, why are balance sheet amounts not changed from time to time to reflect changing market values? The answer is that a balance sheet is prepared under the assumption that the business for which it is prepared is a *going concern,* and as a going concern its assets are not for sale, in fact, cannot be sold without disrupting the business. Therefore, since the assets are for use in the business and are not for sale, their current market values are generally not relevant.

The *going-concern concept* applies in most instances. However, if a business is about to be sold or liquidated, the going-concern concept and the cost principle do not apply in the preparation of its statements. In such cases amounts other than costs are more useful and informative.

From the foregoing discussion of the cost principle and the going-concern concept it is obvious that in most instances a balance sheet does not show the amounts at which the listed assets can be sold or replaced. Nor does it show the "worth" of the business for which it was prepared, since some of the listed assets may be salable for much more or much less than their balance sheet amounts.

The balance sheet equation

■ A balance sheet is so called because its two sides must always balance; the assets must equal liabilities plus owner equity. This equality may be expressed in equation form as follows:

$$\text{Assets} = \text{Liabilities} + \text{Owner Equity}$$

When balance sheet equality is expressed in equation form, the resulting equation is called the *balance sheet equation.* It is also known as the *accounting equation,* since all double-entry accounting is based on it. And, like any mathematical equation, its elements may be transposed and the equation expressed:

$$\text{Assets} - \text{Liabilities} = \text{Owner Equity}$$

The equation in this form illustrates the residual nature of owner equity; an owner's claims are secondary to those of his creditors.

Effects of trans- actions on the accounting equation

■ A business transaction is an exchange of goods or services, and business transactions affect the elements of the accounting equation. However, regardless of what transactions a business completes, its accounting equation always remains in balance and its assets always equal the combined claims of its creditors and its owner or owners. This may be demonstrated with the transactions of Owen Real Estate Agency which follow.

On the first day of July, Larry Owen invested $5,000 in a real estate agency and began business as a real estate agent. After the investment, the one asset of the new business and the equity of Owen in the one asset is shown by the following equation:

Assets	=	Owner Equity
Cash, $5,000	=	Larry Owen, Capital, $5,000

After its first transaction the Owen Real Estate Agency has one asset, cash, $5,000. It has no liabilities; therefore, the equity of Owen in this business is $5,000.

To continue the Owen Real Estate Agency illustration, after investing $5,000 cash, (1) Owen used $300 to pay the rent for three months in advance on an office, (2) $3,000 to buy an automobile that he planned to use only for business purposes, and (3) $1,000 to buy office furniture. The effects of these three transactions on the accounting equation are shown in Illustration 1–3. Observe that the equation remains in balance after each transaction.

	Cash	+	Prepaid Rent	+	Automobile	+	Office Equipment	=	Larry Owen, Capital
	$5,000								$5,000
(1)	−300		+$300						
	$4,700		$300						$5,000
(2)	−3,000				+$3,000				
	$1,700		$300		$3,000				$5,000
(3)	−1,000						+$1,000		
	$ 700	+	$300	+	$3,000	+	$1,000	=	$5,000

Assets = Owner Equity

Illustration 1–3

The nature of the Owen Real Estate Agency assets was changed by the three transactions, the effects of which are shown in Illustration 1–3. After their completion only $700 of the concern's original $5,000 cash remains; however, in exchange for the cash the business acquired three new assets: (1) the right to occupy office space for three months, (2) an automobile, and (3) office furniture.

Continuing the illustration, assume that Owen found it necessary to have some additional equipment in his office. He felt that he should conserve the business cash; consequently, he purchased on credit or on account from Standard Supply Company office furniture costing $350 (transaction No. 4). The effects of this transaction on the agency assets and equities are shown in color in Illustration 1–4.

The assets were increased by purchase of the additional office equipment; however, owner equity remained unchanged because Standard Supply Company acquired a claim against the assets equal to the asset increase. The claim of or the amount owed Standard Supply Company is known as an account payable.

At this stage assume that Larry Owen realized he had one piece of office equipment for which he had no need. Assume further that he was able to sell the equipment to Dale Hall for the $150 it cost. Mr. Hall paid $100 in cash on delivery and promised to pay the $50 balance at a

	Assets					=	Liabili-ties	+	Owner Equity
	Cash +	Prepaid Rent +	Automobile +	Office Equip-ment	=	Accounts Payable	+	Larry Owen, Capital	
	$5,000							$5,000	
(1)	−300	+$300							
	$4,700	$300						$5,000	
(2)	−3,000		+$3,000						
	$1,700	$300	$3,000					$5,000	
(3)	−1,000			+$1,000					
	$ 700	$300	$3,000	$1,000				$5,000	
(4)				+350		+$350			
	$ 700 +	$300 +	$3,000 +	$1,350 =		$350	+	$5,000	

Illustration 1–4

later date. The effects of this transaction (No. 5) on the accounting equation are shown in color in Illustration 1–5.

	Assets						=	Liabili-ties	+	Owner Equity
	Cash +	Accounts Receivable +	Prepaid Rent +	Auto-mobile +	Office Equip-ment	=	Accounts Payable	+	Larry Owen, Capital	
	$5,000								$5,000	
(1)	−300		+$300							
	$4,700		$300						$5,000	
(2)	−3,000			+$3,000						
	$1,700		$300	$3,000					$5,000	
(3)	−1,000				+$1,000					
	$ 700		$300	$3,000	$1,000				$5,000	
(4)					+350		+$350			
	$ 700		$300	$3,000	$1,350		$350		$5,000	
(5)	+100	+$50			−150					
	$ 800 +	$50 +	$300 +	$3,000 +	$1,200 =		$350	+	$5,000	

Illustration 1–5

The sale of the unneeded office equipment was an exchange of office equipment for (1) cash, $100, and (2) a new asset, the right to collect $50 from Dale Hall at a future date. This last asset, the right to collect money from someone to whom goods or services have been sold on credit, is known as an account receivable.

A few days after the foregoing transaction, Dale Hall paid the amount owed (Transaction No. 6); and upon receipt of the money Larry Owen in turn paid Standard Supply Company one half the amount owed to it (No. 7). The effect of these two transactions is shown in Illustration 1–6. Observe that the first, the receipt of cash from Dale Hall, is an exchange

	Assets					= Liabili-ties	+ Owner Equity
	Cash +	Accounts Receivable +	Prepaid Rent +	Auto-mobile +	Office Equip-ment =	Accounts Payable +	Larry· Owen, Capital
	$5,000						$5,000
(1)	−300		+$300				
	$4,700		$300				$5,000
(2)	−3,000			+$3,000			
	$1,700		$300	$3,000			$5,000
(3)	−1,000				+$1,000		
	$ 700		$300	$3,000	$1,000		$5,000
(4)					+350	+$350	
	$ 700		$300	$3,000	$1,350	$350	$5,000
(5)	+100	+$50			−150		
	$ 800	$50	$300	$3,000	$1,200	$350	$5,000
(6)	+50	−50					
	$ 850	0	$300	$3,000	$1,200	$350	$5,000
(7)	−175					−175	
	$ 675 +	0 +	$300 +	$3,000 +	$1,200 =	$175	+ $5,000

Illustration
1–6

of assets; the second results in equal decreases in both assets and liabilities.

Increasing owner equity

The primary objective of a business is to increase owner equity by earning a profit or a net income. The Owen Real Estate Agency will accomplish this objective by selling real estate on a commission basis for its clients. Of course, the business will accomplish this objective only if the commissions earned are greater than the expenses incurred in making the sales.

Commissions earned and expenses incurred affect the elements of an accounting equation. To illustrate their effect, assume that on July 12 Larry Owen sold a house for a client and collected an $850 commission for his services (No. 8). Also, on the last day of July he received the monthly telephone bill in the mail and issued a $20 check for its payment (No. 9). The effects of these two transactions are shown in Illustration 1–7.

Observe carefully the effect of the $850 commission in the Illustration 1–7 equation and note that the commission not only increased the asset, cash, but also caused an $850 increase in owner equity. Owner equity increased because assets increased without any increase in liabilities; or it can be said that owner equity increased because *net assets* increased. Net assets are the excess of assets over liabilities.

Next observe the effect of the $20 telephone expense and note that the effect is opposite from that of a revenue. An expense reduces both net assets and owner equity.

		Assets				=	Liabilities	+	Owner Equity
	Cash +	Accounts Receivable +	Prepaid Rent +	Auto-mobile +	Office Equipment =		Accounts Payable +		Larry Owen, Capital
	$5,000								$5,000
(1)	−300		+$300						
	$4,700		$300						$5,000
(2)	−3,000			+$3,000					
	$1,700		$300	$3,000					$5,000
(3)	−1,000				+$1,000				
	$ 700		$300	$3,000	$1,000				$5,000
(4)					+350		+$350		
	$ 700		$300	$3,000	$1,350		$350		$5,000
(5)	+100	+$50			−150				
	$ 800	$50	$300	$3,000	$1,200		$350		$5,000
(6)	+50	−50							
	$ 850	0	$300	$3,000	$1,200		$350		$5,000
(7)	−175						−175		
	$ 675	0	$300	$3,000	$1,200		$175		$5,000
(8)	+850								+850
	$1,525	0	$300	$3,000	$1,200		$175		$5,850
(9)	−20								−20
	$1,505 +	0 +	$300 +	$3,000 +	$1,200 =		$175 +		$5,830

Illustration
1–7

Then recall that a net income is earned when revenues exceed expenses, and recognize that earning a net income increases both net assets and owner equity.

Classification of balance sheet items

■ The balance sheet shown several pages back was a simple one with few items, and no attempt was made to classify them. However, a balance sheet with a number of items becomes more useful when its assets and liabilities are classified into significant groups, because a reader of a *classified balance sheet* can better judge the adequacy of the different kinds of assets used in the business. He can also better estimate the probable availability of funds to meet the various liabilities as they become due.

Accountants are not in full agreement as to the best way in which to classify balance sheet items. As a result they are classified in several ways; but a common way classifies assets into (1) current assets, (2) long-term investments, (3) plant and equipment, and (4) intangible assets. It classifies liabilities into (1) current liabilities and (2) long-term liabilities.

Of the four asset classifications just listed, only two, current assets and plant and equipment, appear on the balance sheet of Valley Hardware Store, Illustration 1–8 on the next page, because the store is small and has no long-term investments and intangible assets.

Valley Hardware Store
Balance Sheet, December 31, 1972

ASSETS

Current Assets:

Cash..	$ 1,050	
Notes receivable	300	
Accounts receivable	3,961	
Merchandise inventory	10,248	
Prepaid insurance.......................................	109	
Office supplies...	46	
Stores supplies	145	
Total Current Assets.............................		$15,859

Plant and Equipment:

Office equipment.......................................	$ 1,500		
Less accumulated depreciation	300	$ 1,200	
Store equipment	$ 3,200		
Less accumulated depreciation	800	2,400	
Buildings..	$25,000		
Less accumulated depreciation	7,400	17,600	
Land...		4,200	
Total Plant and Equipment.....................			25,400
Total Assets.......................................			$41,259

LIABILITIES

Current Liabilities:

Notes payable..	$ 3,000	
Accounts payable.......................................	2,715	
Wages payable	112	
Total Current Liabilities		$ 5,827

Long-Term Liabilities:

First mortgage payable, secured by a mortgage on land and buildings................		10,000
Total Liabilities...................................		$15,827

OWNER EQUITY

Samuel Jackson, capital, January 1, 1972...........		$23,721
Net income for the year ended December 31, 1972	$ 7,711	
Less withdrawals for personal expenses	6,000	
Excess of income over withdrawals		1,711
Samuel Jackson, capital, December 31, 1972		25,432
Total Liabilities and Owner Equity		$41,259

Illustration
1–8

Current assets

The assets listed on a balance sheet under the current asset caption are primarily those to which current creditors (current liabilities) may look for payment. As presently defined, current assets consist of cash and assets that are reasonably expected to be realized in cash or be sold or consumed within a short period, usually one year. The accounts and notes receivable of Illustration 1–8 are expected to be realized in cash, the merchandise (merchandise inventory) is expected to be sold, and the prepaid insurance and supplies are to be consumed.

Such things as prepaid insurance, office supplies, and store supplies are called prepaid expenses. They were purchased for use in the business and will be consumed within a relatively short period of time, and when consumed become expenses. The American Institute of Certified Public Accountants through one of its committees says: "Prepaid expenses are not current assets in the sense that they will be converted into cash but in the sense that, if not paid in advance, they would require the use of current assets during the operating cycle." [1] This means that if the prepaid expense items were not already owned, current assets would be required for their purchase during the operating cycle, which for most concerns is one year.

Long-term investments

The second balance sheet classification is long-term investments. Stocks, bonds, and promissory notes that will be held for more than one year appear under this classification. Also, such things as land held for future expansion but not now being used in the business appear here.

Plant and equipment

Plant assets are relatively long-lived assets that are held for use in the production or sale of other assets or services, for example, items of equipment, buildings, and land. The key words in the foregoing sentence are "long-lived" and "held for use in the production or sale of other assets or services." Land held for future expansion, as mentioned in the previous paragraph, is not a plant asset because it is not being used to produce or sell other assets, goods, or services.

The words "Plant and equipment" are commonly used as a balance sheet caption; but more complete captions are "Property, plant, and equipment" and "Land, buildings, and equipment." However, all three captions are long and unwieldy; and as a result, items of plant and equipment will be called plant assets in this book.

The order in which plant assets are listed within the balance sheet classification is not uniform; however, it is often from the ones of least permanent nature to those of most permanent nature.

Plant assets, with the exception of land, wear out or *depreciate* through use and the passage of time, and the amount they depreciate each month or year is an expense. The plant assets of Illustration 1–8 are shown at cost less *accumulated depreciation*. The accumulated depreciation is the share of each asset's cost that has been charged off to depreciation expense or the amount the asset has been depreciated from the time of its purchase to the balance sheet date. Depreciation is discussed in more detail beginning in Chapter 3.

---

[1] *Accounting Research and Terminology Bulletins, Final Edition* (New York: American Institute of Certified Public Accountants, 1961), p. 20.

Intangible assets

Intangible assets are assets having no physical nature, their value being derived from the rights conferred upon their owner by possession. Goodwill, patents, and trademarks are examples.

Current liabilities

Current liabilities are debts or other obligations that must be paid or liquidated within a short time, usually one year, and whose payment or liquidation will require the use of current assets. Common current liabilities are notes payable, accounts payable, wages payable, taxes payable, interest payable, and unearned revenues. The order of their listing within the classification is not uniform. Often notes payable are listed as the first current liability because notes receivable are listed first after cash in the current asset section. (A promissory note payable is an unconditional promise in writing to pay on demand or at a fixed or determinable future date a definite sum of money. They are discussed and described in more detail in Chapter 9.)

Unearned revenues, none of which are shown in Illustration 1–8, are normally the last items in the current liability section. They result from transactions in which money is received for goods or services to be delivered at a future date. Subscriptions received in advance by a publisher, rent received in advance by a landlord, and payments received for future delivery of merchandise are examples. Each is a liability, an obligation to deliver goods or services at a future date. Each is classified as a current liability because current assets will normally be required in its liquidation. For example, payments for future delivery of merchandise will be earned and the obligation for delivery will be liquidated by delivering merchandise, a current asset.

Long-term liabilities

The second main liability classification is long-term liabilities. Liabilities that are not due and payable for a comparatively long period, usually more than one year, are listed under this classification. Common long-term liability items are mortgages payable, bonds payable, and notes payable due more than a year after the balance sheet date.

Owner equity on the balance sheet

■ The terms owner equity, proprietorship, net worth, and capital are often used synonymously. All four indicate the equity, in the assets, of the owner or owners of a business. Of the four, owner equity, proprietorship, and capital are considered the better terms because the phrase "net worth" seems to indicate that the amount shown is the net or exact "worth" of the owner's equity. Actually the amount shown may or may not be the equity's "worth" because when assets are purchased, they are recorded at cost; and in most cases until sold or consumed in the business operations, cost remains the basis upon which they are accounted for even though their "worth" may change. Thus, if a building lot is bought for $20,000, its purchase is recorded at $20,000 and the lot remains on the records at that amount even though a year later it may be sold for $30,000. The lot remains on the records at $20,000 until sold; and the change in its "worth" along with the resulting change in its owner's "net worth" is not recorded until a sale is completed.

The manner of reporting owner equity on a balance sheet depends upon the type of business for which the balance sheet is prepared. A business may be a single proprietorship, a partnership, or a corporation.

Single proprietorship

When a business is owned by one person, it is called a single proprietorship and the owner's equity may be reported on the balance sheet as follows:

OWNER EQUITY

James Gibbs, capital, January 1, 1972		$ 13,152
Net income for the year .... $ 3,753		
Withdrawals for personal expenses 4,800		
Excess of withdrawals over earnings	1,047	
James Gibbs, capital, December 31, 1972		$12,105

The just illustrated manner of presenting owner equity shows the increase and decrease resulting from earnings and withdrawals. Some accountants prefer to put these details on a supplementary schedule attached to the balance sheet and called a statement of owner equity. When such a statement is prepared, owner equity is shown on the balance sheet as follows:

OWNER EQUITY

James Gibbs, capital (see schedule attached) ...... $ 12,105

Partnership

When two or more people own a business as partners, changes in their equities resulting from earnings and withdrawals are normally shown on a supplementary statement attached to the balance sheet and only the amount of each partner's equity and the total equities are shown on the balance sheet itself, as follows:

PARTNERS' EQUITIES

James Smith, capital .... $ 16,534	
Robert Burns, capital 18,506	
Total Partners' Equities	$ 35,040

Corporation

Corporations are created under and are regulated by state and federal laws, and these laws require that a distinction be made between the amount invested in a corporation by its owners (its stockholders) and the increase or decrease in that investment due to losses and gains. As a result, the equity of the owners or stockholders in a corporation's assets is commonly shown on its balance sheet as follows:

STOCKHOLDERS' EQUITY

Capital stock	$500,000	
Retained earnings..	63,450	
Total Stockholders' Equity		$563,450

The amount shown after "Capital stock" represents the stockholders' investment in the corporation, and the amount shown after "Retained earnings" is the increase in the equity resulting from retaining earnings in the business.

Partnerships and corporations are discussed in more detail later in this text.

Arrangement of balance sheet items

■ The balance sheet of Illustration 1–2, with the liabilities and owner equity placed to the right of the assets, is called an *account form balance sheet*. Such an arrangement emphasizes that assets equal liabilities plus owner equity. Account form balance sheets are often reproduced on a double page with the assets on the left-hand page and the liabilities and owner equity on the right-hand page.

The balance sheet of Illustration 1–8 is called a *report form balance sheet*. Its items are arranged vertically and better fit a single page. Both forms are commonly used, and neither is preferred.

Classification of income statement items

■ An income statement, like a balance sheet, is more useful with its items classified. However, the classifications used depend upon the type of business for which the statement is prepared and the nature of its costs and expenses; consequently, a discussion of this is deferred to Chapter 5, after more income statement items are introduced.

Accounting concepts introduced with proprietorships

■ The accounting records and reports of single proprietorships are normally less complicated and require an understanding of fewer special terms than do those of either partnerships or corporations. Consequently, single proprietorships are used in the next few chapters to introduce additional accounting concepts and business record keeping. Partnerships and corporations are then discussed in some detail beginning in Chapter 15.

Questions for class discussion

1. Define accounting.
2. How does a businessman use accounting information?
3. Why do the states license certified public accountants?
4. Differentiate between a public accountant and a certified public accountant.

5. What is the American Institute of Certified Public Accountants?
6. What is the purpose of an audit? What does a certified public accountant do when he makes an audit?
7. A public accountant may provide management advisory services. Of what does this consist?
8. What do the tax services of a public accountant include beyond preparing and filing tax returns?
9. What is a private accountant? A public accountant?
10. Differentiate between accounting and bookkeeping.
11. What does an income statement show?
12. As the word is used in accounting, what is a revenue? An expense?
13. Why is the period of time covered by an income statement of extreme significance?
14. What does a balance sheet show?
15. Define (1) asset, (2) liability, (3) equity, and (4) owner equity.
16. Give a synonym for owner equity.
17. What is the cost principle of accounting? Why is such a principle necessary?
18. A business shows office stationery on its balance sheet at its $50 cost, although the stationery can be sold for not more than $0.25 as scrap paper. What accounting principle and concept justify this?
19. What is the balance sheet equation? Why is it of importance to the accounting student?
20. What is a classified balance sheet?
21. What are the characteristics of a current asset? What are the characteristics of an asset classified as plant and equipment?
22. What are current liabilities? Long-term liabilities?
23. Is it possible for a transaction to affect one asset item without affecting any other asset, liability, or owner equity item? Is it possible for a transaction to increase or decrease a single liability without affecting any other asset, liability, or owner equity item?

Class exercises

Exercise 1–1

Determine—

a) The equity of the owner in a business having $34,532 of assets and $9,311 of liabilities.

b) The liabilities of a business having $26,575 of assets and in which the owner has a $19,415 equity.

c) The assets of a business having $6,312 of liabilities and in which the owner has a $12,434 equity.

Exercise 1–2

Describe a transaction that will—

a) Increase an asset and increase owner equity.

b) Increase an asset and decrease an asset.

c) Increase an asset and increase a liability.

d) Decrease an asset and decrease a liability.

e) Decrease an asset and decrease owner equity.

Exercise 1-3

Prepare a form with the following four columnar headings: (1) Transaction, (2) Assets, (3) Liabilities, and (4) Owner Equity. List each of the transactions that follow by letter on a separate line in the first column and indicate the effect of each on the assets, liabilities, and owner equity by writing in the proper columns a plus (+) sign to indicate an increase, a minus (−) sign to show a decrease, and a zero to indicate no effect.

a) A dentist invested cash and equipment in a dental practice.
b) Pulled a tooth for a patient and immediately collected cash for the service.
c) Purchased additional equipment on credit for use in the practice.
d) Paid the dental assistant's wages.
e) Completed dental work on credit for a patient.
f) Paid for the equipment purchased in Transaction (*c*).
g) The patient of Transaction (*e*) paid for the work of that transaction.

Exercise 1-4

On January 1 of the current year Ottis Orr began the practice of law, and on December 31 his records showed the following revenue and expenses for the year. From the information, prepare an income statement showing Mr. Orr's net income for the year. Head the statement Ottis Orr, Attorney.

Legal fees earned	$18,400	Utilities expense	$ 600
Rent expense	1,200	Depreciation expense,	
Salaries expense	4,200	office equipment	300

Exercise 1-5

On December 31, at the end of his first year of law practice, Ottis Orr's accounting records showed the following assets, liabilities, and owner equity:

Accounts payable	$ 200	Office equipment (cost,	
Accounts receivable	1,000	$2,500, less accumulated	
Cash	800	depreciation, $300)	$2,200
Law library	2,400	Ottis Orr, capital	5,100
Note payable (due in two years)	1,200	Prepaid office rent	100

The $5,100 amount shown is Mr. Orr's year-end equity in the law practice. He began the year with a $5,000 investment in the practice. The practice earned $12,100 during the year, and Mr. Orr had withdrawn $1,000 of the earnings each month for personal living expenses. From the foregoing information, prepare a classified December 31 balance sheet.

Problems   **Problem 1-1**

Dale Cobb began a real estate agency on January 1 of the current year by investing $10,000 in cash. On December 31 the records of the agency, called Desert Real Estate Agency, showed the following alphabetically listed items:

Accounts payable..	$	300
Accounts receivable..		850
Advertising expense..		800
Building..	$24,000	
Less accumulated depreciation	1,200	22,800
Cash		400
Commissions earned..		23,250
Dale Cobb, capital...		10,450
Depreciation expense, building		1,200
Depreciation expense, office equipment...........................		300
Land		8,000
Mortgage payable..		24,000
Office equipment	$ 3,000	
Less accumulated depreciation	300	2,700
Office supplies		50
Office supplies expense		100
Salaries expense...		4,800
Salaries payable		50
Utilities expense		600

Required:

1. Select the revenue and expenses from the items and complete an income statement for the agency.

2. Use the remainder of the items plus the following information to prepare a classified December 31 balance sheet. The $10,450 amount listed is Dale Cobb's end-of-the-year equity in the agency. The agency earned a $15,450 net income and Mr. Cobb withdrew $15,000 of that amount for personal living expenses.

Problem 1–2

Roy Hale began the practice of dentistry and during a short period completed these transactions in the name of the practice:

a) Sold for $7,250 a personal investment in RCA stock and deposited $7,000 of the proceeds in a bank account opened in the name of the practice.

b) Purchased for $22,500 a small building to be used as an office. He paid $5,000 in cash and signed a mortgage contract to pay the balance over a period of years.

c) Purchased dental supplies for cash, $200.

d) Took dental equipment, which he had purchased while in college, from home for use in the practice. The equipment had a $250 fair value.

e) Purchased additional dental equipment from Dental Supply Company on credit, $3,500.

f) Paid the local paper $20 for a small advertising announcement of the opening of the practice.

g) Completed dental work for Fred Ball and immediately collected $25 for the work done.

h) Paid Dental Supply Company a $700 installment on the amount owed.

i) Completed $150 additional work for Fred Ball, for which the patient paid $50 in cash and promised to pay the balance within a few days.

j) Paid the dental assistant's wages, $100.

k) Fred Ball paid $50 of the amount owed.

l) Roy Hale withdrew $50 from the bank account of the practice to pay personal expenses.

Required:

1. Arrange the following asset, liability, and owner equity titles in an equation like Illustration 1–7: Cash; Accounts Receivable; Dental Supplies; Dental Equipment; Building; Accounts Payable; Mortgage Payable; and Roy Hale, Capital.
2. Show by additions and subtractions, as in Illustration 1–7, the effects of each transaction on the assets, liabilities, and owner equity. Show new totals after each transaction.

Problem 1–3

Dean Fall owns and operates Service Plumbing Shop. At the beginning of this month the shop had the following assets: cash, $815; plumbing supplies, $1,240; tools, $965; and trucks, $2,780. It also owed a $155 debt to Plumbing Supply Company for supplies previously purchased. During a short period the shop completed these transactions:

a) Paid the rent on the shop space for two months in advance, $200.
b) Purchased tools for cash, $25.
c) Purchased plumbing supplies on credit from Plumbing Supply Company, $150.
d) Completed repair work for Will Dant and received $50 cash in payment therefor.
e) Completed repair work for George Tell on credit, $125.
f) Paid Plumbing Supply Company the amount owed at the beginning of the month.
g) George Tell paid the $125 he owed.
h) Gave tools carried in the accounting records at $100 plus $175 in cash for new tools priced at $275.
i) Purchased plumbing supplies on credit from Plumbing Supply Company, $200.
j) Paid for advertising that had appeared in the local paper, $15.
k) Mr. Fall wrote a $50 check on the bank account of the shop to pay a personal expense.
l) Paid for the supplies purchased in Transaction (*c*).

Required:

1. Arrange the following asset, liability, and owner equity items in an equation like Illustration 1–7: Cash; Accounts Receivable; Prepaid Rent; Plumbing Supplies; Tools; Trucks; Accounts Payable; Dean Fall, Capital.
2. Enter the beginning-of-the-month assets and liability under the item names of the equation and determine the beginning owner equity and enter it.
3. Show by additions and subtractions the effects of the transactions on the equation as in Illustration 1–7. Show new totals after each transaction.

Problem 1–4

On October 1 of the current year Gary Hall opened Gary's Shoe Repair Shop, and during the month he completed these transactions:

a) Transferred $500 from a personal savings account to a checking account opened in the name of the business.
b) Paid the rent on the shop space for one month, $80. (Treat as an expense.)
c) Signed a lease with Shoe Machinery Company for the installation and use

of shoe repair equipment. The lease provided for a $60 monthly rental. Paid the first month's rent. (Treat as an expense.)

d) Purchased a showcase, chairs, and other shop furniture on credit from Store Fixtures, Inc., $400.

e) Purchased shop supplies for cash, $125.

f) Cash shoe repair revenue for the first half of the month, $180.

g) Paid for advertising that had appeared in the local newspaper, $25.

h) Paid Store Fixtures, Inc. $100 of the amount owed to it.

i) Cash shoe repair revenue for the last half of the month, $335.

j) Gary Hall used $85 of the shop supplies in repairing shoes during the month. (Record the expense by reducing the shop supplies and Gary Hall's equity in the business.)

k) The shop furniture depreciated $10 during the month. (Record the expense by reducing the shop furniture and the owner's equity. The direct reduction of shop furniture is not the proper way to handle this transaction; however, it will suffice until the proper method is introduced in Chapter 3.)

Required:

1. Arrange the following asset, liability, and owner equity titles in an equation like Illustration 1–7: Cash; Shop Supplies; Shop Furniture; Accounts Payable; and Gary Hall, Capital. Then show by additions and subtractions the effects of the transactions on the elements of the equation. Show new totals after each transaction.

2. Analyze the information in the last column of the equation and prepare an October income statement for the shoe repair shop.

3. Prepare an October 31 balance sheet for the shop. Under plant and equipment, show the shop furniture at its $400 cost less $10 accumulated depreciation.

Alternate problems

Problem 1–1A

Paul Pentz, D.D.S., began the practice of dentistry with a $4,000 investment on January 1 of the current year. On December 31 the records of the practice showed the following alphabetically arranged items:

Accounts payable		$ 200
Accounts receivable		2,300
Cash		900
Depreciation expense, office equipment		800
Mortgage payable, office equipment		4,000
Office equipment	$9,600	
Less accumulated depreciation, office equipment	800	8,800
Office supplies		400
Office supplies expense		700
Paul Pentz, capital		8,150
Professional fees earned		25,500
Property taxes payable		50
Rent expense, office space		2,400
Salaries expense		5,400
Taxes expense		50

Required:

1. Select the revenue and expenses from the list of items and prepare an income statement for the practice. Head the statement Paul Pentz, D.D.S.
2. Use the remainder of the items plus this additional information to prepare a classified December 31 balance sheet. The $8,150 amount listed is Paul Pentz's end-of-the-year equity in the practice. The practice earned a $16,150 net income during the year, and Dr. Pentz withdrew $1,000 per month for personal living expenses.

Problem 1–2A

Carl Cole, fresh out of law school, completed these transactions during a short period of time:

a) Began the practice of law by investing $1,500 in cash and a law library having a $500 fair value.
b) Paid two months' rent in advance on suitable office space, $300.
c) Purchased office equipment, $300, and office supplies, $100, from Office Outfitters for cash.
d) Completed legal work for Gale Clark and collected $100 cash therefor.
e) Purchased additional office equipment from Office Outfitters on credit, $800.
f) Paid the semimonthly salary of the office secretary, $200.
g) Completed legal work for Valley Realty Company on credit, $250.
h) Paid Office Outfitters one half the amount owed from Transaction *(e)*.
i) Valley Realty Company paid for the work of Transaction *(g)*.
j) Carl Cole withdrew $200 from the practice for personal living expenses.
k) Completed legal work for Security Bank on credit, $150.
l) Paid the monthly telephone bill, $25.

Required:

1. Arrange the following asset, liability, and owner equity titles in an equation like Illustration 1–7: Cash; Accounts Receivable; Prepaid Rent; Office Supplies; Office Equipment; Legal Library; Accounts Payable; and Carl Cole, Capital.
2. Show by additions and subtractions, as in Illustration 1–7, the effects of each transaction on the assets, liabilities, and owner equity. Show new totals after each transaction.

Problem 1–3A

Joe Sharp owns and operates Sharp TV Shop. At the beginning of the month the shop had these assets: cash, $2,300; repair supplies, $1,050; tools, $825; and truck, $1,100. It owed a debt to Electronics Sales, $150, for repair supplies previously purchased. During a short time the shop completed these transactions:

a) Purchased repair supplies for cash, $20.
b) Paid the rent on the shop space for three months in advance, $450.
c) Purchased repair supplies from Electronics Sales on credit, $100.
d) Gave the old company truck and $1,500 in cash for a new company truck.
e) Completed repair work for Walter Keller and collected $35 cash therefor.
f) Completed repair work for Gary Nash on credit, $65.
g) Paid Electronics Sales the amount owed at the beginning of the month.
h) Gary Nash paid for the work of Transaction *(f)*.

i) Paid for gas and oil placed in the truck during the past month, $25.
j) Purchased additional repair supplies from Electronics Sales on credit, $75.
k) Completed repair work for Carl Hall on credit, $40.
l) Joe Sharp wrote a check on the bank account of the shop to pay a personal expense, $60.

Required:
1. Arrange the following asset, liability, and owner equity titles in an equation like Illustration 1–7: Cash; Accounts Receivable; Prepaid Rent; Repair Supplies; Tools; Trucks; Accounts Payable; Joe Sharp, Capital.
2. Enter the beginning assets and liability under the proper titles of the equation. Determine Joe Sharp's beginning equity and enter it.
3. Show by additions and subtractions, as in Illustration 1–7, the effects of the transactions on the elements of the equation. Show new totals after each transaction.

Problem 1–4A

On August 1 of the current year Dale Graw began a new business that he called Desert Realty, and during August he completed these transactions:
a) Transferred $800 from his personal savings account to a checking account opened in the name of Desert Realty.
b) Paid the rent for one month on space to be used as an office, $150. (Treat as an expense.)
c) Purchased office equipment for cash, $200.
d) Purchased office supplies, $50, and office equipment, $450, from Office Supply Company on credit.
e) Sold a house for a client and collected a $650 cash commission for the service.
f) Paid for advertising that had appeared in the local paper, $85.
g) Sold a building lot for a client and collected a $100 cash commission.
h) Paid Office Supply Company $250 of the amount owed it.
i) Paid the telephone bill for August, $45.
j) By the end of August one half the office supplies purchased in Transaction (*d*) had been used. (Record the expense by reducing the office supplies and Dale Graw's equity in the business.)
k) The office equipment depreciated $10 during August. (Record the expense by reducing the office equipment and the owner's equity. The direct reduction in the asset is not the proper way to handle this transaction; however, it will suffice until the proper method is introduced in Chapter 3.)

Required:
1. Arrange the following asset, liability, and owner equity titles in an equation like Illustration 1–7: Cash; Office Supplies; Office Equipment; Accounts Payable; and Dale Graw, Capital. Then show by additions and subtractions the effects of the transactions on the elements of the equation. Show new totals after each transaction.
2. Analyze the information in the last column of the equation and prepare an August income statement for Desert Realty.
3. Prepare an August 31 balance sheet for the business. Under plant and equipment, show the office equipment at its cost less the $10 accumulated depreciation.

Early this year Walter Nash began a new business, called Quick Delivery Service, with a motorcycle having a $500 fair market value and $100 in cash. He has kept no accounting records and now, at the year-end, has engaged you to determine the service's net income or loss for the year. You find that Quick Delivery Service has a year-end bank balance of $760; there is $15 in the office cashbox; and The Bon, a local department store, owes the concern $110 for delivering packages during the past month. The concern still has the motorcycle, but it has depreciated $100 during the year. In addition it has a new delivery truck that cost $3,000, has depreciated $150 since its purchase, and on which the delivery service still owes the finance company $1,700. When the truck was purchased, Mr. Nash borrowed $1,000 from his father-in-law for the down payment. The loan was made in the name of the delivery service and was interest free. It has not been repaid. Finally, Mr. Nash has withdrawn $100 per week from the business (48 weeks) to be used for personal living expenses.

Did the business earn a profit or incur a loss during the year? Present figures to prove your answer.

Chapter 2

Recording transactions

■ Transactions are the raw material of the accounting process, a process which consists of identifying transactions, recording them, and summarizing their effects on periodic reports for the use of management and other decision makers.

Some years ago almost all concerns used pen and ink in recording transactions; but today only small concerns use this method, concerns small enough that their bookkeeping can be done by one person working as bookkeeper a part of his or her day. Larger, modern concerns use electric bookkeeping machines, punched cards, punched paper tape, and magnetic tape in recording transactions.

Nevertheless, most students begin their study of accounting by learning a double-entry accounting system based on pen and ink; and there are several reasons for this. First, since accounting reports evolved from and are based on double entry, the effective use of these reports requires some understanding of the system. Second, there is little lost motion from learning the system, since almost everything about it is applicable to machine methods. Primarily the machines replace pen and ink as the recording medium, taking the drudgery out of the recording process. And last, for the student who will start, manage, or own a small business, one small enough to use a pen-and-ink system, the system applies as it is taught.

Accounts ■ The transactions of a business cause increases and decreases in its assets, liabilities, and owner equity; and a concern using an accounting system based on pen and ink or electric bookkeeping machines uses *accounts* in making a record of these increases and decreases. A number of accounts are normally required, with a separate one being used for summarizing the increases and decreases in each asset, liability, and owner equity item for which an individual record is desired.

In its most simple form an account looks like the letter "T," is called a "T-account," and appears as follows:

(Place for the Name of the Item Recorded in This Account)

(Left side)	(Right side)

Note that the "T" gives the account a left side, a right side, and a place for the name of the asset, liability, or owner equity item, the changes in which are recorded therein.

When a T-account is used in recording increases and decreases in an item, the increases are placed on one side of the account and the decreases on the other. For example, if the increases and decreases in the cash of Owen Real Estate Agency of the previous chapter are recorded in a T-account, they appear as follows:

Cash

Investment	5,000	Payment of rent	300
Sale of equipment	100	Purchase of automobile	3,000
Collection from Hall	50	Purchase of furniture	1,000
Receipt of commission	850	Payment on account payable	175
		Payment of telephone bill	20

The reason for putting the increases on one account side and the decreases on the other is that this makes it possible to summarize quickly all the transactions that have affected the account over a period of time and to learn their aggregate effect.

For example, the increases in Owen Real Estate Agency cash were:

Investment	$5,000
Sale of unneeded equipment to Dale Hall	100
Collection of balance owed by Hall	50
Receipt of a commission	850
Sum of the increases	$6,000

And the decreases were:

Payment of office rent	$ 300
Purchase of automobile	3,000
Purchase of furniture for cash	1,000
Payment on an account payable	175
Payment of telephone bill	20
Sum of the decreases	$4,495

Therefore, the aggregate effect of the increases and decreases may be learned by subtracting the decreases from the increases, as follows:

Sum of the increases	$6,000
Sum of the decreases	4,495
Balance of cash remaining	$1,505

The subtraction indicates that the gross effect of Owen Real Estate Agency's cash transactions was a net reduction in its cash from $5,000 (the investment) to $1,505.

When accounting terminology is used to express the foregoing, it is said that after transactions are recorded in a T-account, they may be summarized and their net effect determined by adding (called "footing") the items on the increases side, adding ("footing") the items on the decreases side, and subtracting the sum of the decreases from the sum of the increases to ascertain the *balance* of the account. The balance of an account is the difference between its increases and decreases.

The ledger ■ A business may use from two dozen to several thousand accounts in recording its transactions, with each account placed on a separate page in a bound or loose-leaf book, or on a separate card in a tray of cards. If the accounts are kept in a book, the book is called a *ledger;* and if the accounts are kept on cards in a file tray, the tray of cards is a ledger. Actually, as used in accounting, the word ledger means a group of accounts.

Accounts commonly used ■ The specific accounts used by a business in recording its transactions vary from one concern to another, depending upon the assets owned, the debts owed, and the information to be secured from the accounting records. Nevertheless, although the specific accounts vary, the following are common.

Asset accounts

If useful records of a concern's assets are to be kept, an individual account is needed for the increases and decreases in each kind of asset owned. Some of the more common assets for which accounts are maintained are:

CASH. Increases and decreases in cash are recorded in an account called "Cash." The cash of a business consists of money or any media of exchange that a bank will accept at face value for deposit. It includes coins, currency, checks, postal and express money orders, and money on deposit in a bank or banks. Increases and decreases in both the cash on hand in the store or office and that on deposit in the bank are recorded in the same account.

NOTES RECEIVABLE. A formal written promise to pay a definite sum of money at a fixed future date is called a promissory note. When amounts due from others are evidenced by promissory notes, the notes are known as *notes receivable* and are recorded in a Notes Receivable account.

ACCOUNTS RECEIVABLE. Goods and services are commonly sold to customers on the basis of oral or implied promises of future payment. Such sales are known as "sales on credit" or "sales on account"; and the oral or implied promises to pay are known as accounts receivable. Accounts receivable are increased by sales on credit and are decreased by customer payments. Since it is necessary to know the amount currently owed by each customer, a separate record must be kept of each customer's purchases and payments. However, a discussion of the manner in which this separate record is kept is deferred until Chapter 6, and for the moment all increases and decreases in accounts receivable are recorded in a single account called Accounts Receivable.

PREPAID INSURANCE. Fire, liability, and other types of insurance protection are normally paid for in advance. The amount paid is called a "premium" and may give protection from loss for from one to five years. As a result, a large portion of each premium is an asset for a considerable time after payment. When insurance premiums are paid, the asset "prepaid insurance" is increased by the amount paid; and the increase is normally recorded in an account called "Prepaid Insurance." Day by day, insurance premiums expire. Consequently, at intervals the insurance policies are examined; the insurance that has expired is calculated; and the balance of the Prepaid Insurance account is reduced accordingly.

OFFICE SUPPLIES. Stamps, stationery, paper, pencils, and like items are known as office supplies. They are assets when purchased, and continue to be assets until consumed. As they are consumed, the amounts consumed become expenses. Increases and decreases in the asset "office supplies" are commonly recorded in an account called "Office Supplies."

STORE SUPPLIES. Wrapping paper, cartons, bags, string, and similar items used by a store are known as store supplies. Increases and decreases in store supplies are usually recorded in an account of that name.

OTHER PREPAID EXPENSES. As previously stated, prepaid expenses are items that are assets at the time of purchase but become expenses as they are consumed or used. Prepaid insurance, office supplies, and store supplies are examples. Other examples are prepaid rent, prepaid taxes, and prepaid wages. Each type of prepaid expense is normally accounted for in a separate account which carries the name of the item, the increases and decreases of which are recorded therein.

EQUIPMENT ACCOUNTS. Increases and decreases in such things as typewriters, desks, chairs, and office machines having long lives are commonly recorded in an account called "Office Equipment." Likewise, changes in the amount of counters, showcases, shelves, cash registers, and like items used by a store are recorded in an account called "Store Equipment." And a company that owns and uses such things as lathes, drill presses, and the like records the increases and decreases in these items in an account called "Machinery and Equipment."

BUILDINGS. A building used by a business in carrying on its operations may be a store, garage, warehouse, or factory; but regardless of use, an account called "Buildings" is commonly employed in recording the increases and decreases in the buildings owned by a business and used in carrying on its operations.

LAND. An account called "Land" is commonly used in recording increases and decreases in the land owned by a business. Although land and the buildings placed upon it are inseparable in physical fact, it is usually desirable to account for land and its buildings in separate accounts, because buildings depreciate or wear out, but land does not.

Liability accounts

Most companies do not have as many liability accounts as asset accounts; however the following are common:

NOTES PAYABLE. Increases and decreases in amounts owed because of promissory notes given to creditors are accounted for in an account called "Notes Payable."

ACCOUNTS PAYABLE. An account payable is an amount owed to a creditor which resulted from an oral or implied promise to pay. Most accounts payable result from the purchase of merchandise, supplies, equipment, and services on credit. Since it is necessary to know the amount owed each creditor, an individual record must be kept of the purchases from and payments to each. However, a discussion of the manner in which this individual record is kept is deferred until Chapter 6, and for the moment all increases and decreases in accounts payable are recorded in a single Accounts Payable account.

OTHER SHORT-TERM PAYABLES. Wages payable, taxes payable, and interest payable are illustrations of other short-term liabilities for which individual accounts must be kept.

MORTGAGE PAYABLE. A mortgage payable is a long-term debt for which the creditor has a secured prior claim against some one or more of the debtor's assets. The mortgage gives its holder, the creditor, the right to force the sale of the mortgaged assets through a foreclosure if the mortgage debt is not paid when due. An account called "Mortgage Payable" is commonly used in recording the increases and decreases in the amount owed on a mortgage.

Owner equity accounts

Many transactions affect owner equity in a single proprietorship business, either increasing it or decreasing it. These transactions include the owner's investment, his withdrawals of cash and other assets for personal use, revenues earned, and expenses incurred. Of these, the more numerous and, from a managerial viewpoint, the more important are the revenue and expense transactions.

In the previous chapter where the effects of transactions on the elements of the accounting equation were shown, all increases and decreases in owner equity, including revenues and expenses, were placed in a single column under the name of the owner. The single column helped to simplify the material, but it did not readily provide information as to each kind of increase and decrease. A single owner equity account would have the same disadvantage. Consequently, in order that information as to the various kinds of increases and decreases in owner equity can readily be secured, numerous owner equity accounts are used—a different one for each kind of increase or decrease. Among these accounts are the following:

CAPITAL ACCOUNT. When a person invests in a business of his own, his investment is recorded in an account carrying his name and the word "Capital." For example, an account called "Larry Owen, Capital" is used in recording the investment of Larry Owen in his real estate agency. In addition to the original investment, the Capital account is also used in recording any permanent increases or decreases in owner equity.

WITHDRAWALS ACCOUNT. Usually a man invests in a business to earn profits or a net income; and normally he expects the income to be large enough to pay his personal living expenses. However, often before income is earned or before it is known that income has been earned, a businessman finds it necessary to withdraw from his business money or other assets for personal living expenses. These withdrawals reduce in equal amounts both assets and owner equity; but they are not a salary nor an expense of the business even though they are in cash and may be at a fixed weekly or monthly amount. They are not a salary because a man cannot make a legally binding employer-employee contract with himself. Law and custom recognize this; and as a result such withdrawals are recorded in an account carrying the name of the proprietor and the word "Withdrawals." For example, an account called "Larry Owen, Withdrawals" is used to record the withdrawals of Larry Owen from his real estate agency. The Withdrawals account is also known as the "Personal" account or "Drawing" account.

REVENUE AND EXPENSE ACCOUNTS. Revenues increase and expenses decrease owner equity. Actually, over a period of time owner equity is increased or decreased by the difference between revenues earned and expenses incurred. It is increased when revenues exceed expenses and decreased when expenses exceed revenues. When revenues exceed expenses, a profit or net income is earned; and when expenses exceed revenues, a loss or net loss is incurred.

Making revenues exceed expenses is the primary objective of a business manager or owner, and to accomplish this an owner or manager must have rather detailed information as to the amount of each kind of revenue earned and each kind of expense incurred. And, this information is secured by providing in the ledger a separate account for each kind of revenue and expense and then, as transactions are completed, by recording in the separate accounts the amount of each kind of revenue earned and each kind of expense incurred.

Recording revenues and expenses in separate accounts requires a number of accounts in any business. In addition, all concerns do not have the same revenues and expenses; and consequently, it is impossible to list all revenue and expense accounts to be encountered. However, Revenue from Repairs, Commissions Earned, Fees Earned, Rent Earned, and Interest Earned are common examples of revenue accounts; and Advertising Expense, Store Supplies Used, Depreciation of Store Equipment, Office Salaries, Office Supplies Used, Rent Expense, Heating and Lighting Expense, Utilities Expense, and Insurance Expense are common examples of expense accounts. It should be noted that the kind of revenue or expense recorded in each above-mentioned account is evident from its title. This is generally true of such accounts.

Debit and credit
■ As previously stated, a T-account has a left side and a right side; however, in accounting the left side is called the *debit* side, abbreviated "Dr."; and the right side is called the *credit* side, abbreviated "Cr." Furthermore, when amounts are entered on the left side of an account, they are called *debits,* and the account is said to be *debited;* and when amounts are entered on the right side, they are called credits, and the account is said to be *credited.* Likewise, the difference between the total debits and the total credits recorded in an account is the account balance and may be either a *debit balance* or a *credit balance.* It is a debit balance when the sum of the debits exceeds the sum of the credits, and a credit balance when the sum of the credits exceeds the sum of the debits, and an account is said to be *in balance* when its debits and credits are equal.

The words "to debit" and "to credit" should not be confused with "to increase" and "to decrease." To debit means simply to enter an amount on the left side of an account, to credit means to enter an amount on the right side, and either may be an increase or a decrease. This may readily be seen by examining the way in which the investment of Larry Owen is recorded in his Cash and Capital accounts which follow:

Cash	Larry Owen, Capital
Investment 5,000	Investment 5,000

When Owen invested $5,000 in his real estate business, both the business cash and Owen's equity were increased. Observe in the foregoing accounts that one increase, the increase in cash, is recorded on the left or debit side of the Cash account; while the other increase, the increase in owner equity, is recorded on the right or credit side. The transaction is recorded in this manner because of the mechanics of *double-entry accounting.*

Mechanics of double-entry accounting ■ The mechanics of double-entry accounting are such that every transaction affects and is recorded in two or more accounts with equal debits and credits. Transactions are so recorded because equal debits and credits offer a means of proving the recording accuracy. The proof is, if every transaction is recorded with equal debits and credits, then the sum of the debits in the ledger must equal the sum of the credits.

The person who first devised double-entry accounting based the system on the accounting equation, $A = L + OE$, and he assigned the recording of increases in assets to the debit sides of asset accounts. He then recognized that the goal of equal debits and credits was possible only if increases in liabilities and owner equity were recorded on the opposite or credit sides of liability and owner equity accounts, or he recognized that if increases in assets were to be recorded as debits, then increases and decreases in all accounts would have to be recorded as follows:

Assets		=	Liabilities		+	Owner Equity	
Debit for Increases	Credit for Decreases		Debit for Decreases	Credit for Increases		Debit for Decreases	Credit for Increases

From the foregoing T-accounts it is possible to formulate rules for recording transactions under a double-entry system. The rules are:

1. Increases in assets are debited to asset accounts; consequently, decreases must be credited.
2. Increases in liability and owner equity items are credited to liability and owner equity accounts; consequently, decreases must be debited.

At this stage, the beginning student will find it helpful to memorize these rules.

The trial balance ■ When a business uses a double-entry system, the equality of the debits and credits in its ledger is periodically tested by preparing a *trial balance*. How a trial balance is prepared and the exact nature of its proof are discussed later in this chapter.

Transactions illustrating the rules of debit and credit ■ The following Owen Real Estate Agency transactions illustrate the application of debit and credit rules and show how transactions are recorded in the accounts. The number preceding each transaction is used throughout the illustration to identify the transaction as it appears in the accounts. Note that most of the transactions are the same ones used in Chapter 1 to illustrate the effects of transactions on the accounting equation.

1. Larry Owen invested $5,000 in a real estate agency.
2. He paid three months' office rent in advance, $300.
3. Paid $3,000 for a business automobile.
4. Purchased office equipment for cash, $1,000.
5. Purchased on credit from Standard Supply Company office supplies, $60, and office equipment, $350.
6. Sold unneeded office equipment to Dale Hall, $100 cash and $50 to be paid at a later date.
7. Collected $50 from Dale Hall.
8. Paid Standard Supply Company $175 of the amount owed for supplies and equipment.
9. Sold a house and collected an $850 commission.
10. Paid the secretary's salary for the first two weeks of the month, $100.
11. Signed a contract to manage an apartment building for $50 per month. Collected the management fee for the last half of July and the month of August, a month and a half, $75.
12. Paid the secretary's salary for the second two weeks of July, $100.
13. Larry Owen withdrew $200 from the business for his personal use.
14. Paid the monthly telephone bill, $20.
15. Paid for gas and oil used in the agency car, $25.
16. Paid for newspaper advertising that had appeared, $60.

Before a transaction can be recorded, it must be analyzed into its debit and credit elements. The analysis consists of (1) determining what asset, liability, or owner equity items are increased or decreased by the transaction and then (2) applying the rules of debit and credit to determine the debit and credit effects of the increases or decreases. An analysis of each of the following transactions is given in order to demonstrate the process.

1. On July 1 of the current year, Larry Owen invested $5,000 in a real estate agency.

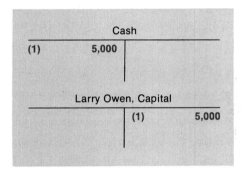

Analysis of the transaction: The transaction increased the agency's cash and at the same time it increased the equity of Owen in the business. Increases in assets are debited, and increases in owner equity are credited. Consequently, Cash should be debited and Larry Owen, Capital should be credited for $5,000.

2. Paid the office rent for three months in advance, $300.

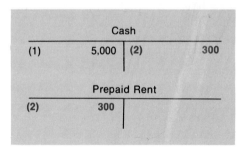

Cash

(1)	5,000	(2)	300

Prepaid Rent

(2)	300		

Analysis of the transaction: The asset prepaid rent, the right to occupy the office for three months, is increased; and the asset cash is decreased. Increases in assets are debited and decreases are credited. Therefore, debit Prepaid Rent and credit Cash for $300.

3. Paid $3,000 for an automobile to be used for business purposes.

Cash

(1)	5,000	(2)	300
		(3)	3,000

Automobile

(3)	3,000		

Analysis of the transaction: The asset automobile is increased, and the asset cash is decreased. Debit Automobile and credit Cash for $3,000.

4. Purchased office equipment for cash, $1,000.

Cash

(1)	5,000	(2)	300
		(3)	3,000
		(4)	1,000

Office Equipment

(4)	1,000		

Analysis of the transaction: The asset office equipment is increased; and the asset cash is decreased. Debit Office Equipment and credit Cash for $1,000.

5. Purchased office equipment, $350, and office supplies, $60, from Standard Supply Company on credit.

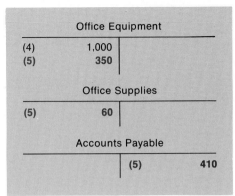

Office Equipment		
(4)	1,000	
(5)	350	

Office Supplies		
(5)	60	

Accounts Payable		
	(5)	410

Analysis of the transaction: This transaction increased the assets office equipment and office supplies; but it also increased the liabilities by granting Standard Supply Company a claim against the business. Increases in assets are debits and increases in liabilities are credits; therefore, debit Office Equipment for $350 and Office Supplies for $60 and credit Accounts Payable for $410.

6. Sold unneeded office equipment to Dale Hall at its $150 cost; $100 in cash and $50 to be paid at a later date.

Cash			
(1)	5,000	(2)	300
(6)	100	(3)	3,000
		(4)	1,000

Accounts Receivable		
(6)	50	

Office Equipment			
(4)	1,000	(6)	150
(5)	350		

Analysis of the transaction: The assets cash and the right to collect from Dale Hall (an account receivable) increased, and the asset office equipment decreased. Debit Cash and Accounts Receivable for the increases and credit Office Equipment for the decrease.

7. Collected $50 from Dale Hall.

Cash			
(1)	5,000	(2)	300
(6)	100	(3)	3,000
(7)	50	(4)	1,000

Accounts Receivable			
(6)	50	(7)	50

Analysis of the transaction: One asset was increased and the other decreased. Debit Cash for $50 to record the increase in cash, and credit Accounts Receivable $50 to record the decrease in the account receivable, or the decrease in the right to collect from Dale Hall.

8. Paid Standard Supply Company $175 of the amount owed.

Cash			
(1)	5,000	(2)	300
(6)	100	(3)	3,000
(7)	50	(4)	1,000
		(8)	175

Accounts Payable			
(8)	175	(5)	410

Analysis of the transaction: Payments to creditors decrease in like amounts both assets and liabilities. Decreases in liabilities are debited, and decreases in assets are credited. Debit Accounts Payable and credit Cash.

9. Sold a house and collected a commission, $850.

Cash			
(1)	5,000	(2)	300
(6)	100	(3)	3,000
(7)	50	(4)	1,000
(9)	850	(8)	175

Commissions Earned			
		(9)	850

Analysis of the transaction: This revenue transaction increased both assets and owner equity. Increases in assets are debits, and increases in owner equity are credits. Therefore, Cash is debited; and in order to show the nature of the increase in owner equity, the owner equity account Commissions Earned is credited.

10. Paid the secretary's salary for the first two weeks in the month, $100.

Cash			
(1)	5,000	(2)	300
(6)	100	(3)	3,000
(7)	50	(4)	1,000
(9)	850	(8)	175
		(10)	100

Office Salaries Expense			
(10)	100		

Analysis of the transaction: The secretary's salary is an expense that decreased both assets and owner equity. Debit the account Office Salaries Expense to show the decrease and the nature of the decrease in owner equity; and credit Cash to show the decrease in the asset.

11. Signed a contract to manage an apartment building for $50 per month and collected the management fee for one and a half months in advance, $75.

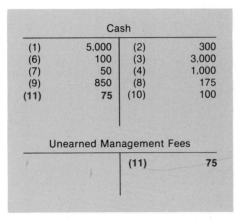

Cash			
(1)	5,000	(2)	300
(6)	100	(3)	3,000
(7)	50	(4)	1,000
(9)	850	(8)	175
(11)	75	(10)	100

Unearned Management Fees			
		(11)	75

Analysis of the transaction: This transaction increased the asset cash and will result in an increase in owner equity as the fee is earned. However, acceptance of the fee in advance of its being earned created a liability for Owen Real Estate Agency, the liability or obligation to manage the apartment building for the next month and a half. Consequently, debit Cash and credit and increase the liability account Unearned Management Fees. (This transaction will be dealt with again in the next chapter.)

12. Paid the secretary's salary for the second two weeks of the month, $100.

Cash			
(1)	5,000	(2)	300
(6)	100	(3)	3,000
(7)	50	(4)	1,000
(9)	850	(8)	175
(11)	75	(10)	100
		(12)	100

Office Salaries Expense			
(10)	100		
(12)	100		

Analysis of the transaction: An expense that decreased assets and owner equity. Debit Office Salaries Expense and credit Cash.

13. Larry Owen withdrew $200 for his personal use.

Cash			
(1)	5,000	(2)	300
(6)	100	(3)	3,000
(7)	50	(4)	1,000
(9)	850	(8)	175
(11)	75	(10)	100
		(12)	100
		(13)	200

Larry Owen, Withdrawals			
(13)	200		

Analysis of the transaction: This transaction reduced in equal amounts both assets and owner equity. However, since the withdrawal is not a salary or an expense, it is debited to the Withdrawals account. Consequently, debit Larry Owen, Withdrawals and credit Cash.

14. Paid the monthly telephone bill, $20.
15. Paid for gas and oil used in the agency car, $25.
16. Paid for newspaper advertising that had appeared, $60.

Cash				Analysis of the transactions: The foregoing expense transactions are alike in that each decreased cash; they differ in each case as to the kind of expense involved. Consequently, in recording them, Cash is credited and a different expense account, one showing the nature of the expense in each case, is debited.
(1)	5,000	(2)	300	
(6)	100	(3)	3,000	
(7)	50	(4)	1,000	
(9)	850	(8)	175	
(11)	75	(10)	100	
		(12)	100	
		(13)	200	
		(14)	20	
		(15)	25	
		(16)	60	

Telephone Expense	
(14)	20

Gas, Oil, and Repairs	
(15)	25

Advertising Expense	
(16)	60

The accounts and the equation

■ In Illustration 2–1 on the opposite page the foregoing transactions of Owen Real Estate Agency are shown in the accounts, with the accounts brought together and classified under the elements of an accounting equation.

Preparing a trial balance

■ As previously stated, in a double-entry accounting system every transaction is recorded with equal debits and credits so that the equality of the debits and credits may be tested as a proof of the recording accuracy. This equality is tested at intervals by preparing a trial balance.

A trial balance is prepared by (1) determining the balance of each account in the ledger, (2) listing in their ledger order the accounts having balances, with the debit balances in one column and the credit balances in another (as in Illustration 2–2), (3) adding the debit balances, (4) adding the credit balances, and then (5) comparing the sum of the debit balances with the sum of the credit balances.

Illustration 2–2 shows a trial balance of the Owen Real Estate Agency ledger. It was prepared from the accounts in Illustration 2–1. Note that its column totals are equal, or in other words, the trial balance is in balance.

Assets	=	Liabilities	+	Owner Equity

Cash

(1)	5,000	(2)	300
(6)	100	(3)	3,000
(7)	50	(4)	1,000
(9)	850	(8)	175
(11)	75	(10)	100
		(12)	100
		(13)	200
		(14)	20
		(15)	25
		(16)	60

Accounts Receivable

(6)	50	(7)	50

Prepaid Rent

(2)	300

Office Supplies

(5)	60

Automobile

(3)	3,000

Office Equipment

(4)	1,000	(6)	150
(5)	350		

Accounts Payable

(8)	175	(5)	410

Unearned Management Fees

		(11)	75

Larry Owen, Capital

		(1)	5,000

Larry Owen, Withdrawals

(13)	200

Commissions Earned

		(9)	850

Office Salaries Expense

(10)	100
(12)	100

Telephone Expense

(14)	20

Gas, Oil, and Repairs

(15)	25

Advertising Expense

(16)	60

Illustration
2–1

Owen Real Estate Agency
Trial Balance, July 31, 19—

Cash	$1,095	
Prepaid rent	300	
Office supplies	60	
Automobile	3,000	
Office equipment	1,200	
Accounts payable		$ 235
Unearned management fees		75
Larry Owen, capital		5,000
Larry Owen, withdrawals	200	
Commissions earned		850
Office salaries expense	200	
Telephone expense	20	
Gas, oil, and repairs	25	
Advertising expense	60	
Totals	$6,160	$6,160

Illustration
2–2

■ If when a trial balance is prepared it does not balance—the two columns are not equal—errors have been made either in recording transactions, in determining the account balances, in copying the balances on the trial balance, or in adding the trial balance columns. On the other hand, if a trial balance balances, it is assumed that no errors have been made. However, a trial balance that balances is not absolute proof of accuracy. Errors may have been made that did not affect the equality of its columns. For example, an error in which a correct debit amount is debited to the wrong account or a correct credit amount is credited to the wrong account will not cause a trial balance to be out of balance. Likewise, an error in which a wrong amount is both debited and credited to the right accounts will not cause a trial balance to be out of balance. Consequently, a trial balance in balance is considered only presumptive proof of recording accuracy.

A standard account form

■ T-accounts like the ones just described are commonly used in teaching and are also commonly used by accountants in solving problems. In either case details are eliminated by their use and the student or accountant can concentrate on ideas. However, such accounts are not used in business for recording transactions. In business, accounts like the one of Illustration 2–3 may be used.

An examination of the Illustration 2–3 account will reveal it is like a T-account in that it has two sides and a place for the name of the item recorded therein. However, it differs in that each side is divided into

Cash   ACCOUNT NO. 1

DATE	EXPLANATION	F.	DEBIT	DATE	EXPLANATION	F.	CREDIT
1972 July 1		1	5 000 00	1972 July 1		1	3 00 00
				3		1	3 00 00
				3		1	1 00 00

Illustration
2–3

columns for recording specific additional information, as indicated by the column headings.

Need for a journal

■ It is possible to record transactions by entering debits and credits directly in the accounts, as was done earlier in this chapter. However, when this is done and an error is made, the error is difficult to locate. It is difficult to locate because even with a transaction having only one debit and one credit, the debit is entered on one ledger page or card and the credit on another, and there is nothing to link the two together.

Consequently, to link together the debits and credits of each transaction and to provide in one place a complete record of each transaction, it is the universal practice in pen-and-ink systems to record all transactions in a *journal* and then to copy the debit and credit information about each transaction from the journal to the ledger accounts.

The linked together debit and credit record of each transaction in a journal is important when errors are made, since the record makes it possible to trace the debits and credits into the accounts and to see that they are equal and properly recorded.

Each transaction entered in a journal is recorded with a separate *journal entry*, and the process of recording transactions in a journal is called *journalizing transactions*. Also, since transactions are recorded in a journal as the first or original step in their recording and their debit and credit information is copied from the journal to the ledger as a second or last step, a journal is called *a book of original entry* and a ledger *a book of final entry*.

The General Journal

■ The simplest and most flexible type of journal is a *General Journal*. It provides for each transaction places for recording (1) the transaction date, (2) the names of the accounts involved, (3) an explanation of the transaction, (4) the account numbers of the accounts to which the transaction's debit and credit information is copied, and (5) the transaction's debit and credit effect on the accounts named. A standard ruling for a general journal page with two of the transactions of Owen Real Estate Agency recorded therein is shown in Illustration 2–4.

GENERAL JOURNAL				PAGE 1
DATE	ACCOUNT TITLES AND EXPLANATION	FO-LIO	DEBIT	CREDIT
1972 July 9	Cash		100.00	
	Accounts Receivable		50.00	
	Office Equipment			150.00
	Sold unneeded office equipment at cost.			
11	Cash		50.00	
	Accounts Receivable			50.00
	In full of amount owed.			

Illustration 2–4

■ To record transactions in a General Journal:

1. The year is written in small figures at the top of the first column.
2. The month is written on the first line in the first column. The year and the month are not repeated except at the top of a new page or at the beginning of a new month or year.
3. The day of each transaction is written in the second column on the first line of the transaction.
4. The names of the accounts to be debited and credited and an explanation of the transaction are written in the Account Titles and Explanation column. The name of the account debited is written first, beginning at the left margin of the column. The name of the account credited is written on the following line, indented about one inch. The explanation is placed on the next line, indented about a half inch from the left margin. The explanation should be short but sufficient to explain the transaction and set it apart from every other transaction.
5. The debit amount is written in the Debit column opposite the name of the account to be debited. The credit amount is written in the Credit column opposite the account to be credited.
6. A single line is skipped between each journal entry to set the entries apart.

At the time transactions are recorded in the General Journal, nothing is entered in the Folio column. However, when the debits and credits are copied from the journal to the ledger, the account numbers of the ledger accounts to which the debits and credits are copied are entered in the Folio column. The use of the Folio column is discussed in more detail later in this chapter.

The first entry in Illustration 2–4 records the sale of unneeded office equipment by Owen Real Estate Agency, and three accounts are involved. When a transaction involves three or more accounts and is recorded with a general journal entry, *a compound entry* is required. A compound entry is one involving three or more accounts.

■ The process of copying journal entry information and transferring it from the journal to the ledger is called *posting*. Normally, near the end of a day all transactions recorded in the journal that day are posted to the ledger. In the posting procedure, journal debits are copied and become ledger account debits and journal credits are copied and become ledger account credits.

The posting procedure for a journal entry is shown in Illustration 2–5, and it may be described as follows. To post a journal entry:

1. Find in the ledger the account named in the debit of the entry to be posted.
2. Enter on the debit side of this account (*a*) the date of the entry as

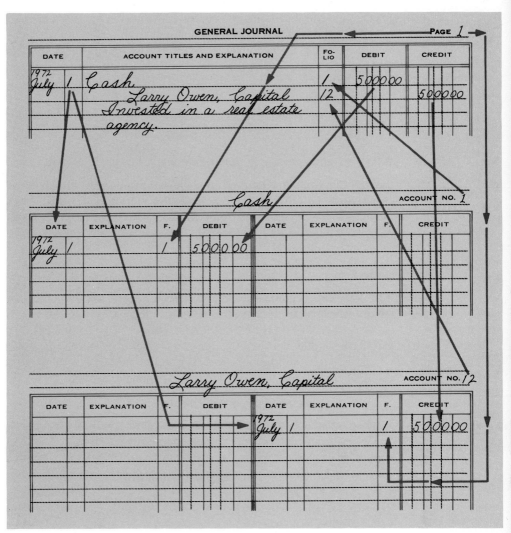

Illustration 2–5

shown in the journal, (b) the page number of the journal from which the entry is being posted, and (c) the debit amount.

3. Enter in the Folio column of the journal the account number of the account to which the amount was posted.

4. Repeat the foregoing steps for the credit of the entry, with the exception that the entry date, journal page number, and credit amount are entered on the credit side of the account.

Observe that the last step (step 3) in the posting procedure for either the debit or the credit of an entry is to insert the account number in the Folio column of the journal. Inserting the account number in the journal Folio column serves two purposes: (1) The account number in the journal and the journal page number in the account act as a cross-reference when it is desired to trace an amount from one record to the other. And, (2) writing the account number in the journal as a last step in posting indicates that posting is completed. If posting is interrupted, the bookkeeper, by examining the journal Folio column, can easily see where posting stopped.

Account numbers and journal page numbers are often called *posting reference numbers*. The reason for this is obvious.

Book-keeping techniques

■ Periods and commas in dollar amounts

When amounts are entered in a journal or a ledger, commas to indicate thousands of dollars and periods to separate dollars and cents are not necessary because the ruled lines accomplish this purpose. However, when statements are prepared on unruled paper, the periods and commas are necessary.

Dollar signs

Dollar signs are not used in journals or ledgers, but they are required on the financial reports prepared on unruled paper. On the reports, a dollar sign is placed (1) before the first amount in each column of figures and (2) before the first amount appearing after a ruled line that indicates an addition or a subtraction. Reexamine Illustration 1–8 on page 14 for examples of the use of dollar signs on a financial report.

Omission of zeros in the cents columns

When an amount to be entered in a ledger or a journal is an amount of dollars and no cents, some bookkeepers will use a dash in the cents column in the place of two zeros to indicate that there are no cents. They feel that the dash is easier and more quickly made than the two zeros. This is a matter of choice in journal and ledger entries. However, on financial reports the two zeros are preferred because they are neater in appearance.

Often in this text, where space is limited, exact dollar amounts are used in order to save space. Obviously, in such cases, neither zeros nor dashes are used to show that there are no cents involved.

Questions for class discussion

1. What is an account? What is a ledger?
2. What determines the number of accounts a business will use?
3. What are the meanings of the following words and terms: (1) debit, (2) to debit, (3) credit, and (4) to credit?
4. If increases in assets were recorded as credits rather than as debits, how would increases in liabilities and owner equity be recorded? Why?
5. Does debit always mean increase and credit always mean decrease?

6. A transaction is to be entered in the accounts. How do you determine the accounts in which amounts are to be entered? How do you determine whether a particular account is to be debited or credited?

7. Why is a double-entry accounting system so called?

8. An accounting student in his first lessons confused the words "debit" and "credit." He consistently recorded debits on the right side of accounts and credits on the left side. What difficulty, if any, did he experience in recording transactions and preparing a trial balance? Would you recommend that he change his procedure? Why?

9. Give the rules of debit and credit for (1) asset accounts and (2) liability and owner equity accounts.

10. Why is the rule of debit and credit the same for both liability and owner equity accounts?

11. List the steps in the preparation of a trial balance.

12. What is the reason for preparing a trial balance?

13. Why is the trial balance considered to be only presumptive proof of recording accuracy? What types of errors are not revealed by a trial balance?

14. Is it possible to record transactions directly in the ledger accounts? What is gained by first recording transactions in a journal and then posting to the accounts?

15. In recording transactions in a journal, which is written first, the debit or the credit? How far is the name of the account credited indented? How far is the explanation indented?

16. What is a compound entry?

17. Are dollar signs used in journal entries? In the accounts?

18. If a period is not used in a journal debit to separate dollars from cents, what accomplishes this purpose?

19. Define or describe each of the following:

   a) Journal.
   b) Ledger.
   c) Book of original entry.
   d) Book of final entry.
   e) Folio column.
   f) Posting.
   g) Footing.
   h) Posting reference numbers.

20. Entering in the Folio column of the journal the account number to which an amount was posted is the last step in posting the amount. What is gained by making this the last step?

Class exercises

Exercise 2–1

Place the following T-accounts on a sheet of ordinary notebook paper: Cash; Accounts Receivable; Shop Supplies; Shop Equipment; Accounts Payable; Roger Ross, Capital; Revenue from Repairs; and Rent Expense. Then record the following transactions by entering debits and credits directly in the T-accounts. Use the transaction letters to identify the amounts in the accounts.

a) Roger Ross opened a TV repair shop, called Ross TV Service, by investing $800 in the business.

b) Paid the rent for one month on the shop space, $100.

c) Purchased shop supplies for cash, $50.

d) Purchased shop supplies, $75, and shop equipment, $200, on credit from Electronics, Inc.

e) Repaired the TV set of Jim Martti and collected $40 for the service.

f) Paid Electronics, Inc., $200 of the amount owed it.

g) Repaired the TV set of Don Parker on credit, $50.

h) Purchased additional shop equipment on credit from Electronics, Inc., $60.

i) Don Parker paid for the repair work of Transaction (g).

Exercise 2-2

After recording the transactions of Exercise 2-1, prepare a trial balance for Ross TV Service. Use the current date.

Exercise 2-3

A careless bookkeeper prepared the following trial balance for Small Repairs Service. It does not balance, and you have been asked to prepare a corrected trial balance. In examining the concern's journal and ledger you discover the following: (1) The debits to the Cash account total $7,625 and the credits total $5,125. (2) A $100 receipt from a customer in payment of his account was not posted to the Accounts Receivable account. (3) A $50 payment to a creditor was entered in the journal but was not posted to any account. (4) The first two digits in the balance of the Revenue from Services account, as shown on the trial balance prepared by the bookkeeper, were transposed in copying the account balance from the ledger to the trial balance.

SMALL REPAIRS SERVICE
Trial Balance, August 31, 19—

Cash		$2,600
Accounts receivable	$3,400	
Office supplies		150
Office equipment	1,600	
Accounts payable	450	
Wages payable	100	
Gary Moxley, capital	2,650	
Revenue from services		6,500
Rent expense	1,200	
Advertising expense		50
Totals	$9,400	$9,300

Exercise 2-4

On a sheet of ordinary notebook paper rule a general journal form like in Illustration 2-4 in your text. After completing the form, record the following transactions in the journal.

Oct. 3 James Carr invested $1,000 in cash and tools having a $600 fair market value in a new business.

5 Purchased additional tools for cash, $200.

Exercise 2-5

Prepare a form on notebook paper having the following three column headings: (1) Error, (2) Amount Out of Balance, and (3) Column Having Larger Total. Then for each of the following errors: (1) list the error by letter in the first column, (2) tell the amount it will cause the trial balance to be out of balance in the second column, and (3) tell in the third column which trial balance column will have the larger total as a result of the error. If an error does not affect the trial balance, write "none" in each of the last two columns.

a) A $25 debit to the Cash account was not posted.

b) A $50 debit to Store Supplies was debited to Store Equipment.

c) A $40 debit to Salaries Expense was debited to the account twice.

d) A $20 debit to Office Supplies was debited to Revenue from Sales.

e) A $45 credit to Accounts Payable was posted as a $54 credit.

f) A $10 debit to Office Supplies was posted as a $100 debit.

Problems   **Problem 2–1**

a) Barry Nash opened an air-conditioning service and repair shop and began business by investing $1,000 in cash and the following additional assets: office equipment, $350; tools, $500; and truck, $1,200. He called his business Coolair Service Company, and during a short period completed the following transactions:

b) Paid the rent for three months in advance on the shop space, $300.

c) Purchased $150 of repair supplies on credit from Tri-City Supply Company.

d) Traded a typewriter carried in the accounting records at $50 for additional tools.

e) Purchased for cash a new typewriter to replace the one traded, $160.

f) Paid for radio advertising announcing the opening of the shop, $35.

g) Completed repair work for George Thomas and received $60 cash in full payment therefor.

h) Completed repair work for Ralph Sims, $175. Accepted $100 in cash and a promise to pay the balance within a short period.

i) Completed repair work for Walter Rice on credit, $85.

j) Ralph Sims paid the amount owed from Transaction (h).

k) Paid Tri-City Supply Company one half the amount owed to it.

l) Paid the utility bills, $15.

m) Mr. Nash withdrew $100 from the cash of the business to be used for personal living expenses.

Required:

1. Set up the following T-accounts: Cash; Accounts Receivable; Repair Supplies; Prepaid Rent; Office Equipment; Tools; Truck; Accounts Payable; Barry Nash, Capital; Barry Nash, Withdrawals; Revenue from Repairs; Advertising Expense; and Utilities Expense.

2. Record the transactions by entering debits and credits directly in the T-accounts. Use the transaction letters to identify each debit and credit amount.

3. Prepare a trial balance using the current date.

Problem 2–2

Kent Sims has just begun the operation of a cleaning and pressing business. During the past few days he completed the following transactions:

Oct. 1 Sold 100 shares of personally owned General Electric Company stock for $9,500 and deposited $9,000 of the proceeds in a checking account opened in the name of his business, Ideal Cleaners.

2 Paid the rent for three months in advance on the cleaning plant building, $600.

2 Purchased $7,500 of cleaning equipment, giving $5,000 in cash and a $2,500 promissory note.

3 Purchased $150 of cleaning supplies and $650 of additional cleaning equipment from Cortez Supply Company on credit.

4 Delivered cleaning to customers and collected cash in full payment therefor, $110.

4 Delivered cleaning to Modern Motel on credit, $50.

5 Paid the wages of the employees, $200.

5 Paid Cortez Supply Company $500 of the amount owed to it.

6 Modern Motel paid the $50 it owed.

Required:

1. Open the following accounts: Cash; Accounts Receivable; Cleaning Supplies; Prepaid Rent; Cleaning Equipment; Notes Payable; Accounts Payable; Kent Sims, Capital; Revenue from Cleaning; and Wages Expense.

2. Prepare general journal entries to record the transactions; post to the accounts; and prepare a trial balance as of October 6.

Problem 2–3

Thomas Howe owns and operates Cactus Realty, and on September 1, 19—, a trial balance of the concern's ledger appeared as follows:

CACTUS REALTY
Trial Balance, September 1, 19—

Cash	$ 1,190	
Office supplies	145	
Office equipment	2,465	
Automobile	2,700	
Land	5,000	
Building	22,000	
Mortgage payable		$20,000
Thomas Howe, capital		13,500
Totals	$33,500	$33,500

During September Mr. Howe completed the following transactions:

a) Purchased $50 of office supplies and $150 of office equipment from Valley Supply Company on credit.

b) Sold a house and collected a $1,250 commission from the sale.

c) Paid Valley Supply Company the amount owed to it.

d) Sent a $75 check to the local newspaper in payment for advertising that had appeared.

e) Purchased a typewriter from Valley Supply Company on credit, $225.

f) Mr. Howe took the old company typewriter, carried in the accounting records at $75, home for permanent use of his high school children as a practice typewriter.

g) Sold a house and collected a $950 commission from the sale.
h) Completed property management services for George Ruston on credit and billed him for the work done, $100.
i) Mr. Howe withdrew $400 from the company bank account to pay personal living expenses.
j) Received payment in full from George Ruston for the services billed in Transaction (h).
k) Paid the salary of the office clerk, $250.
l) Gave $1,000 in cash and the old company car for a new company car.
m) Sent a $50 check to the local newspaper for advertising that had appeared.
n) Paid the telephone bill, $35.

Required:
1. Open the following T-accounts: Cash; Accounts Receivable; Office Supplies; Office Equipment; Automobile; Land; Building; Accounts Payable; Mortgage Payable; Thomas Howe, Capital; Thomas Howe, Withdrawals; Commissions Earned; Property Management Fees; Advertising Expense; Salaries Expense; Telephone Expense.
2. Enter the September 1 trial balance amounts in the accounts, identifying each amount by writing the abbreviation "Bal." before it.
3. Record the transactions by entering debits and credits directly in the T-accounts. Use the transaction letters to identify each debit and credit amount.
4. Prepare a September 30 trial balance.

Problem 2–4

Neal Able, a young lawyer, completed the following transactions during October of the current year:

Oct. 1 Began the practice of law by investing $1,200 in cash and a law library having a fair value of $800.
1 Paid two months' rent in advance on suitable office space, $200.
2 Purchased $1,200 of office equipment, paying $200 in cash and giving a promissory note payable for the balance.
3 Purchased $45 of office supplies and $175 of office equipment from Office Supply Company on credit.
6 Completed legal work for James Mohr and collected $50 in full payment therefor.
10 Paid insurance premiums totaling $95 on several policies taken out in the name of the practice.
15 Completed legal work for First State Bank on credit and billed it $300 for the work done.
15 Paid the salary of the part-time legal secretary, $150.
18 Paid Office Supply Company for the items purchased from it on October 3.
25 Received a $300 check from First State Bank for the legal work completed on October 15.
28 Neal Able withdrew $200 from the bank account of the law practice to be used for personal expenses.
30 Billed First State Bank for additional legal work completed on credit, $150.
31 Paid the legal secretary's salary, $150.

Oct. 31   Paid $5 interest expense and a $100 installment due on the note payable.

31   Paid the monthly utility bills, $25.

Required:

1. Open the following accounts: Cash; Accounts Receivable; Prepaid Rent; Office Supplies; Prepaid Insurance; Office Equipment; Legal Library; Notes Payable; Accounts Payable; Neal Able, Capital; Neal Able, Withdrawals; Revenue from Law Practice; Salaries Expense; Utilities Expense; and Interest Expense.
2. Prepare general journal entries to record the transactions, post to the accounts, and prepare a trial balance under the name of Neal Able, Attorney.

Problem 2–5

On October 1 George Hunter began a business he called Modern Cabinet Shop, and he completed the following transactions during the month:

Oct.   1   Cashed three mature United States savings bonds and deposited the $3,000 proceeds in a checking account of the shop.

2   Paid $180 for three months' rent in advance on the shop building.

3   Purchased $2,500 of shop machinery, giving $1,000 in cash and a promissory note payable for the balance.

5   Purchased $1,500 of shop supplies from Northside Planing Mill on credit.

9   Collected cash on delivery of $350 of cabinet work to Ralph Watson.

13   Completed and delivered cabinet work to David McKeen on credit, $400.

15   Paid the wages of the shop workmen, $325.

15   Paid Red Ball Delivery Service $35 for delivery services rendered during the first half of the month.

18   Paid Northside Planing Mill $750 of the amount owed to it.

20   George Hunter took $40 of shop supplies home for use in repairing his carport.

23   Received a $400 check from David McKeen for the cabinet work delivered on October 13.

25   George Hunter withdrew $150 from the business to be used for his personal living expenses.

28   Collected cash on the delivery of $450 of cabinet work.

31   Paid Red Ball Delivery Service $25 for cabinet work delivered by the company during the last half of the month.

31   Paid the wages of the shop workmen, $300.

31   Paid the light and power bill, $40.

Required:

1. Open the following accounts: Cash; Accounts Receivable; Prepaid Rent; Shop Supplies; Shop Machinery; Notes Payable; Accounts Payable; George Hunter, Capital; George Hunter, Withdrawals; Revenue from Cabinet Work; Delivery Expense; Wages Expense; and Light and Power Expense.
2. Prepare general journal entries to record the transactions, post to the accounts, and prepare a trial balance.

Problem 2–1A

a) Barry Nash opened a television repair shop and began business by investing $1,200 in cash and the following assets: repair supplies, $450; tools, $300; and truck, $200. He called his business Ready TV Service, and during a short period completed the following transactions:

b) Paid $25 for newspaper advertising announcing the opening of the shop.

c) Paid the rent for two months in advance on the shop space, $200.

d) Purchased a desk, chair, and filing cabinet from Tri-City Supply Company on credit, $175.

e) Traded the old truck for additional tools.

f) Purchased for cash a secondhand truck to replace the one traded, $750.

g) Completed repair work for Walter Ruston and received $50 in full payment therefor.

h) Completed repair work for Walter Rice on credit, $75.

i) Completed repair work for Ralph Sims, $125. Accepted $80 in cash and a promise to pay the balance in few days.

j) Paid Tri-City Supply Company $100 of the amount owed to it.

k) Ralph Sims paid the amount he owed.

l) Paid the utility bills, $20.

m) Mr. Nash wrote a $65 check on the bank account of the business in payment of a personal expense.

Required:

1. Set up the following T-accounts: Cash; Accounts Receivable; Repair Supplies; Prepaid Rent; Office Equipment; Tools; Truck; Accounts Payable; Barry Nash, Capital; Barry Nash, Withdrawals; Revenue from Repairs; Advertising Expense; and Utilities Expense.

2. Record the transactions by entering debits and credits directly in the T-accounts. Use the transaction letters to identify each debit and credit amount.

3. Prepare a trial balance using the current date.

Problem 2–2A

Kent Sims has just begun operating a cleaning and pressing plant he calls De Luxe Cleaners. During the first week in operation he completed the following transactions:

Sept. 21   Sold 100 personally owned shares of General Motors stock for $8,750 and deposited $8,500 of the proceeds in a checking account opened in the company name.

21   Purchased $8,000 of cleaning equipment, giving $6,000 in cash and a $2,000 promissory note payable.

21   Paid the rent for two months in advance on the cleaning plant building, $300.

22   Purchased $350 of additional cleaning equipment and $200 of cleaning supplies from Cortez Supply Company on credit.

23   Delivered $175 of cleaning to customers for cash.

24   Delivered $25 of cleaning to Modern Motel on credit.

Sept. 26 Paid Cortez Supply Company $300 of the amount which was owed to it.

26 Collected the $25 owed by Modern Motel.

27 Paid the wages of the employees, $150.

Required:

1. Open the following accounts: Cash; Accounts Receivable; Cleaning Supplies; Prepaid Rent; Cleaning Equipment; Notes Payable; Accounts Payable; Kent Sims, Capital; Revenue from Cleaning; and Wages Expense.
2. Prepare general journal entries to record the transactions; post to the accounts; and prepare a trial balance as of September 27.

Problem 2–3A

Thomas Howe began a real estate agency called Apex Realty Company, and during a short period completed the following transactions:

a) Began business by investing $10,000.
b) Purchased the small office building and office equipment of Cactus Realty Company, consisting of office equipment, $2,000; building, $12,000; and land, $4,000. Gave $8,000 in cash and signed a mortgage contract agreeing to pay the balance over a period of years.
c) Took his personal automobile, which had a fair market value of $2,500, for permanent and exclusive use in the business.
d) Earned and collected a $1,300 commission from the sale of a house.
e) Purchased $75 of office supplies and $250 additional office equipment from Valley Supply Company on credit.
f) Paid the salary of the office clerk, $110.
g) Completed property management services for George Ruston on credit and billed him for the services performed, $60.
h) Paid Valley Supply Company the amount owed to it.
i) Received $60 from George Ruston in payment for the services billed in Transaction (*g*).
j) Purchased $65 of office supplies from Valley Supply Company on credit.
k) Earned and collected a $750 commission from the sale of property.
l) Paid the salary of the office clerk, $110.
m) Paid for newspaper advertising that had appeared, $85.
n) Paid the telephone bill, $25.
o) Mr. Howe wrote a check on the bank account of the realty company in payment of a personal expense, $250.

Required:

1. Open the following T-accounts: Cash; Accounts Receivable; Office Supplies; Office Equipment; Automobile; Land; Building; Accounts Payable; Mortgage Payable; Thomas Howe, Capital; Thomas Howe, Withdrawals; Commissions Earned; Property Management Fees; Advertising Expense, Salaries Expense; and Telephone Expense.
2. Record the transactions by entering debits and credits directly in the T-accounts. Use the transaction letters to identify each debit and credit amount.
3. Prepare a trial balance.

Problem 2–4A

Neal Able began the practice of law and completed the following transactions during September of the current year:

Sept. 1 Began the practice of law by investing the legal library acquired during his college years. The library had a fair value of $500.

2 Sold 50 shares of Republic Steel stock for $1,350 and deposited $1,250 of the proceeds in a bank account opened in the name of the law firm, Neal Able, Attorney.

2 Rented office space, paying $300, the first three months' rent in advance.

2 Purchased $1,500 of office equipment, paying $300 in cash and signing a promissory note payable for the balance.

3 Paid the premiums on several insurance policies taken out in the name of the law practice, $85.

5 Purchased $55 of office supplies and $115 of office equipment from Office Supply Company on credit.

8 Completed legal work for John Morehead and collected $150 in full payment therefor.

12 Completed legal work for First State Bank on credit and billed it $250 for the work done.

15 Paid the salary of the part-time legal secretary, $120.

15 Paid Office Supply Company for the items purchased on September 5.

22 Received $250 from First State Bank in payment for the legal work billed on September 12.

27 Neal Able wrote a $150 check on the bank account of the law practice in payment of the rent on his apartment.

30 Billed First State Bank for additional legal work completed on credit, $100.

30 Paid $5 interest and a $150 installment due on the note payable of the third September 2 transaction.

30 Paid the legal secretary's salary, $120.

30 Paid the utility bills of the month, $20.

Required:

1. Open the following accounts: Cash; Accounts Receivable; Prepaid Rent; Office Supplies; Prepaid Insurance; Office Equipment; Legal Library; Notes Payable; Accounts Payable; Neal Able, Capital; Neal Able, Withdrawals; Revenue from Law Practice; Salaries Expense; Utilities Expense; and Interest Expense.

2. Prepare general journal entries to record the transactions, post to the accounts, and prepare a trial balance in the name of Neal Able, Attorney.

Problem 2–5A

During October George Hunter began a small business that he called A-1 Cabinet Shop, and during the month he completed the following transactions:

Oct. 1 Withdrew $4,000 from his personal savings account and deposited it in a checking account opened in the name of A-1 Cabinet Shop.

1 Paid $1,200 in cash for new shop machinery.

2 Rented a shop building, paying three months' rent in advance, $195.

Oct. 3 Purchased $800 of shop supplies from Northside Planing Mill on credit.

5 Bought $1,500 of additional shop machinery, giving $750 in cash and a promissory note payable for the balance.

8 Delivered $350 of cabinet work to a customer and collected cash on delivery.

10 Mr. Hunter took $50 of shop supplies home for use in repairing his carport.

13 Completed and delivered cabinet work to Gary Keen on credit, $450.

15 Paid the employees' wages for the first half of the month, $340.

18 Sent Northside Planing Mill a check in full payment for the supplies purchased on October 3.

23 Received a $200 check in partial payment for the cabinet work delivered to David McKeen on October 13.

25 Collected $400 for cabinet work delivered to Robert Shell today.

28 Mr. Hunter withdrew $150 from the business to be used to pay certain of his personal living expenses.

31 Paid Motor Delivery Service $45 for delivery services rendered during October.

31 Paid the light and power bill, $50.

31 Paid the wages of the employees for the last half of the month, $350.

Required:

1. Open the following accounts, numbering them beginning with 1: Cash; Accounts Receivable; Prepaid Rent; Shop Supplies; Shop Machinery; Notes Payable; Accounts Payable; George Hunter, Capital; George Hunter, Withdrawals; Revenue from Cabinet Work; Delivery Expense; Wages Expense; and Light and Power Expense.

2. Prepare general journal entries to record the transactions, post to the accounts, and prepare a trial balance.

Decision problem 2–1, The Dock
Ted Moss has just completed the first summer's operation of The Dock, a concession on a lake at which he rents boats and sells sandwiches, soft drinks, and candy. He began the summer's operations with $1,800 in cash and a five-year lease on a boat dock and small building on the lake. The lease calls for a $600 annual rental, although the concession is open only from May 15 to September 15. On opening day Mr. Moss paid the first year's rent and also purchased six boats at $150 each, paying cash. He estimated the boats would have a five-year life, after which he could sell them for $25 each.

During the summer he purchased food, soft drinks, and candy costing $3,250, all of which was paid for by the summer's end, excepting food costing $75 which was purchased during the last week's operations. He also paid electric bills, $65, and the wages of a part-time helper, $750, and he withdrew $100 each week, 17 weeks, from the cash of the concession to pay his personal living expenses.

He took in $1,430 in boat rentals during the summer and sold $7,570 of food and drinks, all of which was collected in cash, except $100 he had not collected from Small Company for supplying food and drinks for an employees' party.

When he closed for the summer, he was able to return to the soft drink company several cases of soft drinks for which he received a $40 cash refund. However, he had to take home for consumption by his family a number of candy bars and some hamburger and buns which cost $15 and could have been sold for $25.

Prepare an income statement for The Dock showing revenues, expenses, and net income for the summer. Also, prepare a balance sheet showing assets, liabilities, and owner equity as of September 15, the summer's end. (T-accounts may prove helpful in organizing the summer's transactions of The Dock.)

Decision problem 2–2, The Hobby Shop

Several weeks ago Jerry Peek opened a new business called The Hobby Shop, for which he decided to keep the accounting records himself. He has now recorded some one hundred transactions, prepared a trial balance that will not balance, and has come to you for help. You learn that some years ago Jerry took the beginning course in accounting while in college, but over the years the exact procedural details seem to have slipped away. When he began the records for his shop, he did remember that accounts had an increases side and a decreases side, but he could not remember which was which nor why. So, having learned to read from left to right, he decided to make the left sides of all accounts the increases sides and the right sides the decreases sides. Also he dimly recalled that revenues increased and expenses decreased owner equity, so he decided to record revenues and expenses directly in his Capital account. And finally, he decided to dispense with a journal and to enter transactions directly in the accounts and thus avoid writing much the same thing in both a journal and the ledger.

Tell Jerry Peek which side of each kind of account is the increases side and which is the decreases side. Explain why increases in assets are recorded on one side of asset accounts, while increases in liability and owner equity items must be recorded on the opposite side of liability and owner equity accounts. Also, explain the purpose of the journal record to Mr. Peek and list the changes you would make in his accounting procedures, telling why you would make each change.

Chapter 3

Adjusting the accounts and preparing the statements

■ The life of a business normally spans a long interval of time, which for accounting purposes is divided into units of equal length, called *accounting periods*. Accounting periods may be any length, such as monthly periods or quarterly periods, but accounting periods one year in length are the most common.

At the end of each accounting period in the life of a business, financial reports are prepared to show the success of the business during the period and its financial position at the period end. These reports always include an income statement and a balance sheet. Both are prepared primarily from information accumulated in the accounts of the business.

Need for adjustments before the statements are prepared ■ An income statement prepared at the end of an accounting period should reflect as nearly as they can be measured the revenues realized during the period and the amount of each expense incurred in realizing the revenues. Likewise, a balance sheet prepared at that time should show as fairly measured as possible the amounts of the various assets, liabilities, and the owner's equity.

Occasionally, at the end of a period, statements reflecting proper amounts may be prepared directly from the accounts just as soon as all transactions are recorded. However, this is unusual. Normally, several

59

account balances as they appear on the end-of-the-period trial balance do not show proper statement amounts because of the expiration of costs brought about by the passage of time. For example, the second item on the trial balance of Owen Real Estate Agency, as prepared

Owen Real Estate Agency
Trial Balance, July 31, 19—

Cash	$1,095	
Prepaid rent	300	
Office supplies	60	
Automobile	3,000	
Office equipment	1,200	
Accounts payable		$ 235
Unearned management fees		75
Larry Owen, capital		5,000
Larry Owen, withdrawals	200	
Commissions earned		850
Office salaries expense	200	
Telephone expense	20	
Gas, oil, and repairs	25	
Advertising expense	60	
Totals	$6,160	$6,160

Illustration
3–1

first in Chapter 2 and reproduced again as Illustration 3–1, is "Prepaid rent, $300." This $300 represents the rent for three months paid in advance on July 1. On July 31, $300 is not the balance sheet amount for this asset because one month's rent, or $100, has expired and become an expense and only $200 remains as an asset. Likewise, a portion of the office supplies as represented by the $60 debit balance in the Office Supplies account has been used, and the automobile and office equipment have begun to wear out and depreciate. Obviously, then, the end-of-the-period balances of the Prepaid Rent, Office Supplies, Automobile, and Office Equipment accounts as they appear on the trial balance simply do not reflect the proper amounts for preparing the July 31 statements. The balance of each and also the balances of the Office Salaries Expense and Management Fees Earned accounts must be *adjusted* before they will show proper amounts for the July 31 statements.

Adjusting the accounts

■ **Prepaid expenses**

As the name implies, a prepaid expense is an expense that has been paid for in advance of its use. At the time of payment an asset is acquired that will be used or consumed and as it is used or consumed, it will become an expense. For example:

On July 1 Owen Real Estate Agency paid three months' rent in advance and thus obtained the right to occupy a rented office for the following three months. On July 1 this right was an asset valued at its $300 cost; but day by day the agency occupied the office; and each day a portion of the prepaid rent expired and became an expense. On July 31 one month's rent, valued at one third of $300, or $100, had expired. Consequently, if the agency's July 31 accounts are to reflect proper asset and expense amounts, the following adjusting entry is required:

July	31	Rent Expense	100.00	
		Prepaid Rent		100.00
		To record the expired rent.		

Posting the adjusting entry has the following effect on the accounts:

Prepaid Rent				Rent Expense		
July 1	300	July 31	100	July 31	100	

After the entry is posted, the Prepaid Rent account with a $200 balance and the Rent Expense account with a $100 balance show proper statement amounts.

To continue, early in July, Owen Real Estate Agency purchased some office supplies and placed them in the office for use; and each day the secretary used a portion. The amount used or consumed each day was an expense that daily reduced the assets and Owen's equity. However, the daily reductions were not recognized in the accounts because day-by-day information as to amounts used and remaining was not needed and because bookkeeping labor could be saved if only a single amount, the total used during the entire month, was recorded.

Consequently, if on July 31 the accounts are to reflect proper statement amounts, it is necessary to record the office supplies used during the month. However, to do this, it is first necessary to learn the amount used; and to learn the amount used, it is necessary to count or inventory the unused supplies remaining and to deduct the amount remaining from the amount purchased. If, for example, $45 of unused supplies remain on hand in the office, then $15 ($60 − $45 = $15) of supplies have been used, and the following entry is required to record the supplies used:

July	31	Office Supplies Used	15.00	
		Office Supplies		15.00
		To record the supplies used.		

The effect of the foregoing adjusting entry on the accounts is:

Office Supplies				Office Supplies Used	
July 5	60	July 31	15	July 31	15

Often, unlike in the two previous examples, items that are prepaid expenses at the time of purchase are both bought and fully consumed within a single accounting period. For example, a company pays its rent in advance on the first day of each month. Each month the amount paid results in a prepaid expense that is entirely consumed before the month's end and before the end of the accounting period. In such cases, it is best to ignore the fact that an asset results from each prepayment. In such cases bookkeeping labor, an end-of-the-accounting-period adjustment, can be saved if each amount paid is recorded as an expense at the time of payment.

Other prepaid expenses that are handled in the same manner as prepaid rent and office supplies are prepaid insurance, store supplies, and factory supplies.

Depreciation

When a business buys a building or an item of equipment, it in effect buys a "quantity of usefulness"; and day by day as the asset is used in carrying on the business operations, a portion of this "quantity of usefulness" is consumed or expires. In accounting, this expiration of a plant asset's "quantity of usefulness" is known as *depreciation.*

Depreciation is an expense just like the expiration of prepaid rent is an expense. For example, if a company purchases and installs a machine at a total cost of $1,200 and the machine is expected to be worn out and valueless at the end of 10 years, the company has purchased a $1,200 quantity of usefulness that on a straight-line basis expires and becomes an expense at the rate of $120 per year ($1,200 ÷ 10 = $120). Actually, the primary difference between depreciation and the expiration of a prepaid expense like rent or insurance is that since it is often impossible to determine in advance just how long a plant asset will last, the amount it depreciates each accounting period is commonly only an estimate.

Estimating and apportioning depreciation can be simple, as in the foregoing example, or it can become complex. A discussion of more complex situations is unnecessary at this point and is deferred to Chapter 11. However, to illustrate the recording of depreciation, assume that —

On July 31 Owen Real Estate Agency estimated its automobile had depreciated $35 and its office equipment $10 during July. In both cases the depreciation reduced the assets and increased expenses. To record the depreciation the following adjusting entries are required:

July	31	Depreciation Expense, Automobile...................	35.00	
		Accumulated Depreciation, Automobile		35.00
		To record the July depreciation.		
	31	Depreciation Expense, Office Equipment..........	10.00	
		Accumulated Depreciation, Office Equipment..		10.00
		To record the July depreciation.		

The effect of the entries on the accounts is:

Automobile			Depreciation Expense, Automobile		
July 3	3,000		July 31	35	

Accumulated Depreciation, Automobile					
		July 31	35		

Office Equipment				Depreciation Expense, Office Equipment	
July 3	1,000	July 9	150	July 31	10
5	350				

Accumulated Depreciation, Office Equipment					
		July 31	10		

Carefully observe the accumulated depreciation accounts in the example just given. Normally, a decrease in an asset is recorded with a credit to the account in which the asset is recorded. However, note in the accounts just shown that this procedure is not followed in recording depreciation. Rather, depreciation is recorded in *contra accounts* such as the Accumulated Depreciation, Automobile and the Accumulated Depreciation, Office Equipment accounts. (A contra account is an account the balance of which is subtracted from the balance of an associate account to show a more proper amount for the items recorded in the associated account.)

There are two good reasons for using contra accounts in recording depreciation. First, at its best, depreciation is only an estimate; and, second, the use of contra accounts better preserves the facts in the lives of plant assets. For example, in this case the asset account, Automobile, preserves in the accounts a record of the auto's historical cost, and the Accumulated Depreciation, Automobile account shows its accumulated depreciation to date.

A better understanding of the latter point, along with an appreciation of why the word "accumulated" is used in the account name, can be gained when it is pointed out that depreciation is recorded at the end of each accounting period in a plant asset's life. As a result, at the end of the fourth month in the life of Owen Real Estate Agency's automobile, the Automobile account and its related accumulated depreciation account will look like this:

Automobile		Accumulated Depreciation, Automobile	
July 3	3,000	July 31	35
		Aug. 31	35
		Sept. 30	35
		Oct. 31	35

And the automobile's cost and four months' accumulated depreciation will be shown on the agency's October 31 balance sheet thus:

Automobile	$3,000	
Less accumulated depreciation	140	$2,860

Accumulated depreciation accounts are sometimes found in ledgers and on statements under titles such as "Allowance for Depreciation, Store Equipment" or the totally unacceptable caption, "Reserve for Depreciation, Office Equipment." However, newer terminology is "Accumulated Depreciation, Store Equipment" and "Accumulated Depreciation, Office Equipment." The newer terminology is better because it is more descriptive.

Accrued expenses

Most expenses are recorded during an accounting period at the time they are paid. However, when a period ends there may be a few expenses that have been incurred but have not been paid and recorded because payment is not yet due. These unpaid and unrecorded expenses for which payment is not due are called *accrued expenses*. Earned but unpaid salaries and wages are a common example. To illustrate:

Owen Real Estate Agency has a secretary who is paid $10 per day or $50 per week for a five-day week that begins on Monday and ends on Friday. Her wages are due and payable every two weeks on Friday night; and during July they were paid on the 12th and 26th and recorded as follows:

Cash			Office Salaries Expense		
	July 12	100	July 12	100	
	26	100	26	100	

If the calendar for July appears as illustrated and the secretary worked on Monday, Tuesday, and Wednesday, July 29, 30, and 31, then at the close of business on Wednesday, July 31, she has earned three days' wages that are not paid and recorded because they are not yet due. However, this $30 of earned but unpaid wages is just as much a part of the July expenses as the $200 of wages that have been paid. Furthermore, on July 31, the unpaid wages are a liability. Consequently, if the agency's accounts are to show the correct amount of secretary's wages for July and all liabilities owed on July 31, then an adjusting entry like the following must be made:

JULY						
S	M	T	W	T	F	S
	1	2	3	4	5	6
7	8	9	10	11	12	13
14	15	16	17	18	19	20
21	22	23	24	25	26	27
28	29	30	31			

July	31	Office Salaries Expense	30.00	
		Salaries Payable..		30.00
		To record the earned but unpaid wages.		

The effect of the entry on the accounts is:

Office Salaries Expense			Salaries Payable	
July 12	100			July 31	30
26	100			
31	30			

Unearned revenues

An unearned revenue results when payment is received for goods or services in advance of their delivery. For instance, on July 16 Owen Real Estate Agency entered into an agreement to manage an apartment building for a $50 monthly fee, and on that date received $75 in advance for its services for the remainder of July and the month of August, which it recorded as follows:

July	16	Cash...	75.00	
		Unearned Management Fees		75.00
		Received a $75 management fee in advance.		

Acceptance of the fee in advance increased the agency's cash and created for it a liability, the obligation to manage the apartment building for the next month and a half. However, by managing the building July 16 through the 31st, the agency discharged $25 of the liability and earned that much revenue. Consequently, on July 31 the following entry is required to make the accounts show the proper statement amounts:

July	31	Unearned Management Fees............................	25.00	
		Management Fees Earned.........................		25.00
		To record the fees earned.		

Posting the entry has this effect on the accounts:

Unearned Management Fees				Management Fees Earned		
July 31	25	July 16	75		July 31	25

The effect of posting the foregoing entry is to transfer the $25 earned portion of the fees from the liability account to the revenue account. It reduces the liability and records as a revenue the $25 that has been earned.

Before proceeding, note that the foregoing advance payment of $75 to Owen Real Estate Agency for property management services was a prepaid expense to the apartment owner and would be treated as such in the accounting records of the apartment building.

Accrued revenues

An accrued revenue is a revenue that has been earned but has not been collected because payment is not due. For example, assume that on July 21 Owen Real Estate Agency signed an additional management contract and took over management of another apartment building for a $2 per day fee, payable at the end of each two months. Under this assumption, by July 31 the agency has managed the building for 10 days and has earned $20 for its services. Therefore, if its accounts are to show proper statement amounts, the following entry is required:

July	31	Accounts Receivable	20.00	
		Management Fees Earned.........................		20.00
		To record management fees that have accrued.		

Posting the entry has this effect on the accounts:

Accounts Receivable				Management Fees Earned		
July 9	50	July 11	50		July 31	25
31	20				31	20

■ The adjustment process just described arises from recognition that the operation of a business results in a continuous stream of transactions, some of which benefit several accounting periods. And, the objective of the process is to allocate to each accounting period that portion of a transaction from which the period benefits. For example, if a revenue like a property management fee is earned over several accounting periods, the adjustment process apportions and credits to each period its fair share. Likewise, if an expense payment like that for rent or insurance benefits several periods, the adjustment process charges a fair share to each benefiting period.

■ A trial balance prepared before adjustments is known as an *unadjusted trial balance,* or simply a trial balance. One prepared after adjustments is known as an *adjusted trial balance;* and a July 31 adjusted trial balance for Owen Real Estate Agency appears in Illustration 3-2.

Owen Real Estate Agency
Adjusted Trial Balance, July 31, 19—

Cash	$1,095	
Accounts receivable	20	
Prepaid rent	200	
Office supplies	45	
Automobile	3,000	
Accumulated depreciation, automobile		$ 35
Office equipment	1,200	
Accumulated depreciation, office equipment		10
Accounts payable		235
Salaries payable		30
Unearned management fees		50
Larry Owen, capital		5,000
Larry Owen, withdrawals	200	
Commissions earned		850
Management fees earned		45
Office salaries expense	230	
Telephone expense	20	
Gas, oil, and repairs	25	
Advertising expense	60	
Rent expense	100	
Office supplies used	15	
Depreciation expense, automobile	35	
Depreciation expense, office equipment	10	
Totals	$6,255	$6,255

Illustration
3-2

■ At the end of an accounting period the items on an adjusted trial balance show proper balance sheet and income statement amounts; and, consequently, the adjusted trial balance may be used in preparing the statements. This is an easy task as an examination of Illustrations 3-3 and 3-4 will show. All that is required is a rearrangement of the revenue and expense items into an income statement as in Illustration 3-3 and a rearrangement of the asset, liability, and owner equity items into a balance sheet as in Illustration 3-4.

Owen Real Estate Agency
Adjusted Trial Balance, July 31, 19—

Cash	$1,095	
Accounts receivable	20	
Prepaid rent	200	
Office supplies	45	
Automobile	3,000	
Accumulated depreciation, automobile		$ 35
Office equipment	1,200	
Accumulated depreciation, office equipment		10
Accounts payable		235
Salaries payable		30
Unearned management fees		50
Larry Owen, capital		5,000
Larry Owen, withdrawals	200	
Commissions earned		850
Management fees earned		45
Office salaries expense	230	
Telephone expense	20	
Gas, oil, and repairs	25	
Advertising expense	60	
Rent expense	100	
Office supplies used	15	
Depreciation expense, automobile	35	
Depreciation expense, office equipment	10	
Totals	$6,255	$6,255

PREPARING THE INCOME STATEMENT
FROM THE ADJUSTED TRIAL BALANCE

Owen Real Estate Agency
Income Statement for Month Ended July 31, 19—

Revenues:		
Commissions earned	$850	
Management fees earned	45	
Total revenues		$895
Operating expenses:		
Office salaries expense	$230	
Telephone expense	20	
Gas, oil, and repairs	25	
Advertising expense	60	
Rent expense	100	
Office supplies used	15	
Depreciation expense, automobile	35	
Depreciation expense, office equipment	10	
Total operating expenses		495
Net Income		$400

Illustration
3–3

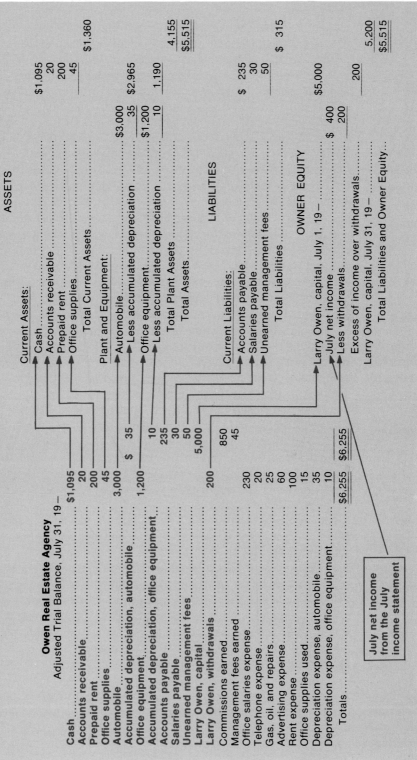

Owen Real Estate Agency
Adjusted Trial Balance, July 31, 19—

Cash	$1,095	
Accounts receivable	20	
Prepaid rent	200	
Office supplies	45	
Automobile	3,000	
Accumulated depreciation, automobile		$ 35
Office equipment	1,200	
Accumulated depreciation, office equipment		10
Accounts payable		235
Salaries payable		30
Unearned management fees		50
Larry Owen, capital		5,000
Larry Owen, withdrawals	200	
Commissions earned		850
Management fees earned		45
Office salaries expense	230	
Telephone expense	20	
Gas, oil, and repairs	25	
Advertising expense	60	
Rent expense	100	
Office supplies used	15	
Depreciation expense, automobile	35	
Depreciation expense, office equipment	10	
Totals	$6,255	$6,255

Owen Real Estate Agency
Balance Sheet, July 31, 19—

ASSETS

Current Assets:

Cash		$1,095	
Accounts receivable		20	
Prepaid rent		200	
Office supplies		45	
Total Current Assets			$1,360

Plant and Equipment:

Automobile	$3,000		
Less accumulated depreciation	35	$2,965	
Office equipment	$1,200		
Less accumulated depreciation	10	1,190	
Total Plant Assets			4,155
Total Assets			$5,515

LIABILITIES

Current Liabilities:

Accounts payable	$ 235	
Salaries payable	30	
Unearned management fees	50	
Total Liabilities		$ 315

OWNER EQUITY

Larry Owen, capital, July 1, 19—			$5,000
July net income	$ 400		
Less withdrawals	200		
Excess of income over withdrawals			200
Larry Owen, capital, July 31, 19—			5,200
Total Liabilities and Owner Equity			$5,515

July net income
from the July
income statement

Illustration
3–4

When the statements are prepared from an adjusted trial balance, the income statement is normally prepared first because the net income, as calculated on the income statement, is needed in completing the balance sheet's owner equity section. Observe in Illustration 3-4 how the net income from the income statement is combined with the withdrawals, and the excess of income over withdrawals, $200, is added to Owen's July 1 capital to show the amount of his July 31 equity.

Need for financial statements

■ Owen Real Estate Agency operated with 23 accounts and completed 16 transactions during July, about as small and simple as a business operation can be. Actually, for managerial purposes it is so small, its owner needs little in the way of accounting reports, since he can carry most of the facts and figures in his head. However, few businesses are so small. Most complete hundreds or thousands of transactions each day, and in such concerns the transactions must be summarized and their effects set out in financial reports if a manager is to comprehend what has and is occurring in the business operations. Likewise, an investor, banker, or other person outside the business who has no direct contact with its operations must depend on financial reports.

Making statement information comparable

■ Thus far the reason given for end-of-the-period adjustments has been "to make the accounts show proper statement amounts." This is a good reason, but a better reason is to make the information on the statements comparable from period to period. For example, Owen Real Estate Agency paid its rent for three months in advance on July 1 and debited the $300 payment to Prepaid Rent. Then at the end of July it transferred $100 of this amount to its Rent Expense account and the $100 appeared on its July income statement as the July rent expense. At the end of August it will transfer another $100 to rent expense and at the end of September it will transfer the third $100, with the result that the amounts shown for rent expense on its July, August, and September income statements will be comparable month by month.

An unsatisfactory alternate procedure would be to debit the entire $300 to Rent Expense at the time of payment and permit the entire amount to appear on the July income statement as rent expense for July. However, if this were done, the July income statement would show $300 of rent expense and the August and September statements would show none, and the income statements of the three months would not be comparable. In addition the July net income would be understated $200 and the net incomes of August and September would be overstated $100 each, and a person seeing only the fluctuations in net income might draw an incorrect conclusion.

Matching revenues and expenses

■ From the need for financial statement information that is comparable period after period has grown the *matching principle* of accounting. Under this principle, the revenues and expenses shown on an income statement must be matched. By this is meant that when an income statement is prepared at the end of an accounting period, it should show all revenues earned during the period, and matched against the revenues (deducted therefrom) should be all the expenses incurred in earning the revenues.

Cash and accrual bases of accounting

■ For income tax purposes an individual or a business in which inventories are not a factor may report income on either a cash basis or an accrual basis. Under the cash basis no adjustments are made for prepaid, unearned, and accrued items. Revenues are reported as being earned in the accounting period in which they are received in cash; expenses are deducted from revenues in the accounting period in which cash is disbursed in their payment; and as a result, net income is the difference between revenue receipts and expense disbursements. Under the accrual basis, on the other hand, adjustments are made for accrued and deferred (prepaid and unearned) items. Under this basis revenues are credited to the period in which earned, expenses are matched with revenues, and no consideration is given to when cash is received and disbursed, with the result that net income is the difference between revenues earned and the expenses incurred in earning the revenues.

Needless to say, although the cash basis of accounting is satisfactory for individuals and small concerns in which accrued and deferred items are not important, it is not satisfactory for most concerns since it results in accounting reports that are not comparable from period to period. Consequently, most businesses keep their records on an accrual basis.

Disposing of accrued items

■ **Accrued expenses**

Several pages back the July 29, 30, and 31 accrued wages of Owen Real Estate Agency's secretary were recorded as follows:

July	31	Office Salaries Expense..................................	30.00	
		Salaries Payable..		30.00
		To record the earned but unpaid wages.		

When these wages are paid on Friday, August 9, the following entry is required:

Aug.	9	Salaries Payable..	30.00	
		Office Salaries Expense	70.00	
		Cash..		100.00
		Paid two weeks' wages.		

The first debit in the foregoing entry cancels the liability for the three days' wages accrued on July 31, and the second debit records the wages of August's first seven working days as an expense of the August accounting period. The credit records the amount paid the secretary.

Accrued revenues

On July 21 Owen Real Estate Agency entered into an agreement to manage an apartment building for $2 per day payable every two months, and on July 31 the following entry was made to record the first 10 days' revenue earned under this contract:

July	31	Accounts Receivable	20.00	
		Management Fees Earned.........................		20.00
		To record management fees that have accrued.		

On August 31 this additional entry will be made to record the 31 days' revenue earned during August:

Aug.	31	Accounts Receivable	62.00	
		Management Fees Earned.........................		62.00
		To record 31 days' accrued management fees.		

And when payment is received on September 21, the following entry will be made:

Sept.	21	Cash...	124.00	
		Accounts Receivable		82.00
		Management Fees Earned.........................		42.00
		To record the receipt of management fees earned.		

The first credit in the foregoing entry records the collection of the fees accrued at the ends of July and August, and the second credit records as revenue the fees earned during the first 21 days of September.

Correcting errors

■ When an error is discovered in either the journal or the ledger, it must be corrected. Such an error is never erased, for this seems to indicate an effort to conceal something. However, the exact method of correction will vary with the nature of the error and the stage in the accounting procedures at which it is discovered.

If an error is discovered in a journal entry before the error is posted, it may be corrected by ruling a single line through the incorrect amount or account name and writing in above the correct amount or account name. Likewise, a posted error or an error in posting in which only the amount is wrong may be corrected in the same manner. However, when a posted error involves a wrong account, it is considered best to correct the error with a correcting journal entry. For example, the following journal entry to record the purchase of office supplies was made and posted:

Oct.	14	Office Furniture and Fixtures..........................	15.00	
		Cash...		15.00
		To record the purchase of office supplies.		

Obviously, the debit of the entry is to the wrong account; consequently, the following entry is needed to correct the error:

Oct.	17	Office Supplies	15.00	
		Office Furniture and Fixtures.....................		15.00
		To correct the entry of October 14 in which the Office Furniture and Fixtures account was debited in error for the purchase of office supplies.		

The debit of the second entry correctly records the purchase of supplies, and the credit cancels the error of the first entry. Note the full explanation of the correcting entry. The explanation of a correcting entry should always be full and complete so that anyone can see exactly what has occurred.

Arrangement of the accounts in the ledger ■ Early in this chapter it was pointed out that asset, liability, owner equity, revenue, and expense amounts are classified and arranged on the statements in such a manner as to make the statements more useful. Likewise, accounts are classified and logically arranged in the ledger. A logical ledger arrangement has two purposes: (1) it aids in locating any account and (2) it aids in preparing the statements. Obviously, statements can be prepared with the least difficulty if accounts are arranged in the ledger in the order of their statement appearance. This arrangement causes the accounts to appear on the adjusted trial balance in their statement order, which in turn aids in rearranging the adjusted trial balance items into a balance sheet and an income statement. Consequently, the balance sheet accounts beginning with the first current asset, cash, and ending with the owner equity accounts appear first in the ledger. These are followed by the revenue and expense accounts in order of their income statement appearance.

Questions for class discussion

1. Why must certain of the accounts of a business be adjusted at the end of an accounting period before statements are prepared?
2. A concern that operates with monthly accounting periods prepaid its rent for three months in advance on June 1, debiting the $450 paid to its

Prepaid Rent account, and on June 30 it made an adjusting entry to record the expired rent. What effect did this adjusting entry have on the accounts?

3. A prepaid expense is an asset at the time of its purchase or prepayment. When is it best to ignore this and record the prepayment as an expense? Why?

4. What is a contra account? Give an example.

5. What contra account is used in recording depreciation? Why is such an account used?

6. What is an accrued expense? Give an example.

7. How does an unearned revenue arise? Give an example of an unearned revenue.

8. What is the balance sheet classification of an unearned revenue?

9. What is an accrued revenue? Give an example.

10. The adjustment process results from recognizing that some transactions benefit several accounting periods. What is the objective of the process?

11. When the statements are prepared from an adjusted trial balance, why should the income statement be prepared first?

12. Why should the income statements of a concern be comparable from period to period?

13. When are a concern's revenues and expenses matched?

14. Differentiate between the cash and the accrual bases of accounting.

15. What is the usual order in which accounts are arranged in the ledger?

Class exercises

Exercise 3–1

Assume that the Prepaid Insurance account has an $847 debit balance at the end of an accounting period before the adjustment for insurance expired and give the required year-end adjusting entry under each of the following unrelated assumptions: (a) An examination of insurance policies shows $621 of insurance expired. (b) An examination of policies shows $325 of unexpired insurance.

Exercise 3–2

Give the year-end adjusting entry required by each of the following:

a) Depreciation on delivery equipment was estimated at $385 for the accounting period.

b) The Repair Supplies account had a $135 balance on January 1; $420 of repair supplies were purchased during the year; and a year-end inventory showed $110 of unconsumed supplies on hand.

c) Four employees in the shop earn a total of $100 per day for a five-day week that begins on Monday and ends on Friday. They were paid for the week ended Friday, December 27, and all four worked full days on Monday and Tuesday, December 30 and 31.

d) Three months' property taxes, estimated at $285, have accrued but are unrecorded at the accounting period end.

Exercise 3–3

Assume that the required adjustments of Exercise 3–2 were not made at the end of the accounting period and tell for each adjustment the effect of its omission on the income statement and balance sheet prepared at that time.

Exercise 3-4

Determine the amounts indicated by the question marks in the columns below. The amounts in each column constitute a separate problem.

	(a)	(b)	(c)	(d)
Supplies on hand on January 1	$213	$142	$325	$?
Supplies purchased during the year......................	475	537	?	452
Supplies consumed during the year......................	?	462	622	395
Supplies remaining at the year-end	238	?	254	204

Exercise 3-5

Apex Realty Company manages office and apartment buildings and credits the revenue earned for this service to an account called Management Fees Earned. On November 1 it received $900 from Dale Gabe, a client who was leaving on a world tour. The $900 paid in advance for six months' management of Gabe's real estate properties and was credited to an account called Unearned Management Fees. Give the entry to record receipt of the $900 and the adjusting entry required on December 31, the end of the yearly accounting period. Also tell how the $900 or portions of it would appear on the year-end statements.

Problems   **Problem 3-1**

On December 31, at the end of a yearly accounting period, the following information for adjustments was available:

a) The prepaid insurance account showed these amounts:

Prepaid Insurance	
Jan. 1 Balance	64.00
May 1	210.00
Nov. 1	270.00

The January 1 balance represents the unexpired premium on a one-year policy purchased on May 1 of the previous year. The May 1 debit resulted from paying the premium on a one-year policy, and the November 1 debit represents the cost of a three-year policy.

b) The office supplies account showed these amounts:

Office Supplies	
Jan. 1 Balance	115.25
Mar. 10 Purchase	155.50
Oct. 5 Purchase	62.00

The December 31 year-end inventory of office supplies showed $95.75 of unused supplies on hand.

c) The company owns and occupies a building that was completed and occupied for the first time on April 1 of the current year. The company had previously occupied rented quarters. The building cost $192,000, has an estimated 40-year useful life, and is not expected to have any salvage value at the end of its life.

d) The company rents portions of the space in its building to two tenants. Tenant A agreed beginning on September 1 to rent a small amount of space at $50 per month, and on that date he paid six months' rent in advance. The $300 payment was credited to the Unearned Rent account.

e) Tenant B pays $75 rent per month on the space he occupies. During the months of June through November he paid his rent each month on the first day of the month and the amounts paid were credited to the Rent Earned account. However, he has recently experienced financial difficulties and has not as yet paid his rent for the month of December.

f) The company has two office employees who earn $20 and $25 per day, respectively. They are paid each Friday for a five-day workweek that begins on Monday. They were paid last Friday and have worked Monday and Tuesday, December 30 and 31 of this week.

Required:
Prepare adjusting entries for each of the foregoing units of information.

Problem 3–2

Pinetop Realty operates with annual accounting periods that end each December 31. At the end of this year, after all transactions were recorded, a trial balance of the concern's ledger appeared as follows:

PINETOP REALTY
Trial Balance, December 31, 19 —

Cash	$ 3,145	
Prepaid insurance	380	
Office supplies	335	
Office equipment	2,975	
Accumulated depreciation, office equipment		$ 615
Automobile	3,645	
Accumulated depreciation, automobile		1,150
Accounts payable		75
Unearned management fees		450
Jerry Knott, capital		6,140
Jerry Knott, withdrawals	9,000	
Sales commissions earned		17,460
Office salaries expense	4,500	
Advertising expense	565	
Rent expense	1,200	
Telephone expense	145	
Totals	$25,890	$25,890

Required:
1. Open the accounts of the trial balance plus these additional ones: Accounts Receivable; Office Salaries Payable; Management Fees Earned; Insurance Expense; Office Supplies Used; Depreciation Expense, Office Equipment;

and Depreciation Expense, Automobile. Enter the trial balance amounts in the accounts.

2. Use the following information to prepare and post adjusting entries:
   a) Insurance expired during the year, $260.
   b) An office supplies inventory showed $120 of unused office supplies on hand at the year-end.
   c) Estimated depreciation of office equipment, $295; and (d) of automobile, $575.
   e) Before departing on a world tour James Green entered into a contract with Pinetop Realty for the management of his apartment building. He paid the management fee for six months in advance, beginning on November 1, and the amount paid, $450, was credited to the Unearned Management Fees account.
   f) On December 1 Pinetop Realty entered into a contract and began managing an office building for a $50 monthly fee. The contract specified that payments for this service were to be made quarterly with the first payment becoming due on March 1 of next year.
   g) The one office employee is paid every two weeks, and on December 31 five days' wages at $18 per day have accrued.

3. Prepare an adjusted trial balance, an income statement, and a classified balance sheet.

Problem 3–3

The following trial balance was taken from the ledger of Red Ball Moving and Storage Company at the end of its annual accounting period:

RED BALL MOVING AND STORAGE COMPANY
Trial Balance, December 31, 19—

Cash	$ 2,460	
Accounts receivable	680	
Prepaid insurance	1,340	
Office supplies	210	
Office equipment	1,540	
Accumulated depreciation, office equipment		$ 320
Trucks	13,800	
Accumulated depreciation, trucks		2,630
Buildings	38,300	
Accumulated depreciation, buildings		10,900
Land	8,000	
Accounts payable		875
Unearned storage fees		685
Mortgage payable		20,000
Gary Ball, capital		18,490
Gary Ball, withdrawals	8,400	
Revenue from moving services		42,995
Storage fees earned		2,960
Office salaries expense	4,200	
Truck drivers' wages	18,410	
Gas, oil, and repairs	2,515	
Totals	$99,855	$99,855

Required:

1. Open the accounts of the trial balance plus these additional accounts: Wages Payable; Insurance Expense; Office Supplies Used; Depreciation Expense, Office Equipment; Depreciation Expense, Trucks; and Depreciation Expense, Buildings. Enter the trial balance amounts in the accounts.
2. Use this information to prepare and post adjusting journal entries:
   a) An examination of insurance policies showed $840 of insurance expired.
   b) An inventory of office supplies showed $45 of unused supplies on hand at the year-end.
   c) Estimated depreciation of office equipment, $115; (d) trucks, $2,450; and (e) buildings, $1,800.
   f) The company follows the practice of crediting the storage fees of customers who pay in advance to the Unearned Storage Fees account. Of the amount credited to this account during the year, $415 had been earned by the year-end.
   g) There were accrued storage fees earned but unrecorded in the accounts and uncollected at the year-end that totaled $110.
   h) There were $225 of accrued truck drivers' wages at the year-end.
3. After posting the adjusting entries, prepare an adjusted trial balance, an income statement, and a classified balance sheet.

Problem 3-4

In the first pair of money columns below is the trial balance of Ross Rental Service and in the second pair of columns is its adjusted trial balance. Analyze the trial balances and prepare the adjusting journal entries made by the concern.

ROSS RENTAL SERVICE
Trial Balance and Adjusted Trial Balance, December 31, 19—

	Trial Balance		Adjusted Trial Balance	
Cash	$ 3,250	....	$ 3,250	....
Accounts receivable	375	....	435	....
Prepaid rent	150	....	....	....
Prepaid insurance	365	....	90	....
Office supplies	135	....	50	....
Office equipment	1,180	....	1,180	....
Accumulated depreciation, office equipment	....	$ 265	....	$ 375
Rental equipment	18,400	....	18,400	....
Accumulated depreciation, rental equipment	....	5,550	....	8,500
Notes payable	....	5,000	....	5,000
Interest payable	....	....	....	50
Accounts payable	....	145	....	145
Unearned rental fees	....	420	....	220
Wages payable	....	....	....	40
Roger Ross, capital	....	8,495	....	8,495
Roger Ross, withdrawals	9,600	....	9,600	....
Rental fees earned	....	19,475	....	19,735
Rent expense	1,650	....	1,800	....
Wages expense	3,560	....	3,600	....
Telephone and utilities	385	....	385	....
Interest expense	300	....	350	....
Insurance expense	....	....	275	....
Office supplies used	....	....	85	....
Depreciation expense, office equipment	....	....	110	....
Depreciation expense, rental equipment	....	....	2,950	....
Totals	$39,350	$39,350	$42,560	$42,560

Problem 3–5

At the end of its annual accounting period, after all transactions were recorded, Travel Trailer Park prepared the following trial balance from its ledger:

TRAVEL TRAILER PARK

Trial Balance, December 31, 19 —

Cash	$ .2,590	
Prepaid insurance	615	
Office supplies	125	
Office equipment	1,250	
Accumulated depreciation, office equipment		$ 325
Building and improvements	65,000	
Accumulated depreciation, building and improvements		7,200
Land	90,000	
Accounts payable		215
Unearned rent		500
Mortgage payable		120,000
Joseph Marcelle, capital		24,070
Joseph Marcelle, withdrawals	12,000	
Rent earned		32,350
Wages expense	4,120	
Utilities expense	340	
Telephone expense	180	
Property taxes expense	1,840	
Interest expense	6,600	
Totals	$184,660	$184,660

Required:

1. Open the accounts of the trial balance plus these: Accounts Receivable; Wages Payable; Property Taxes Payable; Interest Payable; Insurance Expense; Office Supplies Expense; Depreciation Expense, Office Equipment; and Depreciation Expense, Building and Improvements.
2. Use the following information to prepare and post adjusting journal entries:
    a) An examination of insurance policies showed $450 of insurance expired.
    b) An inventory of office supplies showed $40 of unused supplies on hand.
    c) Estimated depreciation on office equipment $110; and (d) on the building and improvements $2,150.
    e) The concern follows the practice of crediting the Unearned Rent account for rents paid in advance by tenants, and an examination revealed that one half of the $500 balance of this account had been earned by the year-end.
    f) A tenant is two months in arrears with his rent payments, and this $100 of accrued revenue was unrecorded at the time the trial balance was prepared.
    g) The one employee works a five-day week at $20 per day. He was paid last week but he has worked four days this week for which he has not been paid.

h) Two months' property taxes expense, totaling $300, has accrued but is unrecorded.

i) One month's interest on the mortgage, $600, has accrued but is unrecorded.

3. After posting the adjusting entries prepare an adjusted trial balance, an income statement, and a classified balance sheet.

Alternate problems

Problem 3–1A

The following information for adjustments was available on December 31, at the end of the annual accounting period. Prepare an adjusting journal entry for each unit of information.

a) An examination of insurance policies showed the following three policies:

Policy No.	Date of Purchase	Life of Policy	Cost
21221-003	November 1 of previous year	3 years	$240
A-1234567	May 1 of current year	3 years	180
565656565	June 1 of current year	1 year	120

Prepaid Insurance was debited for the cost of each policy at the time of its purchase.

b) The Office Supplies account had an $85.50 balance at the beginning of the year, $390.25 of office supplies were purchased during the year, and an inventory of unused supplies on hand at the year-end totaled $75.

c) The two office employees each earn $20 per day and are paid each Friday for a workweek that begins on Monday. This year December 31 falls on Thursday and both employees worked Monday, Tuesday, Wednesday, and Thursday.

d) The company owns a building that it completed and occupied for the first time on May 1 of the current year. The building cost $168,000, has an estimated 40-year life, and is not expected to have any salvage value at the end of that time.

e) The company occupies most of the space in its building but it also rents space to two tenants. One tenant agreed beginning on November 1 to rent a small amount of space at $75 per month, and on that date he paid six months' rent in advance. The amount paid was credited to the Unearned Rent account.

f) The second tenant whose rent is also $75 per month paid his rent on the first of each month August through November, and the amounts paid were credited to Rent Earned. However, he has not paid his December rent, although he has said on several occasions that he would do so the next day.

Problem 3–2A

A trial balance of the ledger of Mesa Realty at the end of its annual accounting period appeared as follows:

MESA REALTY
Trial Balance, December 31, 19—

Cash	$ 3,145	
Prepaid insurance	380	
Office supplies	335	
Office equipment	2,975	
Accumulated depreciation, office equipment		$ 615
Automobile	3,645	
Accumulated depreciation, automobile		1,150
Accounts payable		75
Unearned management fees		450
Jerry Knott, capital		6,140
Jerry Knott, withdrawals	9,000	
Sales commissions earned		17,460
Office salaries expense	4,500	
Advertising expense	565	
Rent expense	1,200	
Telephone expense	145	
Totals	$25,890	$25,890

Required:

1. Open the accounts of the trial balance plus these additional accounts: Accounts Receivable; Office Salaries Payable; Management Fees Earned; Insurance Expense; Office Supplies Used; Depreciation Expense, Office Equipment; and Depreciation Expense, Automobile. Enter the trial balance amounts in the accounts.

2. Use the following information to prepare and post adjusting entries:
   a) An examination of insurance policies showed $315 of insurance expired at the period end.
   b) An inventory of unused office supplies showed $115 of supplies on hand.
   c) The year's depreciation on the office equipment was estimated at $300 and (d) on the automobile at $625.
   e) and (f) Mesa Realty has just begun to offer property management services and has signed two contracts with clients. In the first contract (e) it agreed to manage an apartment building for a $60 monthly fee payable at the end of each quarter. The contract was signed on October 15, and two and a half months' fees have accrued. In the second contract (f) it agreed to manage an office building beginning on November 1. The contract called for a $150 monthly fee, and the client paid the fees for the first three months in advance at the time the contract was signed. The amount paid was credited to the Unearned Management Fees account.
   g) The one office employee is paid weekly, and on December 31 four days' wages at $17.50 per day have accrued.

3. Prepare an adjusted trial balance, an income statement, and a classified balance sheet.

Problem 3-3A

A trial balance taken from the ledger of G-B Moving and Storage Service at the end of its annual accounting period carried these items:

G-B MOVING AND STORAGE SERVICE
Trial Balance, December 31, 19—

Cash	$ 2,460	
Accounts receivable	680	
Prepaid insurance	1,340	
Office supplies	210	
Office equipment	1,540	
Accumulated depreciation, office equipment		$ 320
Trucks	13,800	
Accumulated depreciation, trucks		2,630
Buildings	38,300	
Accumulated depreciation, buildings		10,900
Land	8,000	
Accounts payable		875
Unearned storage fees		685
Mortgage payable		20,000
Gary Ball, capital		18,490
Gary Ball, withdrawals	8,400	
Revenue from moving services		42,995
Storage fees earned		2,960
Office salaries expense	4,200	
Truck drivers' wages	18,410	
Gas, oil, and repairs	2,515	
Totals	$99,855	$99,855

Required:
1. Open the accounts of the trial balance and these additional accounts: Wages Payable; Insurance Expense; Office Supplies Used; Depreciation Expense, Office Equipment; Depreciation Expense, Trucks; and Depreciation Expense, Buildings. Enter the trial balance amounts in the accounts.
2. Use this information to prepare and post adjusting journal entries:
   a) An examination of insurance policies showed $915 of insurance expired.
   b) An office supply inventory showed $55 of unused office supplies on hand at the period end.
   c) Estimated depreciation of office equipment, $130; (d) trucks, $2,875; and (e) buildings, $2,100.
   f) The company credits the storage fees of customers who pay in advance to the Unearned Storage Fees account. Of the $685 credited to this account during the year, $385 had been earned by the year-end.
   g) Accrued storage fees earned but unrecorded in the accounts and uncollected at the year-end totaled $140.

h) There were $285 of accrued truck drivers' wages at the year-end.
3. After posting the adjusting journal entries, prepare an adjusted trial balance, an income statement, and a classified balance sheet.

Problem 3–4A

Analyze the trial balance and adjusted trial balance of Martti Delivery Service which follow and prepare the adjusting journal entries made by the concern.

MARTTI DELIVERY SERVICE
Trial Balance and Adjusted Trial Balance, December 31, 19—

	Trial Balance		Adjusted Trial Balance	
Cash	$ 1,340	....	$ 1,340	....
Accounts receivable	650	....	700	....
Prepaid rent	100	....	....	....
Prepaid insurance	565	....	115	....
Office supplies	115	....	40	....
Office equipment	875	....	875	....
Accumulated depreciation, office equipment	....	$ 125	....	$ 210
Delivery equipment	8,450	....	8,450	....
Accumulated depreciation, delivery equipment	....	1,890	....	3,310
Accounts payable	....	130	....	130
Salaries and wages payable	....	....	....	140
Unearned delivery fees	....	310	....	160
James Martti, capital	....	7,845	....	7,845
James Martti, withdrawals	8,400	....	8,400	....
Delivery fees earned	....	20,350	....	20,550
Rent expense, office	550	....	600	....
Office salaries expense	3,540	....	3,600	....
Telephone expense	185	....	185	....
Office supplies used	....	....	75	....
Depreciation expense, office equipment	....	....	85	....
Rent expense, garage	550	....	600	....
Truck drivers' wages	4,120	....	4,200	....
Gas, oil, and repairs	1,210	....	1,210	....
Insurance expense, delivery trucks	....	....	450	....
Depreciation expense, delivery equipment	....	....	1,420	....
Totals	$30,650	$30,650	$32,345	$32,345

Decision problem 3–1, Sunny Trailer Park   Ted Baker purchased Sunny Trailer Park on October 1 of the current year and has operated it three months without keeping formal accounting records. However, he has deposited all receipts in the bank and has kept an accurate check stub record of his payments, an analysis of which follows:

	Receipts	Payments
Investment...	$20,000	
Purchased Sunny Trailer Park:		
Land $42,500		
Building and improvements 54,000		
Office equipment 1,000		
Total.. $97,500		
Less mortgage assumed................................... 80,000		
Cash paid...		$17,500
Insurance premiums..		1,260
Office supplies purchased..................................		120
Wages paid...		900
Utilities paid..		135
Property taxes paid...		1,320
Personal withdrawals of cash by owner..........................		1,500
Trailer space rentals collected	5,850	
Totals...	$25,850	$22,735
Balance of cash..		3,115
Totals...	$25,850	$25,850

Mr. Baker wants an accrual basis income statement for income tax purposes for the three-month period ending December 31 and has asked you for help. A few questions on your part reveal the following:

The building and improvements were estimated to have 30 years of remaining useful life when purchased, and at the end of that time will have to be wrecked. It is estimated that the sale of salvaged materials will just pay the wrecking costs and the cost of clearing the site. The office equipment is in good condition. When he purchased it, Mr. Baker estimated he would use it for four years from the date of purchase and would then trade it in on new equipment of a like nature. He thought $200 was a fair estimate of what he would receive for the old equipment when traded in on the new equipment at the end of the four-year period.

The $1,260 payment for insurance was for two policies taken out on October 1 and giving protection for three years beginning on that date. Mr. Baker estimates that one third of the office supplies purchased have been used. He also says that he has one employee who earns $15 per day for a five-day week that ends on Friday. The employee was last paid on Friday, December 27, and has worked on Monday and Tuesday, December 30 and 31, but has not been paid. The property tax payment represents one year's taxes that were paid on November 15 for the tax year beginning on October 1, the day Mr. Hall purchased the trailer park.

Included in the $5,850 of space rentals is $300 received from a tenant who paid his rent for six months in advance beginning on December 1. Also, two tenants have not paid their December rent. The total amount due from both is $100.

The mortgage requires the payment of 6% interest annually on the beginning principal balance and a $4,000 annual payment on the principal.

Prepare an accrual basis income statement for Sunny Trailer Park for the

three-month period ending December 31. Also prepare a December 31 classified balance sheet.

Decision problem 3–2, Lakeside Realty

Terry Allen is a real estate agent operating under the business name of Lakeside Realty. He collects a 6% commission on the selling price of each property
he sells. During the second quarter of this year he had five houses listed with
his agency, of which he successfully sold four, but the fifth (No. 4 in the following list) was sold by a rival agent. Mr. Allen's normal business expenses
include operating an automobile, advertising, and office expenses. The car used
in the business cost $4,840 two years ago. Mr. Allen operates the car 50% for
business and 50% for personal uses. He expects to get $1,000 for the car when
he trades it in on a new one in two years.

Since individual houses are named and described in the advertising, it is easy
to keep a record of advertising expense by houses. A record of the five houses
listed during the second quarter, the dates on which they were first listed, advertising expense by months on each, and dates of sale follow:

House	Sales Price	Date Listed	Advertising Expense by Months			Date Sold
			April	May	June	
1	$25,000	March 27	$ 50	$ 60		May 10
2	18,500	March 31	75	40	$ 65	June 22
3	28,000	April 7	15			April 12
4	35,000	April 10	55	80	25	
5	22,500	May 15		20	35	June 20
			$195	$200	$125	

Other agency expenses paid by Mr. Allen were:

Expenses	April	May	June	Totals
Gas, oil, and normal car maintenance (total amounts paid)	$ 55	$ 50	$ 65	$ 170
Office rent	100	100	100	300
Secretary's salary	350	350	350	1,050
Office supplies	10	15	10	35
Telephone	35	45	30	110
Totals	$550	$560	$555	$1,665

Prepare an income statement showing the agency's net income for the second
quarter. Would it be possible to construct monthly income statements for the
agency? Describe and discuss any difficulties that would be encountered in preparing such statements. Would it be possible to construct an income statement
showing the net income from the sale of each house? Describe any difficulties
that would be encountered in preparing such a statement.

Chapter 4

Balance column accounts, the work sheet, and clearing the accounts

■ Since they have definite debit and credit sides, accounts like those in the previous two chapters help a beginning student to understand debits and credits. However, when such accounts are used and it becomes necessary to know the balance of an account, the balance must be calculated; and this is at times inconvenient. Consequently, since a student should by now have some understanding of debits and credits, it is time to introduce a more convenient and more commonly used kind of account, the *balance column account*.

Balance column account

■ Illustration 4–1 shows a balance column account. Such an account differs from the accounts in the previous chapters in that its debit and credit columns are placed side by side and a third or Balance column is provided for the account's current balance. In this Balance column the account's new balance is entered each time the account is debited or credited. For example, in Illustration 4–1 the account was debited to record the purchase of office equipment on July 3, and with this entry its balance became $1,000. On July 5 the account was debited again and its new $1,350 balance entered; and on July 9 it was credited for $150 and its balance reduced to $1,200.

Office Equipment				ACCOUNT NO.	7
DATE	EXPLANATION	FO-LIO	DEBIT	CREDIT	BALANCE
1972 July 3		1	1 000 00		1 000 00
5		1	350 00		1 350 00
9		1		150 00	1 200 00

Illustration 4-1

The convenience of a Balance column in an account is obvious—at any time it shows at a glance the current balance of the account.

When a balance column account like that of Illustration 4-1 is used, the heading of the Balance column does not tell whether the balance is a debit balance as, for example, it would normally be for an asset account or a credit balance as it would normally be for a liability. However, this does not create a problem because an account is always assumed to have its normal kind of balance, unless the contrary is indicated in the account.

The normal balance of an account

Since its column headings do not tell the nature of an account's balance and the balance is always assumed to be the normal kind for that account, unless otherwise indicated, it follows that an accountant must know the normal balance of any account. Fortunately this is not difficult because the balance of an account normally results from recording in it a larger sum of increases than decreases. Consequently, if increases are recorded as debits, the account normally has a debit balance; and if increases are recorded as credits, the account normally has a credit balance. Or, increases are recorded in an account in each of the following classes as shown and its normal balance is:

Type of Account	Increases Are Recorded as—	And the Normal Balance Is—
Asset	Debits	Debit
Contra asset	Credits	Credit
Liability	Credits	Credit
Owner equity:		
Capital	Credits	Credit
Withdrawals	Debits	Debit
Revenue	Credits	Credit
Expense	Debits	Debit

An account with an opposite from normal kind of balance

When an unusual transaction causes an account to have a balance that is opposite from its normal kind of balance, this opposite from normal kind of balance is indicated in the account by entering it in red or by entering it in black and encircling the amount as in the customer account shown in Illustration 4–2.

The account of Illustration 4–2 is an account receivable, and when it has a balance, the balance is normally a debit. However, in this instance the customer made an error and overpaid his account, changing its normal debit balance to a $9 credit balance. Notice how this is shown by encircling the $9 amount. (Individual customer accounts or individual accounts receivable are discussed in more detail beginning in Chapter 6.)

F. M. Pope					
1114 First Avenue, Portland, Oregon			ACCOUNT NO.		
DATE	EXPLANATION	FO-LIO	DEBIT	CREDIT	BALANCE
1972 May 4		16	123 00		123 00
14	*Overpaid account*	17		132 00	(9 00)

Illustration
4–2

An account without a balance

When a posting to a balance column account causes the account to have no balance, some bookkeepers place a –0– in the Balance column on the line of the posting. Others and bookkeeping machines write 0.00 in the Balance column to indicate the account does not have a balance.

Need for a work sheet
■ In the accounting procedures described in the previous chapter, at the end of an accounting period, as soon as all transactions were recorded, recall that (1) adjusting entries were entered in the journal and posted to the accounts and (2) then an adjusted trial balance was prepared and used in making an income statement and balance sheet. Furthermore, for a small business these are satisfactory procedures.

However, if a company has more than a very few accounts and adjustments, errors in adjusting the accounts and constructing the statements are less apt to be made if an additional step is inserted in the procedures. The additional step is the preparation of a *work sheet*. When a work sheet is prepared, it is prepared before the statements are constructed and before the adjusting entries are entered in the journal and posted. Actually, the work sheet is a tool for bringing together in an orderly manner the information used in preparing the statements and in making adjusting entries and clearing entries. (Clearing entries are discussed in more detail later in this chapter.)

A work sheet differs from a balance sheet or an income statement in that it is normally prepared with a pencil. It is a tool of the accountant upon which he (1) achieves the effect of adjusting the accounts before entering the adjustments in the accounts, (2) sorts the adjusted account balances into columns according to whether they are used in preparing the income statement or balance sheet, and (3) calculates and proves the mathematical accuracy of the net income. A work sheet is not for publication or management's use, and preparing it with a pencil makes changes and corrections easy as its preparation progresses.

Preparing a work sheet

■ Owen Real Estate Agency of the previous chapters does not have sufficient accounts or adjustments to warrant use of a work sheet. However, since its transactions and adjustments are familiar, they may be used to illustrate the preparation of a work sheet.

During July, Owen Real Estate Agency completed a number of transactions; and on July 31, after these transactions were recorded but **before any adjusting entries were prepared and posted,** a trial balance of its ledger appeared as in Illustration 4–3.

Owen Real Estate Agency
Trial Balance, July 31, 19—

Cash	$1,095	
Prepaid rent	300	
Office supplies	60	
Automobile	3,000	
Office equipment	1,200	
Accounts payable		$ 235
Unearned management fees		75
Larry Owen, capital		5,000
Larry Owen, withdrawals	200	
Commissions earned		850
Office salaries expense	200	
Telephone expense	20	
Gas, oil, and repairs	25	
Advertising expense	60	
Totals	$6,160	$6,160

Illustration 4–3

Notice that the illustrated trial balance is an **unadjusted trial balance.** The accounts have not been adjusted for expired rent, supplies consumed, depreciation, and et cetera. Nevertheless, this unadjusted trial balance is the starting point in preparing a work sheet, and it is copied in the first two money columns of the work sheet form.

The work sheet illustrated

■ Note that the work sheet shown in Illustration 4–4 has five pairs of money columns and that the first pair is labeled "Trial Balance." In this first pair of columns is copied the unadjusted trial balance of Owen Real Estate Agency. Often when a work sheet is prepared, the trial balance is prepared for the first time in its first two money columns.

Owen Real Estate Agency
Work Sheet for Month Ended July 31, 19—

ACCOUNT TITLES	TRIAL BALANCE Dr.	TRIAL BALANCE Cr.	ADJUSTMENTS Dr.	ADJUSTMENTS Cr.	ADJUSTED TRIAL BALANCE Dr.	ADJUSTED TRIAL BALANCE Cr.	INCOME STATEMENT Dr.	INCOME STATEMENT Cr.	BALANCE SHEET Dr.	BALANCE SHEET Cr.
Cash	1,095.00				1,095.00				1,095.00	
Prepaid rent	300.00			(a)100.00	200.00				200.00	
Office supplies	60.00			(b)15.00	45.00				45.00	
Automobile	3,000.00				3,000.00				3,000.00	
Office equipment	1,200.00				1,200.00				1,200.00	
Accounts payable		235.00				235.00				235.00
Unearned management fees		75.00	(f)25.00			50.00				50.00
Gary Owen, capital		5,000.00				5,000.00				5,000.00
Gary Owen, withdrawals	200.00				200.00				200.00	
Commissions earned		850.00				850.00		850.00		
Office salaries expense	200.00		(e)30.00		230.00		230.00			
Telephone expense	20.00				20.00		20.00			
Gas, oil and repairs	25.00				25.00		25.00			
Advertising expense	60.00				60.00		60.00			
	6,160.00	6,160.00								
Rent expense			(a)100.00		100.00		100.00			
Office supplies used			(b)15.00		15.00		15.00			
Dep. expense, automobile			(c)35.00		35.00		35.00			
Accum. depr., automobile				(c)35.00		35.00				35.00
Dep. expense, office equip			(d)10.00		10.00		10.00			
Accum. depr., office equip				(d)10.00		10.00				10.00
Salaries payable				(e)30.00		30.00				30.00
Management fees earned				(f)45.00		45.00		45.00		
Accounts receivable			(f)20.00		20.00				20.00	
			235.00	235.00	6,255.00	6,255.00	495.00	895.00	5,760.00	5,360.00
Net Income							400.00			400.00
							895.00	895.00	5,760.00	5,760.00

Illustration
4-4

The second pair of work sheet columns is labeled "Adjustments," and the adjustments are entered in these columns. In the work sheet shown in Illustration 4–4 the adjustments are, with one exception, the same as those for which adjusting journal entries were prepared and posted in the previous chapter, prior to the construction of the statements. The one exception is the last one, (f), in which the two adjustments affecting the Management Fees Earned account are combined into one compound adjustment. The reason they are combined is that they both result in credits to the same account.

Note that the adjustments on the illustrated work sheet are keyed together with letters. When a work sheet is prepared, after it and the accounting statements are completed, the adjusting entries still have to be entered in the journal and posted to the ledger. At that time the key letters help identify each adjustment's related debits and credits. Explanations of the adjustments on the illustrated work sheet are:

Adjustment (a): To adjust for the rent expired.
Adjustment (b): To adjust for the office supplies consumed.
Adjustment (c): To adjust for depreciation of the automobile.
Adjustment (d): To adjust for depreciation of the office equipment.
Adjustment (e): To adjust for the accrued secretary's salary.
Adjustment (f): To adjust for the unearned and accrued revenue.

Each adjustment on the Owen Real Estate Agency work sheet required that one or two additional account names be written in below the original trial balance. These accounts did not have balances when the trial balance was prepared and, consequently, were not listed in the trial balance. Often, when a work sheet is prepared, the effects of the adjustments are anticipated; and any additional accounts required are provided without amounts in the body of the trial balance.

When a work sheet is prepared, after the adjustments are entered in the Adjustments columns, the columns are totaled to prove the equality of the adjustments.

The third set of work sheet columns is labeled "Adjusted Trial Balance." In constructing a work sheet each amount in the Trial Balance columns is combined with its adjustment in the Adjustments columns if there is an adjustment and is entered in the Adjusted Trial Balance columns. For example, in Illustration 4–4 the Prepaid Rent account has a $300 debit balance in the Trial Balance columns. This $300 debit is combined with the $100 credit in the Adjustments columns to give the Prepaid Rent account a $200 debit balance in the Adjusted Trial Balance columns. Rent Expense has no balance in the Trial Balance columns, but it has a $100 debit in the Adjustment columns. Therefore, no balance combined with a $100 debit gives Rent Expense a $100 debit in the Adjusted Trial Balance columns. Cash, Automobile, and several other accounts have trial balance amounts but no adjustments. As a result, their trial balance amounts are carried unchanged into the Adjusted Trial Balance columns. Notice that the result of combining the amounts in the Trial Balance columns with the amounts in the Adjustments columns is an adjusted trial balance in the Adjusted Trial Balance columns.

After the amounts in the Trial Balance columns are combined with the amounts in the Adjustments columns and carried to the Adjusted Trial Balance columns, the Adjusted Trial Balance columns are added to prove their equality. Then, after equality is proved, the amounts in these columns are sorted to the proper Balance Sheet or Income Statement columns according to the statement on which they will appear. This is an easy task that requires only two decisions: (1) is the item to be sorted a debit or a credit and (2) on which statement does it appear. As to the first decision, an adjusted trial balance debit amount must be sorted to either the Income Statement debit column or the Balance Sheet debit column and a credit amount must go into either the Income Statement credit or Balance Sheet credit column. In other words, debits remain debits and credits remain credits in the sorting process. As to the second decision, it is only necessary in the sorting process to remember that revenues and expenses appear on the income statement and assets, liabilities, and owner equity items go on the balance sheet.

After the amounts are sorted to the proper columns, the columns are totaled; and at this point, the difference between the debit and credit totals of the Income Statement columns is the net income or loss. The difference is the net income or loss because revenues are entered in the credit column and expenses in the debit column. If the credit column total exceeds the debit column total, the difference is a net income; and if the debit column total exceeds the credit column total, the difference is a net loss. In the illustrated work sheet, the credit column total exceeds the debit column total, and the result is a $400 net income.

On the Owen Real Estate Agency's work sheet, after the net income is determined in the Income Statement columns, it is added to the total of the Balance Sheet credit column. The reason for this is that with the exception of the balance of the Capital account, the amounts appearing in the Balance Sheet columns are "end-of-the-period" amounts. Therefore, it is necessary to add the net income to the Balance Sheet credit column total to make the Balance Sheet columns equal. Adding the income to this column has the effect of adding it to the Capital account.

Had there been a loss, it would have been necessary to add the loss to the debit column. This is because losses decrease owner equity, and adding the loss to the debit column has the effect of subtracting it from the Capital account.

Balancing the Balance Sheet columns by adding the net income or loss is a proof of the accuracy with which the work sheet has been prepared. When the income or loss is added in the Balance Sheet columns, and the addition makes these columns equal, it is assumed that no errors have been made. However, if the addition does not make the columns equal, it is proof that an error or errors have been made. The error or errors may have been either mathematical or an amount may have been sorted to a wrong column.

Although balancing the Balance Sheet columns with the net income or loss is a proof of the accuracy with which a work sheet has been prepared, it is not an absolute proof. These columns will balance even when errors have been made if the errors are of a certain type. For example, an expense carried into the Balance Sheet debit column or an asset carried into the debit column of the income statement section will cause both of these columns to have incorrect totals. Likewise, the net income will be incorrect. However, when such an error is made, the Balance Sheet columns will still balance, but with the incorrect amount of income. Because of this, when a work sheet is prepared, care must be exercised in sorting the adjusted trial balance amounts into the correct Income Statement or Balance Sheet columns.

Work sheet and the financial statements

■ As previously stated, the work sheet is a tool of the accountant and is not for management's use or publication. However, as soon as it is completed, the accountant uses it in preparing the income statement and balance sheet that are given to management. To do this he rearranges the items in the work sheet's Income Statement columns into a formal income statement and he rearranges the items in the Balance Sheet columns into a formal balance sheet.

Work sheet and adjusting entries

■ When a work sheet is used in preparing the statements, both the work sheet and statements are prepared before the accounts are adjusted. As a result, after the work sheet and statements are completed, it is still necessary to prepare and post adjusting journal entries. Fortunately this is an easy task because the adjusting entries may be taken directly from the work sheet's Adjustments columns. When adjusting entries are taken from these columns, a journal entry is made for each adjustment appearing in the columns. Furthermore, to make the entries still easier, at the time the work sheet is prepared each adjustment's debits and credits are keyed together with a letter.

As for the adjusting entries for the work sheet of Illustration 4–4, they are the same as the entries given in the previous chapter, with the exception of the entry for adjustment (f). Here a compound entry having a $25 debit to Unearned Management Fees, a $20 debit to Accounts Receivable, and a $45 credit to Management Fees Earned is used.

Work sheet and clearing entries

■ In addition to being an information source for adjusting entries, the work sheet, as is explained later, is also a source of information for clearing entries, which are the entries that clear and close the revenue and expense accounts.

Need for clearing entries ■ At the end of an accounting period, clearing entries clear the revenue and expense accounts of their balances. These accounts are cleared because:

a) An income statement reports the revenues and expenses of a single accounting period and is prepared from the amounts recorded in the revenue and expense accounts.

b) Consequently, these accounts must begin each new accounting period with zero balances if their end-of-the-period balances are to reflect only a single period's transactions.

Clearing entries that are posted to the revenue and expense accounts at the end of an accounting period cause the revenue and expense accounts to begin the new period with zero balances.

In addition to providing zero balances, clearing entries also summarize a period's revenues and expenses and transfer the difference, the net income or loss, from the revenue and expense accounts to the owner's Capital account. This too is necessary because:

a) Revenues increase owner equity and expenses decrease it.

b) But throughout an accounting period these increases and decreases are recorded in revenue and expense accounts rather than in the owner's Capital account.

c) Consequently, clearing entries are necessary at the end of a period to transfer the net effect of the revenue and expense increases and decreases to the owner's Capital account.

Clearing entries illustrated ■ At the end of July, after its work sheet and statements were prepared and its adjusting entries posted but before its accounts were cleared, the owner equity accounts of Owen Real Estate Agency had balances as shown in Illustration 4–5. (An account's Balance column heading as a rule does not tell the nature of an account's balance. However, in Illustration 4–5 and in the illustrations immediately following, the nature of each account's balance is shown by means of a color overprint. The authors feel the student needs this extra help until such time as he becomes more familiar with the normal balances of different accounts.)

Observe in Illustration 4–5 that Owen's Capital account shows only its $5,000 July 1 balance. This is not the amount of Owen's equity on July 31; clearing entries are required to make this account show the July 31 equity.

Note also the third account in Illustration 4–5, the Income Summary account. This account is used only at the end of the accounting period in summarizing and clearing the revenue and expense accounts.

Larry Owen, Capital

Date	Explanation	Debit	Credit	Balance
July 1			5,000	5,000

Larry Owen, Withdrawals

Date	Explanation	Debit	Credit	Balance
July 26		200		200

Income Summary

Date	Explanation	Debit	Credit	Balance

Commissions Earned

Date	Explanation	Debit	Credit	Balance
July 12			850	850

Management Fees Earned

Date	Explanation	Debit	Credit	Balance
July 31			45	45

Office Salaries Expense

Date	Explanation	Debit	Credit	Balance
July 12		100		100
26		100		200
31		30		230

Telephone Expense

Date	Explanation	Debit	Credit	Balance
July 31		20		20

Gas, Oil, and Repairs

Date	Explanation	Debit	Credit	Balance
July 31		25		25

Advertising Expense

Date	Explanation	Debit	Credit	Balance
July 31		60		60

Rent Expense

Date	Explanation	Debit	Credit	Balance
July 31		100		100

Office Supplies Used

Date	Explanation	Debit	Credit	Balance
July 31		15		15

Depreciation Expense, Automobile

Date	Explanation	Debit	Credit	Balance
July 31		35		35

Depreciation Expense, Office Equipment

Date	Explanation	Debit	Credit	Balance
July 31		10		10

Illustration
4–5

Clearing revenue accounts

Before clearing entries are posted, revenue accounts have credit balances; consequently, to clear a revenue account an entry debiting the account and crediting Income Summary is required. Owen Real Estate Agency has two revenue accounts, and the compound entry to clear them is:

July	31	Commissions Earned	850.00	
		Management Fees Earned	45.00	
		Income Summary		895.00
		To clear the revenue accounts.		

Posting the entry has the effect shown in the accounts of Illustration 4–6.

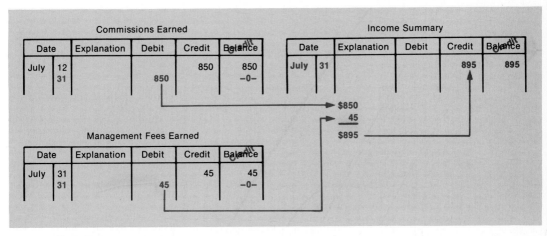

Illustration
4–6

Note that the entry clearing the revenue accounts has a dual effect: (1) it clears the accounts of their balances and (2) transfers the balances in total to the credit side of the Income Summary account.

Clearing expense accounts

Before clearing entries are posted, expense accounts have debit balances; consequently, to clear a concern's expense accounts a compound entry debiting the Income Summary account and crediting each individual expense account is required. Owen Real Estate Agency has eight expense accounts, and the compound entry to clear them is:

July	31	Income Summary..	495.00	
		Office Salaries Expense		230.00
		Telephone Expense.....................................		20.00
		Gas, Oil, and Repairs.................................		25.00
		Advertising Expense....................................		60.00
		Rent Expense		100.00
		Office Supplies Used		15.00
		Depreciation Expense, Automobile.............		35.00
		Depreciation Expense, Office Equipment......		10.00
		To clear the expense accounts.		

Posting this entry has the effect shown in Illustration 4–7 on the next page. Note again that the effect is a dual one: (1) it clears the expense accounts of their balances and (2) transfers the account balances in a total to the debit side of the Income Summary account.

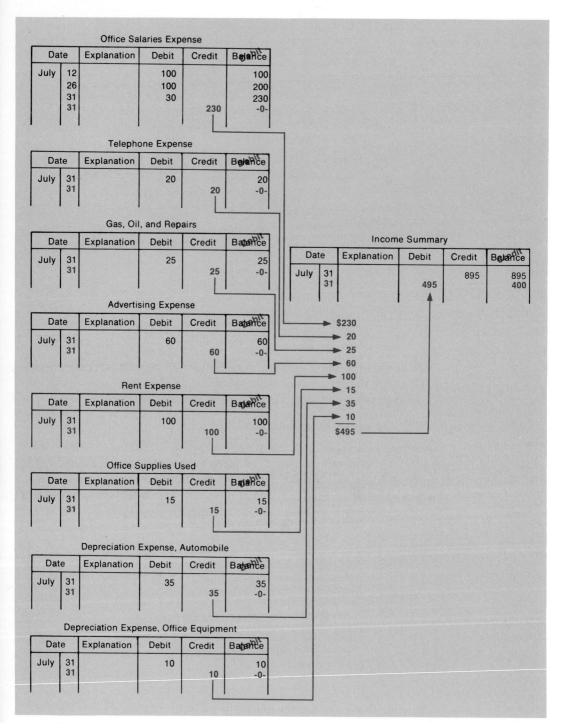

Office Salaries Expense

Date		Explanation	Debit	Credit	Balance
July	12		100		100
	26		100		200
	31		30		230
	31			230	-0-

Telephone Expense

Date		Explanation	Debit	Credit	Balance
July	31		20		20
	31			20	-0-

Gas, Oil, and Repairs

Date		Explanation	Debit	Credit	Balance
July	31		25		25
	31			25	-0-

Advertising Expense

Date		Explanation	Debit	Credit	Balance
July	31		60		60
	31			60	-0-

Rent Expense

Date		Explanation	Debit	Credit	Balance
July	31		100		100
	31			100	-0-

Office Supplies Used

Date		Explanation	Debit	Credit	Balance
July	31		15		15
	31			15	-0-

Depreciation Expense, Automobile

Date		Explanation	Debit	Credit	Balance
July	31		35		35
	31			35	-0-

Depreciation Expense, Office Equipment

Date		Explanation	Debit	Credit	Balance
July	31		10		10
	31			10	-0-

Income Summary

Date		Explanation	Debit	Credit	Balance
July	31			895	895
	31		495		400

$230
20
25
60
100
15
35
10
$495

Illustration
4–7

Clearing the Income Summary account

After a concern's revenue and expense accounts are cleared and their balances transferred to the Income Summary account, the balance of the Income Summary account is equal to the net income or loss. When revenues exceed expenses, there is a net income and the Income Summary account has a credit balance. On the other hand, when expenses exceed revenues, there is a loss and the account has a debit balance. But, regardless of the nature of its balance, the Income Summary account is cleared and its balance, the amount of the net income or loss, is transferred to the Capital account.

Owen Real Estate Agency earned $400 during July; consequently, after its revenue and expense accounts are cleared, its Income Summary account has a $400 credit balance, and the account is cleared and this balance is transferred to the Larry Owen, Capital account with an entry like this:

July	31	Income Summary	400.00	
		Larry Owen, Capital................................,		400.00
		To clear the Income Summary account.		

Posting this entry has the following effect on the accounts:

Income Summary					Larry Owen, Capital			
Date	Debit	Credit	Balance		Date	Debit	Credit	Balance
July 31		895	895		July 1		5,000	5,000
31	495		400		31		400	5,400
31	400		-0-					

Observe again that the clearing entry serves a dual purpose: (1) it clears the Income Summary account and (2) transfers the balance of the account, the amount of the net income in this case, to the Capital account.

Clearing the Withdrawals account

At the end of an accounting period the debit balance of the Withdrawals account shows the amount the owner's equity was reduced during the period by withdrawals of cash and other assets for personal use, and this debit balance is closed to the Capital account with an entry like this:

		July	31	Larry Owen, Capital..	200.00	
				Larry Owen, Withdrawals		200.00
				To close the Withdrawals account.		

Posting the entry has this effect on the accounts:

Larry Owen, Withdrawals					Larry Owen, Capital			
Date	Debit	Credit	Balance		Date	Debit	Credit	Balance
July 26	200		200		July 1		5,000	5,000
31		200	-0-		31		400	5,400
					31	200		5,200

After the entry clearing the Withdrawals account is posted, observe that the two reasons for making clearing entries are accomplished: (1) all revenue and expense accounts have zero balances and (2) the net effect of the period's revenue, expense, and withdrawal transactions on the owner's equity is shown in his Capital account.

Sources of clearing entry information

■ After adjusting entries have been posted, information for the clearing entries may be taken from the individual revenue and expense accounts; however, the work sheet provides this information in a more convenient form. For example, if the Owen Real Estate Agency work sheet on page 91 is examined, it will be seen that every account having a balance extended into the Income Statement debit column has a debit balance in the ledger and must be credited in clearing. Now compare the amounts in this column with the compound clearing entry on page 97 and observe how the column amounts and their account titles are a source of information for the entry. Observe also that if the work sheet is used as an information source for the entry, it is not even necessary to add the entry's individual credit amounts in order to learn the amount of the debit—the debit amount can be taken from the work sheet column total.

In addition to the foregoing, observe also that the work sheet's Income Statement credit column is a convenient information source for the compound entry that clears the revenue accounts.

The accounts after clearing

■ At this stage, after both adjusting and clearing entries have been posted, the Owen Real Estate Agency accounts appear as in Illustration 4–8 on the next several pages. Observe in the illustration that the asset, liability, and the owner's Capital accounts show their end-of-the-period balances. Observe also that the revenue and expense accounts are clear of balances and are ready for recording the new accounting period's revenues and expenses.

Cash

ACCOUNT NO. 1

DATE	EXPLANATION	FO-LIO	DEBIT	CREDIT	BALANCE
1972 July 1		1	5000 00		5000 00
1		1		300 00	4700 00
3		1		3000 00	1700 00
3		1		1000 00	700 00
9		1	100 00		800 00
11		1	50 00		850 00
11		1		175 00	675 00
12		2	850 00		1525 00
12		2		100 00	1425 00
16		2	75 00		1500 00
26		2		100 00	1400 00
26		2		200 00	1200 00
31		2		20 00	1180 00
31		2		25 00	1155 00
31		2		60 00	1095 00

Accounts Receivable

ACCOUNT NO. 2

DATE	EXPLANATION	FO-LIO	DEBIT	CREDIT	BALANCE
1972 July 9		1	50 00		50 00
11		1		50 00	—0—
31		3	20 00		20 00

Prepaid Rent

ACCOUNT NO. 3

DATE	EXPLANATION	FO-LIO	DEBIT	CREDIT	BALANCE
1972 July 1		1	300 00		300 00
31		3		100 00	200 00

Illustration
4–8

Office Supplies   ACCOUNT NO. 4

DATE	EXPLANATION	FO-LIO	DEBIT	CREDIT	BALANCE
1972 July 5		1	60 00		60 00
31		3		15 00	45 00

Automobile   ACCOUNT NO. 5

DATE	EXPLANATION	FO-LIO	DEBIT	CREDIT	BALANCE
1972 July 3		1	3000 00		3000 00

Accumulated Depreciation, Automobile   ACCOUNT NO. 6

DATE	EXPLANATION	FO-LIO	DEBIT	CREDIT	BALANCE
1972 July 31		3		35 00	35 00

Office Equipment   ACCOUNT NO. 7

DATE	EXPLANATION	FO-LIO	DEBIT	CREDIT	BALANCE
1972 July 3		1	1000 00		1000 00
5		1	350 00		1350 00
9		1		150 00	1200 00

Accumulated Depreciation - Office Equipment   ACCOUNT NO. 8

DATE	EXPLANATION	FO-LIO	DEBIT	CREDIT	BALANCE
1972 July 31		3		10 00	10 00

Accounts Payable   ACCOUNT NO. 9

DATE	EXPLANATION	FO-LIO	DEBIT	CREDIT	BALANCE
1972 July 5		1		410 00	410 00
11		1	175 00		235 00

Illustration
4–8
Continued

Salaries Payable   ACCOUNT NO. 10

DATE	EXPLANATION	FO-LIO	DEBIT	CREDIT	BALANCE
1972 July 31		3		30 00	30 00

Unearned Management Fees   ACCOUNT NO. 11

DATE	EXPLANATION	FO-LIO	DEBIT	CREDIT	BALANCE
1972 July 16		2		75 00	75 00
31		3	25 00		50 00

Larry Owen, Capital   ACCOUNT NO. 12

DATE	EXPLANATION	FO-LIO	DEBIT	CREDIT	BALANCE
1972 July 1		1		5000 00	5000 00
31		3		400 00	5400 00
31		3	200 00		5200 00

Larry Owen, Withdrawals   ACCOUNT NO. 13

DATE	EXPLANATION	FO-LIO	DEBIT	CREDIT	BALANCE
1972 July 26		2	200 00		200 00
31		3		200 00	—0—

Income Summary   ACCOUNT NO. 14

DATE	EXPLANATION	FO-LIO	DEBIT	CREDIT	BALANCE
1972 July 31		3		895 00	895 00
31		3	495 00		400 00
31		3	400 00		—0—

Illustration
4–8
Continued

Commissions Earned   ACCOUNT NO. 15

DATE	EXPLANATION	FO-LIO	DEBIT	CREDIT	BALANCE
1972 July 12		2		850 00	850 00
31		3	850 00		—0—

Management Fees Earned   ACCOUNT NO. 16

DATE	EXPLANATION	FO-LIO	DEBIT	CREDIT	BALANCE
1972 July 31		3		45 00	45 00
31		3	45 00		—0—

Office Salaries Expense   ACCOUNT NO. 17

DATE	EXPLANATION	FO-LIO	DEBIT	CREDIT	BALANCE
1972 July 12		2	100 00		100 00
26		2	100 00		200 00
31		3	30 00		230 00
31		3		230 00	—0—

Telephone Expense   ACCOUNT NO. 18

DATE	EXPLANATION	FO-LIO	DEBIT	CREDIT	BALANCE
1972 July 31		2	20 00		20 00
31		3		20 00	—0—

Gas, Oil, and Repairs   ACCOUNT NO. 19

DATE	EXPLANATION	FO-LIO	DEBIT	CREDIT	BALANCE
1972 July 31		2	25 00		25 00
31		3		25 00	—0—

Illustration
4–8
Continued

Advertising Expense — ACCOUNT NO. 20

DATE	EXPLANATION	FOLIO	DEBIT	CREDIT	BALANCE
1972 July 31		2	60 00		60 00
31		3		60 00	—0—

Rent Expense — ACCOUNT NO. 21

DATE	EXPLANATION	FOLIO	DEBIT	CREDIT	BALANCE
1972 July 31		3	100 00		100 00
31		3		100 00	—0—

Office Supplies Used — ACCOUNT NO. 22

DATE	EXPLANATION	FOLIO	DEBIT	CREDIT	BALANCE
1972 July 31		3	15 00		15 00
31		3		15 00	—0—

Depreciation Expense, Automobile — ACCOUNT NO. 23

DATE	EXPLANATION	FOLIO	DEBIT	CREDIT	BALANCE
1972 July 31		3	35 00		35 00
31		3		35 00	—0—

Depreciation Expense, Office Equipment — ACCOUNT NO. 24

DATE	EXPLANATION	FOLIO	DEBIT	CREDIT	BALANCE
1972 July 31		3	10 00		10 00
31		3		10 00	—0—

Illustration
4–8
Concluded

The post-clearing trial balance

■ It is easy to make errors in adjusting and clearing the accounts. Consequently, after all adjusting and clearing entries are posted, a new trial balance is prepared to retest the equality of the accounts. This new, after-clearing trial balance is called a *post-clearing trial balance,* and for Owen Real Estate Agency appears as in Illustration 4–9.

Illustration
4-9

Owen Real Estate Agency
Post-Clearing Trial Balance, July 31, 19—

Cash	$1,095	
Accounts receivable	20	
Prepaid rent	200	
Office supplies	45	
Automobile	3,000	
Accumulated depreciation, automobile		$ 35
Office equipment	1,200	
Accumulated depreciation, office equipment		10
Accounts payable		235
Salaries payable		30
Unearned management fees		50
Larry Owen, capital		5,200
Totals	$5,560	$5,560

Compare Illustration 4–9 with the accounts having balances in Illustration 4–8. Note that only asset, liability, and the owner's Capital accounts have balances in Illustration 4–8, and that these are the only accounts that appear on the post-clearing trial balance of Illustration 4–9. The revenue and expense accounts have been cleared and have zero balances at this point.

Matters of terminology

■ Clearing entries, closing entries

Clearing entries are also called closing entries. They are so called because after the revenue and expense accounts are cleared, they are also closed and have no balances. Thus far these entries have been called clearing entries because this title is a little more descriptive of what the entries do. However, from this point on the phrases closing entries and clearing entries, closed account and cleared account, and post-closing trial balance and post-clearing trial balance will be used interchangeably.

Temporary proprietorship accounts

Revenue and expense accounts plus the Income Summary and Withdrawals accounts are called *temporary proprietorship accounts*. A moment's thought will reveal the reason for this is that in a sense the items recorded in these accounts are only temporarily recorded therein. At the end of each accounting period the items, through the account balances, are in a sense transferred out and on to the owner or proprietor's Capital account.

Real and nominal accounts

Balance sheet accounts are commonly called *real accounts,* presumably because the items recorded in these accounts exist in objective form. Likewise, income statement accounts are called *nominal accounts* because the items recorded in these accounts exist in name only.

Working papers

As an aid in their work, accountants prepare numerous memoranda, analyses, notes, and informal papers that serve as a basis for the more formal reports given to management or to their clients. These analyses, notes, and memoranda are called "working papers" and are invaluable tools of the accountant. The work sheet of this chapter is a so-called working paper. Others will be discussed from time to time.

The accounting cycle

■ The life of a business is divided into accounting periods; and each period is a recurring accounting cycle, beginning with transactions recorded in a journal and ending with a post-closing trial balance. All steps in the cycle have now been discussed, and a knowledge of accounting requires that each step be understood and its relation to the others seen. The steps in the order of their occurrence are:

1. *Journalizing* .... Analyzing and recording transactions in a journal.

2. *Posting* .... Copying the debits and credits of journal entries into the ledger accounts.

3. *Preparing a trial balance* ...... Summarizing the ledger accounts and testing the recording accuracy.

4. *Constructing a work sheet* .... Affecting the adjustments without making entries in the accounts. Then sorting the account balances into balance sheet and income statement accounts and finally determining the income or loss.

5. *Preparing the statements* .... Rearranging the work sheet information into a balance sheet and an income statement.

6. *Adjusting the ledger accounts* .... Preparing adjusting journal entries from information in the Adjustments columns of the work sheet and posting the entries in order to bring the account balances up to date.

7. *Closing the temporary proprietorship accounts* .... Preparing and posting entries to close the temporary proprietorship accounts and transfer the net income or loss to the Capital account.

8. *Preparing a post-closing trial balance* .... Proving the accuracy of the adjusting and closing procedure.

■ In order to shorten the material presented, textbooks commonly use problems and illustrations in which businesses operate with accounting periods one month in length. In actual practice monthly accounting periods are seldom if ever used. An occasional business will close its books every three or every six months; however, most operate with annual accounting periods or accounting periods one year in length.

Any accounting period of 12 consecutive months is known as a *fiscal year*. A fiscal year or annual accounting period may coincide with the calendar year or it may follow the *natural business year*. The natural business year of a company begins and ends when the company's business activity is at its lowest point. For example, in the automobile sales business the natural business year begins October 1, just before the new models are brought out, and ends the following September 30. When accounting periods follow the natural business year, the books are closed when inventories are at their lowest point and business activity is at its lowest ebb.

**Questions
for class
discussion**

1. A balance column account is more convenient than the kind of account described in earlier chapters. Why?

2. A work sheet is a tool of the accountant upon which he accomplishes three tasks. What are these tasks?

3. Is it possible to complete the statements and adjust and clear the accounts without preparing a work sheet? What is gained by preparing a work sheet?

4. At what stage in the accounting process is a work sheet prepared?

5. From where are the amounts that are entered in the Trial Balance columns of a work sheet obtained?

6. Why are the adjustments in the Adjustments columns of a work sheet keyed together with letters?

7. What is the result of combining the amounts in the Trial Balance columns with the amounts in the Adjustments columns of a work sheet?

8. Why must care be exercised in sorting the items in the Adjusted Trial Balance columns to the proper Income Statement of Balance Sheet columns?

9. In extending the items in the Adjusted Trial Balance columns of a work sheet, what would be the result of extending: (*a*) an expense into the Balance Sheet debit column; (*b*) a liability into the Income Statement credit column; and (*c*) a revenue into the Balance Sheet debit column? Would each of these errors be automatically detected on the work sheet? Which would be automatically detected? Why?

10. Why are revenue and expense accounts called "temporary proprietorship accounts"?

11. What two purposes are accomplished by recording closing entries?

12. What accounts are affected by closing entries? What accounts are not affected?

13. Explain the difference between adjusting and closing entries.

14. What is the purpose of the Income Summary account?

15. Why is a post-closing trial balance prepared?

16. A bookkeeping student's post-closing trial balance listed "Depreciation expense, building, $672." What did this indicate?

Exercise 4–1

The following alphabetically arranged accounts and balances appeared on the trial balance of Fast Repair Shop. Without changing their alphabetical arrangement, list the accounts on a sheet of notebook paper in the form of a trial balance, being sure that the amounts entered in the debit and credit columns are equal. All accounts have normal balances.

Accounts payable	$ 250
Accounts receivable	270
Accumulated depreciation, repair equipment	1,120
Advertising expense	225
Cash	855
Dale Howard, capital	3,425
Dale Howard, withdrawals	5,200
Prepaid insurance	215
Rent expense	960
Repair equipment	4,220
Repair supplies	1,550
Revenue from repairs	13,475
Wages expense	4,775

Exercise 4–2

The following item amounts are from a work sheet's Adjustments columns. From the information prepare adjusting journal entries. Use December 31 of the current year as the date.

	Adjustments	
	Debit	*Credit*
Prepaid insurance		(a) 360
Office supplies		(b) 180
Accumulated depreciation, office equipment		(c) 115
Accumulated depreciation, delivery equipment		(d) 2,210
Office salaries expense	(e) 30	
Truck drivers' wages	(e) 265	
Insurance expense, office equipment	(a) 65	
Insurance expense, delivery equipment	(a) 295	
Office supplies expense	(b) 180	
Depreciation expense, office equipment	(c) 115	
Depreciation expense, delivery equipment	(d) 2,210	
Salaries and wages payable		(e) 295
Totals	3,160	3,160

Exercise 4–3

The following items appeared in the Income Statement columns of a work sheet prepared for a business owned by Carl Dale. Under the assumption that Mr. Dale had withdrawn $7,200 from the business during the accounting period of the work sheet, prepare entries to close the revenue, expense, Income Summary, and withdrawals accounts of the business. Use December 31 as the date.

	Income Statement	
	Debit	Credit
Revenue from services	....	15,485
Wages expense	4,800	....
Rent expense	960	....
Advertising expense	225	....
Insurance expense	165	....
Repair supplies used	1,170	....
Depreciation expense, repair equipment	650	....
	7,970	15,485
Net income	7,515	
	15,485	15,485

Exercise 4–4

Following is a list of trial balance accounts and their balances. To save you time, the balances are in one- and two-digit numbers; however, to increase your skill in sorting adjusted trial balance amounts to the proper work sheet columns, the accounts are listed in alphabetical order.

TRIAL BALANCE ACCOUNTS AND BALANCES

Accounts payable	$ 2	Perry Price, withdrawals	$ 2
Accounts receivable	4	Prepaid insurance	3
Accumulated depreciation, shop equipment	3	Revenue from services	19
		Shop equipment	10
Advertising expense	1	Shop supplies	4
Cash	5	Unearned revenue	3
Notes payable	2	Utilities expense	2
Perry Price, capital	10	Wages expense	8

Required:
1. Prepare a work sheet form on ordinary notebook paper and enter the trial balance accounts and amounts on the work sheet in their alphabetical order.
2. Complete the work sheet using the following information:
    a) Estimated depreciation on shop equipment, $2.
    b) Expired insurance, $1.
    c) Unused shop supplies on hand per inventory, $1.
    d) An examination showed that $2 of the amount listed as unearned revenue had been earned by the work sheet date.
    e) Accrued wages, $1.

Problems   Problem 4–1

On November 30 of the current year, at the end of the shop's annual accounting period, a trial balance of the ledger of TV Tim, a television repair shop owned by Tim Gage, carried the following amounts:

TV TIM
Trial Balance, November 30, 19—

Cash	$ 975	
Prepaid insurance	240	
Repair supplies	1,425	
Repair equipment	7,215	
Accumulated depreciation, repair equipment		$ 1,050
Accounts payable		260
Tim Gage, capital		4,535
Tim Gage, withdrawals	5,200	
Revenue from repairs		15,135
Wages expense	4,760	
Rent expense	900	
Advertising expense	265	
Totals	$20,980	$20,980

Required:

1. Enter the trial balance amounts in the Trial Balance columns of a work sheet and complete the work sheet using the following information:
   a) Expired insurance, $185.
   b) An inventory of repair supplies showed $310 of unused supplies on hand.
   c) Estimated depreciation of repair equipment, $725.
   d) Wages earned by the one employee but unpaid on the trial balance date, $80.
2. From the work sheet prepare an income statement and a balance sheet.
3. From the work sheet prepare adjusting journal entries and compound closing entries.

Problem 4–2

On November 1 of the current year John Howe opened Quick Service Repair Shop, and during the month completed the following transactions:

Nov. 1 Withdrew $1,000 from his personal savings account and deposited it in an account opened in the name of the shop.

1 Paid the rent on the shop space for one month, $100.

1 Paid the premium on a one-year insurance policy, $96.

2 Signed a lease for the installation and use of shoe repair equipment. The lease called for a monthly rental of $40. Paid the first month's rent.

4 Purchased on credit from Shop Equipment Company a showcase, chairs for the shop, and other shop furniture, $500.

5 Purchased shop supplies for cash, $90.

8 Paid for advertising on the local radio station, $25.

15 Cash shoe repair revenue for the first half of the month, $72.

20 Paid Shop Equipment Company $100 on account.

30 Cash shoe repair revenue for the last half of the month, $134.

Required work for November:

1. Open the following accounts: Cash; Prepaid Insurance; Shop Supplies; Shop Furniture; Accumulated Depreciation, Shop Furniture; Accounts

Payable; John Howe, Capital; John Howe, Withdrawals; Income Summary; Shoe Repair Revenue; Shop Rent; Equipment Rent; Advertising Expense; Insurance Expense; Shop Supplies Used; and Depreciation Expense, Shop Furniture.

2. Prepare and post journal entries to record the November transactions.
3. Prepare a trial balance in the Trial Balance columns of a work sheet, and complete the work sheet using the following information:
   a) One month's insurance has expired.
   b) An inventory of shop supplies shows $40 of supplies on hand.
   c) Estimated depreciation of shop furniture, $10
4. Prepare a November income statement and a balance sheet as of November 30.
5. Prepare and post adjusting and compound closing entries.
6. Prepare a post-closing trial balance.

During December John Howe completed the following additional transactions for Quick Service Repair Shop:

Dec. 1 Paid the rent on the shop space, $100.
   1 Paid the December rent on the shop equipment.
   4 Purchased on credit from Shop Equipment Company additional chairs for the shop, $125.
   8 Purchased shop supplies for cash, $160.
   15 Cash shoe repair revenue for the first half of the month, $280.
   18 Paid for newspaper advertising that had appeared, $40.
   23 Paid Shop Equipment Company $400 on account.
   30 Withdrew $200 to be used for personal living expenses.
   31 Cash shoe repair revenue for the second half of the month, $305.

Required work for December:

1. Prepare and post journal entries to record the December transactions.
2. Prepare a trial balance in the Trial Balance columns of a work sheet, and complete the work sheet using the following information:
   a) One month's insurance has expired.
   b) An inventory of shop supplies shows $65 of supplies on hand.
   c) Estimated depreciation of shop furniture, $12.
3. Prepare a December income statement and a December 31 balance sheet.
4. Prepare and post adjusting and compound closing entries.
5. Prepare a post-closing trial balance.

Problem 4–3

(If the working papers that accompany this text are not used, omit this problem.)

The ledger of Quick Delivery Service, showing account balances as of December 31, the end of the current accounting period, appears in the booklet of working papers. All accounts with balances have normal kinds of balances.

Required:

1. Prepare a trial balance of the ledger in the Trial Balance columns of a work sheet form and complete the work sheet using the following information:
   a) Insurance expired on the office equipment, $60; and on the delivery equipment, $420.
   b) An inventory of office supplies shows $110 of unused office supplies on hand.

c) Estimated depreciation on office equipment, $125; and (*d*) on delivery equipment, $2,125.

e) Three stores entered into contracts with Quick Delivery Service in which they agreed to pay a fixed fee for having packages delivered. Two of the stores made advance payments on their contracts, and the amounts paid were credited to Unearned Delivery Service Revenue. An examination of their contracts shows that $250 of the $450 they paid in advance was earned by the accounting period end. The contract of the third store provides for a $100 monthly fee to be paid at the end of each month's service. It was signed on December 15, and a half month's revenue has accrued but is unrecorded.

f) Office salaries, $60; and truck drivers' wages, $320, have accrued.

2. Prepare an income statement and a classified balance sheet.
3. Prepare and post adjusting and closing journal entries.
4. Prepare a post-clearing trial balance.

Problem 4–4

A trial balance of the ledger of Gleaming Janitorial Service at the end of its annual accounting period appeared as follows:

GLEAMING JANITORIAL SERVICE
Trial Balance, December 31, 19—

Cash	$ 650	
Accounts receivable	210	
Prepaid insurance	525	
Prepaid rent	150	
Cleaning supplies	815	
Cleaning equipment	2,750	
Accumulated depreciation, cleaning equipment		$ 1,410
Trucks	6,680	
Accumulated depreciation, trucks		1,790
Accounts payable		110
Unearned janitorial revenue		225
Jack Gleam, capital		6,435
Jack Gleam, withdrawals	6,600	
Janitorial revenue		18,245
Wages expense	8,650	
Rent expense	400	
Gas, oil, and truck repairs	785	
Totals	$28,215	$28,215

Required:

1. Enter the trial balance amounts in the Trial Balance columns of a work sheet form and complete the work sheet using the following information:
   a) Expired insurance, $395.
   b) The cleaning service rents garage and equipment storage space. At the beginning of the accounting period three months' rent was prepaid as shown by the debit balance in the Prepaid Rent account. Rents for the months April through November were paid on the first day of each

month and debited to the Rent Expense account. The December rent was unpaid on the trial balance date.

c) An inventory of cleaning supplies showed $145 of cleaning supplies on hand.

d) Estimated depreciation on cleaning equipment, $320; and (e) on the trucks, $845.

f) On November 1 the janitorial service contracted to clean the office of Desert Insurance Agency for $75 per month. The insurance agency paid in advance for three months' service, and the amount paid was credited to the Unearned Janitorial Revenue account. The janitorial service also entered into a contract and began cleaning the office of Cactus Realty on December 15. By the month-end a half month's revenue, $50, had been earned on this contract but it was unrecorded.

g) Employees' wages amounting to $115 had accrued but were unrecorded on the trial balance date.

2. From the work sheet prepare an income statement and a classified balance sheet.

3. Prepare adjusting and closing entries from the work sheet.

Alternate problems

Problem 4–1A

The following trial balance was taken from the ledger of Local Moving and Storage Service at the end of its annual accounting period:

LOCAL MOVING AND STORAGE SERVICE
Trial Balance, October 31, 19 –

Cash	$ 1,855	
Accounts receivable	515	
Prepaid insurance	1,280	
Office supplies	225	
Office equipment	1,480	
Accumulated depreciation, office equipment		$ 310
Trucks	14,200	
Accumulated depreciation, trucks		2,720
Building	34,800	
Accumulated depreciation, building		10,400
Land	6,000	
Accounts payable		345
Unearned storage fees		630
Mortgage payable		15,000
Tom Mills, capital		20,735
Tom Mills, withdrawals	9,600	
Revenue from moving services		41,880
Storage fees earned		3,120
Office salaries expense	4,250	
Advertising expense	365	
Truck drivers' wages	17,940	
Gas, oil, and truck repairs	2,630	
Totals	$95,140	$95,140

Required:

1. Enter the trial balance amounts in the Trial Balance columns of a work sheet form and complete the work sheet using the following information:

   a) Expired insurance, $865.

   b) An office supplies inventory shows $85 of unused office supplies on hand.

   c) Estimated depreciation of office equiment, $125; (*d*) trucks, $2,640; and (*e*) building, $1,500.

   f) The company credits the storage fees of customers who pay in advance to the Unearned Storage Fees account. Of the amount credited to this account during the year, $445 has been earned by the accounting period end. Also there are $135 of accrued storage fees earned but unrecorded and uncollected at the period end.

   g) Of the $365 debited to the Advertising Expense account, $100 represents the cost of several hundred calendars imprinted with advertising that were received on October 20 and are to be distributed to prospective customers beginning on December 1 in the new accounting period.

   h) There are $160 of accrued but unpaid truck drivers' wages at the accounting period end.

2. Prepare an income statement and a classified balance sheet.
3. Prepare adjusting and closing entries from the work sheet.

Problem 4–3A

(If the working papers that accompany this text are not used, omit this problem.)

The ledger of Go-Go Delivery Service, showing account balances as of December 31, the end of the current annual accounting period, appears in the booklet of working papers. All accounts with balances have normal kinds of balances.

Required:

1. Prepare a trial balance of the ledger in the Trial Balance columns of a work sheet form and complete the work sheet using the following information:

   a) The delivery service entered into contracts with three stores during November and December in which it agreed to deliver packages for each store for a fixed fee. The contract of one store, signed on December 10, provides for a $90 monthly fee, payable on the 10th of each month after service is rendered. On December 31, $60, two thirds of the first month's fee, has been earned but is unrecorded. The other two stores made advance payments on their contracts, and the delivery service credited the amounts paid to its Unearned Delivery Service Revenue account. An examination of the contracts of these stores shows that $175 of the $450 paid has been earned by the accounting period end.

   b) Insurance expired on the office equipment, $50; and on the delivery equipment, $510.

   c) An inventory of office supplies shows $85 of unused office supplies on hand.

   d) Estimated depreciation on office equipment, $150; and (*e*) on delivery equipment, $2,350.

   f) Fifty dollars of office salaries and $300 of truck drivers' wages have accrued but are unrecorded.

2. Prepare an income statement and a classified balance sheet.
3. Prepare and post adjusting and closing entries.
4. Prepare a post-clearing trial balance.

Problem 4–4A

A-1 Janitorial Service operates with annual accounting periods that end each December 31, and on that date of the current year the following trial balance was taken from its ledger:

A-1 JANITORIAL SERVICE
Trial Balance, December 31, 19—

Cash	$ 1,080	
Accounts receivable	515	
Cleaning supplies	645	
Prepaid insurance	720	
Cleaning equipment	3,235	
Accumulated depreciation, cleaning equipment		$ 1,470
Trucks	7,395	
Accumulated depreciation, trucks		2,115
Accounts payable		165
Unearned janitorial revenue		200
Jeffro Jenkins, capital		6,940
Jeffro Jenkins, withdrawals	7,200	
Janitorial revenue		22,895
Wages expense	11,850	
Advertising expense	335	
Gas, oil, and repairs	695	
Miscellaneous expenses	115	
Totals	$33,785	$33,785

Required:

1. Enter the trial balance on a work sheet form and complete the work sheet using the following information:

   a) The year-end cleaning supplies inventory showed $125 of unused cleaning supplies on hand.

   b) Expired insurance for the year, $515.

   c) Estimated depreciation of cleaning equipment, $345; and (*d*) of trucks, $1,225.

   e) During December A-1 Janitorial Service entered into two contracts to provide cleaning services on a fixed-fee basis. The first contract, on which services began on December 1, called for a $100 monthly fee. The customer paid for the first two months' service in advance, and the amount paid was credited to the Unearned Janitorial Revenue account. The second contract called for a $150 monthly fee payable after services are rendered. One half of a month's services had been rendered on this contract by December 31, but the amount earned was unrecorded at the time the trial balance was prepared.

f) Wages totaling $125 had accrued by the trial balance date but were unpaid and unrecorded.

g) The $335 balance in the Advertising Expense account resulted from $235 in payments to the local paper for advertising that had appeared and $100 for ball-point pens with advertising imprinted thereon. The pens were to be given to customers and prospective customers in the new year.

2. Prepare an income statement and a classified balance sheet from the work sheet.
3. Prepare adjusting and closing entries from the work sheet.

Decision problem 4–1, Mr. Clean, Janitorial Service

The bookkeeper of Mr. Clean, Janitorial Service was taken seriously ill during the annual closing of the concern's books. Homer Cobb, the owner of the service, is sure the bookkeeper prepared a work sheet, income statement, and balance sheet. However, he has only the income statement and cannot find either the work sheet or balance sheet. He does have a trial balance that he prepared from the ledger accounts; he says no one owes him for work done; and he wants you to prepare adjusting and closing entries from the following trial balance and income statement so he can post them to the ledger. He would also like for you to prepare a year-end balance sheet.

Mr. Clean, Janitorial Service
Trial Balance, December 31, 19—

Cash	$ 895	
Prepaid insurance	425	
Cleaning supplies	815	
Cleaning equipment	2,980	
Accumulated depreciation, cleaning equipment		$ 1,435
Trucks	6,110	
Accumulated depreciation, trucks		2,565
Building	11,500	
Accumulated depreciation, building		3,475
Land	3,500	
Accounts payable		115
Unearned janitorial revenue		250
Homer Cobb, capital		14,455
Homer Cobb, withdrawals	6,500	
Janitorial revenue		26,635
Wages expense	14,995	
Advertising expense	285	
Gas, oil, and repairs	775	
Property taxes expense	150	
Totals	$48,930	$48,930

MR. CLEAN, JANITORIAL SERVICE
Income Statement for Year Ended December 31, 19 —

Revenue:

Janitorial revenue $26,785

Operating expenses:

Wages expense	$15,135	
Advertising expense...	285	
Gas, oil, and repairs...	775	
Property taxes expense	180	
Insurance expense..	295	
Cleaning supplies used	630	
Depreciation expense, cleaning equipment..................	315	
Depreciation expense, trucks.....................................	850	
Depreciation expense, building	300	
Total operating expenses		18,765
Net Income..		$ 8,020

Decision problem 4–2, Walt's TV Service

Walter Nash opened Walt's TV Service on January 1 of this year; and now, at the year-end, he has asked your help in determining his financial position. He says that business has been fairly good for the first year, but the bank has begun to dishonor his checks, his creditors are dunning him and he is unable to pay, and he just cannot understand why he is in such a position.

You find the accounting records, such as they are, have been kept by Mrs. Nash, who has had no formal training in record keeping. However, she has prepared for your inspection the following statement of cash receipts and disbursements:

WALT'S TV SERVICE
Cash Receipts and Disbursements
For Year Ended December 31, 19 —

Receipts:

Investment...	$ 5,000	
From customers..	27,250	$32,250

Disbursements:

Rent expense...	$ 1,300	
Repair equipment	3,000	
Insurance expense..	350	
Delivery truck expense	4,250	
Repair parts and supplies..	5,900	
Wages expense	17,500	32,300
Bank overdraft..		$ (50)

You find no errors in the statement and you ascertain the following additional facts:

1. Mrs. Nash has a list of customers who owe a total of $600 for TV repair work done on credit.

2. The lease contract for the shop space runs for five years and requires rent payments of $100 per month. It also stipulates that rents for the first and last months under the lease must be paid in advance. All required payments were made on time.

3. The repair equipment cost $3,000 and has a five-year useful life, after which it will be valueless.

4. The premiums on two insurance policies were paid on January 1. One premium was for $80 and purchased protection for one year. The other premium was for $270 and purchased three years' protection.

5. The delivery truck expense consists of $3,600 paid for the truck on January 1, plus $650 paid for gas, oil, and minor repairs to the truck. Mr. Nash expects to use the truck for four years, after which he thinks he will get $800 for it as a trade-in on a new truck.

6. In addition to the $5,900 of repair parts and supplies paid for during the year, Mr. Nash's creditors are dunning him for $700 for parts and supplies purchased and delivered, but not paid for. Also, an inventory shows there are $1,500 of unused repair parts and supplies on hand.

7. The $17,500 of wages expense consists of $7,100 paid the shop's one employee plus $200 per week withdrawn by Mr. Nash for personal living expenses. In addition, $50 is owed the one employee on December 31 for wages earned since the last payday.

Prepare a balance sheet showing the financial position of Walt's TV Service as of December 31 and prepare an income statement showing the results of its first year's operations.

Chapter 5

Accounting for a merchandising concern

■ The accounting records and reports of Owen Real Estate Agency, as described in previous chapters, are those of a service enterprise. Other service enterprises are laundries, taxicab companies, barber and beauty shops, theaters, and golf courses. Each performs a service for a commission or fee, and the net income of each is the difference between fees or commissions earned and operating expenses.

A merchandising concern, on the other hand, whether a wholesaler or retailer, earns revenue by selling goods or merchandise, and a net income results when revenue from sales exceeds the cost of the goods sold plus operating expenses, as the following condensed income statement shows:

A. Merchant
Condensed Income Statement

Revenue from sales..	$10,000
Cost of goods sold...	6,000
Gross profit from sales	$ 4,000
Operating expenses	3,000
Net Income...	$ 1,000

The merchant of the foregoing income statement sold for $10,000, goods that cost $6,000, and thereby earned a $4,000 gross profit from sales, from which he subtracted $3,000 of operating expenses to show a $1,000 net income.

Gross profit from sales, as shown on the foregoing income statement, is the "profit" before operating expenses are deducted; and accounting for the factors that enter into its calculation differentiates the accounting of a merchandising concern from that of a service enterprise.

Gross profit from sales is determined by subtracting the cost of whatever goods were sold from the revenue resulting from their sale; but before the subtraction can be made, both revenue from sales and cost of goods sold must be determined.

Revenue from sales

■ Revenue from sales consists of gross proceeds from merchandise sales less returns, allowances, and discounts. It is commonly reported on an income statement as follows:

Nelson Hardware Company		
Income Statement for Year Ended December 31, 19—		
Revenue from sales:		
Gross sales...		$78,750
Less: Sales returns and allowances...............	$650	
Sales discounts	750	1,400
Net sales		$77,350

Gross sales

The item, Gross sales, $78,750, on the foregoing partial income statement is the total cash and credit sales made by the company during the year. Cash sales were "rung up" on a cash register as each sale was completed, and at the end of each day the register total showed the amount of that day's cash sales, which was recorded with an entry like this:

Nov.	3	Cash...	205.00	
		Sales		205.00
		To record the day's cash sales.		

In addition an entry like this was used to record credit sales:

Nov.	3	Accounts Receivable	45.00	
		Sales		45.00
		Sold merchandise on credit.		

As a result, at the year-end the $78,750 credit balance of the company's Sales account showed the total of its cash and credit sales for the year.

Sales returns and allowances

In most stores a customer is permitted to return any unsatisfactory merchandise he has purchased; or he is sometimes allowed to keep the unsatisfactory goods and is given an allowance or an amount off its sales price. Either way, returns and allowances result from dissatisfied customers; consequently, it is important for management to watch returns and allowances and their relation to sales. Information as to returns and allowances is supplied by the Sales Returns and Allowances account when each return or allowance is recorded as follows:

Nov.	4	Sales Returns and Allowances.........................	20.00	
		Accounts Receivable (or Cash)..................		20.00
		Customer returned unsatisfactory merchandise.		

Sales discounts

When goods are sold on credit, the terms of payment are always made definite so there will be no misunderstanding as to the amount and time of payment. The terms normally appear on the invoice or sales ticket and are part of the sales agreement. Exact terms granted usually depend upon the custom of the trade. In some trades it is customary for invoices to become due and payable 10 days after the end of the month in which the sale occurred. Invoices in these trades carry terms, "n/10 EOM." In other trades invoices become due and payable 30 days after the invoice date and carry terms of "n/30." This means that the net amount of the invoice is due 30 days after the invoice date.

When credit periods are long, creditors usually grant discounts, called *cash discounts,* for early payments. This practice reduces the amount invested in accounts receivable and tends to decrease losses from uncollectible accounts. When discounts for early payment are granted, they are made part of the credit terms and appear on the invoice as, for example, "Terms: 2/10, n/60." Terms of 2/10, n/60 mean that the credit period is 60 days but that the debtor may deduct 2% from the invoice amount if payment is made within 10 days after the invoice date. The 10-day period is known as the discount period.

Since at the time of a sale it is not known if the customer will pay within the discount period and take advantage of a cash discount, sales discounts cannot be recorded until the customer pays. For example, on November 12, Nelson Hardware Company sold $100 of merchandise to a customer on credit, terms 2/10, n/60, and recorded the sale as follows:

Nov.	12	Accounts Receivable	100.00	
		Sales		100.00
		Sold merchandise, terms 2/10, n/60.		

At the time of the foregoing sale the customer had a choice. He could receive credit for paying the full $100 by sending Nelson Hardware Company a $98 check any time before November 22. Or he could wait 60 days, until January 11, and pay the full $100. If he elected to pay by November 22 and take advantage of the cash discount, Nelson Hardware Company would record the receipt of his $98 check as follows:

Nov.	22	Cash..	98.00	
		Sales Discounts	2.00	
		Accounts Receivable		100.00
		Received payment for the November 12		
		sale less the discount.		

Sales discounts are accumulated in the Sales Discounts account until the end of an accounting period when their total appears on the income statement as a deduction from gross sales. This is logical. A sales discount is an "amount off" the regular price of goods that is granted for early payment. Such discounts reduce revenue from sales, so it is only logical to deduct their total from gross sales.

Cost of goods sold
■ An automobile dealer or an appliance store, both of which make a limited number of sales each day, can easily refer to their records at the time of each sale and record the cost of the car or appliance sold. A drugstore, on the other hand, would find this difficult. For instance, if a drugstore sells a customer a tube of toothpaste, a box of aspirin, and a magazine, it can easily record with a cash register the sale of these items at marked selling prices; but it would find it difficult to maintain records that would enable it to also "look up" and record as "cost of goods sold" the costs of the items sold. As a result, stores such as drug, grocery, and others selling a volume of low-priced items make no effort to record the cost of the goods sold at the time of each sale. Rather, they wait until the end of an accounting period, take a physical inventory, and from the inventory and their accounting records determine at one time the cost of all goods sold during the period.

The end-of-the-period inventories taken by drug, grocery, hardware, or like stores in order to learn the cost of the goods they have sold are called *periodic inventories;* and the system used by such stores in accounting for cost of goods sold is known as a *periodic inventory system.* Such a system is described and discussed in this chapter. The system used by a car or appliance dealer to record the cost of each car or appliance sold depends on a *perpetual inventory record* of cars or appliances in stock, and as a result is known as a *perpetual inventory system of accounting for goods on hand and sold*. It is discussed in Chapter 10.

Cost of goods sold, periodic inventory system

■ As previously said, a store using a periodic inventory system makes no effort to determine and record the cost of items sold as they are sold. Rather, it waits until the end of an accounting period and determines at one time the cost of all the goods it sold during the period. And to do this, it must have information as to (1) the cost of the merchandise it had on hand at the beginning of the period, (2) the cost of the merchandise it purchased during the period, and (3) the cost of the unsold goods on hand at the period end. With this information a store can, for example, determine the cost of the goods it sold during a period as follows:

Cost of goods on hand at beginning of period	$ 2,000
Cost of goods purchased during the period	28,000
Goods available for sale during the period	$30,000
Unsold goods on hand at the period end	1,000
Cost of goods sold during the period	$29,000

The store of the foregoing calculation had $2,000 of merchandise at the beginning of the accounting period, and during the period it purchased an additional $28,000. Consequently, it had available and could have sold $30,000 of merchandise. However, $1,000 of this merchandise was on hand unsold at the period end; therefore, the cost of the goods it sold during the period was $29,000.

A reexamination of the foregoing calculation will show that three factors enter into calculating cost of goods sold: (1) the cost of the goods on hand at the beginning, (2) the cost of the goods purchased, and (3) the cost of the unsold goods on hand at the end. The sum of the first two is the amount of goods that were for sale, and by subtracting the last, the cost of the unsold goods on hand at the end, cost of goods sold is determined.

Merchandise inventories

The merchandise on hand at the beginning of an accounting period is called the *beginning inventory* and that on hand at the end is the *ending inventory*. Furthermore, since accounting periods follow one after another, the ending inventory of one period always becomes the beginning inventory of the next.

When a periodic inventory system is in use, cost of goods on hand at the end of an accounting period, the ending inventory, is determined by (1) physically counting the items on the shelves in the store and in the stock room, (2) multiplying the count for each kind of goods by its cost, and (3) adding the costs of the different kinds.

After the cost of the ending inventory is determined in the manner just described, it appears on the income statement as a subtraction in the cost of goods sold section. Also, by means of a closing entry, it is posted to an account called *Merchandise Inventory,* where it remains throughout the succeeding accounting period as a record of the inventory at the end of the period ended and the beginning of the succeeding period.

It should be emphasized at this point that entries are made in the Merchandise Inventory account only at the end of each accounting period; the entries are closing entries; and furthermore, since some goods are soon sold and other goods purchased, the account does not long show the amount of goods on hand. Rather, as soon as goods are sold or purchased, the account balance becomes a historical amount, the amount of goods that were on hand at the end of the last period and the beginning of the new period.

Cost of merchandise purchased

When a periodic inventory system is in use, cost of merchandise purchased is determined by subtracting from purchases any discounts, returns, and allowances and then adding any freight charges on purchases. However, before examining this calculation it is best to see how the amounts involved are accumulated.

Under a periodic inventory system, when merchandise is bought for resale, its cost is debited to an account called *Purchases,* as follows:

Nov.	5	Purchases	1,000.00	
		Accounts Payable..................................		1,000.00
		Purchased merchandise on credit, terms 2/10, n/30.		

The Purchases account has as its sole purpose the accumulation of the cost of all merchandise bought for resale during an accounting period. The account does not at any time show whether the purchased merchandise is on hand or has been disposed of through sale or other means.

If a credit purchase like that in the entry just given is subject to a cash discount, payment within the discount period results in a credit to *Purchases Discounts,* as in the following entry:

Nov.	12	Accounts Payable..	1,000.00	
		Purchases Discounts.............................		20.00
		Cash...		980.00
		Paid for the purchase of November 5 less the discount.		

When purchase discounts are involved, it is important that every invoice on which there is a discount be paid within the discount period, so that no discounts are lost. On the other hand, good cash management requires that no invoice be paid until the last day of its discount period. Consequently, to ensure that no discount is lost for lack of payment within the discount period, but that no invoice is paid before the end of the discount period, every invoice must be filed in such a way that it automatically comes to the attention of the company treasurer or other disbursing officer on the last day of its discount period. A simple way to do this is to provide a file with 31 folders, one for each day in a month. Then after an invoice is recorded, it is placed in the file folder of the last day of its discount period. For example, if an invoice is dated November 2, with terms of 2/10, n/30, the last day of its discount period is November 12, and such an invoice would be filed in folder number 12. Then on November 12 this invoice, together with any other invoices in the same folder, would be removed and paid or refiled for payment on a later date.

Sometimes merchandise received from suppliers for a variety of reasons is not acceptable and must be returned or, if kept, is kept only because the supplier grants an allowance or reduction in its price. When merchandise is returned, the purchaser "gets his money back"; but from a managerial point of view more is involved. Buying merchandise, receiving and inspecting it, deciding that the merchandise is unsatisfactory, and returning it is a costly procedure that should be held to a minimum; and the first step in holding it to a minimum is to know the amount of returns and allowances. Therefore, to make this information available to management, returns and allowances on purchases are commonly recorded in an account called *Purchases Returns and Allowances,* as follows:

Nov.	8	Accounts Payable..	65.00	
		Purchases Returns and Allowances............		65.00
		Returned defective merchandise.		

Sometimes a manufacturer or wholesaler pays freight, express, or other transportation costs on merchandise he sells and the total cost of the goods to the purchaser is the amount paid the manufacturer or wholesaler. Other times the purchaser must pay transportation costs; and when he does, such charges are a proper addition to the cost of the goods purchased and may be recorded with a debit to the Purchases account. However, more complete information is obtained if such costs are debited to an account called *Freight-In,* as follows:

Nov.	24	Freight-In	22.00	
		Cash		22.00
		Paid express charges on merchandise purchased.		

When an income statement is prepared at the end of an accounting period, the balances of the Purchases, Purchases Returns and Allowances, Purchases Discounts, and Freight-In accounts are combined on it as follows to show *net cost of purchases:*

Purchases..		$48,650
Less: Purchases returns and allowances.......... $275		
Purchases discounts 550	825	
Net purchases...		$47,825
Add: Freight-in		1,100
Net cost of purchases................................		$48,925

Cost of goods sold

The last item in the foregoing calculation, net cost of purchases, is the cost of the merchandise purchased during the accounting period, and it is combined on the income statement with the beginning and ending inventories to arrive at cost of goods sold as follows:

Cost of goods sold:			
Merchandise inventory, January 1, 19—................			$ 7,750
Purchases..		$48,650	
Less: Purchases returns and allowances...... $275			
Purchases discounts 550		825	
Net purchases...		$47,825	
Add: Freight-in		1,100	
Net cost of purchases................................			48,925
Goods available for sale			$56,675
Merchandise inventory, December 31, 19—............			8,950
Cost of goods sold..			$47,725

Inventory losses

Under a periodic inventory system any goods lost through shrinkage, spoilage, or shoplifting is automatically included in cost of goods sold. For example, assume a store actually lost $500 of merchandise to shoplifters during a year. This caused its year-end inventory to be $500 less than it otherwise would have been, since these goods were not available for inclusion in the year-end count. Consequently, since the year-end inventory was $500 smaller because of the loss, the cost of the goods the store sold was $500 greater.

Many stores are troubled with shoplifting; and although under a periodic inventory system the cost of such losses is automatically included in cost of goods sold, it is often important to know their extent. Consequently, a way to estimate shoplifting losses is described in Chapter 10.

Income
statement
of a
merchan-
dising
concern

■ A classified income statement for a merchandising concern has three sections: (1) a revenue section, (2) a cost of goods sold section, and (3) an operating expenses section. The first two have already been discussed in this chapter, but note in Illustration 5–1 how they are brought together to show gross profit from sales.

Nelson Hardware Company
Income Statement for Year Ended December 31, 19—

Revenue:			
Gross sales			$78,750
Less: Sales returns and allowances		$ 650	
Sales discounts		750	1,400
Net sales			$77,350
Cost of goods sold:			
Merchandise inventory, January 1, 19—		$ 7,750	
Purchases	$48,650		
Less: Purchases returns and allowances $275			
Purchases discounts 550	825		
Net purchases	$47,825		
Add: Freight-in	1,100		
Net cost of purchases		48,925	
Goods available for sale		$56,675	
Merchandise inventory, December 31, 19—		8,950	
Cost of goods sold			47,725
Gross profit from sales			$29,625
Operating expense:			
Selling expenses:			
Sales salaries	$ 8,200		
Rent expense, selling space	4,800		
Advertising expense	900		
Freight-out and delivery expense	1,350		
Store supplies used	425		
Depreciation expense, store equipment	775		
Total selling expenses		$16,450	
General and administrative expenses:			
Office salaries	$ 3,100		
Rent expense, office space	600		
Expired insurance	65		
Office supplies used	125		
Depreciation expense, office equipment	160		
Total general and administrative expenses		4,050	
Total operating expenses			20,500
Net Income			$ 9,125

Illustration
5–1

Observe also in Illustration 5–1 how operating expenses are classified as either "Selling expenses" or "General and administrative expenses." Selling expenses include expenses of storing and preparing goods for sale, promoting sales, actually making sales, and if there is not a delivery department separate from the selling departments, the expenses of delivering goods to customers. General and administrative expenses include the general office, accounting, personnel, and credits and collections expenses.

Sometimes an expenditure should be divided or prorated part to selling expenses and part to general and administrative expenses. Nelson Hardware Company divided the rent on its store building in this manner, as an examination of Illustration 5–1 will reveal. However, it did not prorate its insurance expense because the amount involved was so small the company felt the extra exactness did not warrant the extra work.

When an expense such as rent or heating and lighting is not prorated, it is a common practice to classify the expense as either a general and administrative expense or as a selling expense depending upon whether the office or the store occupies the greater amount of space. For example, if selling activities occupy more space than the office and rent is not prorated, it is only fair to classify it as a selling expense.

Work sheet of a merchandising concern ■ A concern selling merchandise, like a service-type company, uses a work sheet in bringing together the end-of-the-period information needed in preparing its income statement, balance sheet, and adjusting and clearing entries. Such a work sheet, that of Nelson Hardware Company, is shown in Illustration 5–2.

Note in Illustration 5–2 that the merchandising accounts are stressed by the use of color. This is done because the remainder of the accounts receive the same work sheet treatment as do the accounts of a service-type concern; and since this was fully discussed in Chapter 4, only the treatment of the merchandising accounts needs consideration here.

Trial Balance columns

The Trial Balance columns of the Nelson Hardware Company's work sheet, Illustration 5–2, show the balances of the company's accounts as of December 31, 19—. The account balances were taken from the company's ledger on that date and indicate that—

1. The January 1 beginning-of-the-year inventory was $7,750.
2. Sales totaling $78,750 were made during the year.
3. Customers returned $650 of goods they purchased.
4. Sales discounts totaling $750 were granted during the year.
5. The year's purchases of merchandise amounted to $48,650.
6. Merchandise purchases totaling $275 were returned.
7. Purchases discounts totaling $550 were taken during the year.
8. Freight charges totaling $1,100 were paid on goods purchased.

Adjustments columns and Adjusted Trial Balance columns

Generally none of the merchandising accounts require adjustments. Consequently, no adjustments appear opposite these accounts in the

Nelson Hardware Company
Work Sheet for Year Ended December 31, 19—

Account Titles	Trial Balance Dr.	Trial Balance Cr.	Adjustments Dr.	Adjustments Cr.	Adjusted Trial Balance Dr.	Adjusted Trial Balance Cr.	Income Statement Dr.	Income Statement Cr.	Balance Sheet Dr.	Balance Sheet Cr.
Cash	2,400				2,400				2,400	
Accounts receivable	3,300				3,300				3,300	
Merchandise inventory	7,750				7,750		7,750	8,950	8,950	
Prepaid insurance	195			(a) 65	130				130	
Store supplies	590			(b) 425	165				165	
Office supplies	185			(c) 125	60				60	
Store equipment	7,910				7,910				7,910	
Accumulated depreciation, store equipment		3,200		(d) 775		3,975				3,975
Office equipment	1,590				1,590				1,590	
Accumulated depreciation, office equipment		250		(e) 160		410				410
Accounts payable		1,700				1,700				1,700
George Nelson, capital		14,095				14,095				14,095
George Nelson, withdrawals	4,800				4,800				4,800	
Sales		78,750				78,750		78,750		
Sales returns and allowances	650				650		650			
Sales discounts	750				750		750			
Purchases	48,650				48,650		48,650			
Purchases returns and allowances		275				275		275		
Purchases discounts		550				550		550		
Freight-in	1,100				1,100		1,100			
Sales salaries	8,200				8,200		8,200			
Rent expense, selling space	4,800				4,800		4,800			
Advertising expense	900				900		900			
Freight-out and delivery expense	1,350				1,350		1,350			
Office salaries	3,100				3,100		3,100			
Rent expense, office space	600				600		600			
	98,820	98,820								
Expired insurance			(a) 65		65		65			
Store supplies used			(b) 425		425		425			
Office supplies used			(c) 125		125		125			
Depreciation expense, store equipment			(d) 775		775		775			
Depreciation expense, office equipment			(e) 160		160		160			
			1,550	1,550	99,755	99,755	79,400	88,525	29,305	20,180
Net income							9,125			9,125
							88,525	88,525	29,305	29,305

Illustration 5–2

Adjustments columns and the unadjusted trial balance amounts are carried directly into the Adjusted Trial Balance columns.

Income Statement columns

In any company the accounts that appear on its income statement are those whose balances are carried into the Income Statement columns of its work sheet; and in a merchandising concern these are the (1) revenue, (2) cost of goods sold, and (3) operating expense accounts. (The work sheet treatment of the operating expense accounts was discussed in Chapter 4 and needs no further consideration here.)

REVENUE ACCOUNTS. The Sales account is the primary revenue account of a merchandising concern. It is credited throughout each accounting period for the selling price of goods sold, and always reaches the end of the period with a credit balance, which is carried into the work sheet's Income Statement credit column.

Sales returns and allowances and sales discounts are in effect negative sales; and although the Sales Returns and Allowances and Sales Discounts accounts are classified as revenue accounts, they are really negative revenue accounts. Throughout each accounting period they are debited for returns, allowances, and discounts and both reach the period end with debit balances which are carried into the Income Statement debit column, where in effect the returns, allowances, and discounts are subtracted from the sales when the debit column total is subtracted from the credit column total in arriving at net income.

COST OF GOODS SOLD ACCOUNTS. When a work sheet is prepared for a company selling merchandise, (1) the debit balances of its Merchandise Inventory, Purchases, and Freight-In accounts are carried into the Income Statement debit column; (2) the credit balances of the Purchases Returns and Allowances and Purchases Discounts accounts are carried into the Income Statement credit column; after which (3) the dollar amount of the ending inventory is entered directly in both the Income Statement credit column and Balance Sheet debit column.

It is easy to understand why the balances of the Merchandise Inventory, Purchases, and Freight-In accounts are carried into the Income Statement debit column—the balances are debit balances and they enter into the calculation of the net income. Likewise, it is easy to understand why the credit balances of the Purchases Returns and Allowances and Purchases Discounts accounts are carried into the Income Statement credit column—they are in effect subtractions from Purchases in the debit column. However, the reasons for the work sheet treatment of the ending inventory are not so apparent and require the following explanations:

First: Note that there are two inventories to be dealt with on the work sheet of a company selling merchandise—the beginning-of-the-period inventory and the end-of-the-period inventory.

Second: At the end of a period, before closing entries are posted, it is the beginning inventory amount that appears in the accounts as the debit balance of the Merchandise Inventory account; and it is this beginning inventory amount that is entered in the Trial Balance debit column opposite the account title, Merchandise Inventory, and is carried into the Adjusted Trial Balance and Income Statement debit columns.

Third: Before closing entries are posted, the dollar amount of the ending inventory does not appear in any account. As was explained earlier, the ending inventory is determined at the end of each period by counting the items of unsold merchandise on hand, multiplying the count for each kind by its cost, and adding the dollar amounts of the several kinds to determine the number of dollars of inventory.

Fourth: As soon as the number of dollars of ending inventory is determined, it is entered directly on the work sheet in both the Income Statement credit column and the Balance Sheet debit column. It is thus entered for three reasons: (1) After the other income statement items (including the operating expenses) have been carried into the Income Statement columns, it is necessary to enter the amount of the ending inventory if the difference between the two columns is to equal the net income or loss. (2) Entering the ending inventory in the Income Statement credit column puts this amount on the work sheet in position to become part of one of the closing entries and thus be taken into the accounts as the historical record of the inventory on hand at the end of the period. (Closing entries for a company selling merchandise are discussed in more detail later.) And finally, (3) since the amount of the ending inventory is an end-of-the-period asset, entering it in the Balance Sheet debit column puts this item in position to be added to the other end-of-the-period assets and to appear on the balance sheet.

Completing the work sheet

After the various income statement and balance sheet amounts of a company selling merchandise are sorted and entered in the proper columns of its work sheet, the columns are totaled and the work sheet is completed in the usual way.

Preparing the statements; adjusting entries

■ As in a service-type concern, the work sheet of a company selling merchandise is a tool for bringing together information needed in preparing the financial statements. The income statement is prepared from information in the Income Statement columns, the balance sheet from the Balance Sheet columns, and no essentially new techniques are required in the preparation of either.

Likewise, no new techniques are required in preparing and posting adjusting entries. Each adjustment in the work sheet's Adjustments columns requires an adjusting entry that is journalized and posted in the usual manner.

Closing entries ■ The Income Statement columns of its work sheet provide the information needed by a merchandising concern in making its closing entries, just as in a service enterprise. Furthermore, an examination of the following closing entries and the work sheet of Illustration 5–2, from which they were prepared, will show these closing entries are prepared in the same way as are those of a service-type company. In both types of companies the Income Summary account is debited for the work sheet's Income Statement debit column total and each account having an item in the column is credited. Then, each account having an item in the Income Statement credit column is debited and the Income Summary account is credited for the column total. And so on, as was explained in Chapter 4.

Dec.	31	Income Summary...	79,400.00	
		Merchandise Inventory..............................		7,750.00
		Sales Returns and Allowances...................		650.00
		Sales Discounts		750.00
		Purchases		48,650.00
		Freight-In..		1,100.00
		Sales Salaries..		8,200.00
		Rent Expense, Selling Space....................		4,800.00
		Advertising Expense................................		900.00
		Freight-Out and Delivery Expense..............		1,350.00
		Office Salaries		3,100.00
		Rent Expense, Office Space		600.00
		Expired Insurance...................................		65.00
		Store Supplies Used................................		425.00
		Office Supplies Used		125.00
		Depreciation Expense, Store Equipment.....		775.00
		Depreciation Expense, Office Equipment....		160.00
		To close the temporary proprietorship accounts having debit balances.		
	31	Merchandise Inventory...............................	8,950.00	
		Sales	78,750.00	
		Purchases Returns and Allowances................	275.00	
		Purchases Discounts	550.00	
		Income Summary		88,525.00
		To close the temporary proprietorship accounts having credit balances and to set up the ending inventory.		
	31	Income Summary...	9,125.00	
		George Nelson, Capital.............................		9,125.00
		To close the Income Summary account.		
	31	George Nelson, Capital.................................	4,800.00	
		George Nelson, Withdrawals		4,800.00
		To close the Withdrawals account.		

Closing entries and the inventory

■ Although there is nothing new about the closing entries of a merchandising concern, their effect on the Merchandise Inventory account should be observed.

Before closing entries were posted, the Merchandise Inventory account of Nelson Hardware Company showed in its $7,750 debit balance the amount of the company's beginning-of-the-period inventory,[1] as follows:

Merchandise Inventory					ACCOUNT NO. *114*	
DATE	EXPLANATION	FO-LIO	DEBIT	CREDIT	BALANCE	
197A Dec. 31		63	7 7 5 0 00		7 7 5 0 00	

Then, when the first closing entry was posted, its $7,750 credit to the Merchandise Inventory account had the effect of clearing the beginning inventory from the account, as follows:

Merchandise Inventory					ACCOUNT NO. *114*	
DATE	EXPLANATION	FO-LIO	DEBIT	CREDIT	BALANCE	
197A Dec. 31		63	7 7 5 0 00		7 7 5 0 00	
197B Dec. 31		77		7 7 5 0 00	-0-	

After this, when the second closing entry was posted, its $8,950 debit to Merchandise Inventory put back into the account the amount of the ending inventory, as follows, where the amount remains throughout the succeeding year as the debit balance of the account and as a historical record of the amount of inventory on hand at the end of 197B and the beginning of 197C.

Merchandise Inventory					ACCOUNT NO. *114*	
DATE	EXPLANATION	FO-LIO	DEBIT	CREDIT	BALANCE	
197A Dec. 31		63	7 7 5 0 00		7 7 5 0 00	
197B Dec. 31		77		7 7 5 0 00	-0-	
31		77	8 9 5 0 00		8 9 5 0 00	

[1] The date of the beginning inventory, 197A, is intended to convey the idea that the $7,750 beginning inventory amount was posted to this account at the end of the preceding year.

Taking the ending inventory

■ As previously stated, when a periodic inventory system is in use, the dollar amount of the ending inventory is determined by (1) physically counting the items of unsold merchandise remaining in the store at the accounting period end, (2) multiplying the count for each kind of item by its cost, and (3) adding the costs for all the items. The first step, counting the items, is called taking an inventory.

Counting unsold merchandise at the end of an accounting period is often a difficult task; and unless great care is exercised, items may be omitted from the count or they may be counted more than once. Because of this, inventories are commonly taken at night, on holidays, and on weekends; or the store is closed for business in order to take the inventory.

A store's salesclerks who are familiar with the store and its merchandise are usually best equipped to make an inventory count. Before the count is started, the merchandise should be straightened and arranged in an orderly fashion on the shelves and in the showcases. Items are less apt to be counted twice or omitted if prenumbered inventory tickets like the one shown in Illustration 5–3 are used in making the count. If inventory tickets are used, at the start of the count a sufficient number of tickets, at least one for each type of product on hand, is issued to each department in the store. When the inventory count is made, a clerk counts the quantity of each product and from the count and the price tag attached to the merchandise fills in the information on the inventory ticket. He then initials the ticket and attaches it to the counted items. A department head or other responsible person usually examines

Illustration 5–3

and recounts a sufficient proportion of the items to ensure an accurate count. In each department, after the clerks complete the count, the department is examined for uncounted items. At this stage, inventory tickets are attached to all counted items. Consequently, any products without tickets attached are uncounted. After all items are counted and tickets attached, the tickets are removed and sent to the accounting department for completion of the inventory. To ensure that no ticket is lost or left attached to merchandise, all the prenumbered tickets issued are accounted for when the tickets arrive in the accounting department.

In the accounting department, the information on the tickets is copied on inventory summary sheets, and the sheets are completed by multiplying the number of units of each product by its unit cost. This gives the dollar amount of each product on hand, and the total for all products is the amount of the inventory.

For many years it has been a common practice to price inventory items at *cost or market, whichever is lower.* "Cost" is the actual price that was paid for an item when it was purchased. "Market" is the price that would have to be paid if the item were being purchased on the inventory date. In other words, "market" is the replacement cost of the item. For example, on the inventory summary sheet of Illustration 5–4, the Ajax claw hammers are valued at cost because their $1 cost price is below their $1.25 market price. Likewise, the Sharp hand saws are valued at market because their $2.90 market price is below their $3 cost price.

INVENTORY SUMMARY SHEET

Item	Quantity on Hand	Date Purchased	Sales Price	Cost Price	Market Price	Inventory Value
Ajax claw hammers	4	12-12	1 50	1 00	1 25	4 00
Sharp hand saws	2	11-3	4 50	3 00	2 90	5 80
Danley 24-inch levels	2	9-14	5 50	3 50	3 50	7 00

Illustration
5–4

■ A concern's inventory should include all goods owned by the business and held for sale, regardless of where the goods may be located at the time of the inventory. In the application of this rule, there are generally no problems with respect to most items. For most items all that is required is to see that they are counted, that nothing is omitted, and that nothing is counted more than once. However, goods in transit from a manufacturer or wholesaler, goods sold but not delivered, goods on consignment, and obsolete and damaged goods do require special attention.

When goods are in transit on the inventory date, the purchase should be recorded and the goods should appear on the purchaser's inventory if title has passed to the purchaser. The general rule as to the passing of title is: if the buyer is responsible for paying the freight charges, title passes as soon as the goods are loaded aboard the means of transportation; if the seller is to pay the freight charges, title passes when the goods arrive at their destination.

Goods on consignment are goods shipped by their owner (known as the consignor) to another person or firm (called the consignee) who is to sell the goods for the owner. Consigned goods belong to the consignor and should appear on his inventory.

Damaged goods and goods that have deteriorated or become obsolete should not be placed on the inventory if they are not salable. If such goods are salable but at a reduced price, they should be placed on the inventory at a conservative estimate of their realizable value (sale price less the cost of making the sale). This causes the accounting period in which the goods are damaged, deteriorated, or become obsolete to suffer the resultant loss.

■ Merchandise purchased that does not meet specifications on delivery, goods received in damaged condition, goods received that were not ordered, goods received short of the amount ordered and billed, and invoice errors are matters for adjustment between the buyer and seller. In some cases the buyer can make the adjustment, and in others the adjustment is a subject for negotiation between the buyer and the seller. When there are invoice errors or when goods are received that were not ordered, the buyer may make the adjustment. If he does, he must notify the seller of his action, and commonly he does this by sending a *debit memorandum* or a *credit memorandum*.

For instance, in checking an invoice for merchandise purchased from Eugene Manufacturing Company, Salem Department Store discovered an invoice error, the correction of which reduced the invoice total from $85 to $75. Since an invoice error does not require negotiation, Salem Department Store notified Eugene Manufacturing Company of the error by mailing it the debit memorandum shown in Illustration 5–5. A debit memorandum was sent because correction of the error reduced the amount of Salem Department Store's debt to Eugene Manufacturing Company from $85 to $75, and to reduce an account payable a debit is required.

Debit Memorandum

Salem Department Store

Salem, Oregon

To: Eugene Manufacturing Company
2590 Chula Vista Street
Eugene, Oregon

Date: December 5, 19--

WE DEBIT YOUR ACCOUNT AS FOLLOWS:

Error in addition on your invoice
No. C-113. Invoice totals $75
rather than the $85 shown.. $10.00

SALEM DEPARTMENT STORE

Frank Hatte

Manager, Purchasing Department

Illustration
5-5

In recording this purchase, Salem Department Store could debit Purchases and credit Accounts Payable for $85 and then immediately record the debit memorandum by debiting Accounts Payable and crediting Purchases for $10. However, a better way would be to mark the correction on the invoice, attach a copy of the debit memorandum to show that Eugene Manufacturing Company had been notified, and then debit Purchases and credit Accounts Payable for the corrected amount of the invoice, $75.

Some adjustments, such as merchandise received in damaged condition or merchandise not meeting specifications, normally require negotiations between the buyer and seller. In such cases the buyer may debit Purchases for the full invoice amount and enter into negotiations with the seller for a return or a price adjustment. If the seller agrees to a return or adjustment, he notifies the buyer with a credit memorandum. This memorandum is a credit memorandum to the seller because the return or adjustment reduces the amount of his account receivable with the buyer. For example, Salem Department Store purchased a number of items from Novelty Supply Company, totaling $100. When the merchandise arrived, five ceramic figurines were found to have been improperly packed and were consequently damaged in transit. Salem Department Store recorded the full amount of the invoice by debiting Purchases and crediting Accounts Payable for $100. It then entered into negotiations for an adjustment equal to the value of the broken figurines. Novelty Supply Company agreed to the adjustment and notified Salem Department Store with the credit memorandum shown in Illustration 5–6.

CREDIT MEMORANDUM

Novelty Supply Company
PORTLAND, OREGON

NUMBER L·364

DATE December 12, 19--

TO Salem Department Store

   1451 High Street

   Salem, Oregon

WE CREDIT YOUR ACCOUNT AS FOLLOWS

5 ceramic figurines damaged in transit and returned $18.00

T. A. Briggs
Sales Manager

Illustration
5–6

Since Salem Department Store debited Purchases and credited Accounts Payable for the full amount of the original invoice, it records the credit memorandum by a debit to Accounts Payable and a credit to Purchases Returns and Allowances for $18.

A debit or credit memorandum may originate with either party to a transaction. The memorandum gets its name from the action of the party originating it. If the originator debits, he sends a debit memorandum. If the originator credits, he sends a credit memorandum.

Dispensing with the Adjusted Trial Balance columns	■ Thus far, because using such columns makes learning easier, all illustrated work sheets have had Adjusted Trial Balance columns. However, the experienced accountant commonly omits these columns from his work sheet in order to reduce the time and effort required in its preparation. When he does so, after he has entered the adjustments in the Adjustments columns, he combines the adjustment amounts with the trial balance amounts and sorts the combined amounts directly into the Income Statement and Balance Sheet columns in a single operation. In other words, he simply eliminates the adjusted trial balance from his work sheet.
Code numbers as a means of identifying accounts	■ The account numbering scheme used in the chapters before this has been a simple one in which the accounts have been numbered consecutively. Such a scheme is satisfactory in a small business. However, in a larger more complicated accounting system, account numbers commonly become code numbers that not only identify accounts but also tell their statement classifications. For example, in one numbering system three-digit numbers with each digit having a significant meaning are used. In this system the first digit in each account number tells the major balance sheet or income statement classification of the account to which it is assigned. For example, account numbers with first digits of 1, numbers 111 to 199, are assigned to asset accounts, and liability accounts are assigned numbers with the first digits of 2, numbers 211 to 299. When this system is used, main balance sheet and income statement account classifications are assigned the following numbers:

111 to 199 are assigned to asset accounts.
211 to 299 are assigned to liability accounts.
311 to 399 are assigned to owner equity accounts.
411 to 499 are assigned to sales or revenue accounts.
511 to 599 are assigned to cost of goods sold accounts.
611 to 699 are assigned to operating expense accounts.
711 to 799 are assigned to other revenue and expense accounts.

When accounts are assigned code numbers having several digits, all of the digits have a significant meaning. In the system under discussion where the first digit indicates the main balance sheet or income statement classification, the second and third digits further classify the account. For example, the second digits under each of the following main classifications indicate the subclassification shown:

111 to 199. Asset accounts
    111 to 119. Current asset accounts (second digits of 1)
    121 to 129. Long-term investment accounts (second digits of 2)
    131 to 139. Plant asset accounts (second digits of 3)
    141 to 149. Intangible asset accounts (second digits of 4)

211 to 299. Liability accounts
    211 to 219. Current liability accounts (second digits of 1)

221 to 229. Long-term liability accounts (second digits of 2)

611 to 699. Operating expense accounts
    611 to 629. Selling expense accounts (second digits of 1 and 2)
    631 to 649. Delivery expense accounts (second digits of 3 and 4)
    651 to 669. General administrative expense accounts (second digits of 5 and 6)

The third digit in each number further classifies the account. For example, in the system under discussion, all selling expense accounts, which have account numbers with first digits of 6 and second digits of 1 and 2, are further classified as follows:

611 to 699. Operating expense accounts
    611 to 629. Selling expense accounts
        611. Sales salaries (third digit of 1)
        612. Advertising (third digit of 2)
        613. Depreciation of store equipment (third digit of 3)

Questions for class discussion

1. How does a merchandising concern earn revenue?
2. What is gross profit from sales?
3. What is a cash discount? If terms are 2/10, n/60, what is the length of the credit period? What is the length of the discount period?
4. How and when is cost of goods sold determined in a store using a periodic inventory system?
5. May a store sell goods at a price above their cost and still suffer a loss? How?
6. Why should a concern be interested in the amount of its sales returns and allowances?
7. Since total sales returns and allowances is subtracted from the balance of the Sales account on the income statement, why not save the effort of this subtraction by debiting each return or allowance to the Sales account?
8. If a concern may return for full credit all unsatisfactory merchandise purchased, why should it be interested in the amount returned?
9. Which of the following are debited to the Purchases account of a grocery store: (a) the purchase of a cash register; (b) the purchase of a roll of wrapping paper; (c) the purchase of advertising space in a newspaper; and (d) the purchase of a case of tomato soup?
10. At the end of an accounting period which inventory, the beginning inventory or the ending, appears on the trial balance?
11. Why is the amount of the ending inventory entered in the work sheet's Income Statement credit column? Why is it entered in the Balance Sheet debit column?
12. What effect do closing entries have on the Merchandise Inventory account?
13. Why are inventory tickets used in taking a physical inventory?
14. When applied to an inventory item and used in the phrase, "cost or market, whichever is lower," what is the meaning of the words (a) cost and (b) market?

15. During a year a company purchased merchandise costing $22,000. What was the company's cost of goods sold if there were:
    a) No beginning or ending inventories?
    b) A beginning inventory of $10,000 and no ending inventory?
    c) A beginning inventory of $8,000 and an ending inventory of $9,500?
    d) No beginning inventory and an ending inventory of $7,000?
16. In counting the merchandise on hand at the end of an accounting period, a clerk failed to count, and consequently omitted from the inventory, all the merchandise on one shelf. If the cost of the merchandise on the shelf was $100, what was the effect of the omission on (a) the balance sheet and (b) the income statement?
17. Suppose that the omission of the $100 from the inventory (Question 16) was not discovered. What would be the effect on the balance sheet and income statement prepared at the end of the next accounting period?
18. When a three-digit account numbering system like the one described in this chapter is in use, which digit of an account's number is the most significant?

Class exercises

Exercise 5–1

Sport Shop purchased $1,200 of merchandise, terms 2/10, n/60, from Blue Company and paid for the merchandise within the discount period. (a) Give without dates the entries made by Sport Shop to record the purchase and payment and (b) give without dates the entries made by Blue Company to record the sale and collection.

Exercise 5–2

The following items, with expenses condensed to conserve space, appeared in the Income Statement columns of University Store's December 31, 197B, work sheet. From the information prepare a 197B income statement for University Store.

	Income Statement Debit	Income Statement Credit
Merchandise inventory	10,000	9,000
Sales		60,000
Sales returns and allowances	500	
Sales discounts	1,000	
Purchases	34,500	
Purchases returns and allowances		300
Purchases discounts		700
Freight-in	1,500	
Selling expenses	8,000	
General and administrative expenses	6,000	
	61,500	70,000
Net income	8,500	
	70,000	70,000

Exercise 5-3

PART 1. Assume that University Store of Exercise 5-2 is owned by Gary Fall and prepare entries to close the store's revenue, expense, and Income Summary accounts.

PART 2. Rule a balance-column Merchandise Inventory account on notebook paper, and under the date, December 31, 197A, enter the $10,000 beginning inventory of Exercise 5-2 as its balance. Then post to the account the portions of the closing entries that affect this account. (Post first the credit that removes the beginning inventory amount from the account.)

Exercise 5-4

Copy the following tabulation and fill in the missing amounts. Indicate a loss by placing a minus sign before the amount. Each horizontal row of figures is a separate problem situation.

Sales	Beginning Inventory	Net Purchases	Ending Inventory	Cost of Goods Sold	Gross Profit	Expenses	Net Income or Loss
85,000	50,000	40,000	?	55,000	?	20,000	?
90,000	35,000	?	45,000	50,000	?	25,000	15,000
125,000	50,000	?	40,000	?	55,000	35,000	20,000
?	40,000	70,000	35,000	?	40,000	35,000	?
100,000	40,000	65,000	?	60,000	?	25,000	?
70,000	30,000	?	35,000	40,000	?	?	10,000
?	40,000	50,000	30,000	?	40,000	?	−5,000
85,000	?	50,000	35,000	?	30,000	?	10,000

Exercise 5-5

Following is a list of trial balance accounts and their balances. To simplify the problem and to save time, the balances are in numbers of not more than two digits. However, in order to increase your skill in sorting adjusted trial balance amounts to the proper Income Statement and Balance Sheet columns of a work sheet, the accounts are listed in alphabetical order.

TRIAL BALANCE ACCOUNTS AND BALANCES

Accounts payable	$ 2	Merchandise inventory	$ 4
Accounts receivable	3	Prepaid insurance	3
Accumulated depreciation,		Purchases	10
store equipment	2	Purchases discounts	1
Advertising expense	4	Salaries expense	5
Cash	2	Sales	30
Freight-in	1	Sales returns	2
Gary Green, capital	13	Store equipment	9
Gary Green, withdrawals	2	Store supplies	3

Required:

Prepare a work sheet form on ordinary notebook paper and copy the trial balance accounts and amounts on the work sheet without changing their alphabetical arrangement. Then complete the work sheet using the following information:

a) Estimated depreciation on store equipment, $1.
b) Ending merchandise inventory, $2.
c) Expired insurance, $2.
d) Accrued salaries payable, 3.
e) Ending inventory of store supplies, $1.

Problems **Problem 5–1**

Prepare general journal entries to record the following transactions:

Oct. 1 Purchased merchandise on credit, terms 2/10, n/30, $750.
 1 Paid ONC Truck Line $35 for freight charges on the foregoing shipment of merchandise.
 5 Sold merchandise on credit, terms 2/10, 1/15, n/60, $300.
 8 Purchased on credit a new typewriter for office use, terms n/10 EOM, $225.
 9 Purchased merchandise on credit from Phoenix Company, terms 2/10, n/60, $600.
 11 Received a $50 credit memorandum from Phoenix Company for merchandise purchased on October 9 and returned for credit.
 12 Sold merchandise for cash, $45.
 15 Purchased office supplies on credit, terms n/10 EOM, $85.
 16 Received a credit memorandum for unsatisfactory office supplies purchased on October 15 and returned, $25.
 17 Sold merchandise on credit, terms 2/10, 1/15, n/60, $425.
 18 Issued a credit memorandum to the customer of October 17 who returned $25 of the merchandise he had purchased.
 19 Paid for the merchandise purchased on October 9, less the return and the discount.
 20 The customer who purchased merchandise on October 5 walked into the store and paid for his purchase of that date less the applicable discount.
 27 Received payment for the merchandise sold on October 17, less the return and applicable discount.
 31 Paid for the merchandise purchased on October 1.

Problem 5–2

(*If the working papers that accompany this text are not used, omit this problem.*)

The work sheet of Valley Sales, completed through the Adjusted Trial Balance columns, is reproduced in the booklet of working papers.

Required:

1. Sort the work sheet's adjusted trial balance amounts into the proper Income Statement and Balance Sheet columns, enter the ending inventory amount, $15,880, in the Income Statement credit column and Balance Sheet debit column, and complete the work sheet.
2. From the work sheet prepare an income statement that is complete through the calculation of gross profit from sales.
3. Prepare compound closing entries from the work sheet.
4. Post those portions of the closing entries that affect the Merchandise In-

ventory account. Post first the credit that clears the beginning inventory from the account.

Problem 5–3

The following trial balance was taken from the ledger of Universal Sales at the end of its annual accounting period:

UNIVERSAL SALES

Trial Balance, December 31, 19—

Cash	$ 1,525	
Accounts receivable	1,115	
Merchandise inventory	14,540	
Store supplies	675	
Prepaid insurance	220	
Store equipment	9,890	
Accumulated depreciation, store equipment		$ 3,210
Accounts payable		2,225
Earl Dale, capital		17,045
Earl Dale, withdrawals	7,800	
Sales		74,415
Sales returns and allowances	310	
Sales discounts	1,145	
Purchases	41,320	
Purchases returns and allowances		435
Purchases discounts		790
Freight-in	565	
Sales salaries	11,435	
Rent expense	6,000	
Advertising expense	815	
Heating and lighting expense	765	
Totals	$98,120	$98,120

Required:
1. Enter the trial balance on a work sheet form and complete the work sheet using the following information:
   a) Ending store supplies inventory, $145.
   b) Expired insurance, $120.
   c) Estimated depreciation on store equipment, $910.
   d) Accrued sales salaries payable, $165.
   e) Ending merchandise inventory, $16,040.
2. Prepare an income statement complete through the calculation of gross profit from sales.
3. From the work sheet prepare compound closing entries.
4. Open a Merchandise Inventory account and enter the $14,540 beginning inventory amount as its balance. Then post the portions of the closing entries that affect this account, posting first the credit that clears the beginning inventory from the account.

Problem 5–4

A trial balance of Campus Shop carried the following items at the end of an annual accounting period:

CAMPUS SHOP
Trial Balance, December 31, 19—

Cash	$ 1,190	
Merchandise inventory	12,655	
Store supplies	780	
Office supplies	145	
Prepaid insurance	235	
Store equipment	9,835	
Accumulated depreciation, store equipment		$ 3,370
Office equipment	1,775	
Accumulated depreciation, office equipment		750
Accounts payable		4,145
Larry Dunn, capital		20,550
Larry Dunn, withdrawals	5,400	
Sales		67,705
Sales returns and allowances	1,510	
Purchases	40,235	
Purchases returns and allowances		515
Purchases discounts		245
Freight-in	915	
Sales salaries	12,230	
Rent expense, selling space	4,950	
Advertising expense	830	
Office salaries	3,910	
Rent expense, office space	550	
Telephone expense	135	
Totals	$97,280	$97,280

Required:

1. Copy the trial balance amounts into the Trial Balance columns of a work sheet form and complete the work sheet using the following information:
   a) Ending store supplies inventory, $135; and (b) office supplies inventory, $55.
   c) Expired insurance, $120.
   d) Estimated depreciation on store equipment, $990; and (e) on office equipment, $215.
   f) Accrued sales salaries, $205; and accrued office salaries, $45.
   g) Campus Shop allocates one tenth of its rent expense to the office and the remainder to selling space. Rent for the month of December had accrued but was unpaid and unrecorded on the trial balance date.
   h) Ending merchandise inventory, $11,610.
2. Prepare a classified income statement for the shop.
3. Prepare compound closing entries.
4. Open a Merchandise Inventory account and enter the $12,655 beginning inventory amount as its balance. Then post the portions of the closing entries that affect this account, posting first the credit that clears the beginning inventory from the account.

Problem 5–5

The following trial balance was taken from the ledger of University Store at the end of its annual accounting period:

UNIVERSITY STORE
Trial Balance, December 31, 19—

Cash	$ 1,275	
Merchandise inventory	13,145	
Store supplies	820	
Office supplies	275	
Prepaid insurance	315	
Office equipment	1,850	
Accumulated depreciation, office equipment		$ 645
Store equipment	9,780	
Accumulated depreciation, store equipment		3,135
Accounts payable		1,540
Carl Holt, capital		14,185
Carl Holt, withdrawals	8,400	
Sales		77,385
Sales returns and allowances	960	
Purchases	41,480	
Purchases returns and allowances		365
Purchases discounts		915
Freight-in	570	
Sales salaries	9,245	
Rent expense, selling space	4,320	
Advertising expense	575	
Delivery expense	240	
Heating and lighting expense	885	
Office salaries	3,555	
Rent expense, office space	480	
Totals	$98,170	$98,170

Required:
1. Enter the trial balance in the Trial Balance columns of a work sheet form and complete the work sheet using the following information:
   a) Store supplies inventory, $185; and (b) office supplies inventory, $125.
   c) Expired insurance, $245.
   d) Estimated depreciation on office equipment, $210; and (e) on store equipment, $970.
   f) Accrued sales salaries, $165; and accrued office salaries, $45.
   g) Ending merchandise inventory, $14,750.
2. Prepare a classified income statement and a classified balance sheet.
3. Prepare adjusting and compound closing entries.
4. Open a Merchandise Inventory account and enter the $13,145 beginning inventory amount as its balance. Then post those portions of the closing entries that affect this account.

Alternate problems

Problem 5–1A

Prepare general journal entries to record the following transactions:

Oct. 1 Purchased merchandise on credit, terms 1/10, n/30, $650.
    3 Sold merchandise for cash, $60.

Oct. 6 Purchased office equipment on credit, terms n/10 EOM, $150.
8 Purchased merchandise on credit from ABC Company, terms 2/10, n/60, $585.
8 Paid Rapid Freight Company $40 for freight charges on the foregoing purchase of merchandise.
12 Received a $35 credit memorandum from ABC Company for merchandise purchased on October 8 and returned for credit.
13 Sold merchandise on credit, terms 2/10, 1/15, n/60, $400.
15 Purchased office supplies on credit, terms n/10 EOM, $65.
16 Sold merchandise on credit, terms 2/10, 1/15, n/60, $545.
17 Received a credit memorandum for unsatisfactory office supplies purchased on October 15 and returned for credit, $15.
18 Issued a $45 credit memorandum to the customer who purchased merchandise on October 16 and returned a portion for credit.
18 Paid for the merchandise purchased on October 8, less the return and the discount.
26 Received payment for the merchandise sold on October 16, less the return and the applicable discount.
28 The customer of October 13 walked into the store and paid for his purchase of that date, less the applicable discount.
31 Paid for the merchandise purchased on October 1.

Problem 5–3A

The following trial balance was taken from the ledger of Desert Supply House at the end of its annual accounting period:

DESERT SUPPLY HOUSE
Trial Balance, December 31, 19—

Cash	$ 870	
Merchandise inventory	14,540	
Store supplies	810	
Prepaid insurance	295	
Store equipment	8,865	
Accumulated depreciation, store equipment		$ 3,340
Accounts payable		4,110
Paul Ross, capital		20,805
Paul Ross, withdrawals	6,000	
Sales		69,225
Sales returns and allowances	725	
Sales discounts	1,225	
Purchases	42,540	
Purchases returns and allowances		385
Purchases discounts		210
Freight-in	885	
Sales salaries	12,560	
Rent expense	7,200	
Advertising expense	925	
Utilities expense	635	
Totals	$98,075	$98,075

Required:

1. Copy the trial balance into the Trial Balance columns of a work sheet form and complete the work sheet using the following information:
    a) Ending inventory of store supplies, $175.
    b) Expired insurance, $180.
    c) Estimated depreciation of store equipment, $980.
    d) Accrued sales salaries payable, $215.
    e) Ending merchandise inventory, $12,990.
2. Prepare an income statement completed through the calculation of gross profit from sales.
3. Prepare compound closing entries from the work sheet.
4. Open a Merchandise Inventory account and enter the $14,540 beginning inventory amount as its balance. Then post the portions of the closing entries that affect this account, posting first the credit that clears the beginning inventory from the account.

Problem 5-4A

The following trial balance was taken from the ledger of The Man's Shop at the end of its annual accounting period:

THE MAN'S SHOP
Trial Balance, December 31, 19—

Cash	$ 2,215	
Merchandise inventory	12,655	
Store supplies	795	
Office supplies	170	
Prepaid insurance	345	
Store equipment	9,140	
Accumulated depreciation, store equipment		$ 1,320
Office equipment	1,490	
Accumulated depreciation, office equipment		265
Accounts payable		2,590
Gary Hall, capital		16,135
Gary Hall, withdrawals	7,800	
Sales		75,810
Sales returns and allowances	810	
Purchases	40,980	
Purchases returns and allowances		315
Purchases discounts		785
Freight-in	720	
Sales salaries	9,155	
Rent expense, selling space	5,400	
Advertising expense	785	
Office salaries	4,160	
Rent expense, office space	600	
Totals	$97,220	$97,220

Required:

1. Enter the trial balance on a work sheet form and complete the work sheet using the following information:

a) Ending store supplies inventory, $155; and (b) ending office supplies inventory, $60.

c) Expired insurance, $215.

d) Estimated depreciation on store equipment, $875; and (e) on office equipment, $145.

f) Accrued sales salaries, $110; and accrued office salaries, $35.

g) The Man's Shop charges 10% of its total rent expense to the office and the remainder to selling space; and its lease contract calls for a total annual rent equal to 9% of its annual net sales with minimum monthly payments of $500 each month. The store had made all of its $500 monthly payments during the year but it has not recorded the additional accrued rent.

h) Ending merchandise inventory, $13,880.

2. Prepare a classified income statement.

3. Prepare compound closing entries.

4. Open a merchandise inventory account and enter the $12,655 beginning inventory amount as its balance. Then post those portions of the closing entries that affect this account.

Decision problem 5–1, Westgate Shop

PART 1. You have just been hired as the bookkeeper of Westgate Shop, a store owned by Sid Hall. In your preliminary examination of the store's records you find that the store never bothers to take advantage of cash discounts, although it could earn a 2% discount on all purchases, since its suppliers all grant terms of 2/10, n/60. The store does not take advantage of discounts because to do so it would, in the words of the owner, Ted Hall, "have to be constantly borrowing money from the bank," and he is opposed to this. The store's sales, purchases, and inventories remain about at the same levels throughout the year, and a typical annual income statement shows the following:

Sales	$250,000
Cost of goods sold	150,000
Gross profit from sales	$100,000
Operating expenses	80,000
Net Income	$ 20,000

Prepare a statement to show Mr. Hall how much he could increase the store's annual net income by borrowing sufficient money at 6% per year to take advantage of all cash discounts.

PART 2. Assume that Mr. Hall has agreed that the store should take advantage of all discounts. However, you discover that the store's previous bookkeeper followed the practice of putting all invoices approved for payment in a file marked "To Be Paid." Then, each day the bookkeeper searched through the file to find the invoices due for payment that day. You recognize that if discounts are to be taken on all invoices on the last day of the discount period, discounts are certain to be missed under such a filing system, because in searching through the file, invoices will occasionally be overlooked on the last day of the discount period. Consequently, describe a system for filing invoices that

you would use and that would reduce the chances of an invoice being overlooked on the last day of its discount period.

The following preliminary income statement was prepared for use of the
management of Western Sales before the concern's accounts were closed for
the year-end:

WESTERN SALES

Income Statement for Year Ended December 31, 19—

Sales...		$268,350
Cost of goods sold:		
Merchandise inventory, January 1, 19—	$ 17,550	
Net cost of purchases	182,400	
Goods available for sale.......................................	$199,950	
Merchandise inventory, December 31, 19—	18,800	
Cost of goods sold		181,150
Gross profit on sales...		$ 87,200
Operating expenses		61,000
Net Income		$ 26,200

There were no returns and allowances, but the following errors were discovered by the public accounting firm engaged to conduct the annual audit:
1. A $500 purchase invoice, dated December 27, was received on December
    31 and recorded. The goods were shipped on the invoice date. Western
    Sales was responsible for the freight charges which it had paid and re-
    corded on January 2 when the goods arrived. (Since both the invoice and
    the freight charges were recorded, their amounts are included in net cost
    of purchases as listed in the preliminary income statement.) The goods
    were not included in the inventory, since they had not arrived on the in-
    ventory date.
2. A $350 purchase of merchandise was received on December 31 and in-
    cluded in the inventory. The invoice arrived on January 2, but had not
    been recorded. The seller was responsible for the freight charges.
3. A $750 purchase invoice, dated December 28, did not arrive until Jan-
    uary 2 and had not been recorded. Western Sales was responsible for and
    had paid and recorded the freight charges on the shipment of the invoice
    when it arrived on January 2. The goods were not included in the inven-
    tory, since they were in transit on the inventory date.
4. A sales invoice for $1,350, dated December 31, had been recorded. The
    terms of the sale required delivery of the goods to the buyer. The goods
    cost $900, had been set aside in the warehouse on December 31, and were
    excluded from the inventory, but had not been shipped.
5. A sales invoice for $1,200, dated December 31, had not been recorded.
    The merchandise was shipped on December 31 under terms requiring West-
    ern Sales to deliver the goods to the buyer. Western Sales had prepaid

the freight charges on the shipment but had not recorded the payment. The goods cost $850, were excluded from the inventory, and were delivered to the buyer on January 2.

6. A $600 item of office equipment, received on December 31, was erroneously recorded as a purchase of merchandise and included in the inventory.

7. There was an error in totaling an inventory sheet, which caused a $200 understatement of the inventory total as given on the preliminary income statement.

Tell which of the foregoing invoice amounts should be included and which should be excluded from sales, purchases, and ending inventory. Tell how you would correct each error. Also, prepare a corrected income statement for the concern.

Chapter 6

Columnar journals and subsidiary ledgers

■ The General Journal described in previous chapters is a flexible journal in which it is possible to record any transaction. However, since each debit and credit entered in such a journal must be posted individually, using a General Journal to record all the transactions of a business results in the expenditure of too much posting labor.

Reducing posting labor ■ Several ways have been devised to reduce this posting labor. One way takes advantage of the fact that like transactions always result in debits and credits to the same accounts. For example, all sales on credit are alike in that they result in debits to Accounts Receivable and credits to Sales. Consequently, if advantage is taken of this and a company's credit sales for, say, a month are recorded in a Sales Journal like Illustration 6–1 at the top of the next page, labor is saved by waiting until the end of the month, totaling the sales recorded in the journal, and debiting Accounts Receivable and crediting Sales for the total.

Sales Journal

Date	Account Debited	Invoice Number	F	Amount
Oct. 1	James Henry...	307	✔	200.00
7	Albert Smith	308	✔	100.00
12	John Wright..	309	✔	150.00
15	Paul Roth	310	✔	225.00
22	Sam Moore...	311	✔	125.00
25	Frank Booth	312	✔	50.00
28	Sam Moore...	313	✔	175.00
31	Total—Accounts Receivable, Dr.; Sales, Cr....			1,025.00
				(113/411)

Total is posted at the end of the month.

Accounts Receivable	113		
Date	Debit	Credit	Balance
Oct. 31	1,025.00		1,025.00

Sales		411	
Date	Debit	Credit	Balance
Oct. 31		1,025.00	1,025.00

Illustration 6–1

Only seven sales are recorded in the journal of Illustration 6–1. However, if the seven sales are assumed to represent, say 700 charge sales, the labor saved by posting only one debit to Accounts Receivable and one credit to Sales for their total rather than 700 debits and 700 credits can better be appreciated.

Since the journal of Illustration 6–1 has columns for recording the date, the customer's name, invoice number, and the amount of each charge sale, it is called a *columnar journal*. Only charge sales can be recorded in it, and they are recorded daily with the information about each sale being placed on a separate line. Normally the information about each sale is taken from the sales ticket or invoice prepared at the time of the sale. However, before discussing the journal further, the subject of *subsidiary ledgers* must be introduced.

Subsidiary ledgers
■ The one Accounts Receivable account used thus far does not readily tell how much each customer bought and paid for or how much each customer owes. As a result, a business selling on credit must maintain additional accounts receivable, one for each customer, to provide this information. These individual customer accounts are in addition to the Accounts Receivable account used thus far and are normally kept in a book or file tray, called a *subsidiary ledger,* that is separate and distinct from the book or tray containing the financial statement accounts.

Also, to distinguish the two, the book or tray containing the customer accounts is called the *Accounts Receivable Ledger,* while that containing the financial statement accounts is known as the *General Ledger.*

Observe in Illustration 6–2 how the idea of keeping the customer accounts in one ledger and the financial statement accounts in a different ledger, kept in a different book or file tray, is shown by putting the customer accounts in one double-ruled box and the general ledger accounts in a different box.

Before going on, note again in Illustration 6–2 that the individual customer accounts in the subsidiary Accounts Receivable Ledger do not replace the Accounts Receivable account described in previous chapters but are in addition to it. The Accounts Receivable account of previous chapters must still be maintained in the General Ledger where it serves three functions: (1) it shows the total amount owed by all customers; (2) it helps keep the General Ledger a balancing ledger in which debits equal credits; and (3) it offers a means of proving the accuracy of the customer accounts in the subsidiary Accounts Receivable Ledger. The last two functions are discussed in more detail later in this chapter.

Posting the Sales Journal

■ When a Sales Journal like that of Illustration 6–2 is used, the individual sales recorded in the journal are posted each day to the proper customer accounts in the Accounts Receivable Ledger. These daily postings keep the customer accounts up to date, which is important in granting credit. It is important because when a customer asks for credit, the person responsible for granting it should know the amount currently owed by the customer, as well as his promptness in meeting past obligations. The source of this information is the customer's account; and if it is not up to date, an incorrect decision may be made.

Note the check marks in the Sales Journal's Folio column. They indicate that the sales recorded in the journal were individually posted to the customer accounts in the Accounts Receivable Ledger. Check marks rather than account numbers are used because the customer accounts commonly do not have numbers. Rather, as an aid in locating individual accounts, they are alphabetically arranged in the Accounts Receivable Ledger, with new accounts being added in their proper alphabetical positions as required. Consequently, numbering the accounts is impractical, since many numbers would have to be changed each time new accounts are added.

In addition to the daily postings to customer accounts, at the end of the month the Sales Journal's Amount column is totaled and the total is debited to Accounts Receivable and credited to Sales. The credit records the month's revenue from charge sales, and the debit records the resulting increase in accounts receivable. Furthermore, since both of these accounts are in the General Ledger, posting a debit to one and an equal credit to the other helps maintain the equality of debits and credits in the ledger.

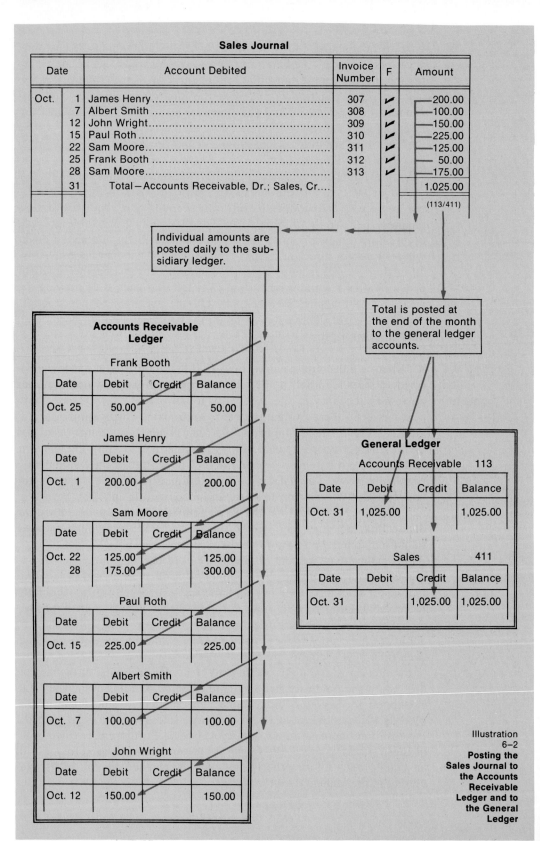

Sales Journal

Date		Account Debited	Invoice Number	F	Amount
Oct.	1	James Henry.....................................	307	✔	200.00
	7	Albert Smith	308	✔	100.00
	12	John Wright.....................................	309	✔	150.00
	15	Paul Roth.......................................	310	✔	225.00
	22	Sam Moore......................................	311	✔	125.00
	25	Frank Booth	312	✔	50.00
	28	Sam Moore......................................	313	✔	175.00
	31	Total—Accounts Receivable, Dr.; Sales, Cr....			1,025.00
					(113/411)

Individual amounts are posted daily to the subsidiary ledger.

Total is posted at the end of the month to the general ledger accounts.

Accounts Receivable Ledger

Frank Booth

Date	Debit	Credit	Balance
Oct. 25	50.00		50.00

James Henry

Date	Debit	Credit	Balance
Oct. 1	200.00		200.00

Sam Moore

Date	Debit	Credit	Balance
Oct. 22	125.00		125.00
28	175.00		300.00

Paul Roth

Date	Debit	Credit	Balance
Oct. 15	225.00		225.00

Albert Smith

Date	Debit	Credit	Balance
Oct. 7	100.00		100.00

John Wright

Date	Debit	Credit	Balance
Oct. 12	150.00		150.00

General Ledger

Accounts Receivable   113

Date	Debit	Credit	Balance
Oct. 31	1,025.00		1,025.00

Sales   411

Date	Debit	Credit	Balance
Oct. 31		1,025.00	1,025.00

Illustration 6–2
Posting the Sales Journal to the Accounts Receivable Ledger and to the General Ledger

Sales taxes ■ Many cities and states require retailers to collect sales taxes from their customers and periodically remit these taxes to the city or state treasurer. When a columnar Sales Journal is used, a record of taxes collected can be obtained by adding special columns as shown in Illustration 6–3.

Sales Journal

Date	Account Debited	Invoice Number	F	Accounts Receivable Debit	Sales Taxes Payable Credit	Sales Credit
Dec. 1	D. R. Horn..........	7-1698		103.00	3.00	100.00

Illustration
6–3

In posting a journal like Illustration 6–3, the individual amounts in the Accounts Receivable column are posted daily to customer accounts in the Accounts Receivable Ledger and the column total is posted at the end of the month to the Accounts Receivable account. The individual amounts in the Sales Taxes Payable and Sales columns are not posted. However, at the end of the month the total of the Sales Taxes Payable column is credited to the Sales Taxes Payable account and the total of the Sales column is credited to Sales.

A concern making cash sales upon which sales taxes are collected may add a special Sales Taxes Payable column in its Cash Receipts Journal. The Cash Receipts Journal is discussed later in this chapter.

Sales invoices as a Sales Journal ■ To save labor, many companies do not enter charge sales in a Sales Journal. These companies post each sales invoice total directly to the customer's account in a subsidiary Accounts Receivable Ledger. Copies of the invoices are then bound in numerical order in a binder; and at the end of the month, all the invoices of that month are totaled on an adding machine and a general journal entry is made debiting the Accounts Receivable account and crediting Sales for the total. In effect, the bound invoice copies act as a Sales Journal. Such a procedure eliminates the labor of entering each invoice in a Sales Journal and is known as direct posting of sales invoices.

Controlling accounts ■ When a company maintains an Accounts Receivable account in its General Ledger and puts its individual customer accounts in a subsidiary ledger, the Accounts Receivable account is said to control the subsidiary ledger and is called a *controlling account*. The extent of the control is such that after all posting is completed, if no errors were made, the sum of all of the customer account balances in the subsidiary Accounts Receivable Ledger will equal the balance of the Accounts Receivable controlling account in the General Ledger. This equality is also a proof of the customer account balances.

Posting principle of controlling accounts and subsidiary ledgers

■ As was demonstrated with the Sales Journal, the posting principle under which a subsidiary ledger and its controlling account operate requires that (1) the controlling account must be debited periodically for an amount or amounts equal to the sum of the debits to its subsidiary ledger. Also (2) the controlling account must be credited periodically (discussed later) for an amount or amounts equal to the sum of the credits to its subsidiary ledger accounts. Debiting the controlling account for the sum of the debits to its subsidiary ledger and crediting the controlling account for the sum of the credits brings the balance of the controlling account up to date, and if no errors were made, also makes this balance equal to the sum of the balances in the subsidiary ledger.

Proving the balances of a subsidiary ledger

■ As a result of the principle under which a subsidiary ledger and its controlling account operate, the balance of a controlling account may be used to prove the accuracy of the accounts in its subsidiary ledger. The proof is, if the sum of the account balances in the subsidiary ledger equals the balance of the controlling account, the subsidiary ledger accounts are assumed to be correct. For example, to prove the account balances in a subsidiary Accounts Receivable Ledger, a trial balance of the General Ledger and a schedule of accounts receivable (Illustration 6–4) are prepared. The trial balance includes the balance of the Accounts Receivable account; and if the trial balance is in balance, the Accounts Receivable controlling account is assumed to be correct. Also, if the sum of the account balances listed on the schedule of accounts receivable equals the balance of the Accounts Receivable controlling account, they too are assumed to be correct.

Sloan Novelty Company
Schedule of Accounts Receivable
December 31, 19—

A. B. Dean	$ 75
Frank Fish	125
T. M. Johnson	250
W. C. Nagle	160
John Roak	100
Sam Warren	140
Total Accounts Receivable	$850

Illustration 6–4

A schedule of accounts receivable is prepared by listing the names of the customers who owe the company and the amounts owed by each. Also, a simple adding machine list, rather than a formal schedule, is often used to prove the account balances in a subsidiary ledger.

Other columnar journals

■ Only sales on credit may be recorded in the sales journals described thus far; and as a result, if a company takes full advantage of the fact that like transactions always result in debits and credits to the same accounts, it must use several columnar journals in addition to a Sales Journal. These are a Cash Receipts Journal, a Purchases Journal, a Cash Disbursements Journal, and perhaps others. Also, and regardless of the columnar journals used, there are always a few miscellaneous transactions plus adjusting, closing, and correcting entries that cannot be recorded in any columnar journal, and for these a General Journal must be provided.

Cash Receipts Journal

■ A Cash Receipts Journal designed to save the maximum of posting labor through posting column totals must be a multicolumn journal. A multicolumn journal is necessary because although all cash receipts are alike in that they result in debits to Cash, they differ as to sources and, consequently, as to the accounts credited when cash is received from different sources. For example, if the cash receipts of a mercantile concern are classified as to sources, they normally fall into three groups: (1) cash from charge customers in payment of their accounts, (2) cash from cash sales, and (3) cash from miscellaneous sources. Note in the Cash Receipts Journal of Illustration 6–5 how a special column is provided for entering the credits resulting when cash is received from each of these sources. Also, note the special columns for the debits to Sales Discounts and to Cash.

Cash from charge customers

When cash received from a charge customer in payment of his account is recorded in a columnar Cash Receipts Journal like Illustration 6–5, the customer's name is entered in the Account Credited column; the amount credited to his account is entered in the Accounts Receivable credit column; and the debits to Sales Discounts and Cash are entered in the journal's last two columns.

Give close attention to the Accounts Receivable credit column in the journal of Illustration 6–5. Observe that (1) only credits to customer accounts are entered in this column; (2) the individual credits are posted daily to the customer accounts in the subsidiary Accounts Receivable Ledger; and (3) the column total is posted at the month end to the credit of the Accounts Receivable controlling account. This is the normal recording and posting procedure when controlling accounts and subsidiary ledgers are used. When such accounts and ledgers are used, transactions are normally entered in a journal column, the individual amounts are posted to the subsidiary ledger accounts, and the column total is posted to the controlling account. Note that this recording and posting procedure keeps the controlling account balance equal to the sum of the balances in its subsidiary ledger.

Cash Receipts Journal

Date	Account Credited	Explanation	F	Sundry Accounts Credit	Accts. Rec. Credit	Sales Credit	Sales Disc. Debit	Cash Debit
Oct. 6	Sales	Cash sales	✔			400.00		400.00
10	James Henry........	Invoice, 10/1	✔		200.00		4.00	196.00
13	Sales	Cash sales	✔			390.00		390.00
17	Albert Smith	Invoice, 10/7	✔		100.00		2.00	98.00
18	Notes Payable......	Note to bank	211	1,000.00				1,000.00
20	Sales	Cash sales	✔			450.00		450.00
20	John Wright	Invoice, 10/12......	✔		150.00		3.00	147.00
25	Paul Roth............	Invoice, 10/15......	✔		225.00		4.50	220.50
27	Sales	Cash sales	✔			398.50		398.50
31	Totals			1,000.00	675.00	1,638.50	13.50	3,300.00
				(✔)	(113)	(411)	(413)	(111)

Individual amounts in the Sundry Accounts credit and Accounts Receivable credit columns are posted daily.

Total is not posted.

Totals posted at the end of the month.

Accounts Receivable Ledger

James Henry

Date	Debit	Credit	Balance
Oct. 1	200.00		200.00
10		200.00	-0-

Paul Roth

Date	Debit	Credit	Balance
Oct. 15	225.00		225.00
25		225.00	-0-

Albert Smith

Date	Debit	Credit	Balance
Oct. 7	100.00		100.00
17		100.00	-0-

John Wright

Date	Debit	Credit	Balance
Oct. 12	150.00		150.00
20		150.00	-0-

General Ledger

Cash   111

Date	Debit	Credit	Balance
Oct. 31	3,300.00		3,300.00

Accounts Receivable   113

Date	Debit	Credit	Balance
Oct. 31	1,025.00		1,025.00
31		675.00	350.00

Notes Payable   211

Date	Debit	Credit	Balance
Oct. 18		1,000.00	1,000.00

Sales   411

Date	Debit	Credit	Balance
Oct. 31		1,025.00	1,025.00
31		1,638.50	2,663.50

Sales Discounts   413

Date	Debit	Credit	Balance
Oct. 31	13.50		13.50

Illustration
6–5

Posting the Cash Receipts Journal to the Accounts Receivable Ledger and to the General Ledger

Cash sales

In an average company cash sale amounts are accumulated each day on one or more cash registers and their total is recorded by means of a journal entry at the end of the day. All of these entries are alike; all have repetitive debits to Cash and repetitive credits to Sales.

When cash sales are recorded in a Cash Receipts Journal like that of Illustration 6–5, the repetitive debits to Cash are entered in the Cash debit column and a special column headed "Sales credit" is provided for the repetitive credits to Sales. By entering each day's cash sales in the Sales column, the cash sales of a month may be posted at the month's end in a single amount, the column total. (Although cash sales are normally recorded daily from the cash register reading, the cash sales of Illustration 6–5 are recorded only once each week in order to shorten the illustration.)

At the time daily cash sales are recorded in the Cash Receipts Journal, some bookkeepers, as in Illustration 6–5, place a check mark in the Folio column to indicate that no amount is individually posted from that line of the journal. Other bookkeepers use a double check (✔✔) to distinguish amounts not posted from amounts posted to customer accounts.

Miscellaneous receipts of cash

Most cash receipts come from customer collections and cash sales. However, cash is occasionally received from other sources such as, for example, the sale for cash of an unneeded plant asset, or a promissory note is given to a bank in order to borrow money. For miscellaneous receipts such as these the Sundry (or Miscellaneous) Accounts credit column is provided in the Cash Receipts Journal.

Posting the Cash Receipts Journal

■ As previously stated, the individual items in the Cash Receipts Journal's Accounts Receivable column are posted daily as credits to the customer accounts named in the Account Credited column. These items must be posted daily so that the accounts receivable ledger accounts show for each customer the current amount owed.

In an average company, the items in the Sundry Accounts credit column are few and are posted to a variety of general ledger accounts. As a result, postings are less apt to be omitted if these items are also posted daily. Furthermore, if the individual items in both the Sundry Accounts and the Accounts Receivable columns are posted daily, only the column totals remain to be posted at the end of the month.

The amounts in the Accounts Receivable, Sales, Sales Discounts, and Cash columns are posted as column totals at the end of the month. However, since the transactions recorded in any journal must result in equal debits and credits to general ledger accounts, the debit and credit equality in a columnar journal such as the Cash Receipts Journal is proved by *crossfooting* or cross adding the column totals before they are posted at the end of the month. In crossfooting, the debit column totals are added together, the credit column totals are added together, and the two sums are compared for equality. For example, if the debit column totals of the Cash Receipts Journal in Illustration 6–5 are added and the credit column totals are added, the two sums appear as follows:

Debit Columns		Credit Columns	
Sales discounts debit	$ 13.50	Sundry accounts credit	$1,000.00
Cash debit	3,300.00	Accounts receivable credit	675.00
		Sales credit	1,638.50
Total	$3,313.50	Total	$3,313.50

And since the sums are equal, the debits in the journal are assumed to equal the credits.

After the debit and credit equality is proved by crossfooting, the totals are posted. The Accounts Receivable column total is posted to the credit of the Accounts Receivable controlling account in the General Ledger; the Sales column total is posted to the credit of the Sales account; the Sales Discounts column total is posted to the debit of the Sales Discounts account; and the Cash column total is posted to the debit of the Cash account. Since individual items in the Sundry Accounts column are posted daily, this column total is not posted. This posting procedure is demonstrated in Illustration 6–5.

Posting items daily from the Sundry Accounts column of the Cash Receipts Journal with a delayed posting of the offsetting totals causes the General Ledger to be out of balance throughout the month. However, this is of no consequence because the offsetting totals are posted before a trial balance is prepared.

The Cash Receipts Journal's Folio column is used only for daily postings from the Sundry Accounts and Accounts Receivable columns. The account numbers appearing in the Folio column indicate items posted to the General Ledger from the Sundry Accounts column; and the check marks indicate either that an item like a day's cash sales was not posted or that an item was posted to the subsidiary Accounts Receivable Ledger. The total of the Sundry Accounts column is not posted. Note in Illustration 6–5 the check mark below this column. The check mark indicates that when the journal was posted, this column total was not posted. The account numbers of the accounts to which the Accounts Receivable, Sales, Sales Discounts, and Cash column totals of Illustration 6–5 were posted are indicated in parentheses below each column.

Miscellaneous credits to accounts receivable ■ Credits to accounts receivable occur when merchandise previously sold on credit is returned. A company having few such returns records them in a General Journal with an entry like the following:

Oct.	17	Sales Returns and Allowances	412	17.50	
		Accounts Receivable – George Ball	113/✔		17.50
		Returned defective merchandise.			

The debit of the foregoing entry is posted to the Sales Returns and Allowances account; and the credit is posted to both the Accounts Receivable controlling account and to the customer's account. Note the account number and the check, 113/✔, in the Folio column on the credit line. This indicates that both the Accounts Receivable controlling account in the General Ledger and the George Ball account in the Accounts Receivable Ledger were credited for $17.50.

Many beginning students, upon their first encounter with a general journal entry like the foregoing, think that posting two credits, a credit to Accounts Receivable and another to the George Ball account, with only one debit to Sales Returns and Allowances will cause the trial balance to be out of balance. However, this is not true because the balance of the George Ball account does not appear on the trial balance. Rather, it appears on the schedule of accounts receivable and is proved by comparing the schedule's total with the balance of the Accounts Receivable controlling account.

Companies having sufficient sales returns can save posting labor by recording them in a special Sales Returns and Allowances Journal like that of Illustration 6–6. Note that this is in keeping with the generally

Sales Returns and Allowances Journal

Date		Account Credited	Explanation	Credit Memo No.	F	Amount
Oct.	7	Robert Moore...........	Defective mdse............	203	✔	10.00
	14	James Warren	Defective mdse............	204	✔	12.00
	18	T. M. Jones..............	Not ordered	205	✔	6.00
	23	Sam Smith...............	Defective mdse............	206	✔	18.00
	31	Sales Returns and Allow., Dr.; Accounts Rec., Cr.				46.00
						412/113

Illustration
6–6

recognized idea that a company can design and use a special journal for any class of like transactions in which there are within the class sufficient transactions to warrant the journal. When a Sales Returns and Allowances Journal is used to record returns, the individual amounts entered in the journal are posted daily to the credit of each affected customer account. At the end of the month, the journal total is posted to both the debit of the Sales Returns and Allowances account and the credit of the Accounts Receivable controlling account.

Occasionally a customer is unable to pay his account when due. In such cases, a promissory note is sometimes given by the customer to secure an extension of time on the amount due. The note does not pay the debt, but it does change its form from an informal promise to pay to a formal written promise to pay, and the change must be reflected in the accounting records because informal promises appear on the balance sheet as accounts receivable, while formal written promises appear as notes receivable. A general journal entry to record the receipt of a note to gain an extension on an account appears as follows:

Oct.	19	Notes Receivable	112	239.50	
		Accounts Receivable—D. A. Root..........	113/✔		239.50
		Received a 60-day note in settlement			
		of the account			

Accounts payable

■ As with accounts receivable, the one Accounts Payable account used thus far does not show how much is owed each creditor. One way to secure this information is to maintain an individual account for each creditor in a subsidiary Accounts Payable Ledger controlled by an Accounts Payable controlling account in the General Ledger. If maintained, the controlling account, subsidiary ledger, and columnar journal techniques demonstrated thus far with accounts receivable apply to these accounts payable. The only difference is that a Purchases Journal, Cash Disbursements Journal, and perhaps a Purchases Returns and Allowances Journal are used in recording the transactions affecting the accounts. However, this difference is not great, since the new journals operate in the same manner as the journals described thus far. All have columns for the repetitive debits and credits of like transactions and all save posting labor through the posting of column totals.

The Purchases Journal and its posting

■ A one-column Purchases Journal is very similar to the Sales Journal previously described, and both journals operate in the same manner. The information recorded in the Purchases Journal usually includes the date of each entry, the creditor's name, the invoice date, terms, and the amount of the purchase. This information is recorded from approved purchase invoices; and its use, in the main, is apparent. The invoice date and the terms together indicate the date on which payment is due.

The one-column Purchases Journal is posted in the same manner as a Sales Journal: (1) The individual amounts in the Amount column are posted daily to the subsidiary Accounts Payable Ledger and (2) the column total is debited at the end of the month to the Purchases account and credited to the Accounts Payable controlling account. This posting is demonstrated in Illustration 6–7.

The Cash Disbursements Journal and its posting

■ The Cash Disbursements Journal, like the Cash Receipts Journal, has columns that make it possible to post repetitive debits and credits in column totals. The repetitive debits and credits of cash payments are debits to the Accounts Payable controlling account and credits to both Purchases Discounts and Cash. In most companies the purchase of merchandise for cash is not common; therefore, a Purchases column is

Purchases Journal

Date		Account Credited	Date of Invoice	Terms	F	Amount
Oct.	3	Horn Supply Company..............	10/2	n/30	✔	350.00
	5	Acme Mfg. Company	10/5	2/10, n/30	✔	200.00
	13	Wycoff & Company..................	10/10	n/30	✔	150.00
	20	Smith and Company................	10/19	2/10, n/30	✔	300.00
	25	Acme Mfg. Company	10/24	2/10, n/30	✔	100.00
	27	A. Evans and Son...................	10/27	1/10, n/30	✔	50.00
	29	H. A. Green Company..............	10/28	2/10, n/60	✔	175.00
	31	Total—Purchases, Dr.; Accounts Payable, Cr.				1,325.00

(511/212)

Individual amounts are posted daily.

Total is posted at the end of the month.

Accounts Payable Ledger

Acme Mfg. Company

Date	Debit	Credit	Balance
Oct. 5		200.00	200.00
15	200.00		-0-
25		100.00	100.00

A. Evans and Son

Date	Debit	Credit	Balance
Oct. 27		50.00	50.00

H. A. Green Company

Date	Debit	Credit	Balance
Oct. 29		175.00	175.00

Horn Supply Company

Date	Debit	Credit	Balance
Oct. 3		350.00	350.00

Smith and Company

Date	Debit	Credit	Balance
Oct. 20		300.00	300.00

Wycoff & Company

Date	Debit	Credit	Balance
Oct. 13		150.00	150.00

General Ledger

Accounts Payable 212

Date	Debit	Credit	Balance
Oct. 31		1,325.00	1,325.00

Purchases 511

Date	Debit	Credit	Balance
Oct. 12	25.00		25.00
31	1,325.00		1,350.00

Illustration
6-7
Posting the Purchases Journal

not needed and a cash purchase is recorded as on line 2 of Illustration 6–8. However, although cash purchases are commonly treated as on line 2, it should be pointed out that any company having many such purchases would find it advantageous to place a Purchases column in its Cash Disbursements Journal.

Note that the Cash Disbursements Journal of Illustration 6–8 has a column headed "Check No." In order to gain control over cash disbursements, all such disbursements (excepting petty cash disbursements, which are discussed in Chapter 8) should be made by check. The checks should be prenumbered by the printer and they should be entered in the journal in numerical order with each check's number in the column headed "Check No." This makes it possible to scan the numbers in the column for omitted checks.

When a Cash Disbursements Journal has a column for check numbers and checks are entered in it in numerical order, it is often called a Check Register. The reason for the name is obvious.

A Cash Disbursements Journal or Check Register like Illustration 6–8 is posted as follows. The individual amounts in the Sundry Accounts column are posted daily to the debit of the general ledger accounts named in the Account Debited column; and the individual amounts in the Accounts Payable column are posted daily to the subsidiary Accounts Payable Ledger to the debit of the creditors named in the Account Debited column. At the end of the month, after the column totals are crossfooted to prove their equality, the Accounts Payable column total is posted to the debit of the Accounts Payable controlling account; the Purchases Discounts column total is posted to the credit of the Purchases Discounts account; and the Cash column total is posted to the credit of the Cash account. Since the items in the Sundry Accounts column are posted individually, this column total is not posted. Posting of the Cash Disbursements Journal is demonstrated in Illustration 6–8.

When several special journals are used, it is necessary to indicate in the account Folio column before each posted amount the journal as well as the page number of the journal from which the amount was posted. The journal is indicated by using its initial or initials. Because of this, items posted from the Cash Disbursements Journal carry the initial "D" before their journal page number in the Folio columns. Likewise, items from the Cash Receipts Journal carry the letter "R," those from the Sales Journal carry the initial "S," items from the Purchases Journal carry the initial "P," and from the General Journal, the letter "G."

Miscellaneous debits to creditor accounts

■ A company having sufficient purchases returns and allowances may use a Purchases Returns and Allowances Journal similar to the Sales Returns and Allowances Journal previously illustrated. However, if it has only a few such returns and allowances it will record them with a general journal entry like the following:

Cash Disbursements Journal

Date		Ch. No.	Payee	Account Debited	F	Sundry Accounts Debit	Accts. Pay. Debit	Pur. Disc. Credit	Cash Credit
Oct.	3	105	L. & N. Railroad...	Freight-In	514	18.50			18.50
	12	106	East Sales Co	Purchases	511	25.00			25.00
	15	107	Acme Mfg. Co.....	Acme Mfg. Co.......	✓		200.00	4.00	196.00
	15	108	Jerry Hale..........	Salaries Expense...	611	86.00			86.00
	20	109	Horn Supply Co...	Horn Supply Co.....	✓		75.00		75.00
	29	110	Smith and Co......	Smith and Co	✓		300.00	6.00	294.00
	31		Totals...........			129.50	575.00	10.00	694.50
						(✓)	(212)	(513)	(111)

Individual amounts in the Sundry Accounts debit column and Accounts Payable debit column are posted daily.

Totals posted at the end of the month.

Accounts Payable Ledger

Acme Mfg. Company

Date	Debit	Credit	Balance
Oct. 5		200.00	200.00
15	200.00		-0-
25		100.00	100.00

Horn Supply Company

Date	Debit	Credit	Balance
Oct. 3		350.00	350.00
20	75.00		275.00

Smith and Company

Date	Debit	Credit	Balance
Oct. 20		300.00	300.00
29	300.00		-0-

General Ledger

Cash   111

Date	Debit	Credit	Balance
Oct. 31	3,300.00		3,300.00
31		694.50	2,605.50

Accounts Payable   212

Date	Debit	Credit	Balance
Oct. 31		1,325.00	1,325.00
31	575.00		750.00

Purchases   511

Date	Debit	Credit	Balance
Oct. 12	25.00		25.00
31	1,325.00		1,350.00

Purchases Discounts   513

Date	Debit	Credit	Balance
Oct. 31		10.00	10.00

Freight-In   514

Date	Debit	Credit	Balance
Oct. 3	18.50		18.50

Salaries Expense   611

Date	Debit	Credit	Balance
Oct. 15	86.00		86.00

Illustration
6–8
Posting the Cash Disbursements Journal

Oct.	8	Accounts Payable—Medford Mfg. Company...	212/✓	32.00	
		Purchases Returns and Allowances.........	512		32.00
		Returned defective merchandise.			

Sometimes a note is issued in gaining a time extension on an account with a creditor. The note changes the form of the liability and is recorded with a general journal entry like the following:

Oct.	24	Accounts Payable—Springfield Company	212/✓	500.00	
		Notes Payable....................................	211		500.00
		Gave a 30-day, 6% note.			

Purchase and sale of assets used in the business

■ When single-column purchases and sales journals are used, only purchases and sales of merchandise may be recorded in these journals. This is because the column total of the Purchases Journal is debited to the Purchases account; the column total of the Sales Journal is credited to the Sales account; and purchases and sales of assets other than merchandise do not affect either of these accounts. However, every company must purchase assets for use in the business; and when these assets are no longer needed, they may be sold. If the purchase or sale is for cash, the transaction is recorded in one of the cash journals. But if the purchase or sale is on credit, the transaction must be recorded in either the General Journal or, in cases where assets are purchased and such a journal is used, a multicolumn Purchases Journal similar to that shown in Illustration 6–9.

Purchases Journal

Date		Account Credited	F	Accts. Payable Credit	Purchases Debit	Store Supplies Debit	Office Supplies Debit
Oct.	2	Marsh Wholesale Company.........		154.10	154.10		
	2	Office Supply Company.............		18.75			18.75

Illustration
6–9

Some companies save posting labor by using a multicolumn Purchases Journal like Illustration 6–9. Note that the journal has one credit column and in this case three debit columns; more debit columns could be added. The credit column is used to record the amounts credited to each creditor; and the items purchased are recorded in the debit columns. Such a journal is sometimes known as an "Accounts Payable Register."

In companies using an ordinary one-column Purchases Journal rather than a multicolumn Purchases Journal, purchases of assets for use in the business are recorded in the General Journal with an entry like the following:

Oct.	29	Office Supplies	119	23.75	
		Accounts Payable—Ace Supply Co..........	212/✓		23.75
		Bought office supplies.			

Questions for class discussion

1. How do columnar journals save posting labor?
2. How do columnar journals take advantage of the fact that for any single class of transactions either the debit or the credit of each transaction is always to the same account?
3. What functions are served by the Accounts Receivable controlling account?
4. Why should sales to charge customers and receipts of cash from charge customers be recorded and posted daily?
5. A company has the following numbers of accounts with balances:

   a) Asset accounts including the Accounts Receivable account but not the individual customer accounts 25
   b) Customer accounts... 500
   c) Liability accounts including the Accounts Payable account but not the individual creditor accounts 10
   d) Creditor accounts 20
   e) Owner equity accounts including income statement accounts... 20

   Total 575

   How many items appear on the trial balance of this company? What in addition to a trial balance is used to prove the account balances of this company?
6. How is a schedule of accounts payable prepared? How is it used to prove the balances of the creditor accounts in the Accounts Payable Ledger? What may be substituted for a formal schedule?
7. How is the equality of a controlling account and its subsidiary ledger accounts maintained?
8. Describe how copies of a company's sales invoices may be used as a Sales Journal.
9. After all posting is completed, the balance of the Accounts Receivable controlling account does not agree with the sum of the balances in the Accounts Receivable Ledger. If the trial balance is in balance, where is the error apt to be?
10. How is a multicolumn journal crossfooted? Why is a multicolumn journal crossfooted?
11. How is it possible to tell from which journal a particular amount in a ledger account was posted?
12. When a general journal entry is used to record a returned charge sale, the

credit of the entry must be posted twice. Does this cause the trial balance to be out of balance? Why or why not?

13. Both credits to customer accounts and credits to miscellaneous accounts are individually posted from a Cash Receipts Journal like that of Illustration 6–5. Why not place both kinds of credits in the same column and thus save journal space?

Class exercises

Exercise 6–1

A concern uses a one-column Sales Journal, a one-column Purchases Journal, a Cash Receipts Journal, a Cash Disbursements Journal, and a General Journal. List the following transactions by letter and opposite each letter give the name of the journal in which each transaction should be recorded.

a) Purchased merchandise on credit.
b) Purchased office supplies on credit.
c) Purchased office equipment for cash.
d) Returned merchandise purchased on credit.
e) Sold merchandise for cash.
f) Sold merchandise on credit.
g) Gave a customer credit for merchandise purchased on credit and returned.
h) A customer paid for merchandise previously purchased on credit.
i) Paid a creditor.
j) Paid sales salaries.
k) Recorded adjusting and closing entries.

Exercise 6–2

At the end of November the Sales Journal of ABC Company showed the following sales on credit:

SALES JOURNAL

Date		Account Debited	Invoice Number	F	Amount
Nov.	2	John Mohr...............................	345		300.00
	9	Jerry Dale.............................	346		250.00
	16	Gary Ball..............................	347		200.00
	27	John Mohr.............................	348		100.00
	30	Total.................................			850.00

The company had also recorded the return of merchandise with the following entry:

Nov.	18	Sales Returns and Allowances................	50.00	
		Accounts Receivable—Gary Ball......		50.00
		Customer returned merchandise.		

Required:

1. On a sheet of notebook paper open a subsidiary Accounts Receivable Ledger having an account for each customer listed in the Sales Journal. Post to the customer accounts the entries of the Sales Journal and also the portion of the general journal entry that affects a customer's account.
2. Open a General Ledger having an Accounts Receivable controlling account, a Sales account, and a Sales Returns and Allowances account. Post the sales journal total and the portions of the general journal entry that affect these accounts.
3. Prove the subsidiary ledger accounts with a schedule of accounts receivable.

Exercise 6–3

Sierra Company, a company that posts its sales invoices directly and then binds the invoices to make them into a Sales Journal, had the following sales during October:

Oct.	3	Robert Hall	$ 800
	6	Carl Fetter	1,100
	11	Taylor Gordon...	1,600
	18	Carl Fetter	2,200
	21	Taylor Gordon...	700
	27	Walter Scott	1,500
		Total	$7,900

Required:

1. On a sheet of notebook paper open a subsidiary Accounts Receivable Ledger having a T-account for each customer with an invoice bound in the foregoing Sales Journal. Post the invoices to the subsidiary ledger.
2. Give the general journal entry to record the end-of-the-month total of the Sales Journal.
3. Open an Accounts Receivable controlling account and a Sales account and post the general journal entry.
4. Prove the subsidiary Accounts Receivable Ledger with a schedule of accounts receivable.

Exercise 6–4

A company that records credit sales in a one-column Sales Journal and records sales returns in its General Journal made the following errors. List each error by letter, and opposite each letter tell when the error will be discovered:

a) Correctly recorded a $75 sale in the Sales Journal but posted it to the customer's account as a $750 sale.

b) Made an addition error in totaling the Amount column of the Sales Journal.

c) Posted a sales return recorded in the General Journal to the Sales Returns and Allowances account and to the Accounts Receivable account but did not post to the customer's account.

d) Posted a sales return to the Accounts Receivable account and to the customer's account but did not post to the Sales Returns and Allowances account.

e) Made an addition error in determining the balance of a customer's account.

Exercise 6–5

Following are the condensed journals of a merchandising concern. The journal column headings are incomplete in that they do not indicate whether the columns are debit or credit columns.

Required:

1. Prepare T-accounts on a sheet of ordinary notebook paper for the following general ledger and subsidiary ledger accounts. Separate the accounts of each ledger group as follows:

General Ledger Accounts	*Accounts Receivable Ledger Accounts*
Cash	A. Able
Accounts Receivable	B. Best
Prepaid Insurance	C. Call
Store Equipment	
Notes Payable	
Accounts Payable	
Sales	*Accounts Payable Ledger Accounts*
Sales Returns	Company One
Sales Discounts	Company Two
Purchases	Company Three
Purchases Returns	
Purchases Discounts	

2. Without referring to any of the illustrations showing complete column headings for the journals, post the following journals to the proper T-accounts.

SALES JOURNAL		SALES RETURNS AND ALLOWANCES JOURNAL		PURCHASES JOURNAL	
Account	Amount	Account	Amount	Account	Amount
A. Able	1,000	B. Best	300	Company One...	1,200
B. Best...........	1,500	C. Call..............	200	Company Two...	1,400
C. Call	2,000		500	Company Three.	1,600
	4,500				4,200

GENERAL JOURNAL

......	...	Accounts Payable — Company Three........	300.00	
		Purchases Returns.........................		300.00

CASH RECEIPTS JOURNAL

Account	Sundry Accounts	Accounts Receivable	Sales	Sales Discounts	Cash
A. Able.............................	....	1,000	......	20	980
Cash Sales	....	....	1,450	....	1,450
Notes Payable	2,000	....	......	....	2,000
Cash Sales	....	....	1,650	....	1,650
C. Call.............................	....	1,500	......	30	1,470
Store Equipment	150	....	......	....	150
	2,150	2,500	3,100	50	7,700

CASH DISBURSEMENTS JOURNAL

Account	Sundry Accounts	Accounts Payable	Purchases Discounts	Cash
Prepaid Insurance	100	....	....	100
Company Two....................................	....	1,400	28	1,372
Company Three..................................	....	1,300	26	1,274
Store Equipment................................	500	....	....	500
	600	2,700	54	3,246

Problems **Problem 6–1**

Northwest Sales Company completed the following transactions:

Oct. 1 Issued Check No. 516 to Alpha Realty in payment of the October rent, $600.

2 Received merchandise and an invoice dated September 30, terms 2/10, n/60, from Valley Supply Company, $975.

4 Received merchandise and an invoice dated October 1, terms 2/10, n/60, from North Manufacturing Company, $1,050.

5 Purchased store equipment on credit from Store Outfitters, terms n/10 EOM, $350.

6 Received a $125 credit memorandum from Valley Supply Company for unsatisfactory merchandise received on October 2 and returned.

9 Issued Check No. 517 to Valley Supply Company in payment of its September 30 invoice, less the return and discount.

Oct. 10   Received a $25 credit memorandum from Store Outfitters for unsatisfactory store equipment purchased on October 5 and returned.

10   Sold merchandise on credit to Dale Hall, Invoice No. 905, $550. (Terms of all sales are 2/10, n/60.)

11   Sold merchandise on credit to Walter Nash, Invoice No. 906, $800.

11   Issued Check No. 518 to North Manufacturing Company in payment of its October 1 invoice, less the discount.

14   Received merchandise and an invoice dated October 10, terms 1/10, n/30, from Mesa Sales Company, $775.

15   Cash sales for the first half of the month, $2,165. (Cash sales are normally recorded daily from the cash register readings; however, they are recorded only twice in this problem in order to shorten the problem.)

15   *Post to the customer and creditor accounts and also post any amounts that should be posted as individual amounts to the general ledger accounts.*

18   Sold merchandise on credit to Terry Blue, Invoice No. 907, $865.

19   Sold merchandise on credit to Dale Hall, Invoice No. 908, $650.

20   Received a $539 check from Dale Hall in payment of the October 10 sale.

21   Received a $784 check from Walter Nash in payment of the October 11 sale.

23   Sold store equipment at cost for cash, $25.

24   Received merchandise and an invoice dated October 21, terms 2/10, n/60, from North Manufacturing Company, $950.

25   Borrowed $2,000 from First State Bank by giving a note payable.

28   Sold merchandise on credit to Walter Nash, Invoice No. 909, $565.

29   Received a $637 check from Dale Hall in payment of the October 19 sale.

31   Issued Check No. 519 to North Manufacturing Company in payment of its October 21 invoice, less the discount.

31   Issued Check No. 520, payable to Payroll, in payment of the monthly sales salaries, $1,250.

31   Cash sales for the last half of the month, $2,230.

31   *Post to the customer and creditor accounts and also post any amounts that should be posted as individual amounts to the general ledger accounts.*

31   *Total the journals and make the month-end postings.*

Required:

1. Open the following general ledger accounts: Cash; Accounts Receivable; Store Equipment; Notes Payable; Accounts Payable; Sales; Sales Discounts; Purchases; Purchases Returns and Allowances; Purchases Discounts; Sales Salaries; and Rent Expense.

2. Open the following subsidiary accounts receivable ledger accounts: Terry Blue; Dale Hall; and Walter Nash.

3. Open these subsidiary accounts payable ledger accounts: Mesa Sales Company; North Manufacturing Company; Store Outfitters; and Valley Supply Company.

4. Prepare a Sales Journal, a one-column Purchases Journal, a Cash Receipts

Journal, a Cash Disbursements Journal, and a General Journal similar to the ones illustrated in this chapter.

5. Enter the transactions in the journals and post when instructed to do so.
6. Prepare a trial balance of the General Ledger and prove the subsidiary ledgers with schedules of accounts receivable and accounts payable.

Problem 6-2

Valley Sales Company completed the following credit transactions:

Dec. 3 Purchased $935 of merchandise from Mesa Wholesale Company.

5 Purchased $75 of office supplies from Store and Office Suppliers.

9 Purchased $1,245 of merchandise from Boswell and Boswell.

11 Purchased $120 of store supplies and $650 of merchandise from Phoenix Wholesale Company.

15 Purchased a desk and chair for the office from Store and Office Suppliers, $225.

19 Purchased $985 of merchandise from Phoenix Wholesale Company.

23 Purchased $110 of store supplies and $65 of office supplies from Store and Office Suppliers.

26 Purchased $450 of merchandise from Boswell and Boswell.

28 Purchased $735 of merchandise from Mesa Wholesale Company.

Required:

1. Prepare a General Journal and a multicolumn Purchases Journal similar to Illustration 6-9. Enter the foregoing transactions in the journals.
2. Open the required general ledger and accounts payable ledger accounts and post the journals.

Problem 6-3

Webster Supply Company completed the following transactions during February of the current year:

Feb. 2 Received merchandise and an invoice dated January 30, terms 2/10, n/30, from Globe Manufacturing Company, $1,535.

3 Purchased store equipment from Ryan Equipment Company, n/10 EOM, $585.

3 Sold merchandise on credit to Rice and Son, $950. (Terms of all credit sales are 2/10, n/60. Number sales invoices beginning with 617.)

4 Sold merchandise on account to Tyler and Vance, $1,265.

5 Received merchandise and an invoice dated February 3, terms 1/10, n/60, from F. M. Pope, Inc., $1,690.

6 Received a credit memorandum from Globe Manufacturing Company for unsatisfactory merchandise received from it on February 2 and returned, $135.

7 Received a credit memorandum from Ryan Equipment Company for store equipment received on February 3 and returned, $60.

7 Cash sales for the first week of February, $1,445.

7 *Post to the customer and creditor accounts and also post any amounts that should be posted as individual amounts to the general ledger accounts. (Normally such items are posted daily; but to shorten the problem, you are asked to post them only once each week.)*

Feb. 9 Issued Credit Memorandum No. 102 to Tyler and Vance for defective merchandise sold on February 4 and returned, $115.

9 Sent Globe Manufacturing Company Check No. 312 in payment of its invoice of January 30, less the return and discount.

11 Sold merchandise on credit to Bruce Sawyer, Inc., $1,595.

12 Received a check from Rice and Son in payment of the sale of February 3, less the discount.

13 Received a check from Tyler and Vance in payment of the sale of February 4, less the return and discount.

14 Received merchandise and an invoice dated February 11, terms 2/10, n/60, from Western Supply Company, $1,850.

14 Issued Check No. 313, payable to Payroll, in payment of the sales salaries for the first half of the month, $815. Cashed the check and paid the employees.

14 Cash sales for the week ended February 14, $1,395.

14 *Post to the customer and creditor accounts and also post any amounts that should be posted as individual amounts to the general ledger accounts.*

16 Issued Credit Memorandum No. 103 to Bruce Sawyer, Inc., for defective merchandise sold on February 11 and returned, $45.

17 Received merchandise and an invoice dated February 14, terms 2/10, n/60, from Western Supply Company, $1,450.

18 Received merchandise and an invoice dated February 16, terms 1/10, n/60, from F. M. Pope, Inc., $435.

18 Sold merchandise to Rice and Son on credit, $650.

21 Received a check from Bruce Sawyer, Inc., in payment of the sale of February 11, less the return and discount.

21 Sent Western Supply Company Check No. 314 in payment of its invoice of February 11, less the discount.

21 Cash sales for the week ended February 21, $1,425.

21 *Post to the customer and creditor accounts and also post any amounts that should be posted as individual amounts to the general ledger accounts.*

24 Sent Western Supply Company Check No. 315 in payment of its invoice of February 14, less the discount.

25 Borrowed $4,000 by giving Valley National Bank a 60-day, 6% promissory note payable.

26 Sold merchandise to Bruce Sawyer, Inc., on credit, $915.

27 Sold merchandise to Tyler and Vance on credit, $1,085.

28 Issued Check No. 316 to *The Gazette* for advertising expense, $375.

28 Issued Check No. 317 payable to Payroll for sales salaries, $815. Cashed the check and paid the employees.

28 Received a check from Rice and Son in payment of the February 18 sale, less the discount.

28 Cash sales for the last week of the month, $1,345.

28 *Post to the customer and creditor accounts and also post any amounts that should be posted as individual amounts to the general ledger accounts.*

28 *Make the month-end postings from the journals.*

Required:

1. Open the following general ledger accounts: Cash; Accounts Receivable; Store Equipment; Notes Payable; Accounts Payable; Sales; Sales Returns and Allowances; Sales Discounts; Purchases; Purchases Returns and Allowances; Purchases Discounts; Advertising Expense; and Sales Salaries.
2. Open the following accounts receivable ledger accounts: Bruce Sawyer, Inc.; Rice and Son; and Tyler and Vance.
3. Open the following accounts payable ledger accounts; Globe Manufacturing Company; F. M. Pope, Inc.; Ryan Equipment Company; and Western Supply Company.
4. Prepare a one-column Sales Journal, a one-column Purchases Journal, a Sales Returns and Allowances Journal, a Cash Receipts Journal, a Cash Disbursements Journal, and a General Journal similar to the ones illustrated in this chapter.
5. Enter the foregoing transactions in the journals and post when instructed to do so.
6. Prepare a trial balance and schedules of the accounts receivable and accounts payable.

Problem 6-4

(*If the working papers that accompany this text are not being used, omit this problem.*)

Assume that Small Sales Company operates with annual accounting periods that end each January 31, that it is now the last week of February of the current year, and you have just been hired as the company's bookkeeper. The previous bookkeeper has journalized the transactions for the first three weeks of February and has posted those entry portions that would be posted as individual amounts. An examination of the journals and ledgers of the company as they appear in the booklet of working papers will reveal this.

During the last week of the month the following transactions were completed by the company:

Feb. 23 Received merchandise and an invoice dated February 20, terms 2/10, n/60, from Arizona Supply Company, $900.

23 Sold merchandise on credit to Albert Getty, Invoice No. 716, $850. The terms of all sales are 2/10, n/60.

25 Received a check from Albert Getty in full of the sale of February 16, less the normal 2% discount.

26 Purchased several items of store supplies on credit from Store Supply Company, terms n/10 EOM, $85.

27 Issued Check No. 723 to pay the Southwest Wholesale Company invoice of February 17, less the discount.

28 Douglas Murphy, the proprietor, issued Check No. 724 to himself, the proceeds to be used for personal living expenses, $150.

28 Issued Check No. 725 to Public Utility Company in payment of the February gas and electric bill, $113. (Debit Utilities Expense.)

28 Issued Check No. 726, payable to Payroll, in payment of the sales salaries for the last two weeks of the month, $345. Cashed the check and paid the employees.

28 Cash sales for the last half of the month, $715. (Cash sales are usually

recorded daily, but are recorded only twice each month in this problem to reduce the repetitive transactions.)

Required for February:

1. Record the transactions for the last week of February.
2. Post to the customer and creditor accounts and also post any amounts that should be posted as individual amounts to the general ledger accounts. (Normally these amounts are posted daily; but they are posted only twice each month in this problem in order to simplify the problem.)
3. Make the month-end column-total postings from the journals.
4. Prepare a February 28 trial balance and schedules of accounts receivable and accounts payable.
5. Double rule the date and amount columns of the columnar journals so that they may be used to record the March transactions.

Small Sales Company completed the following transactions in March:

Mar. 2 Issued Check No. 727 to Apex Realty in payment of the March rent, $250.

2 Mailed Check No. 728 to Arizona Supply Company in full of its invoice of February 20, less the discount.

3 Received a check from Robert Johnson in full of the sale of February 21, less the discount.

5 Received a check from Albert Getty in full of the sale of February 23, less the discount.

6 Sold merchandise on credit to George Mohr, Invoice No. 717, $650.

7 Purchased merchandise from Western Manufacturing Company, invoice dated March 4, terms 2/10, n/60, $450.

9 Sold the local Y.M.C.A. a roll of wrapping paper (store supplies) at cost for cash, $18.

10 Issued Check No. 729 to Store Supply Company in payment for the items purchased on February 26.

11 Received merchandise and an invoice dated March 9 from Southwest Wholesale Company, terms 2/10, n/60, $750.

12 Sold merchandise on credit to Robert Johnson, Invoice No. 718, $950.

14 Mailed Western Manufacturing Company Check No. 730 in payment of its invoice of March 4, less the discount.

14 Issued Check No. 731, payable to Payroll, in payment of the biweekly sales salaries, $320. Cashed the check and paid the employees.

14 Cash sales for the first half of the month, $765.

14 *Post to the customer and creditor accounts and also post any amounts that should be posted as individual amounts to the general ledger accounts.*

16 Received a check from George Mohr in full of the March 6 sale, less the discount.

19 Mailed Check No. 732 to Southwest Wholesale Company in full of its March 9 invoice, less the discount.

21 Received a check from Robert Johnson in full of the March 12 sale, less the discount.

23 Sold merchandise on credit to James Scott, Invoice No. 719, $865.

24 Sold merchandise on credit to George Mohr, Invoice No. 720, $985.

Mar. 26 Received merchandise and an invoice dated March 23, terms 2/10, n/60, from Western Manufacturing Company, $915.

28 Issued Check No. 733, payable to Payroll, in payment of the bi-weekly sales salaries, $320. Cashed the check and paid the employees.

29 Received a credit memorandum from Western Manufacturing Company for defective merchandise received on March 26 and returned, $111.

31 Issued Check No. 734 to Public Utility Company in payment of the March gas and electric bill, $112.

31 Cash sales for the last half of the month, $820.

31 *Post to the customer and creditor accounts and also post any amounts that should be posted as individual amounts to the general ledger accounts.*

31 *Make the month-end column-total postings from the journals.*

Required for March:
1. Record the transactions in the journals and post at the points indicated.
2. Prepare a March 31 trial balance and schedules of accounts receivable and payable.

Problem 6–5

On the next page is a columnar journal of Bit Different Company, a journal unlike any described in your text and designed to test your understanding of the posting principles of columnar journals.

Required:
1. Open a General Ledger having T-accounts as follows: Cash; Store Supplies; Store Equipment; Accounts Payable; Purchases; Purchases Returns; Purchases Discounts; Sales Salaries; and Rent Expense.
2. Open a subsidiary Accounts Payable Ledger having these accounts: Horn Supply Company; Lee Company; and Swing Wholesale Company.
3. Post the special journal, prepare a trial balance of the General Ledger, and prove the subsidiary ledger with a schedule of accounts payable. (The Cash account will have a credit balance in the trial balance.)

Alternate problems

Problem 6–1A

East Bay Sales Company completed the following transactions:

Oct. 2 Sold merchandise on credit to Terry Blue, Invoice No. 671, $850. (Terms of all sales are 2/10, n/60.)

3 Received merchandise and an invoice dated October 2, terms 2/10, n/60, from Mesa Sales Company, $1,150.

4 Borrowed $2,500 from Guaranty Bank by giving a note payable.

5 Purchased store equipment on credit from Store Outfitters, terms n/10 EOM, $545.

(*Problem continues on page 183.*)

Problem 6-5 — continued

CASH DISBURSEMENTS, PURCHASES, AND PURCHASES RETURNS JOURNAL

	Debit Columns								Credit Columns			
Store Supplies	Sales Salaries	Purchases	Accts. Payable	Sundry Accts.	Date	Account Titles and Explanations	F	Sundry Accts.	Accts. Payable	Pur. Discount	Cash
.....	.....	.....	.....	500.00	Dec. 1	Rent Expense		.....	.....	.....	500.00
75.00	.....	525.00	.....	.....	2	Horn Supply Company		.....	600.00	.....	.....
.....	.....	850.00	.....	.....	5	Lee Co.		.....	850.00	.....	.....
.....	.....	.....	600.00	.....	10	Horn Supply Company		.....	.....	12.00	588.00
.....	.....	.....	100.00	.....	13	Lee Co. – Purchases Returns		100.00	.....	.....	.....
.....	.....	.....	750.00	.....	14	Lee Company		.....	.....	15.00	735.00
.....	.....	1,200.00	.....	.....	15	Swing Wholesale Company		.....	1,200.00	.....	.....
.....	750.00	.....	.....	.....	15	Salaries for first half of month		.....	.....	.....	750.00
.....	.....	.....	.....	175.00	18	Store Equipment		.....	.....	.....	175.00
50.00	.....	1,100.00	.....	.....	23	Horn Supply Company		.....	1,150.00	.....	.....
.....	.....	.....	1,200.00	.....	24	Swing Wholesale Company		.....	.....	24.00	1,176.00
.....	750.00	.....	.....	.....	31	Salaries for last half of month		.....	.....	.....	750.00
125.00	1,500.00	3,675.00	2,650.00	675.00				100.00	3,800.00	51.00	4,674.00

Oct. 6 Sold merchandise on credit to Dale Hall, Invoice No. 672, $600.

8 Received a credit memorandum from Store Outfitters for unsatisfactory store equipment returned, $135.

9 Received merchandise and an invoice dated October 6, terms 2/10, n/60, from Valley Supply Company, $1,285.

11 Sold merchandise on credit to Walter Nash, Invoice No. 673, $750.

12 Received an $833 check from Terry Blue in payment of the October 2 sale.

12 Issued Check No. 922 to Mesa Sales Company in payment of its October 2 invoice, less the discount.

13 Received a credit memorandum from Valley Supply Company for unsatisfactory merchandise received on October 9 and returned, $85.

15 Issued Check No. 923 to Hill Realty Company in payment of one month's rent on the store building, $500.

15 Issued Check No. 924, payable to Payroll, in payment of sales salaries for the first half of the month, $550.

15 Cash sales for the first half of the month, $2,115. (Cash sales are normally recorded daily from the cash register readings; however, they are recorded only twice in this problem in order to shorten the problem.)

15 *Post to the customer and creditor accounts and also post any amounts that should be posted as individual amounts to the general ledger accounts.*

16 Issued Check No. 925 to Valley Supply Company in payment of the October 6 invoice, less the return and the discount.

17 Sold merchandise on credit to Terry Blue, Invoice No. 674, $700.

20 Received a $735 check from Walter Nash in payment of the October 11 sale.

21 Received merchandise and an invoice dated October 18, terms 2/10, n/60 from Mesa Sales Company, $900.

22 Sold unneeded store equipment for cash at cost, $35.

24 Received merchandise and an invoice dated October 22, terms 2/10, n/60 from North Manufacturing Company, $615.

27 Received a $686 check from Terry Blue in payment of the October 17 sale.

27 Sold merchandise to Walter Nash on credit, Invoice No. 675, $495.

28 Issued Check No. 926 to Mesa Sales Company in payment of the October 18 invoice, less the discount.

31 Issued Check No. 927, payable to Payroll, in payment of sales salaries for the last half of the month, $550.

31 Cash sales for the last half of the month, $2,295.

31 *Post to the customer and creditor accounts and post any amounts that should be posted as individual amounts to the general ledger accounts.*

31 *Total the journals and make the month-end postings.*

Required:

1. Open the following general ledger accounts: Cash; Accounts Receivable; Store Equipment; Notes Payable; Accounts Payable; Sales; Sales Discounts; Purchases; Purchases Returns and Allowances; Purchases Discounts; Sales Salaries; and Rent Expense.

2. Open the following accounts receivable ledger accounts: Terry Blue; Dale Hall; and Walter Nash.
3. Open these accounts payable ledger accounts: Mesa Sales Company; North Manufacturing Company; Store Outfitters; and Valley Supply Company.
4. Prepare a Sales Journal, one-column Purchases Journal, Cash Receipts Journal, Cash Disbursements Journal, and General Journal like the ones in this chapter.
5. Enter the transactions in the journals and post when instructed to do so.
6. Prepare a trial balance of the General Ledger and prove the subsidiary ledgers with schedules of accounts receivable and accounts payable.

Problem 6–2A

During a short period a company completed the following credit transactions:

Nov. 3   Purchased merchandise from Boswell and Boswell, $1,175.
8   Purchased merchandise, $845, and store supplies, $110, from Mesa Wholesale Company.
12   Purchased merchandise, $360, store supplies, $85, and office supplies, $20, from Phoenix Wholesale Company.
15   Purchased on credit two typewriters for office use from Store and Office Suppliers, $560.
18   Purchased office supplies, $90, and store supplies, $60, from Mesa Wholesale Company.
25   Purchased merchandise from Boswell and Boswell, $2,110.
28   Purchased store supplies from Store and Office Suppliers, $45.

Required:

1. Prepare a General Journal and a multicolumn Purchases Journal similar to the ones illustrated in this chapter. Enter the transactions in the journals.
2. Open the required general ledger and accounts payable ledger accounts and post the journals.

Problem 6–3A

Munzel Sales Company completed the following transactions during February of the current year:

Feb. 2   Sold merchandise on credit to Tyler and Vance, $1,250. (Terms of all sales are 2/10, n/30. Number sales invoices beginning with 758.)
2   Sold merchandise on credit to Bruce Sawyer, Inc., $1,500.
3   Received merchandise and an invoice dated January 31, terms 2/10, n/60, from Globe Manufacturing Company, $2,800.
4   Issued Check No. 522 to *The Journal* in payment for advertising, $185.
5   Received store equipment and an invoice dated February 3, terms n/10 EOM, from Ryan Equipment Company, $650.
7   Cash sales for the first week of February, $1,200.
7   *Post to the customer and creditor accounts and also post any amounts that should be posted as individual amounts to the general ledger accounts. (Normally such items are posted daily; but to shorten the problem, you are asked to post them only once each week.)*
8   Issued Credit Memorandum No. 123 to Bruce Sawyer, Inc., for

defective merchandise sold on February 2 and returned for credit, $400.

Feb. 9   Sold unneeded store equipment at cost for cash, $140.

10   Sold merchandise on credit to Rice and Son, $800.

10   Received merchandise and an invoice dated February 6, terms 1/10, n/60, from Western Supply Company, $1,850.

10   Sent Check No. 523 to Globe Manufacturing Company in full of the invoice of January 31, less the discount.

12   Received a check from Tyler and Vance in full payment of the sale of February 2, less the discount.

12   Received a check from Bruce Sawyer, Inc., in full payment of the sale of February 2, less the return and the discount.

14   Cash sales for the week ended February 14, $1,450.

14   *Post to the customer and creditor accounts and also post any amounts that should be posted as individual amounts to the general ledger accounts.*

15   Sold merchandise on credit to Rice and Son, $900.

15   Issued Check No. 524, payable to Payroll, in payment of the sales salaries for the first half of the month, $600. Cashed the check and paid the employees.

17   Issued Credit Memorandum No. 124 to Rice and Son for defective merchandise purchased on February 15 and returned, $150.

18   Sold merchandise on credit to Bruce Sawyer, Inc., $1,300.

18   Received merchandise and an invoice dated February 15, terms 2/10, n/30, from F. M. Pope, Inc., $3,500.

20   Received a check from Rice and Son in full of the sale of February 10, less the discount.

21   Cash sales for the week ended February 21, $1,550.

21   *Post to the customer and creditor accounts and also post any amounts that should be posted as individual amounts to the general ledger accounts.*

22   Received merchandise and an invoice dated February 18, terms 1/10, n/60, from Western Supply Company, $1,250.

22   Received merchandise and an invoice dated February 18, terms 2/10, n/60, from Globe Manufacturing Company, $2,650.

23   Received a credit memorandum from F. M. Pope, Inc., $350. The merchandise covered by the memorandum did not meet specifications and had been returned.

24   Received a check from Rice and Son in full of the invoice of February 15, less the return and the discount.

24   Sent F. M. Pope, Inc., Check No. 525 in full of the invoice of February 15, less the return and the discount.

25   Sold merchandise on credit to Tyler and Vance, $1,175.

27   Borrowed $5,000 from the United States National Bank by giving a 60-day, 6% note payable.

28   Sent Globe Manufacturing Company Check No. 526 in full of the invoice of February 18, less the discount.

28   Issued Check No. 527 payable to Payroll for sales salaries, $600. Cashed the check and paid the employees.

28   Cash sales for the week ended February 28, $1,225.

28   *Post to customer and creditor accounts and also post any amounts*

that should be posted as individual amounts to general ledger accounts.

Feb. 28 *Crossfoot the journals and make the month-end postings.*

Required:

1. Open the following general ledger accounts: Cash: Accounts Receivable; Store Equipment; Notes Payable; Accounts Payable; Sales; Sales Returns and Allowances; Sales Discounts, Purchases; Purchases Returns and Allowances; Purchases Discounts; Advertising Expense; and Sales Salaries.
2. Open the following subsidiary accounts receivable ledger accounts: Bruce Sawyer, Inc.; Rice and Son; and Tyler and Vance.
3. Open the following subsidiary accounts payable ledger accounts: Globe Manufacturing Company; F. M. Pope, Inc.; Ryan Equipment Company; and Western Supply Company.
4. Prepare a Sales Journal, a Sales Returns and Allowances Journal, a Purchases Journal, a Cash Receipts Journal, a Cash Disbursements Journal, and a General Journal similar to the ones illustrated in this chapter.
5. Enter the transactions in the journals and post when instructed to do so.
6. Prepare a trial balance and schedules of accounts receivable and accounts payable.

Decision problem 6–1, Driftwood Sales

The bookkeeper of Driftwood Sales was in an accident while driving home from work on July 12 and is unconscious in the hospital; and the store's owner has approached you for help in filing his second quarter state sales tax return, which is due today, July 15.

The state in which Driftwood Sales is located requires retailers to collect a 3% tax on all retail sales except on those to governmental units, such as school districts and cities. The tax is payable on the 15th of the month following the end of each quarter, and the retailer must make good the deficiency when the total amount collected from customers is less than 3% of net taxable sales.

An examination of the ledger of Driftwood Sales shows the following account balances as of March 31, the end of the first quarter, and June 30, the end of the second quarter:

	March 31	June 30
Sales taxes payable	$ 1,843.60	$ 1,999.25
Sales	64,568.40	71,214.80
Sales returns and allowances	1,472.65	1,582.25
Sales tax expense	19.25	19.25

A carbon copy of the first quarter tax return filed by Driftwood Sales on April 14 shows the payment of $1,862.85 sales tax. Its General Journal shows this entry on April 14:

| Apr. | 14 | Sales Tax Expense | 19.25 | |
| | | Sales Tax Payable | | 19.25 |

Supplementary records show nontaxable sales and returns for the first and second quarters as follows:

	First Quarter	Second Quarter
Sales	$1,216.30	$2,615.65
Sales returns and allowances	215.55	238.10

Prepare in good form with all items properly labeled a calculation showing the second quarter sales tax liability of Driftwood Sales and the amount of the deficiency in its second quarter collections. Give in general journal form the entries to record the deficiency and the payment of the second quarter tax.

Decision problem 6–2, Valley Building Materials

Cecil Elwood worked in the post office in Kings Valley for 20 years, until his aunt died, leaving him $40,000. After sitting around for a year, doing little aside from watching his bank balance dwindle, he opened a retail building materials store six months ago, calling it Valley Building Materials. At the time he began the business, Kings Valley had no such store and it appeared to Mr. Elwood that such a venture would be profitable.

He began business by transferring $25,000 from his savings account to a checking account opened in the name of the business. He immediately bought for cash store equipment costing $4,000, which he expected to use for 10 years, after which it would be worn out and valueless. He also bought a stock of merchandise costing $15,000, which he paid for with cash; and he paid the rent for six months in advance on the store building, $1,500.

He estimated that like stores in neighboring communities marked their goods for sale at prices averaging 40% above cost. In other words, an item costing $10 was marked for sale at $14. In order to get his store off to a good start, he decided to mark his merchandise for sale at 35% above cost, and he thought this would still leave him a net income equal to 10% on the cost of goods sold.

Since Kings Valley is a farming community, Mr. Elwood granted liberal credit terms, telling his creditworthy customers to pay "when the crops are in." His suppliers granted Mr. Elwood the normal 30-day credit period on merchandise purchased.

Today, December 1, six months after opening his store, Mr. Elwood has come to you for advice. He thinks business has been excellent. He has paid his suppliers for all purchases when due and owes only for the purchases, $8,500, made during the last 30 days and for which payment is not due. He has replaced his inventory four times during the six months, and an income statement he has prepared shows $21,000 gross profit and a $6,800 net income. However, you note that he has not charged any depreciation on his equipment. He says he has a full stock of merchandise which cost $15,000 and his customers owe him $20,500. In addition to the rent paid in advance, he has paid all his other expenses, $12,700, with cash.

Nevertheless, Mr. Elwood doubts the validity of his own gross profit and net income figures, since he started business with $25,000 in cash and now has only $800 in the bank and owes $8,500 for merchandise purchased on credit.

Did Mr. Elwood actually meet his profit expectations? If so, explain to him the apparent paradox of adequate income and a declining cash balance. Back your explanation with a six months' income statement, a December 1 balance sheet, and a statement accounting for the $800 December 1 cash balance.

Chapter 7

Internal control

■ In a small business the owner-manager commonly controls the entire operation through his personal supervision and his direct participation in the affairs and activities of the business. For example, he commonly buys all the assets, goods, and services bought by the business, personally hires and closely supervises all employees, negotiates all contracts, and signs all checks. As a result, as he signs checks, for example, he knows from personal contact and observation that the assets, goods, and services for which the checks pay were received by the business. However, as a business grows it becomes increasingly difficult to maintain this personal contact, and at some point it becomes necessary for a manager to delegate responsibilities and rely for control on *internal control procedures* rather than personal contact.

Internal control ■ The methods and procedures adopted by a business to control its operations are collectively known as a *system of internal control*. In a properly designed system the procedures encourage adherence to prescribed managerial policies, promote operational efficiencies, protect the business assets from waste, fraud, and theft, and ensure accurate and reliable accounting data.

Internal control methods and procedures vary from company to company, depending on such factors as the nature of the business and its size. However, some broad principles of internal control are as follows:[1]

Responsibilities should be clearly established

Good internal control necessitates that responsibilities be clearly established. Furthermore, in a given situation or for a given task, one person should be made responsible. When responsibility is shared and something goes wrong, it is difficult to determine who was at fault. For example, when two salesclerks share the same cash drawer and there is a shortage, it is normally impossible to tell which clerk is at fault. Each will tend to blame the other, and neither can prove that the responsibility is not his. In such a situation each clerk should be assigned a separate cash drawer or one of the clerks should be given responsibility for making all change.

Adequate records should be maintained

Good records provide a means of control by placing responsibility for the care and protection of assets, but poor records invite laxity and often theft. When a company has poor accounting control over its assets, dishonest employees soon become aware of this and are quick to take advantage.

Assets should be insured and employees bonded

Assets should be covered by adequate casualty insurance, and employees who handle cash and negoitable assets should be bonded. Bonding not only provides a means for recovery if a loss occurs but it also tends to prevent losses, since a bonded employee is less apt to take assets for his personal use if he knows he must deal with a bonding company when the shortage is revealed.

Record keeping and custody should be separated

A fundamental principle of internal control requires that the person who has access to or is responsible for an asset should not maintain the accounting record for that asset. When this principle is observed, the custodian of an asset, knowing that a record of the asset is being kept by another person, is not apt to either misappropriate the asset or waste it; and the record keeper, who does not have access to the asset, has no reason to falsify his record. Furthermore, if the asset is to be misappropriated and the theft concealed in the records, collusion is necessary.

Responsibility for related transactions should be divided

Responsibility for a divisible transaction or a series of related transactions should be divided between individuals or departments in such a manner that the work of one acts as a check on that of another. This

---

[1] *Internal Control* (New York: American Institute of Certified Public Accountants, 1959), p. 6.

does not mean there should be duplication of work. Each employee or department should perform an unduplicated portion, but in such a manner that the work of one acts as a check on that of another. For example, responsibility for placing orders, receiving the merchandise, and paying the vendors should not be given to one individual or department. To do so is to invite laxity in checking the quality and quantity of goods received, and carelessness in verifying the validity and accuracy of invoices. It also invites the purchase of goods for an employee's personal use and the payment of fictitious invoices.

Personnel should be rotated

Whenever possible, employees should be rotated in their job assignments. This has a number of advantages. In the first place, an employee is less apt to be careless or to intentionally commit a wrong when he knows his action will likely be brought to light when job assignments are changed. Also, an employee who has handled a number of assignments in his department is usually more capable at any one job because he understands how that job fits into the work of the department. And finally, the work of a department does not cease when an employee who performs a key operation is ill or absent. Other employees can take his place.

Mechanical devices should be used whenever practicable

Cash registers, check protectors, time clocks, and mechanical counters are examples of control devices that should be used whenever practicable. A cash register with a locked-in tape makes a record of each cash sale, a check protector by perforating the amount of a check into its face makes it almost impossible to change the amount, and a time clock registers the exact time an employee arrived on the job and when he departed.

Employees should be informed

An internal control system will not function as it should unless the employees cooperate and perform their tasks competently and in the prescribed manner. When employees do not understand the need for certain procedures or feel the procedures cause them unnecessary work, they will often avoid the procedures and, thus, destroy the effectiveness of the entire system. Consequently, when an internal control system is installed, it should be designed to cause the employees the least amount of work and inconvenience, and the reasons for its prescribed procedures should be fully explained.

The system should be under constant review

An internal control system, no matter how well designed, cannot be expected to function properly without constant examination and review. An examination or audit may disclose that prescribed procedures are not being followed or that better control or better work at less cost will be gained with a change in the procedures. Large companies commonly maintain a staff of internal auditors who constantly review their company's internal control system to see that it is functioning properly and its procedures are being followed.

Where internal control is needed

■ Internal control procedures apply to all assets owned by a business and to every phase of its operations. However, such procedures are particularly important in transactions involving cash receipts and disbursements and in the purchase of assets, goods, and services. As a result, purchasing procedures and cash disbursements are used in this chapter to introduce the subject and controlling cash receipts is discussed in the next chapter.

To appreciate the need for control over purchasing procedures and cash disbursements, assume that every employee in a large store has and exercises the authority to buy merchandise for resale by the store and that no business forms and procedures are provided to keep a record of purchases. Under such conditions there would be nothing but confusion as to what had been ordered and received; and there would also be errors, duplications, shortages, and payments for goods not received, plus unlimited opportunities for fraud through kickbacks to dishonest employees and through the payment of fictitious invoices.

Controlling purchases in a large store

■ In a large store, due to the size of the task but also to gain control, it is necessary to divide the responsibilities connected with purchasing merchandise and other assets among several departments. These are commonly the departments requesting that merchandise or other assets be purchased, the purchasing department, the receiving department, and the accounting department. It is also necessary to coordinate and control the responsibilities of these departments with business papers, a list of which follows. An explanation of each paper with its use will show how a large concern may gain control over its purchases.

	Business Paper	Prepared by	Sent to
1.	Purchase requisition	Selling department manager desiring that merchandise be purchased	Purchasing department
2.	Purchase order	Purchasing department	Vendor and the accounting department
3.	Invoice	Company selling the merchandise	Accounting department
4.	Receiving report	Receiving department	Purchasing, accounting, and requisitioning departments
5.	Invoice approval form	Accounting department	Attached to invoice in the accounting department

Purchase requisition

A large store is normally divided into selling departments and service departments, with each department under the supervision of a manager.

The selling departments sell different types of merchandise, and the service departments perform services for the selling department; and in such a store the purchasing department is a service department responsible for buying for all departments.

In making purchases, the purchasing department generally cannot know firsthand the merchandise needs of all the selling departments; therefore, the responsibility for keeping an adequate supply of the right kinds of merchandise in each department is usually delegated to each department manager. However, the department managers cannot be permitted to purchase directly from supply sources because if each manager were permitted to deal directly with wholesalers and manufacturers, the amount of merchandise purchased and the resulting liabilities could not be controlled. Therefore, in order to gain control over purchases and resulting liabilities, department managers are commonly required to place all orders through the purchasing department. In such cases the function of the several department managers in the purchasing procedure is to inform the purchasing department of their needs. Each manager performs this function by preparing in triplicate a purchase requisition, Illustration 7–1, listing the merchandise de-

Courtesy Tops Business Forms

Illustration
7–1

sired. The original and a duplicate copy of the purchase requisition are sent to the purchasing department. The third copy is retained by the requisitioning department as a check on the purchasing department.

Purchase order

The purchase order is a business form used by the purchasing department in placing an order with a manufacturer or wholesaler. It authorizes the supplier to ship the merchandise ordered and takes the place of a typewritten letter placing the order. A sample purchase order is shown in Illustration 7–2.

PURCHASE ORDER   NO. **4238**

THE EUGENE MANUFACTURING COMPANY
2590 Chula Vista Street · Eugene, Oregon

DATE
F.O.B.
SHIP BY
TERMS

TO   SHIP TO

PLEASE SHIP THE FOLLOWING   DATE REQUIRED

QUANTITY	✓	DESCRIPTION	PRICE	PER	AMOUNT

IMPORTANT
OUR ORDER NUMBER MUST APPEAR ON INVOICES AND PACKAGES. ACKNOWLEDGE IF UNABLE TO SHIP ON TIME.   ORDERED BY

Illustration
7–2

Courtesy Tops Business Forms

On receipt of a purchase requisition from a selling department, the purchasing department prepares four or more copies of the purchase order. The copies are distributed as follows:

Copy 1 Copy 1, the original copy, is sent to the supplier as a request to purchase and as authority to ship the merchandise listed.

Copy 2 Copy 2, with a copy of the purchase requisition attached, is sent to the accounting department where it will ultimately be used in approving the invoice of the purchase for payment.

Copy 3 Copy 3 is sent to the department issuing the requisition to acknowledge the requisition and tell the action taken.

Copy 4 Copy 4 is retained on file by the purchasing department.

Invoice

An invoice is an itemized statement of goods bought and sold. It is prepared by the seller or *vendor,* and to the seller it is a sales invoice. However, when the same invoice is received by the buyer or *vendee*, it becomes a purchase invoice to the buyer. Invoices used in manufacturing and wholesaling are of the general type shown in Illustration 7–3.

Illustration
7–3

Courtesy Tops Business Forms

In the purchasing procedure, upon receipt of a purchase order, the manufacturer or wholesaler receiving the order ships the ordered merchandise to the buyer and mails a copy of the invoice covering the shipment. The goods are delivered to the buyer's receiving department, and the invoice is sent directly to the buyer's accounting department.

Receiving report

Most large companies maintain a special department assigned the duty of receiving all merchandise or other assets purchased. As each shipment is received, counted, and checked, the receiving department prepares four or more copies of a receiving report. On this report are listed the quantity, description, and condition of the items received. The original copy is sent to the accounting department; the second copy to the department that requisitioned the merchandise; the third copy is sent to the purchasing department; and the fourth copy is retained on file in the receiving department. The copies sent to the purchasing and requisitioning departments act as notification of the arrival of the goods. An example of a receiving report is shown in Illustration 7–4.

Received from	Receiving Report	No. 4383
		Date
		Purchase Order No.
		Supplier's Invoice No.
		Received via

Quantity	Description	Condition

Counted and inspected by

Illustration
7–4

Courtesy Tops Business Forms

Invoice approval form

When the receiving report arrives in the accounting department, the accounting department then has in its possession copies of the—

1. Requisition listing the items requisitioned.
2. Purchase order that lists the merchandise ordered.
3. Invoice showing quantity, description, unit price, and total of the goods shipped by the seller.
4. Receiving report that lists quantity and condition of the items received.

With the information on these papers, the accounting department is in position to approve the invoice for entry on the books and ultimate payment. In approving the invoice, the accounting department checks and compares the information on all the papers. To facilitate the checking procedure and to ensure that no step is omitted, an invoice approval form (Illustration 7-5) is commonly used. The invoice approval form may be a separate business paper that is attached to the invoice, or the information shown on the illustrated form may be stamped directly on the invoice with a rubber stamp.

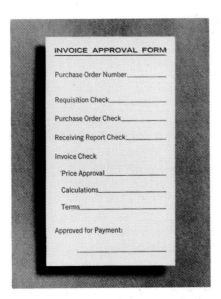

INVOICE APPROVAL FORM

Purchase Order Number_____

Requisition Check_____

Purchase Order Check_____

Receiving Report Check_____

Invoice Check

   Price Approval_____

   Calculations_____

   Terms_____

Approved for Payment:

Illustration
7-5

As each step in the checking procedure is completed, the clerk making the check initials the invoice approval form. Initials in each space on the form indicate:

1. Requisition Check.............. The items on the invoice agree with the requisition and were requisitioned.

2. Purchase Order Check........ The items on the invoice agree with the purchase order and were ordered.
3. Receiving Report Check...... The items on the invoice agree with the receiving report and were received.
4. Invoice Check:

   Price Approval .... The invoice prices are the agreed prices.

   Calculations .... The invoice has no mathematical errors.

   Terms .... The terms are the agreed terms.

Recording the invoice

After the invoice is checked and approved, the purchase requisition, purchase order, receiving report, and the invoice approval form, if a stamp is not used, are attached to the invoice. It is then ready for final approval, recording, and payment. However, before going into this, a system for controlling cash disbursements, called a *voucher system,* should be discussed.

The voucher system

■ A voucher system consists of vouchers and the procedures built around vouchers that are used to gain control over the incurrence and payment of obligations that result in cash disbursements. In a small business, one in which the owner-manager signs all checks and knows from personal contact and observation that the assets, goods, and services for which the checks pay were actually received, such a system is not needed. However, in a large business this personal contact with all phases of the business is impossible; and as a result, the person who signs checks must depend on an internal control system, such as a voucher system, to tell him that an obligation is a proper obligation and should be paid.

The voucher

■ The dictionary defines the word "voucher" as a paper that certifies to the truthfulness of something. This is a satisfactory accounting definition. In accounting a voucher is a business paper on which a transaction is summarized, its correctness certified, and its recording and payment approved.

Vouchers vary somewhat from company to company; but in general, they are so designed that the invoice, bill, or other documents from which they are prepared are attached to and folded inside the voucher. This makes for ease in filing. The inside of a voucher is shown in Illustration 7–6 and the outside in Illustration 7–7. All information entered on a voucher except the payment date and paying check number is entered at the time the voucher is prepared. Information as to payment is written in later when the voucher is actually paid.

Illustration
7–6
**Inside of a
Voucher**

Voucher No. 767

VALLEY SUPPLY COMPANY
Eugene, Oregon

Date _Oct. 1, 19--_
Pay to _A.B. Seay Wholesale Company_
City _Salem_   State _Oregon_

For the following: (attach all invoices and supporting papers)

Date of Invoice	Terms	Invoice Number and Other Details	Amount
Sept. 30, 19--	2/10, n/60	Invoice No. C-11756 Less Discount Net Amount Payable	800.00 16.00 784.00

Payment Approved

M. O. Neal
Auditor

**The
voucher
system and
control**

■ A voucher system gains control over cash disbursements by providing a routine which (1) permits only specific departments and individuals to incur obligations that will result in cash disbursements; (2) establishes procedures for incurring such obligations and for their verification, approval, and recording; and (3) permits checks to be issued only in payment of properly verified, approved, and recorded obligations. Furthermore, every obligation must be recorded at the time it is incurred and every purchase is treated as an independent transaction, complete in itself, even though a number of purchases may be made from the same company during a month or other billing period.

When a voucher system is in use, control over cash disbursements begins with the incurrence of obligations that will result in cash disbursements. Only specified departments and individuals are authorized to incur such obligations, and the kind each may incur is limited. For

Voucher No. _767_

ACCOUNTING DISTRIBUTION

Account Debited	Amount
Purchases	800.00
Freight-In	
Store Supplies	
Office Supplies	
Sales Salaries	

Due Date _____ October 10, 19-- _____

Pay to _ A.B Seay Wholesale Co. _
City _____ Salem _____
State _____ Oregon _____

Total Vouch. Pay.Cr.	800.00

Summary of Charges:
Total Charges _____ 800.00 _____
Discount _____ 16.00 _____
Net Payment _____ 784.00 _____

Record of Payment:
Paid _____
Check No. _____

Illustration
7–7
**Outside of
a Voucher**

example, only the purchasing department may incur obligations by purchasing merchandise, small assets, and supplies.

Further control is gained by establishing a more or less inflexible routine to be followed in incurring each kind of obligation, providing within the routine for the production of business papers at each step, and providing a means of bringing these papers together, checking them, and using them as a basis for approving the transaction for recording and payment.

Take the purchase of merchandise, for example, and recall how a department manager desiring the purchase of merchandise for his department must complete a purchase requisition and send it to the purchasing department. The purchasing department then issues a purchase order to a vendor who ships the merchandise to the purchaser's receiving department and mails an invoice to the accounting department. The receiving department counts and examines the merchandise and reports to the accounting department on a receiving report. The accounting department then has in its possession:

1. A copy of the requisition listing the items requested.
2. A purchase order listing the merchandise ordered.
3. An invoice showing the goods shipped by the seller.
4. A receiving report listing the items received.

With the information on these business papers the accounting department is in a position to approve the invoice for entry on the books and ultimate payment. In approving the invoice, clerks in the accounting department check and compare the information on these papers, noting the completion of each step on the invoice approval form. Then, after the checking and comparing procedure is completed, a voucher is prepared. This is a simple task requiring only that a clerk type the required information in the proper blank spaces of a voucher form. The information is taken from the invoice and its supporting documents. After the voucher is completed, the invoice and its supporting documents are attached to and folded inside the voucher. The voucher is then sent to the desk of the chief clerk or auditor who makes an additional check, approves the accounting distribution, and approves the voucher for recording.

After being approved and recorded a voucher is filed until its due date, when it is sent to the office of the company cashier or other disbursing officer for payment. Here the person responsible for issuing checks depends upon the approved voucher and its supporting documents to tell him the obligation is a proper obligation, properly incurred, and should be paid. For example, the purchase requisition and purchase order attached to the voucher tell him the purchase was authorized, the receiving report tells him the items were received, and the invoice approval form tells him the invoice was checked for errors. Also, he knows there is little chance for fraud, unless all the documents were stolen and the signatures forged, or there was collusion.

The Vouchers Payable account ■ When a voucher system is in use, an account called Vouchers Payable replaces the Accounts Payable account of previous chapters. As a result, when merchandise is purchased, the voucher covering the purchase is recorded with a debit to Purchases and a credit to Vouchers Payable. Likewise, when a plant asset is purchased, a debit to the proper asset account and a credit to Vouchers Payable results. Furthermore, when any voucher is paid, its payment results in a debit to Vouchers Payable and a credit to Cash.

The voucher system and expenses ■ The substitution of the Vouchers Payable account for the Accounts Payable account, as described in the previous paragraph, is a small procedural change. However, the use of the new account in recording expenses, such as telephone expense, represents a somewhat greater

Date	Voucher No.	Payee	When and How Paid		Vouch- ers Payable Credit	Pur- chases Debit	Freight- In Debit	
			Date	Check No.				
19— Oct. 1	767	A. B. Seay Co.	10/9	753	800 00	800 00		1
1	768	Daily Sentinel	10/9	754	53 00			2
2	769	Seaboard Supply Co.	10/12	756	235 00	155 00	10 00	3
6	770	George Smith	10/6	734	65 00			4
6	771	Frank Jones	10/6	735	62 00			5
6	772	George Roth	10/6	736	70 00			6
30	998	First National Bank	10/30	972	505 00			33
								34
30	999	Pacific Telephone Co.	10/30	973	18 00			35
31	1000	Tarbell Wholesale Co.			235 00	235 00		36
31	1001	Office Equipment Co.	10/31	974	195 00			37
31		Totals			5,079 00	2,435 00	156 00	38
					(213)	(511)	(514)	39
								40
								41

Illustration
7–8

change. To understand this change, recall that under a voucher system, in order to gain control over cash disbursements, every obligation that will result in a cash disbursement must be approved for payment and recorded as a liability (vouchers payable) at the time it is incurred. As a result, when the monthly telephone bill is received, it is verified and any long-distance calls are approved, a voucher is then prepared, and the telephone bill is attached to and folded inside the voucher. The voucher is then recorded in the same way as a voucher for the purchase of merchandise, with the only difference being that the recording entry results in a debit to Telephone Expense rather than to Purchases. A check is then issued in payment of the voucher.

Requiring that an expense payment be approved and recorded as a voucher payable at the time it is incurred helps ensure that every expense payment is approved when information for its approval is available. Often invoices, bills, and statements for such things as equipment repairs are received weeks after the work is done; and if no record of the repairs exist, it is difficult at that time to determine whether the invoice or bill is a correct statement of the amount owed. Also, if no records exist, it is possible for a dishonest employee to arrange with an outsider for more than one payment of an obligation, for payment of excessive amounts, and for payment for goods and services not received, all with kickbacks to the dishonest employee.

	Selling Expenses Controlling Dr.			General Expenses Controlling Dr.			Miscellaneous Accounts Debit		
	Acct. Code	Folio	Amount Debit	Acct. Code	Folio	Amount Debit	Account Name	Folio	Amount Debit
1									
2	612	✔	53 00						
3							Store Supplies	117	70 00
4				651	✔	65 00			
5	611	✔	62 00						
6	611	✔	70 00						
33							Notes Payable	211	500 00
34							Interest Expense	721	5 00
35				655	✔	18 00			
36									
37							Office Equipment	134	195 00
38			837 00			716 00			935 00
39			(600)			(650)			(✔)
40									
41									

Recording vouchers ■ When a voucher system is in use, vouchers are recorded in a Voucher Register. Since vouchers are prepared for the purchase of all assets, goods, and services and in payment of all expenses, a Voucher Register is an expanded purchases journal, one in which all purchases and every expense that requires a cash disbursement are recorded. As such it replaces the purchases journals described in the previous chapter.

Voucher Registers vary somewhat from company to company; but in general, they provide columns for the date, creditor's name, voucher number, and a record of voucher payments. In addition, there is a Vouchers Payable credit column and several debit columns. Exact debit columns provided vary from company to company. However, in merchandising concerns a debit column is always provided for recording merchandise purchases; and in all companies, so long as space is available, special debit columns are provided in order that posting labor may be saved by posting column totals. In addition, a Miscellaneous Accounts debit column is provided for those debits that do not occur often.

All information about each voucher that is entered in the register, with the exception of that entered in the columns used in recording the voucher's payment, is entered as soon as each voucher is approved for recording. The information as to payment date and the number of the paying check is entered later as each voucher is paid.

Sometimes a company, such as the one whose Voucher Register is shown in Illustration 7–8, places its expense accounts in subsidiary expense ledgers and maintains only expense controlling accounts in its General Ledger. When this is done, the usual controlling-account-subsidiary-ledger technique of posting column totals to the controlling accounts and posting individual amounts from the columns to the subsidiary expense ledgers is followed.

If individual amounts are to be posted from expense columns such as those shown in Illustration 7–8, it is necessary to indicate in the Voucher Register at the time each voucher is recorded, the subsidiary ledger account to which the amount is to be posted. The account could be indicated by placing its name in an account name column. However, often there is not sufficient room for such a column; and as in Illustration 7–8, the individual subsidiary ledger expense accounts to which amounts are to be posted are commonly indicated by using account identifying code numbers. (It might be wise at this time for the student to review the discussion of code numbers in Chapter 5.) When a code number is used to identify the subsidiary ledger account to which an amount is to be posted, the code number is entered in the "Acct. Code" column at the time the amount is recorded.

A Voucher Register such as that shown in Illustration 7–8 is posted as follows. At the end of each month the columns are totaled and cross-footed to prove their equality. After this, the Vouchers Payable column total is credited to the Vouchers Payable account, the Purchases column total is debited to Purchases, and the Freight-In column total is debited to Freight-In. The individual amounts in these columns are not posted.

The Selling Expense and General Expense column totals are debited to these general ledger controlling accounts; and the individual amounts in the columns are debited to the subsidiary expense ledger accounts indicated by the code numbers in the "Acct. Code" columns.

The individual amounts in the Miscellaneous Accounts column are debited to the accounts named; and the column total is not posted. If voucher register space is limited, account code numbers and an account code number column may be used in this section instead of account names and an Account Name column.

The unpaid vouchers file ■ When a voucher system is in use, some vouchers are paid as soon as they are recorded, while others have to be filed until their due dates. Generally vouchers that are not due are filed in an unpaid vouchers file under the dates on which they will be paid. This aids in taking cash discounts because it automatically brings a voucher to the disbursing officer's attention on its due date. Under this system a discount is seldom missed because a voucher's due date was overlooked.

When a voucher system is installed, the Vouchers Payable account and the file of unpaid vouchers are substituted for the Accounts Payable controlling account and subsidiary Accounts Payable Ledger. In effect the unpaid vouchers file is a subsidiary ledger of creditors' accounts. Likewise, the Vouchers Payable account is in effect a controlling account controlling both the unpaid vouchers file and the vouchers listed as unpaid in the Voucher Register. Consequently, after posting is completed, the balance of the Vouchers Payable account should equal the sum of the unpaid vouchers in the unpaid vouchers file.

This equality is verified after posting is completed each month by preparing a schedule or adding machine list of the unpaid vouchers in the unpaid vouchers file and comparing its total with the balance of the Vouchers Payable account. Likewise, the unpaid vouchers in the file are compared with the unpaid vouchers shown in the Voucher Register's record of payments column. Since the number of each paying check and the payment date are entered in the Voucher Register's payments column as each voucher is paid, the vouchers in the register without check numbers and payment dates should be the same as those in the unpaid vouchers file.

The voucher system Check Register

■ Under a voucher system, checks drawn in payment of vouchers are recorded in a Check Register that is nothing more than a simplified Cash Disbursement Journal. It is simplified because under a voucher system no obligation is paid until a voucher covering the payment is prepared and recorded, and no check is drawn except in payment of a specific voucher. Consequently, all checks drawn result in debits to

Check Register

Date		Payee	Voucher No.	Check No.	Vouchers Payable Debit	Purchases Discounts Credit	Cash Credit
19—							
Oct.	1	C. B. & Y. RR Co.	765	728	14.00		14.00
	3	Frank Mills	766	729	73.00		73.00
	3	Ajax Wholesale Co.	753	730	250.00	5.00	245.00
	4	Normal Supply Co.	747	731	100.00	2.00	98.00
	5	Thomas McGinnin	763	732	43.00		43.00
	6	Giant Equipment Co.	759	733	342.00		342.00
	6	George Smith	770	734	65.00		65.00
	6	Frank Jones	771	735	62.00		62.00
	30	First National Bank	998	972	505.00		505.00
	30	Pacific Telephone Co.	999	973	18.00		18.00
	31	Office Equipment Co.	1001	974	195.00		195.00
	31	Totals			6,468.00	28.00	6,440.00
					(213)	(512)	(111)

Illustration 7–9
The Voucher System Check Register

Vouchers Payable and credits to Cash, unless a discount must be recorded, and then there are credits to both Purchases Discounts and to Cash. As a result, a voucher system Check Register needs at most three money columns. It needs columns for debits to Vouchers Payable, credits to Purchases Discounts, and credits to Cash. Such a Check Register is shown in Illustration 7–9.

Not only is the design of a Check Register used with a voucher system simplified, its posting is also easier. No amounts are posted individually; all amounts are posted in column totals at the end of the month. In posting, the Vouchers Payable debit column total is debited to the Vouchers Payable account and the Purchases Discounts and Cash column totals are credited to these accounts.

Purchases returns ■ A company with a well-organized and properly functioning routine for handling purchases makes most of its returns before vouchers are prepared. However, occasionally an item must be returned after the voucher recording its purchase has been prepared and entered. In such cases the return may be recorded with a general journal entry similar to the following:

Nov.	5	Vouchers Payable	15.00	
		Purchases		15.00
		Returned defective merchandise.		

In addition to the entry, a reference to the entry is made in the Payments columns of the Vouchers Register, on the upper half of the line for the voucher on which the return is made. The reference is made small enough so that the check number of the paying check and the date of the voucher's payment can be entered on the same line. Also, the amount of the return is deducted on the voucher and the credit memorandum and other documents verifying the return are attached to the voucher. Then, when the voucher is paid, a check is drawn for its corrected amount.

Notice that the return of the entry just given is credited directly to the Purchases account. This is optional; a Purchases Returns and Allowances account may be maintained, and returns credited to it. However, when a company has only a few returns during an accounting period that are immaterial in total, it may choose to credit them directly to the Purchases account.

Other internal control procedures ■ Internal control procedures apply to every phase of a company's operations from purchases through sales, cash receipts, cash disbursements, and the control of plant assets. Many of these procedures are discussed in later chapters. However, the way in which a company can gain control over purchases discounts should be discussed here.

Recall that thus far the following entries in general journal form have been used in recording the receipt and payment of an invoice for merchandise purchased:

Nov.	2	Purchases	1,000.00	
		Accounts (or Vouchers) Payable		1,000.00
		Purchased merchandise, terms 2/10, n/60.		
	12	Accounts (or Vouchers) Payable	1,000.00	
		Purchases Discounts		20.00
		Cash		980.00
		Paid the invoice of November 2.		

The invoice of the foregoing entries was recorded at its gross, $1,000, amount, and this is perhaps the way in which most invoices are recorded. However, well-managed companies follow the practice of taking all offered cash discounts; and in many of these companies invoices are recorded at their net, after discount amounts. For example, if a company that records invoices at net amounts purchases merchandise having a $1,000 invoice price, terms 2/10, n/60, on receipt of the goods it deducts the offered $20 discount from the gross invoice amount and records the purchase in its Voucher Register with debits and credits:

Nov.	1	Purchases	980.00	
		Vouchers Payable		980.00
		Purchased merchandise on credit.		

If the voucher for this purchase is paid within the discount period (all vouchers should be so paid), the check register entry to record the payment has a debit to Vouchers Payable and a credit to Cash for $980. However, if payment is not made within the discount period and the discount is lost, an entry like the following must be made in the General Journal when the voucher is paid:

Dec.	31	Discounts Lost	20.00	
		Vouchers Payable		20.00
		To record the discount lost.		

In addition to the foregoing entry a notation is placed in the When and How Paid column of the Voucher Register on the line of the voucher on which the discount was lost. The notation might read "See G.J., P. 35" or something similar. It refers a person examining the records to the general journal entry recording the discount lost, and makes it easy to trace the entire transaction. Also, a notation of the discount lost is placed on the voucher and a check for the full $1,000 invoice amount is drawn in its payment and entered in the Check Register.

Advantage of the net method

When invoices are recorded at gross amounts, the amount of discounts taken is deducted from the balance of the Purchases account on the income statement to arrive at the cost of merchandise purchased. However, when invoices are recorded at gross amounts, if through oversight or carelessness discounts are lost, the amount of discounts lost does not appear in any account or on the income statement and may not come to the attention of management. On the other hand, when purchases are recorded at net amounts, the amount of discounts taken does not appear on the income statement; but the amount of discounts lost is called to management's attention through the appearance on the income statement of the expense account, Discounts Lost, as in the condensed income statement of Illustration 7–10.

XYZ Company
Income Statement for Year Ended December 31, 19—

Sales	$100,000
Cost of goods sold	60,000
Gross profit from sales	$ 40,000
Operating expenses	28,000
Income from operations	$ 12,000
Other revenues and expenses:	
Discounts lost	150
Net Income	$ 11,850

Illustration
7–10

Of the two methods, recording invoices at their net amounts probably supplies management with the more valuable information, the amount of discounts lost through oversight, carelessness, or other cause. It also gives management better control over the work of the people responsible for taking cash discounts; because if discounts are lost, someone must explain why. As a result, few discounts are lost through carelessness.

In passing it should be observed that when a voucher system is in use and invoices are recorded at net amounts, the Check Register needs only one money column. Only one money column is needed because discounts are not recorded and each check entered in the register results in a debit to Vouchers Payable and an equal credit to Cash. Therefore, the amount of each check may be entered in a register column and the total may be debited to Vouchers Payable and credited to Cash.

Trade discounts ■ Cash discounts, just discussed, are granted for prompt payment of invoices. Trade discounts have no relation to payments. A trade discount is a deduction from a list or catalog price and is used in determining the actual selling price of goods. Trade discounts are commonly used by manufacturers and wholesalers to avoid frequent republication of catalogs when selling prices change. If selling prices change, catalog prices can be adjusted by merely issuing a new list of discounts to be applied to the catalog prices.

Trade discounts may be stated as a single percentage or as a chain of percentages. For example, a single discount of 40% off the listed catalog price may be granted, or discounts of 20%, 10%, and 10% may be granted. If a single 40% discount is granted, the selling price of the goods is calculated:

List or catalog price	$1,000
Less trade discount of 40%	400
Selling price	$ 600

If a chain of discounts such as 20%, 10%, and 10% is given, the selling price is calculated:

List or catalog price	$1,000
Less the 20% discount	200
Amount remaining	$ 800
Less first 10% discount	80
Amount remaining	$ 720
Less second 10% discount	72
Selling price	$ 648

Trade discounts are not entered in the accounts; only selling prices are used. For example, the sale of the chain discount calculation just given is recorded in general journal form as follows:

Dec.	10	Accounts Receivable – Blue Company	648.00	
		Sales		648.00
		Sold merchandise on account.		

Transportation terms

■ Invoice terms commonly designate the party responsible for transportation charges. Terms are usually either "FOB Shipping Point" or "FOB Destination."

FOB shipping point

The letters "FOB" are an abbreviation for "free on board." Terms "FOB Shipping Point" mean that the seller will place the goods on board the means of transportation at the factory or shipping point free of charges and the buyer must pay transportation costs from there.

FREIGHT IS PAID BY BUYER ON RECEIPT OF GOODS. If terms are FOB shipping point, the buyer is responsible for transportation charges. Consequently, if he pays the charges on receipt of the goods, the amount paid the transportation company is recorded with a debit to Freight-In and a credit to Cash.

FREIGHT IS PREPAID BY SHIPPER. Sometimes although terms are FOB shipping point, the seller will prepay transportation costs, adding the amount to the invoice. When the shipment is by parcel post, it is not possible to do otherwise; but commonly when the shipment is by other means, the seller will prepay the charges as a convenience to the buyer. For example, Trenton Company sold Manley Sales Company $1,000 of goods, terms 2/10, n/60, FOB shipping point; and as a convenience prepaid $75 of freight charges on the shipment. If Manley Sales Company records invoices at their gross amounts and does not have a voucher system, it should make an entry like the following to record the invoice of this purchase:

Nov.	3	Purchases	1,000.00	
		Freight-In	75.00	
		Accounts Payable — Trenton Company........		1,075.00
		Purchased merchandise on credit.		

In a case such as this, when a discount is granted for prompt payment, the discount is applicable only to the merchandise purchased. Consequently, if Manley Sales Company pays this invoice within the discount period, it may take a $20 discount ($1,000 × 0.02 = $20) and record the payment with an entry like this:

Nov.	9	Accounts Payable — Trenton Company..............	1,075.00	
		Purchases Discounts		20.00
		Cash..		1,055.00
		Paid invoice, less the discount.		

FOB destination

This means "free on board" means of transportation to destination and the seller is to pay the freight.

SELLER PAYS THE FREIGHT. When terms are FOB destination and the seller prepays the transportation costs, as he should, the buyer need only record the purchase when the goods arrive and pay the seller at the proper time.

SELLER DOES NOT PREPAY THE CHARGES. When terms are FOB destination and the seller fails to prepay the transportation costs, the buyer must pay the charges on receipt of the goods and deduct the payment from the amount owed the seller. For example, Manley Sales Company purchased $1,000 of goods from Phoenix Company, terms 2/10, n/60, FOB destination. If the seller failed to prepay the $50 of freight on the shipment, Manley Sales Company would record the purchase and freight payment as follows:

Nov.	3	Purchases	1,000.00	
		Accounts Payable — Phoenix Company		1,000.00
		Purchased merchandise on credit.		

Exercise 7–3

A company purchased from Alpha Company merchandise having a $1,000 list price, less a chain trade discount of 20%, 10%, and 5%; and it purchased from Beta Company merchandise having a $1,000 list price, less a 35% trade discount. Under the assumption the company records invoices at gross amounts, give the entries to record the purchases. Use the current date. Assume the company has a voucher system.

Exercise 7–4

Prepare general journal entries to record the following transactions for a company that has a voucher system and records invoices at gross amounts:

Nov. 6 Received from Gamma Company $600 of merchandise and an invoice dated November 4, terms 2/10, n/60, FOB factory. Gamma Company had prepaid the freight charges and added the amount, $50, to the invoice, bringing the invoice total to $650.

8 Received a $100 credit memorandum from Gamma Company for unsatisfactory merchandise from the November 6 purchase that was returned for credit after the voucher was prepared and recorded.

14 Mailed a check to Gamma Company in payment of the November 4 invoice, less the return and the discount.

Problems **Problem 7–1**

Northwest Company received quotations from two different manufacturers for several items of merchandise. The quotations were:

From Alpha Company: List price $1,000, less 20%, 10%, and 10%, FOB Alpha Company's factory, 1/10, n/30.

From Beta Company: List price $1,000, less 35%, FOB Beta Company's factory, 2/10, n/30.

Northwest Company accepted the best offer, including the cash discount, and completed the following transactions:

Nov. 3 Received the merchandise and an invoice dated November 1. The vendor had prepaid the freight charges, $50, as a service to Northwest Company and had added the amount to the invoice. Northwest Company prepared Voucher No. 567 authorizing payment of the invoice and filed it for payment on the last day of the discount period.

9 Northwest Company received a $100 credit memorandum (invoice price) for merchandise from the foregoing shipment which was returned after the voucher was recorded. It recorded the memorandum, reduced the total of Voucher No. 567, attached the memorandum to the voucher, and in error filed it for payment on the last day of the invoice's credit period.

Dec. 1 Discovered the discount had been lost on the invoice of Voucher No. 567, made the necessary entry or entries, and mailed a check for the amount owed.

Required:

1. Prepare general journal entries to record the transactions under the assumption Northwest Company records invoices at gross amounts.

2. Prepare a second set of entries to record the transactions under the assumption the company records invoices at net amounts.
3. Under the contrary assumptions that Voucher No. 567 was correctly filed on November 9, was paid on November 11, and the discount was earned, (a) give the entry to record its payment under the assumption the company records invoices at gross amounts. Then (b) give the entry to record payment under the assumption the company records invoices at net amounts.

Problem 7–2

On October 31 the credit balance of Kenton Company's Sales account showed it had sold $12,000 of merchandise during the month. The company had begun October with a $6,500 merchandise inventory and ended it with a $7,000 inventory, and it had incurred $3,610 of operating expenses during the month. It had also recorded these transactions:

Oct. 3 Prepared Voucher No. 111 payable to Basset Company for merchandise having a $2,800 invoice price, terms 2/10, n/30, invoice dated October 1.

8 Prepared Voucher No. 112 payable to Doberman Company for merchandise having a $2,000 invoice price, terms 2/10, n/30, invoice dated October 6.

9 Received a $300 credit memorandum (invoice price) from Basset Company for merchandise received on October 3 and returned for credit. (The company has few returns.)

14 Prepared Voucher No. 113 payable to Collie Company for merchandise having a $3,500 invoice price, terms 2/10, n/30, invoice dated October 12.

16 Issued Check No. 115 in payment of the invoice of Voucher No. 112, less the discount.

22 Issued Check No. 118 in payment of the invoice of Voucher No. 113, less the discount.

31 Discovered that Voucher No. 111 had been filed in error for payment on this date. Issued Check No. 123 in its payment, making all necessary entries.

Required:
1. Under the assumption that Kenton Company records invoices at gross amounts, (a) prepare general journal entries to record the transactions and (b) prepare an October income statement for the company.
2. Under the assumption that Kenton Company records invoices at net amounts, (a) prepare a second set of general journal entries to record the transactions and (b) prepare a second income statement for the company.

Problem 7–3

Huron Company completed these transactions affecting vouchers payable:

Nov. 1 Prepared Voucher No. 911 payable to Drylake Company for merchandise having a $750 invoice price, invoice dated October 28, terms FOB destination, 2/10, n/30.

5 Prepared Voucher No. 912 payable to Hillside Company for merchandise having a $1,150 invoice price, invoice dated November 3, terms FOB shipping point, 2/10, n/60. The vendor had prepaid the freight charges, $50, adding the amount to the invoice and bringing its total to $1,200.

Nov. 6 Received a credit memorandum for merchandise having a $250 invoice price. The merchandise was received on November 1, Voucher No. 911, and returned for credit.

10 Prepared Voucher No. 913 payable to Ontario Realty for one month's rent, $700. (Charge $600 to Rent Expense, Selling Space, Account No. 611; and charge $100 to Rent Expense, Office Space, Account No. 651.) Issued Check No. 910 in payment of the voucher.

13 Issued Check No. 911 in payment of Voucher No. 912.

18 Prepared Voucher No. 914 payable to Office Supply Co. for the purchase of office equipment having a $250 invoice price, terms n/10 EOM.

22 Prepared Voucher No. 915 payable to Valley Sales for office supplies having a $100 invoice price, invoice dated November 21, terms n/10 EOM.

25 Prepared Voucher No. 916 payable to Brunswick Company for merchandise having an $850 invoice price, invoice dated November 22, terms FOB shipping point, 2/10, n/60. The vendor had prepaid the freight charges, $30, adding the amount to the invoice and bringing its total to $880.

27 Discovered that Voucher No. 911 had been filed in error for payment on the last day of its credit period rather than on the last day of its discount period, causing the discount to be lost. Issued Check No. 912 in payment of the voucher, making all necessary entries. (Do not forget the return.)

30 Prepared Voucher No. 917 payable to Payroll for sales salaries, Account No. 612, $900; and office salaries, Account No. 652, $450. Issued Check No. 913 in payment of the voucher. Cashed the check and paid the employees.

Required:

1. Assume Huron Company records vouchers at gross amounts. (*a*) Prepare a Voucher Register, a Check Register, and a General Journal and record the transactions. (*b*) Prepare a Vouchers Payable account and post those portions of the Journal and register entries that affect this account. (*c*) Prove the balance of the Vouchers Payable account by preparing a schedule of unpaid vouchers.

2. Assume Huron Company records vouchers at net amounts. (*a*) Prepare a second Voucher Register, Check Register, and General Journal and record the transactions. (*b*) Prepare a second Vouchers Payable account and post those portions of the entries that affect this account. (*c*) Prove the balance of the Vouchers Payable account by preparing a schedule of unpaid vouchers.

Problem 7–4

Dean Sales Company uses a voucher system in which it records invoices at gross amounts, and during November it completed these transactions affecting vouchers payable:

Nov. 1 Prepared Voucher No. 801 payable to East Company for merchandise having an $800 invoice price, terms 2/10, n/60.

2 Prepared Voucher No. 802 payable to *The Journal* for advertising (Account No. 618), $60. Issued Check No. 801 in payment of the voucher.

Nov. 5 Prepared Voucher No. 803 payable to Sharp Realty for one month's rent, $500. (Charge Rent Expense, Selling Space [Account No. 611] with $450 and Rent Expense, Office Space [Account No. 651] with $50.) Issued Check No. 802 in payment of the voucher.

8 Issued Check No. 803 in payment of Voucher No. 801, less the discount.

10 Prepared Voucher No. 804 payable to Vale Supply Company for store supplies, $75, terms n/10 EOM.

13 Prepared Voucher No. 805 payable to West Company for merchandise having a $1,000 invoice price, terms 2/10, n/60.

17 Prepared Voucher No. 806 payable to Office Outfitters for office equipment, $400, terms n/10 EOM.

20 Issued Check No. 804 in payment of Voucher No. 805, less the discount.

23 Prepared Voucher No. 807 payable to North Sales Company for merchandise having a $650 invoice price, FOB factory, terms 2/10, n/60.

23 Prepared Voucher No. 808 payable to Valley Express for freight on the merchandise received from North Sales Company, $40. Issued Check No. 805 in payment of the voucher.

30 Prepared Voucher No. 809 payable to Payroll for sales salaries (Account No. 612), $750; and office salaries (Account No. 652), $350. Issued Check No. 806 in payment of the voucher. Cashed the check and paid the employees.

Required:

1. Prepare a Voucher Register and a Check Register similar to the ones illustrated in this chapter.
2. Prepare a General Ledger having these accounts (the number after each account is its code number): Cash, 111; Store Supplies, 115; Office Equipment, 137; Vouchers Payable, 212; Purchases, 511; Purchases Discounts, 513; Freight-In, 514; Selling Expenses Control, 600; and General Expenses Control, 650.
3. Prepare a subsidiary Selling Expenses Ledger having these accounts: Rent Expense, Selling Space, 611; Sales Salaries, 612; and Advertising, 618.
4. Prepare a subsidiary General Expenses Ledger having these accounts: Rent Expense, Office Space, 651; and Office Salaries, 652.
5. Enter the transactions in the registers and post at the end of the month.
6. Prove the balance of the Vouchers Payable account by preparing a schedule of unpaid vouchers. Prove the balance of the Selling Expenses Control account by preparing a schedule of the subsidiary Selling Expenses Ledger; and prove the balance of the General Expenses Control account by preparing a schedule of the General Expenses Ledger.

Problem 7–5

Deeplake Company records invoices carrying cash discounts at their net amounts, and during October it completed these transactions:

Oct. 1 Prepared Voucher No. 611 payable to Hill Manufacturing Co. for merchandise having a $1,400 invoice price, invoice dated September 27, terms FOB destination, 2/10, n/30.

3 Prepared Voucher No. 612 payable to Gamma Realty for one month's

rent, $600. (Charge Rent Expense, Selling Space, Account No. 611, with $500 and Rent Expense, Office Space, Account No. 651, with $100.) Issued Check No. 608 in payment of the voucher.

Oct. 5 Prepared Voucher No. 613 payable to Alpha Supply Company for store supplies having a $50 invoice price, invoice dated October 5, terms 2/10, n/30.

6 Received a credit memorandum for merchandise having a $200 invoice price; the merchandise was received on October 1, Voucher No. 611, and returned for credit.

10 Prepared Voucher No. 614 payable to *The Daily News* for advertising (Account No. 618), $75. Issued Check No. 609 in payment of the voucher.

11 Prepared Voucher No. 615 payable to Wright Sales Company for merchandise having a $1,250 invoice price, invoice dated October 9, terms FOB shipping point, 2/10, n/60. The vendor had prepaid the freight charges, $40, adding the amount to the invoice and bringing its total to $1,290.

14 Prepared Voucher No. 616 payable to Business Machines Co. for office equipment having a $350 invoice price, terms n/10 EOM.

15 Issued Check No. 610 in payment of Voucher No. 613.

19 Issued Check No. 611 in payment of Voucher No. 615.

24 Prepared Voucher No. 617 payable to Wright Sales Company for merchandise having an $800 invoice price, invoice dated October 22, terms FOB shipping point, 2/10, n/60. The vendor had prepaid the freight, $25, adding the amount to the invoice and bringing the total to $825.

27 Discovered that Voucher No. 611 had been filed in error for payment on the last day of its credit period rather than the last day of its discount period. Made an entry to record the discount lost and issued Check No. 612 in payment of the voucher as adjusted for the return and the discount lost.

31 Prepared Voucher No. 618 payable to Payroll for sales salaries (Account No. 612), $800; and office salaries (Account No. 652), $500. Issued Check No. 613 in payment of the voucher. Cashed the check and paid the employees.

Required:

1. Prepare a Voucher Register similar to the one illustrated in this chapter, a one-money-column Check Register, and a General Journal.

2. Prepare a General Ledger having these accounts (the number after each account is its code number): Cash, 111; Store Supplies, 115; Office Equipment 137; Vouchers Payable, 212; Purchases, 511; Freight-In, 514; Selling Expenses Control, 600; General Expenses Control, 650; and Discounts Lost, 711.

3. Prepare a subsidiary Selling Expenses Ledger with these accounts: Rent Expense, Selling Space, 611; Sales Salaries, 612; and Advertising, 618.

4. Prepare a subsidiary General Expenses Ledger with these accounts: Rent Expense, Office Space, 651; and Office Salaries, 652.

5. Record the transactions in the journal and registers and post.

6. Prove the balance of the Vouchers Payable account by preparing a schedule of unpaid vouchers. Prove the balances of the Selling Expenses Control

account and General Expenses Control account by preparing schedules of the accounts in each of the expense ledgers.

Problem 7–1A

Gamma Company quoted West Sales Company a $1,000 list price, less 20%, 20%, and 10%, FOB its factory, 2/10, n/60, for several items of merchandise. Delta Company quoted a $1,000 list price, less 40% and 5%, FOB its factory, 1/10, n/60, for the same items. West Sales Company accepted the best offer, including the cash discount, and completed the following transactions:

Oct. 10 Received the merchandise and an invoice dated October 8. The vendor had prepaid the freight charges, $40, as a service to the vendee and had added the amount to the invoice. West Sales Company prepared Voucher No. 789 authorizing payment of the invoice.

15 Received a $50 credit memorandum (invoice price) for merchandise returned from the foregoing shipment after the voucher was prepared. Recorded the memorandum, reduced the voucher total, attached the memorandum to the voucher, and refiled it for payment on the last day of the discount period.

18 Issued a check in payment of Voucher No. 789.

Required:

1. Prepare general journal entries to record the transactions under the assumption the company records invoices at gross amounts.
2. Prepare a second set of entries to record the transactions under the assumption the company records invoices at net amounts.
3. Assume that after the credit memorandum was recorded, rather than being filed for payment on the last day of the discount period, the voucher was filed in error for payment on the last day of the credit period, and give the entry or entries needed to pay the invoice (*a*) when it is recorded at its gross amount and (*b*) when it is recorded at its net amount.

Problem 7–2A

Zest Sales Company had a $6,000 merchandise inventory on October 1 and a $5,000 inventory on October 31; during October it made $12,000 of sales and incurred $3,590 of operating expenses; and during the month it completed these transactions:

Oct. 2 Prepared Voucher No. 201 for the purchase of merchandise having a $2,500 invoice price, invoice dated October 1, terms 2/10, n/30.

6 Received a $500 credit memorandum for merchandise having that invoice price which was received on October 2 and returned after Voucher 201 was recorded. The company has few returns, and they are immaterial in total.

8 Prepared Voucher No. 202 for the purchase of merchandise having a $3,000 invoice price, invoice dated October 6, terms 2/10, n/30.

14 Prepared Voucher No. 203 for the purchase of merchandise having a $1,500 invoice price, invoice dated October 13, terms 2/10, n/30.

Oct. 16 Issued Check No. 206 in payment of the invoice of Voucher No. 202, less the discount.

23 Issued Check No. 210 in payment of the invoice of Voucher No. 203, less the discount.

31 Discovered that Voucher No. 201 had been filed in error for payment on this date. Issued Check No. 215 in its payment, making all necessary entries.

Required:

1. Under the assumption that Zest Sales Company records invoices at gross amounts, (a) prepare general journal entries to record the transactions and (b) prepare an October income statement for the company.

2. Under the assumption that Zest Sales Company records invoices at net amounts, (a) prepare a second set of general journal entries to record the transactions and (b) prepare a second income statement for the company.

Problem 7–4A

Eastgate Company uses a voucher system in which it records invoices at gross amounts, and during November it completed these transactions:

Nov. 1 Prepared Voucher No. 751 payable to Tipton Sales Company for merchandise having a $1,200 invoice price, terms FOB shipping point, 2/10, n/60. Tipton Sales Company had prepaid the freight, $50, and added the amount to the invoice, bringing its total to $1,250.

4 Prepared Voucher No. 752 payable to KXYZ Radio for advertising (Account No. 618), $100. Issued Check No. 748 in payment of the voucher.

8 Issued Check No. 749 in payment of Voucher No. 751, less the discount.

12 Prepared Voucher No. 753 payable to Alpha Supply Company for store supplies, $65, terms n/10 EOM.

16 Prepared Voucher No. 754 payable to Office Supply Company for the purchase of office equipment, $500, terms n/10 EOM.

20 Prepared Voucher No. 755 payable to Mesa Sales Company for merchandise having a $650 invoice price, terms 2/10, n/60, FOB destination.

24 Prepared Voucher No. 756 payable to Woods Realty for one month's rent, $450. (Charge Rent Expense, Selling Space [Account No. 611] with $400 and Rent Expense, Office Space [Account No. 651] with $50.) Issued Check No. 750 in payment of the voucher.

26 Prepared Voucher No. 757 payable to City Sales for the purchase of merchandise having a $1,000 invoice price, terms 2/10, n/60, FOB shipping point.

26 Prepared Voucher No. 758 payable to Union Truck Line for freight on the City Sales purchase of the previous transaction, $35. Issued Check No. 751 in payment of the voucher.

27 Issued Check No. 752 in payment of Voucher No. 755, less the discount.

30 Prepared Voucher No. 759 payable to Payroll for sales salaries (Account No. 612), $600; and office salaries (Account No. 652), $400. Issued Check No. 753 in payment of the voucher. Cashed the check and paid the employees.

Required:

1. Prepare a Voucher Register and a Check Register similar to the ones illustrated in this chapter.
2. Prepare a General Ledger having these accounts (the number after each account is its code number): Cash, 111; Store Supplies, 115; Office Equipment, 137; Vouchers Payable, 212; Purchases, 511; Purchases Discounts, 513; Freight-In, 514; Selling Expenses Control, 600; and General Expenses Control, 650.
3. Prepare a subsidiary Selling Expenses Ledger having these accounts: Rent Expense, Selling Space 611; Sales Salaries, 612; and Advertising, 618.
4. Prepare a subsidiary General Expenses Ledger having these accounts: Rent Expense, Office Space, 651; and Office Salaries, 652.
5. Enter the transactions in the registers and post at the end of the month.
6. Prove the balance of the Vouchers Payable account by preparing a schedule of unpaid vouchers. Prove the balance of the Selling Expenses Control account by preparing a schedule of the subsidiary Selling Expenses Ledger; and prove the balance of the General Expenses Control account by preparing a schedule of the General Expenses Ledger.

Problem 7–5A

Newport Company records invoices carrying discounts at their net amounts, and during November it completed these transactions:

Nov. 1 Prepared Voucher No. 501 payable to Payroll for sales salaries (Account No. 612), $750; and office salaries (Account No. 652), $450. Issued Check No. 501 in payment of the voucher. Cashed the check and paid the employees.

    2 Prepared Voucher No. 502 payable to Dale Manufacturing Co. for merchandise having a $950 invoice price, invoice dated October 31, terms FOB destination, 2/10, n/30.

    4 Prepared Voucher No. 503 payable to *The Gazette* for advertising (Account No. 618), $80. Issued Check No. 502 in payment of the voucher.

    8 Prepared Voucher No. 504 payable to Beta Supply Company for store supplies having a $100 invoice price, invoice dated November 7, terms 2/10, n/30.

    9 Received a credit memorandum for merchandise having a $150 invoice price. The merchandise was received on November 2, Voucher No. 502, and returned for credit.

    12 Prepared Voucher No. 505 payable to Hill Supply Company for office equipment having a $250 invoice price, terms n/10 EOM.

    15 Prepared Voucher No. 506 payable to Gale Sales Company for merchandise having a $1,100 invoice price, invoice dated November 13, terms FOB shipping point, 2/10, n/60. The vendor had prepaid the freight charges, $35, adding the amount to the invoice and bringing its total to $1,135.

    15 Prepared Voucher No. 507 payable to Lake Realty for one month's rent, $750. (Charge $650 to Rent Expense, Selling Space, Account No. 611; and charge $100 to Rent Expense, Office Space, Account No. 651.) Issued Check No. 503 in payment of the voucher.

    17 Issued Check No. 504 in payment of Voucher No. 504.

    23 Issued Check No. 505 in payment of Voucher No. 506.

Nov. 25 Prepared Voucher No. 508 payable to Gale Sales Company for merchandise having a $1,000 invoice price, invoice dated November 21, terms FOB shipping point, 2/10, n/60. The vendor had prepaid the freight charges, adding the amount, $45, to the invoice and bringing its total to $1,045.

  30 Discovered that Voucher No. 502 had been filed in error for payment on the last day of the credit period rather than the last day of the discount period. Made an entry to record the discount lost and issued Check No. 506 in payment of the voucher as adjusted for the return and discount lost.

Required:
1. Prepare a Voucher Register similar to the one illustrated in this chapter, a one-money-column Check Register, and a General Journal.
2. Prepare a General Ledger having these accounts (the number after each account is its code number): Cash, 111; Store Supplies, 115; Office Equipment, 137; Vouchers Payable, 212; Purchases, 511; Freight-In, 514; Selling Expenses Control, 600; General Expenses Control, 650; and Discounts Lost, 711.
3. Prepare a subsidiary Selling Expenses Ledger with these accounts: Rent Expense, Selling Space, 611; Sales Salaries, 612; and Advertising, 618.
4. Prepare a subsidiary General Expenses Ledger with these accounts: Rent Expense, Office Space, 651; and Office Salaries, 652.
5. Record the transactions in the journal and registers and post.
6. Prove the balance of the Vouchers Payable account by preparing a schedule of unpaid vouchers. Prove the balances of the subsidiary expense ledgers by preparing a schedule of selling expenses and a schedule of general expenses.

Decision problem 7–1, Builders' Supply Company

A year ago, upon the death of his father, Lee Allen took over the management of his father's business, Builders' Supply Company. At the time he took over, Lee recognized his knowledge of accounting was limited, since he had taken only one course in elementary accounting in college and had not bothered to learn much. However, he reasoned that if the balance of the company's Cash account increased, the company was progressing satisfactorily. Consequently, he watched with enthusiasm the growth of the concern's cash balance from $3,200 when he took over to $17,500 at the end of his first year as manager; and when he received the following income statement covering the year's operations, he was shocked to learn the company had suffered a $4,000 loss during the year.

You are an accountant, and Lee has asked you to explain how it is possible for Builders' Supply Company to suffer a loss during a year in which there was such a gratifying increase in its cash. Assume that the company's accounts receivable decreased $6,500 during the year but its accounts payable total did not change. There were no accrued salaries and wages at the beginning of the year, but $300 of the year's salaries and wages expense consisted of salaries and wages earned but unpaid at the year's end. The advertising expense was paid in cash. And finally, the company had the same number of dollars invested in

BUILDERS' SUPPLY COMPANY
Income Statement for Year Ended December 31, 19—

Revenue:
Sales.. $228,000

Cost of goods sold:
Merchandise inventory, January 1, 19— .... $ 29,000
Purchases 159,000

Goods for sale... $188,000
Merchandise inventory, December 31, 19— 25,000

Cost of goods sold 163,000
Gross profit from sales...................................... $ 65,000

Operating expenses:
Salaries and wages expense .... $ 59,900
Advertising expense 1,200
Supplies expense.. 400
Depreciation expense, equipment......................... 5,000
Depreciation expense, building............................. 2,500

Total operating expenses............................... 69,000
Net Loss.. $ (4,000)

supplies at the beginning and end of the year. Back your explanation with a statement accounting for the company's increase in cash.

Decision problem 7–2, Steel Supply Company

Steel Supply Company fabricates structural steel beams to customers' specifications for bridges and large buildings. It purchases flat rolled steel and angles from steel mills and places the steel in an enclosed storage area which is in charge of a storage area keeper. The company has a good system of internal control for purchases; and from invoices and receiving reports, its accounting department keeps a record of the number of tons of steel purchased and placed in the storage area. Also, when steel is needed for fabrication in the plant, a requisition must be prepared and signed by the plant superintendent or a foreman. The requisition shows the kinds and amounts of steel needed in the plant and the customer's job on which it is to be used. The steel is issued to the plant by the storage area keeper, but first it is weighed and its weight is entered on the requisition. The requisition is then sent to the accounting department where the cost of the steel is charged to the proper customer's job and the inventory record of steel in the storage area is reduced by the weight of the steel issued.

The steel issued to the plant is cut into proper shapes and to the proper size and is used in fabricating the beams specified in customers' orders. The plant superintendent is ultimately responsible for the cutting and for controlling waste. Studies in like plants have shown that an average of 8% of the steel issued for use in fabricating customers' orders is wasted due to cutting odd sizes and shapes. Steel Supply Company accumulates this waste at the back door of its plant until the pile gets sufficiently large as to "get in the way." The plant superintendent then calls a local scrap dealer who hauls it away, weighs it, and mails a check payable to Steel Supply Company, which is endorsed by the company treasurer and deposited.

Records in the accounting department show that 21,200 tons of steel were issued to the plant for fabricating customers' orders. Freight records show that 18,655 tons of finished beams were shipped to customers, and records in the treasurer's office show the company received $45,150 from the sale of 1,505 tons of scrap.

Point out any poor internal control practices of the company and suggest corrective measurers. Does there appear to be any discrepancy in the company's records? If so, how much money is involved and how could the discrepancy be explained?

Chapter 8

Cash and accounts receivable

■ Cash has universal usefulness, small bulk for high value, and no special identification marks by which its ownership may be established; consequently procedures for controlling cash transactions are very important to a business owner; but they are equally as important to the employees responsible for handling cash, since a good system of internal control enables the employees to prove their work was done accurately and honestly.

Internal control for cash

■ A good system of internal control for cash should provide adequate procedures for protecting both cash receipts and cash disbursements, and in these procedures three basic principles should always be observed. First, there should be a separation of duties so that the people responsible for handling cash and for its custody are not the same people who keep the cash records. Second, all cash receipts should be deposited in the bank, intact, each day. Third, all payments should be made by check. The one exception to the last principle is that small disbursements may be made in cash from a petty cash fund. The petty cash fund is discussed in more detail later in this chapter.

The reason for the first of the foregoing principles is that a division of duties necessitates collusion between two or more people if cash is to be embezzled and the theft concealed in the accounting records. The second, requiring that all receipts be deposited intact each day, prevents an employee from making personal use of the money for a few days before depositing it. And, requiring that all receipts be deposited intact and all payments be made by check provides a separate and external record of all cash transactions that may be used to prove the company's own records.

The exact procedures used to achieve control over cash vary from company to company and depend upon such things as company size, number of employees, cash sources, and so on; consequently, the procedures described below are only illustrative of some that are in use.

Cash sales

Cash from cash sales should be rung up on a cash register at the time of each sale. To help ensure that correct amounts are rung up, each cash register should be so placed that customers can see the amounts rung up, and the clerks should be required to ring up each sale before wrapping the merchandise. Also, each cash register should have a locked-in tape on which the amount of each sale and total sales are printed by the register.

Good cash control, as previously stated, requires a separation of custody for cash from record keeping for cash; and for cash sales this separation begins with the cash register. The salesclerk who has access to the cash in the register should not have access to its locked-in tape. At the end of each day the salesclerk is usually required to count the cash in his register and to turn the cash and its count over to an employee in the cashier's office. The second employee, the one in the cashier's office, like the salesclerk, has access to the cash and should not have access to the register tape or other accounting records. A third employee, commonly from the accounting department, removes the tape from the register, compares its total with the cash turned over to the cashier's office, and uses the tape's information as a basis for the entry recording cash sales.

Since the employee from the accounting department who has access to the register tape does not have access to cash, he cannot take any. Likewise, since the salesclerk and the employee from the cashier's office do not have access to the cash register tape, they cannot take cash without the shortage being revealed.

Control of cash received through the mail

Control of cash coming in through the mail begins with a mail clerk who opens the mail and makes a list in triplicate of the money received. The list should give each sender's name, the purpose for which the money was sent, and the amount. One copy of the list is sent to the cashier with the money, the second copy goes to the bookkeeper, and the third copy is kept by the mail clerk. The cashier deposits the money in the bank, and the bookkeeper uses his copy for entries in the Cash

Receipts Journal. Then, if the bank balance is reconciled (discussed later) by a fourth person, errors or fraud by the mail clerk, the cashier, or bookkeeper will be detected. Errors will be detected because the cash deposited and the records of three people must agree; and fraud is impossible, unless there is collusion. The mail clerk must report all receipts or customers will question their account balances. The cashier must deposit all receipts because the bank balance must agree with the bookkeeper's cash balance. The bookkeeper and the person reconciling the bank balance do not have access to cash and, therefore, have no opportunity to withhold any.

Cash disbursements

To gain control over cash disbursements, all disbursements should be made by check, excepting those from petty cash. If authority to sign checks is delegated to some person other than the business owner, that person should not have access to the accounting records. This helps prevent a fraudulent disbursement being made and concealed in the accounting records.

All checks should be prenumbered by the printer and should be entered in the Check Register or Cash Disbursements Journal in numerical order. This makes it possible to scan the numbers in the Check Number column for omitted checks. If a check is spoiled in writing, many concerns require that it be entered in the disbursements journal or register in numerical order with the words "spoiled check" in the Payee column and no amounts in the money columns. The spoiled check is then marked "void" and is attached to its check stub or is filed.

In a small business the owner-manager who signs checks usually knows from personal contact and observation that the items for which the checks pay were received by the business. However, this is impossible in a large business, and in a large business internal control procedures such as those described in the previous chapter should be used to tell the person who signs checks that the obligations for which the checks pay are proper obligations, properly incurred, and should be paid.

The petty cash fund

■ Petty cash payments are excluded from the all-payments-by-check rule because every business must make many small payments for items such as postage, express charges, collect telegrams, and small items of supplies. If each such payment is made by check, many checks for immaterial amounts are written, which is both time consuming and expensive. Therefore, to avoid writing checks for small amounts, a *petty cash fund* is established, and such payments are made from this fund.

When a petty cash fund is established, an estimate is made of the total small payments likely to be disbursed during a short period, usually not more than a month. A check is drawn and debited to the Petty Cash account for an amount slightly in excess of this estimate; the check is cashed; and the money is turned over to a member of the office staff who is designated *petty cashier* and who is responsible for the petty cash and for making payments therefrom.

The petty cashier usually keeps the petty cash in a locked box in the office safe. As each disbursement is made, a *petty cash voucher* or a *petty cash receipt,* Illustration 8–1, is completed. Each petty cash

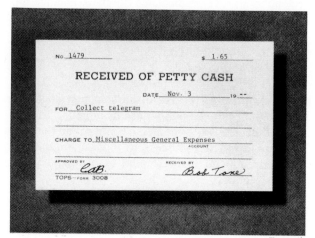

Courtesy Tops Business Forms

Illustration
8–1

voucher acts as a receipt and is signed by the person receiving payment. As each payment is made, the paid voucher is entered in the *Petty Cash Record* (Illustration 8–3) and then placed with the remaining money in the petty cashbox. Under this system, the petty cashbox should always contain paid vouchers and money equal to the amount of the fund.

Each disbursement reduces the money and increases the sum of the vouchers in the petty cashbox. When the money is nearly exhausted, the fund is reimbursed. To reimburse the fund, the petty cashier presents the paid petty cash vouchers to the company cashier who stamps each voucher "paid" so that it may not be reused, retains the vouchers, and gives the petty cashier a check for their sum. When this check is cashed and the proceeds returned to the petty cashbox, the money in the box is restored to its original amount and the fund is ready to begin anew the cycle of its operations.

**Petty cash
fund
illustrated**
■ To avoid writing numerous checks for small amounts, a company established a petty cash fund, designating one of its office clerks, Alice Smith, petty cashier. A check for $20 was drawn, cashed, and the proceeds turned over to this clerk. The entry to record the check is shown in Illustration 8–2. The effect of the entry was to transfer $20 from the regular Cash account to the Petty Cash account.

The Petty Cash account is debited when the fund is established but is not debited or credited again unless the size of the fund is changed. If the fund is exhausted and reimbursements occur too often, the fund should be increased. This results in an additional debit to the Petty Cash account and a credit to the regular Cash account for the amount of the increase. If the fund is too large, part of its cash should be returned to general cash.

Cash Disbursements Journal

Date	Ch. No.	Payee	Account Debited	F	Sundry Accts. Debit	Cash Credit
Nov. 1	58	Alice Smith, Petty Cashier	Petty Cash........		20.00	20.00

Illustration
8–2

During the first month of the illustrated fund's operation, the following petty cash payments were made:

Nov.	3	Collect telegram .... $ 1.65
	7	Purchased paper clips... .50
	12	Express on purchases... 1.75
	18	Postage on sale.. 1.80
	19	Dinner for employee working overtime....................................... 1.60
	20	Purchased postage stamps... 5.00
	21	Express on purchases... 2.80
	24	Cleaning windows 1.00
	27	Repair of typewriter 2.50
		Total $18.60

As each amount was disbursed, a petty cash voucher or receipt was signed by the person receiving payment. Each voucher was then recorded in the Petty Cash Record and placed in the petty cashbox. The Petty Cash Record with the paid vouchers entered is shown in Illustration 8–3.

Commonly, as in this illustration, the Petty Cash Record is a supplementary record and not a book of original entry. A book of original entry is a journal or register from which postings are made. A supplementary record is one in which information is summarized but not posted. Rather, the summarized information is used as a basis for an entry in a regular journal or register, which is posted.

To continue the illustration, on November 27, after the last of the foregoing payments was made, only $1.40 in money remained in the fund. The petty cashier recognized that this would probably not cover another payment, so she gave her $18.60 of paid petty cash vouchers to the company cashier in exchange for an $18.60 check to replenish the fund. On receiving the check, she ruled and balanced her Petty Cash Record (see Illustration 8–3), entered the amount of the replenishing check, cashed the check, and was ready to begin anew payments from the fund.

Petty Cash Record

Date	Explanation	Voucher No.	Receipts	Payments	Distribution of Payments			Miscellaneous Payments	
					Postage	Freight-In	Misc. General Expense	Account	Amount
Nov. 1	Established fund (Ch. No. 58).....		20.00						
3	Collect telegram.....	1		1.65			1.65		
7	Purchased paper clips.....	2		.50				Office supplies.......	.50
12	Express on purchases.....	3		1.75		1.75			
18	Postage on sale.....	4		1.80				Delivery expense...	1.80
19	Overtime meals.....	5		1.60			1.60		
20	Purchased postage stamps.....	6		5.00	5.00				
21	Express on purchases.....	7		2.80		2.80			
24	Cleaning windows.....	8		1.00			1.00		
27	Repair of typewriter.....	9		2.50			2.50		
27	Totals.....		20.00	18.60	5.00	4.55	6.75		2.30
	Balance.....			1.40					
	Totals.....		20.00	20.00					
Nov. 27	Balance.....		1.40						
27	Replenished fund (Ch. No. 106)..		18.60						

Illustration
8–3

The reimbursing check was recorded in the Cash Disbursements Journal with the entry of Illustration 8–4. Information for this entry was secured from a summarization of the entries in the Petty Cash Record. Commonly, as previously stated, the Petty Cash Record is a supplementary record and not a book of original entry; therefore, if petty cash payments are to get to the ledger accounts, an entry like that of Illustration 8–4 is required.

Cash Disbursements Journal

Date	Ch. No.	Payee	Account Debited	F	Sundry Accts. Debit	Cash Credit
Nov. 1	58	Alice Smith, Petty Cashier	Petty Cash........		20.00	20.00
Nov. 27	106	Alice Smith, Petty Cashier	Postage		5.00	
			Freight-In.........		4.55	
			Misc. Gen. Expenses		6.75	
			Office Supplies..		.50	
			Delivery Expense		1.80	18.60

Illustration 8–4

Observe the debits of the entry in Illustration 8–4. All are to accounts affected by payments from the fund. Note that such an entry is necessary to get debits into the accounts for amounts paid from a petty cash fund. Consequently, petty cash must be reimbursed at the end of each accounting period, as well as at any time the money in the fund is low. If the fund is not reimbursed at the end of each accounting period, the asset petty cash is overstated and the expenses and assets of the petty cash payments are understated on the financial statements.

Occasionally, at the time of a petty cash expenditure a petty cashier will forget to secure a receipt; and by the time the fund is reimbursed, she will have forgotten the expenditure. This causes the fund to be short. If at reimbursement time the petty cash fund is short and no errors or omitted entries can be found, the shortage is entered in the Petty Cash Record as a payment in the Miscellaneous Payments column. It is then recorded as an expense in the reimbursing entry with a debit to the Cash Over and Short account discussed in the next section.

Cash over and short ■ Regardless of care exercised in making change, customers are sometimes given too much change or are shortchanged. As a result, at the end of a day the actual cash from a cash register is commonly not equal to the cash sales "rung up" on the register. When this occurs and, for example, actual cash as counted is $557 but the register shows cash sales of $556, the entry in general journal form to record sales and the overage is:

Nov.	23	Cash..	557.00	
		Cash Over and Short.............................		1.00
		Sales		556.00
		Day's cash sales and overage.		

If, on the other hand, cash is short, less cash than the amount of sales shown on the register, the entry to record the sales and shortage is:

Nov.	24	Cash..	621.00	
		Cash Over and Short....................................	4.00	
		Sales		625.00
		Day's cash sales and shortage.		

Over a period of time cash overages should about equal cash shortages. However, customers are more prone to report instances in which they are given too little change; therefore, amounts of cash short are apt to be greater than amounts of cash over, and the Cash Over and Short account normally reaches the end of the accounting period with a debit balance. When it does so, the balance represents an expense, which may appear on the income statement, at the end, as one of the items in the other revenue and expense section. Or if the amount is small, it may be combined with other miscellaneous expenses and appear as part of the item, miscellaneous expenses. When Cash Over and Short reaches the end of the period with a credit balance, the balance represents revenue and normally appears on the income statement as part of the item, miscellaneous revenues.

The voucher system and petty cash

■ Obviously a petty cash fund must be maintained when a voucher system is in use because the issuance of a check under a voucher system is even more difficult, time consuming, and expensive than when a Cash Disbursements Journal is used. Fortunately, the voucher system does not materially affect the operation of a petty cash fund. If the fund is started after a voucher system is in operation, a voucher debiting Petty Cash is prepared and recorded. A check is then drawn and cashed in its payment, and the proceeds are turned over to the petty cashier. The fund then operates in the usual manner until it must be replenished. When the fund is replenished, a voucher is prepared and approved for the amount of the replenishing check. The debits listed on the voucher are obtained in the usual manner from the petty cash record. After the replenishing voucher is recorded, a check is drawn in its payment and cashed; the proceeds are given to the petty cashier; and the fund is ready to begin anew the cycle of its operations.

■ Every month banks furnish each commercial depositor a statement of his account. The statement shows: (1) the amount on deposit at the beginning of the month, (2) checks and any other amounts deducted from the account, (3) deposits and any other amounts added to the account, and (4) the account balance at the end of the month, according to the records of the bank. If all receipts are deposited and all payments are made by check, the bank statement becomes a device for proving the depositor's cash records. A bank statement is shown in Illustration 8-5.

MERCHANT'S NATIONAL BANK
Eugene, Oregon

STATEMENT OF ACCOUNT

BALANCE BROUGHT FORWARD		STATEMENT OF BALANCE		CHECKS RETURNED
Date	Balance	Date	Balance	
9/30/72	1,578.00	10/31/72	1,753.00	9

Valley Hardware Company
10th and Pine Sts.
Eugene, Oregon

CHECKS IN DETAIL				DEPOSITS	DATE	BALANCE
58 00					10 2	1520 00
120 00		200 00			10 5	1200 00
				240 00	10 6	1440 00
				150 00	10 10	1490 00
25 00		75 00		180 00	10 18	1670 00
					10 23	1610 00
10 00		50 00			10 25	1575 00
		135 00		100 00	10 28	1555 00
		20 00			10 30	1753 00
				198 00		

If no error is reported within ten days this account will be considered correct.

Illustration
8-5

Banks commonly mail each depositor a bank statement soon after the end of each month. Included in the envelope with the statement are the depositor's *canceled checks* and any debit or credit memoranda that have affected the account. The checks returned are the ones the bank has paid during the month. They are called "canceled checks" because they are canceled by stamping or punching to show that they have been paid. During any month, in addition to the checks the depositor has drawn, the bank may deduct from the depositor's account amounts for service charges, printing checks, items deposited that are uncollectible, and for errors. The bank notifies the depositor of each such deduction with a debit memorandum. A copy of the memorandum is always included with the monthly statement. The bank may also add amounts to the depositor's account for errors and for amounts collected for the depositor. A credit memorandum is used to notify of any such additions.

Need for reconciling the bank balance

Normally, when the bank statement arrives, the balance of cash as shown by the statement does not agree with the balance shown by the depositor's accounting records. In order to prove the accuracy of both the depositor's records and those of the bank, it is necessary to reconcile and account for any differences between the two balances.

Numerous things may cause the bank statement balance to differ from the depositor's book balance of cash. Some of the more common are:

1. *Outstanding Checks.* These are checks that have been drawn by the depositor and deducted on the depositor's records but have not reached the bank for payment and deduction.
2. *Unrecorded Deposits.* Concerns often make deposits at the end of each business day, after the bank has closed. These deposits are made in the bank's night depository and are not recorded by the bank until the next business day. Consequently, if a deposit is placed in the night depository the last day of the month, it does not appear on the bank statement for that month.
3. *Charges for Service and Uncollectible Items.* A bank often deducts amounts from a depositor's account for services rendered and for items deposited that it is unable to collect. Insufficient funds checks are the most common of the latter. The bank notifies the depositor of each such deduction with a debit memorandum. If the item is material in amount, the memorandum is mailed to the depositor on the day of the deduction. Furthermore, in a well-managed company, each such deduction is entered in the Cash Disbursements Journal or the Voucher Register on the day the memorandum is received. However, occasionally there are unentered amounts near the end of the month.
4. *Collections.* Banks often act as collecting agents for their depositors, collecting for a small fee promissory notes and other items. When an item such as a promissory note is collected, the bank usually adds the proceeds to the depositor's account and sends a credit memorandum as notification of the transaction. As soon as the memorandum is received, an entry should be made in the Cash Receipts Journal. Occasionally, there are unentered amounts near the end of the month.
5. *Errors.* Regardless of care and systems of internal control for automatic error detection, both the bank and the depositor make errors that affect the bank balance. Occasionally, these errors are not discovered until the balance is reconciled.

Steps in reconciling the bank balance

The steps in reconciling the bank balance are:

1. Compare the deposits listed on the bank statement with deposits shown in the accounting records. Note any discrepancies and discover which is correct. List any errors or unrecorded items.
2. When canceled checks are returned by the bank, they are in a stack in the order in which the bank paid them and also in the order of their listing on the bank statement. While the checks are in this order, compare each with its bank statement listing. Note any discrepancies or errors.
3. Rearrange the returned checks in numerical order, the order in which they were written. Secure the previous month's reconciliation and determine if any checks outstanding at the end of the previous month are still outstanding. If there are any, list them. Also, see that any deposits that were unrecorded by the bank at the end of the previous month have been recorded.
4. Insert among the canceled checks any bank memorandum according to their dates. Compare each check with its entry in the Cash Disbursements Journal or Check Register. Note for correction any discrepancies, and list any unpaid checks or unrecorded memorandum.
5. Prepare a reconciliation of the bank statement balance with the book balance of cash. Such a reconciliation is shown in Illustration 8-6.
6. Determine if any debits or credits appearing on the bank statement are unrecorded in the books of account. Make journal entries to record them.

Illustration of a bank reconciliation

■ To illustrate a bank reconciliation assume that Valley Hardware Company found the following when it attempted to reconcile its bank balance of October 31. The bank balance as shown by the bank statement was $1,753, and the cash balance according to the accounting records was $1,370. Check No. 124 for $150 and Check No. 126 for $200 were outstanding and unpaid by the bank. A $120 deposit, placed in the bank's night depository after banking hours on October 31, was unrecorded by the bank. Among the returned checks was a credit memorandum showing the bank had collected a note receivable for the company on October 30, crediting the proceeds, $200 less a $2 collection fee, to the company account. Also returned with the bank statement was an NSF (not sufficient funds) check for $20. This check had been received from a customer, Frank Jones, on October 25, and had been included in that day's deposit. The collection of the note and the return of the NSF check were unrecorded on the company books. In addition, a check for $25 drawn by Valley Haberdashery was among the canceled checks returned. This check had been charged in error to the account of Valley Hardware Company. The statement reconciling these amounts is shown in Illustration 8-6.

A bank reconciliation helps locate any errors made by either the bank or the depositor; discloses any items which have been entered on the

Valley Hardware Company
Bank Reconciliation as of October 31, 19—

Book Balance of Cash.........................$1,370		Bank Statement Balance		$1,753
Add:		Add:		
Proceeds of note less		Deposit of 10/31 ....$120		
collection fee............................ 198		Valley Haberdashery check		
	$1,568	charged in error 25		145
				$1,898
Deduct:		Deduct:		
NSF check of Frank Jones 20		Outstanding checks:		
		No. 124............................$150		
		No. 126............................ 200		350
Reconciled Balance $1,548		Reconciled Balance		$1,548

Illustration
8–6

company books but have not come to the bank's attention; and discloses items that should be recorded on the company books but are unrecorded on the date of the reconciliation. For example, in the reconciliation illustrated, the reconciled cash balance, $1,548, is the true cash balance. However, at the time the reconciliation is completed, Valley Hardware Company's accounting records show a $1,370 book balance. Consequently, entries must be made to adjust the book balance, increasing it to the true cash balance. This requires two entries, the first in general journal form is:

Nov.	2	Cash...	198.00	
		Collection Expense	2.00	
		Notes Receivable		200.00
		To record the proceeds and collection charge of a note collected by the bank.		

The foregoing entry is self-explanatory. The bank collected a note receivable, deducted a collection fee, and deposited the difference to the Valley Hardware Company account. The entry increases the amount of cash on the books, records the collection expense, and reduces notes receivable.

The second entry is:

Nov.	2	Accounts Receivable—Frank Jones	20.00	
		Cash...		20.00
		To charge back the NSF check received from Frank Jones.		

This entry records the NSF check returned as uncollectible. The check was received from Jones in payment of his account and was deposited as cash. The bank, unable to collect the check, deducted $20 from the Valley Hardware account, making it necessary for the company to reverse the entry made when the check was received. After recording the returned check, the company will endeavor to collect the $20 from Jones. If after all legal means of collection have been exhausted and the company is still unable to collect, the amount will be written off as a bad debt.

ACCOUNTS RECEIVABLE

■ Most of the problems encountered in recording transactions with customers have already been discussed. However, the matter of *bad debts* and a few miscellaneous matters need attention.

Bad debts ■ When goods and services are sold on credit, there are almost always a few customers who do not pay. The accounts of such customers are called bad debts and are a loss and expense of selling on credit.

It might be asked: Why do merchants sell on credit if bad debts result? The answer is, of course, that merchants sell on credit in order to increase total sales and profits. Merchants are willing to take a reasonable loss from bad debts in order to increase sales and profits. Therefore, bad debt losses are an expense of selling on credit, an expense incurred in order to increase sales. Also, if revenues and expenses are matched, bad debt losses must be matched against the sales they helped produce.

Matching bad debt losses with sales ■ A bad debt loss results from an error in judgment, an error in granting credit and making a sale to a customer who will not pay. Consequently, a bad debt loss is incurred at the moment credit is granted and a sale is made to such a customer. Of course the merchant making such a sale does not know at the time of the sale that he has incurred a loss. Actually, he normally will not be sure of the loss for as much as a year or more, after he has exhausted every means of collecting. Nevertheless, final recognition a year or so later does not change the time of the loss — the loss occurred at the moment of the sale.

When it is recognized that a bad debt loss occurs at the moment of a sale to a customer who will not pay and that a merchant cannot be sure the customer will not pay until a year or more after the sale, it follows that if bad debt losses are matched with the sales they helped produce, they must be matched on an estimated basis. The allowance method of accounting for bad debts does just that.[1]

Allowance method of accounting for bad debts ■ Under the allowance method of accounting for bad debts, an estimate is made at the end of each accounting period of the total bad debts that are expected to result from the period's sales, and an allowance is provided for the resulting loss. This has two advantages: (1) the estimated loss is charged to the period in which the revenue is recognized,

---

[1] *Basic Concepts and Accounting Principles Underlying Financial Statements* (New York: American Institute of Certified Public Accountants, 1970), pp. 61–62.

and (2) the accounts receivable appear on the balance sheet at their estimated realizable value, a more informative balance sheet amount.

Estimating bad debts

In making the year-end estimate of bad debts that are expected to result from the year's sales, companies commonly assume that "history will repeat." For example, over the past several years Alpha Company has experienced bad debt losses equal to one half of 1% of its charge sales, and during the past year its charge sales were $300,000. Consequently, if history repeats, Alpha Company can expect $1,500 of bad debt losses to result from the year's sales ($300,000 $\times$ 0.005 = $1,500).

Recording the estimated bad debts loss

Under the allowance method of accounting for bad debts, the estimated bad debts loss is recorded at the end of each accounting period with a work sheet adjustment and an adjusting entry. For example, Alpha Company will record its $1,500 estimated bad debts loss with a work sheet adjustment and an adjusting entry like the following:

Dec.	31	Bad Debts Expense..	1,500.00	
		Allowance for Doubtful Accounts..............		1,500.00
		To record the estimated bad debts.		

The debit of the foregoing entry causes the estimated bad debts loss to appear on the income statement of the year in which the sales were made; and as a result, this estimated $1,500 expense of selling on credit is matched with the $300,000 of revenue it helped to produce.

Bad debt losses normally appear on the income statement as an administrative expense rather than as a selling expense. They appear as an administrative expense because granting credit is usually not a responsibility of the sales department; and therefore since the sales department is not responsible for granting credit, it should not be held responsible for bad debt losses. The sales department is usually not given responsibility for granting credit because it is feared the sales department would at times be swayed in its judgment of a credit risk by its desire to make a sale.

Bad debts in the accounts

If at the time the foregoing bad debts adjusting entry is posted, Alpha Company has $20,000 of accounts receivable, the Accounts Receivable and Allowance for Doubtful Accounts accounts will show the following balances:

Accounts Receivable		Allowance for Doubtful Accounts	
Dec. 31 20,000			Dec. 31 1,500

The bad debts adjusting entry reduces the accounts receivable to their estimated realizable value. However, note that the credit of the entry is to the contra account, Allowance for Doubtful Accounts, rather than to the Accounts Receivable controlling account.

It is necessary to credit the estimated bad debts loss to the contra account rather than the Accounts Receivable account because at the time of the adjusting entry it is not known for certain just which customers will fail to pay. (The total loss from bad debts can be estimated from past experience, but the exact customers who will not pay cannot be known until every means of collecting from each has been exhausted.) Consequently, since the bad accounts are not identifiable at the time the adjusting entry is made, they cannot be removed from the subsidiary Accounts Receivable Ledger; and the Allowance for Doubtful Accounts account must be credited instead of the controlling account. The allowance account must be credited because to credit the controlling account without removing the bad accounts from the subsidiary ledger would cause the controlling account balance to differ from the sum of the balances in the subsidiary ledger.

Allowance for doubtful accounts on the balance sheet

When the balance sheet is prepared, the balance of the Allowance for Doubtful Accounts account is subtracted thereon from the balance of the Accounts Receivable account to show the amount that is expected to be realized from the accounts, as follows:

ASSETS

Current Assets:		
Cash		$11,300
Accounts receivable	$20,000	
Less allowance for doubtful accounts	1,500	18,500
Merchandise inventory		27,200
Prepaid expenses		1,100
Total Current Assets		$58,100

Writing off a bad debt

When an allowance for doubtful accounts is provided, accounts deemed uncollectible are written off against this allowance. For example, after spending a year trying to collect, Alpha Company finally concluded the $100 account of George Vale was uncollectible and made the following entry to write it off:

Jan.	23	Allowance for Doubtful Accounts	100.00	
		Accounts Receivable — George Vale		100.00
		To write off the uncollectible account of George Vale.		

Posting the entry had this effect on the accounts:

Accounts Receivable				Allowance for Doubtful Accounts			
Dec. 31	20,000	Jan. 23	100	Jan. 23	100	Dec. 31	1,500

Two points should be observed in the foregoing entry and accounts. First, although bad debts are an expense of selling on credit, the Allowance for Doubtful Accounts account rather than an expense account is debited in the write-off. The allowance account is debited because the expense was recorded at the end of the period in which the sale occurred. At that time, the loss was foreseen, and the expense was recorded in the estimated bad debts adjusting entry.

Second, although the write-off removed the amount of the account from the ledgers, it did not affect the estimated realizable amount of Alpha Company's accounts receivable, as the following tabulation shows:

	Before Write-off	After Write-off
Accounts receivable	$20,000	$19,900
Less allowance for doubtful accounts	1,500	1,400
Estimated realizable accounts receivable	$18,500	$18,500

Bad debts written off seldom equal the allowance provided

The uncollectible accounts from a given year's sales seldom, if ever, exactly equal the allowance provided for their loss. If accounts written off are less than the allowance provided, the Allowance for Doubtful Accounts account reaches the end of the year with a credit balance. On the other hand, if accounts written off exceed the allowance provided, the allowance account reaches the period end with a debit balance, which is then eliminated with the new bad debts adjusting entry. In either case no harm is done if the allowance provided is approximately equal to the bad debts written off and is neither continually excessive nor insufficient.

Often when the addition to the allowance for doubtful accounts is based on a percentage of sales, the passage of several accounting periods is required before it becomes apparent the percentage is either too large or too small. In such cases when it becomes apparent the percentage is incorrect, a change in the percentage should be made.

Bad debt recoveries ■ Frequently an error in judgment is made in regard to a customer's ability to pay his past-due account. As a result, accounts written off as uncollectible are later sometimes collected in full or in part. If an account is written off as uncollectible and later the customer pays part or all of the amount previously written off, the payment should be shown in the customer's account for future credit action. It should be shown because when a customer fails to pay and his account is written off, the customer's credit standing is impaired; and later when the customer pays the amount previously written off, the payment helps restore the credit standing. When an account previously written off as a bad debt is collected, two entries are made. The first reinstates the customer's account balance and has the effect of reversing the original write-off. The second entry records the collection of the reinstated account.

For example, if George Vale, whose account was written off by Alpha Company (page 239) on January 23, pays in full on August 15, the entries in general journal form to record the bad debt recovery are:

Aug.	15	Accounts Receivable—George Vale..................	100.00	
		Allowance for Doubtful Accounts...............		100.00
		To reinstate the account of George Vale written off on January 23.		
	15	Cash...	100.00	
		Accounts Receivable—George Vale...........		100.00
		In full of account.		

The cash collection just illustrated would normally be recorded in a Cash Receipts Journal. However, beginning at this point and continuing through the remainder of the text, almost all entries will be given in general journal form to simplify the illustrations. The student should realize that a company would make such entries in a Cash Receipts Journal or other appropriate journal if it made use of such.

Other bases for estimating bad debts

■ As previously explained, the relationship between charge sales and past bad debt losses is often used in estimating losses from uncollectible accounts. Too, when the proportion of credit sales to cash sales remains about the same, total sales rather than charge sales may be used. Likewise, in companies where about the same percentage of accounts receivable prove uncollectible each year, a percentage of the year-end balance of the Accounts Receivable account may be set up as the estimated bad debts expense.

Aging accounts receivable

■ In estimating bad debt losses, many companies age their accounts receivable. This consists of preparing a schedule of accounts receivable with the accounts listed and their balances entered in columns according to age. Such a schedule appears as in Illustration 8–7. After a schedule showing account ages is prepared, responsible and experienced executives of the sales and credit departments examine each account listed thereon and from experience and by judgment decide which are probably uncollectible. Normally, the majority of accounts appearing on the schedule are current and not past due; these are examined for possible losses but receive less scrutiny than past-due accounts. The older accounts are more apt to prove uncollectible; these receive the greatest attention. After decisions are made as to which accounts are probably uncollectible, the allowance for bad debts is adjusted to provide for them.

Schedule of Accounts Receivable by Age					
Customer's Name	Not Due	1 to 30 Days Past Due	31 to 60 Days Past Due	61 to 90 Days Past Due	Over 90 Days Past Due
Charles Abbot	45.00				
Frank Allen	53.00				
George Arden			14.00		
Paul Baum					27.00

Illustration 8–7

To illustrate this adjustment, assume that a company has $60,000 of accounts receivable at the end of an accounting period and in aging these accounts its executives estimate that accounts totaling $1,950 are probably uncollectible. Assume further that the company has a $250 credit balance in its allowance account. Under these assumptions the company will make the following adjusting entry to increase the balance of the allowance account to the amount needed to provide for the estimated uncollectible accounts:

Dec.	31	Bad Debts Expense	1,700.00	
		Allowance for Doubtful Accounts..............		1,700.00
		To increase the allowance for doubtful accounts to $1,950.		

The $1,700 credit of the illustrated entry increases the balance of the allowance account to the $1,950 needed to provide for the estimated bad debts. If it had been assumed that the allowance account had a $150 debit balance before adjustment, rather than the assumed $250 credit balance, it would have been necessary to increase the entry amounts to $2,100 ($150 + $1,950) in order to bring the account balance up to the required amount.

Aging accounts receivable and increasing the allowance for doubtful accounts to an amount sufficient to provide for the accounts deemed uncollectible has two things in its favor. (1) When accounts receivable are aged, an excessive or an inadequate provision for bad debts in one period is automatically adjusted in the next; and as a result, the balance of the allowance account never builds up to an excessive amount, as sometimes happens when it is increased each period by a percent of sales. (2) The aging method also normally provides a better balance sheet figure than does the percent of sales method, a figure closer to realizable value. However, the aging method may not as closely match revenues and expenses as the percent of sales method.

Direct write-off of bad debts

■ Since the allowance method of accounting for bad debts results in a better matching of revenues and expenses, it is the method that should be used in most cases. However, under certain circumstances another method, called the *direct write-off method,* may be used. Under the direct write-off method, when it is decided that an account is uncollectible, it is written off directly to the Bad Debts Expense account with an entry like this:

Nov.	23	Bad Debts Expense	52.50	
		Accounts Receivable – Dale Hall		52.50
		To write off the uncollectible account		
		of Dale Hall.		

The debit of the entry charges the bad debt loss directly to the current year's Bad Debts Expense account, and the credit removes the balance of the uncollectible account from the subsidiary ledger and controlling account.

If an account previously written off directly to the Bad Debts Expense account is later collected in full, the following entries in general journal form are used to record the bad debt recovery.

Mar.	11	Accounts Receivable – Dale Hall	52.50	
		Bad Debts Expense		52.50
		To reinstate the account of Dale Hall		
		previously written off.		
	11	Cash...	52.50	
		Accounts Receivable – Dale Hall		52.50
		In full of account.		

The entry to reinstate the Dale Hall account assumes collection in the year following the write-off and that the Bad Debts Expense account has a debit balance from other write-offs during the year. If the account has no balance from other write-offs and no write-offs are expected, the credit of the entry could be to a revenue account called, for example, Bad Debt Recoveries.

Direct write-off mismatches revenues and expenses

Since a bad debt loss occurs at the moment of a sale to a customer who will not pay but the bad debt cannot be identified until as much as a year or more later when every effort to collect has failed, it follows that the direct write-off method commonly mismatches revenues and expenses. It mismatches revenues and expenses because the revenue from a bad debt sale appears on the income statement of one year while the expense of the loss is deducted on the income statement of the following or a later year.

When direct write-off is permissible

Although the direct write-off method commonly fails in the matching process, it may still be used in situations where its use does not materially affect reported net income. For example, it may be used in a store where substantially all sales are for cash and bad debt losses from a few charge sales are immaterial in relation to total sales and net income. In such a store the use of direct write-off comes under *the accounting principle of materiality*. (Under the accounting principle of materiality it is held that a strict adherence to any accounting principle, in this case the matching principle, is not required when adherence is relatively difficult or expensive and the lack of adherence does not materially affect reported net income. Or in other words, failure to adhere is permissible when the failure does not produce an error or misstatement sufficiently large as to influence a financial statement reader's judgment of a given situation.)

Other factors affecting accounts receivable

■ Overpayment of an account

Customers occasionally fail to take earned discounts or in some other manner overpay their accounts. Because of this, customer accounts with credit balances are not uncommon. When there are customer accounts with credit balances in the Accounts Receivable Ledger, the balance of the Accounts Receivable controlling account should not appear on the balance sheet as the amount of accounts receivable. In such cases, because assets and liabilities should not be offset, the accounts in the Accounts Receivable Ledger having debit balances should be added and their sum placed on the balance sheet as the amount of accounts receivable. At the same time the accounts having credit balances should be added and their sum placed on the balance sheet as a current liability under a caption such as, for example, "Credit balances in customer accounts."

Sales to and purchases from the same firm

If goods are sold to and purchases are made from the same firm, two accounts should be kept, and their balances should not be offset. In such cases the amount receivable should appear on the balance sheet as part of the accounts receivable and the amount payable should appear as part of the accounts payable.

Miscellaneous accounts receivable

If the caption "Accounts receivable" appears on the balance sheet without any further descriptive words or limitations, only amounts due from regular trade debtors should be included under the designation. Accounts receivable from stockholders or company officers, in the case of a corporation, or from employees should be shown separately, unless these accounts arose from sales that are collectible in accordance with the company's regular selling terms. Loans and advances to stockholders, officers, and employees may be shown as current assets under a suitable descriptive title if there is evidence that the amounts will be collected within the period normally allotted for the collection of current assets; otherwise, they should appear at the end of the asset section as, for example, "Other assets—accounts receivable from officers and employees."

Questions for class discussion

1. Why should the bookkeeper of a company not be given the responsibility for receiving cash for the company nor the responsibility for signing checks or making cash disbursements in any other way?
2. What is meant by the phrase "all receipts should be deposited intact"?
3. Why should all cash receipts be deposited intact on the day of receipt?
4. Why are some cash payments made from a petty cash fund? Why are not all payments made by check?
5. What is a petty cash voucher? When a petty cash voucher is prepared, who signs it?
6. Explain how a petty cash fund operates.
7. Why must a petty cash fund be reimbursed at the end of each accounting period?
8. What are two results of reimbursing the petty cash fund?
9. Is the Petty Cash Record a book of original entry?
10. What is a bank statement? What kind of information appears on a bank statement?
11. What is the meaning of the phrase "to reconcile"?
12. Why are the bank statement balance of cash and the depositor's book balance of cash reconciled?
13. What occurs when revenues and expenses are properly matched?
14. At what point in the selling-collecting procedures of a company does a bad debt loss occur?
15. Why does the direct write-off method of accounting for bad debt losses commonly fail in matching revenues and expenses?
16. George Jacks purchased $50 of merchandise from Company A and another $50 from Company B. He did not pay either company and one year later, on February 28, both wrote off his uncollectible accounts. Company A used the direct write-off method, and Company B used the allowance method. Give the write-off entries.
17. In estimating bad debt losses it is commonly assumed that "history will repeat." How is the assumption that "history will repeat" used in estimating bad debt losses?

18. A company has charge sales for a year amounting to $484,000. What amount of bad debt losses may the company expect to experience from these sales if its past bad debt loss record shows losses equal to one fourth of 1% of charge sales?

19. What is a contra account? Why are estimated bad debt losses credited to a contra account rather than to the Accounts Receivable controlling account?

20. Classify the following accounts: (*a*) Accounts Receivable, (*b*) Allowance for Doubtful Accounts, and (*c*) Bad Debts Expense.

Class exercises

Exercise 8–1

On October 28 a company established a $40 petty cash fund, appointing one of its office clerks, June Nash, petty cashier. The fund was reimbursed on November 25 for the following expenditures: freight-in, $18.50; postage, $10; office supplies, $4; and miscellaneous expenses, $5.25. Give in general journal form the entry to establish the fund and the entry to reimburse it.

Exercise 8–2

Southside Shop deposits all receipts intact on the day received and makes all payments by check; and on November 30, after all posting was completed, its Cash account showed a $1,510 debit balance; but its November 30 bank statement showed only $1,299 on deposit in the bank on that day. Prepare a bank reconciliation for the shop, using the following information:

a) Outstanding checks, $200.

b) Included with the November canceled checks returned by the bank was a $4 debit memorandum for bank services.

c) Check No. 512, returned with the canceled checks, was correctly drawn for $24 in payment of the telephone bill and was paid by the bank on November 7, but it had been erroneously entered in the Cash Disbursements Journal and debited to the Telephone Expense account as though it were for $42.

d) The November 30 cash receipts, $425, were placed in the bank's night depository after banking hours on that date and were unrecorded by the bank at the time the November bank statement was mailed.

Exercise 8–3

Prepare in general journal form any entries that Southside Shop should make as a result of its having prepared the bank reconciliation of the previous exercise.

Exercise 8–4

On December 31, 1972, a company estimated it would lose as bad debts an amount equal to one fourth of 1% of its $844,000 of 1972 charge sales, and it provided an addition to its allowance for doubtful accounts equal to that amount. On the following April 7 it decided the $310 account of Harry Bang was uncollectible and wrote it off as a bad debt. On August 10 Harry Bang unexpectedly paid the amount previously written off. Give the required entries in general journal form to record these transactions.

Exercise 8–5

At the end of each year a company ages its accounts receivable and increases its allowance for doubtful accounts by an amount sufficient to provide for the estimated uncollectible accounts, and at the end of last year it estimated it would be unable to collect $2,300 of its total accounts receivable. (*a*) Give the entry to increase the allowance account under the assumption it had a $150 credit balance before adjustment. (*b*) Give the entry under the assumption that the Allowance for Doubtful Accounts account had a $100 debit balance before adjustment.

Problems

Problem 8–1

Brier Sales Company completed the following transactions involving petty cash during December of the current year:

Dec. 3 Drew Check No. 135 to establish a $25 petty cash fund. Appointed Joan Hall, one of the office clerks, petty cashier.

4 Paid $3.85 express charges on a purchase of merchandise delivered by the express company.

7 Paid Ben Franklin Press $8 for printing advertising circulars.

8 Paid a college student $2.50 for delivering the advertising circulars to prospective customers.

11 Purchased postage stamps, $5.

12 Paid $4.25 express charges on a purchase of merchandise delivered by the express company.

12 Drew Check No. 152 to reimburse the petty cash fund; and because the fund had been so rapidly exhausted, made the check sufficiently large to increase the size of the fund to $50.

14 Paid $5.10 express charges on a purchase of merchandise delivered by the express company.

17 Purchased postage stamps, $8.

18 The proprietor, Jack Hall, signed a petty cash voucher and took $1 from the petty cash fund for coffee money.

20 Paid $5 for repairs to a typewriter.

23 Paid $1.35 for a collect telegram.

26 Paid $3.80 express charges on a purchase of merchandise delivered by the express company.

28 Purchased postage stamps, $5.

31 Drew Check No. 172 to reimburse the petty cash fund at the end of the accounting period. There was $19.75 in cash in the fund and the cashier could not account for the shortage.

Required:

Record the foregoing transactions in a Petty Cash Record and, where required, in a Cash Disbursements Journal similar to the ones described in this chapter. Balance and rule the Petty Cash Record at the time of each reimbursement. Skip a line between the entries in the Cash Disbursements Journal to set them apart.

Problem 8–2

A company established a petty cash fund, appointing one of its office clerks, Mary Wren, petty cashier. It then completed these transactions:

Oct. 2 Received, cashed, and placed the $25 proceeds of Check No. 781 in the petty cash drawer of the office safe.
3 Paid $5 to have the office windows washed.
8 Paid $4.65 express on a shipment of merchandise purchased.
11 Purchased carbon paper and paper clips, $3.85.
17 Purchased postage stamps, $5.
23 Paid $4.25 for minor repairs to an office chair.
23 Received Check No. 804 to replenish the fund, $22.75.
Nov. 1 Paid express charges on merchandise purchased, $4.35.
5 Paid $1.50 for the delivery of a package to a customer.
9 Paid $3.95 express charges on a purchase of merchandise.
14 Paid $2 for the delivery of a package to a customer.
18 Paid $2.25 for a collect telegram.
24 Purchased postage stamps, $8.
24 After purchasing the foregoing stamps Mary Wren found she had only $1.95 in money in her petty cash fund and she could not account for the shortage. Consequently, she prepared a petty cash voucher for the amount of the shortage, had it approved by her employer, and recorded it in her Petty Cash Record. She then exchanged her paid and approved petty cash vouchers for a $23.05 check, No. 852, to replenish the fund.

Required:

1. Prepare a Petty Cash Record and a Cash Disbursements Journal and open the following T-accounts: Cash; Petty Cash; Office Supplies; Postage; Freight-In; Miscellaneous General Expenses; Delivery Expense; and Cash Over and Short.
2. Enter the check establishing the fund in the Petty Cash Record and in the Cash Disbursements Journal. Post the journal entry.
3. Enter the October transactions in the Petty Cash Record, balance the record, and enter the replenishing check in both the Petty Cash Record and Cash Disbursements Journal. Skip a line between entries in the Cash Disbursements Journal. Post the disbursements journal entry.
4. Repeat the foregoing instructions for the November transactions.

Problem 8–3

The following information was available to reconcile Abbott Company's book and bank statement balances of cash as of December 31:

a) The December 31 cash balance according to the accounting records was $2,782, and the bank statement balance for that date was $2,653.60.
b) Two checks, No. 722 for $103.50 and No. 726 for $93.85, were outstanding on November 30 when the book and bank statement balances were

last reconciled. Check No. 726 was returned with the December canceled checks but Check No. 722 was not.

c) Check No. 803 for $79.75 and Check No. 805 for $73.60, both written and entered in the Cash Disbursements Journal in December, were not among the canceled checks returned.

d) When the December checks were compared with entries in the Cash Disbursements Journal, it was found that Check No. 751 had been correctly drawn for $183 in payment for store supplies but was entered in the Cash Disbursements Journal in error as though it were drawn for $138.

e) Two debit memoranda and a credit memorandum were included with the returned checks and were unrecorded at the time of the reconciliation. The credit memorandum indicated that the bank had collected a $500 note receivable for the company, deducted a $2 collection fee, and credited the balance to the company's account. One of the debit memoranda was for $32 and had attached to it a NSF check in that amount that had been received from a customer, Dale Hill, in payment of his account. The second debit memorandum was for a special printing of checks and was for $16.75.

f) The December 31 cash receipts, $789.50, had been placed in the bank's night depository after banking hours on that date and did not appear on the bank statement.

Required:

Prepare (*a*) a December 31 bank reconciliation for the company and (*b*) the entries in general journal form required to adjust the company's book balance of cash to the reconciled balance.

Problem 8–4

Little Service Company reconciled its book and bank statement balances on October 31 with two checks, No. 716 for $142 and No. 717 for $275 outstanding. The following information is available for the November 30 reconciliation:

Little Service Company 17th and High Streets	Statement of account with UNITED STATES NATIONAL BANK		
Date	Checks and Other Debits	Deposits	Balance
Nov. 1	Balance brought forward		1,912.00
2	275.00		1,637.00
3	218.00	312.00	1,731.00
5	302.00		1,429.00
9	737.00		692.00
12	75.00 132.00		485.00
14		551.00	1,036.00
18	284.00		752.00
21		512.00	1,264.00
28	343.00	472.00	1,393.00
29	43.00 NSF		1,350.00
30	3.00 SC	995.00 CM	2,342.00
Code: CM Credit Memorandum DM Debit Memorandum	NSF Not sufficient funds check SC Service charge		

FROM THE CASH RECEIPTS JOURNAL				FROM THE CASH DISBURSEMENTS JOURNAL			

FROM THE CASH RECEIPTS JOURNAL

Date			Cash Debit
Nov. 3			312.00
14			551.00
21			512.00
28			472.00
30			247.00
30			2,094.00

FROM THE CASH DISBURSEMENTS JOURNAL

Check Number			Cash Credit
718			218.00
719			320.00
720			75.00
721			737.00
722			132.00
723			136.00
724			284.00
725			343.00
726			53.00
			2,298.00

FROM THE GENERAL LEDGER
Cash

Date	Explanation	F	Debit	Credit	Balance
Oct. 31	Balance	✔			1,495.00
Nov. 30		R-8	2,094.00		3,589.00
30		D-9		2,298.00	1,291.00

Check No. 719 was correctly drawn for $302 in payment for office equipment; however, the bookkeeper misread the amount and entered it in both the Sundry Accounts debit and Cash credit columns of the Cash Disbursements Journal as though it were for $320.

The NSF check was received from a customer, Willie Hale, in payment of his account. Its return is unrecorded. The credit memorandum resulted from a $1,000 note collected for Little Service Company by the bank. The bank had deducted a $5 collection fee. The collection is not recorded.

Required:
1. Prepare a November 30 bank reconciliation for the company.
2. Prepare in general journal form the entries needed to adjust the book balance of cash to the reconciled balance.

Problem 8–5

On January 1, 197A, a company's Allowance for Doubtful Accounts account had a $2,050 credit balance, and during the year it completed these transactions:

Feb. 12 Wrote off the $315 account of West Company. The company had gone out of business leaving no assets to be attached.

Apr. 5 Wrote off the $275 uncollectible account of Charles Gage.

12 Reinstated and recorded the collection of the $80 account of Walter Nash upon the unexpected receipt of that amount from him. The account had been written off two years earlier.

July   7   Collected from his receiver in bankruptcy 10% of the $650 owed by George Hale. Wrote off the remainder as uncollectible.

Oct. 14   Received $100 from Charles Gage in partial payment of the account written off on April 5. Mr. Gage stated in a letter with the payment that business had improved and he expected to pay the balance of his debt in the near future.

Dec. 27   Used a compound entry to write off the following accounts: Robert Short, $235; Andrew Woods, $340; and Hall and Keller, $410.

      31   Provided an addition to the allowance for doubtful accounts equal to one half of 1% of the $438,000 of 197A charge sales.

      31   Closed the 197A Bad Debts Expense account.

Required:

1. Open accounts for Allowance for Doubtful Accounts, Bad Debts Expense, and Income Summary; and enter the $2,050 balance in the Allowance for Doubtful Accounts account.

2. Prepare general journal entries to record the transactions and post the entry portions that affect the three accounts opened.

3. Give the alternate bad debts adjusting entry that the company would have made under the assumptions that, rather than providing an addition to its allowance for doubtful accounts equal to one half of 1% of its 197A charge sales, it aged its accounts, estimated that accounts totaling $1,875 were probably uncollectible, and increased its allowance for doubtful accounts to provide for them.

Alternate problems

Problem 8–1A

W. A. Kern, owner of Kern Sales and Service, established a petty cash fund on the advice of his accountant, and during the fund's first month the following transactions were completed:

Nov. 2   Drew a $50 check, No. 562, payable to Jane Hill, petty cashier, and delivered the check plus the Petty Cash Record to Miss Hill.

       4   Eight dollars of petty cash funds were used to purchase postage stamps.

       5   Paid $4.35 express charges on a purchase of merchandise delivered by the express company.

       8   Paid the delivery truck driver of Snowhite Laundry $2.50 upon delivery of a package of shirts Mr. Kern had dropped off at the laundry and asked that they be laundered for him and delivered to the office.

      11   Paid $5 for minor repairs to the office typewriter.

      13   Paid $3.95 express charges on a purchase of merchandise.

      15   Gave Mrs. Kern, wife of the proprietor, $5 for cab fare and other personal expenses.

      18   Paid Speedy Delivery $2.50 to deliver merchandise to a customer.

      23   Paid $1.85 for a collect telegram.

      27   Paid $4.15 express charges on a special order of merchandise shipped to a customer.

      30   Drew Check No. 591 to reimburse the fund for expenditures and a $0.50 shortage.

Required:

Prepare a Petty Cash Record and a Cash Disbursements Journal similar to the ones illustrated in this chapter and record the transactions. Balance and rule the Petty Cash Record before entering the replenishing check. Skip a line between the checks entered in the Cash Disbursements Journal.

Problem 8–2A

A company established a petty cash fund, appointing one of its office clerks, Abby Todd, petty cashier. Miss Todd then completed these transactions:

Nov. 2 Received, cashed, and placed the proceeds of a $30 check, No. 815, in the petty cash drawer of the office safe.
  3 Paid $3.75 express charges on a shipment of merchandise purchased.
  7 Paid $4.50 for minor repairs to an office typewriter.
  8 Paid $1 for the delivery of merchandise to a customer.
  11 Paid $5 to have the office windows washed.
  15 Paid $6.50 express charges on a shipment of merchandise purchased.
  21 Purchased postage stamps, $5.
  25 Purchased carbon paper for office use, $2.50.
  28 Received replenishing Check No. 882 for $28.25 from the company cashier in exchange for the paid petty cash vouchers.
Dec. 2 Paid $2.50 for the delivery of merchandise to a customer.
  6 Paid $5.25 express charges on a shipment of merchandise purchased.
  12 Paid $2.75 for delivery of a collect telegram.
  15 Paid $7.50 express charges on a shipment of merchandise purchased.
  20 Purchased postage stamps, $10.
  20 After purchasing the foregoing postage stamps, the petty cashier found she had only $1.50 in money in the petty cash fund. Consequently, she prepared a petty cash voucher for the amount of the shortage, had it approved by her employer, and recorded it in her Petty Cash Record. She then exchanged the paid and approved petty cash vouchers for a $28.50 check, No. 985, to replenish the fund.

Required:

1. Prepare a Petty Cash Record and a Cash Disbursements Journal and open the following T-accounts: Cash; Petty Cash; Office Supplies; Postage; Freight-In; Miscellaneous General Expenses; Delivery Expense; and Cash Over and Short.
2. Enter the check establishing the fund in the Petty Cash Record and in the Cash Disbursements Journal. Post the journal entry.
3. Enter the November transactions in the Petty Cash Record, balance the record, and enter the replenishing check in both the Petty Cash Record and Cash Disbursements Journal. Skip a line between entries in the Cash Disbursements Journal. Post the disbursements journal entry.
4. Repeat the foregoing instructions for the December transactions.

Problem 8–3A

The following information was available for reconciling May Company's November 30 book balance of cash with its bank statement balance of that date:

a) After all posting was completed on November 30, the company's Cash account had a $2,614 debit balance but its bank statement showed a $3,240 balance.

b) Checks No. 721 for $102 and No. 726 for $197 were outstanding on the October 31 bank reconciliation. Check No. 726 was returned with the November canceled checks, but Check No. 721 was not.

c) In comparing the canceled checks returned with the bank statement with the entries in the Cash Disbursements Journal it was found that Check No. 801 for the purchase of office equipment was correctly drawn for $258 but was entered in the Cash Disbursements Journal as though it were for $285. It was also found that Check No. 835 for $125 and Check No. 837 for $50, both drawn in November, were not among the canceled checks returned with the statement.

d) A credit memorandum enclosed with the bank statement indicated that the bank had collected a $1,000 noninterest-bearing note for the concern, deducted a $5 collection fee, and had credited the remainder to the concern's account.

e) A debit memorandum with a $126 NSF check received from a customer, David Green, attached was among the canceled checks returned.

f) Also among the canceled checks was a $5 debit memorandum for bank services. None of the memoranda had been recorded.

g) The November 30 cash receipts, $542, were placed in the bank's night depository after banking hours on that date and their amount did not appear on the bank statement.

Required:
1. Prepare a bank reconciliation for the company.
2. Prepare entries in general journal form to adjust the company's book balance of cash to the reconciled balance.

Problem 8–4A

Trailer Service Company reconciled its bank balance on November 30 with two checks, No. 808 for $262 and No. 813 for $93 outstanding. The following information is available for the December 31 reconciliation:

Trailer Service Company 1475 North Main Street		Statement of account with THE FIRST NATIONAL BANK		
Date	Checks and Other Debits		Deposits	Balance
Dec. 1	Balance brought forward			1,834.00
2	262.00			1,572.00
3	225.00		223.00	1,570.00
5	306.00			1,264.00
6	846.00			418.00
12			945.00	1,363.00
15	51.00	117.00		1,195.00
22			649.00	1,844.00
28	321.00		748.00	2,271.00
30	240.00 NSF			2,031.00
31	1.00 SC		498.00 CM	2,528.00
Code: CM Credit Memorandum DM Debit Memorandum		NSF Not sufficient funds check SC Service charge		

FROM THE CASH RECEIPTS JOURNAL				FROM THE CASH DISBURSEMENTS JOURNAL			
Date			Cash Debit	Check Number			Cash Credit
Dec. 3			223.00	814			306.00
12			945.00	815			225.00
22			649.00	816			846.00
28			748.00	817			51.00
31			319.00	818			117.00
31			2,884.00	819			312.00
				820			129.00
				821			163.00
							2,149.00

FROM THE GENERAL LEDGER
Cash

Date	Explanation	F	Debit	Credit	Balance
Nov. 30	Balance	✔			1,479.00
Dec. 31		R-9	2,884.00		4,363.00
31		D-9		2,149.00	2,214.00

Check No. 819 was correctly drawn for $321 in payment for store equipment purchased; however, the bookkeeper misread the amount and entered it in both the Sundry Accounts debit and Cash credit columns as though it were for $312. The bank paid and deducted the correct amount.

The NSF check was received from a customer, Jerry Mays, in payment of his account. Its return was unrecorded. The credit memorandum resulted from a $500 note which the bank had collected for the company, deducted a $2 collection fee, and deposited the balance in the company's account. The collection was not recorded.

Required:
1. Prepare a bank reconciliation for Trailer Service Company.
2. Prepare in general journal form the entries needed to bring the company's book balance of cash into agreement with the reconciled balance.

Problem 8–5A

A company's Allowance for Doubtful Accounts account had a $2,115 credit balance on January 1, 197A. During the year it completed these transactions:

Mar. 2 Learned that Earl Hall had gone out of business, leaving no assets to attach. Wrote off his $420 uncollectible account as a bad debt.

Apr. 14 Reinstated and recorded the collection of the $115 account of Harry Kane upon the receipt of that amount from him. The account had been written off almost two years previously.

June 7 Wrote off the $165 uncollectible account of David Earl.

July 12 Learned of the bankruptcy of Larry Vale. Made a claim on his receiver in bankruptcy for the $750 owed by Mr. Vale, and on October 3 received a $75 check from the receiver. A letter accompanying the check stated that the $75 was all that would be paid. Recorded receipt of the $75 and wrote off the remainder as uncollectible.

Oct. 15   David Earl whose account was written off on June 7 walked into the office today and paid $65 of the amount written off. He stated that business had improved and he expected to pay the balance shortly.

Dec. 28   Made a compound entry to write off the following accounts: George Small, $345; Terry Wells, $435; and James Tarr, $385.

    31   Provided an addition to the allowance for doubtful accounts equal to one fourth of 1% of the $864,000 of 197A charge sales.

    31   Closed the Bad Debts Expense account.

Required:

1. Open accounts for Allowance for Doubtful Accounts, Income Summary, and Bad Debts Expense; and enter the $2,115 balance in the Allowance for Doubtful Accounts account.
2. Prepare general journal entries to record the transactions and post the entry portions that affect the accounts opened.
3. Give the alternate bad debts adjusting entry that the company would have made under the assumptions that rather than providing an addition to its allowance for doubtful accounts equal to one fourth of 1% of its 197A charge sales, it aged its accounts, estimated that accounts totaling $2,255 were probably uncollectible, and increased its allowance for doubtful accounts to provide for them.

Decision problem 8–1, Junior Accountant I

You have just been hired by a public accounting firm as a junior accountant, and in their training program you have been asked for solutions to these problems:

PROBLEM 1. Miss Emma, the bookkeeper at Dawson's Department Store, will retire next week after over 40 years with the company, having been hired by the father of the store's present owner. She has always been a very dependable employee, and as a result has been given more and more responsibilities over the years. Actually, for the past 15 years she has "run" the store's office, keeping the books, verifying invoices, and issuing checks in their payment, which in the absence of the store's owner, George Dawson, she could sign. In addition, at the end of each day the store's salesclerks turn over their daily cash receipts to Miss Emma, who after counting the money and comparing the amounts with the cash register tapes, which she is responsible for removing from the cash registers, makes the Cash Receipts Journal entry to record cash sales and then deposits the money in the bank. She also reconciles the bank balance each month with her book balance of cash.

Mr. Dawson, the store's owner, realizes he cannot expect a new bookkeeper to accomplish as much in a day as Miss Emma does; and since the store is not large enough to warrant more than one office employee, he recognizes he must take over some of Miss Emma's duties when she retires. He already places all orders for merchandise and supplies and closely supervises all employees and does not want to add more to his duties than necessary.

Discuss the foregoing situation from an internal control point of view, pointing out which of Miss Emma's tasks should be taken over by Mr. Dawson and which can be assigned to the new bookkeeper with safety.

PROBLEM 2. Gary Hale owns and operates Vista Theater, acting both as its manager and its projectionist. The theater has not been too profitable of late; and this morning at breakfast, while discussing ways to cut costs, his wife suggested that he discharge the theater's doorman whose job is to collect and destroy the tickets sold by the cashier, and that he permit the cashier to collect an admission from each patron without issuing a ticket. This, Mrs. Hale pointed out, would result in a double savings, the wages of the doorman and, also, since there would be no one to take up tickets, rolls of prenumbered tickets would not have to be purchased. Mr. Hale said he could not do this unless Mrs. Hale would take over the cashier's job.

Discuss the wife's suggestion and her husband's counter proposal from an internal control point of view. You may assume the cashier is a college student and that cashiers change frequently, since the job interferes with dating.

Decision problem 8–2, The Man's Shop

The Man's Shop has been in operation five years. Its owner, Ned Moss, has been aggressive in expanding the shop's clientele. Three years ago he liberalized the shop's credit policy in an effort to increase sales. Sales have increased, but now Mr. Moss is concerned with the effects of the more liberal credit policy. Bad debts written off (the store uses the direct write-off method) have increased materially during the past two years, and now he wonders if the sales increase justifies the substantial bad debt losses which he is certain have resulted from the more liberal credit policy.

The store earns a 40% gross profit on sales; its operating expenses (excluding bad debts) are 30% of sales; and during the past five years it had the following credit sales and bad debts.

Year	Credit Sales	Bad Debts Written Off	Losses by Year of Sales
1	$ 80,000	$ 80	$ 480
2	90,000	540	450
3	120,000	720	1,920
4	150,000	2,400	2,250
5	160,000	2,400	2,720

The last column in the sales and bad debts summary results from reclassifying bad debt losses by the years in which the merchandise was sold; consequently, the $2,720 of fifth-year losses includes $1,680 of estimated bad debts in present accounts receivable.

Prepare a schedule showing the following in columns by years: credit sales, cost of goods sold, gross profit on sales, operating expenses, income before bad debts, bad debts incurred, and net income. Then below the net income figures show for each year bad debts written off as a percentage of sales followed on the next line by bad debts incurred as a percentage of sales. Also, prepare a report to Mr. Moss answering his concern about the new credit policy and recommending any changes you consider desirable in his accounting for bad debts.

Accounting for notes and interest

■ Some companies sell merchandise on the installment plan and commonly take promissory notes from their customers. Others, such as dealers in farm machinery, likewise often take notes. However, when companies in which the credit period is long are excepted, note transactions in comparison to other transactions are not too numerous. Nevertheless, many companies in which such transactions are not common will at one time or another accept a note from a customer or will give a note to a creditor. Consequently, one interested in accounting must have some knowledge of promissory notes.

Promissory notes
■ A promissory note is an unconditional promise in writing to pay on demand or at a fixed or determinable future date a definite sum of money. In the note shown in Illustration 9-1 Hugo Brown promises to pay Frank Black or his order a definite sum of money at a fixed future date. Hugo Brown is the *maker* of the note; Frank Black is the *payee*. To Hugo Brown the illustrated note is a *note payable*, a liability; and to Frank Black the same note is a *note receivable*, an asset.

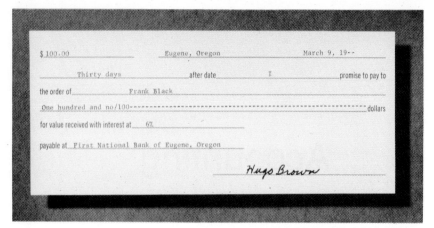

Illustration
9–1
**A Promissory
Note**

The illustrated Hugo Brown note bears interest at 6%. Interest is a charge for the use of money. To a borrower, interest is an expense; to a lender, it is a revenue. A note may be interest bearing or it may be noninterest bearing. If a note bears interest, the rate or the amount of interest must be stated on the note. Interest is usually stated as a percentage of the note's *principal*. If a note is noninterest bearing, no interest is collected unless the note is not paid when due. If a noninterest-bearing note is not paid when due, interest at the full legal rate may be collected from the *maturity date* until the date of final payment. The maturity date is the date upon which the note is due and payable.

Calculating interest ■ Unless otherwise stated, the rate of interest on a note is the rate charged for the use of the principal for one year. The formula for callating interest is:

$$\begin{matrix} \text{Principal} \\ \text{of the} \\ \text{Note} \end{matrix} \times \begin{matrix} \text{Rate of} \\ \text{Interest} \end{matrix} \times \begin{matrix} \text{Time of the} \\ \text{Note Expressed} \\ \text{in Years} \end{matrix} = \text{Interest}$$

For example, interest on a $1,000, 6%, one-year note is calculated:

$$\$1,000 \times \frac{6}{100} \times 1 = \$60$$

In business, most note transactions involve a period less than a full year, and this period is usually expressed in days. When the time of a note is expressed in days, the actual number of days elapsing, not including the day of the note's date but including the day on which it falls due are counted. For example, a 90-day note, dated July 10, is due on October 8. This October 8 maturity date is calculated as follows:

Number of days in July... 31
Minus the date of the note... 10
Gives the number of days the note runs in July 21
Add the number of days in August 31
Add the number of days in September.................................. 30
Total through September 30 82
Days in October needed to equal the time of the note, 90 days,
    also the due date of the note – October.............................. 8
      Total time the note runs in days...................................... 90

    Occasionally, the time of a note is expressed in months. In such cases, the note matures and is payable in the month of its maturity on the same day of the month as its date. For example, a note dated July 10 and payable three months after date is payable on October 10.

    In calculating interest, banks and businessmen usually consider a year to have just 360 days. This simplifies most interest calculations. It makes the interest calculation on a 90-day, 5%, $1,000 note as follows:

$$\text{Principal} \times \text{Rate} \times \frac{\text{Exact Days}}{360} = \text{Interest}$$

or

$$\$1,000 \times \frac{5}{100} \times \frac{90}{360} = \text{Interest}$$

or

$$\$\cancel{1,000} \times \frac{5}{\cancel{100}} \times \frac{\cancel{90}}{\cancel{360}} = \frac{25}{2} = \$12.50$$

Likewise, the interest calculation on a $1,200, 60-day, 6% note is:

$$\$\cancel{1,200} \times \frac{\cancel{6}}{\cancel{100}} \times \frac{\cancel{60}}{\cancel{360}} = \$12.00$$

Sixty-day, 6% method

  ■ An examination of the preceding calculation shows the interest on $1,200 at 6% for 60 days to be $12. Twelve dollars is 1%, or 0.01, of $1,200; and as in this case, the interest on any note that runs exactly 60 days and earns interest at exactly 6% is always 1% of the note's principal. This is because 60 days are ⅙ of one year, and ⅙ of 6% is 1%.

    Therefore, it is evident that to compute the interest on any given principal at exactly 6% for exactly 60 days, it is only necessary to multiply the principal by 1%, or 0.01. And, to multiply a principal by 0.01, the decimal point is moved two places to the left in the principal. For example, the interest on $757 for 60 days at 6% is:

$$\$757 \times 0.01 = \$7.57$$

Six-day, 6% counterpart ■ Six days are $\frac{1}{10}$ of 60 days. Therefore, interest at 6% on a given principal for six days is $\frac{1}{10}$ of 1%, or 0.001; and to compute interest on a given principal at 6% for six days, it is only necessary to move the decimal point three places to the left in the principal. For example, the interest on $1,200 at 6% for six days is:

$$\$1,200 \;\times\; 0.001 \;=\; \$1.20$$

The 60-day, 6% method or its six-day, 6% counterpart may be used for any combination of days. However, either has its greatest advantage when the time is either exactly 60 days, or exactly six days, or an even combination or fraction of one or the other. For example, interest on $800 at 6% for 45 days is $6, and is calculated as follows:

Interest on $800 for 60 days at 6% is (point off two places) $8.
Forty-five days are exactly $\frac{3}{4}$ of 60 days.
Therefore, the interest for 45 days is $\frac{3}{4}$ of the interest for 60 days, or is $\frac{3}{4} \times \$8 = \$6$.

Likewise, the interest on $500 at 6% for 42 days is $3.50, and it is calculated:

Interest on $500 for six days at 6% is (point off three places) $0.50.
Forty-two days are the equivalent of seven six-day periods.
Therefore, interest for 42 days is seven times the interest for six days, or is $7 \times \$0.50 = \$3.50$.

The 60-day, 6% method and its six-day, 6% counterpart may be used for other interest rates. For example, 8% is 1 and $\frac{1}{3}$ times 6%; and to calculate interest at 8%, make the calculation at 6% and add $\frac{1}{3}$. Likewise, 4% is $\frac{2}{3}$ of 6%; consequently, to calculate interest at 4%, make the calculation at 6% and take $\frac{2}{3}$ of the result.

Actually, these short-cut methods can be used for any combination of days or for any rate of interest. However, any saving made by their use is lost when the calculation becomes complex.

NOTES PAYABLE

■ Notes payable result from the purchase of an asset with a note or from gaining an extension of time on an open account; and they frequently arise when money is borrowed from a bank.

Purchasing an asset with a note ■ Giving a note to purchase an asset is not a common transaction. Occasionally, when the purchase price is high or the credit period is long, a note is given instead of making the purchase on open account. The entry for such a transaction is:

Oct.	14	Store Equipment..	1,600.00	
		Notes Payable..		1,600.00
		Purchased display refrigerator with a one-year, 6% note.		

Usually, all notes payable are recorded in a single Notes Payable account. If several notes are issued, each may be identified in the account by writing the payee's name in the Explanation column on the line of the entry recording the note's issuance or payment. If a company issues many notes, an unusual situation, a supplementary record called a Notes Payable Register may be used for recording the details of each note.

Note given to secure an extension of time on an account ■ A note may be given to secure an extension of time on an open account. For example, George Brock cannot pay his open account with Ajax Company when it becomes due and the company agrees to accept Brock's 60-day, 6%, $350 note in settlement of the open account. Brock will record the transaction in his General Journal with the following entry:

Aug.	23	Accounts Payable—Ajax Company...................	350.00	
		Notes Payable.......................................		350.00
		Gave a 60-day, 6% note in settlement of our open account.		

Observe that the note does not pay the debt; it merely changes its form from an account payable to a note payable. Ajax Company prefers the note to the open account because in case of default and a lawsuit to collect, the note improves its legal position, since the note is written evidence of the debt and its amount.

When the note becomes due, Brock gives Ajax Company a check for $353.50 and records the payment of the note and its interest with an entry as follows:

Oct.	22	Notes Payable..	350.00	
		Interest Expense	3.50	
		Cash..		353.50
		Paid our note with interest.		

Recording a bank loan ■ In lending money, banks distinguish between *loans* and *discounts*. With either a loan or a discount, the bank lends money. However, in case of a loan, the bank collects interest when the loan is repaid; while in case of a discount, it deducts interest at the time the loan is made. To illustrate loans and discounts, assume that Henry Green wishes to borrow approximately $1,000 for 60 days at 6%.

A loan

In a loan transaction the bank will lend Green $1,000 in exchange for his signed promissory note. The note will read: "Sixty days after date I promise to pay $1,000 with interest at 6%," and Green will record the transaction as follows:

Sept.	10	Cash..	1,000.00	
		Notes Payable.......................................		1,000.00
		Gave the bank a 60-day note.		

When the note and interest are paid, Green makes the following entry:

Nov.	9	Notes Payable...	1,000.00	
		Interest Expense	10.00	
		Cash..		1,010.00
		Paid our 60-day, 6% note.		

Observe in case of the loan transaction that interest is paid at the time the loan is repaid.

A discount

If, contrary to the situation described in the previous paragraphs, it is the practice of Green's bank to deduct interest at the time a loan is made, the bank will *discount* Green's $1,000 note. If it discounts the note at 6% for 60 days, it will deduct from the face amount of the note 60 days' interest at 6%, which is $10, and will give Green the difference, $990. The $10 of deducted interest is called *bank discount,* and the $990 are the *proceeds* of the discounted note. Green will record the transaction as follows:

Sept.	10	Cash..	990.00	
		Interest Expense	10.00	
		Notes Payable.......................................		1,000.00
		Discounted a $1,000 note at 6%.		

When the note matures, Green will pay the bank just the face amount of the note, $1,000, and will record the transaction like this:

Nov.	9	Notes Payable...	1,000.00	
		Cash..		1,000.00
		Paid our discounted note.		

Since interest is deducted in a discount transaction at the time the loan is made, the note used in such a transaction must state that only the principal amount is to be paid at maturity. Such a note may read: "Sixty days after date I promise to pay $1,000 with no interest," and is commonly called a noninterest-bearing note. However, banks are not in business to lend money interest free; and interest is paid in a discount transaction; but since it is deducted at the time the loan is made, the note used must state that no additional interest is to be collected at maturity. Of course it can be argued in the case of the discounted Green note that the bank collected $10 interest at maturity for the use of $990, and your authors would not disagree with this.

NOTES RECEIVABLE

■ With the exception of companies selling on the installment plan and other companies in which the credit period is long, notes receivable are not common. However, in enterprises in which the credit period is long, notes are preferred to open accounts because a note may be readily turned into cash before it is due by discounting or selling it to a bank. Notes are also preferred because a note represents a written acknowledgment by the debtor of both the debt and its amount. Also, notes are preferred because they generally earn interest.

Recording the receipt of a note ■ Notes receivable are recorded in a single Notes Receivable account. Each note may be identified in the account by writing the name of the maker in the Explanation column on the line of the entry recording its receipt or payment. Only one account is needed because the individual notes are on hand; and the maker, rate of interest due date, and other information may be learned by examining each note. However, if note transactions are numerous, a supplementary record may be maintained to record the details of each note. This supplementary record is called a Notes Receivable Register, and as such does not change the regular journal and ledger record of notes.

A note received at the time of a sale is recorded as follows:

Dec.	5	Notes Receivable	650.00	
		Sales		650.00
		Sold merchandise, terms six-month, 6% note.		

When a note is taken in granting an extension on a past-due open account, the creditor usually attempts to collect part of the past-due account in cash. This reduces the debt and requires the acceptance of a note for a smaller amount. For example, Symplex Company agrees to accept $232 in cash and a $500, 60-day, 6% note from Joseph Cook in settlement of his $732 past-due account. When Symplex receives the cash and note, the following entry is made:

Oct.	5	Cash	232.00	
		Notes Receivable	500.00	
		Accounts Receivable—Joseph Cook...........		732.00
		Received cash and a note in settlement of		
		an account.		

Observe that the foregoing entry changes the form of $500 of the debt from an account receivable to a note receivable.

When Cook pays the note, this entry is made:

Dec.	4	Cash	505.00	
		Notes Receivable		500.00
		Interest Earned		5.00
		Collected the Joseph Cook note.		

Dishonored notes receivable

■ Occasionally, the maker of a note either cannot or will not pay his note at maturity. When a note's maker refuses to pay at maturity, the note is said to be *dishonored*. Dishonoring a note does not relieve the maker of his obligation, and every legal means should be made to collect. However, collection may require lengthy legal proceedings.

The Notes Receivable account balance should show only the amount of notes that have not matured. Therefore, a dishonored, past-due note is always removed from the Notes Receivable account and charged back to the account of its maker. For example, Symplex Company holds a $700, 6%, 60-day note of George Jones. At maturity, Mr. Jones dishonors the note. To remove the dishonored note from its Notes Receivable account, the company makes the following entry:

Oct.	14	Accounts Receivable—George Jones	707.00	
		Interest Earned		7.00
		Notes Receivable		700.00
		To charge the account of George Jones for		
		his dishonored $700, 6%, 60-day note.		

Charging a dishonored note back to the account of its maker serves two purposes. It removes the amount of the note from the Notes Receivable account, leaving in the account only notes that have not matured; and it records the dishonored note in the maker's account. The second purpose is important because if in the future the maker of the dishonored note again applies for credit, his account will show all past dealings, including the dishonored note.

Observe in the foregoing entry, which charged back the dishonored note of George Jones, that the Interest Earned account is credited for interest earned even though it was not collected. The reason for this is that George Jones owes both the principal and the interest, and his account should reflect the full amount owed.

Discounting notes receivable

■ Many businessmen prefer a note receivable to an open account because a note may be discounted or sold to a bank. Discounting enables the businessman to turn a note into cash without waiting until it matures. To discount a note, the owner endorses and delivers the note to the bank in exchange for cash. The bank then collects the maturity value of the note from its maker at maturity.

If the credit reputation of a note's endorser is good, a bank is usually willing to accept and discount a note because the endorser, by his endorsement, agrees to pay the note at maturity if it is not paid by the maker. This means that the endorser makes himself *contingently liable* for payment of the note. His *contingent liability* depends upon the note's dishonor by its maker. If the maker pays, the endorser has no liability. However, if the maker dishonors the note, then the endorser's contingent liability becomes a real liability. Because contingent liabilities sometimes become actual liabilities, they may affect the credit standing of the one contingently liable. Consequently, when a note is discounted, the contingent liability should appear in the accounts and on the balance sheet of the person or company discounting the note.

Aside from recording the contingent liability, discounting a noninterest-bearing note receivable is similar to discounting one's own note payable. This is because the maker of a noninterest-bearing note is not required to pay interest on such a note. Consequently, the bank discounting a noninterest-bearing note collects only the amount of the note's principal at maturity; and as a result it bases the amount of its discount on the note's principal.

To illustrate, on April 6, Symplex Company received a noninterest-bearing, 60-day, $800 note, dated April 5, from Frank Brown in granting an extension on his account. The maturity date of this note is June 4, and if Symplex Company discounts the note at its bank on April 20, the bank must wait until June 4 to collect the $800 from Brown. This 45 days is called the *discount period,* and is calculated as follows:

Number of days in April	30
Date of discount	20
Days discounted in April	10
Days note discounted in May	31
Days note discounted in June	4
Days in discount period	45

In this situation, the bank plans to collect $800 from Frank Brown in 45 days, which is three fourths of 60 days. Furthermore, if the bank's discount rate is 6%, it will deduct a $6 discount from the $800 maturity value of the note ($800 × 0.01 × $\frac{3}{4}$ = $6), and Symplex Company will receive $800 less $6, or $794, for the note. The $794 is called the *proceeds of the note.* The $6 discount is interest expense to Symplex Company.

It records the transaction:

Apr.	20	Cash..	794.00	
		Interest Expense	6.00	
		Notes Receivable Discounted		800.00
		Discounted the Brown note.		

The foregoing credit to *Notes Receivable Discounted* records the contingent liability of Symplex. After the entry is posted, the Notes Receivable and Notes Receivable Discounted accounts appear as follows:

Notes Receivable		Notes Receivable Discounted	
(Brown note) 800			(Brown note) 800
(Jones note) 500			

If a balance sheet is prepared before the maturity date of the foregoing discounted note, the balances of both the Notes Receivable and Notes Receivable Discounted accounts may appear on it as follows:

Current Assets:			
Cash..		$2,500	
Notes receivable..	$1,300		
Less notes receivable discounted..........................	800	500	
Accounts receivable		4,000	
Merchandise inventory..		8,000	
Total Current Assets..		$15,000	

Showing "Notes receivable discounted" on the balance sheet as a subtraction from "Notes receivable" indicates the contingent liability to a balance sheet reader. The contingent liability may also be shown by means of a balance sheet footnote. If Symplex Company followed this practice, it would show the amount of its notes receivable in the current asset section of its balance sheet at $500 followed by an asterisk or other indication of a footnote. It would then place a footnote at the bottom of the balance sheet saying, for example: "Symplex Company is contingently liable for $800 of notes receivable discounted."

Payment of a discounted note by the maker ■ When a note is discounted at a bank, the bank takes possession of the note in exchange for money. The bank will if possible collect the note from the maker at maturity. If the maker pays, it is only necessary for the one who discounted the note to remove the contingent liability from his books. If, for example, Frank Brown pays the note discounted by Symplex Company, Symplex will make the following entry:

June	7	Notes Receivable Discounted	800.00	
		Notes Receivable		800.00
		To remove the contingent liability of the		
		Brown note.		

In this example, the effect of the entry is to balance the Notes Receivable Discounted account and to remove the amount of the paid $800 note from the Notes Receivable account as follows:

Notes Receivable		Notes Receivable Discounted	
(Brown note) 800	(Brown note) 800	(Brown note) 800	(Brown note) 800
(Jones note) 500			

Dishonor of a discounted note

■ If it is able to do so, a bank always collects a discounted note directly from the maker; and the one who discounted the note will not hear from the bank if the note is paid at maturity. However, if a discounted note is dishonored, the bank will notify at once the one who endorsed and discounted the note.

If the bank is unable to collect a discounted note from its maker at maturity, it will normally *protest* the note and look to the endorser or endorsers for payment. Protesting a dishonored note fulfills one of the legal requirements necessary to hold endorsers liable. To protest a note, a *notice of protest* is prepared and mailed to each endorser. A notice of protest is a statement, usually attested by a notary public, that says the note was duly presented to the maker for payment and payment was refused. The cost of protesting a negotiable instrument is called a *protest fee*. The bank will look to the one who discounted a dishonored note for payment of both its maturity value and the protest fee.

For example, suppose that instead of paying the $800 note previously illustrated, Frank Brown dishonors it. As soon as the note is dishonored, the bank notifies Symplex Company by mailing a notice of protest and a letter asking payment of the note's maturity value and the protest fee. Symplex Company must pay both. If the protest fee is, say, $3, Symplex will pay the bank $803. In recording the payment, Symplex charges the note and protest fee back to the account of Frank Brown as follows:

June	5	Accounts Receivable—Frank Brown..................	803.00	
		Cash..		803.00
		To charge the account of Brown with his dishonored note and the protest fee.		

The dishonor changed Symplex's contingent liability to a real liability; and upon payment of the dishonored note both the real liability and the contingent liability ended. The entry just given records the payment of the real liability. The following entry is made to remove the contingent liability from the books:

June	5	Notes Receivable Discounted	800.00	
		Notes Receivable		800.00
		To remove the contingent liability of the dishonored Frank Brown note.		

Of course, upon receipt of the $803, the bank will deliver to Symplex the dishonored note. Symplex Company will then make every legal effort to collect from Brown, not only the maturity value of the note and protest fee but also interest on the maturity value and protest fee from the date of dishonor until the date of final settlement. However, it may not be able to collect, and after exhausting every legal means to do so, it may have to write the account off as a bad debt. Normally in such cases no additional interest is taken onto the books before the write-off.

Discounting an interest-bearing note

■ Discounting an interest-bearing note receivable differs slightly from discounting a noninterest-bearing note. This is because when a bank discounts an interest-bearing note, it will collect from the maker at maturity both the note's principal and interest on the principal, which together are called the note's *maturity value*. As a result and as is customary, the bank bases its discount on this maturity value. For example, on September 19 Symplex Company discounts at 6% the $600, 4%, 90-day note of Carl Snow which is dated August 20.

The maturity value of this note is $606, calculated as follows:

Principal of the note $600
Interest on $600 for 90 days at 4% 6
Maturity value $606

If the bank discounts this note on September 19, it is discounting it for 60 days, calculated as follows:

Time of the note in days..		90
Less time held by Symplex:		
Number of days in August..................................	31	
Date of note...	20	
Days held in August...	11	
Days held in September	19	
Total days held..		30
Discount period..		60

This method of calculating the discount period differs from the one illustrated on page 265. However, either method gives the same result and is equally satisfactory.

Then since the bank bases the amount of its discount on the maturity value of the note, as is customary, and since its discount rate is 6%, it will in discounting the note deduct 60 days' interest at 6% from the maturity value of the note and will give Symplex Company the proceeds, $599.94. This is calculated:

Maturity value of the note... $606.00
Less interest on $606 at 6% for 60 days (point off two places)................... 6.06
Proceeds $599.94

Note in this case that the proceeds are $0.06 less than the face amount of the note. Consequently, Symplex will record the transaction as follows:

Sept.	19	Cash..	599.94	
		Interest Expense	.06	
		Notes Receivable Discounted		600.00
		Discounted the Carl Snow note for 60 days		
		at 6%.		

In making the above entry, Symplex in effect offsets the $6 of interest it would have earned by holding the note to maturity against the $6.06 discount charged by the bank and records only the difference, the $0.06 excess of expense.

In the situation just described the proceeds of the discounted note were less than the principal, and the difference was recorded as interest expense. When the proceeds exceed the principal, the difference is credited to Interest Earned. For example, suppose that Symplex Company held the Carl Snow note and discounted it on October 19 rather than on September 19. If the note is discounted on October 19 at 6%, the discount period is 30 days, the discount is $3.03, and the proceeds of the note are $602.97, calculated as follows:

Maturity value of the note.. $606.00
Less interest on $606 at 6% for 30 days...................... 3.03
Proceeds... $602.97

In this case the proceeds exceed the principal, and the transaction is recorded as follows:

Oct.	19	Cash..	602.97	
		Notes Receivable Discounted		600.00
		Interest Earned		2.97
		Discounted the Carl Snow note at 6% for		
		30 days.		

In either case, the bank collects the maturity value of the discounted note from Carl Snow at maturity. If within a day or so after the maturity date, Symplex does not receive notice of dishonor, it assumes that the note was paid and makes a general journal entry to cancel its contingent liability.

Discounted interest-bearing note dishonored at maturity

■ If the Carl Snow note previously illustrated is dishonored at maturity, the bank will demand payment from Symplex of—

The maturity value of the note:
Principal... $600.00
Interest... 6.00 $606.00
Protest fee (assumed amount) 2.50
    Total $608.50

Symplex must pay the $608.50. In recording the payment, it charges this amount to the account of Carl Snow in the manner shown on page 267; in addition, it should cancel its contingent liability.

When Symplex Company receives the dishonored note from the bank, it should make every legal effort to collect its maturity value, the protest fee, and interest on both from the date of maturity. For example, if 30 days after the dishonor, Carl Snow pays the maturity value of the dishonored note, the protest fee, and interest, he should pay:

Maturity value	$606.00
Protest fee	2.50
Interest on $608.50 at 4% for 30 days	2.03
Total	$610.53

This is recorded by Symplex Company:

Dec.	18	Cash	610.53	
		Accounts Receivable—Carl Snow		608.50
		Interest Earned		2.03
		Dishonored note and protest fee collected with interest.		

Interest on the dishonored Carl Snow note illustrated is calculated at 4% from the date of maturity and is at the rate stated on the note. In some cases, regardless of the rate stated, interest at the maximum legal rate is collected on the maturity value and protest fee from the date of maturity. The maximum legal rate varies from 8 to 12% in the various states.

Collecting an out-of-town note

■ A promissory note is a *negotiable instrument;* and a negotiable instrument is a document to which title is readily changed, usually by endorsement and delivery, but sometimes by delivery only. Negotiable instruments readily pass from hand to hand without question because negotiable instrument laws have been written to encourage this. No effort will be made here to go into the legal aspects of negotiable instruments. That is reserved for a course in business law. For the purpose of this discussion, it is sufficient to point out that a *holder in due course* of a negotiable instrument, or one who under certain circumstances receives a negotiable instrument from a holder in due course, has the legal right to collect the instrument without proving the existence of a debt. A holder in due course is one who gives something of value for a negotiable instrument before maturity without knowledge of defects in the title of previous holders.

These legal aspects sometimes cause a problem in collecting notes. The holder of a note will not part with it without receiving payment, since he does not wish to part with the evidence of indebtedness. Likewise, the maker will not pay his note without gaining possession of it, because he must pay again if the original holder transfers the note, even after receiving payment, to a holder in due course or to one with the same rights.

No problem is involved in collecting a note when both parties to the transaction live in the same city. The holder can present the note directly to its maker for payment. However, when the parties live in different cities, a problem does arise in the exchange of cash for possession of a note. This problem is usually overcome by using a bank as an agent to collect an out-of-town note. To illustrate, Symplex Company of Eugene, Oregon, holds the $1,000, 6%, 60-day note of Sam Small of Longview, Washington. When the note nears maturity, Symplex delivers the note to its Eugene bank for collection. The Eugene bank forwards the note to a Longview, Washington, correspondent bank, and the Longview bank notifies Sam Small that it has the note for collection. When Small pays the Longview bank, he receives possession of the note. The Longview bank transmits the proceeds of the note to the Eugene bank, and the Eugene bank credits the proceeds, less a collection fee, to the Symplex Company bank account.

Only one entry is needed to record the collection of an out-of-town note through a bank. This is made when the bank notifies that it has credited the proceeds less the collection fee. No entry is made when the note is delivered to the bank for collection. At that time it is not known if the note will be paid or dishonored. Until the note is paid, there is no change in the relationship of the parties. For example, when the Sam Small note is paid, the bank notifies Symplex that it has deposited the proceeds less the collection fee to Symplex's bank account. Symplex then makes the following entry:

Oct.	17	Cash..	1,008.00	
		Collection Expense	2.00	
		Notes Receivable		1,000.00
		Interest Earned		10.00
		Proceeds of the Sam Small note less collection charge.		

End-of-the-period adjustments

■ **Accrued interest expense**

Interest accrues daily on all interest-bearing notes; consequently, if any notes payable are outstanding at the end of an accounting period, their accrued interest should be calculated and recorded. For example, a company gave its bank a $5,000, 60-day, 6% note on December 13 to borrow that amount of money. If the company's accounting period ends on December 31, by then 18 days' or $15 interest has accrued on this note and may be recorded with a work sheet adjustment and the following adjusting entry:

Dec.	31	Interest Expense	15.00	
		Interest Payable		15.00
		To record accrued interest on a note payable.		

The adjusting entry causes the $15 accrued interest to appear on the income statement as an expense of the period benefiting from 18 days' use of the money. It also causes the interest payable to appear on the balance sheet as a current liability.

PAYING ACCRUED INTEREST THAT HAS BEEN RECORDED. When the foregoing note becomes due in the next accounting period, its payment may be recorded as follows:

Feb.	11	Notes Payable..	5,000.00	
		Interest Expense	35.00	
		Interest Payable	15.00	
		Cash..		5,050.00
		Paid a $5,000 note and its interest.		

The foregoing $15 debit to Interest Payable records payment of the interest accrued at the end of the previous period.

Discount on notes payable

When a note payable is discounted at a bank, interest based on the principal of the note is deducted and this interest is normally recorded as interest expense. Furthermore, since most such notes run for 30, 60, or 90 days, the deducted interest is usually an expense of the period in which it is deducted. However, when the time of a note extends beyond a single accounting period, an adjusting entry is required. For example, on December 11, 197A, a company discounted at 6% its own $6,000, 60-day, noninterest-bearing note payable and recorded the transaction as follows:

197A				
Dec.	11	Cash...	5,940.00	
		Interest Expense	60.00	
		Notes Payable.....................................		6,000.00
		Discounted our noninterest-bearing, 60-day note at 6%.		

If this company operates with accounting periods that end each December 31, 20 days' interest on this note, or $20 of the $60 of discount, is an expense of the 197A accounting period and 40 days' interest or $40 is an expense of 197B. Consequently, if revenues and expenses are matched, the company must make the following December 31, 197A, adjusting entry:

197A				
Dec.	31	Discount on Notes Payable	40.00	
		Interest Expense		40.00
		To set up as a contra liability the interest applicable to 197B.		

The adjusting entry removes from the Interest Expense account the $40 of interest that is applicable to 197B, leaving in the account the $20 that is an expense of 197A. The $20 then appears on the 197A income statement as an expense, and the $40 is carried to the 197A balance sheet where, if this is the only note the company has outstanding, it is deducted from notes payable as follows:

Current Liabilities:
    Notes payable $6,000.00
    Less discount on notes payable 40.00 $5,960.00

Putting discount on notes payable on the balance sheet as a contra liability results in showing as a liability on the balance sheet date the amount of money received in discounting the note plus the accrued interest on the note to the balance sheet date. In this example $5,940 was received in discounting the note and the accrued interest on the note to December 31 amounts to $20, which together total $5,960, and which is the amount actually owed the bank on December 31.

The foregoing treatment of discount on notes payable is in line with the recommendations of the American Institute of Certified Public Accountants. Nevertheless, a different treatment is occasionally encountered, one in which discount on notes payable is called "prepaid interest" and is placed on the balance sheet as a current asset. Income tax rules allow this treatment; however, it cannot be justified in theory, for any attempt to prepay interest does nothing more than reduce the amount borrowed and increase the effective rate of interest on the loan.

ACCOUNTING FOR DISCOUNT ON NOTES PAYABLE IN THE NEW PERIOD. The $40 interest set out as discount on notes payable in the previous paragraphs becomes an expense early in 197B. Consequently, sooner or later it must be taken from the Discount on Notes Payable account and returned to the Interest Expense account. Some accountants make this return with a *reversing entry* that is made as the last step in the end-of-the-accounting-period work and is dated the first day of the new accounting period. Such a reversing entry appears as follows:

197B Jan.	1	Interest Expense	40.00	
		Discount on Notes Payable		40.00
		To reverse the adjusting entry that set out discount on notes payable.		

Observe that the foregoing reversing entry is debit for credit and credit for debit the reverse of the adjusting entry it reverses, and that is where it gets its name. Also, observe that it returns the $40 interest to the expense account so that it will appear on the 197B income statement as an expense without further ado.

Some accountants, rather than making a reversing entry, wait until the end of the new accounting period and handle a reversal like the above with a work sheet adjustment and an adjusting entry, as follows:

197B				
Dec.	31	Interest Expense	40.00	
		Discount on Notes Payable		40.00
		To return to the expense account interest applicable to 197B.		

Note that the reversing entry and the adjusting entry are identical, except as to their dates. Either may be used, since they both accomplish the same objective.

Accountants who make reversing entries normally prepare a work sheet, the year-end statements, adjusting and closing entries, and a post-closing trial balance. They then examine the work sheet and reverse any entries the reversal of which will expedite future accounting. In this case the reversal makes it unnecessary at the end of 197B for the accountant to search back through the records to see if the $40 of discount on notes payable has become an expense.

Accrued interest on notes receivable

Notes received from customers usually earn interest: and if any such notes are outstanding at the accounting period end, their accrued interest should be calculated and recorded. For example, on December 11 a company accepted a $3,000, 60-day, 6% note from a customer in granting an extension on a past-due account. If the company's accounting period ends on December 31, by then $10 interest has accrued on this note and should be recorded with a work sheet adjustment and the following adjusting entry:

Dec.	31	Interest Receivable.......................................	10.00	
		Interest Earned		10.00
		To record accrued interest on a note receivable.		

The adjusting entry causes the interest earned to appear on the income statement of the period in which it was earned. It also causes the interest receivable to appear on the balance sheet as a current asset.

COLLECTING INTEREST PREVIOUSLY ACCRUED. When the foregoing note is collected, the transaction may be recorded as follows:

Feb.	9	Cash..	3,030.00	
		Interest Earned		20.00
		Interest Receivable..................................		10.00
		Notes Receivable		3,000.00
		Received payment of a note and its interest.		

The entry's credit to Interest Receivable records collection of the interest accrued at the end of the previous period.

Discount on notes receivable

When a bank discounts a customer's note, it deducts interest in advance; but since most such notes are short term, the interest is normally earned before the end of the accounting period. Consequently, when a customer's note is discounted, most banks credit the interest collected to Interest Earned, as follows:

197A					
Dec.	16	Notes Receivable	4,000.00		
		Interest Earned		40.00	
		Cash..			3,960.00
		Discounted a customer's $4,000 note at 6% for 60 days.			

If the bank's accounting period ends on December 31, by that time $10 of the foregoing $40 interest has been earned and should appear on its 197A income statement as revenue, and $30 should be deferred until 197B. Consequently, the following adjusting entry is required:

197A				
Dec.	31	Interest Earned	30.00	
		Discount on Notes Receivable		30.00
		To remove the unearned interest from the revenue account.		

The foregoing entry causes $10 of the interest on the discounted note to appear on the bank's 197A income statement as revenue and $30 to appear on its balance sheet as a deduction from notes receivable.

Since the bank has many notes to account for, in a case such as this it will usually return the $30 to the Interest Earned account with a reversing entry.

Notes and interest on the statements
■ Short-term notes receivable are a current asset, and their total normally appears on the balance sheet under the caption "Notes receivable." Short-term notes payable are a current liability, and their total normally appears on the balance sheet as "Notes payable."

Interest earned, interest expense, and collection expense appear on the income statement under the heading "Other revenues and expenses." Since "other revenues and expenses" are not revenues and expenses from regular operations, they appear at the end of the statement as an addition to and a deduction from operating income, as in Illustration 9–2.

E-Z Paint Company
Income Statement for Year Ended December 31, 19—

Sales...	$410,000
Cost of goods sold:	
Operating income..	$ 51,500
Other revenues and expenses:	
Interest earned.. $1,200	
Interest expense... 900	
Addition to operating income	300
Net Income...	$ 51,800

Illustration
9–2

Questions for class discussion

1. Define:
   a) Promissory note.
   b) Payee of a note.
   c) Maturity date.
   d) Dishonored note.
   e) Notice of protest.
   f) Holder in due course.
   g) Discount period of a note.
   h) Maker of a note.
   i) Principal of a note.
   j) Maturity value.
   k) Contingent liability.
   l) Protest fee.

2. What distinction do banks make between discounts and loans?

3. Distinguish between bank discount and cash discount.

4. What are the due dates of the following notes?
   a) Ninety-day note dated June 10.
   b) Sixty-day note dated May 13.
   c) Ninety-day note dated November 12.

5. Calculate interest on the following amounts:
   a) $2,162 at 6% for 60 days.
   b) $2,500 at 6% for 24 days.
   c) $3,000 at 6% for 66 days.
   d) $3,000 at 4% for 30 days.
   e) $6,000 at 8% for 60 days.
   f) $3,212 at 4% for 90 days.
   g) $1,000 at 3% for 120 days.
   h) $1,800 at 7% for 54 days.

6. James Thumb borrows from two different banks. From the first he borrows by giving his $1,000, 60-day, 6% note. From the second he borrows by discounting his $1,000, 60-day, noninterest-bearing note at 6%. (a) Give the entries in general journal form to record the two loans on the books of Thumb. (b) Give the entries in general journal form to record the payments of the loans. (c) How do the entries differ in the two situations? (d) Which method of making loans favors the bank?

7. B. A. Lee purchased $500 worth of merchandise from Mesa Manufacturing Company, terms 2/10, n/30. Lee could not pay the account when due and secured an extension of time from Mesa by giving a 60-day, 6% note in the amount of $500. Lee paid the note in full when due. Record this series of transactions in T-accounts (a) on the books of Lee and (b) on the books of Mesa.

8. On December 10, S. A. Starns received from a customer a $1,200, 60-day, 5% note dated December 8. On December 26, he discounted the note at 6%. The note was not protested at maturity. Give the required entries in general journal form on the books of Starns.

9. If the following accounts and balances appear in a ledger:

Notes Receivable		Notes Receivable Discounted	
Bal.	8,500	Bal.	5,200

a) How many dollars of notes receivable are in the hands of the company?
b) How many dollars of notes have been discounted?
c) What is the contingent liability of the company?

Class exercises

Exercise 9–1

PART 1. On October 5 Lake Sales borrowed $5,000 from Security Bank by giving a 60-day, 6% note payable. The loan was repaid on December 4. Give the required entries.

PART 2. On December 8 Lake Sales borrowed $5,000 from First State Bank by discounting its own $5,000, noninterest-bearing, 60-day note payable at 6%. The loan was repaid on February 6. Give the entries to record the loan and its payment.

Exercise 9–2

Prepare entries in general journal form to record the following:

June 10 Sold merchandise to Jerry Hall, $950, terms 2/10, n/60.
Aug. 15 Received $150 in cash and an $800, 60-day, 6% note dated August 14 in granting a time extension on the amount due from Jerry Hall.
26 Discounted the Jerry Hall note at the bank at 6%.
Oct. 16 Since notice protesting the Jerry Hall note had not been received, assumed it paid and canceled the discount liability.

Exercise 9–3

Prepare entries in general journal form to record these transactions:

Aug. 15 Accepted a $2,400, 60-day, 5% note dated August 13 from Dale Small in granting a time extension on his past-due account.
19 Discounted the Dale Small note at the bank at 6%.
Oct. 13 Received notice protesting the Dale Small note. Paid the bank the maturity value of the note plus a $2 protest fee and canceled the discount liability.
Nov. 11 Received a check from Dale Small paying the maturity value of his dishonored note, the protest fee, and interest at 5% on both for 30 days beyond maturity.

Exercise 9–4

Prepare entries in general journal form to record these transactions:

Mar. 4 Accepted a $500, 60-day, 6% note dated this day from Earl Kane in granting a time extension on his past-due account.
May 3 Earl Kane dishonored his note when presented for payment.
Dec. 27 After exhausting all legal means of collecting, wrote off the debt of Earl Kane against the allowance for doubtful accounts.

Exercise 9–5

On July 12 Valley Company sold Robert Young merchandise having a $1,500 catalog list price, less 20% and 5%, 2/10, n/60. Young was unable to pay and was granted a time extension on receipt of his 60-day, 6% note dated September 15. Valley Company held the note until October 9, when it discounted the note at its bank at 6%. The note was not protested. Answer these questions:

1. How many dollars of trade discount were granted on this sale?
2. How many dollars of cash discount could Young have earned?
3. What was the maturity date of the note?
4. How many days were in the discount period?
5. How much bank discount did the bank deduct?
6. What were the proceeds of the note?
7. What was the last entry made by Valley Company in recording the transactions growing out of this sale and collection?

Problems

Problem 9–1

PART 1.   On September 7 Western Sales sold Carl Albert $3,600 of merchandise, terms 2/10, n/60. On November 10 it accepted Albert's $3,600, 60-day, 6% note dated that day in granting an additional 60 days on the amount owed. On November 25 Western Sales discounted the Albert note at 6%. The note was paid at maturity.

Required:
Prepare general journal entries to record the transactions (*a*) first on the books of Western Sales and then (*b*) on the books of Carl Albert.

PART 2.   On December 4 Western Sales accepted an $1,800, 5%, 60-day note dated December 2 from Carl Moss in granting a time extension on his past-due account. On December 8 Western Sales discounted the note at 6%, and on February 1 received notice that it had been dishonored. The concern paid the bank the maturity value of the note plus a $3 protest fee, and on March 4 received a check from Carl Moss paying the maturity value of the note, the protest fee, and interest at 5% on both for 30 days beyond maturity.

Required:
Prepare general journal entries to record the transactions (*a*) first on the books of Western Sales and then (*b*) on the books of Carl Moss.

Problem 9–2

Prepare entries in general journal form to record the following transactions:

Jan.   3   Sold merchandise to Gary Small, $1,450, terms 2/10, n/30.
Feb.   6   Accepted $250 in cash and a $1,200, 60-day, 5% note dated February 6 from Gary Small in settlement of his past-due account.
      12   Discounted the Gary Small note at 6% at the bank.
Apr.   9   Since notice protesting the Gary Small note had not been received, assumed the note paid and canceled the discount liability.
May 19   Accepted an $1,800, 60-day, 6% note, dated May 17, from Fred Green in granting an extension of his past-due open account.
      29   Discounted the Fred Green note at 6% at the bank.
July 17   Received notice protesting the Fred Green note. Paid the note's

maturity value plus a $2 protest fee and canceled the discount liability.

Aug. 16   Received a check from Fred Green paying the maturity value of his dishonored note, the protest fee, and interest on both at 6% for 30 days beyond maturity.

Oct.   5   Accepted a $1,500, 60-day, 6% note dated October 4 from Jack Quinn in granting an extension on the amount owed by him.

Nov. 27   Sent the Jack Quinn note to Security Bank for collection.

Dec.   5   Received a credit memorandum from Security Bank which represented the proceeds of the Jack Quinn note less a $2 collection fee.

Problem 9–3

Prepare general journal entries to record these transactions:

Dec.   4   Accepted $250 in cash and a $1,400, 60-day, 6% noted dated December 2 from Dale Zeff in settlement of his past-due open account.

      7   Accepted a $2,100, 60-day, 6% note dated this day from Ted Brown in granting a time extension on his past-due account.

   10   Borrowed money from First State Bank by discounting a $6,000, 60-day, noninterest-bearing note payable at 6%.

   14   Discounted the Dale Zeff note at the bank at 6%.

   16   Borrowed money from Security Bank by giving a $4,000, 60-day, 6% note.

   31   Made an adjusting entry to record the accrued interest on the Ted Brown note.

   31   Made an adjusting entry to record the accrued interest on the note given Security Bank.

   31   Made an adjusting entry to remove from the Interest Expense account the interest on the note given First State Bank that is chargeable to the new accounting period.

   31   Made an entry dated January 1 to reverse the foregoing entry and to return the interest to the Interest Expense account.

Jan. 30   Sent the Ted Brown note to First State Bank for collection.

Feb.   1   Received notice protesting the Dale Zeff note. Paid the bank the note's maturity value plus a $3 protest fee. Canceled the discount liability.

      8   Paid the note discounted on December 10.

      8   Received a credit memorandum representing the proceeds of the Ted Brown note less a $3 collection fee.

   14   Paid the note given Security Bank on December 16.

Mar.   2   Received a check from Dale Zeff paying the maturity value of his dishonored note, the protest fee, and interest on both at 6% for 30 days beyond maturity.

Problem 9–4

Prepare general journal entries to record these transactions:

Oct.   4   Sold merchandise to Earl Potts, $2,025, terms 2/10, n/30.

Nov.   5   Accepted $225 in cash and an $1,800, 60-day, 5% note dated today from Earl Potts in settlement of the October 4 sale.

      7   Accepted a $1,600, 60-day, 6% note dated November 5 from Walter Nash in granting a time extension on his past-due account.

   11   Discounted the Earl Potts note at the bank at 6%.

Nov. 25 Borrowed money from Guaranty Bank by giving a $4,000, 60-day, 6% note payable.

Dec. 7 Accepted a $500, 60-day, 6% note dated this day from Frank Kosh in granting a time extension on his past-due account.

11 Discounted the Walter Nash note at 6% at the bank.

16 Borrowed money by discounting a $4,000, 60-day, noninterest-bearing note payable at First State Bank at 6%.

31 Made an adjusting entry to record the accrued interest on the note given Guaranty Bank on November 25.

31 Made an adjusting entry to record the accrued interest on the Frank Kosh note.

31 Made an adjusting entry to remove from the Interest Expense account the interest on the note discounted on December 16 that is chargeable to the new accounting period.

31 Made a reversing entry dated January 1 to return the interest on the note discounted on December 16 to the Interest Expense account.

Jan. 5 Received notice that Walter Nash had dishonored the note discounted on December 11. Paid the bank the maturity value of the note plus a $3 protest fee. Canceled the discount liability.

6 Since notice protesting the Earl Potts note had not been received, assumed it paid and canceled the discount liability.

24 Paid the note given Guaranty Bank on November 25.

Feb. 5 Frank Kosh dishonored his $500 note on which interest was accrued on December 31. Recorded the additional accrued interest on the note and charged the note and its interest back to the account of the maker.

10 Received a check from Walter Nash paying the maturity value of his dishonored note, the protest fee, and interest on both for 36 days beyond maturity.

14 Paid the note discounted on December 16.

Dec. 31 Wrote off the account of Frank Kosh against the allowance for doubtful accounts.

Alternate problems

Problem 9–1A

PART 1. On July 5 Valley Sales sold Carl Lee $1,475 of merchandise, terms 2/10, n/60. Carl Lee could not pay the account when due, and on September 10 he gave Valley Sales $275 in cash and a 60-day, 6%, $1,200 note dated that day for the balance. Valley Sales held the note until September 28 and then discounted it at the bank at 6%. The note was not protested at maturity.

PART 2. On October 22 Valley Sales sold Robert Gregg $1,500 of merchandise, terms 2/10, n/60. Robert Gregg could not pay the account, and on January 2 gave Valley Sales a $1,500, 60-day, 6% note dated that day to gain an extension on the amount owed. When the note was presented for payment on March 3, it was dishonored. The following December 28, after having exhausted every legal means to collect, Valley Sales wrote off the debt as uncollectible.

Required:

1. Prepare entries in general journal form to record the Part 1 transactions (*a*) first on the books of Valley Sales and (*b*) then on the books of Carl Lee.
2. Prepare entries in general journal form to record the Part 2 transactions (*a*) first on the books of Valley Sales and (*b*) then on the books of Robert Gregg.

Problem 9–2A

Prepare entries in general journal form to record these transactions:

Jan. 2 Sold merchandise to Larry Davis, $2,650, terms 2/10, n/30.

Feb. 6 Accepted $250 in cash and a $2,400, 60-day, 5% note dated this day from Larry Davis in settlement of the January 2 sale.

12 Discounted the Larry Davis note at 6% at Guaranty Bank.

Apr. 10 Since notice protesting the Larry Davis note had not been received, assumed the note had been paid and canceled the discount liability.

May 18 Accepted a $1,600, 60-day, 6% note dated May 17 in granting an extension on the past-due account of David Hall.

June 1 Discounted the David Hall note at 6% at Guaranty Bank.

July 17 Received notice protesting the David Hall note. Paid the bank the maturity value of the note plus a $3 protest fee and canceled the discount liability.

Aug. 22 Received a check from David Hall paying the maturity value of his dishonored note plus the protest fee and interest at 6% on both for 36 days beyond maturity.

Sept. 5 Accepted a $2,500, 6%, 30-day note dated September 3 from Dale Evans in granting an extension on the amount owed by him.

Oct. 1 Sent the Dale Evans note to Guaranty Bank for collection.

5 Received a credit memorandum from Guaranty Bank which represented the proceeds of the Dale Evans note less a $2 collection fee.

Problem 9–3A

Prepare general journal entries to record these transactions:

Nov. 8 Accepted a $1,600, 60-day, 6% note dated this day from Dale Baker in granting an extension on the due date of his account balance.

17 Accepted a $2,600, 6%, 60-day note dated this day from Fred Kirk in granting a time extension on the amount owed by him.

26 Discounted the Dale Baker note at 6% at the bank.

29 Discounted the Fred Kirk note at 6% at the bank.

Dec. 7 Gave Guaranty Bank a $5,000, 60-day, 6% note payable to borrow that amount of money.

11 Discounted a $4,500, 60-day, noninterest-bearing note payable at 6% at Security Bank.

31 Made an adjusting entry to record the accrued interest on the note given Guaranty Bank on December 7.

31 Made an adjusting entry to remove from the Interest Expense account the interest on the note discounted at Security Bank on December 11 that is chargeable to the new accounting period.

31 Made a reversing entry dated January 1 to return to the Interest Expense account the interest on the Security Bank note.

Jan. 8 Received notice protesting the Dale Baker note. Paid the bank the maturity value of the note plus a $3 protest fee and canceled the discount liability.

Jan. 19 Since notice protesting the Fred Kirk note had not been received, assumed it paid and canceled the discount liability.

Feb. 5 Paid the note given Guaranty Bank on December 7.

9 Paid the note discounted at Security Bank on December 11.

18 Received a check from Dale Baker paying the maturity value of his dishonored note, the protest fee, and interest on both at 6% for 42 days beyond maturity.

Problem 9–4A

Prepare general journal entries to record the following transactions:

Jan. 5 Sold merchandise to James Bond, $750, terms 2/10, n/60.

15 Discounted our own $3,000, 30-day, noninterest-bearing note payable at the bank at 6% for 30 days.

17 Sold merchandise to Fred Small, $1,500, terms 2/10, n/60.

Feb. 14 Paid the note discounted on January 15.

Mar. 15 Received $250 in cash and accepted a $500, 60-day, 6% note dated March 14 for the merchandise sold James Bond on January 5.

16 Sold merchandise to Harry Bean, $1,700, terms 2/10, n/60.

25 Accepted a $1,500, 60-day, 6% note dated March 24 from Fred Small in granting an extension on the due date of the January 17 sale.

26 Discounted the James Bond note at 6% at the bank.

Apr. 17 Discounted the Fred Small note at 6% at the bank.

18 Borrowed $2,500 from Guaranty Bank by giving a 60-day, 6% note payable.

May 17 Since notice protesting the James Bond note had not been received, assumed it paid and canceled the discount liability.

24 Received notice protesting the Fred Small note discounted on April 17. Paid the bank the maturity value of the note plus a $4 protest fee and canceled the discount liability.

26 Accepted a $1,700, 60-day, 6% note dated May 25 in granting a time extension on the amount owed by Harry Bean on the March 16 sale.

31 Discounted the Harry Bean note at 6% at the bank.

June 17 Paid the note given the bank on April 18.

23 Received a check from Fred Small paying the maturity value of his dishonored note, the protest fee and interest on both for 30 days beyond maturity at 6%.

July 25 Received notice protesting the Harry Bean note discounted on May 31. Paid the bank the maturity value of the note plus a $4 protest fee. Canceled the discount liability.

Dec. 28 Wrote off the Harry Bean debt against the allowance for doubtful accounts.

Decision problem 9–1, Farm Machinery Company

Farm Machinery Company manufactures a line of farm machinery which it sells through retail implement dealers. The company has not been in business too many years and is attempting to compete with larger and better established agricultural machinery manufacturers.

The company's machines are somewhat less cumbersome and less complicated and, therefore, less expensive than those of its competitors. Nevertheless, the unit prices are fairly substantial, and because of the custom in the industry, generous credit terms must be provided. Sales are made to dealers on credit at terms of 10% in cash, and the balance due three months after the date of sale. Dealers customarily give about the same terms to farmers, but since many credit extensions up to nine months are often given, the dealers must then also be given a longer period in which to pay Farm Machinery Company.

A number of other problems in financing have arisen. The company would like to schedule production uniformly over the year, but because of seasonal sales and the small cash inflow during certain months, it has had difficulty securing the necessary funds to operate uniformly over a 12-month period. Dealers also complain that customers should be given a longer credit period in order to meet competition. It is believed that sales could be increased 20% if credit terms were extended to nine months.

Sales for the past year were distributed as follows:

January	$30,000	May	$90,000	September	$20,000
February	40,000	June	70,000	October	10,000
March	60,000	July	50,000	November	10,000
April	80,000	August	40,000	December	20,000

At a dealers' meeting in December Tom Burton, the founder and major owner of Farm Machinery Company, proposed the following plan:
1. Dealers ask customers to give noninterest-bearing notes for the amounts due after the 10% down payments. These notes would run for nine months from dates of sales.
2. Dealers would endorse to the manufacturer customer notes up to the amounts due the company on each month's sales beyond the 10% paid in cash.
3. The company could then discount these notes at its bank at 6%.

Prepare a report expressing your opinion of Tom Burton's proposal including the following:
1. Should dealers prefer the proposed credit plan over the current plan? Should the plan be acceptable to farmers? Should the bank be willing to discount the farmers' notes when presented by Farm Machinery Company?
2. Assume that sales will increase 20% under the new credit plan and that cash requirements to cover production and other cash operating costs are 60% of sales, how much cash will be needed each month if production is equalized over the year?
3. Would you recommend the adoption of Tom Burton's plan? Explain.

Chapter 10

Inventories and cost of goods sold

■ A merchandising business earns revenue by selling merchandise, and for such a concern the phrase *merchandise inventory* is used to describe the aggregate of the items of tangible personal property it holds for sale. As a rule the items for sale are sold within one year; consequently, the inventory is a current asset, usually the largest current asset on a merchandising concern's balance sheet.

Matching merchandise costs with revenues

■ The American Institute of Certified Public Accountants has said: "A major objective of accounting for inventories is the proper determination of income through the process of matching appropriate costs against revenues."[1] The matching process referred to is one with which the student is already somewhat familiar. It consists of determining how much of the total cost of the goods that were for sale during a period should be deducted from the period's revenue from sales and how much should be carried forward as inventory to be matched against a future period's revenue.

The cost of the goods that were for sale during an accounting period may be determined from the accounting records by adding to the cost

---

[1] *Accounting Research and Terminology Bulletins, Final Edition* (New York: American Institute of Certified Public Accountants, 1961), p. 28.

of the beginning inventory the net cost of the goods purchased during the period. But, since most concerns do not keep a record of the cost of the goods sold during a period, in most concerns cost of goods sold cannot be determined from accounting records but must be ascertained by separating *goods for sale* into *goods sold* and *goods unsold*.

In separating goods available for sale into its components of goods sold and goods not sold, the key problem is that of assigning a cost to the goods not sold or to the ending inventory. However, it should be constantly borne in mind that the procedures for assigning a cost to the ending inventory are also the means of determining cost of goods sold. Cost of goods sold and ending inventory are opposite sides of the same coin, because whatever portion of the cost of goods for sale is assigned to the ending inventory, the remainder goes into cost of goods sold.

Assigning a cost to the ending inventory

■ Assigning a cost to the ending inventory normally involves two problems: (1) determining the quantity of each product on hand and (2) pricing the products.

The quantity of unsold merchandise on hand at the end of an accounting period is usually determined by a physical inventory. Physical inventories and the way in which such inventories are taken were discussed in Chapter 5; consequently, it is only necessary to repeat that in a physical inventory the unsold merchandise is counted, weighed, or otherwise measured to determine the units, pounds, gallons, board feet, or other measure of each product on hand.

After an inventory is counted, weighed, or otherwise measured, the units are priced. Generally, inventories are priced at cost.[2] However, as previously stated, a departure from cost is sometimes necessary when goods have been damaged or have deteriorated. Likewise, a departure from cost is sometimes necessary when replacement costs for inventory items are less than the amounts actually paid for the items when they were purchased. This last point is discussed in more detail later in this chapter under the heading, "Cost or market, the lower."

Accounting for an inventory at cost

■ Pricing an inventory at cost is not difficult when costs remain fixed. However, when identical items were purchased during an accounting period at different costs, a problem arises as to which costs apply to the ending inventory and which apply to the goods sold. There are at least four acceptable ways of assigning costs to goods in the ending inventory and to goods sold. They are: (1) specific invoice prices; (2) weighted average cost; (3) first-in, first-out; and (4) last-in, first-out.

To illustrate the four, assume that a company has on hand at the end of an accounting period 12 units of Article X. Also, assume that the company began the year and purchased Article X during the year as follows:

---

[2] *Ibid.*, p. 28. *Basic Concepts and Accounting Principles Underlying Financial Statements* (New York: American Institute of Certified Public Accountants, 1970), p. 80.

```
Jan.   1   Opening inventory ......... 10 units @ $10.00  =  $100.00
Mar. 13   Purchased ................... 15 units @   11.50  =   172.50
Aug. 17   Purchased ................... 20 units @   12.50  =   250.00
Nov. 10   Purchased ................... 10 units @   12.00  =   120.00
               Total .......................... 55 units              $642.50
```

Specific invoice prices

When it is possible to identify each item in an inventory with a specific purchase and its invoice, specific invoice prices may be used to assign costs to the inventory and to the goods sold. For example, if for purposes of illustration it is assumed that 6 of the 12 remaining units of Article X were from the November purchase and 6 were from the August purchase, the costs are assigned to the inventory and goods sold by means of specific invoice prices as follows:

```
Total cost of 55 units available for sale.....................................   $642.50
Less final inventory priced by means of specific invoices:
   6 units from the November purchase at $12.00 each............... $72.00
   6 units from the August purchase at $12.50........................... 75.00
   12 units in ending inventory ................................................     147.00
Cost of goods sold ................................................................   $495.50
```

Weighted average

Under this method prices for the units in the beginning inventory and in each purchase are weighted by the number of units in the beginning inventory and in each purchase and are averaged to find the weighted average cost per unit as follows:

```
10 units @ $10.00   =   $100.00
15 units @   11.50   =    172.50
20 units @   12.50   =    250.00
10 units @   12.00   =    120.00
55                              $642.50
$642.50  ÷  55  =  $11.682, weighted average cost per unit
```

After the average cost per unit is determined, this weighted average is used to assign costs to the inventory and the units sold as follows:

```
Total cost of 55 units available for sale..................................... $642.50
Less ending inventory priced on a weighted average cost basis:
   12 units at $11.682 each....................................................... 140.18
Cost of goods sold ................................................................. $502.32
```

First-in, first-out

In a merchandising business clerks are usually instructed to sell the oldest merchandise first. Consequently, when this instruction is followed, merchandise tends to flow out on a first-in, first-out basis. When first-in, first-out is applied in pricing an inventory, it is assumed that costs also follow this pattern, and as a result, the cost of the last items received are assigned to the ending inventory and the remaining costs are assigned to goods sold. When first-in, first-out, or *Fifo* as it is often called from its first letters, is used, costs are assigned to the inventory and to the goods sold as follows:

Total cost of 55 units available for sale		$642.50
Less ending inventory priced on a basis of Fifo:		
10 units from the November purchase at $12.00 each	$120.00	
2 units from the August purchase at $12.50 each	25.00	
12 units in the ending inventory		145.00
Cost of goods sold		$497.50

Last-in, first-out

Under this method of inventory pricing, commonly called *Lifo,* the costs of the last goods received are matched with revenue from sales. The theoretical justification for this is that a going concern must at all times keep a certain amount of goods in stock; consequently, when goods are sold, replacements are purchased. Thus it is a sale that causes the replacement of goods; and if costs and revenues are matched, replacement costs should be matched with the sales that induced the acquisitions.

Under Lifo, costs are assigned to the 12 remaining units of Article X and to the goods sold as follows:

Total cost of 55 units available for sale		$642.50
Less ending inventory priced on a basis of Lifo:		
10 units in the beginning inventory at $10.00 each	$100.00	
2 units from the first purchase at $11.50 each	23.00	
12 units in the ending inventory		123.00
Cost of goods sold		$519.50

Notice that this method of matching costs and revenue results in the final inventory being priced at the cost of the oldest 12 units.

Comparison of methods

In a stable market where prices remain unchanged, the inventory pricing method is of little importance, because when prices are unchanged over a period of time, all methods give the same cost figures. However, in a changing market where prices are rising and falling, each method may give a different result. This may be seen by comparing the costs for the units of Article X sold as calculated by the several methods just discussed. These costs are:

Based on specific invoice prices	$495.50
Based on weighted average invoice prices	502.32
Based on Fifo	497.50
Based on Lifo	519.50

All four pricing methods are used; and each under certain circumstances has its advantages. Specific invoice prices exactly match costs and revenue; average invoice prices tend to smooth out price fluctuations; Fifo tends to associate costs and the merchandising ideal of selling the oldest merchandise first; and when prices are rising, as in most of the years since World War II, Lifo has certain tax advantages. However, since the method used may affect the amounts of reported ending inventory and cost of goods sold, a company should show on its statements by means of footnotes or other manner the pricing method used. Also, accountants are of the opinion that a company should select for use the method that best reflects its periodic net income.

Tax effect of Lifo

During periods of rising prices Lifo offers a tax advantage to its users. This advantage arises because when compared with other commonly used methods the application of Lifo results in assigning greatest amounts of costs to goods sold. This in turn results in the smallest reported net incomes and income taxes.

The use of Lifo is not limited to concerns in which goods are actually sold on a last-in, first-out basis. A concern may choose Lifo even though it actually sells goods on a first-in, first-out basis, or on an average basis, as in the case of an oil dealer who pumps new purchases of oil into a storage tank before exhausting his old inventory.

Consistency ■ Often a company's reported net income can be either increased or decreased simply by changing its method of inventory pricing. Consequently, although accountants hold that a company may use any accepted method that fairly reflects its periodic income, they insist that the company consistently follow the chosen method.

Often there are several acceptable ways of handling any transaction or accounting problem. Inventory pricing methods are one example, and the several methods of calculating depreciation as discussed in the next chapter are another. Accountants hold that when there are several acceptable methods or procedures that may be followed in a given situation, a concern may choose any one so long as the chosen method or procedure fairly reflects periodic income and is consistently followed thereafter. Consistency is a fundamental principle of accounting. Accountants strive for consistency so that there will be a high degree of comparability in the statements prepared period after period.

In their desire for consistency, however, accountants do not hold that a method once chosen can never be changed. Rather, they agree that if upon additional consideration it is decided that a different acceptable method from the one in use will better reflect periodic income, a change may be made. But in such a case accountants insist that adequate disclosure of the change and its effects be reported in the company's statements.

Elements of inventory cost ■ The American Institute of Certified Public Accountants has said: "As applied to inventories, cost means in principle the sum of the applicable expenditures and charges directly or indirectly incurred in bringing an article to its existing condition and location."[3] Therefore, the cost of an inventory item includes the invoice price, less the discount, plus any additional incidental costs necessary to put the goods into place and condition for sale. The additional incidental costs include import duties, freight and transportation, storage, insurance while being stored or transported, plus any other applicable costs, such as those incurred during an aging process.

If incurred, any of the foregoing enter into the cost of an inventory. However, in pricing an inventory, most concerns do not take into consideration the incidental costs of acquiring merchandise. They price the inventory on the basis of invoice prices only, and treat all incidental costs of acquiring goods as expenses of the period in which incurred.

Although not correct in theory, treating incidental costs as expenses of the period in which incurred is commonly permissible and often best. In theory a share of each incidental cost should be assigned to every unit purchased, thus causing a portion of each to be carried forward in the inventory to be matched against the revenue of the period in which the inventory is sold. However, the expense of computing costs on such a precise basis usually outweighs any benefit from the extra accuracy. Consequently, when possible, most concerns take advantage of the accounting principle of materiality and treat such costs as expenses of the period in which incurred.

Cost or market, the lower

■ Over the years, the traditional rule for pricing an inventory has been "the lower of cost or market." This rule gained its wide acceptance because it placed an inventory on the balance sheet at a conservative figure—the lower of what the inventory cost or its replacement cost on the balance sheet date.

The argument advanced in support of this conservatism was that if the replacement cost of an inventory item had declined, then its selling price would probably have to be reduced, and since this might result in a loss, the loss should be anticipated and taken in the year of the price decline. It was a good argument; however, since selling prices do not always exactly and quickly follow cost prices, the application of the rule often resulted in misstating net income in the year of a price decline and again in the succeeding year. For example, suppose that a firm purchased merchandise costing $1,000; marked it up to a $1,500 selling price; and sold one half of the goods. The gross profit on the goods sold would be calculated as follows:

Sales	$750
Cost of goods sold	500
Gross profit	$250

However, if the $500 replacement cost of the unsold goods had de-

---

[3] *Ibid.*, p. 28.

clined to $450 on the inventory date, an income statement based upon the traditional application of cost or market would show:

Sales..		$750
Cost of goods sold:		
Purchases	$1,000	
Less ending inventory........................	450	550
Gross profit		$200

The $450 would be a conservative balance sheet figure for the unsold goods. However, if these goods were sold at their full price early in the following year, the $450 inventory figure would have the erroneous effect of deferring $50 of income to the second year's income statement as follows:

Sales..	$750
Cost of goods sold:	
Beginning inventory.............................	450
Gross profit	$300

Merchants are prone to be slow in marking down goods; they normally try to sell merchandise at its full price if possible. Consequently, the illustrated situation was not uncommon. For this reason the lower of cost or market rule has been modified in recent years as follows for situations in which replacement costs are below actual costs.[4]

1. Goods should be placed on an inventory at cost, even though replacement cost is lower, if there has not been and there is not expected to be a decline in selling price.
2. Goods should at times be placed on an inventory at a price below their cost but above their replacement cost. For example, suppose the cost of an item that is normally bought for $20 and sold for $30 declines from $20 to $16, and its selling price declines from $30 to $27. The normal profit margin on this item is one third of its selling price. If this normal margin is applied to $27, the item should be placed on the inventory at two thirds of $27, or at $18. This is below cost but above replacement cost.
3. At times, goods should be placed on an inventory at a price below replacement cost. For example, assume that the goods described in the preceding paragraph can only be sold for $18.50 and that the disposal costs are estimated at $3. In this case the goods should be placed on the inventory at $15.50, a price below their replacement cost of $16.

Conservatism

■ Balance sheet conservatism was once considered one of the first principles of accounting. The objective of such conservatism was to place each item on the balance sheet at a conservative figure. This in

---

[4]*Ibid.*, pp. 30 and 31.

itself was commendable; but it was often carried too far and resulted not only in the misstatement of asset values but also in unconservative income statements. For example, as shown in the foregoing paragraphs, when prices are falling, the blind application of the unmodified lower of cost or market rule to inventories may result in a conservative balance sheet figure for inventories; but it may also result in an improper deferring of net income and in inaccurate income statements. Likewise, the too rapid write-off of plant assets to depreciation, not uncommon in the past, in order to place these assets on the balance sheet at conservative figures resulted not only in the misstatement of the asset values but also in the overstatement of expenses and in misleading income statements. Consequently, today accountants recognize that balance sheet conservatism does not outweigh other factors. Today, accountants favor practices that result in a fair statement of net income period after period.

Inventory errors

■ An error in determining the end-of-the-period inventory will cause misstatements in cost of goods sold, gross profit, reported net income, the current assets, and owner equity. Also, since the ending inventory of one period is the beginning inventory of the next, the error will carry forward and cause misstatements in the succeeding period's cost of goods sold, gross profit, and reported net income. Furthermore, since the amount involved in an inventory is often large, the error and misstatements can be material without being readily apparent.

To illustrate the effects of an inventory error, assume that in each of 1972, 1973, and 1974 a company had $100,000 in sales. If the company maintained a $20,000 inventory throughout the period and made $60,000 in purchases in each of the years, its cost of goods sold each year was $60,000 and its annual gross profits were $40,000. However, assume the company incorrectly calculated its December 31, 1972, inventory at $18,000 rather than $20,000. The error would have the effects shown in Illustration 10–1.

	1972		1973		1974	
Sales		$100,000		$100,000		$100,000
Cost of goods sold:						
Beginning inventory	$20,000		$18,000*		$20,000	
Purchases	60,000		60,000		60,000	
Goods for sale	$80,000		$78,000		$80,000	
Ending inventory	18,000*		20,000		20,000	
Cost of goods sold		62,000		58,000		60,000
Gross profit		$ 38,000		$ 42,000		$ 40,000

*Should have been $20,000.

Illustration
10–1

Observe in Illustration 10–1 that the $2,000 understatement of the December 31, 1972, inventory caused a $2,000 overstatement in 1972 cost of goods sold and a $2,000 understatement in gross profit and net income. Also, since the ending inventory of 1972 became the beginning inventory of 1973, the error caused an understatement in the 1973 cost of goods sold and a $2,000 overstatement in gross profit and net income. However, by 1974 the error had no effect.

In Illustration 10–1 the December 31, 1972, inventory is understated. Had it been overstated instead of understated, it would have caused opposite results – the 1972 net income would have been overstated and the 1973 income understated.

It is sometimes argued that a mistake in taking a year-end inventory is not too serious, since the error it causes in reported net income the first year is exactly offset by an opposite error in the second. However, such reasoning is unsound because it fails to consider that management, creditors, and owners base many important decisions on fluctuations in reported net income. Consequently, such mistakes should be avoided, and they may be avoided if care is exercised and procedures such as those outlined at the end of Chapter 5 are used in taking an inventory.

Perpetual inventories

■ Concerns selling a limited number of products of relatively high value often keep perpetual or book inventories. Also, large concerns that process their accounting data electronically or with punched cards commonly keep such records.

A perpetual or book inventory based on pen and ink makes use of a subsidiary record card for each product in stock. On these individual cards, one for each kind of product, the number of units received is recorded as units are received; the number of units sold is recorded as units are sold; and after each receipt or sale, the balance remaining on hand is recorded. (An inventory record card for ¼ H.P. Electric Motors is shown in Illustration 10–2.) At any time, each perpetual inventory

| Item ¼ H.P. Electric Motors | | | | | | | Location in stock room Bin 8 | | |
| Maximum 25 | | | | | | | Minimum 5 | | |

| Date | Received | | | Sold | | | Balance | | |
	Units	Cost	Total	Units	Cost	Total	Units	Cost	Balance
1/1							10	10.00	100.00
1/5				5	10.00	50.00	5	10.00	50.00
1/8	20	10.50	210.00				5	10.00	
							20	10.50	260.00
1/10				3	10.00	30.00	2	10.00	
							20	10.50	230.00

Illustration 10–2
Inventory Record Card

card tells the balance on hand of any one product; and the total of all cards is the amount of the inventory.

The January 10 sale on the card of Illustration 10–2 indicates that the perpetual inventory of which this card is a part is kept on a first-in, first-out basis. Observe that this sale is recorded as being from the oldest units in stock. Perpetual inventories may also be kept on a last-in, first-out basis. When this is done, each sale is recorded as being from the last units received in stock, until these are exhausted, then sales are from the next to last, and so on.

When a concern keeps perpetual inventory records, it normally also makes a once-a-year physical count of each kind of goods in stock in order to check the accuracy of its book inventory records.

Perpetual inventories not only tell the amount of inventory on hand at any time but they also aid in controlling the total amount invested in inventory. Each perpetual inventory card may have on it the maximum and minimum amounts of that item that should be kept in stock. By keeping the amount of each item within these limits, an oversupply or an undersupply of inventory is avoided.

Periodic and perpetual inventory systems

■ A system of inventory accounting like that described in Chapter 5 is normally based upon periodic, physical inventories and is known as a periodic inventory system. As was explained in Chapter 5, cost of goods sold is determined under such a system by adding net cost of purchases to beginning inventory and subtracting the ending inventory. When such a system is used, an inventory is necessary in order to determine ending goods on hand and cost of goods sold.

Under a perpetual inventory system, cost of goods sold during a period, as well as the ending inventory, may be determined from the accounting records without a physical inventory. Under such a system an account called "Merchandise" takes the place of and is used for recording the information entered in the periodic inventory system accounts, "Purchases" and "Merchandise Inventory." The "Merchandise" account is a controlling account that controls the numerous perpetual inventory cards described in previous paragraphs.

When merchandise is purchased by a concern using a perpetual inventory system, the acquisition is recorded as follows:

Jan.	8	Merchandise...	210.00	
		Accounts Payable – Blue Company............		210.00
		Purchased merchandise on account.		

In addition to the entry debiting the purchase to the Merchandise account, entries are also made on the proper perpetual inventory cards in the Received columns to show the kinds of merchandise bought. (See Illustration 10–2.)

When a sale is made, since the inventory cards show the cost of each item sold, it is possible to record both the sale and the cost of the goods sold. For example, if goods that according to the inventory cards cost $30 are sold for $50, cost of goods sold and the sale may be recorded as follows:

Jan.	10	Accounts Receivable – George Black................	50.00	
		Cost of Goods Sold......................................	30.00	
		Sales		50.00
		Merchandise...		30.00
		Sold merchandise on account.		

In addition to the entry just given which credits the Merchandise account for the cost of the goods sold, the goods sold are entered in the Sold columns of the proper inventory cards.

Note the debit to Cost of Goods Sold in the entry just given. If this account is debited at the time of each sale for the cost of the goods sold, the debit balance of the account will show at the end of the accounting period the cost of all goods sold during the period.

Note also the Merchandise account as it appears in the two entries just given. If this account is debited for the cost of merchandise purchased and credited for the cost of merchandise sold, at the end of an accounting period its debit balance will show the cost of the unsold goods on hand, the ending inventory.

If cost of goods sold, as well as sales, is to be recorded in a columnar Sales Journal, an additional column is required.

Periodic inventory systems are more common than perpetual inventory systems in retail and wholesale concerns. However, perpetual inventory systems are not uncommon in concerns selling goods having a high unit cost.

Estimated inventories

■ Retail method

Good management requires that income statements be prepared more often than once each year, usually monthly or quarterly; and inventory information is necessary for these statements. However, taking a physical inventory in a retail store is both time consuming and expensive. Consequently, many retailers use the so-called *retail inventory method* to estimate inventories for monthly or quarterly statements. These monthly or quarterly statements are called *interim* or "in between" statements, since they are prepared in between the regular year-end statements.

ESTIMATING AN ENDING INVENTORY BY THE RETAIL METHOD. When the retail method is used to estimate an end-of-an-interim-period inventory, a store's records must show the amount of inventory it had at the beginning of the period both *at cost* and *at retail*. At cost for an inventory means just that, while "at retail" means the amount of the inventory at the marked selling prices of the inventory items.

In addition to the beginning inventory, the records must also show the amount of goods purchased during the period both at cost and at retail plus the net sales at retail. The last item is easy; it is the balance of the Sales account less returns and discounts. Then, with this information the interim inventory is estimated as follows: (1) The amount of goods that were for sale during the period both at cost and at retail is first computed. Next, (2) "at cost" is divided by "at retail" to obtain a cost ratio. Then, (3) sales (at retail) are deducted from goods for sale (at retail) to arrive at the ending inventory (at retail). And finally, (4) the ending inventory at retail is multiplied by the cost ratio to reduce it to a cost basis. These calculations are shown in Illustration 10–3.

		At Cost	At Retail
(1)	Goods available for sale:		
	Beginning inventory..	$20,500	$ 34,500
	Net purchases...	39,500	65,500
	Goods available for sale....................................	$60,000	$100,000
(2)	Cost ratio: $60,000 ÷ $100,000 = 60%)		
(3)	Sales at retail...		70,000
	Ending inventory at retail		$ 30,000
(4)	Ending inventory at cost ($30,000 × 60%)	$18,000	

Illustration 10–3

The essence of Illustration 10–3 is: (1) This store had $100,000 of goods (at marked selling prices) for sale during the period. (2) These goods cost 60% of the $100,000 at which they were marked for sale. (3) The store's records (its Sales account) showed that $70,000 of these goods were sold, leaving $30,000 of merchandise unsold and presumably in the ending inventory. Therefore, (4) since cost in this store is 60% of retail, the cost of this ending inventory is $18,000.

An ending inventory calculated as in Illustration 10–3 is an estimate that is arrived at by deducting sales (goods sold) from goods for sale. Inventories estimated in this manner are satisfactory for interim statements, but for year-end statements, or at least once each year, a store should take a physical inventory.

USING THE RETAIL METHOD TO REDUCE A PHYSICAL INVENTORY TO A COST BASIS. Items for sale in a retail store normally have price tickets attached that show selling prices. Consequently, when a retail store takes a physical inventory, it commonly takes the inventory at the marked selling prices of the inventoried items. It then reduces the total of this inventory to a cost basis by applying its cost ratio. It does this because the selling prices are readily available and the application of the cost ratio eliminates the need to look up the invoice price of each inventoried item.

For example, assume that the store of Illustration 10–3, in addition to estimating its inventory by the retail method, also takes a physical inventory at the marked selling prices of the inventoried goods. Assume further that the total of this physical inventory is $29,600. Under these assumptions the store may arrive at a cost basis for this inventory, without having to look up the cost of each inventoried item, simply by applying its cost ratio to the $29,600 inventory total as follows:

$$\$29,600 \times 60\% = \$17,760$$

The $17,760 cost figure for this store's ending physical inventory is a satisfactory figure for year-end statement purposes. It is also acceptable to the Bureau of Internal Revenue for tax purposes.

INVENTORY SHORTAGES.   An inventory determined as in Illustration 10–3 is an estimate of the amount of goods that should be on hand; but since it is arrived at by deducting sales from goods for sale, it does not reveal any actual shortages due to breakage, loss, or theft. However, the amount of such shortages may be determined by first estimating an inventory as in Illustration 10–3 and then taking a physical inventory at marked selling prices.

For example, by means of the Illustration 10–3 calculations, it was estimated the store of this discussion had a $30,000 ending inventory at retail. However, in the previous section it was assumed that this same store took a physical inventory and had only $29,600 of merchandise on hand. Therefore, if this store should have had $30,000 of goods in its ending inventory as determined in Illustration 10–3, but had only $29,600 when it took a physical inventory, it must have had a $400 inventory shortage at retail or a $240 shortage at cost ($400 × 60% = $240).

MARKUPS AND MARKDOWNS.   The calculation of a cost ratio is often not as simple as that shown in Illustration 10–3, because many stores not only have a *normal markup* that they apply to items purchased for sale but also make *additional markups* and *markdowns*. A normal markup is the normal amount or percentage that is applied to the cost of an item to arrive at its selling price. For example, if a store's normal markup is 50% on cost and it applies this normal markup to an item that cost $10, it will mark the item for sale at $15. Normal markups appear in the calculation of a store's cost ratio as the difference between net purchases at cost and at retail.

Additional markups are markups made in addition to normal markups. Stores commonly give goods of outstanding style or quality such additional markups, because they can get a higher than normal price for such goods. They also commonly mark down for a clearance sale any slow-moving merchandise.

When a store using the retail inventory method makes additional markups and markdowns it must keep a record of them. It then uses the information in calculating its cost ratio and in estimating an interim inventory as in Illustration 10–4.

Goods available for sale:	At Cost	At Retail
Beginning inventory	$18,000	$27,800
Net purchases	34,000	50,700
Additional markups		1,500
Goods available for sale	$52,000	$80,000
Cost ratio: $52,000 ÷ $80,000 = 65%		
Sales at retail		$54,000
Markdowns		2,000
Total sales and markdowns		$56,000
Ending inventory at retail ($80,000 less $56,000)		$24,000
Ending inventory at cost ($24,000 × 65%)	$15,600	

Illustration
10–4

Observe in Illustration 10–4 that the store's $80,000 of goods for sale at retail were reduced $54,000 by sales and $2,000 by markdowns, a total of $56,000. (To understand the markdowns, visualize this effect of a markdown: The store had an item for sale during the period at $25. The item did not sell, and to move it the manager marked its price down from $25 to $20. By this act he reduced the amount of goods for sale in the store at retail by $5, and by a number of such markdowns goods for sale at retail in the store of Illustration 10–4 were reduced $2,000.) Now back to Illustration 10–4. The store's $80,000 of goods for sale were reduced $54,000 by sales and $2,000 by markdowns, leaving an estimated $24,000 ending inventory at retail. Therefore, since "cost" is 65% of "retail," the ending inventory at "cost" is $15,600.

Observe also in Illustration 10–4 that markups enter into the calculation of the cost ratio, but markdowns do not. It has long been customary in using the retail inventory method to add additional markups but to ignore markdowns in computing the percentage relation between goods for sale at cost and at retail. The justification for this was and is that a more conservative figure for the ending inventory results, a figure that approaches "cost or market, the lower." A further discussion of this phase of the retail inventory method is reserved for a more advanced text.

Gross profit method

Often retail price information about beginning inventory, purchases, and markups is not kept. In such cases the retail inventory method cannot be used. However, if a company knows its normal gross profit margin; has information at cost in regard to its beginning inventory, net purchases, and freight-in; and knows the amount of its sales and sales returns, the company can estimate its ending inventory by the gross profit method.

For example, on March 27, the inventory of a company was destroyed by a fire. The company's average gross profit rate during the past five or six years has been 30% of net sales, and on the date of the fire the company's accounts showed the following balances:

Sales	$31,500
Sales returns	1,500
Inventory, January 1, 19—	12,000
Net purchases	20,000
Freight-in	500

Since the March 27 inventory was totally destroyed by fire, it was necessary for insurance purposes to estimate the inventory by the gross profit method as shown in Illustration 10–5.

Illustration 10–5

Goods available for sale:		
Inventory, January 1, 19—		$12,000
Net purchases	$20,000	
Freight-in	500	20,500
Goods available for sale		$32,500
Less estimated cost of goods sold:		
Sales	$31,500	
Sales returns	1,500	
Net sales	$30,000	
Less estimated gross profit (30% of $30,000)	9,000	
Estimated cost of goods sold		21,000
Estimated March 27 inventory		$11,500

To understand Illustration 10–5, recall that in a normal situation an ending inventory is subtracted from goods for sale to determine cost of goods sold. Then observe in Illustration 10–5 that the opposite subtraction is made. In Illustration 10–5 estimated cost of goods sold is subtracted from goods for sale to arrive at the ending inventory.

In addition to its use in insurance cases, as in this illustration, the gross profit method is also commonly used by accountants in checking on the probable accuracy of a physical inventory taken and priced in the normal way.

Questions for class discussion

1. What is meant by the statement: "The inventory is turned over every 60 days"?

2. Why may it be said that ending inventory and cost of goods sold are opposite sides of the same coin?

3. Give the meanings of the following when applied to inventory:
   a) First-in, first-out.
   b) Fifo.
   c) Last-in, first-out.
   d) Lifo.
   e) Cost.
   f) Market.
   g) Cost or market, the lower.
   h) Perpetual inventory.
   i) Physical inventory.
   j) Book inventory.

4. If prices are rising, will the "Lifo" or the "Fifo" method of inventory valuation result in the higher gross profit?
5. May a company change its inventory pricing method at will?
6. Why do accountants require consistency in the application of accounting methods?
7. What are the elements of an inventory cost?
8. Why are incidental costs commonly ignored in pricing an inventory?
9. What is meant when it is said that inventory errors "correct themselves"?
10. If inventory errors "correct themselves," why be concerned when such errors are made?
11. What is a "regular markup"? A "markdown"?

Class exercises

Exercise 10-1

A concern began a year and purchased Product Z as follows:

Jan. 1	Beginning inventory......	10 units	@	$ 9.20	=	$ 92
Feb. 5	Purchased...................	40 units	@	10.00	=	400
June 8	Purchased...................	20 units	@	10.60	=	212
Aug. 3	Purchased...................	30 units	@	11.20	=	336
Dec. 9	Purchased...................	20 units	@	11.00	=	220
	Total......................	120 units				$1,260

Required:
Under the assumption the ending inventory consisted of 30 units, 10 from each of the last three purchases, determine the share of the $1,260 cost of the units for sale that should be assigned to the ending inventory and to goods sold under each of the following additional assumptions: (a) costs are assigned on the basis of specific invoice prices, (b) costs are assigned on a weighted average cost basis, (c) costs are assigned on the basis of Fifo, and (d) costs are assigned on the basis of Lifo.

Exercise 10-2

During an accounting period a company sold $78,000 of merchandise at marked retail prices. At the period end the following information was available from its records:

	At Cost	At Retail
Beginning inventory	$15,000	$21,000
Net purchases	55,000	74,000
Additional markups..		5,000
Markdowns...		2,000

Use the retail method to estimate what the store's ending inventory at cost would be.

Exercise 10-3

Assume that in addition to estimating its ending inventory by the retail method, the store of Exercise 10–2 also took a physical inventory at the marked selling prices of the inventory items. Assume further that the total of this physical inventory at marked selling prices was $19,500. Then (a) determine the amount of this inventory at cost and (b) determine the store's inventory shrinkage from breakage, theft, or other cause at retail and at cost.

Exercise 10-4

On January 1 a company had a $17,000 inventory at cost. During the first quarter of the year it purchased $65,000 of merchandise, returned $500, and paid freight charges on merchandise purchased totaling $3,500. During the past several years the company's gross profit on sales has averaged 35%. Under the assumption the company had $100,000 of sales during the first quarter of the year, use the gross profit method to estimate its end of the first quarter inventory.

Exercise 10-5

A company had $80,000 in sales during each of 197A, 197B, and 197C. It purchased merchandise costing $50,000 in each of the three years and in addition maintained a $10,000 inventory from the beginning to the end of the three-year period. However, at the end of 197A it made an error that caused its December 31, 197A, inventory to appear on its statements at $11,000, rather than the correct $10,000 amount.

Required:
1. State the actual amount of the company's gross profit in each of the years.
2. Prepare a comparative income statement, like the one illustrated in this chapter, showing the effect of this error on the company's cost of goods sold and gross profit for each of the three years.

Problems **Problem 10-1**

A concern that sells a single product began an accounting period with 300 units of the product, costing $50 each, and it made successive purchases of the product as follows:

Feb. 2 400 units @ $60 each
May 14 500 units @ 70 each
Aug. 2 400 units @ 80 each
Oct. 7 400 units @ 60 each

Required:
1. Prepare a calculation showing the number and total cost of the units for sale during the period.
2. Assume the concern had 500 units of the product in its December 31, end of the period periodic inventory and prepare calculations to show the portions of the total cost of the units for sale during the period that should be assigned

to ending inventory and to units sold (*a*) first on a Fifo basis, (*b*) then on a Lifo basis, and (*c*) finally on a weighted average cost basis.

Problem 10–2

A concern that keeps perpetual inventory records completed the following transactions involving Item ABX during January:

Jan. 1 Balance of Item ABX: 12 units costing $6 each.
     4 Received 20 units costing $7 each.
     9 Sold 10 units.
     15 Sold 15 units.
     19 Received 20 units costing $8 each.
     24 Sold 5 units.
     29 Sold 16 units.

Required:

1. Under the assumption the concern keeps its records on a Fifo basis, enter the beginning balance and the transactions on a perpetual inventory record card like the one illustrated in this chapter.
2. Under the assumption the concern keeps its inventory records on a Lifo basis, enter the beginning inventory and the transactions on a second inventory record card.
3. Assume the 16 units sold on January 29 were sold to Harry Kane at $12 each, and prepare a general journal entry to record the sale and the cost of the goods sold on a Lifo basis.

Problem 10–3

Apex Sales markets a single product that it sold at $10 per unit throughout the year just ended. Sales totaled 8,500 units during the year, and the company began the year and purchased the product as follows:

January 1 inventory	1,000 units at $5.60 per unit
Purchases:	
Feburary 5	1,000 units at $6.00 per unit
April 28	3,000 units at $6.20 per unit
August 22	4,000 units at $6.50 per unit
October 15	1,000 units at $7.00 per unit

Required:

Under the assumption the company incurred operating expenses totaling $2 per unit in marketing the 8,500 units of product, prepare three separate income statements for the concern. In the first show last year's results with the ending inventory based on Fifo, in the second use Lifo, and in the third base the ending inventory on a weighted average cost.

Problem 10–4

Campus Shop takes a year-end physical inventory at marked selling prices and reduces the total to a cost basis for year-end statement purposes. It also uses the retail method to estimate the amount of inventory it should have at the end of a year, and by comparison determines any inventory shortages due to shoplifting or other cause. At the end of the current year the following information was available to make the calculations:

	At Cost	At Retail
Sales		$117,340
Sales returns		1,870
January 1 inventory	$12,210	18,100
Purchases	83,385	119,900
Purchases returns	1,415	1,950
Additional markups		2,450
Markdowns		1,530
December 31 physical inventory		20,950

Required:
1. Use the retail method to estimate the shop's year-end inventory at cost.
2. Use the retail method to reduce the shop's year-end physical inventory to a cost basis.
3. Prepare a schedule showing the inventory shortage at cost and at retail.

Problem 10-5

On Monday morning November 12, the manager of Tops Store unlocked the store to learn that thieves had broken in over the weekend and stolen the entire inventory of the store. The following information for the period, January 1 through November 11, was available to establish the amount of the loss:

Sales	$139,550
Sales returns	1,050
Purchases	92,240
Purchases returns	510
Freight on purchases	870

The store had a $32,600 inventory on January 1 of the year of the theft, and it had earned an average 32% gross profit on sales during the past five years.

Required:
Prepare a statement showing the estimated amount of the store's loss.

Problem 10-6

A company that sells a single product began its 197A accounting period with 200 units of this product, costing $50 each, in its inventory. It also ended each of 197A, 197B, and 197C with 200 units of the product in its inventory. During these years it made sales as follows:

197A sales, 1,000 units at an average price of $115 per unit
197B sales, 1,000 units at an average price of $133 per unit
197C sales, 1,000 units at an average price of $138 per unit

During these years the company made successive purchases of the product as follows:

197A Purchases				197C Purchases		
200 units @ $55	=	$11,000		200 units @ $70	=	$14,000
200 units @ 50	=	10,000		400 units @ 65	=	26,000
300 units @ 60	=	18,000		200 units @ 65	=	13,000
300 units @ 65	=	19,500		200 units @ 75	=	15,000
1,000		$58,500		1,000		$68,000

197B Purchases		
500 units @ $60	=	$30,000
300 units @ 70	=	21,000
200 units @ 70	=	14,000
1,000		$65,000

Required:

1. Prepare three comparative income statements for the company, one for each year. Place each year's statement on four-column paper, showing in the first two columns the sales, calculation of cost of goods sold, and gross profit under the assumption the company priced its ending inventory on a Fifo basis, and showing in the second two columns the sales, cost of goods sold, and gross profit under the assumption the company priced its ending inventory on a Lifo basis.
2. Answer these questions: (*a*) Which inventory pricing method results in the smaller annual income for the company? (*b*) Which better synchronizes costs and revenues?

Alternate problems

Problem 10–1A

PART 1. The information which follows is available from a store's records:

	At Cost	At Retail
Year's sales		$221,560
Sales returns		2,345
January 1 inventory	$ 21,540	32,950
Purchases	146,490	219,735
Purchases returns	980	1,470
Additional markups		5,785
Markdowns		1,285

Required:

Using the retail method, prepare a calculation estimating the store's year-end inventory.

PART 2. The following information is available from a store's records:

January 1 inventory at cost	$ 42,850
Purchases	123,900
Purchases returns	1,200
Freight-in	2,680
Sales	189,900
Sales returns	3,400
Average gross profit rate	32%

The gross profit rate is an average for the past five years. The remaining figures are for a six-month period, January 1 through June 30.

Required:
Using the gross profit method, calculate the store's June 30 inventory.

Problem 10–2A

The perpetual inventory record card of Item XYZ showed the following transactions:

Jan. 1 Balance 5 units costing $5 each.
    2 Received 10 units costing $5.40 each.
    6 Sold 3 units.
  10 Sold 8 units.
  14 Received 8 units costing $6 each.
  18 Sold 3 units.
  28 Sold 4 units.

Required:
1. Assume the inventory record card for Item XYZ is kept on a Fifo basis and enter the beginning balance and transactions on the card.
2. Assume the inventory record card for Item XYZ is kept on a Lifo basis and enter the beginning balance and transactions on a second card.
3. Assume the four units sold on January 28 were sold on credit at $7.50 each to Lee Hale. Give the entry to record the sale and cost of goods sold on a Lifo basis.

Problem 10–3A

Beta Company began 197A with 100 units of the one product it sells. During the year it sold 850 units of the product at $200 per unit. The costs of the beginning inventory and purchases made during the year were as follows:

January 1 inventory	100 units @ $121 each
Purchases:	
January 28	300 units @ $120 each
April 29	200 units @ 125 each
July 27	300 units @ 129 each
December 2	100 units @ 132 each

Required:
Prepare three separate 197A income statements for Beta Company that are complete through the calculation of gross profit on sales. On the first income statement use an ending inventory based on Fifo, on the second use an ending inventory based on Lifo, and on the third use an inventory based on a weighted average cost.

Problem 10–4A

The following information is available from University Store's records at the end of the current year:

	At Cost	At Retail
January 1 inventory	$ 18,500	$ 28,450
Purchases	143,880	217,180
Purchases returns	1,180	1,820
Additional markups		4,190
Markdowns		2,110
Sales		220,120
Sales returns		1,830

University Store takes a year-end physical inventory at marked selling prices and reduces the total to a cost basis for statement purposes by an application of the retail method. This physical inventory totaled $27,200 at the end of the current year. However, the store also always estimates its year-end inventory by the retail method and by a comparison determines the amount of inventory shortage, if any.

Required:
1. Prepare a calculation to estimate the amount of the store's year-end inventory.
2. Use the store's cost ratio to reduce the amount of its year-end physical inventory to a cost basis.
3. Prepare a schedule showing the amount of inventory shrinkage at cost and at retail.

Problem 10–5A

The building occupied by Valley Sales burned on April 23; and everything except the accounting records, which were in a fireproof vault, was destroyed. You have been asked to prepare a claim for the inventory loss. The following information is available:

Merchandise inventory, January 1	$23,400
Sales January 1 through April 23	94,730
Sales returns for same period	2,230
Purchases from January 1 through April 23	61,520
Purchases returns for same period	1,260
Freight-in for same period	2,660
Average gross profit rate for past four years	34%

Required:
Prepare a statement showing an estimate of the store's April 23 inventory.

Decision problem 10–1, Family Shoe Store

Family Shoe Store suffered extensive damage from water and smoke and a small amount of fire damage on the night of October 27. The store carried adequate insurance, and next morning the insurance company's claims agent arrived to inspect the damage. After completing his survey, the agent agreed with Dan Kelley, the store's owner, that the inventory could be sold to a company specializing in fire sales for about one fifth its cost. The agent offered Mr. Kelley $20,000 in full settlement for the damage to the inventory. He suggested that Mr. Kelley accept the offer and said he had authority to deliver at once a check for the amount of the damage. He pointed out that a prompt settlement would provide funds to replace the inventory in time for the store to participate in the Christmas shopping season.

Mr. Kelley felt the loss might exceed $20,000, but he recognized that a time-consuming physical count and inspection of each item in the inventory would be necessary to establish the loss more precisely; and he was reluctant to take the time for the inventory, since he was anxious to get back into business before the Christmas rush, the season making the largest contribution to his annual profit. Yet he was also unwilling to take a substantial loss on the insurance settlement; so he asked for and received a 24-hour period in which to consider the insurance company offer, and he immediately went to his records for the following information:

	At Cost	At Retail
a) January 1 inventory..	$ 28,400	$ 45,600
Purchases, January 1 through October 27	173,100	279,100
Net sales, January 1 through October 27		281,300

b) On March 10 the remaining inventory of winter footwear was marked down from $10,000 to $8,000, and placed on sale in the annual end-of-the-winter-season sale. Three fourths of the shoes were sold; the markdown on the remainder was canceled, and the shoes were returned to their regular retail prices.

c) In June a special line of imported Italian shoes proved very popular, and 80 high-styled pairs were marked up from their normal $20 retail price to $25 per pair. Sixty pairs were sold at this higher price, and on August 1 the markup on the remaining 20 pairs was canceled and they were returned to their regular $20 per pair price.

d) Between January 1 and October 27 markdowns totaling $1,200 were taken on several odd lots of shoes.

Recommend whether or not you think Mr. Kelley should accept the insurance company's offer. Show all computations in good form.

Decision problem 10–2, City Center Furniture Store

City Center Furniture Store has been in business four years, during which it has earned a 34% average annual gross profit on sales. However, the night before last, on June 3, it suffered a disastrous fire that destroyed its entire inventory, and Josh Green, the store's owner, has filed a $53,320 inventory loss claim with the store's insurance company. When asked on what he based his claim, he replied that during the day before the fire he had marked every item in his store down 20% in preparation for his annual summer clearance sale, and during the marking-down process he had also taken an inventory of the merchandise in the store. Furthermore, he said, "It's a big loss, but every cloud has a silver lining, because I am giving you fellows (the insurance company) the benefit of the 20% markdown in filing this claim."

When it was explained to Mr. Green that he would have to back his loss claim with more than his word as to the amount of the loss, he produced the following information from his pre-sale inventory and his accounting records, which fortunately were in a fireproof vault and were not destroyed in the fire.

1. The store's accounts were closed on December 31 of last year.
2. After all posting was completed, the accounts showed these June 3 balances.

Sales	$193,970
Sales returns	5,470
Purchases	123,900
Purchases returns	1,250
Freight-in	2,730
Merchandise inventory (January 1, balance)	42,920

3. Mr. Green's pre-fire inventory totaled $66,650.

From the information given, present figures to show the amount of loss suffered by Mr. Green. Show how Mr. Green arrived at the amount of his loss claim. Can his pre-sale inventory be used to substantiate the amount of his actual loss? If so, use the pre-sale inventory figure to substantiate the actual loss amount.

Chapter 11

Plant and equipment

■ Assets that are used in the production or sale of other assets or services and that have a useful life longer than a single accounting period are classified for balance sheet purposes as *plant and equipment* or as *fixed assets*. The phrase "fixed assets" has been used in accounting literature for many years in referring to items of plant and equipment, and it was once commonly used as a balance sheet caption. However, as a caption it is rapidly disappearing from published balance sheets, being replaced by the more descriptive "plant and equipment" or the more complete "property, plant, and equipment" or by "land, buildings, and equipment."

Use in the production or sale of other assets or services is the characteristic that distinguishes a plant asset from an item of merchandise or an investment. An office machine or a factory machine held for sale by a dealer is merchandise to the dealer. Likewise, land purchased and held for future expansion but presently unused is classified for balance sheet purposes as a long-term investment. Neither should be classified as plant and equipment until put to use in the production or sale of other assets or services.

A productive or service life longer than one accounting period distinguishes an item of plant and equipment from an item of supplies. An item of supplies may be consumed in a single accounting period; and if consumed, its cost is charged to the period of consumption. The productive life of a plant asset, on the other hand, is longer than one period. A plant asset contributes to production for several periods; and if revenues and expenses are matched, its cost must be allocated to these periods on some fair basis.

Cost of plant and equipment

■ The cost of an item of plant and equipment includes all normal and reasonable expenditures necessary to get the asset in place and ready to use. For example, the cost of a factory machine includes its invoice price, less any discount for cash, plus freight, unpacking, and assembling. Cost also includes any special concrete base or foundation, electrical or power connections, and adjustments needed to place the machine in operation. In short, the cost of a plant asset includes all normal, necessary, and reasonable costs incurred in getting the asset ready to produce.

A cost must be normal and reasonable as well as necessary if it is to be properly included in the cost of a plant asset. For example, if a machine is damaged by being dropped in unpacking, repairs should not be added to its cost but should be charged to an expense account. Likewise, a fine paid for moving a heavy machine on city streets without proper permits is not part of the cost of the machine; although if secured, the cost of the permits would be part of the machine's cost.

After being purchased but before being put to use, a plant asset must sometimes be repaired, reconditioned, or remodeled before it meets the needs of the purchaser. In such a case the repairing, remodeling, or reconditioning expenditures are part of the cost of the asset and should be charged to the asset account. Furthermore, depreciation charges should not begin until the asset is ready for use.

When a plant asset is constructed or manufactured by a concern for its own use, cost includes the costs of materials and labor used plus a reasonable amount of overhead or indirect expenses such as heat, lights, power, and depreciation on the machinery used in constructing or manufacturing the asset. Cost also includes architectural and design fees, building permits, and insurance during construction. Insurance during construction is included because it is necessary to get the asset ready to produce or be used. Needless to say, insurance on the same asset after it has been placed in production is an expense.

When land is purchased for a plant or building site, its cost includes the amount paid for the land plus real estate commissions, escrow and legal fees, fees for examining and insuring the title, and any accrued property taxes paid by the purchaser. Cost also includes expenditures for surveying, clearing, grading, draining, and landscaping. All are part of the cost of the land. Furthermore, any assessments incurred at the time of purchase or later for such things as the installation of streets, sewers, and sidewalks should be debited to the Land account since they add a more or less permanent value to the land.

Land purchased as a building site sometimes has an old building that must be removed. In such cases the entire purchase price, including the amount paid for the to-be-removed building, should be charged to the Land account. Also, the cost of removing the old building, less any amounts recovered through the sale of salvaged materials, should be charged to this account.

Land used as a building site is assumed to have an unlimited life and is therefore not subject to depreciation. However, buildings and land improvements such as driveways, parking lots, fences, and lighting systems are subject to depreciation. Consequently, land, building, and land improvement costs should not be recorded in the same account. At least two accounts should be used, one for land and a second for buildings and land improvements; but three accounts, one for land, a second for buildings, and a third for land improvements, would be better.

Often land, buildings, and equipment are purchased together for one lump sum. When this occurs, the purchase price must be apportioned among the assets on some fair basis, since some of the assets depreciate and some do not. A fair basis may be tax-assessed values or appraised values. For example, assume that land independently appraised at $30,000 and a building appraised at $70,000 are purchased together for $90,000. The cost may be apportioned on the basis of appraised values as follows:

	Appraised Value	Percent of Total	Apportioned Cost
Land	$ 30,000	30%	$27,000
Building	70,000	70%	63,000
Totals	$100,000	100%	$90,000

Nature of depreciation

■ When a plant asset is purchased, in effect an amount or quantity of usefulness that will contribute to production throughout the life of the asset is acquired. Furthermore, since the life of any plant asset (other than land) is limited, this quantity of usefulness is also limited and will in effect be consumed over the asset's useful life. Therefore, depreciation, as the term is used in accounting, is nothing more than the expiration of a plant asset's amount of usefulness, and the recording of depreciation is a process of allocating and charging the cost of this usefulness to the accounting periods that benefit from the asset's use.

For example, when a company purchases an automobile to be used by one of its salesmen in making calls, it in effect purchases a quantity of usefulness, a quantity of transportation for the salesman. The cost of this quantity of usefulness is the cost of the car less whatever will be received for it when sold or traded in at the end of its useful life. And, recording depreciation on the car is a process of allocating the cost of this usefulness to the accounting periods that benefit from the car's use. It is not the recording of physical deterioration nor recording the decline in the car's market value.

The foregoing is in line with the pronouncements of the American Institute of Certified Public Accountants which has described depreciation as follows:

The cost of a productive facility is one of the costs of the services it renders during its useful economic life. Generally accepted accounting principles require that this cost be spread over the expected useful life of the facility in such a way as to allocate it as equitably as possible to the periods during which services are obtained from the use of the facility. This procedure is known as depreciation accounting, a system of accounting which aims to distribute the cost or other basic value of tangible capital assets, less salvage (if any), over the estimated useful life of the unit . . . in a systematic and rational manner. It is a process of allocation, not of valuation.[1]

Productive life of a plant asset

■ The productive or service life of a plant asset is the period of time its owner uses it in producing or selling other assets or services. This may not be the same as the asset's potential life. For example, typewriters have a potential 10- or 12-year life; however, if a company finds from a production-cost view that it is wise to trade its old typewriters on new ones every three years, in this company typewriters have a three-year service life. Furthermore, in this business the cost of new typewriters less their trade-in value, in other words the cost of their quantity of usefulness should be charged to depreciation expense over this three-year period.

At the time of purchase a plant asset's productive life must be predicted so that its depreciation may be allocated to the several periods in which it will be used. Predicting or estimating service life is sometimes difficult because several factors are often involved. Wear and tear and the action of the elements determine the useful life of some assets. However, two additional factors, *inadequacy* and *obsolescence,* often need be considered. When a business acquires plant assets, it should acquire assets of a size and capacity to take care of its foreseeable needs. However, a business often grows more rapidly than anticipated; and in such cases plant assets may become too small for the productive demands of the business long before they wear out. When this happens, inadequacy is said to have taken place. Inadequacy cannot easily be predicted. Obsolescence, like inadequacy, is also difficult to foretell because the exact occurrence of new inventions and improvements normally cannot be predicted; yet new inventions and improvements often cause an asset to become obsolete and make it wise to discard the obsolete asset long before it wears out.

A company that has previously used a particular type of asset may estimate the service life of a new asset of like kind from past experience. A company without previous experience with a particular asset must depend upon the experience of others or upon engineering studies and judgment. The Internal Revenue Service publishes information giving estimated service lives for hundreds of new assets. Many businessmen refer to this information in estimating the life of a new asset.

---

[1] *Accounting Research and Terminology Bulletins, Final Edition* (New York: American Institute of Certified Public Accountants, 1961), p. 76.

Salvage value ■ When a plant asset has a salvage value, the cost of its quantity of usefulness is the asset's cost minus its salvage value.

The salvage value of a plant asset is the portion of its cost that is recovered at the end of its productive life. Some assets such as typewriters, trucks, and automobiles are traded in on similar new assets at the end of their service lives. The salvage values of such assets are their trade-in values. Other assets may have no trade-in value and little or no salvage value. For example, at the end of its service life, some machinery can be sold only as scrap metal.

When the disposal of a plant asset involves certain costs, as in the wrecking of a building, the salvage value is the net amount realized from the sale of the asset. The net amount realized is the amount received for the asset less its disposal cost.

Obviously, when a plant asset is purchased, its exact salvage value is difficult to estimate. Yet, salvage value must be reasonably estimated so that depreciation can be estimated and recorded.

Allocating depreciation ■ Many methods of allocating a plant asset's total depreciation to the several accounting periods in its service life have been suggested and are used. Four of the more common are the *straight-line method,* the *units-of-production method,* the *declining-balance method,* and the *sum-of-the-years'-digits method.*

Straight-line method

When the straight-line method is used in allocating depreciation, the cost of the depreciating asset minus its estimated salvage value is divided by the estimated number of accounting periods in the asset's productive life. The result is the estimated amount the asset depreciates each period. For example, if a machine costs $550, has an estimated service life of five years, and an estimated $50 salvage value, its depreciation per year by the straight-line method is $100 and is calculated as follows:

$$\frac{\text{Cost} - \text{Salvage}}{\substack{\text{Service Life} \\ \text{in Years}}} = \frac{\$550 - \$50}{5} = \$100$$

Note that the straight-line method allocates an equal share of the cost of an asset's quantity of usefulness or an equal share of its total depreciation to each accounting period in its life.

Units-of-production method

The primary purpose of recording depreciation is to charge each accounting period in which an asset is used with a fair share of its depreciation. The straight-line method charges an equal share to each period; and when plant assets are used about the same amount in each accounting period, this method rather fairly allocates total depreciation. However, in some lines of business the use of certain plant assets varies greatly from accounting period to accounting period. For example, a contractor may use a particular piece of construction equipment for a month and then not use it again for many months. For such an asset, since use and contribution to revenue may not be uniform from period to period, the units-of-production method often more fairly allocates depreciation than does the straight-line method.

When the units-of-production method is used in allocating depreciation, the cost of an asset's quantity of usefulness is divided by the estimated units of product it will produce during its entire service life. This division gives depreciation per unit of product. Then the amount the asset depreciates in any one accounting period is determined by multiplying the units of product produced in that period by depreciation per unit. Units of product may be expressed as units of product or in any other unit of measure such as hours of use or miles driven. For example, a delivery truck costing $4,800 is estimated to have an $800 salvage value. If it is also estimated that during the truck's service life it will be driven 50,000 miles, the depreciation per mile, or the depreciation per unit of product, is $0.08. This is calculated as follows:

$$\frac{\text{Cost} \; - \; \text{Salvage Value}}{\begin{array}{c}\text{Estimated Units of}\\ \text{Production}\end{array}} = \begin{array}{c}\text{Depreciation per}\\ \text{Unit of Product}\end{array}$$

or

$$\frac{\$4,800 \; - \; \$800}{50,000 \text{ Miles}} = \$0.08 \text{ per Mile}$$

If these estimates are correct and the truck is driven 20,000 miles during its first year, depreciation for the first year is $1,600. This is 20,000 miles at $0.08 per mile. If the truck is driven 15,000 miles in the second year, depreciation for the second year is 15,000 times $0.08, or $1,200.

Declining-balance method

The Internal Revenue Code permits depreciation methods for tax purposes which result in higher depreciation charges during the early years of a plant asset's life. The declining-balance method is one of these. Under the declining-balance method, depreciation of up to twice the straight-line rate, without considering salvage value, may be applied each year to the declining book value of a new plant asset having an estimated life of three years or more. If this method is followed and twice the straight-line rate is used, the amount charged each year as depreciation expense on a plant asset is determined by (1) calculating a straight-line depreciation rate for the asset without considering the asset's salvage value; (2) doubling this rate; and then (3) at the end of each year in the asset's life, applying this doubled rate to the asset's remaining book value. (The book value of a plant asset is its cost less accumulated depreciation; it is the value shown for the asset on the books.)

If this method is used to charge depreciation on a $10,000 new asset that has an estimated five-year life and no salvage value, these steps are followed: (Step 1) A straight-line depreciation rate is calculated by dividing 100% by five (years) to determine the straight-line annual depreciation rate of 20%. Next (Step 2) this rate is doubled; and then (Step 3) annual depreciation charges are calculated as in the following table:

Year	Annual Depreciation Calculation	Annual Depreciation Expense	Remaining Book Value
1st year	40% of $10,000	$4,000.00	$6,000.00
2d year	40% of 6,000	2,400.00	3,600.00
3rd year	40% of 3,600	1,440.00	2,160.00
4th year	40% of 2,160	864.00	1,296.00
5th year	40% of 1,296	518.40	777.60

Under the declining-balance method the book value of a plant asset never reaches zero; consequently, when the asset is sold, exchanged, or scrapped, any remaining book value is used in determining the gain or loss on disposal.

In passing it should be observed that if an asset has a salvage value, the asset may not be depreciated beyond its salvage value. For example, if instead of no salvage value the foregoing $10,000 asset has an estimated $1,000 salvage value, depreciation for its fifth year is limited to $296, the amount required to reduce the asset's book value to its salvage value.

Sum-of-the-years'-digits method

Under this reducing fraction method, the years in an asset's service life are added and their sum becomes the denominator of a series of fractions used in allocating total depreciation to the periods in the asset's service life. The numerators of the fractions are the years in the asset's life in their reverse order.

For example, if the sum-of-the-years'-digits method is used in allocating depreciation on a machine costing $7,000, having an estimated five-year life and an estimated $1,000 salvage value, the sum of the years' digits in the asset's life is calculated:

$$1 + 2 + 3 + 4 + 5 = 15$$

and then annual depreciation charges are calculated as follows:

Year	Annual Depreciation Calculation	Annual Depreciation Expense
1st year	5/15 of $6,000	$2,000
2d year	4/15 of 6,000	1,600
3rd year	3/15 of 6,000	1,200
4th year	2/15 of 6,000	800
5th year	1/15 of 6,000	400
		$6,000

When either declining-balance or sum-of-the-years'-digits depreciation is used and accounting periods do not coincide with the years in an asset's life, additional calculations are necessary if depreciation is to be properly charged. For example, assume that the machine for which sum-of-the-years'-digits depreciation was calculated above is placed in use on April 1 and the annual accounting periods of the company owning the machine end on December 31. Under these assumptions the machine will be in use three fourths of a year during the first accounting period in its life; and as a result, this period should be charged with $1,500 depreciation ($2,000 × $\frac{3}{4}$ = $1,500). Likewise, the second accounting period should be charged with $1,700 depreciation [($\frac{1}{4}$ × $2,000) + ($\frac{3}{4}$ × $1,600) = $1,700], and like calculations should be used for the remaining periods in the asset's life.

The reducing charge methods (both the declining-balance and the sum-of-the-years'-digits method) are advocated by an increasing number of accountants who claim that their use results in a more equitable "use charge" for long-lived plant assets than other methods. These accountants point out, for example, that as assets grow older, repairs and maintenance increase. Therefore, when smaller amounts of depreciation computed by a reducing charge method are added to increasing repair costs, a more equitable total expense charge to match against revenue results. Also, they point out that as an asset grows older, in some instances its ability to produce revenue is reduced. For example, rentals from an apartment building are normally higher in the earlier years of its life but will decline as the building becomes less attractive and less modern. Certainly in such cases, a more reasonable allocation of cost would provide heavier depreciation charges in the earlier years and lighter charges in the later years of the asset's life.

The foregoing are sound reasons for the use under applicable conditions of reducing charge methods of allocating depreciation. However, a tax reason rather than sound accounting theory is probably more responsible for the increase in their popularity. The tax reason may be described as follows: Reducing charge methods of allocating depreciation normally result in the greatest amounts of depreciation expense during the early years of an asset's use. This in turn means smaller taxable incomes and taxes; and in effect it also means the interest-free use for a period of time of the amounts that would otherwise be paid in taxes under, for example, a straight-line method. Of course, these interest-free amounts must in effect be repaid in higher taxes during later years of the asset's use.

Recording depreciation

■ Depreciation on the several classes of a company's plant assets is recorded at the end of each accounting period by means of adjusting entries. This was discussed in an earlier chapter and needs no further amplification here.

■ In order to present as clearly as possible all the facts concerning the plant assets of a business, both the cost of such assets and their accumulated depreciation by functional classes are commonly shown on the balance sheet. For example, the plant assets of a merchandising concern may be shown as follows:

Plant Assets:		
Store equipment	$ 4,000	
Less accumulated depreciation	1,500	$ 2,500
Office equipment	$ 1,800	
Less accumulated depreciation	600	1,200
Building	$16,000	
Less accumulated depreciation	1,820	14,180
Land		3,000
Total Plant Assets		$20,880

When plant assets are shown in this manner, a balance sheet reader can see both the cost and the accumulated depreciation to the balance sheet date for each class of assets, and a much better picture is obtained than if only net undepreciated costs are given. When both costs and accumulated depreciation are shown, the reader can tell not only something of the physical adequacy of the assets but also something of their age. For example, $50,000 of assets with $45,000 accumulated depreciation are quite different from $5,000 of new assets. Yet, the net undepreciated cost is the same in both cases.

Financial statement readers who have never studied accounting sometimes mistakenly think that the amounts shown on a balance sheet as accumulated depreciation represent funds accumulated to buy new plant assets when present assets wear out and must be discarded. However, an informed reader recognizes that accumulated depreciation represents that portion of an asset's cost that has been charged off to depreciation expense during its life. He also knows that accumulated depreciation accounts are contra accounts having credit balances that cannot be used to buy anything. Furthermore, he knows that if a concern has cash with which to buy assets, it is shown on the balance sheet as a current asset "Cash."

■ From the discussion thus far the student should recognize that the recording of depreciation is not primarily a valuing process, rather it is a process of allocating the costs of plant assets to the several accounting periods that benefit from their use. Furthermore, he should recognize that because the recording of depreciation is an allocating process rather than a valuing process, balance sheets show for plant assets unallocated costs or undepreciated costs rather than market values.

The fact that balance sheets show undepreciated costs rather than market values seems to disturb many beginning accounting students. It should not. When a balance sheet is prepared, normally the company for which it is prepared has no intention of selling its plant assets; consequently, the market values of these assets are of no great significance. The student should recognize that when a balance sheet is prepared, it is under the assumption the company for which it is prepared is a going concern that will continue in business long enough to recover the costs of its plant assets through the sale of its products.

The assumption that a company is a going concern that will continue in business long enough to recover its plant asset costs through the sale of its products is known in accounting as the *going-concern concept.* It is a concept the student or any balance sheet reader should bear in mind as he reads a balance sheet.

Recovering the cost of plant assets ■ A company that earns a profit or breaks even (neither earns a profit nor suffers a loss) eventually recovers the cost of its plant assets through the sale of its products. This is best explained with a condensed income statement like that of Illustration 11–1.

Even Steven Company
Income Statement for Year Ended December 31, 19—

Sales		$100,000
Cost of goods sold	$60,000	
Rent expense	10.000	
Salaries expense	25,000	
Depreciation expense	5,000	
Total		100,000
Net Income		$ 0

Illustration 11–1

Even Steven Company broke even during the year of the illustrated income statement; but in breaking even it also recovered $5,000 of the cost of its plant assets through the sale of its products. It recovered the $5,000 because of the $100,000 that flowed into the company from sales only $95,000 flowed out to pay for goods sold, rent, and salaries. No funds flowed out for depreciation expense; and as a result, the company recovered this $5,000 portion of the cost of its plant assets through the sale of its products. Furthermore, if the company remains in business for the life of its plant assets, either breaking even or earning a profit, it will during the life of the plant assets recover their entire cost in this manner.

At this point students commonly ask, "Where is the recovered $5,000?" The answer is that the company may have the $5,000 in the bank. If it does, its bank balance increased $5,000 during the year. However, the money may also have flowed out to increase merchandise inventory, to buy additional equipment, to pay off a debt, or it may have been withdrawn for personal use by the business owner. In short, the cash may still be in the bank or it may have been used for any purpose for which a business uses cash, and only an examination of its balance sheets as of the beginning and end of the year will show this.

Discarding and selling a plant asset

■ Sooner or later a plant asset wears out, becomes obsolete, or becomes inadequate; and when this occurs, the asset is discarded. If its service life and salvage value estimates were correct, the discarded asset may be sold for its salvage value. For example, a small drill press costing $900 and having an estimated four-year service life and an estimated $100 salvage value depreciates $200 each year of its life. At the end of its fourth and last year the drill press has a $100 book value, and the accounts that show its accounting history and book value appear as follows:

Machinery		Accumulated Depreciation, Machinery	
Jan. 2, '69	900	Dec. 31, '69	200
		Dec. 31, '70	200
		Dec. 31, '71	200
		Dec. 31, '72	200

If at the end of its fourth year the drill press is discarded and sold for its book value, the entry to record the sale is:

Jan.	2	Cash...	100.00	
		Accumulated Depreciation, Machinery..............	800.00	
		Machinery...		900.00
		Sold machinery at book value.		

In the entry just given the debit to the accumulated depreciation account and the credit to the Machinery account remove the machine's cost from the accounts and end its accounting history.

Discarding and selling plant assets at a gain or a loss

■ Exactly estimating salvage value or exactly estimating service life is not easy. Normally one estimate or the other is incorrect. Consequently, when a plant asset is discarded and sold, and either its salvage value or service life was incorrectly estimated, a book gain or a book loss is incurred. For example, if the drill press previously illustrated as having an estimated $100 salvage value is sold at the end of its service life for only $60, a $40 book loss is incurred. The entry to record the sale at a loss is:

Jan.	2	Cash...	60.00	
		Loss on the Sale of Plant Assets......................	40.00	
		Accumulated Depreciation, Machinery..............	800.00	
		Machinery...		900.00
		Sold a drill press at a loss.		

Or assume that the drill press is sold at the end of its service life for $125. If the machine is sold for $125, a $25 book gain is made. This is recorded:

Jan.	2	Cash..	125.00	
		Accumulated Depreciation, Machinery..............	800.00	
		Machinery		900.00
		Gain on the Sale of Plant Assets................		25.00
		Sold a drill press at a profit.		

To illustrate further, assume that an error is made in estimating service life and the drill press previously illustrated wears out and must be discarded at the end of the third year in its estimated four-year service life. At that time the asset has a $300 book value; this is its $900 cost less three years' depreciation totaling $600. If the drill press is sold at the end of its third year for its estimated $100 salvage value, the entry to record the sale is:

Jan.	2	Cash..	100.00	
		Loss on the Sale of Plant Assets.....................	200.00	
		Accumulated Depreciation, Machinery..............	600.00	
		Machinery		900.00
		Sold a drill press at a loss.		

If, on the other hand, the estimated life of the drill press is too short, the machine will be in use after the end of its estimated service life. Normally, in such a situation, no depreciation is charged for the years after the end of the estimated life, and the asset is carried on the books at its salvage value. When the asset is finally discarded, a gain or loss is recorded if the asset is sold for more or less than its salvage value.

Plant asset gains and losses on the income statement ■ When a plant asset is sold, it is normally sold at either a gain or loss. These gains and losses are recorded at the time of each sale in either a gain or loss account; and at the end of each period these accounts are closed to Income Summary, and their balances appear on the income statement, at the very end, in a section called "Extraneous gains and losses." Here gains are added and losses are subtracted from income from operations.

Discarding plant assets because of damage ■ Occasionally, before the end of its service life, a plant asset may be wrecked in an accident or destroyed by fire; and in such cases a loss occurs. If an uninsured asset is totally destroyed in an accident such as a fire, the entry to record the loss is:

Jan.	3	Loss from Fire	500.00	
		Accumulated Depreciation, Machinery..............	400.00	
		Machinery		900.00
		To record the accidental destruction of machinery.		

If the loss is partially covered by insurance, the money received from the insurance company is debited to Cash and the loss is less. The entry to record an accidental loss partially covered by insurance is:

Jan.	3	Cash...	350.00	
		Loss from Fire	150.00	
		Accumulated Depreciation, Machinery..............	400.00	
		Machinery		900.00
		To record the destruction of machinery and the receipt of insurance compensation.		

Depreciation for partial years

■ In most of the illustrations thus far it has been assumed that the assets were purchased and discarded at either the beginning or end of an accounting period. This is an assumption that seldom occurs. Businessmen normally buy assets when needed and sell or discard these assets when they are no longer usable or needed; and the purchases and sales are normally made without regard for time. Because of this, depreciation must often be calculated for partial years. For example, a truck costing $2,600 and having an estimated five-year service life and a $600 estimated salvage value is purchased on October 8, 1968. If the yearly accounting period ends on December 31, depreciation for three months must be recorded on this truck on that date. Three months are three twelfths of a year. Consequently, the three months' depreciation is calculated:

$$\frac{\$2,600 - \$600}{5} \times \frac{3}{12} = \$100$$

In this illustration, depreciation is calculated for a full three months, even though the asset was purchased on October 8. Depreciation is an estimate; therefore calculation to the nearest full month is usually considered sufficiently accurate. This means that depreciation is usually calculated for a full month on assets purchased before the 15th of the month. Likewise, depreciation for the month in which an asset is purchased is normally disregarded if the asset is purchased after the middle of the month.

The entry to record depreciation for three months on the truck purchased on October 8 is:

Dec.	31	Depreciation Expense, Delivery Trucks..................	100.00	
		Accumulated Depreciation, Delivery Trucks......		100.00
		To record depreciation for three months on		
		the delivery truck.		

On December 31, 1969, and at the end of each of the following three years, a journal entry to record a full year's depreciation on this truck is made. The entry is:

Dec.	31	Depreciation Expense, Delivery Trucks..................	400.00	
		Accumulated Depreciation, Delivery Trucks......		400.00
		To record depreciation for one year on the		
		delivery truck.		

After the December 31, 1972, depreciation entry is recorded, the accounts showing the history of this truck appear as follows:

Delivery Trucks		Accumulated Depreciation, Delivery Trucks	
Oct. 8, '68 2,600		Dec. 31, '68 100	
		Dec. 31, '69 400	
		Dec. 31, '70 400	
		Dec. 31, '71 400	
		Dec. 31, '72 400	

If this truck is disposed of during 1973, two entries must be made to record the disposal. The first records 1973 depreciation to the date of disposal, and the second records the actual disposal. For example, assume that the truck is sold for $900 on June 24, 1973. To record the disposal, depreciation for six months (depreciation to the nearest full month) must first be recorded. The entry for this is:

June	24	Depreciation Expense, Delivery Trucks..................	200.00	
		Accumulated Depreciation, Delivery Trucks......		200.00
		To record depreciation for one-half year on		
		the delivery truck.		

After making the entry to record depreciation to the date of sale, a second entry to record the actual sale is made. This entry is:

June	24	Cash...	900.00	
		Accumulated Depreciation, Delivery Trucks	1,900.00	
		Delivery Trucks		2,600.00
		Gain on the Sale of Plant Assets....................		200.00
		To record the sale of a delivery truck.		

Plant asset records ■ Business concerns commonly divide their plant assets into functional groups and provide separate asset and accumulated depreciation accounts for each group. For example, a store will normally provide an Office Equipment account and an Accumulated Depreciation, Office Equipment account, as well as a Store Equipment account and an Accumulated Depreciation, Store Equipment account. In short, the store will normally have a separate plant asset account and a separate accumulated depreciation account for each functional group of assets it owns. Furthermore, all transactions affecting any one of the functional groups are recorded in the asset and the accumulated depreciation accounts of that group. For example, the purchase, depreciation, exchange, or sale of all office equipment is recorded in the one office equipment and its related accumulated depreciation account.

Some years ago the functional general ledger plant asset accounts and their related accumulated depreciation accounts were often the only plant asset records maintained by any but larger concerns. However, today because of income tax regulations any business that reports a deduction from income for depreciation or reports a gain or loss on a plant asset sale must be able to substantiate such items with detailed records. No specific kind of records is required, but normally each general ledger plant asset account and its related accumulated depreciation account become controlling accounts controlling detailed subsidiary records. For example, the Office Equipment account and the Accumulated Depreciation, Office Equipment account control a subsidiary ledger having a separate record for each individual item of office equipment. Likewise, the Store Equipment account and its related Accumulated Depreciation, Store Equipment account become controlling accounts controlling a subsidiary store equipment ledger. Often these subsidiary ledger records are kept on plant asset record cards.

To illustrate these plant asset records, assume that a concern's office equipment consists of just one desk and a chair. The general ledger record of these assets is maintained in the Office Equipment controlling account and the Accumulated Depreciation, Office Equipment controlling account. Since in this case there are only two assets, only two subsidiary record cards are needed. The general ledger and subsidiary ledger record of these assets appear as in Illustration 11–2 on the following two pages.

The information given on the subsidiary plant asset record cards is in the main self-evident. Note how the balance of the general ledger account, Office Equipment, is equal to the sum of the balances in the asset record section of the two subsidiary ledger cards. The general ledger account controls this section of the subsidiary ledger. Note also how the Accumulated Depreciation, Office Equipment account controls the depreciation record section of the cards. The disposition section at the bottom of the card is used to record the final disposal of the asset. When the asset is discarded, sold, or exchanged, a note telling of the final dis-

			Office Equipment			ACCOUNT NO. 132
DATE	EXPLANATION	FO-LIO	DEBIT	CREDIT	BALANCE
1970 July 2	Desk and chair	G-1	185 00		185 00

			Accumulated Depreciation, Office Equipment			ACCOUNT NO. 132A
DATE	EXPLANATION	FO-LIO	DEBIT	CREDIT	BALANCE
1970 Dec. 31		G-23		4 50	4 50
1971 Dec. 31		G-42		9 00	13 50
1972 Dec. 31		G-65		9 00	22 50

Illustration
11–2

Plant Asset
No. 1

SUBSIDIARY PLANT ASSET AND DEPRECIATION RECORD

Item _Office chair_

General Ledger
Account _Office Equipment_

Description _Office chair_

Mfg. Serial No. _____

Purchased
from _Office Equipment Co._

Where Located _Office_

Person Responsible for the Asset _Office Manager_
Estimated Life _12 years_ Estimated Salvage Value _$4.00_
Depreciation per Year _$3.00_ per Month _$0.25_

Date	Explanation	F	Asset Record			Depreciation Record		
			Dr.	Cr.	Bal.	Dr.	Cr.	Bal.
July 2, '70		G1	40.00		40.00			
Dec. 31, '70		G23					1.50	1.50
Dec. 31, '71		G42					3.00	4.50
Dec. 31, '72		G65					3.00	7.50

Final Disposition of the Asset _____

Illustration
11–2
Continued

position is entered here. The card is then removed from the subsidiary ledger and filed for future reference.

Plant assets of low cost ■ Because individual plant asset records are expensive to keep, many concerns establish a minimum, say $25, and do not keep such records for assets costing less than the minimum. Rather, they charge the cost of

Plant Asset
No. 2

SUBSIDIARY PLANT ASSET AND DEPRECIATION RECORD

General Ledger
Item Desk   Account Office Equipment
Description Office desk

Purchased
Mfg. Serial No.   from   Office Equipment Co.
Where Located   Office
Person Responsible for the Asset Office Manager
Estimated Life 20 years   Estimated Salvage Value $25.00
Depreciation per Year $6.00 per Month $0.50

Date	Explanation	F	Asset Record			Depreciation Record		
			Dr.	Cr.	Bal.	Dr.	Cr.	Bal.
July 2, '70		G1	145.00		145.00			
Dec. 31, '70		G23					3.00	3.00
Dec. 31, '71		G42					6.00	9.00
Dec. 31, '72		G65					6.00	15.00

Final Disposition of the Asset

such assets directly to an expense account at the time of purchase; and if about the same amount is expended for such assets each year, this is an acceptable procedure.

Questions for class discussion

1. What are the characteristics of an asset classified as a plant asset?
2. What is the balance sheet classification of land held for future expansion? Why is such land not classified as a plant asset?
3. What in general is included in the cost of a plant asset?
4. A company asked for bids from several machine shops for the construction of a special machine. The lowest bid was $12,500. The company decided to build the machine for itself and did so at a total cash outlay of $10,000. It then recorded the machine's construction with a debit to Machinery for $12,500, a credit to Cash for $10,000, and credit to Gain on the Construction of Machinery for $2,500. Was this a proper entry? Discuss.
5. As used in accounting, what is the meaning of the term depreciation?
6. Does the recording of depreciation cause a plant asset to appear on the balance sheet at market value? What is accomplished by recording depreciation?
7. Is it possible to keep a plant asset in such an excellent state of repair that recording depreciation is unnecessary?
8. A company has just purchased a machine that has a potential life of 15 years. However, the company's management believes that the development of a more efficient machine will make it necessary to replace the just-

purchased machine in eight years. What period of useful life should be used in calculating depreciation on this machine?

9. A building estimated to have a useful life of 30 years was completed at a cost of $85,000. It was estimated that at the end of the building's life it would be wrecked at a cost of $1,000 and that materials salvaged from the wrecking operation would be sold for $2,000. How much straight-line depreciation should be charged on the building?

10. Define the following terms as used in accounting for plant assets:

   a) Trade-in value.   *c)* Book value.   *e)* Inadequacy.

   b) Market value.   *d)* Salvage value.   *f)* Obsolescence.

11. Does the balance of the account, Accumulated Depreciation, Machinery, represent funds accumulated to replace the machinery as it wears out? Tell in your own words what the balance of such an account represents.

12. What is the essence of the going-concern concept of a business?

13. Explain how a concern that breaks even recovers the cost of its plant assets through the sale of its products. Where are the funds thus recovered?

14. Straight-line depreciation assigns an equal share of the cost of a plant asset's amount of usefulness to each accounting period in which the asset is used. Describe a situation in which this might not be a fair basis of allocation. Name a more fair basis for the situation described.

Class exercises

Exercise 11–1

A machine was purchased for $2,500, terms 2/10, n/60, FOB factory. The invoice was paid within the discount period along with $135 freight charges. The machine required a special concrete base and power connections costing $265, and $170 was paid a millwright to assemble the machine and get it into operation. Also, raw materials costing $50 were consumed in adjusting the machine so that it would produce a satisfactory product. The product produced while the adjustments were being made was not salable. Prepare a schedule to show the cost of the machine.

Exercise 11–2

Three machines were purchased for $8,640 at an auction sale of a bankrupt company's machinery. The purchaser paid $400 to transport the machines to his factory. Machine No. 1 was twice as big and weighed twice as much as Machine No. 2. Machines 2 and 3 were approximately equal in size and weight. The machines had the following appraised values and installation costs:

	Machine No. 1	Machine No. 2	Machine No. 3
Appraised values	$5,000	$4,000	$3,000
Installation costs..................	300	200	150

Determine the cost of each machine for accounting purposes.

Exercise 11–3

A machine was installed in a factory at a $16,500 cost. Its useful life was estimated at five years or 50,000 units of product with a $1,500 trade-in value. During its second year the machine produced 12,000 units of product. Determine the machine's second-year depreciation with depreciation calculated in each of the following ways: (*a*) straight-line basis, (*b*) units-of-production basis, (*c*) declining-balance basis at twice the straight-line rate, and (*d*) sum-of-the-years'-digits basis.

Exercise 11–4

A machine cost $2,000 installed and was estimated to have a four-year life and a $200 trade-in value. Use declining-balance depreciation at twice the straight-line rate to determine the amount of depreciation to be charged against the machine in each of the four years of its life.

Exercise 11–5

A machine was installed on January 6, 197A, at a total cost of $4,800. A full year's depreciation on a straight-line basis was charged against the machine on each of December 31, 197A, 197B, and 197C, under the assumption the machine would have a four-year life and no salvage value. The machine was disposed of on March 31, 197D. (*a*) Give the entry to record the partial year's depreciation on March 31, 197D, and give the entries to record the disposal under each of the following unrelated assumptions: (*b*) the machine was sold for $1,000; (*c*) the machine was sold for $850; and (*d*) the machine was totally destroyed in a fire and the insurance company settled the insurance claim for $750.

Problems   **Problem 11–1**

PART 1.   A machine costing $17,000 was installed in a factory. Its useful life was estimated at four years, after which it would have a $2,000 trade-in value; and it was estimated the machine would produce 75,000 units of product during its life. It actually produced the following numbers of units: year 1, 16,000; year 2, 21,000; year 3, 20,000; and year 4, 18,000.

Required:
1. Prepare a calculation showing the number of dollars of this machine's cost that should be charged to depreciation over its four-year life.
2. Prepare a form with the following column headings:

Year	Straight Line	Units of Production	Declining Balance	Sum of the Years' Digits

Then show the depreciation for each year and the total depreciation for the machine under each depreciation method. Use twice the straight-line rate for the declining-balance method.

PART 2.   A secondhand truck was purchased for $1,950 on March 12, 197A. The next day $135 was paid for building special racks and shelves in the truck and $130 for a new set of tires. The tires were priced at $142, but a $12 trade-in allowance was received for the truck's old tires. Give the entries for the purchase of the truck, payment for the racks and shelves, and payment for the tires.

PART 3.   At the time of purchase it was estimated the foregoing Part 2 truck had a remaining 30,000 miles in its service life and that it would have a $415 trade-in value at the end of its life. During 197A the truck was driven 7,000 miles; and between January 1, 197B, and October 10, 197B, it was driven an additional 9,000 miles. On the latter date it was retired from service. Give the entries to record the 197A and 197B depreciation. Also, give the entries to record the retirement under each of the following unrelated assumptions: (*a*) The truck was sold on October 10, 197B, for $1,300. (*b*) It was totally destroyed in a wreck, and the insurance company paid $1,000 in full settlement of the loss claim.

Problem 11–2

Company X and Company Y are identical in almost every respect. Both began business on January 2 of last year with store equipment costing $25,000, having a 10-year life, and a $5,000 salvage value; neither added to its equipment during the year; and both purchased merchandise as follows:

Jan. 2	100 units @	$50 each
Mar. 17	200 units @	48 each
June 29	300 units @	55 each
Oct. 10	200 units @	58 each
Dec. 18	100 units @	60 each

At the year-end, before recording depreciation, their ledgers showed the following revenues and expenses:

	Company X	*Company Y*
Sales	$80,000	$80,000
Salaries expense	15,000	15,000
Rent expense	3,000	3,000
Other expenses	500	500

However, Company X decided to use declining-balance depreciation at twice the straight-line rate, while Company Y chose straight-line depreciation. Also, Company X priced its 150-unit ending inventory on a Lifo basis, while Company Y used Fifo for its 150-unit inventory.

Required:

1. Prepare an income statement for each company showing last year's results.
2. Prepare a schedule accounting for the difference in their net incomes.

Problem 11–3

A company purchased five machines during 197A, 197B, and 197C, and has used four ways to allocate depreciation on the machines. Information about the machines follows:

Machine Number	Placed in Use on	Cost	Estimated Life	Salvage Value	Depreciation Method
1	Oct. 2, 197A	$ 6,000	8 years	$ 400	Straight line
2	June 28, 197A	20,000	8 years	2,000	Sum of the years' digits
3	Apr. 12, 197B	36,000	60,000 units	3,000	Units of production
4	Aug. 29, 197B	24,000	8 years	4,000	Declining balance
5	June 30, 197C	?	10 years	2,000	Declining balance

Twice the straight-line rate was used for declining-balance depreciation. Machine No. 3 produced 6,000 units of product in 197B and 8,400 units in 197C. Machine No. 5 had an invoice price of $29,500, 2/10, n/60, FOB factory. The invoice was paid on the last day of the discount period, June 29, but the company had to borrow $20,000 in order to do so (90-day, 8% note). The loan was repaid on September 27. Freight charges on Machine No. 5 were $240, and the machine was placed on a special concrete base that cost $475. It was assembled and installed by the company's own employees. Their wages during the installation period amounted to $375. Payments for the freight charges, the concrete base, and the employees' wages were made on July 2.

Required:
1. Prepare a form with the following columnar headings:

Machine Number	Amount to Be Charged to Depreciation	197A Depreciation	197B Depreciation	197C Depreciation

Enter the machine numbers in the first column and complete the information opposite each machine's number. Total the columns.
2. Prepare entries to record all transactions involving the purchase of Machine No. 5, including the note transactions.
3. Prepare an entry to record the 197C depreciation on the machines.

Problem 11–4

Service Market completed the following plant asset transactions over a two-year period:

197A

Jan. 3 Purchased on credit a Superior scale from Alpha Equipment Company for $265. The serial number of the scale was B-23452, its service life was estimated at 10 years, and its trade-in value at $25.

5 Purchased on credit a Coldaire refrigerated display case from Alpha Equipment Company for $3,200. The serial number of the display case was 00–23234, its service life was estimated at eight years, and its trade-in value at $800.

Apr. 7 Purchased on credit a Regal cash register for $323 from Beta Equipment Company. The serial number of the cash register was 3–32564, its service life was estimated at eight years, and its trade-in value at $35.

Dec. 31 Recorded the 197A depreciation on the store equipment.

197B

Oct. 28 Sold the Regal cash register to Thomas Seay for $250 cash.

28 Purchased on credit a new King cash register from Beta Equipment Company for $360. The serial number of the cash register was XXX-12435, its service life was estimated at 10 years, and its trade-in value at $48.

Dec. 31 Recorded the 197B depreciation on the store equipment.

Required:
1. Open general ledger accounts for Store Equipment and Accumulated Depreciation, Store Equipment. Prepare as needed a subsidiary plant asset ledger card for each item of equipment owned by Service Market.

2. Prepare general journal entries to record the plant asset transactions completed by Service Market, and post to the proper general ledger and subsidiary ledger accounts.

3. Prove the December 31, 197B, balances of the Store Equipment and Accumulated Depreciation, Store Equipment accounts by preparing from the subsidiary plant asset ledger cards a list showing the cost and accumulated depreciation of each store equipment item owned by Service Market on that date.

Problem 11–5

Timber Manufacturing Company was organized early in January of the current year; and in making your audit of the company's records at the end of its first year, you have discovered that the company's bookkeeper has debited an account called "Land, Buildings, and Equipment" for what he thought was the cost of the company's new factory. The account has a $761,225 debit balance made up of the following items:

Cost of land and old building purchased as the site of the company's plant (appraised value of the land, $100,000, and of an old building on the site, $10,000)	$105,000
Attorney's fee for title search to assure a clear title to the land	500
Cost of removing old building from site	4,000
Cost of grading plant site	500
Architect's fee for planning new building	16,500
Cost of new building (Contract price, $372,000; but in lieu of cash, the contractor accepted a number of bonds which Timber Manufacturing Company had purchased as a temporary investment while waiting for the building's completion. The cost of the bonds, $380,000, had been debited to an account called Temporary Investments. Their fair market value on the day given to the contractor was $372,000.)	380,000
Cost of landscaping the plant site	9,000
Cost of concrete walks and paving the parking lot	5,400
Cost of installing parking lot lights	900
Factory machinery and equipment (including the $1,700 cost of a machine dropped and made useless while being unloaded from a freight car)	216,300
Fine and permit for hauling heavy machinery on city streets (The company was cited for hauling the machinery without a permit and it then secured the permit. The fine was $200 and the cost of the permit was $25.)	225
Cost of machinery installation	21,200
Cost of damaged machine replaced	1,700
Total	$761,225

An examination of the payroll records showed that an account called "Superintendence" had been debited for the plant superintendent's $12,500 salary for the 10-month period, March 1 through December 31. From March 1 through August 31 the superintendent had supervised construction of the factory building. During September and October he supervised installation of the factory machinery.

The bookkeeper had set up an account called "Miscellaneous Revenues" and had credited it for the $500 proceeds from the sale of materials salvaged from the old building removed from the plant site and for $25 from the sale of the wrecked machine.

Required:
1. Prepare a four-column form having column headings for the following plant assets: Land, Land Improvements, Buildings, and Machinery. List the items and sort their amounts to the proper asset columns under the assumption the company's manufacturing operations began on November 1. Show a negative item by enclosing it in parentheses. Total the columns.
2. Under the assumption that none of the accounts used by the bookkeeper had been closed, prepare an entry to remove the foregoing item amounts from the accounts in which they were incorrectly entered and to enter them in the proper accounts.
3. Prepare an entry to record depreciation expense for the partial year. Assume the building and land improvements will have a 30-year life and no salvage value and that the machinery will have a 12-year life and a salvage value equal to 10% of its cost.

Alternate problems

Problem 11–1A

PART 1.   A machine having an estimated four-year life and a $400 salvage value was installed at a total cost of $4,600. It was estimated the machine would produce 60,000 units of product during its life. It actually produced the following numbers: year 1, 12,000; year 2, 17,000; year 3, 18,000; and year 4, 13,000.

Required:
1. Prepare a calculation to show the total number of dollars of this machine's cost that should be charged to depreciation during its four-year life.
2. Prepare a form with the following column headings:

Year	Straight Line	Units of Production	Declining Balance	Sum of the Years' Digits

Then enter on the form the depreciation for each year and the total depreciation on the machine under each depreciation method. Use twice the straight-line rate for declining-balance depreciation.

PART 2.   A secondhand machine was purchased for $1,845 on January 2, 197A. The next day it was repaired and repainted at a cost of $210 and was installed on a new concrete base that cost $125. It was estimated the machine would have a three-year life and a $380 salvage value. Depreciation was to be charged on a straight-line basis. A full year's depreciation was charged against the machine on December 31, 197A; and on June 27, 197B, the machine was retired from service.

Required:
1. Prepare entries to record the purchase of the machine, the cost of repairing and repainting it, and its installation. Assume cash was paid in each case.
2. Give the entries to record the 197A and 197B depreciation on the machine.
3. Give the entries to record its retirement under each of the following un-

related assumptions: (*a*) The machine was sold for $1,350. (*b*) It was totally destroyed in a fire and the insurance company paid $1,200 in full settlement of the loss claim.

Problem 11–3A

A concern purchased five machines during 197A and 197B. Machine No. 1 was placed in use on October 3, 197A. It cost $26,500, had an estimated six-year life and a $2,500 salvage value, and was depreciated on a straight-line basis. Machine No. 2 was placed in use on November 12, 197A, and was depreciated on a units-of-production basis. It cost $20,000 and it was estimated that it would produce 90,000 units of product during its eight-year life, after which it would have an estimated $2,000 salvage value. It produced 1,200 units in 197A, 8,200 units in 197B, and 19,500 in 197C. Machines 3, 4, and 5 were purchased from a bankrupt firm at auction for $85,800 in cash on March 5, 197B, and were first placed in use on April 2 of that year. Additional information about the machines follows:

Machine Number	Appraised Value	Salvage Value	Estimated Life	Installation Cost	Depreciation Method
3	$40,000	$4,000	8 years	$ 800	Declining balance
4	25,000	2,000	10 years	500	Declining balance
5	45,000	3,000	6 years	1,500	Sum of the years' digits

Required:
1. Prepare a form with the following columnar headings:

Machine Number	Amount to Be Charged to Depreciation	197A Depreciation	197B Depreciation	197C Depreciation

Enter the machine numbers in the first column, complete the information opposite each machine number, and total the columns. Assume that twice the straight-line rate was used for declining-balance depreciation.
2. Prepare entries to record payment for Machines 3, 4, and 5 and for their installation. Assume that cash was paid for the installation on the day the machines were placed in use.
3. Prepare an entry to record the 197C, depreciation on the five machines.

Problem 11–4A

Corona Company completed the following plant asset transactions during a two-year period:

197A
Jan. 7 Purchased on credit from Zippo, Inc., a Zippo calculator, $720. The serial number of the machine was X2X345. Its service life was estimated at eight years with a $144 trade-in value.

  9 Purchased on credit an Accurate typewriter from Office Outfitters for $435. The machine's serial number was MMM-0156, its service life was estimated at five years, and its trade-in value at $135.

Mar. 27 Purchased a Quicko adding machine from Office Outfitters for $385. The serial number of the machine was STM-1176. Its service life was estimated at eight years with a $97 trade-in value.

Dec. 31 Record the 197A depreciation on the office equipment.

197B

June 3 Sold the Accurate typewriter for $365 cash.

      4 Purchased on credit a new Speedy typewriter for $350 from Speedway Typewriter Company. The machine's serial number was MO7781. Its service life was estimated at five years with an $80 trade-in value.

Dec. 31 Recorded the 197B depreciation on the office equipment.

Required:

1. Open Office Equipment and Accumulated Depreciation, Office Equipment accounts plus subsidiary plant asset record cards as needed.
2. Prepare general journal entries to record the foregoing transactions. Post to the general ledger accounts and the subsidiary record cards.
3. Prove the December 31, 197B, balance of the Office Equipment and Accumulated Depreciation, Office Equipment accounts by preparing with totals a schedule showing the cost and accumulated depreciation of each plant asset owned on that date.

Problem 11–5A

Assume you are making the first year-end audit of the records of Holly Manufacturing Company, a company organized in January of the current year; and you have discovered that the company's bookkeeper has debited an account called "Land, Buildings, and Machinery" for what he thought was the cost of the company's new factory. The account has a $822,000 debit balance made up of the following items:

Cost of land and an old building on the land purchased as the site of the company's new factory (appraised value of the land, $80,000, and of the old building, $10,000)	$ 85,500
Attorney's fees resulting from land purchase	500
Escrow and legal fees connected with the land purchase	400
Cost of removing old building from plant site	2,000
Surveying and grading of plant site	1,600
Cost of retaining wall and the placing of tile to drain the site	1,200
Cost of new building (The contract price was $381,900; however, the contractor accepted $79,400 in cash and 30 bonds having a $300,000 par value. The company had purchased the bonds as a temporary investment at the start of construction for $300,000. The market value of the bonds on the day they were given to the contractor was $302,500.)	379,400
Architect's fee for planning building	23,100
Cost of paving parking lot	8,600
Lights for parking lot	400
Landscaping	2,700
Machinery (including the $800 cost of a machine dropped and made useless while being unloaded from a freight car)	312,500
Fine and permit to haul heavy machinery on city streets. The company was cited for hauling machinery without a permit. It then secured the permit. (Fine, $250; cost of permit, $50.)	300
Cost of hauling machinery on city streets	3,000
Cost of replacing damaged machine	800
Total	$822,000

In auditing the company's other accounts it was discovered that the bookkeeper had credited the $300 proceeds from the sale of materials salvaged from the old building removed from the plant site to an account called "Miscellaneous Revenues." He had also credited this account for $50 from the sale of the wrecked machine.

An examination of the payroll records showed that an account called "Superintendence" had been debited for the plant superintendent's $15,000 salary for the 10-month period, March 1 through December 31. From March 1 through August 31 the superintendent had supervised construction of the factory building. During September, October, and November he had supervised installation of the factory machinery. The factory began manufacturing operations on December 1.

Required:
1. Prepare a form having the following four column headings: Land, Land Improvements, Buildings, and Machinery. List the items and sort their amounts to the proper columns. Show a negative amount in parentheses. Total the columns.
2. Under the assumption that the company's accounts had not been closed, prepare an entry to remove the foregoing item amounts from the accounts in which they were incorrectly entered and record them in the proper accounts.
3. The company closes its books annually on December 31. Prepare the entry to record the partial year's depreciation on the plant assets. Assume the building and land improvements are estimated to have 30-year lives and no salvage values and that the machinery is estimated to have a 12-year life and a salvage value equal to 10% of its cost.

Decision problem 11-1, Metropolitan Daily

Metropolitan Daily operates a fleet of 20 trucks which it uses to deliver newspapers to its route carriers throughout the metropolitan area. It buys 10 new trucks every two years and accounts for them on a group basis so as to determine the costs of operating different kinds of trucks. Its standard policy is to replace each group of 10 trucks every four years.

It has just purchased 10 new DM trucks at $4,800 each. The data on the last fleet of DM trucks are as follows (average per truck):

Year	Miles Operated	Repairs and Maintenance
1	20,000	$100
2	18,000	300
3	15,000	500
4	12,000	600

It is expected that the repairs experience of the previous fleet will be repeated for the new fleet. The reduction in mileage each year is largely due to the policy of using new trucks on the longer routes and taking the older trucks off the regular routes and using them as extras. After four years the old trucks are not traded in but are sold to used-car dealers and others at an average of $12\frac{1}{2}$ percent of original cost.

In the past the company has used straight-line depreciation; but its controller has asked you to make a study of other depreciation methods with a comparison of methods to determine which will give the most equitable expense charge for depreciation plus maintenance and repair costs as related to yearly benefits derived from the operation of the trucks. For purposes of this study it may be assumed that benefits derived are in proportion to miles operated.

Required:
1. Prepare a schedule showing in columns by years (*a*) straight-line depreciation, (*b*) repairs and maintenance costs, and (*c*) the sum of depreciation and maintenance costs per year for each of the four years. Then on the next line (*d*) express each year's total costs as a percentage of the four-year total of costs; and finally, on the last line (*e*) express each year's benefits derived as a percentage of the four-year total (miles per year divided by total miles).
2. Prepare similar schedules using in turn units of production, declining balance at twice the straight-line rate, and sum-of-the-years'-digits depreciation.
3. Compare the cost percentages with the benefit percentages on each schedule and write a summary of conclusions, recommending the depreciation method you would use and give the reason for your conclusion.

Decision problem 11–2, Junior Accountant II   It is your last year in college; you are working part time for a local accounting firm; and in your examination of the plant asset accounts of a concern being audited by your firm, you find the following debits and credits in an account called Land and Buildings:

Debits

Jan.	3	Cost of land and buildings acquired for new plant site............................	$ 50,000
	10	Attorney's fee for title search	500
	27	Cost of wrecking old building on plant site...	5,000
Feb.	1	Six months' liability and fire insurance on new building..........................	1,500
June 30		Payment to building contractor on completion of building........................	225,250
July	1	Architect's fee for new building	13,500
	3	City assessment for street improvements	3,500
	14	Cost of landscaping new plant site...	2,000
			$301,250

Credits

Jan. 25	Proceeds from sale of salvaged materials from old building.......................	$ 1,000
July 3	Refund of one month's insurance premium..	250
Dec. 31	Depreciation at 2½% per year...	3,750
31	Balance..	296,250
		$301,250

In consultation with the senior accountant in charge of the audit, you learn that 40 years is a reasonable life expectancy for a building of the type involved and that it is reasonable to assume that there will be no salvage value at the end of the building's life. He also tells you to prepare a schedule with columns headed Date, Description, Total Amount, Land, Buildings, and Other Accounts and to enter the items found in the Land and Buildings account on the schedule, distributing the amounts to the proper columns. He suggests that you show credits on your schedule by enclosing the amounts in parentheses; and finally he suggests that since the accounts have not been closed, you draft any required correcting entry or entries. Assume that an account called Depreciation Expense, Land and Buildings was debited in recording the $3,750 of depreciation.

Chapter 12

Plant and equipment; intangible assets

■ Some of the problems met in accounting for property, plant, and equipment were discussed in the previous chapter. Additional problems involving plant assets and some of the accounting problems encountered with intangible assets are discussed in this chapter.

Accounting for small tools

■ Small tools such as hammers, wrenches, and drills which have low individual costs and are easily lost, broken, or stolen are normally either charged directly to an expense account at the time of purchase or are accounted for on an inventory basis. They are either expensed or accounted for on an inventory basis because it is impracticable to set up individual records and to account for such items on a depreciation basis. If small tools costing about the same amount are purchased each year to replace those lost, broken, or stolen, their costs may be charged directly to an expense account at the time of purchase. However, if the amounts purchased vary greatly from year to year, an inventory basis becomes a more equitable means of accounting for them.

When small tools are accounted for on an inventory basis, the cost of tools on hand at the beginning of a period is represented by a debit balance in the asset account, Small Tools; and as tools are purchased during the period, their cost is debited to this account. At the end of the period a physical inventory of usable tools on hand in the factory is taken; and the inventory amount is subtracted from the end-of-the-period balance of the Small Tools account to determine the cost of tools lost, broken, and stolen during the period. This cost is then charged to an expense account by a work sheet adjustment and an adjusting entry similar to the following:

Dec.	31	Small Tools Expense	200.00	
		Small Tools		200.00
		To record the cost of the tools lost, broken, and stolen.		

The debit of the foregoing entry records as an expense the cost of tools lost, broken, or stolen during the period. The credit reduces the balance of the Small Tools account to the cost of the usable tools on hand.

Since the lives of small tools are relatively short, when an inventory is taken at the end of an accounting period, normally all usable tools are placed on the inventory at cost.

Exchanging plant assets
■ Some plant assets are sold at the ends of their useful lives. Others such as machinery, automobiles, and office equipment may be traded on new, up-to-date assets of a like nature. When a plant asset is traded in on a new plant asset, normally either a book gain or loss is experienced. If the trade-in allowance received is greater than the book value of the traded asset, a book gain is experienced; and if the trade-in allowance is less than the traded asset's book value, a book loss is incurred. When such gains and losses are material in amount, they should be entered in the accounts as gains and losses. Immaterial gains and losses may be absorbed into the cost basis of the new asset.

Recording material gains and losses

When a material gain or loss is experienced on the exchange of a plant asset, the gain or loss should be recognized in the accounts as a gain or a loss. For example, a machine which cost $18,000 and upon which $15,000 depreciation has accumulated is traded in at $5,500 on a new machine of like nature having a $21,000 cash price. The book value of the old machine is $3,000. Therefore, if a $5,500 trade-in allowance is received, there is a $2,500 book gain on the transaction. The book value and gain are calculated:

Cost of old machine	$18,000
Less accumulated depreciation..............................	15,000
Book value	$ 3,000
Trade-in allowance on new machine	$ 5,500
Less book value of old machine	3,000
Book gain on the exchange	$ 2,500

When the exchange is made, the entry to record it is:

Jan.	5	Machinery	21,000.00	
		Accumulated Depreciation, Machinery	15,000.00	
		Machinery		18,000.00
		Gain on the Exchange of Machinery		2,500.00
		Cash		15,500.00
		Exchanged old machine and cash for a new machine of like nature.		

Or to illustrate further, assume that the old $18,000 machine with $15,000 accumulated depreciation is traded in at $1,000 on the new machine having a $21,000 cash price. If the old machine is traded at $1,000, a $2,000 book loss is incurred. The loss is calculated:

Book value of old machine $3,000
Less trade-in allowance on new machine................. 1,000
Book loss on the exchange $2,000

If the old machine is traded at a loss, the entry to record the exchange is:

Jan.	5	Machinery	21,000.00	
		Loss on the Exchange of Machinery	2,000.00	
		Accumulated Depreciation, Machinery	15,000.00	
		Machinery		18,000.00
		Cash		20,000.00
		Exchanged old machine and cash for a new machine of like nature.		

Income tax method of recording plant asset exchanges

When a plant asset is traded in on a new asset of like nature, a book gain or loss on the exchange usually results. However, the Internal Revenue Code does not recognize such gains and losses for tax purposes. According to the Internal Revenue Code, when an old asset is traded in on a new asset of like nature, any book gain or loss on the exchange must be absorbed into the cost of the new asset. This cost basis then becomes for tax purposes the amount that must be used in calculating depreciation on the new asset or any gain or loss on its sale or exchange.

For example, if an old typewriter that cost $180 and upon which $150 depreciation has accumulated is traded in at $45 on the purchase of a new $210 typewriter, the cost basis of the new typewriter for tax purposes is calculated as follows:

Cash paid ($210 less the $45 trade-in allowance) $165
Book value of old typewriter ($180 less $150) 30
Income tax basis of new asset for depreciation, sale, or exchange................. $195

Before going on observe that the cost basis for tax purposes of an asset acquired through an exchange is the sum of (1) the cash given plus (2) the book value of the old traded-in asset. This is the essence of the calculation in every case.

If the income tax basis of the new typewriter is used in recording the exchange just described, the entry is:

Jan.	5	Office Equipment	195.00	
		Accumulated Depreciation, Office		
		Equipment..	150.00	
		Office Equipment		180.00
		Cash..		165.00
		Traded old typewriter and cash for a new typewriter.		

Or to illustrate further, if rather than a $45 trade-in allowance, only a $20 allowance is received when the foregoing typewriter is exchanged, the cost basis of the new typewriter for tax purposes is:

Cash paid ($210 less a $20 trade-in allowance)	$190
Book value of old typewriter ($180 less $150)	30
Income tax basis of new asset for depreciation, sale, or disposal...................	$220

And if this basis is used in recording the typewriter exchange, the entry is:

Jan.	5	Office Equipment	220.00	
		Accumulated Depreciation, Office		
		Equipment..	150.00	
		Office Equipment......................................		180.00
		Cash...		190.00
		Exchanged old typewriter and cash for a new typewriter.		

When an asset having a $30 book value is traded at $45, there is a $15 book gain; likewise, there is a $10 book loss when the asset is traded at $20. However, observe in the foregoing calculations and entries that the application of the tax rule results in the nonrecognition of the gain in the first instance and the loss in the second. When the tax rule is applied, the effect is that the gain and the loss are absorbed into the cost basis of the new asset.

The reason for the tax rule is that it prevents a taxpayer from taking an unfair tax advantage by shifting taxable earnings from one year to the next by means of an arranged book gain or loss on an exchange. (A book loss for a taxpayer, for example, can be arranged if the dealer and the taxpayer agree to reduce by equal amounts both the normal trade-in allowance on the traded asset and the new asset's quoted price.)

At first glance it might seem that nonrecognition of gains and losses works a hardship when errors in estimating depreciation are made. However, this is usually not true. For example, when an asset is exchanged at a loss, the loss may not be counted as a loss for tax purposes; it is in fact added to the cost of the new asset. This causes the new asset to be taken into the records at a higher cost basis, the higher cost basis results in greater depreciation expense throughout the life of the new asset; and the greater depreciation expense offsets the unrecognized loss on the exchange. In the end, through greater depreciation expense, owner equity is reduced by the amount of the exchange loss. Likewise, in the end, through reduced depreciation expense on the new asset, a book gain on an exchange increases owner equity by the amount of the unrecognized gain.

Materiality and the choice of methods

When a plant asset is traded in on a new asset of like nature, there is normally either a book gain or loss on the exchange; but as previously stated, the Internal Revenue Code does not recognize such gains and losses for tax purposes. Consequently, if a gain or a loss is recorded as such at the time of an exchange, two sets of depreciation records must be kept throughout the life of the new asset, one for use in determining net income for accounting purposes and an additional set for determining the depreciation deduction for tax purposes.

Obviously keeping two records is more costly than one. Yet, when an exchange results in a material gain or loss, the gain or loss should be recorded and two sets of records kept. On the other hand, when an exchange results in an immaterial gain or loss, it is permissible to avoid the two sets of records by using the income tax method to record the transaction. The use of the tax method when there is a minor exchange gain or loss is permissible under an accounting principle called the *principle of materiality.*

The principle of materiality holds that strict adherence to any accounting principle is not required if the cost to adhere is proportionally great and the lack of adherence will not materially affect reported periodic net income. For example, if there is a $25 loss in trading an item of office equipment, using the income tax method to record the exchange would not materially affect the average company's statements. On the other hand, recording the loss and thereafter keeping two sets of depreciation records would be costly. Consequently, the income tax method is commonly used in such cases.

Revising depreciation rates ■ An occasional error in estimating the useful life of a plant asset is to be expected. Furthermore, when such an error is discovered, it is corrected by spreading the cost of the asset's remaining quantity of usefulness over its remaining useful life. For example, seven years ago a machine was purchased at a cost of $10,500. At that time the machine was estimated to have a 10-year life with a $500 salvage value. Therefore, it was depreciated at the rate of $1,000 per year [($10,500 — $500) ÷ 10 = $1,000]; and it began its eighth year with a $3,500 book value, calculated as follows:

```
Cost..................................................................... $10,500
Less seven years' accumulated depreciation .............. 7,000
Book value ........................................................ $ 3,500
```

If at the beginning of its eighth year the estimated number of years remaining in this machine's useful life is changed from three to five years, depreciation for each of the machine's remaining years should be recalculated as follows:

$$\frac{\text{Book Value} - \text{Salvage Value}}{\text{Remaining Useful Life}} = \frac{\$3,500 - \$500}{5 \text{ Years}} = \$600 \text{ per Year}$$

And an entry like the following should be used to record depreciation at the end of the machine's eighth and each succeeding year to retirement:

Dec.	31	Depreciation Expense, Machinery.....................	600.00	
		Accumulated Depreciation, Machinery........		600.00
		To record depreciation at the revised rate.		

If depreciation is charged at the rate of $1,000 per year for the first seven years of this machine's life and $600 per year for the next five, depreciation expense is overstated during the first seven years and understated during the next five. However, if a concern has many plant assets, the lives of some will be underestimated and the lives of others will be overestimated at the time of purchase; consequently, such errors will tend to cancel each other out with little or no effect on the income statement. Also, the American Institute of Certified Public Accountants through its Accounting Principles Board has said such corrections are normal and recurring, and it approves the described manner of correction. The described method is also acceptable for determining income subject to federal income taxes.

Repairs and replace-ments
■ Repairs and replacements fall into two groups: (1) ordinary repairs and replacements and (2) extraordinary repairs and replacements.

Ordinary repairs and replacements

Expenditures for ordinary repairs and replacements are necessary to maintain an asset in good operating condition. A building must be painted and its roof repaired or a machine must be reconditioned and small parts replaced. Any expenditures to maintain a plant asset in its normal good state of repair are considered ordinary repairs and replacements. Ordinary repairs and replacements are a current expense and should appear on the current income statement as a deduction from revenues.

Maintenance costs such as those for cleaning, lubricating, and adjusting machinery are also a current expense and are accounted for in the same way as ordinary repairs. Often such costs are combined with ordinary repairs for accounting purposes.

Extraordinary repairs and replacements

Extraordinary repairs and replacements are major repairs and replacements made, not to keep an asset in its normal good state of repair but to extend its useful life beyond that originally estimated. As a rule, the cost of such repairs and replacements should be debited to the repaired asset's accumulated depreciation account under the assumption they make good past depreciation, add to the asset's useful life, and benefit future periods. For example, a machine was purchased for $8,000 and depreciated under the assumption it would last eight years and have no salvage value. As a result, at the end of the machine's sixth year its book value is $2,000, calculated as follows:

Cost of machine	$8,000
Less six years' accumulated depreciation	6,000
Book value	$2,000

If at the beginning of the machine's seventh year it is given a major overhaul that extends its estimated useful life three years beyond the eight originally estimated, the $2,100 cost of the repairs should be recorded with an entry like the following:

Jan.	12	Accumulated Depreciation, Machinery..............	2,100.00	
		Cash (or Accounts Payable)		2,100.00
		To record extraordinary repairs to machinery.		

In addition, depreciation for each of the five years remaining in the machine's life should be calculated as follows:

Book value before extraordinary repairs	$2,000
Extraordinary repairs	2,100
Total	$4,100
Annual depreciation expense for remaining years ($4,100 ÷ 5 years)	$ 820

And, if the machine remains in use for five years after the major overhaul, the five annual $820 depreciation charges will exactly write off its new book value, including the cost of the extraordinary repairs.

Betterments ■ A betterment may be defined as the replacement of an existing asset or asset portion with an improved or superior asset or portion, usually at a cost materially in excess of the replaced item. Replacing the manual controls on a machine with automatic controls, removing an old motor and replacing it with a larger, more powerful one, and replacing a wood shingle roof with a tile roof are illustrations of betterments. Usually a betterment results in a better, more efficient, or more productive asset, but not necessarily one having a longer life.

When a betterment is made, its cost should be debited to the improved asset's account and depreciated over the remaining service life of the asset. Also, the cost and applicable depreciation of the replaced asset or portion should be removed from the accounts. For example, if the motor on a machine is replaced with a faster more powerful one, the cost of the new motor should be debited to the Machinery account and the cost and applicable depreciation on the old motor should be removed from the accounts.

Rearrangement of plant assets

■ The costs of rearranging factory machinery to secure greater efficiency or to reduce production costs should be recorded as an asset if such costs are material and will benefit future accounting periods. Normally costs of rearranging machinery are recorded as a *deferred charge* and are then written off in the manner of a prepaid expense over the several periods that benefit from the rearrangement. For example, if factory machinery is rearranged at a $10,000 cost, the expenditure may be recorded as follows:

Jan.	7	Rearrangement of Machinery	10,000.00	
		Cash (or Accounts Payable)		10,000.00
		To record the cost of rearranging machinery.		

And, if it is assumed the rearrangment will benefit the current and four additional accounting periods (five periods in all), five annual adjusting entries like the following may be used to write off the cost:

Dec.	31	Machinery Rearrangement Expense	2,000.00	
		Rearrangement of Machinery		2,000.00
		To write off one fifth the cost of rearranging factory machinery.		

A deferred charge is in effect a long-term prepaid expense. If on a balance sheet date a concern has deferred charges not previously written off, their amounts should appear on the balance sheet under a special asset classification called "Deferred charges." Normally deferred charges appear on the balance sheet as the last asset classification.

Capital and revenue expenditures

■ A *revenue expenditure* is one that should appear on the current income statement as an expense and a deduction from the period's revenues. Expenditures for ordinary repairs, rent, and salaries are examples.

Expenditures for betterments and for extraordinary repairs that lengthen the estimated life of an asset should appear on the balance sheet as increases in asset book values; and as a result, they are examples of what are called *capital expenditures* or balance sheet expenditures that benefit future periods.

Obviously, care must be exercised to distinguish between capital and revenue expenditures when transactions are recorded; for if errors are made, such errors often affect a number of accounting periods. For instance, an expenditure for a betterment initially recorded in error as an expense overstates expenses in the year of the error and understates net income. Also, since the cost of a betterment should be depreciated over the remaining useful life of the bettered asset, depreciation expense of future periods is understated and net income is overstated.

Natural resources

■ Natural resources such as standing timber, mineral deposits, and oil reserves are known as wasting assets. The distinguishing characteristic of wasting assets is that in their natural state they represent inventories that will be converted into a product by cutting, mining, or pumping. Standing timber, for example, is an inventory of uncut lumber. When it is cut and sawed, it becomes a product to be sold; and one of the costs of the product is the cost of the standing timber from which it was manufactured. However, until cut, it is a noncurrent asset commonly shown on the balance sheet under a caption such as "Timber lands." Or if a mineral deposit or oil reserve, it is commonly shown as "Mineral deposits" or "Oil reserves."

Natural resources are accounted for at cost, and appear on the balance sheet at cost less accumulated depletion. The amount such assets are depleted each year by cutting, mining, or pumping is commonly calculated on a "units-of-production" basis. For example, if a mine having an estimated 500,000 tons of available ore is purchased for $500,000, the depletion charge per ton of ore mined is $1. Furthermore, if 85,000 tons are mined during the first year, the depletion charge for the year is $85,000 and is recorded as follows:

Dec.	31	Depletion of Mineral Deposit...........................	85,000.00	
		Accumulated Depletion, Mineral Deposit.....		85,000.00
		To record depletion of ore body resulting from mining 85,000 tons of ore.		

On the balance sheet prepared at the end of the first year the mine should appear at its $500,000 cost less $85,000 accumulated depletion.

If all of the foregoing 85,000 tons of ore are sold by the end of the first year, the entire $85,000 depletion charge reaches the income statement as the depletion cost of the ore mined and sold. However, if a portion of the 85,000 tons remains unsold at the year-end, the depletion cost of the unsold ore is carried forward on the balance sheet as part of the cost of the unsold ore inventory, a current asset.

Often machinery must be installed or a building constructed in order to exploit a natural resource. The costs of such assets should be recorded in separate plant and equipment accounts, and they should be depreciated over the life of the natural resource with annual depreciation charges that are in proportion to the annual depletion charges. For example, if machinery having a 10-year life is installed in a mine that will be depleted in six years, the machinery should be depreciated over the six-year period. Furthermore, if one eighth of the mine's ore is removed during the first year, one eighth of the machine's total depreciation should be recorded as one of the costs of the ore mined.

Intangible assets ■ Intangible assets are assets having no intrinsic value, their value being derived from the long-term rights conferred by ownership and possession. Patents, copyrights, leaseholds, goodwill, trademarks, and organization costs are examples. Notes and accounts receivable are also intangible in nature, but these appear on the balance sheet as current assets rather than under the intangible assets classification.

All intangible assets are accounted for at cost. Some, like goodwill or a trade name, may have been acquired without cost; and although of great value to a business, they should not appear on its balance sheet unless they were purchased.

For accounting purposes, intangible assets are divided into two classes: (1) those having a limited life either by law, regulation, contract, or their nature; and (2) those having no indicated limit to their existences. Patents, copyrights, and leaseholds are in the first class; and goodwill, trademarks, and organization costs are in the second. The intangibles in the first class, those having limited lives, are *amortized* or systematically written off to expense accounts over their useful lives. Amortization of an intangible is a process similar to the recording of depreciation.

Patents

Patents are granted by the federal government to encourage the invention of new machines and mechanical devices. A patent gives its owner the exclusive right to manufacture and sell a patented machine or device for a period of 17 years. All costs of developing a patented machine or device, or the costs of acquiring the patent rights of others, are debited to an account called "Patents." Patent rights are never conclusive until successfully defended in the courts. Consequently, the costs of a successful lawsuit in defense of a patent should also be debited to the Patents account.

Although a patent gives its owner exclusive rights to the patented device for 17 years, its cost should be amortized or written off over a shorter period if its useful or economic life is estimated to be less than 17 years. For example, if a patent costing $25,000 has an estimated useful life of only 10 years, the following adjusting entry is made at the end of each year in the patent's life:

Dec.	31	Patents Written Off..	2,500.00	
		Patents		2,500.00
		To write off one tenth of patent costs.		

The entry's debit causes $2,500 of patent costs to appear on the annual income statement as one of the costs of the patented product manufactured. The credit directly reduces the balance of the Patents account. Normally, patents are written off directly to the Patents account as in this entry.

Research and development costs

Many concerns maintain a research department charged with developing new products, testing raw materials, testing the company's own products and the products of competitors, and doing pure research. A cost incurred by such a department in testing and in pure research is an expense of the period in which it is incurred. Costs incurred in developing new products, on the other hand, may be capitalized in a Patents or like account or they may be charged to current expense accounts.

Some concerns charge all the costs of operating a research department to current expense accounts and thus expense all testing, research, and product development costs in the year in which the costs are incurred. They do this under the assumption that the costs of maintaining a research department are recurring costs that must be borne period after period if the company is to maintain its competitive position. Other companies use cost accounting to allocate research department costs to testing, to pure research, and to the several products under development. They then capitalize the costs that result in successful new products and write off as a current expense any testing, pure research, and unsuccessful new product costs. Either method is acceptable.

Copyrights

A copyright is granted by the federal government and gives its owner the exclusive right to publish and sell a musical, literary, or artwork for a period of 28 years, with renewal rights for an additional 28 years. Obviously, most copyrights have value for a much shorter time, and their costs should be amortized over the shorter period. Often the only cost of a copyright is the fee paid the Copyright Office; and since this is nominal, it is commonly charged directly to an expense account.

Leaseholds

Property is rented under a contract called a *lease*. The person or company owning the property and granting the lease is called the *lessor*, the person or company securing the right to possess and use the property is called the *lessee*, and the rights granted the lessee under the lease are called a *leasehold*.

Some leases require no advance payment from the lessee but do require monthly rent payments. In such cases a Leasehold account is not needed and the monthly payments are debited to a Rent Expense account. Sometimes a long-term lease is so drawn that the last year's rent must be paid in advance at the time the lease is signed. When this occurs, the last year's advance payment is debited to the Leasehold account where it remains until the last year of the lease, at which time it is transferred to Rent Expense.

Often a long-term lease, one running 20 or 25 years, becomes very valuable after a few years because its required rent payments are much less than current rentals for identical property. In such cases the increase in value of the lease should not be entered on the books since no extra cost was incurred in acquiring it. However, if the property is subleased and the new tenant makes a cash payment for the rights under the old lease, the new tenant should debit the payment to a Leasehold account and amortize or write it off as additional rent expense over the remaining life of the lease.

Leasehold improvements

Long-term leases often require the lessee to pay for any alterations or improvements to the leased property, such as new partitions and store fronts. Normally the costs of the improvements are debited to an account called Leasehold Improvements; and since the improvements become part of the property and revert to the lessor at the end of the lease, their cost should be amortized over the life of the lease or the life of the improvements, whichever is shorter. The amortization entry commonly has a debit to Rent Expense and a credit to Leasehold Improvements.

Goodwill

When a concern so conducts its affairs that its customers are convinced their future dealings with the company will be as completely satisfactory as in the past, when the customers always return to transact with the concern the kind of business it conducts, and when its customers' good reports tend to bring in new customers, that concern is said to have goodwill.

The foregoing is a common description of goodwill; but it is not sufficiently broad for accounting purposes. In accounting, *a business is said to have goodwill when its expected future earnings are greater than the earnings normally realized in its industry*. Above-average earnings and the existence of goodwill may be demonstrated as follows with Companies A and B, both of which are in the same industry:

	Company A	Company B
Net assets (other than goodwill)	$100,000	$100,000
Normal rate of return in this industry	10%	10%
Normal return on net assets	$ 10,000	$ 10,000
Actual net income earned	10,000	15,000
Earnings above average	$ 0	$ 5,000

Company B has above-average earnings for its industry and is said to have goodwill. Its goodwill, as with any concern, may be the result of excellent customer relations, the location of the business, manufacturing efficiency, monopolistic privileges, good employee relations, superior management, or a combination of these factors. However, regardless of what created the goodwill, a prospective investor would normally be willing to pay more for Company B than for Company A if he felt the extra earnings would continue. Thus, goodwill is an asset having value and it can be sold.

Accountants are in general agreement that goodwill should not be recorded unless it is bought or sold. This normally occurs only when a business is purchased in its entirety or when a new combination of partners takes over an existing partnership. When either of these events occur, the goodwill of a business may be valued in many ways. Examples of three follow:

1. The buyer and seller may place an arbitrary value on the goodwill of a business being sold. For instance, a seller may be willing to sell a business having above-average earnings for $115,000 and a buyer may be willing to pay that amount; and if they both agree that the net assets of the business other than its goodwill have a $100,000 fair market value, they are arbitrarily valuing the goodwill at $15,000.

2. Goodwill may be valued at some multiple of that portion of expected earnings which is above average. For example, if a company is expected to have $5,000 each year in above-average earnings, its goodwill may be valued at, say, four times that portion of its earnings which are above average or at $20,000. In this case it may also be said that the goodwill is valued at four years' above-average earnings; but regardless of how it is said, this too is placing an arbitrary value on the goodwill.

3. The portion of a concern's earnings which is above average may be capitalized in order to place a value on its goodwill. For example, if a business is expected to continue to have $5,000 each year in earnings that are above average and the normal rate of return on invested capital in its industry is 10%, the excess earnings may be capitalized at 10% and a $50,000 value may be placed on its goodwill ($5,000 ÷ 10% = $50,000). Note that this values the goodwill at the amount that must be invested at the normal rate of return in order to earn the extra $5,000 each year ($50,000 × 10% = $5,000). It is a satisfactory method if the extra earnings are expected to continue indefinitely. However, since this may not happen, the extra earnings are often capitalized at a rate higher than the normal rate of the industry, say, at twice the normal rate or at 20% in this case. If in this case the extra earnings are capitalized at 20%, the goodwill is valued at $25,000 ($5,000 ÷ 20% = $25,000).

There are other ways to value goodwill; but like the three just described, in a final analysis goodwill is always valued at the price at which a seller is willing to sell and a buyer is willing to buy.

AMORTIZING GOODWILL. It is generally recognized that the benefits derived from purchased goodwill eventually disappear; therefore, the cost of purchased goodwill should be amortized or written off by

Oklahoma Sales Company
Income Statement for Year Ended December 31, 19—

Revenue:			
Sales			$114,750
Less: Sales returns		$ 1,250	
Sales discounts		1,330	2,580
Net sales			$112,170
Cost of goods sold:			
Merchandise inventory, January 1, 19—		$12,530	
Purchases	$69,370		
Less: Purchases returns	$765		
Purchases discounts	980	1,745	
Net purchases	$67,625		
Add: Freight-in	1,840		
Net cost of purchases		69,465	
Goods for sale		$81,995	
Merchandise inventory, December 31, 19—		10,135	
Cost of goods sold			71,860
Gross profit from sales			$ 40,310
Operating expenses:			
Selling expenses:			
Sales salaries	$12,450		
Payroll taxes expense, sales salaries	620		
Rent expense, selling space	4,800		
Freight-out	500		
Advertising expense	2,165		
Personal property taxes, selling	205		
Store supplies used	345		
Insurance expense, selling	215		
Depreciation of store equipment	835		
Total selling expenses		$22,135	
General and administrative expenses:			
Office salaries	$ 3,600		
Payroll taxes expense, office salaries	180		
Rent expense, office space	600		
Personal property taxes, office	20		
Bad debts expense	1,135		
Office supplies used	175		
Insurance expense, office	25		
Depreciation of office equipment	195		
Total general and administrative expenses		5,930	
Total operating expenses			28,065
Income from operations			$ 12,245
Other revenues and expenses:			
Interest earned		$ 185	
Less: Interest expense	$ 60		
Cash short	10	70	
Addition to income from operations			115
Net Income			$ 12,360

Illustration 12–1

systematic charges to income over the period estimated to be benefited. However, a discussion of this is deferred to a more advanced text.

Trademarks and trade names

Proof of prior use of a trademark or a trade name is sufficient under the common law to prove ownership. However, both may be registered at the Patent Office at a nominal cost to prove ownership. Trademarks and trade names are considered to have unlimited lives and as a result are not amortized.

A more complete income statement

■ A number of income statement items have been introduced since this statement was last illustrated in Chapter 5. Consequently, to aid the student in placing these items on an income statement, Illustration 12–1 is presented on the preceding page.

Questions for class discussion

1. Why are small tools accounted for on an inventory basis?
2. When should a gain or loss on the exchange of a plant asset be recorded as such? When is it permissible to absorb such a gain or loss into the cost basis of the new plant asset?
3. When plant assets of like nature are exchanged, what determines the cost basis of the newly acquired asset for federal income tax purposes?
4. When the gain or loss on an exchange of plant assets is immaterial in amount, what advantage results from taking the newly acquired asset into the records at the amount of its cost basis for tax purposes?
5. When an old plant asset is traded in at a book loss on a new asset of like nature, the loss is not recognized for tax purposes. In the end this normally does not work a hardship on the taxpayer. Why?
6. What is the essence of the accounting principle of materiality?
7. If at the end of four years it is discovered that a machine that was expected to have a five-year life will actually have an eight-year life, how is the error corrected?
8. Distinguish between ordinary repairs and replacements and extraordinary repairs and replacements.
9. How should ordinary repairs to a machine be recorded? How should extraordinary repairs be recorded?
10. What is a betterment? How should a betterment to a machine be recorded?
11. Distinguish between revenue expenditures and capital expenditures.
12. What are the characteristics of an intangible asset?
13. In general, how are intangible assets accounted for?
14. Define (a) lease, (b) lessor, (c) leasehold, and (d) leasehold improvement.
15. In accounting, when is a business said to have goodwill?

Class exercises

Exercise 12–1

A truck that cost $4,600 and that had $3,200 of accumulated depreciation recorded against it was traded in on a new truck having a $5,200 list price. An

$1,800 trade-in allowance was received and the balance was paid in cash. Determine (a) the book value of the old truck, (b) the cash given in making the exchange, (c) the book gain on the exchange, (d) the cost basis of the new truck for income tax purposes, and (e) the annual straight-line depreciation on the new truck for tax purposes under the assumption that it will have an estimated four-year life and a $1,200 trade-in value.

Exercise 12–2

A machine that cost $4,000 and on which $3,200 of depreciation had been recorded was disposed of on January 7 of the current year. Give without explanations the entries to record the disposal under each of the following unrelated assumptions:
a) The machine was sold for $700 cash.
b) The machine was sold for $950 cash.
c) The machine was traded in on a new machine having a $5,000 price. A $700 trade-in allowance was received, the balance was paid in cash, and the loss on the exchange was recorded.
d) The income tax method was used to record Transaction (c).
e) A $950 trade-in allowance was received on the old machine when traded in on the new $5,000 machine, the balance was paid in cash, and the gain was recorded.
f) Transaction (e) was recorded by the income tax method.

Exercise 12–3

A machine that cost $12,000 was depreciated on a straight-line basis for six years under the assumption it would have an eight-year life and a $2,000 trade-in value. At that point it was recognized that the machine had four years of remaining useful life, after which it would still have a $2,000 trade-in value.
a) Determine the machine's book value at the end of its sixth year.
b) Determine the total depreciation to be charged against the machine during its remaining years of life.
c) Give the entry to record depreciation on the machine for its seventh year.

Exercise 12–4

A company owns a building that appeared on its balance sheet at the end of last year at its original $246,000 cost less $205,000 accumulated depreciation. The building had been depreciated on a straight-line basis under the assumption it would have a 30-year life and no salvage value. During the first week in January of the current year, major structural repairs were completed on the building at a $64,000 cost. The repairs did not improve the building's usefulness but they did extend its expected life for 10 years beyond the 30 years originally estimated. (a) Determine the building's age on last year's balance sheet date. (b) Give the entry to record the cost of the repairs. (c) Determine the book value of the building after its repairs were recorded. (d) Give the entry to record the current year's depreciation.

Exercise 12–5

Six years ago a company purchased for $1,000,000 the mineral rights to an ore body containing 1,000,000 tons of ore. The company invested an additional $1,000,000 in mining machinery designed to exhaust the mine in 10 years. During the first five years the mine produced 500,000 tons of ore that were sold at a profit. During the sixth year 100,000 tons of ore were mined; but due to technological changes in the manufacturing processes of the customers to whom the ore was normally sold, there was little demand for the ore and it was sold at a $1 per ton loss.

Required:
Under the assumption that the remaining 400,000 tons of ore can be mined and sold at a $1 per ton loss during the next four years and there is no prospect of ever doing better, recommend whether the mine should be closed and the loss stopped or it should be continued in operation at a loss. Cite figures to back your recommendation.

Problems   **Problem 12–1**

The following machines were owned by a concern the accounting periods of which end each December 31.

Asset	Pur- chased	Cost	Estimated Life	Salvage Value	Method of Depreciation	Disposal Date and Details
No. 5	5/2/66	$3,500	5 years	$500	Straight line	Traded 1/5/68 on Asset No. 6, trade-in allowance, $2,000
No. 6	1/5/68	$4,300 less trade-in allowance	5 years	$600	Sum of the years' digits	Sold for $800 on 10/7/72
No. 7	1/9/68	$6,400	4 years	$400	Declining balance*	Traded on Asset No. 8, 1/4/72, trade-in allowance, $900
No. 8	1/4/72	$7,000 less trade-in allowance	12,000 units of product	$500	Units of production†	Sold for $4,000 on 6/3/73

*At twice the straight-line rate.
†Asset No. 8 produced 2,500 units of product in 1972 and 500 before its sale in 1973.

Required:
Prepare general journal entries to record: (1) the purchase of each machine; (2) the depreciation recorded on the first December 31 of each machine's life; and (3) the disposal of each machine. Use the income tax method to record exchanges. (Treat the entries for the first two machines as one series of transactions and those of the next two machines as an unrelated second series. Only one entry is needed to record the exchange of one machine for another.)

Problem 12-2

On January 4, 1965, Greenwood Mill purchased and placed in operation a machine estimated to have a 10-year life and no salvage value. The machine cost $15,000 and was depreciated on a straight-line basis. On December 27, 1968, a $600 device that increased the machine's output by one fourth was added to the machine. The new device made no change in the machine's estimated life and salvage value. During the first week of January, 1972, the machine was completely overhauled at a cost of $4,500 (completed and paid for on January 11). The overhaul added three additional years to the machine's estimated life but did not change its salvage value. On July 3, 1973, the machine was completely destroyed in a fire. The insurance company settled the loss claim for $5,000.

Required:

Prepare entries in general journal form to record: (*a*) the purchase of the machine, (*b*) the 1965 depreciation, (*c*) the addition of the new device, (*d*) the 1969 depreciation, (*e*) the overhauling of the machine, (*f*) the 1972 depreciation, and (*g*) the fire loss and insurance settlement.

Problem 12-3

PART 1.   Valley Company purchased Machine 345 at an installed cost of $12,400 on January 4, 1967, and depreciated the machine on a straight-line basis at the ends of 1967, 1968, 1969, and 1970 under the assumption it would have a 10-year life and a $2,400 salvage value. After more experience with the machine and before recording 1971 depreciation, the company revised its estimate of the machine's remaining life downward from six years to four years and revised the estimate of the machine's salvage value downward from $2,400 to $2,000. On March 27, 1973, after recording 1971, 1972, and part of a year's depreciation for 1973, the company traded Machine 345 on Machine 542. A $2,800 trade-in allowance was received. Machine 542 cost $14,100, less the $2,800 trade-in allowance, and was depreciated on a straight-line basis on December 31, 1973, under the assumption it would have a six-year life and a $2,300 trade-in value.

Required:

Prepare entries to record (*a*) the purchase of Machine 345, (*b*) the 1967 depreciation on the machine, (*c*) the 1971 depreciation on the machine, (*d*) the exchange of Machine 345 for Machine 542, and (*e*) the 1973 depreciation on Machine 542. (Use the income tax method to record the exchange.)

PART 2.   Dale Company paid $500,000 for land having an ore body estimated to contain 2,000,000 tons of ore. The ore was to be removed by stripping, and as a result the land would be worthless after its removal. The company installed machinery costing $160,000, having a 10-year life and no salvage value, and capable of exhausting the mine in 8 years. During the first six months' operations, ending December 31, the company mined 80,000 tons of ore.

Required:

Prepare entries to record (*a*) the purchase of the mineral land, (*b*) the installation of the machinery, (*c*) the first six months' depletion, and (*d*) the first six months' depreciation on the machinery.

Problem 12-4

PART 1. Eight years ago Dale Small leased a store building for a 20-year period. The lease contract requires a $6,000 annual rental payment on each January 1 throughout the life of the lease, and it requires the lessee to pay for all improvements to the leased property. Due to traffic pattern changes the lease has become more valuable, and on January 1 of the current year Mr. Small subleased the property for the remaining period of the lease to Allied Stores. Allied Stores paid Mr. Small $24,000 for his rights under the lease and it also agreed to pay the annual rental charges directly to the building owner. In addition, during the first 12 days of January it remodeled the store front on the leased building at an $8,400 total cost, paying the contractor on January 14. The remodeled store front was estimated to have a life equal to the remaining life of the leased building, 28 years.

Required:

Prepare general journal entries to record Allied Stores' payment for the right to sublease the property, payment of the annual rental charge, and payment for the new store front. Also, prepare end-of-the-first-year adjusting entries to amortize portions of the $24,000 sublease cost and the cost of the new store front.

PART 2. A company completed the following transactions involving the purchase and operation of a secondhand truck:

1970

Jan.   7   Purchased a secondhand truck for $2,650 cash. It was estimated the truck would be used for three years and would then have a $410 trade-in value.

       7   Paid Service Garage $135 for new tires for the secondhand truck and $25 for minor repairs and adjustments to its motor.

Dec. 31   Recorded straight-line depreciation on the truck.

1971

Jan. 12   Installed a hydraulic loader on the truck at a cost of $500. The loader increased the truck's salvage value by $100.

Dec. 31   Recorded depreciation on the truck.

1972

Oct.   3   Traded the secondhand truck on a new truck priced at $4,400. An $800 trade-in allowance was received and the balance was paid in cash. It was estimated the new truck would be used for four years and would then have a $1,000 trade-in value. (Use the income tax method in recording the exchange.)

Dec. 31   Recorded straight-line depreciation on the new truck.

Required:

Prepare general journal entries to record the transactions and end-of-the-period adjustments.

Problem 12-5

Ted Hall wishes to buy an established business and is considering Companies X and Y, both of which have been in business for exactly five years, during which time Company X has reported an average annual net income of $11,835 and Company Y has reported an average of $14,250. However, the incomes are not comparable, since the companies have not used the same accounting procedures. Current balance sheets of the companies show these items:

	Company X	Company Y
Cash	$ 6,700	$ 8,200
Accounts receivable	51,600	58,500
Allowance for doubtful accounts	(3,200)	-0-
Merchandise inventory	71,300	86,100
Store equipment	28,800	25,600
Accumulated depreciation, store equipment	(24,000)	(16,000)
Total Assets	$131,200	$162,400
Current liabilities	$ 62,400	$ 68,900
Owner equity	68,800	93,500
Total Liabilities and Owner Equity	$131,200	$162,400

Company X has used the allowance method in accounting for bad debts and has added to its allowance each year an amount equal to 1% of sales. However, this seems excessive, since an examination shows only $1,500 of its accounts that are probably uncollectible. Company Y, on the other hand, has used the direct write-off method but has been slow to write off bad debts, and an examination of its accounts shows $3,000 of accounts that are probably uncollectible.

During the past five years Company X has priced its inventories on a Lifo basis with the result that its current inventory appears on its balance sheet at an amount that is $12,000 below replacement cost. Company Y has used Fifo, and its ending inventory appears at approximately its replacement cost.

Both companies have assumed eight-year lives and no salvage value in depreciating equipment; however, Company X has used sum-of-the-years'-digits depreciation, while Company Y has used straight line. Mr. Hall is of the opinion that straight-line depreciation has resulted in Company Y's equipment appearing on its balance sheet at approximately its fair market value and that it would have had the same result for Company X.

Mr. Hall is willing to pay what he considers fair market value for the assets of either business, not including cash, but including goodwill measured at four times average annual earnings in excess of 15% on the fair market value of the net tangible assets. He defines net tangible assets as all assets, including accounts receivable, minus liabilities. He will also assume the liabilities of the purchased business, paying its owner the difference between total assets purchased and the liabilities assumed.

Required:
Prepare the following schedules: (*a*) a schedule showing the net tangible assets of each company at their fair market values according to Mr. Hall, (*b*) a schedule showing the revised net incomes of the companies based on Fifo inventories and straight-line depreciation, (*c*) a schedule showing the calculation of each company's goodwill, and (*d*) a schedule showing the amount Mr. Hall would pay for each business.

Problem 12–1A

The accounting periods of the company owning the following machines end each December 31.

Machine No. 63 was purchased on March 25, 1966, at an installed cost of $5,400. Its useful life was estimated at four years with a $600 trade-in value. Straight-line depreciation was recorded on the machine at the ends of 1966 and 1967, and on June 27, 1968, it was traded in on Machine No. 92. A $3,000 trade-in allowance was received.

Machine No. 92 was purchased on June 27, 1968, at an installed cost of $7,000, less the trade-in allowance received on Machine No. 63. Its life was estimated at five years with a $700 trade-in value. Sum-of-the-years'-digits depreciation was recorded on the machine on each December 31 of its life, and on January 4, 1973, it was sold for $1,000.

Machine No. 89 was purchased on January 5, 1968, at an installed cost of $5,000. Its useful life was estimated at five years, after which it would have a $500 trade-in value. Declining-balance depreciation at twice the straight-line rate was recorded on the machine at the ends of 1968, 1969, 1970, and 1971; and on September 26, 1972, it was traded on Machine 127. A $700 trade-in allowance was received.

Machine No. 127 was purchased on September 26, 1972, at a $6,200 installed cost, less the trade-in allowance received on Machine No. 89. It was estimated the new machine would produce 90,000 units of product during its useful life, after which it would have a $600 trade-in value. Units-of-production depreciation was recorded on the machine for the last three months of 1972, a period in which it produced 12,000 units of product. Between January 1 and April 12, 1973, the machine produced 10,000 more units, and on the latter date it was sold for $4,000.

Required:

Prepare general journal entries to record (*a*) the purchase of each machine, (*b*) the depreciation recorded on the first December 31 of each machine's life, and (*c*) the disposal of each machine. Use the income tax method to record exchanges. (Treat the entries for the first two machines as one series of transactions and those of the next two machines as an unrelated second series. Only one entry is needed to record the exchange of one machine for another.)

Problem 12–2A

Prepare general journal entries to record the following transactions of Hayden Mill. Use straight-line depreciation.

1968

Jan. 6 Purchased and placed in operation Machine No. 321 which was estimated to have a six-year life and no salvage value. The machine with its concrete base and special power connections cost $18,000.

Dec. 31 Recorded depreciation on Machine No. 321.

1969

Feb. 18 After a little over 13 months of satisfactory operation, Machine No. 321 was cleaned, inspected, oiled, and painted at a cost of $215.

Dec. 31 Recorded the 1969 depreciation on Machine No. 321

1970

June 28 Added a new device to Machine No. 321 at a cost of $700. The device increased the machine's output by one third but did not change its expected life nor increase its salvage value.

Dec. 31 Recorded the 1970 depreciation on Machine No. 321.

1971

Dec. 31 Recorded the 1971 depreciation on Machine No. 321.

1972

Jan. 9 Repaired and completely overhauled Machine No. 321 at a cost of $4,000. Of this amount $400 was for ordinary repairs and $3,600 was for extraordinary repairs. It was thought that the extraordinary repairs would extend the service life of the machine for two years beyond the six years originally estimated.

Dec. 31 Recorded the 1972 depreciation on Machine 321.

1973

July 9 Machine No. 321 was destroyed in a fire. The insurance company settled the loss claim for $5,000.

Problem 12–3A

PART 1.   Ten years ago Jerry Hern leased the store building at 2310 Main Street for a period of 20 years. His lease contract calls for $7,200 annual rental payments to be paid on each January 1 throughout the life of the lease, and it also provides that the lessee must pay for all additions and improvements to the leased property. The recent construction of a new shopping center across the street has made the location more valuable, and on January 1 Jerry Hern subleased the building to Ted Hall for the remaining 10 years of the lease. Ted Hall paid Jerry Hern $30,000 for the privilege of subleasing the property and in addition agreed to assume and pay to the building owner the $7,200 annual rental charges. During the first 10 days of January Mr. Hall remodeled the store front on the leased building at a cost of $10,000. The store front is estimated to have a life equal to the remaining life of the building, 30 years, and was paid for on January 14.

Required:

Prepare entries in general journal form to record: (*a*) Ted Hall's payment to sublease the building, (*b*) his payment of the annual rental charge to the building owner, and (*c*) payment for the new store front. Also, prepare the adjusting entries required at the end of the first year of the sublease to amortize (*d*) a proper share of the $30,000 cost of the sublease and (*e*) a proper share of the store front cost.

PART 2.   On March 12 of the current year Zeal Company paid $800,000 for mineral land estimated to contain 4,000,000 tons of recoverable ore. It installed machinery costing $120,000, having a 12-year life and no salvage value, and capable of exhausting the mine in 10 years. The machinery was paid for on July 5, three days after mining operations began. During the first six months' operations the company mined 165,000 tons of ore.

Required:

Prepare entries to record (*a*) the purchase of the mineral land, (*b*) the installation of the machinery, (*c*) the first six months' depletion under the assumption that the land will be valueless after the ore is mined, and (*d*) the first six months' depreciation on the machinery.

Problem 12–4A

Prepare general journal entries to record the following transactions involving the purchase and operation of a secondhand truck:

1970

Jan.   5   Purchased a secondhand delivery truck costing $2,850, having an estimated remaining useful life of three years and an $800 trade-in value.

7   Paid Apex Garage for the following:

Repairs to truck's motor................. $20
New battery............................... 30
Gas and oil 8

Total................................... $58

Dec. 31   Recorded straight-line depreciation on the truck.

1971

Jan. 14   Installed a hydraulic loader on the truck at a cost of $450. The loader increased the truck's salvage value by $50.

June 27   Paid Apex Garage for the following:

Minor repairs to motor................... $ 25
Gas and oil 6
New tires 115

Total................................... $146

Oct. 21   Paid for repairs to the hydraulic loader damaged when the driver backed into a loading dock, $65.

Dec. 31   Recorded depreciation on the truck.

1972

Jan. 11   Paid Apex Garage $200 to overhaul the truck's motor, replacing its bearings and rings and extending the truck's useful life for one year beyond the original three years planned. However, it was also estimated that the extra year's operation would reduce the truck's trade-in value to $550.

Dec. 31   Recorded depreciation on the truck.

1973

July   2   Traded the old truck in on a new truck priced at $4,000, less a $750 trade-in allowance for the old truck.

Decision problem 12–1, Joe Dean

Joe Dean plans to buy an established business, and he has narrowed his list to three choices, Companies A, B, and C. All three have been in business for exactly four years and have reported average annual net incomes as follows: Company A, $13,125; Company B, $11,912; and Company C, $20,970. However, since they have used different accounting methods, their reported incomes are not comparable, nor are their current balance sheets which show these items:

	Company A	Company B	Company C
Cash	$ 9,800	$ 12,500	$ 19,400
Accounts receivable	82,500	93,400	97,600
Allowance for doubtful accounts	(6,500)	(1,800)	-0-
Merchandise inventory	94,700	75,600	92,100
Equipment	27,500	30,000	26,000
Accumulated depreciation, equipment	(17,000)	(17,712)	(10,400)
Building	110,000	98,000	105,000
Accumulated depreciation, building	(11,000)	(9,800)	-0-
Land	20,000	20,000	20,000
Goodwill			2,500
Total Assets	$310,000	$300,188	$352,200
Current liabilities	$ 80,000	$ 95,000	$ 85,000
Mortgage payable	85,000	80,000	90,000
Owner equity	145,000	125,188	177,200
Total Liabilities and Owner Equity	$310,000	$300,188	$352,200

Company A has added an amount to its allowance for doubtful accounts each year equal to one half of 1% of sales. These amounts seem to have been excessive, since an analysis shows just $2,000 of the company's accounts receivable that are probably uncollectible. Company B has been more conservative, and its allowance is approximately equal to its uncollectible accounts. Company C has used the direct write-off method in accounting for bad debts; but it has always been slow to recognize a bad debt, and an examination shows accounts totaling $8,500 that are probably uncollectible.

Company B has accounted for its inventories on a Lifo basis; and as a result its current inventory appears on its books as an amount that is $15,000 below replacement cost. Companies A and C have used Fifo, and their inventories are stated at amounts near replacement costs.

The three companies have not added to their plant assets since beginning operations, and all three have assumed 10-year lives and no salvage values in recording depreciation on equipment. However, Company A has used sum-of-the-years'-digits depreciation, Company B has used declining balance at twice the straight-line rate, and Company C has used straight line.

The buildings of the companies are of concrete construction and are comparable in every respect. Companies A and B have recorded straight-line depreciation on their buildings, assuming 40-year lives and no salvage values. However, since its building is of concrete construction and "will last forever," Company C has taken no depreciation on its building.

Mr. Dean is of the opinion that if all three companies had used straight-line depreciation for both buildings and equipment, the resulting book values would approximate market values.

The goodwill on Company C's balance sheet resulted from capitalizing advertising costs during the company's first year in business.

In purchasing a business, Mr. Dean will buy its tangible assets, including the accounts receivable, but not including cash; and he will pay what he thinks is fair market value. He will assume the liabilities of the business and will pay for goodwill measured at four times average annual earnings in excess of a 10% return on net tangible assets, based on first-in, first-out inventories and straight-line depreciation.

Determine the amounts Mr. Dean would be willing to pay for each of Companies A, B, and C. Base the amounts on the following schedules: (*a*) a schedule showing net tangible assets for each company, (*b*) a schedule showing revised and corrected average net incomes, and (*c*) a schedule showing the calculation of each company's goodwill. Base all schedules on first-in, first-out inventories and straight-line depreciation.

Decision problem 12–2, intangible assets

CASE 1. Tiptop Company has spent the last 10 years developing national recognition for its brand name coffee. It has used advertising and other public relations efforts in building the name. However, over the years it has made no effort to distinguish between advertising and public relations designed to build annual sales and those designed to build recognition for the brand name. Underhill Company, on the other hand, recently purchased the going business of a company distributing a nationally known brand of coffee. Included in the purchase price was the payment of $500,000 for the exclusive right to use the company's name for coffee.

What kind of an asset is involved in each case here? Assume that the assets described are of equal value. How will each company show the asset on its balance sheet? Will a statement reader find this confusing when he compares the balance sheets of the two companies? Discuss your response to the last question.

CASE 2. Harry Ball is negotiating for the purchase of a going business to which the following statistics apply:

Assets (exclusive of goodwill)	$135,000
Liabilities	55,000
Current and expected future annual earnings	12,000
Normal earnings rate on net assets for the industry	10%

Does this business have goodwill? If so, how much should Mr. Ball pay for the goodwill?

Chapter 13

Payroll accounting

■ An understanding of payroll records and payroll accounting requires some knowledge of the laws and programs that affect payrolls. Consequently, the more pertinent of these are discussed in the first portion of this chapter before the subject of payroll records is introduced.

The federal Social Security Act

■ The federal Social Security Act provides for a number of programs, two of which materially affect payroll accounting. These are (1) a federal old-age and survivors' benefits program with medical care for the aged and (2) a joint federal-state unemployment insurance program.

Federal old-age and survivors' benefits program

The Social Security Act provides that a qualified worker in a covered industry who reaches the age of 62 and retires shall receive monthly retirement benefits for the remainder of his life, and in addition certain medical benefits after reaching 65. It further provides benefits for the family of a worker covered by the act who dies either before or after reaching retirement age and benefits for covered workers who become disabled. The benefits in each case are based upon the average earnings of the worker during the years of his employment in covered industries.

No attempt will be made here to list or discuss the requirements to be met by a worker or his family to qualify for benefits. In general, any person who works for an employer covered by the act for a sufficient length of time qualifies himself and his family. All companies and individuals who employ one or more persons and are not specifically exempted are covered by the law.

Funds for the payment of old-age, survivors', and medical benefits under the Social Security Act come from payroll taxes. These taxes are imposed under a law called the Federal Insurance Contributions Act and are often called "F.I.C.A. taxes." They are also often called "old-age benefit taxes" or just "social security taxes." These F.I.C.A. taxes are imposed in like amounts on both covered employers and their employees. As presently amended the act provides for a 1972 tax on both employers and their employees amounting to 5.2% of the first $9,000 paid each employee. It also provides for rate increases as follows:

Years	Tax on Employees	Tax on Employers
1973 through 1975	5.65%	5.65%
1976 through 1979	5.85	5.85
1980 through 1986	5.95	5.95
1987 and after	6.05	6.05

The above table shows that rate increases are scheduled. However, probably little effort should be made to remember these rates beyond the one currently in effect, for if history is any indication, Congress will change the future rates (probably increasing them) before they become effective. Furthermore, because changes have been so common in the past, your authors will make no effort to use the current rate in the illustrations and problems but will use an assumed F.I.C.A. tax rate of 5% of the first $9,000 paid each employee during a year. A 5% rate is less than the current rate; however, it makes calculations easy.

The Federal Insurance Contribution Act in addition to setting rates requires that an employer:

1. Withhold from the wages of each employee each payday an amount of F.I.C.A. tax calculated at the current rate. The withholding to continue each payday during the year until the F.I.C.A. tax-exempt point is reached. The tax-exempt point at this writing is $9,000.
2. Pay a payroll tax equal to the amount withheld from the wages of all employees.
3. Periodically remit both the amounts withheld from the employees' wages and the employer's tax to the Internal Revenue Service. (Times of payment are discussed later in this chapter.)
4. Within one month after the end of each calendar quarter, file a tax information return known as Employer's Quarterly Federal Tax Return, Form 941. (See Illustration 13–1.)
5. Furnish each employee before January 31 following each year a Withholding Tax Statement, Form W–2, which tells the employee the amounts of his wages that were subject to F.I.C.A. and federal income taxes and the amounts of such taxes withheld. (A W–2 Form is shown in Illustration 13–2.)
6. Furnish the Internal Revenue Service copies of all the W–2 Forms given the employees.

FORM 941
(Rev. July 1970)
Department of the Treasury
Internal Revenue Service

Employer's Quarterly Federal Tax Return

1. TOTAL WAGES AND TIPS SUBJECT TO WITHHOLDING PLUS OTHER COMPENSATION ➝	3,000	00
2. AMOUNT OF INCOME TAX WITHHELD (If not required write "None")	260	00
3. ADJUSTMENT FOR PRECEDING QUARTERS OF CALENDAR YEAR		
4. ADJUSTED TOTAL OF INCOME TAX WITHHELD ➝	260	00
5. TAXABLE F.I.C.A. WAGES PAID (Item 21) . . $ 3,000 multiplied by 10% = TAX	300	00
6. TAXABLE TIPS REPORTED (Item 22) . . . $ multiplied by 5% = TAX		
7. TOTAL F.I.C.A. TAXES (Item 5 plus Item 6) ➝	300	00
8. ADJUSTMENT (See Instructions)		
9. ADJUSTED TOTAL OF F.I.C.A. TAXES ➝	300	00
10. TOTAL TAXES (Item 4 plus Item 9)	560	00
11a. TOTAL TAXES DEPOSITED FOR THE QUARTER (See Instructions on Page 4) 560.00		
11b. OVERPAYMENT FROM PREVIOUS QUARTER		
11c. TOTAL DEPOSITS (Item 11a plus Item 11b)	560	00
12a. IF ITEM 11c IS LESS THAN ITEM 10, PAY BALANCE DUE TO INTERNAL REVENUE SERVICE	-0-	
12b. IF ITEM 11c IS MORE THAN ITEM 10, ENTER EXCESS HERE ➝ $ AND CHECK IF TO BE: ☐ APPLIED TO NEXT RETURN, OR ☐ REFUNDED.		

13. If not liable for returns in succeeding quarters write "FINAL" here ➤ and enter date of final payment of taxable wages here ➤

Under penalties of perjury, I declare that I have examined this return, including accompanying schedules and statements, and to the best of my knowledge and belief it is true, correct, and complete.

Date April 29, 1972   Signature *John K. Jones*   Title (Owner, etc.) Owner

Employer's name, address, employer identification number, and calendar quarter. (If not correct, please change)

Name (as distinguished from trade name)
John K. Jones   Date quarter ended March 31, 1972
Trade name, if any
Jones Corner Market   Employer Identification No. 12 123123
Address and ZIP code
1212 Main Street, Mesa, Arizona 85201
Entries must be made both above and below this line

Name (as distinguished from trade name)
John K. Jones   Date quarter ended March 31, 1972
Trade name, if any
Jones Corner Market   Employer Identification No. 12 123123
Address and ZIP code
1212 Main Street, Mesa, Arizona 85201

SCHEDULE A—QUARTERLY REPORT OF WAGES TAXABLE UNDER THE FEDERAL INSURANCE CONTRIBUTIONS ACT (FOR SOCIAL SECURITY)
IF WAGES WERE NOT TAXABLE UNDER THE F.I.C.A. MAKE NO ENTRIES BELOW

14. (First quarter only) Number of employees (except household) employed in the pay period including March 12th.	15. Total pages of this return including this page and any pages of Form 941a.	16. Total number of employees listed.
3	1	3

List for each nonagricultural employee the WAGES taxable under the F.I.C.A. which were paid during the quarter. If you pay an employee more than $9,000 in a calendar year, report only the first $9,000 of such wages. In the case of "Tip Income" see instructions on Page 4.

Please be sure to report each employee's name and number exactly as shown on his Social Security card.

17. EMPLOYEE'S SOCIAL SECURITY NUMBER (If number is unknown, see Circular E) 000 00 0000	18. NAME OF EMPLOYEE (Please type or print)	19. TAXABLE F.I.C.A. WAGES Paid to Employee in Quarter (Before deductions) Dollars Cents	20. TAXABLE TIPS REPORTED (See page 4) Dollars Cents
123 12 1234	James Jay Smallwood	1,000 00	
234 23 2345	Robert Thomas Robert	1,000 00	
345 34 3456	Mary Jane Smith	1,000 00	
		3,000 00	

If you need more space for listing employees, use Schedule A continuation sheets, Form 941a.
Totals for this page—Wage total in column 19 and tip total in column 20 ➝

21. TOTAL WAGES TAXABLE UNDER F.I.C.A. PAID DURING QUARTER.
(Total of column 19 on this page and continuation sheets.) Enter here and in Item 5 above . . . $ 3,000 00

22. TOTAL TIPS REPORTED UNDER F.I.C.A. DURING QUARTER. (If no tips reported, write "None.")
(Total of column 20 on this page and continuation sheets.) Enter here and in Item 6 above . . . $ None

SEE "WHERE TO FILE" ON PAGE 2.

Illustration 13–1

7. Keep a record for four years for each employee that shows among other things wages subject to F.I.C.A. taxes and the taxes withheld. (The law does not specify the exact form of the record; but most employers keep individual employee earnings records similar to the one shown later in this chapter.)

1 12 123123 John K. Jones 1212 Main Street, Mesa, Arizona 85201				WAGE AND TAX STATEMENT—1972			
				(For use in States or Cities authorizing combined form)			
Type or print EMPLOYER'S Federal identification number, name, and address above.			Employer's State Identification Number			Copy A— For Internal Revenue Service	
FEDERAL INCOME TAX INFORMATION			SOCIAL SECURITY INFORMATION			STATUS	*
Federal income tax withheld	Wages paid subject to withholding in 1972 ¹	Other compensation paid in 1972 ¹	F.I.C.A. employee tax withheld ³	Total F.I.C.A. wages paid in 1972 ⁴	1. Single 2. Married		
$350.00	$4,000.00		$200.00	$4,000.00	2		**
EMPLOYEE'S social security number ▶ 123 12 1234			Name of State	State Form No.		State income tax withheld	
James Jay Smallwood 319 East Geneva Drive Mesa, Arizona 85201			Name of City	City Form No.		City income tax withheld	

			*See Circ. E for sick pay reporting. **Gross wages for State if different from Federal.
			¹ Includes tips reported by employee. Amount is before payroll deductions or sick pay exclusion.
			² Report salary or other employee compensation which was not subject to withholding.
			  See Circular E.
			³ One-eighth of this amount was withheld to finance the cost of Hospital Insurance
			  Benefits. The remainder is for old-age, survivors, and disability insurance.
			⁴ Includes tips reported by employee.					

Type or print EMPLOYEE'S name and address (including ZIP code) above.			Uncollected Employee Tax on Tips . . . . $				
FORM W-2 Department of the Treasury, Internal Revenue Service			16—44071-1	EMPLOYER: See instructions on back of copy D.			

Illustration
13–2

Observe that the Employer's Quarterly Federal Tax Return, Form 941 (Illustration 13–1) actually has two parts. (It is perforated between the two listings of the employer's name and is designed to be torn into two parts at this point.) On the first part the employer reports (1) total wages subject to withholding, (2) employees' federal income taxes withheld, (3) total wages subject to F.I.C.A. taxes (item 5), and (4) the combined amount of the employees' and employer's F.I.C.A. taxes. The combined employees' and employer's F.I.C.A. taxes are shown as item 5 where it says $3,000 multiplied by 10% = Tax. The 10% is the sum of the assumed 5% F.I.C.A. tax withheld from the employees' wages and the assumed 5% levied on the employer.

On the second half of the quarterly tax return, labeled Schedule A, the employer reports each employee's social security number, name, and his wages subject to F.I.C.A. taxes. This schedule is sent to the Social Security Administration by the Internal Revenue Service. The Social Security Administration posts the information as to each employee's wages to his social security record where it becomes the basis for determining the employee's retirement and survivors' benefits.

Joint federal-state unemployment insurance program

The federal government participates with the states in a joint federal-state unemployment insurance program. Within this joint program each state has established and now administers its own unemployment insurance program under which it pays unemployment benefits to its unemployed workers. The federal government through the Social Security

Administration approves the state programs and pays a portion of their administrative expenses.

The federal money for administering the state programs is raised by a tax imposed under a law called the Federal Unemployment Tax Act. This act levies a payroll tax on employers of one or more people. Note that the tax is imposed on employers only; employees pay nothing; and also that the money from this tax is used for administrative purposes and not to pay benefits.

Historically, in 1935 when the Federal Unemployment Tax Act was first passed, only one state had an unemployment insurance program; consequently, at that time Congress passed certain sections of the Social Security Act and the Federal Unemployment Tax Act with two purposes in view. The first was to induce the individual states to create satisfactory unemployment insurance programs of their own, and the second was to provide funds to be distributed to the states for use in administering the state programs. These acts were successful in accomplishing their first purpose, all states immediately created unemployment programs; and today the acts remain in effect for their second purpose, to provide funds to be distributed to the states, and also to retain a measure of federal control over the several state programs.

THE FEDERAL UNEMPLOYMENT TAX ACT. The Federal Unemployment Tax Act requires employers of one or more employees to—

1. Pay an excise tax equal to 0.5% of the first $4,200 in wages paid each employee. (Times of payment are discussed later in this chapter.)
2. On or before January 31 following the end of each year, file a tax return, called an "Employer's Annual Federal Unemployment Tax Return, Form 940," reporting the amount of tax due.
3. Keep records to substantiate the information on the tax return. (In general the records required by other payroll laws and the regular accounting records satisfy this requirement.)

STATE UNEMPLOYMENT INSURANCE PROGRAMS. While the various state unemployment insurance programs differ in some respects, all have three common objectives. They are:

1. To pay unemployment compensation for limited periods to unemployed individuals. (To be eligible for benefits, an unemployed individual must have worked for a tax-paying employer covered by the law of his state. In general the various state laws cover employers of from one to four or more employees who are not specifically exempted.)
2. To stabilize employment by covered employers. (In all states this is accomplished by a so-called merit-rating plan. Under a merit-rating plan an employer who provides steady employment for his employees gains a merit rating that substantially reduces his state unemployment tax rate.)

3. To establish and operate employment facilities that assist unemployed individuals in finding suitable employment and assist employers in finding employees.

All states support their unemployment insurance programs by placing a payroll tax on employers; a few states place an additional tax on employees. At one time the basic tax rate on employers in all states was an almost uniform 2.7% of the first $3,000 paid each employee, and an employer could gain a merit rating that would reduce this basic rate to zero in some states by keeping his employees employed. State rates now vary, but any state's rate can still be reduced by means of a merit rating. Also, by the end of 1972 all states will probably have increased the amount on which their tax is based to a uniform "first $4,200 paid each employee."

The states also vary as to required reports, but in general all require a tax return and payment of the required tax within one month after the end of each calendar quarter. Also, since the benefits paid an eligible unemployed individual are based upon his earnings, the tax return must usually name each employee and tell his wages.

In addition to reports and payment of taxes, all states require employers to maintain certain payroll records. These vary from state to state; but in general require, among other things, a payroll record for each pay period showing the pay period dates, hours worked, and taxable earnings of each employee. An individual earnings record for each employee is also commonly required, and each earnings record generally must show about the same information required by social security laws. In addition, information as to (1) the date an employee was hired, rehired, or reinstated after a layoff; (2) the date the employee quit, was discharged, or laid off; and (3) the reason for termination is also commonly required.

Withholding employees' federal income taxes

■ With few exceptions, employers of one or more persons are required to calculate, collect, and remit to the federal government the income taxes of their employees. Historically, although the first federal income tax law became effective in 1913, it applied to only a few individuals having high earnings, and it was not until World War II that income taxes were levied on the great masses of wage earners. At that time Congress recognized that many individual wage earners could not be expected to save sufficient money with which to pay their income taxes once each year. Consequently, Congress instituted a system of pay-as-you-go withholding of taxes each payday at their source. This pay-as-you-go withholding of employee income taxes requires an employer to act as a tax collecting agent of the federal government.

The federal income tax to be withheld from an employee's wages is determined by his wages and the number of his exemptions. Each exemption exempts from income tax $700 of an employee's yearly earnings in 1972 and $750 in 1973 and after. For example, an employee with five exemptions and earning less than \$3,500 in 1972 pays no tax (5 × \$700 = \$3,500 exempted). An employee is allowed one exemption for himself, additional exemptions if he or his wife are over 65 or blind, and an exemption for each dependent. Every covered employee is required to furnish his employer an employee's withholding exemption certificate, Illustration 13-3, showing the exemptions to which he is entitled.

Illustration
13-3

Most employers use a wage bracket withholding table similar to the one shown in Illustration 13-4 in determining federal income taxes to be withheld from employee's gross earnings. The illustrated table is applicable when a pay period is one week. Different tables are provided for biweekly, semimonthly, and monthly pay periods; somewhat similar tables are available for determining F.I.C.A. tax withholdings.

Determining the federal income tax to be withheld from an employee's gross wages is quite easy when a withholding table is used. First the employee's wage bracket is located in the first two columns. Then the amount to be withheld is found on the line of the wage bracket in the column showing the exemptions to which the employee is entitled. The column heading numbers refer to the number of exemptions claimed by an employee on his exemption certificate.

In addition to determining and withholding income tax from each employee's wages every payday, employers are required to—

1. Periodically remit the withheld taxes to the Internal Revenue Service. (Times of remittance are discussed later.)
2. Within one month after the end of each quarter, file a report showing the income taxes withheld. This report is the Employer's Quarterly Federal Tax Return, Form 941, discussed previously and shown in

And the wages are—		And the number of withholding exemptions claimed is—										
At least	But less than	0	1	2	3	4	5	6	7	8	9	10 or more
		The amount of income tax to be withheld shall be—										
$100	$105	$13.10	$11.10	$9.10	$7.00	$4.80	$2.80	$1.00	$0	$0	$0	$0
105	110	13.90	11.90	9.90	7.80	5.70	3.60	1.70	0	0	0	0
110	115	14.70	12.70	10.70	8.70	6.50	4.40	2.40	.70	0	0	0
115	120	15.50	13.50	11.50	9.50	7.40	5.30	3.10	1.40	0	0	0
120	125	16.30	14.30	12.30	10.30	8.20	6.10	4.00	2.10	.30	0	0
125	130	17.10	15.10	13.10	11.10	9.10	7.00	4.80	2.80	1.00	0	0
130	135	17.90	15.90	13.90	11.90	9.90	7.80	5.70	3.60	1.70	0	0
135	140	18.70	16.70	14.70	12.70	10.70	8.70	6.50	4.40	2.40	.70	0
140	145	19.50	17.50	15.50	13.50	11.50	9.50	7.40	5.30	3.10	1.40	0
145	150	20.30	18.30	16.30	14.30	12.30	10.30	8.20	6.10	4.00	2.10	.30
150	160	21.50	19.50	17.50	15.50	13.50	11.50	9.50	7.40	5.30	3.10	1.40
160	170	23.10	21.10	19.10	17.10	15.10	13.10	11.10	9.10	7.00	4.80	2.80
170	180	25.00	22.70	20.70	18.70	16.70	14.70	12.70	10.70	8.70	6.50	4.40
180	190	26.90	24.50	22.30	20.30	18.30	16.30	14.30	12.30	10.30	8.20	6.10
190	200	28.80	26.40	24.10	21.90	19.90	17.90	15.90	13.90	11.90	9.90	7.80
200	210	30.70	28.30	26.00	23.60	21.50	19.50	17.50	15.50	13.50	11.50	9.50
210	220	32.60	30.20	27.90	25.50	23.10	21.10	19.10	17.10	15.10	13.10	11.10
220	230	34.50	32.10	29.80	27.40	25.00	22.70	20.70	18.70	16.70	14.70	12.70
230	240	36.40	34.00	31.70	29.30	26.90	24.50	22.30	20.30	18.30	16.30	14.30
240	250	38.30	35.90	33.60	31.20	28.80	26.40	24.10	21.90	19.90	17.90	15.90
250	260	40.20	37.80	35.50	33.10	30.70	28.30	26.00	23.60	21.50	19.50	17.50
260	270	42.10	39.70	37.40	35.00	32.60	30.20	27.90	25.50	23.10	21.10	19.10
270	280	44.10	41.60	39.30	36.90	34.50	32.10	29.80	27.40	25.00	22.70	20.70
280	290	46.20	43.60	41.20	38.80	36.40	34.00	31.70	29.30	26.90	24.50	22.30
290	300	48.30	45.70	43.10	40.70	38.30	35.90	33.60	31.20	28.80	26.40	24.10
300	310	50.40	47.90					35.50	33.10	30.70	28.30	26.00
310	320										30.20	

Illustration
13–4
Wage Bracket
Withholding
Table

Illustration 13–1. It is the same report required for F.I.C.A. taxes.

3. On or before January 31 following each year, give each employee a Withholding Statement, Form W–2, which tells the employee (1) his total wages for the preceding year, (2) wages subject to F.I.C.A. taxes, (3) income taxes withheld, and (4) F.I.C.A. taxes withheld. A copy of this statement must also be given to each terminated employee within 30 days after his last wage payment.

4. On or before January 31 following the end of each year, send the Internal Revenue Service copies of all W–2 forms given employees.

City and state income taxes

■ In addition to deducting employees' federal income taxes, employers in many cities and in three fourths of the states must also deduct employees' city and state income taxes. When this is necessary, the city and state taxes are handled much the same as federal income taxes.

Fair Labor Standards Act

■ The Fair Labor Standards Act, often called the Wages and Hours Law, sets minimum hourly wages and maximum hours of work per week for employees, with certain exceptions, of employers engaged either directly or indirectly in interstate commerce. As amended, the law at this writing generally sets a $1.60 per hour minimum wage and a maximum 40-hour workweek. However, although the act sets a maximum 40-hour workweek, it does not prohibit an employee from working longer hours but provides that if an employee covered by the act works more than 40 hours in one week, he must be paid for the hours in excess of 40 at his regular pay rate plus an overtime premium of at least one half his regular rate. This gives an employee an overtime rate of at least one and one half times his regular hourly rate. The act also requires employers to maintain records for each covered employee similar to the employee's individual earnings record of Illustration 13–9.

Union contracts ■ Although the Wages and Hours Law requires covered employers to pay time and one half for hours worked in excess of 40 in any one week, employers commonly operate under contracts with their employees' union that provide even better terms. For example, union contracts often provide for time and one half for work in excess of eight hours in any one day, time and one half for work on Saturdays, and double time for Sundays and holidays. When an employer is under such a union contract, since the contract terms are better than those of the Wages and Hours Law, the contract terms take precedence over the law.

In addition to specifying working hours and wage rates, union contracts often provide for the collection of employees' union dues by the employer. Such a requirement commonly provides that the employer shall deduct dues from the wages of each employee and remit the amounts deducted to the union. The employer is usually required to remit once each month and to report the name and amount deducted from each employee's pay.

Other payroll deductions ■ In addition to the payroll deductions discussed thus far, employees may individually authorize additional deductions, such as:

1. Deductions to accumulate funds for the purchase of U.S. savings bonds.
2. Deductions to pay health, accident, hospital, or life insurance premiums.
3. Deductions to repay loans from the employer or the employees' credit union.
4. Deductions to pay for merchandise purchased from the company.
5. Deductions for donations to charitable organizations such as Boy Scouts, Girl Scouts, Community Chest, or Red Cross.

Time-keeping ■ Compiling a record of the time worked by each employee is called *timekeeping*. In an individual company the method of compiling such a record depends upon the nature of the business and the number of its employees. In a very small business timekeeping may consist of no more than pencil notations of each employee's working time made in a memorandum book by the manager or owner. On the other hand, in a larger company a time clock or several time clocks are often used to record on clock cards each employee's time of arrival and departure. When time clocks are used, they are placed at the entrances to the office, store, or factory, and a rack for clock cards is provided beside each clock. At the beginning of each payroll period a clock card for each employee similar to Illustration 13–5 is placed in the rack at the entrance

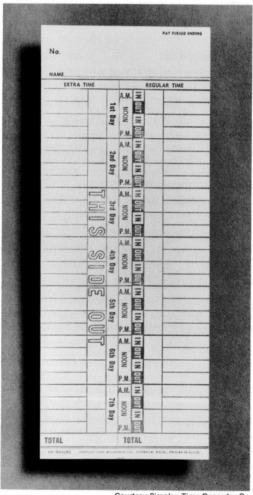

Illustration
13–5

Courtesy Simplex Time Recorder Co.

to be used by the employee. Each day as the employee enters the plant, store, or office, he takes his card from the rack and places it in a slot in the time clock. This actuates the clock to stamp the date and arrival time on the card. The employee then returns the card to the rack and proceeds to his place of work. Upon leaving the plant, store, or office at noon or at the end of the day, the procedure is repeated. The employee takes the card from the rack, places it in the clock, and stamps the time of departure. As a result, at the end of the pay period the card shows the hours the employee was on the job.

The Payroll Register

■ Each pay period the information as to hours worked as compiled on clock cards or otherwise is summarized in a Payroll Register. A pen-and-ink form of such a register is shown in Illustration 13–6. A Payroll Register for use with a bookkeeping machine would be similar. The Illustration 13–6 register is for a weekly pay period and shows the payroll data for each employee on a separate line. The column headings and the data recorded in the columns are in the main self-explanatory.

The columns under the heading "Daily Time" show hours worked each day by each employee. The total of each employee's hours is entered in the column headed "Total Hours." If hours worked include overtime hours, these are entered in the column headed "O.T. Hours."

The column headed "Reg. Pay Rate" is for the hourly pay rate of each employee. Total hours worked multiplied by the regular pay rate equals regular pay; overtime hours multiplied by the overtime premium rate equals overtime premium pay; and regular pay plus overtime premium pay is the gross pay of each employee.

Under the heading "Deductions," the amounts withheld from each employee's gross pay for social security or F.I.C.A. taxes are shown in the column marked "F.I.C.A. Taxes." These amounts are determined by multiplying the gross pay of each employee by the F.I.C.A. tax rate in effect. In this and the remaining illustrations of this chapter an assumed 5% rate is used.

Observe in the F.I.C.A. Taxes column of Illustration 13–6 that there is no F.I.C.A. deduction for the next to last employee, Robert Smith. This is because Smith's cumulative earnings for the year have previously passed the assumed $9,000 tax-exempt point and therefore his wages are no longer subject to tax. (See the discussion for Illustration 13–10 on page 380.)

As previously stated, the income tax withheld from each employee depends upon his gross pay and exemptions. This amount is commonly determined by the use of a wage bracket withholding table and when determined, it is entered in the column headed "Federal Income Taxes."

The column headed "Hosp. Ins." shows the amounts withheld from employees' wages to pay hospital insurance premiums for the employees and their families. The total withheld from all employees is a current liability of the employer until paid to the insurance company.

As previously stated, union contracts commonly require the employer to withhold union dues and to periodically remit the amounts withheld to the union. The total withheld for employees' union dues is

Employee	Clock Card No.	Daily Time							Total Hours	O.T. Hours	Earnings			
		M	T	W	T	F	S	S			Reg. Pay Rate	Reg-ular Pay	O.T. Pre-mium Pay	Gross Pay
Robert Austin	105	8	8	8	8	8			40		2.00	80.00		80.0
Charles Cross	97	8	8	8	8	8	4		44	4	3.00	132.00	6.00	138.0
John Cruz	89	8	8	8	8	8			40		2.50	100.00		100.0
Howard Keife	112	8	8	0	0	0			16		2.50	40.00		40.0
Lee Miller	95	8	8	8	8	8			40		2.50	100.00		100.0
Dale Sears	53	8	8	8	8	8			40		2.00	80.00		80.0
Robert Smith	68	8	8	8	8	8	4		44	4	4.50	198.00	9.00	207.0
George Tucker	74	8	8	8	8	8			40		2.50	100.00		100.0
Totals														845.0

Illustration
13–6

a current liability until paid to the union. The column marked "Union Dues" in the illustrated Payroll Register is for this deduction.

Additional columns may be added to the Payroll Register for deductions that occur sufficiently often to warrant special columns. For example, a company that regularly deducts amounts from its employees' pay for U.S. savings bonds may add a special column for this deduction.

An employee's gross pay less his total deductions is his net pay and is entered in the column headed "Net Pay." The total of this column is the amount to be paid the employees. The numbers of the checks used in paying the employees are entered in the column headed "Check No."

The three columns under the heading "Distribution" are for sorting the various salaries into kinds of salary expense. Here each employee's gross salary is entered in the proper column according to the type of his work. The column totals then tell the amounts to be debited to the salary expense accounts.

Recording the payroll ■ Generally a Payroll Register such as the one shown in Illustration 13–6 is a supplementary memorandum record. As a supplementary record, its information is not posted directly to the accounts but is first

	Deductions				Payment		Distribution		
I.C.A. axes	Federal Income Taxes	Hosp. Ins.	Union Dues	Total Deductions	Net Pay	Check No.	Sales Salaries	Office Salaries	Delivery Salaries
4.00	7.50	3.00		14.50	65.50	893		80.00	
6.90	16.70		2.50	26.10	111.90	894			138.00
5.00	7.00	4.50	1.50	18.00	82.00	895	100.00		
2.00	1.10	4.50	1.50	9.10	30.90	896	40.00		
5.00	9.10	4.50	1.50	20.10	79.90	897	100.00		
4.00	7.50			11.50	68.50	898		80.00	
	21.50	4.50		26.00	181.00	899		207.00	
5.00	11.10	3.00	1.50	20.60	79.40	900	100.00		
31.90	81.50	24.00	8.50	145.90	699.10		340.00	367.00	138.00

recorded with a general journal entry, which is then posted. The entry to record the payroll shown in Illustration 13–6 is:

Nov.	18	Sales Salaries Expense	340.00	
		Office Salaries Expense	367.00	
		Delivery Salaries Expense	138.00	
		F.I.C.A. Taxes Payable		31.90
		Employees' Federal Income Taxes Payable		81.50
		Employees' Hospital Insurance Premiums Payable		24.00
		Employees' Union Dues Payable		8.50
		Accrued Payroll Payable		699.10
		To record the payroll of the week ended November 18.		

The debits of this entry are taken from the Payroll Register's distribution column totals, and they charge the employees' gross earnings to the proper salary expense accounts. The credits to F.I.C.A. Taxes Payable, Employees' Federal Income Taxes Payable, Employees' Hospital Insurance Premiums Payable, and Employees' Union Dues Payable record these amounts as current liabilities. The credit to Accrued Payroll Payable records as a liability the amount to be paid the employees.

Paying the employees ■ Almost every business pays its employees with checks. In a company having but few employees these checks are often drawn on the regular bank account. When this is done, each check is recorded in either a Check Register or a Cash Disbursements Journal. Since each check results in a debit to the Accrued Payroll Payable account, posting labor may be saved by adding an Accrued Payroll Payable debit column to the Check Register or Cash Disbursements Journal. For example, assume that a firm uses a Check Register like that described in Chapter 6, before the introduction of the voucher system. If a firm uses such a register and adds an Accrued Payroll debit column, the entries to pay the employees of the Illustration 13–6 payroll will appear somewhat like those in Illustration 13–7.

		Check Register							
Date	Check No.	Payee	Account Debited	F	Sundry Accounts Debit	Accts. Pay. Debit	Accr. Payroll Debit	Pur. Dis. Credit	Cash Credit
Nov. 18	893	Robert Austin	Accrued Payroll				65.50		65.50
18	894	Charles Cross	"				111.90		111.90
18	895	John Cruz	"				82.00		82.00
18	896	Howard Keife	"				30.90		30.90
18	897	Lee Miller	"				79.90		79.90
18	898	Dale Sears	"				68.50		68.50
18	899	Robert Smith	"				181.00		181.00
18	900	George Tucker	"				79.40		79.40

Illustration 13–7

Although not required by law, most employers furnish each employee an earnings statement each payday. The objective of such a statement is to inform the employee and give him a record of hours worked, gross pay, deductions, and net pay that may be retained. The statement usually takes the form of a detachable paycheck portion that is removed before the check is cashed. A paycheck with a detachable portion showing deductions is reproduced in Illustration 13–8.

Payroll bank account ■ A business with many employees normally makes use of a special payroll bank account in paying its employees. When such an account is used, one check for the amount of the payroll is drawn on the regular bank account and deposited in the special payroll bank account. Individual payroll checks are then drawn on this special payroll account. Because only one check for the payroll is drawn on the regular bank account each payday, a special payroll bank account simplifies reconciliation of the regular bank account. It may be reconciled without considering the payroll checks outstanding, and there may be many of

Robert Austin	40		2.00	80.00		80.00	4.00	7.50	3.00		14.50	65.50
Employee	Total Hours	O.T. Hours	Reg. Pay Rate	Reg-ular Pay	O.T. Prem. Pay	Gross Pay	F.I.C.A. Taxes	In-come Taxes	Hosp. Ins.	Union Dues	Total Deduc-tions	Net Pay

STATEMENT OF EARNINGS AND DEDUCTIONS FOR EMPLOYEE'S RECORDS—DETACH BEFORE CASHING CHECK

THE EUGENE MANUFACTURING COMPANY
2590 Chula Vista Street · Eugene, Oregon

No. 893

PAY TO THE ORDER OF____ Robert Austin _____ DATE November 18, 1972 $ 65.50

----------------Sixty-five dollars and fifty cents----------------

EUGENE MANUFACTURING COMPANY

Merchants National Bank
Eugene, Oregon

James R. Morris

Illustration
13–8

these. Likewise, when the payroll bank account is separately reconciled, only the outstanding payroll checks need be considered.

A company using a special payroll bank account completes the following steps in paying its employees:

1. First, it records the information shown on its Payroll Register in the usual manner with a general journal entry similar to the one illustrated on page 375. This entry causes the sum of the employees' net pay to be credited to the liability account Accrued Payroll Payable.
2. Next, a single check payable to Payroll Bank Account for the amount of the payroll is drawn and entered in the Check Register. This results in a debit to Accrued Payroll Payable and a credit to Cash.
3. Then this check is endorsed and deposited in the payroll bank account. This transfers cash equal to the payroll from the regular bank account to the special payroll bank account.
4. Last, individual payroll checks are drawn on the special payroll bank account and delivered to the employees. These pay the employees and, as soon as all employees cash their checks, exhaust the funds in the special account.

A special Payroll Check Register may be used in connection with a payroll bank account. However, most companies do not use such a register but prefer to enter the payroll check numbers in their Payroll Register, making it act as a Check Register.

Employee's Individual Earnings Record

■ An Employee's Individual Earnings Record, Illustration 13–9, provides for each employee in one record a full year's summary of his working time, gross earnings, deductions, and net pay. In addition it accumulates information that—

1. Serves as a basis for the employer's state and federal payroll tax returns.
2. Tells when an employee's earnings have reached the tax-exempt points for F.I.C.A. and state and federal unemployment taxes.
3. Supplies data for the Withholding Statement, Form W–2, which must be given to the employee at the end of the year.

The payroll information on an Employee's Individual Earnings Record is taken from the Payroll Register. The information as to earnings, deductions, and net pay is first recorded on a single line in the Payroll Register, from where it is posted each pay period to the earnings record.

Illustration
13–9

Payroll taxes levied on the employer

■ Under the previous discussion of the Federal Social Security Act, it was pointed out that F.I.C.A. taxes are levied in like amounts on both employed workers and their employers. A covered employer is required by law to deduct from his employees' pay the amounts of their F.I.C.A. taxes; but in addition, he must himself pay a tax equal to the sum of his employees' F.I.C.A. taxes. Commonly, the tax levied on the employer is recorded at the same time the payroll to which it relates is recorded. Also, since both the employees' taxes and employer's tax are reported on the same tax return and are paid in one amount, the liability for both is normally recorded in the same liability account, the F.I.C.A. Taxes Payable account.

As previously explained, although F.I.C.A. taxes are levied on both covered employers and their employees, employers only are required to pay federal and, usually, state unemployment taxes. Most employers record all three of these payroll taxes with one general journal entry. This entry is normally made at the time the payroll to which the taxes relate is recorded. For example, the entry to record the employer's payroll taxes on the payroll of Illustration 13–6 is:

Nov.	18	Payroll Taxes Expense..................................	46.30	
		F.I.C.A. Taxes Payable		31.90
		State Unemployment Taxes Payable...........		12.15
		Federal Unemployment Taxes Payable		2.25
		To record the employer's payroll taxes.		

The debit of this entry is to the expense account Payroll Taxes Expense. Often this one debit is broken into amounts applicable to each type of salaries and is recorded in several expense accounts such as, for example, Payroll Taxes Expense on Sales Salaries, Payroll Taxes Expense on Office Salaries, and Payroll Taxes Expense on Delivery Salaries. A division such as this makes it possible to classify on the income statement the taxes expense applicable to each type of salaries.

There are three current liability accounts credited in the foregoing entry recording the employer's payroll taxes. The credit to F.I.C.A. Taxes Payable is for $31.90. This amount is equal to and matches the total deduction from the employees' wages in the Payroll Register of Illustration 13–6. It is 5% of $638. The payroll total is $845; but since the amount previously paid in wages to one employee, Robert Smith, exceeds the $9,000 tax-exempt point, the $207 of his current wages is tax-exempt. The fact that Smith's current wages are not subject to F.I.C.A. taxes is determined by the person responsible for completing the Payroll Register by examining the Cumulative Pay column of Smith's individual earnings record.

The $12.15 credit to State Unemployment Taxes Payable in the employer's payroll tax entry is based on the assumption the employer's tax rate is 2.7% of the first $4,200 paid each employee. As previously stated, it is the duty of the one responsible for completing the Payroll Register to check the Cumulative Pay columns of the employees' individual earnings records to see when any employee's earnings reach the tax-exempt point or points and are no longer subject to state and federal unemployment taxes, and when the earnings reach $9,000 and are no longer subject to F.I.C.A. taxes. In the illustrative payroll it is assumed that the employees have cumulative earnings prior to this pay period and earnings subject to the various taxes as shown in Illustration 13–10.

If the employees have prior cumulative earnings as listed in Illustration 13–10, then two employees have earned in excess of $4,200 and their pay is assumed, as in the majority of states, to be exempt from state unemployment taxes. One employee has previously earned $4,150 and only the first $50 of his earnings are subject to the tax, and the wages of the remaining employees are taxable in full. Consequently, the $12.15 credit to State Unemployment Taxes Payable in the entry recording the employer's payroll taxes results from multiplying $450 of wages subject to tax by the assumed 2.7% rate.

Employees' Cumulative Earnings through the Last Pay Period and Earnings Subject to the Various Taxes

Employees	Earnings through Last Pay Period	Earnings This Pay Period	Earnings Subject to—	
			F.I.C.A. Taxes	State and Federal Unemployment Taxes
Robert Austin	$3,252	$ 80.00	$ 80.00	$ 80.00
Charles Cross................	5,246	138.00	138.00	
John Cruz	2,860	100.00	100.00	100.00
Howard Keife.................	1,810	40.00	40.00	40.00
Lee Miller......................	880	100.00	100.00	100.00
Dale Sears....................	2,400	80.00	80.00	80.00
Robert Smith.................	9,115	207.00		
George Tucker..............	4,150	100.00	100.00	50.00
		$845.00	$638.00	$450.00

Illustration 13–10

As the law is presently amended, an employer's federal unemployment tax is based on the first $4,200 in wages paid each employee. Therefore the federal unemployment tax liability in the illustrated journal entry results from multiplying $450 by the 0.5% rate, or is $2.25.

Paying the payroll taxes

■ Federal income and the F.I.C.A. taxes withheld each payday from the employees' pay plus the F.I.C.A. tax imposed on the employer are current liabilities until paid to the United States Treasury Department. The normal method of payment is to deposit the amounts due to the credit of the United States Treasury in a bank authorized to accept such deposits. The depositing procedure results in a punched card which the bank mails to the Internal Revenue Service. On receipt of the card the Internal Revenue Service gives the depositor credit for paying the amount deposited, and the depositor reports on his tax return that he has paid the taxes through a federal deposit or deposits.

Required times of payment depend on the amounts involved. If the sum of the F.I.C.A. taxes plus the employees' income taxes is less than $200 for a quarter, the taxes may be paid when the employer files his Employer's Quarterly Tax Return, Form 941. This return is due on April 30, July 31, October 31, and January 31 following the end of each calendar quarter, and a check for the taxes, if less than $200, may be attached to the return or the taxes may be deposited in a federal depository bank at the time the return is filed. The check or the deposit is recorded in the same manner as a check paying any other liability.

If the taxes exceed $200 in a quarter, after each payday the employer must total the amount of his employees' income and F.I.C.A. taxes withheld since the beginning of the quarter plus his own employer's F.I.C.A. tax. This total, less any deposits already made during the quarter, is the employer's F.I.C.A. and income tax liability. Then (1) if on any of the 7th, 15th, 22d, and last day of any month in the quarter this tax liability reaches $2,000 or more, the entire amount must be deposited to the credit of the United States Treasury within three banking days thereafter. (2) If as of the last day of the first or second month of a quarter the tax liability is less than $2,000 but more than $200, the amount must be deposited on or before the 15th day of the next month, unless a deposit has already been made during the month. For the last month in the quarter the deposit does not have to be made until the end of the next month, or it may be remitted with the quarterly tax return.

A deposit of F.I.C.A. and withheld employees' income taxes in a federal depository bank pays these taxes. Consequently, if at the time an employer files his Employer's Quarterly Tax Return, Form 941, he has paid the taxes reported on the return by means of deposits, he needs only to mail the return to the Internal Revenue Service, and no accounting entries are required.

In most states, when state unemployment taxes are less than $100 per month, they may be paid quarterly. If they exceed $100 per month, some states require monthly payments. This is somewhat similar to the federal procedures; therefore, most employers account for state unemployment taxes in the same manner as F.I.C.A. and employee income taxes.

An employer's federal unemployment tax for the first three quarters of a year must be deposited in a federal depository bank by the last day of the month following each quarter (i.e., on April 30, July 31, and October 31). However, no deposit is required if the tax due for a quarter plus the undeposited tax for previous quarters are $100 or less. The tax for the last quarter of a year plus the undeposited tax for previous quarters must either be deposited or paid with the Employer's Annual Federal Unemployment Tax Return, Form 940, which must be filed on or before January 31 following the end of the tax year. When the form is filed, a check for the tax due may be attached if the tax has not previously been paid by federal deposits. The check or the federal deposits are recorded in the same manner as a check paying any other liability.

Accruing taxes and wages

■ Payroll taxes are levied on wages actually paid; consequently, there is no legal liability for taxes on accrued wages. Nevertheless, both wages and the employer's payroll taxes on the wages are from a theoretical viewpoint expenses of the accounting period in which the wages are earned; and if the income statement is to show all expenses of an accounting period, both accrued wages and the accrued taxes on the wages should be recorded at the end of the period.

To illustrate the entry for accruing wages and taxes on the wages, assume that (1) a company's accounting period ends on June 30, (2) its last pay period ended on June 26, (3) the company employees worked on June 28, 29, and 30 and earned sales salaries of $750 and office salaries of $250 during the three days. The adjusting entry to record these accrued wages and payroll taxes is:

June	30	Sales Salaries	750.00	
		Office Salaries	250.00	
		Payroll Taxes Expense	82.00	
		F.I.C.A. Taxes Payable		50.00
		State Unemployment Taxes Payable		27.00
		Federal Unemployment Taxes Payable		5.00
		Accrued Payroll Payable		1,000.00
		To record the accrued payroll.		

The $82 debit to Payroll Taxes Expense is the sum of the F.I.C.A., federal unemployment, and state unemployment taxes levied on the employer. The amount is based on the assumptions that all the wages were subject to taxes at a 5% F.I.C.A. tax rate, a 0.5% federal unemployment rate, and a 2.7% state unemployment rate.

Although payroll taxes on accrued wages are theoretically an expense of the accounting period in which the wages are earned, often such accrued taxes are not material in amount. Consequently, many accountants apply the rule of materiality and do not accrue such taxes.

Machine methods

■ Manually prepared pen-and-ink records like the ones described in this chapter are found in many small concerns, and very satisfactorily meet their needs. However, concerns having many employees commonly use machines in their payroll work. The machines vary but are usually designed to take advantage of the fact that each pay period much the same information must be entered for each employee in the Payroll Register, on his earnings record, and on his paycheck. The machines take advantage of this and simultaneously print the information in all three places in one operation.

1. What are F.I.C.A. taxes? Who pays these taxes and for what purposes are the funds from F.I.C.A. taxes used?
2. Company A has one employee from whose pay it withholds each week $4.40 of federal income tax and $4.16 of F.I.C.A. tax. Company B has 200 employees from whose pay it withholds each week over $2,000 of employee F.I.C.A. and federal income taxes. When must each of these companies remit these amounts to the Internal Revenue Service?
3. What benefits are paid to unemployed workers from funds raised by the Federal Unemployment Insurance Act? Why was this act passed?
4. Who pays federal unemployment insurance taxes? What is the tax rate?
5. What are the objectives of state unemployment insurance laws? Who pays state unemployment insurance?
6. What is a state unemployment merit rating? Why are such merit ratings granted?
7. What determines the amount that must be deducted from an employee's wages for federal income taxes?
8. What is a wage bracket withholding table? Use the wage bracket withholding table in Illustration 13–4 to find the income tax to be withheld from the wages of an employee with three exemptions who earned $108 in a week.
9. What does the Fair Labor Standards Act require of a covered employer?
10. How is a clock card used in recording the time an employee is on the job?
11. How is a special payroll bank account used in paying the wages of employees?
12. At the end of an accounting period a firm's special payroll bank account has a $162.35 balance because the payroll checks of two employees have not cleared the bank. Should this $162.35 appear on the firm's balance sheet? If so, where?
13. What information is accumulated on an employee's individual earnings record? Why must this information be accumulated? For what purposes is the information used?
14. What payroll taxes are levied on the employer? What taxes are deducted from the wages of an employee?

Exercise 13–1

An employee of a company subject to the Fair Labor Standards Act worked 44 hours during the week ended January 7. His pay rate is $2.50 per hour and his wages are subject to no deductions other than F.I.C.A. and federal income taxes. He claims three income tax deductions. Calculate his regular pay, overtime premium pay, gross pay, F.I.C.A. tax deduction at an assumed 5% rate, income tax deduction (use the wage bracket withholding table of Illustration 13–4), total deductions, and net pay.

Exercise 13–2

On January 6, at the end of its first weekly pay period in the year, the column totals of a company's Payroll Register showed that its sales employees had earned $1,500 and its office employees had earned $500. The employees were to have F.I.C.A. taxes withheld at an assumed 5% rate plus $185 of federal income taxes, $45 of union dues, and $75 of hospital insurance premiums. Calculate the amount of F.I.C.A. taxes to be withheld and give the general journal entry to record the Payroll Register.

Exercise 13–3

Give the general journal entry to record the employer's payroll taxes resulting from the Exercise 13–2 payroll. Assume the company has a merit rating that reduces its state unemployment tax rate to 1.8% of the first $4,200 paid each employee.

Exercise 13–4

The following information as to earnings and deductions for the pay period ended December 21 was taken from a company's payroll records:

Employee's Names	Gross Pay	Earnings to End of Previous Week	Federal Income Taxes	Hospital Insurance Deductions
James Abbott	$125	$2,880	$10.30	$ 4.50
Jane Cotton..............	140	4,085	13.50	
George Green...........	185	8,950	18.30	4.50
Jerry Hall	175	9,010	19.10	4.50
	$625		$61.20	$13.50

Required:
1. Calculate the employees' F.I.C.A. tax withholdings at an assumed rate of 5% on the first $9,000 paid each employee, total deductions, and net pay.
2. Prepare a general journal entry to record the payroll information. Assume all employees work in the office.
3. Prepare a general journal entry to record the employer's payroll taxes resulting from the payroll. Assume a state unemployment tax rate of 1.5% of the first $4,200 paid each employee.

Problems **Problem 13–1**

The column totals of a company's Payroll Register indicated its sales employees had earned $2,000 and its office employees $500 during the pay period ended January 6. The employees were to have F.I.C.A. taxes withheld at an assumed 5% rate, plus $225 of federal income taxes, $110 of group insurance deductions, and $50 of union dues.

Required:
1. Calculate the total of the F.I.C.A. Taxes Payable column in the Payroll Register.

2. Prepare a general journal entry to record the payroll register information.
3. Prepare a general journal entry to record the employer's payroll taxes resulting from the payroll. Assume the company has a merit rating that reduces its state unemployment tax rate to 2.2% of the first $4,200 paid each employee.
4. Under the assumption the company uses special payroll checks and a payroll bank account in paying its employees, give the check register entry (Check No. 815) to transfer funds equal to the payroll from the regular bank account to the payroll bank account.
5. Answer this question: After the check register entry is made and posted, are additional debit and credit entries required to record the payroll checks and pay the employees?

Problem 13-2

The following information was taken from a company's payroll records for the weekly pay period ended December 18:

Employees' Names	Clock Card No.	Daily Time							Pay Rate	Federal Income Taxes	Medi-cal Insur-ance	Union Dues	Earnings to End of Previous Week
		M	T	W	T	F	S	S					
Roy Andrews......	11	8	8	8	8	8	0	0	2.75	10.70	4.75	2.00	2,275
Jerry Dale	12	8	8	8	8	8	0	0	2.75	8.70	4.75	2.00	4,175
Ray Lewis..........	13	8	8	8	8	8	4	0	3.50	19.10	4.75	2.50	7,725
Walter Mohr.......	14	8	8	8	8	8	0	0	4.50	18.30	4.75		8,950
Mary Page..........	15	8	8	8	8	8	4	0	2.50	11.50	3.00		2,910

Required:
1. Enter the relevant information in the proper columns of a Payroll Register and complete the register using a F.I.C.A. tax rate of 5% on the first $9,000 paid each employee. Assume the company is subject to the Fair Labor Standards Act, and also assume the first two employees are salesmen, the third drives the delivery truck, and the last two work in the office.
2. Prepare a general journal entry to record the payroll register information.
3. Make the check register entry (Check No. 234) to transfer funds equal to the payroll from the regular bank account to the payroll bank account under the assumption the company uses special payroll checks and a payroll bank account in paying its employees. Assume the first payroll check is numbered 668 and enter the payroll check numbers in the Payroll Register.
4. Prepare a general journal entry to record the employer's payroll taxes resulting from the payroll. Assume the company has a merit rating that reduces its state unemployment tax rate to 1.5% of the first $4,200 paid each employee.

Problem 13-3

A company subject to the Fair Labor Standards Act accumulated the following payroll information for the weekly pay period ended December 15:

Employees' Names	Clock Card No.	Daily Time							Pay Rate	Income Tax Exemptions	Medical Insurance	Union Dues	Earnings to End of Previous Week
		M	T	W	T	F	S	S					
Paul Baer	22	8	8	8	8	8	0	0	2.90	3	5.00	2.00	2,150
Frank Clift	23	8	8	8	8	8	0	0	2.90	2	5.00	2.00	2,916
Dale Duff.........	24	0	0	8	8	8	0	0	4.50	4	5.00		8,960
June Nash	25	8	8	8	8	9	3	0	2.25	2	5.00	2.00	4,132
Lee Ross..........	26	8	8	8	9	9	0	0	3.50	5	5.00	2.50	7,980

Required:

1. Enter the relevant information in the proper columns of a Payroll Register and complete the register using a F.I.C.A. tax rate of 5% of the first $9,000 paid each employee. Use the wage bracket withholding table of Illustration 13–4 to determine the federal income tax to be withheld from the wages of each employee. Assume the first two employees are salesmen, the second two work in the office, and the last drives the delivery truck.
2. Prepare a general journal entry to record the payroll register information.
3. Make the check register entry to transfer funds equal to the payroll from the regular bank account to the payroll bank account (Check No. 567) under the assumption the company uses special payroll checks and a payroll bank account in paying its employees. Assume the first payroll check is numbered 444 and enter the payroll check numbers in the Payroll Register.
4. Prepare a general journal entry to record the employer's payroll taxes resulting from the payroll. Assume the company has a merit rating that reduces its state unemployment tax rate to 1.8% of the first $4,200 paid each employee.

Problem 13–4

A company has nine employees to each of whom it pays $400 per month on the last day of each month. On June 1 the following accounts and balances appeared in its ledger:

a) F.I.C.A. Taxes Payable, $360. (Since the company's F.I.C.A. and employees' income taxes exceed $200 per month, the balance of this account represents the liability for both the employer and employees' F.I.C.A. taxes for the May 31 payroll only.)
b) Employees' Federal Income Taxes Payable, $350 (liability for May only).
c) Federal Unemployment Taxes Payable, $90 (liability for first five months of the year).
d) State Unemployment Taxes Payable, $144 (liability for April and May).
e) Employees' Group Insurance Payable, $80 (liability for April and May).

During June and July the company completed the following payroll related transactions:

June 12   Issued Check No. 755 payable to Security Bank, a federal depository bank authorized to receive F.I.C.A. and employee income tax payments from employers. The check was for $710 and was in payment of the May F.I.C.A. and employee income taxes.

    30   Prepared a general journal entry to record the June Payroll Register which had the following column totals:

F.I.C.A. Taxes	Federal Income Taxes	Group Insurance Deductions	Total Deductions	Net Pay	Office Salaries	Shop Wages
$180	$350	$40	$570	$3,030	$400	$3,200

June 30   Issued Check No. 828 payable to Payroll Bank Account in payment of the June payroll. Endorsed the check, deposited it in the payroll bank account, and issued payroll checks to the employees.

30   Prepared and posted a general journal entry to record the employer's payroll taxes resulting from the June payroll. The company has a merit rating that reduces its state unemployment tax rate to 2% of the first $4,200 paid each employee.

July 14   Issued Check No. 863 payable to Security Bank. The check was in payment of the June F.I.C.A. and employee income taxes.

14   Issued Check No. 884 payable to Apex Insurance Company. The check was for $120 and was in payment of the April, May, and June employee group insurance premiums.

14   Issued Check No. 895 to the State Tax Commission for the April, May, and June state unemployment taxes. Mailed the check along with the second quarter tax return to the State Tax Commission.

31   Issued Check No. 915 payable to Security Bank. Since the tax liability exceeded $100, the check was in payment of the employer's federal unemployment taxes for the first two quarters of the year.

31   Mailed to the Internal Revenue Service the Employer's Quarterly Tax Return reporting the F.I.C.A. taxes and the employees' federal income tax deductions for the second quarter of the year.

Required:
Prepare the necessary general journal and check register entries to record these transactions.

Alternate problems

Problem 13–1A

On January 7, at the end of the first weekly pay period of the year, the column totals of a company's Payroll Register indicated its sales employees had earned $1,500, its office employees had earned $900, and its delivery employees $400. The employees were to have F.I.C.A. taxes withheld from their wages at an assumed 5% rate plus $290 federal income taxes, $38 group insurance deductions, and $24 of union dues.

Required:
1. Calculate the total of the F.I.C.A. Taxes Payable column in the Payroll Register, and prepare a general journal entry to record the register information.

2. Prepare a general journal entry to record the employer's payroll taxes resulting from the payroll. Assume the company has a merit rating that reduces its state unemployment tax rate to 1.5% of the first $4,200 paid each employee.
3. Under the assumption the company uses a payroll bank account and special payroll checks in paying its employees, give the check register entry (Check No. 745) to transfer funds equal to the payroll from the regular bank account to the payroll bank account.
4. Answer this question: After the check register entry is made and posted, are additional debit and credit entries required to record the payroll checks and pay the employees?

Problem 13-2A

A company's payroll records provided the following information for the weekly pay period ended December 20:

Employees' Names	Clock Card No.	Daily Time							Pay Rate	Federal Income Taxes	Medi-cal Insur-ance	Union Dues	Earnings to End of Previous Week
		M	T	W	T	F	S	S					
Dale Agnew	14	8	8	8	8	8	0	0	4.50	20.30	4.50		8,920
Mary Hall	15	8	8	8	8	8	4	0	2.50	9.50	4.50	1.50	4,140
John Koop..........	16	8	8	8	8	8	0	0	3.00	10.30	4.50	2.00	2,710
Carl Lee	17	8	8	8	8	8	0	0	3.00	12.30	4.50	2.00	3,325
Roy Page	18	8	8	8	8	8	2	0	4.00	20.70	4.50	2.50	8,410

Required:
1. Enter the relevant information in the proper columns of a Payroll Register and complete the register using a F.I.C.A. tax rate of 5% of the first $9,000 paid each employee. Assume the company is subject to the Fair Labor Standards Act, and assume the first two employees work in the office, the next two are salesmen, and the last drives the delivery truck.
2. Prepare a general journal entry to record the payroll register information.
3. Assume the company uses special payroll checks drawn on a payroll bank account in paying its employees, and make the check register entry (Check No. 202) to transfer funds equal to the payroll from the regular bank account to the payroll bank account. Also assume the first payroll check is No. 653 and enter the payroll check numbers in the Payroll Register.
4. Prepare a general journal entry to record the employer's payroll taxes resulting from the payroll. Assume the concern has a merit rating that reduces its state unemployment tax rate to 1.5% of the first $4,200 paid each employee.

Problem 13-3A

The following information for the weekly pay period ended December 17 was taken from the records of a company subject to the Fair Labor Standards Act:

Employees' Names	Clock Card No.	Daily Time M	T	W	T	F	S	S	Pay Rate	Income Tax Exemp-tions	Medi-cal Insur-ance	Union Dues	Earnings to End of Previous Week
Mary Alt..........	21	8	8	8	8	8	0	0	2.50	2			4,130
Harry Bray.......	22	8	8	8	8	8	2	0	4.50	3	4.50		8,920
Jerry Hamm......	23	8	8	8	8	8	0	0	2.80	4	4.50	2.00	2,510
Alex Hunt........	24	8	8	8	8	8	0	0	2.80	2	4.50	2.00	5,650
Gary Sage	25	8	8	8	8	8	4	0	3.00	3	4.50	2.50	2,912

Required:

1. Enter the relevant information in the proper columns of a Payroll Register and complete the register using a F.I.C.A. tax rate of 5% of the first $9,000 paid each employee. Use the wage bracket withholding table of Illustration 13–4 to determine the federal income taxes to be withheld from the wages of the employees. Assume that the first two employees work in the office, the next two are salesmen, and the last drives the delivery truck.
2. Prepare a general journal entry to record the payroll register information.
3. Make the check register entry (Check No. 789) to transfer funds equal to the payroll from the regular bank account to the payroll bank account. As-sume the first payroll check is numbered 901 and enter the payroll check numbers in the Payroll Register.
4. Prepare a general journal entry to record the employer's payroll taxes re-sulting from the payroll. Assume the company has a merit rating that reduces its state unemployment tax rate to 2.5% of the first $4,200 paid each employee.

Problem 13–4A

Mesa Company has eight employees to each of whom it pays $475 per month on the last day of each month. On June 1 the following accounts and balances appeared in its ledger:

F.I.C.A. taxes payable (liability for the employer's and employees' taxes resulting from the May 31 payroll) $380.00

Employees' federal income taxes payable (liability for the May 31 payroll deductions) 375.00

Federal unemployment taxes payable (liability for first five months of the year) 95.00

State unemployment taxes payable (liability for April and May) 114.00

Employees' group insurance payable (liability for April and May)...... 84.00

During June and July the company completed the following payroll related transactions:

June 14   Issued Check No. 816 payable to Guaranty Bank, a federal deposi-tory bank authorized to accept F.I.C.A. and employee income tax payments from employers. The check was for $755 and was in pay-ment of the May F.I.C.A. and employee income taxes.

June 30   Prepared and posted a general journal entry to record the June Payroll Register. The register had the following column totals:

Gross pay	$3,800.00
Employees' F.I.C.A. taxes payable	190.00
Employees federal income taxes payable	375.00
Group insurance deductions	42.00
Total deductions	607.00
Net pay	3,193.00
Sales salaries	3,325.00
Office salaries	475.00

     30   Issued Check No. 863 payable to Payroll Bank Account in payment of the June payroll. Endorsed the check, deposited it in the payroll bank account, and issued payroll checks to the employees.

     30   Prepared and posted a general journal entry to record the employer's payroll taxes resulting from the June 30 payroll. Due to a merit rating the company's state unemployment tax rate was 1.5% of the first $4,200 paid each employee.

July 15   Issued Check No. 871 payable to Guaranty Bank. The check was in payment of the June F.I.C.A. and employee income taxes.

     15   Issued Check No. 912 to the State Tax Commission for the April, May, and June state unemployment taxes. Mailed the check along with the second quarter tax return to the State Tax Commission.

     20   Issued Check No. 933 payable to Security Insurance Company. The check was for $126 and was in payment of the April, May, and June employee group insurance premiums.

     31   Issued Check No. 989 payable to Guaranty Bank. The company's federal unemployment tax for the second quarter plus the undeposited federal unemployment tax for the first quarter exceeded $100; consequently, this check was in payment of the tax for the first two quarters.

     31   Mailed the Internal Revenue Service the Employer's Quarterly Tax Return, Form 941, reporting the F.I.C.A. taxes and the employees' federal income tax deductions for the second quarter.

Required:
Prepare the necessary general journal and check register entries to record these transactions.

Decision problem 13–1, Plastaglas Company   Plastaglas Company manufactures a number of products from plastics. It has 300 full-time employees, all earning $4,200 or more per year. The company's plant and office are located in a state in which the maximum state unemployment tax rate is 2.7% of the first $4,200 paid each employee. However, due to its excellent past employment record, the company has a merit rating that reduces its state unemployment tax rate to from 2.7% to 0.5% of the first $4,200 paid each employee.

    Recently the company secured an order for Christmas toys from a large chain of department stores. The order should be very profitable and will probably be repeated each year. In filling the order Plastaglas Company can stamp out the parts for the toys with present machines and employees. However, it will have to add 50 women to its work force for 40 hours per week for 10 weeks to assemble the toys and pack them for shipment.

The company can hire these women and add them to its own payroll or it can secure their services through Extra Hands, Inc., a company in the business of supplying temporary help. If the temporary help is secured through Extra Hands, Inc., Plastaglas Company will pay Extra Hands, Inc., $3.60 per hour for each hour worked by each person supplied. The people supplied will be employees of Extra Hands, Inc., and it will pay their wages and all taxes on the wages. On the other hand, if Plastaglas Company employs the women and places them on its payroll, it will pay them $2.50 per hour and will also pay the following payroll taxes on their wages: F.I.C.A. tax, 5%; federal unemployment tax, 0.5%; and state unemployment tax, 2.7% of the wages paid the temporary employees. (The state unemployment tax rate will be 2.7% because if the company hires the temporary people and terminates them each year after 10 weeks, it will lose its merit rating.)

Should Plastaglas Company place the temporary help on its own payroll or should it secure their services through Extra Hands, Inc.? Justify your answer.

Chapter 14

Accounting systems: manual, mechanical, and electronic

■ An accounting system consists of the business papers, records, and reports plus the procedures that are used in recording and reporting transactions. Operation of an accounting system begins with the preparation of a business paper, such as an invoice or check, and includes the capture of the data entered on this paper and its flow through the recording, classifying, summarizing, and reporting steps of the system.

Actually, an accounting system is a data processing system, and it may be a manual, a mechanical, or an electronic system, depending upon how data are processed within it.

Manual data processing

■ Thus far this text has described only manually prepared, handposted, pen-and-ink records and procedures; and while such records and procedures are good for introducing a student to accounting, they are not satisfactory for any but a very small business, and even for a small business they may often be improved.

One way to improve any pen-and-ink system is to reduce the number of times the same information is copied and recopied in the records. For example, in the systems described thus far a source document, such as a check or an invoice, is prepared for each transaction. The document is then recorded in a journal, and is later posted to the accounts. This writing-copying-posting procedure accomplishes the recording objective, but it takes time and also offers opportunities for errors at each copying and recopying of the record. Consequently, anything that reduces the number of times the transaction information is copied and recopied improves the system.

Pegboard systems

So-called pegboard systems reduce the number of times accounting information is copied and recopied. There are many such systems on the market. All are designed to process a portion or all the data of a transaction with one writing, and they are called pegboard systems because they depend on a board or other device containing pegs to align and hold together the documents and records used in the system. In addition to the pegboard, all depend upon carbon paper and specially designed forms to produce with one writing the several records of a transaction.

Payroll accounting may be used to show the operation of a pegboard system. Recall from the chapter on payroll accounting that information as to the hours an employee worked, his earnings, deductions, and net pay are entered opposite his name in a Payroll Register, again on his individual earnings record, and again on the detachable stub of his paycheck. Illustration 14–1 shows how the paycheck, earnings record, and Payroll Register may be aligned on a pegboard so that this information can be entered on all three records with one writing.

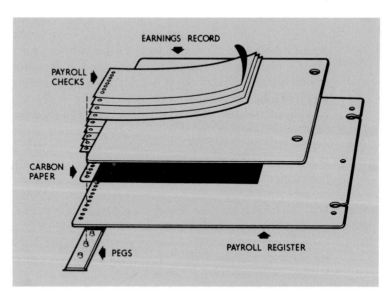

Illustration
14–1

In the pegboard system of Illustration 14–1 the Payroll Register is placed on the pegboard with a sheet of carbon paper face down over it. Next a pad of payroll checks is placed over the carbon paper. The detachable stub of each check is at the check's top (like Illustration 13–8), and the stub has carbon on its back. Also, the checks are fastened together with each check extending one line below the check above in the pad, like shingles on a roof. This "shingling" of the checks causes the employees' earnings and deductions to be entered on separate lines of the Payroll Register, with each employee's payroll information appearing one line below that of the preceding employee.

Before an employee's hours, deductions, and net pay are written on his check stub, his earnings record is slipped under the check and its stub. This makes it possible to enter the payroll information on the check stub, the earnings record, and in the Payroll Register with one writing.

After the payroll information for an employee is entered on his check stub, the check which does not have carbon on its back is completed. The check and stub are then detached, and the procedures are repeated for the next employee.

In addition to payroll records, pegboard systems are available for recording sales, purchases, cash receipts, and cash disbursements. In recording credit sales, for example, the entry on the customer's month-end statement, the posting to his account, and the entry in the Sales Journal are all made with one writing.

In any pegboard system it is usually impossible to enter all the information about a transaction on the source document and in all the records with one writing. Ideally the information that is common to all should be entered with one writing; and the forms should be so designed that the information that is not the same on all the records may be entered on each individual record at the same time the common information is entered.

Mechanical data processing

■ With sufficient time, one or more people can manually process all the accounting data of a business; and if the business is small, such records may serve its purposes very well. However, on a per transaction basis, manually kept records are costly and require much time. Consequently, when there are sufficient transactions, machines are normally employed to reduce costs and speed the data processing.

Cash registers, adding machines, and desk calculators are commonly used machines that speed data processing. Cash registers accumulate totals for cash sales, credit sales, sales taxes, and receipts on account. Adding machines and calculators speed the arithmetical processes and also reduce the expense and annoyance of errors.

Less commonly used data processing machines are electric accounting machines and punched card equipment.

Electric accounting machines

There are many electric accounting machines on the market, some designed for a single task and others for a multiplicity of tasks. No effort will be made to describe all the available machines. In fact only one machine will be discussed, and it for purposes of showing how such machines reduce labor and speed the processing of accounting data.

Illustration 14–2 shows an electric accounting machine which can be used for sales accounting, cash receipts, cash disbursements, accounts payable, payroll, and other accounting applications. No attempt will be made to describe the machine's operation in each of these applications. However, when used in sales accounting, as an example, the machine will produce the invoice for each charge sale, post to the customer's account, update the statement to be sent the customer at the end of the month, and enter the sale in the Sales Journal, all in one operation. Furthermore, it is as proficient in other applications.

Illustration
14–2

Courtesy National Cash Register Company

In sales accounting the current page of the Sales Journal is placed in the machine at the time the operator begins processing a group of sales transactions. In Illustration 14–2 the Sales Journal sheet is on the tray at the back of the machine. Next, after putting the Sales Journal sheet in the machine, the operator will for each charge sale place in the machine's carriage a blank invoice form, the customer's account from the subsidiary Accounts Receivable Ledger, and the statement to be mailed to the customer at the end of the month. After this she picks up in the machine from the customer's account the amount of his previous balance. She then types the customer's name, address, terms, et cetera on the invoice. Then she types on the invoice the commodities sold. For each commodity this consists of a description, the number of units sold, and the unit price. After listing units and unit price for a commodity, the operator depresses a key and the machine multiplies units by unit price and prints the extension. After listing all items, the operator presses another key and the machine totals the invoice and prints the total on the invoice, makes the entry in the Sales Journal, and spaces over and enters the sale and the new balance on the customer's account and on the month-end statement. After this the carriage returns automatically and opens for the removal of the invoice, customer's account, and statement. It also spaces the Sales Journal sheet up one line and is ready for recording the next sale.

In addition to the foregoing, when the operator completes the processing of a day's sales, the machine will print out the dollar total of the invoices processed, which is the day's debit to the Accounts Receivable controlling account. Also, it will print out the total credit to Sales and, if any, the credit to Sales Taxes Payable. Furthermore, if the sales were entered in the machine by departments, it will break down the sales credit into totals by departments.

Punched card accounting

When punched cards are used in accounting, information from an invoice, check, credit memorandum, or other source document is punched into cards with a card punch, called a key punch, like the one shown in Illustration 14–3. Such a punch has a keyboard similar to that of a typewriter and is operated in much the same manner, punching a hole or holes when a key is depressed. After the data from the source document is punched into the cards, the cards can be read by other machines. In each case, when the cards are fed into other machines, the card holes create electrical impulses which cause the machines to sort the cards, post their data to other cards, add, multiply, divide, and subtract, select and summarize, and print accounting reports, all automatically. For example, machines will take the accounts receivable of a concern when punched into cards like the one of Illustration 14–6 on page 401, sort the information, and print a schedule of accounts receivable by age like the one described on page 242. Furthermore, the machine will sort the accounts (cards) at the rate of up to 1,000 cards a minute and automatically print the account amounts in columns by age at the rate of up to 140 cards per minute.

The heart of a punched card accounting system is a series of cards like the one shown in Illustration 14–4. The card shown has 80 vertical columns in which holes may be punched, each column having 12 punching positions, 10 numbered (lines) 0 through 9 and two unnumbered positions in the upper margin. Both alphabetical and numerical infor-

Illustration
14–3

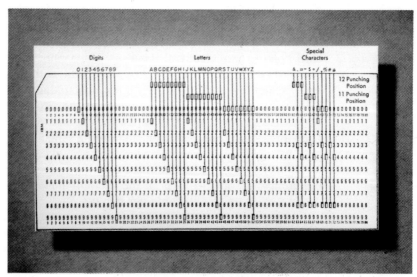

Illustration
14–4

mation may be punched into a card, and some machines will both punch information into a card and print the information on the card. A digit of a number is recorded by punching a hole in one of the columns; for example, a 5 is recorded by punching a hole in one of the columns in the line of 5s. A letter is recorded by punching two holes in one of the columns; for example, the letter Z is recorded by punching a hole in the 0 line and another hole in the same column in the 9 line. (At this point, for a better understanding of how digits and letters are represented by holes in a card, the student should take the information as to which holes represent which digits and letters, as shown in Illustration 14–4, and use this information to interpret the holes punched into the card of Illustration 14–5. If the student does so, he will find in the card of Illustration 14–5 that the two holes punched in column 18 represent an N; the two holes in column 19 represent an E; and so on.)

Illustration 14–5 shows a sales invoice of General Manufacturing Company with one of the cards that would be used in accounting for this sale. The one card has information punched into it as to the customer, branch, salesman, date, and invoice number, plus information as to the quantity, commodity number, and item amount of the first of the six commodities listed on the invoice. In accounting for this sale five additional commodity cards, a total of six commodity cards, one for each product listed on the invoice, are punched. Each card is punched identically as to customer, branch, salesman, date, and invoice number, and differs only as to the quantity of the product sold, commodity number, and item amount. In addition to the six commodity cards, an accounts receivable card as shown in Illustration 14–6 is also punched. All of these cards are produced in one punching operation, with the common information of the cards being reproduced from one card to the next automatically.

The six commodity cards of the Illustration 14–5 invoice are used in posting to the perpetual inventory records, in each case reducing the inventory record of the commodity by the units sold. The posting is done by machine automatically. Also, the commodity cards of this invoice, along with the cards of other invoices for the same period (day, week, or month), are summarized and their total, which is the amount of charge sales for the period, is debited to Accounts Receivable control and credited to Sales.

The accounts receivable card, Illustration 14–6, is filed in the subsidiary Accounts Receivable Ledger. Actually, this card with any other unpaid accounts receivable cards of New Mexico Company become the company's account in the subsidiary Accounts Receivable Ledger.

Observe that the accounting described in the previous two paragraphs is like that described in earlier chapters. The same debits and credits, general ledger accounts, subsidiary ledgers and controlling accounts, and the same accounting principles apply. It differs only in that it is done with cards and machines.

When accounting data are punched into cards, it is possible to secure

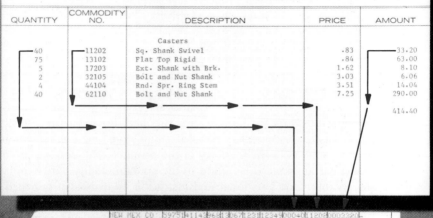
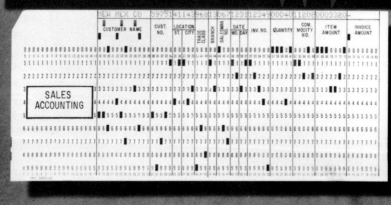

Illustration
14–5

from the cards much more information, at a reasonable cost, than is possible from traditional accounting records. For example, the six commodity cards of the Illustration 14–5 invoice show commodities sold, salesman, branch, city, and customer. Consequently, it is possible to

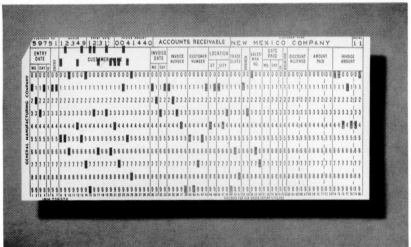

Illustration
14–6

Courtesy International Business Machines Corporation

take these cards and other like cards of a period such as a week or month, sort them by machine, and print reports showing total sales by commodities, by salesman, branches, territories, cities, and customers.

The foregoing discussion is given to introduce the possibilities of punched cards and punched card accounting. It is not intended to be a complete discussion; this must be deferred to a data processing course. Likewise, no effort will be made here to describe the application of punched cards to other phases of accounting. However, the student should recognize that the cards, machines, and methods may be used to do most record-keeping work more rapidly, more accurately, and when there is a sufficient volume of work, more economically than by hand or other machine methods.

Electronic data processing

■ Data are processed in an electric bookkeeping machine when the operator depresses the proper keys, and speed is dependent primarily on the operator's skill, but is at times limited by the mechanical movements of the machine. In a punched card system cards are passed through machines, and holes in the cards result in the completion of electrical circuits which cause the machines to sort the data or to add, multiply, divide, and subtract with punched or printed results. In a punched card operation, data may be processed many times faster than with electric adding, calculating, and bookkeeping machines; however, a punched card system is slow when compared with a system that processes data electronically.

Although newer punched card machines make use of electronics, the phrase "processing data electronically" means using an electronic computer in processing data, with an electronic computer being one or more machines containing from several hundred to more than a thousand transistors and other electronic gadgetry and being capable of, for example, from a few hundred to millions of additions, multiplications, divisions, and subtractions per second, all completed without error in a predetermined sequence according to instructions stored within the machine.

What a computer can do

Before explaining how a computer operates, it might be wise to convey some idea of what a computer can do. For example, before computers were used, a concern with, say, 10,000 or 12,000 employees required five or six days each pay period to complete its payroll records and prepare the paychecks, even though a hundred or more people with desk calculators and other electric machines were used to speed the work. But, today, a computer can do all the calculations, complete the payroll records, and print the checks in a matter of three or four hours.

For another example, a nationally known manufacturer and distributor of electrical appliances uses a computer in filling orders. The orders originate in any one of 53 different sales offices in as many cities, and are filled from one or more of 36 different warehouses scattered throughout the country. The company uses a teletype network to transmit orders from the sales offices to a central computer in Pittsburgh, Pennsylvania. The computer then takes over. It selects the best warehouse to fill the order in terms of proximity to the customer and available inventory. It prices and totals each sale, including any taxes, and updates the perpetual inventory records. In addition, the computer prepares punched cards for all accounting operations, writes the customer's invoice, and prepares punched cards for teletyping shipping instructions for each order to the warehouse selected. And when these punched cards are placed in a teletype in Pittsburgh, they automatically reproduce for each order at the selected warehouse a bill of lading, packing lists, and shipping labels. Furthermore, the company can receive an order in one city, process it, and ship from a selected warehouse in another city in less than an hour.

What a computer does

A computer is a machine, and as a machine it can do nothing without being given a detailed set of instructions called a *program.* However, with a properly prepared program, a computer is a complete data processing system that will accept data through an *input unit,* store and process the data in an *arithmetic-memory unit,* and produce the processed results through an *output unit* in the form of, say, a printed balance sheet. To accomplish all of this and to control all its activities, a computer has a *control unit.* These units are diagrammed in Illustration 14–7.

How a computer operates

To understand how a computer operates, it is necessary to examine the function of each of its units and the computer program.

THE INPUT UNIT. The input unit provides a way to communicate with the computer; in other words, it provides a way to put data into the computer's arithmetic-memory unit and a way to tell the computer how to process the data. Communication may be through an electric typewriter connected to the computer, or by means of punched cards, punched paper tape, magnetic tape, or such things as bank checks imprinted with magnetic ink. However, regardless of whether cards, tape, or other media, the media, through the input unit, transmit data and instructions to the computer's arithmetic-memory unit in the form of electrical impulses. The impulses are in a code language the computer can interpret.

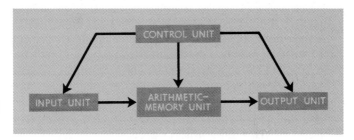

Illustration
14–7

The speed with which the various input media can enter data into the computer's memory varies from a character or two per second for the typewriter to hundreds of thousands of characters per second for magnetic tape.

THE ARITHMETIC-MEMORY UNIT. The arithmetic-memory unit should be viewed as having two sections: an arithmetic section and a memory section.

The arithmetic section manipulates the data stored in the memory section. It performs addition, subtraction, multiplication, and division, and it makes simple yes-or-no decisions, such as: Are the two numbers equal? Has the end of the magnetic tape been reached? Does the card have an X punched in column 73? It performs these operations one at a time, storing the intermediate results in the memory section. And, depending upon the computer's size and cost, its arithmetic section performs these operations at a rate of from a few hundred operations per second for a small machine to several million per second for a large one.

The memory section of the arithmetic-memory unit serves the same purpose as a human's memory, a storage place for data and instructions. However, a computer's memory is more like a file of information than like a person's memory, since each bit of data stored in the computer's memory is stored in a specific location, just as in a file. Furthermore, for a computer to locate information in its memory, it must be told exactly where the information is stored.

Since a computer must be told where to find information in its memory, the memory is divided into cells, with each cell identified by a number, which is the cell's *address* within the memory unit. For example, if the memory unit has 4,000 cells for the storage of data, the cells are numbered from 0000 to 3999 and these numbers are the addresses of the cells.

Each cell in a computer's memory is capable of storing one bit of data, for example, one word or one number of up to, say, 10 digits. Likewise, depending upon its size, a computer may have storage capacity in its memory unit for from 1,000 bits of information for a small unit to 100,000 for a large one, and additional memory may be made available in auxiliary memory files.

THE OUTPUT UNIT. When processing of the data in the computer is finished, it is necessary for the machine to communicate the results. This may be done through various devices, such as an electric typewriter, a line printer, punched cards, magnetic tape, and punched paper tape. As an output device, a typewriter will type out a report at the rate of 10 characters per second, while a line printer, which prints a whole 120-character line of type in one operation, will print up to 800 lines per minute. The punched cards, magnetic tape, and punched paper tape, as output media, require further processing in, for example, a line printer.

THE CONTROL UNIT. The control unit controls the operations of all the computer units. It tells the input device what information or instructions to enter in memory and where (at what numbered addresses) to store the bits of information or instructions. It then reads the stored instructions one at a time and tells the arithmetic section what operation to perform, where in memory to find the required information, and where to store the results. And finally, it controls the output device, telling it what information to print out or punch out and where in memory to find the information.

The foregoing sounds fantastic, but remember the control unit does nothing more than follow, step by step, a detailed set of instructions that have been placed in the computer's memory unit. As previously explained, the instructions are called a program.

THE PROGRAM. In processing data with a computer, both the data to be processed and the program for its processing are placed in the computer's memory section. The control unit then takes from the memory section the first instruction of the program plus the data needed in carrying out this instruction and places both in the arithmetic section. The arithmetic section executes the instruction, whether it be to add, multiply, divide, or compare two numbers for equality, and stores the results back in the memory section. The control unit then places the next instruction and the required data in the arithmetic section, and so on, until the program is completed and the data is processed, all at the rate of from a few hundred to millions of instructions per second.

At this point a typical computer program could be shown, but since a program consists of nothing more than a series of computer instructions expressed in code numbers, such a program would be quite incomprehensible to a beginning student. Furthermore, a typical program commonly contains hundreds or even thousands of individual instructions. Consequently, only a small portion of a program in which the instructions are in words rather than in code numbers is used to show the detail of such a program.

Assume a computer is processing a payroll and has computed and stored in its memory an employee's gross pay and the sum of his deductions. The next step would be to subtract the sum of the deductions from gross pay to arrive at net pay; but for the computer to do this, it must be instructed in detail. It must be told exactly where in memory the numbers representing gross pay and the sum of the deductions are stored and where the number representing net pay is to be stored. Assume the number representing gross pay is stored at memory address 1001, the sum of the deductions at memory address 1002, and net pay is to be stored at memory address 1003. Then, this portion of the program would have these three instructions:

1. Insert in the arithmetic section the number (gross pay) now stored in memory address 1001.
2. Subtract the number (sum of the deductions) stored in memory address 1002 from the contents of the arithmetic section.
3. Store the result of the subtraction (net pay) at memory address 1003.

The foregoing instructions illustrate the detail of a computer program, and a program may contain hundreds or even thousands of such instructions. Nevertheless, a computer is able to execute the instructions in sequence, without error, at a rate of from a few hundred to millions of instructions per second.

At this point it might be asked how a computer can execute thousands or millions of instructions per second when the program it is processing has only a few hundred instructions. The answer is that the computer can be directed to repeat the same set of instructions over and over again, but each time with a new set of data. For example, in completing a payroll, the computer can be programmed to go through the same set of instructions over and over again, but each time with the hours, pay rate, and deductions of a different employee, until all the payroll is processed.

A computer requires a separate program for each job it is to do; and to change a computer from one job to another, it is only necessary to enter a new program in its memory, along with the data to be processed. For example, to change a computer from processing a payroll to processing inventory records, it is only necessary to feed the inventory program and the data of the inventory transactions into the computer's memory with the input device.

YES-OR-NO DECISIONS. One of the most important abilities of a computer is its ability to make yes-or-no decisions, such as, for example: Has the employee's earnings reached the F.I.C.A. tax-exempt point? In processing a payroll, a computer can compare the amount of an employee's year-to-date earnings with the number of dollars representing the tax-exempt point and make a decision such as this. The importance of such a decision is obvious. If the earnings are below the tax-exempt point, the computer must calculate and deduct F.I.C.A. taxes; but if the earnings are beyond this point, the computer is programmed to omit this step.

The ability to compare numbers and make yes-or-no decisions makes it possible for a computer to process data containing exceptions, such as the foregoing F.I.C.A. tax example. However, it should be observed that the computer does not really make decisions. It only makes a comparison in each case, after which it processes the data one way or another, depending upon the result of the comparison. Also, for a computer to do this, a programmer must first design a program for the computer to follow. In designing the program, the programmer must determine in advance what exceptions can occur; he must then devise a set of yes-or-no questions that will isolate each exception, and he must tell the computer how to process each exception. Finally, after all this, the computer can follow through the program's maze of decisions and alternate instructions, rapidly and accurately. However, if it encounters an exception not anticipated in the program, it is helpless and can only process the exception incorrectly or stop.

IMPORTANCE OF THE COMPUTER PROGRAM. The ability to store a program in its memory section and then to race through the program's maze of yes-or-no decisions and alternate instructions is what distinguishes a computer from a punched card calculator or an electric calculator. To appreciate this, desk calculators exist that can do an addition, a multiplication, or division in one millionth of a second, in other words at about the speed of a fast computer. Yet, with all this speed, a calculator of this type cannot be operated much faster than an ordinary calculator, since without a program it must depend upon a person to push its keys telling it what to do.

In conclusion

Computers can process data with incredible speed and heretofore unobtainable accuracy. However, before a computer can do this, a human must think through the procedures the computer will use in processing the data, anticipate every processing exception, and then instruct the computer in great detail as to how to do its job. Consequently, computers are utterly dependent on humans; and rather than being giant brains are nothing but large, fast morons that can do nothing without first being told how. And, too, it always should be remembered that they are probably the fastest machines ever invented for turning out *wrong* answers when fed incorrect data or an inaccurate program.

Computer problem[1] The following short problem is designed to further your understanding of computers. In it you are to punch into IBM cards the data of 18 transactions completed by Phoenix Sales.[2] After the cards are punched, your instructor will arrange a time for you to deliver the cards to the computer center of your school. In the computer center your deck of cards will be combined with an additional deck containing Phoenix Sales' beginning-of-the-period trial balance and the program of instructions for processing your cards. Both decks will then be entered into the computer's arithmetic-memory unit through the input unit, and the computer will update the company's accounts and type out end-of-the-month financial statements reflecting the effects of the transactions.

The beginning-of-the-period trial balance of Phoenix Sales which is punched into the deck of cards containing the program has the accounts and balances shown below. You need do nothing about the trial balance.

PHOENIX SALES
Trial Balance, April 1, 19 –

Cash	$ 1,350	
Accounts receivable (Adam Bell)	750	
Merchandise inventory	11,850	
Store supplies	150	
Store equipment	9,400	
Accumulated depreciation, store equipment		$ 3,500
Accounts payable (Simpson Wholesale Company)		1,000
Gary Ball, capital		19,000
Totals	$23,500	$23,500

During April Phoenix Sales completed these transactions:

Date	Transaction Number	Transaction Description
Apr. 1	111	Issued a $350 check in payment of the April rent.
3	112	Sold merchandise on credit to Fred Grey, $1,500. Terms of all credit sales are 2/10, n/30.
4	113	Received a $735 check from Adam Bell in payment of his account, less a 2% discount.

---

[1] This problem was originally prepared by Professor Robert Robinson, Jr. of Oregon State University and Professor Joseph W. Wilkinson of Arizona State University.

[2] The instructor's solutions manual suggests several ways to assign this portion of the problem.

Date	Transaction Number	Transaction Description
Apr. 5	114	Purchased store supplies on credit from Store Outfitters, Inc., terms n/10 EOM, $125.
8	115	Issued a $50 check to pay for advertising that had appeared in the April 5 issue of the local paper.
9	116	Purchased merchandise on credit from Simpson Wholesale Company, terms n/10 EOM, $1,600.
10	117	Issued a $1,000 check to Simpson Wholesale Company in payment of the amount owed to the company on April 1.
13	118	Received a $1,470 check from Fred Grey in payment of his account, less a 2% discount.
14	119	Purchased $750 of store equipment on credit from Store Outfitters, Inc., terms n/10 EOM.
15	120	Sold merchandise on credit to Carl Dale, $800.
15	121	Paid the semimonthly salaries, $300.
17	122	Discarded fully depreciated store equipment and removed its $400 cost and $400 accumulated depreciation from the accounts.
22	123	Purchased merchandise on credit from Simpson Wholesale Company, n/10 EOM, $1,750.
23	124	Sold merchandise on credit to Fred Grey, $650.
30	125	Paid the semimonthly salaries, $300.
30	126	Cash sales for April, according to the cash register tapes, totaled $3,770.
30	127	Made an adjusting entry to record supplies used during April, $100.
30	128	Made an adjusting entry to record depreciation on store equipment, $75.
30	129	The April 30 merchandise inventory is $10,650. (The computer has been programmed to accept and process the ending inventory information if you include in your deck of cards a card carrying the punched transaction number, 129, the inventory account number, 115, and the inventory amount, $10,650, punched as a debit. See coding and punching instructions which follow.)

Phoenix Sales uses a limited number of accounts. Following is a list with each account name preceded by the account's code number. In each case the code number identifies the account and is also the account's address in the memory unit of the computer. Note that there are neither accounts receivable nor accounts payable controlling accounts. These accounts were omitted to simplify the problem. Consequently, when recording a credit sale, for example, debit the customer's account and credit Sales. Likewise, when recording a payment on account by a customer (see the coding sheet example which follows), debit Cash and Sales Discounts, if any, and credit the customer's account. A similar procedure should be followed for accounts payable, and in both cases the computer is programmed to print out the controlling account amounts.

PHOENIX SALES
Chart of Accounts

111 Cash	212 Store Outfitters, Inc.
112 Adam Bell	311 Gary Ball, Capital
113 Carl Dale	411 Sales
114 Fred Grey	412 Sales Discounts
115 Merchandise Inventory	511 Purchases
116 Store Supplies	611 Rent Expense
121 Store Equipment	612 Salaries Expense
122 Accumulated Depreciation, Store Equipment	613 Advertising Expense
211 Simpson Wholesale Company	614 Depreciation Expense
	615 Supplies Expense

Instruction one

Code the transactions of Phoenix Sales on the coding sheet provided in your booklet of working papers. Skip a line after each transaction on the coding sheet to set the transactions apart.

The purpose of the coding sheet is to help you organize the transaction data into columns and thus make it easier for you to punch this information into the proper columns of IBM cards. (See Instruction two; and remember that the columns in which holes are punched in a card are important, since the computer's interpretation of a card's holes depends upon the location of the holes in the card.)

The columns of the coding sheet are divided into groups that correspond to the columns of a General Journal, and in coding the transactions of Phoenix Sales, you are in effect making general journal entries. However, observe the coding of the company's third transaction in the following illustration, and note these differences:

CODING SHEET

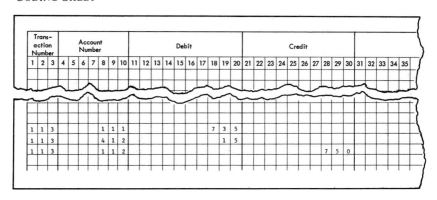

Instead of a date, the transaction number is entered in the first three numbered columns on the line of each debit and credit; and instead of account names, account numbers are used to identify the accounts debited and credited.

In coding the transactions, these rules must be observed for each debit and credit: (1) The transaction number must be entered in columns 1, 2, and 3. (2) The number of the account debited or credited must be entered in columns 8, 9, and 10. (3) A debit amount must be entered with its last digit in column 20. And (4) a credit amount must be entered with its last digit in column 30.

The amounts involved in this problem are in full dollars, which simplifies the coding and card punching. Do not enter zeros to show there are no cents. Also, a thousand dollar amount should be entered without a comma separating hundreds of dollars from thousands of dollars. And finally, explanations are not needed.

As previously stated, the purpose of the coding sheet is to help organize the data into columns and thus make it easier to punch the data into the proper columns of IBM cards. Also, it should be observed that in actual practice a coding sheet is not used. Such a sheet is not needed because an experienced key punch operator can easily punch information into cards while reading directly from a source document, such as an invoice.

Instruction two

After entering the transactions on the coding sheet, secure approximately 50 IBM cards from your bookstore and punch the coded transaction data into cards, using a key punch. In punching the cards: (1) Punch a separate card for each debit and each credit entered on the coding sheet. (2) In each card punch the transaction number in columns 1, 2, and 3. (3) Punch the number of the account debited or credited in columns 8, 9, and 10. (4) If a debit, punch the amount debited so that its last digit is in column 20. And (5) if a credit, punch the amount credited so that its last digit is in column 30.

Instruction three

After punching a card for each debit and each credit on the coding sheet, including a card for the ending inventory, punch these additional cards. (1) Punch your name on a card with the first letter beginning in column 10. If the punching is a team effort, punch on a separate line the name of each team member. This identification card should be placed so that it is the first card in your deck. (2) In addition punch a card with the number 999 in columns 1, 2, and 3. This card should be placed last in your deck.

Instruction four

After completing your cards, arrange with your instructor for their processing on the computer.

Chapter 15

Partnership accounting

■ About half the states have adopted the Uniform Partnership Act to govern the formation and operation of partnerships. This act defines a partnership as "an association of two or more persons to carry on as co-owners a business for profit." A partnership has been further defined as "an association of two or more competent persons under a contract to combine some or all their property, labor, and skills in the operation of a business." And although both of these definitions tell something of its legal nature, a better understanding of a partnership as a form of business organization may be gained by examining some of its characteristics.

Characteristics of a partnership

■ A voluntary association

A partnership is a voluntary association into which a person cannot be forced against his will. This is because a partner is responsible for the business acts of his partners, when the acts are within the scope of the partnership; and too, a partner is unlimitedly liable for the debts of his partnership. Consequently, partnership law recognizes it is only fair that a person be permitted to select the people he wishes to join in a partnership, and normally a person will select only financially responsible people in whose judgment he has respect.

Based on a contract

One advantage of a partnership as a form of business organization is the ease with which it may be begun. All that is required is that two or more competent people agree to be partners. Their agreement becomes a contract and should be in writing, with all anticipated points of future disagreement covered. However, it is just as binding if only orally expressed.

Limited life

The life of a partnership is always limited. Death, bankruptcy, or anything that takes away the ability of one of the partners to contract automatically ends a partnership. In addition, since a partnership is based on a contract, if the contract is for a definite period, the partnership ends with the period's expiration. If the contract does not specify a time period, the partnership ends when the business for which it was created is completed. Or, if no time is stated and the business for which it was created cannot be completed but goes on indefinitely, the partnership may be terminated at will by any one of the partners.

Mutual agency

Normally there is mutual agency in a partnership. This means that under normal circumstances every partner is an agent of his partnership and can bind it to any contract within the apparent scope of its business. For example, a partner in a trading business can bind his partnership to contracts to buy merchandise, lease a store building, borrow money, or hire employees, since these are all within the scope of a trading firm. On the other hand, a partner in a law firm, acting alone, cannot bind his partners to a contract to buy merchandise or rent a store building. These are not within the normal scope of a law firm's business.

Partners among themselves may agree to limit the right of any one or more of the partners to negotiate certain contracts for the partnership. However, although such an agreement is binding on the partners and on outsiders who know of the agreement, it is not binding on outsiders who are unaware of its existence. Outsiders who are unaware of anything to the contrary have a right to assume that each partner has the normal agency rights of a partner.

Mutual agency offers an important reason for care in the selection of partners. Good partners benefit all; but a poor partner can do great damage. Mutual agency plus unlimited liability are the reasons most partnerships have only a few members, with two, three, or four being common numbers of partners.

Unlimited liability

When a partnership is unable to pay its debts, the creditors may satisfy their claims from the personal assets of the partners. Furthermore, if the personal property of a partner is insufficient to meet his share, the creditors may turn to the assets of the remaining partners who are able to pay. Thus, a partner may be called on to pay all the debts of his partnership and is said to have unlimited liability for its debts.

Unlimited liability may be illustrated as follows: Albert and Bates each invested $1,000 in a store to be operated as a partnership venture, under an agreement to share losses and gains equally. Albert has no property other than his $1,000 investment; Bates owns his own home, a farm, and has sizable savings in addition to his investment. The partners rented store space and bought merchandise and fixtures costing $10,000, paying $2,000 in cash and promising to pay the balance at a later date. However, the night before the store opened the building in which it was located burned and the merchandise and fixtures were totally destroyed. There was no insurance, all the partnership assets were lost, and Albert has no other assets. Consequently, the partnership creditors may collect the full $8,000 of their claims from Bates, although Bates may look to Albert for payment of half at a later date, if Albert ever becomes able to pay.

Advantages and disadvantages of a partnership

■ Limited life, mutual agency, and unlimited liability are disadvantages of a partnership. Yet, a partnership has advantages over both the single proprietorship and corporation forms of organization. A partnership has the advantage of being able to bring together more money and skills than a single proprietorship, and is much easier to organize than a corporation. Also, it does not have the corporation's governmental supervision nor its extra burden of taxation, and partners may act freely and without the necessity of stockholders' and directors' meetings, as in a corporation.

Partnership accounting

■ Partnership accounting is exactly like that of a single proprietorship except for transactions affecting owner equity. Here, because ownership rights are divided between two or more partners, there must be:

1. A Capital account for each partner.
2. A Withdrawals account for each partner.
3. An accurate measurement and division of earnings among the partners.

As for the separate Capital and Withdrawals accounts, each partner's Capital account is credited, and asset accounts showing the nature of the assets invested are debited in recording the investment of each partner. Likewise, a partner's withdrawals are debited to his Withdrawals account, and in the end-of-the-period closing procedure the Capital account is credited for a partner's share of the net income. Obviously, these procedures are not new, only the added accounts are new, and they need no further consideration here. However, the matter of dividing earnings among partners does need additional discussion.

Nature of partnership earnings

■ Because, as a member of his partnership, a partner cannot enter into an employer-employee contractual relationship with himself, a partner, like a single proprietor, cannot legally hire himself and pay himself a salary. Law and custom recognize this. Furthermore, law and custom recognize that a partner works for partnership profits and not a salary, and law and custom recognize that a partner invests in a partnership for earnings and not for interest.

Nevertheless, although partners have no legal right to interest on their partnership investments or salaries in payment for their partnership services, it should be recognized that partnership earnings do include a return for services, even though the return is contained within the earnings and is not a salary in a legal sense. Likewise, partnership earnings include a return on invested capital, although the return is not interest in the legal sense of the term.

Furthermore, if partnership earnings are to be fairly shared, it is often necessary to recognize that the earnings do include a return for services and a return on investments. For example, if one partner contributes five times as much capital as another, it is only fair that this be taken into consideration in the method of sharing. Likewise, if the services of one partner are much more valuable than those of another, it is only fair that some provision be made for the unequal service contributions.

Division of earnings ■ The law provides that in the absence of a contrary agreement, all partnership earnings are shared equally. This means that if partners do not agree in advance as to the method of sharing, each partner receives an equal share. Partners may agree in advance to any method of sharing; and if they agree as to the method of sharing earnings but say nothing of losses, losses are shared in the same way as earnings.

Several methods of sharing partnership earnings are employed. All attempt in one way or another to recognize differences in service contributions or in investments, when such differences exist. The following three methods will be discussed here:

1. On a stated fractional basis.
2. Based on the ratio of capital investments.
3. Salary and interest allowances and the remainder in a fixed ratio.

Earnings allocated on a stated fractional basis ■ The easiest way to divide partnership earnings is to give each partner a stated fraction of the total. A division on a fractional basis may provide for an equal sharing if service and capital contributions are equal. An equal sharing may also be provided when the greater capital contribution of one partner is offset by a greater service contribution of another. Or, if the service and capital contributions are unequal, a fixed ratio may easily provide for an unequal sharing. All that is necessary in any case is for the partners to agree as to the fractional share to be given each.

For example, the partnership agreement of Morse and North may provide that each partner is to receive half the earnings; or the agreement may provide for two thirds to Morse and one third to North; or it may provide for three fourths to Morse and one fourth to North. Any fractional basis may be agreed upon as long as the partners feel earnings are thereby fairly shared. For example, assume the agreement of Morse and North provides for a two-thirds and one-third sharing, and earnings for a year are $9,000. After all revenue and expense accounts are closed, if earnings are $9,000, the partnership Income Summary account has a $9,000 credit balance. It is closed and the earnings are allocated to the partners with the following entry:

Dec.	31	Income Summary	9,000.00	
		A. P. Morse, Capital..................................		6,000.00
		R. G. North, Capital.................................		3,000.00
		To close the Income Summary account and allocate the earnings.		

Division of earnings based on the ratio of capital investments

■ If the business of a partnership is of a nature that earnings are closely related to money invested, as in the investment banking business, a division of earnings based on the ratio of partners' investments offers a fair sharing method.

To see how earnings are shared in the investment ratio, assume that Chase, Davis, and Fall have agreed to share earnings in the ratio of their beginning-of-the-year investments. If these are Chase $50,000, Davis $30,000, and Fall $40,000, and if the earnings for the year are $24,000, the respective shares of the partners are calculated as follows:

Step 1:
Chase, capital	$ 50,000
Davis, capital	30,000
Fall, capital	40,000
Total invested	$120,000

Step 2: Share of earnings to Chase $\frac{\$50,000}{\$120,000} \times \$24,000 = \$10,000$

Share of earnings to Davis $\frac{\$30,000}{\$120,000} \times \$24,000 = \$6,000$

Share of earnings to Fall $\frac{\$40,000}{\$120,000} \times \$24,000 = \$8,000$

The entry to allocate the earnings to the partners is then:

Dec.	31	Income Summary...	24,000.00	
		T. S. Chase, Capital.................................		10,000.00
		S. A. Davis, Capital.................................		6,000.00
		R. R. Fall, Capital..................................		8,000.00
		To close the Income Summary account and allocate the earnings.		

Salaries and interest as aids in sharing

■ Sometimes partners' capital contributions are unequal; and sometimes one partner devotes full time to partnership affairs and the other or others devote only part time. Too, in partnerships in which all partners devote full time, the services of one partner may be more valuable than the services of another. When these situations occur and, for example, the capital contributions are unequal, the partners may allocate a portion of the profits to themselves in the form of interest, so as to compensate for the unequal investments. Or when service contributions are unequal, they may use salary allowances as a means of compensating for unequal service contributions. Or when investment and service contributions are both unequal, they may use a combination of interest and salary allowances in an effort to share earnings fairly.

For example, Hill and Dale are partners in a business in which Hill has had much experience and could command a $9,000 annual salary working for another firm of like nature. Dale is new to the business and could expect to earn not more than $6,000 working elsewhere. Furthermore, Hill has invested $15,000 in the business and Dale has invested $5,000. Consequently, the partners have agreed that in order to compensate for the unequal service and capital contributions, they will share losses and gains as follows:

1. A share of the profits equal to interest at 8% is to be allowed on the partners' initial investments.
2. Annual salary allowances of $9,000 per year to Hill and $6,000 per year to Dale are to be allowed.
3. The remaining balance of income or loss is to be shared equally.

Under this agreement a year's $17,700 net income would be shared as in Illustration 15–1.

	Share to Hill	Share to Dale	Income Allocated
Total net income			$17,700
Allocated as interest:			
Hill (8% on $15,000).....................................	$ 1,200		
Dale (8% on $5,000).....................................		$ 400	
Total allocated as interest			1,600
Balance of income after interest allowances...........			$16,100
Allocated as salary allowances:			
Hill...	9,000		
Dale..		6,000	
Total allocated as salary allowances.............			15,000
Balance of income after interest and salary allowances...			$ 1,100
Balance allocated equally:			
Hill...	550		
Dale..		550	
Total allocated equally			1,100
Balance of income.......................................			-0-
Shares of the Partners	$10,750	$6,950	

Illustration
15–1

After the shares in the $17,700 net income are determined, the following entry may be used to close the Income Summary account and carry the net income shares to the partners' Capital accounts. Observe in the entry that the credit amounts may be taken from the first two money columns of the computation of Illustration 15–1.

Dec.	31	Income Summary	17,700.00	
		Robert Hill, Capital		10,750.00
		William Dale, Capital		6,950.00
		To close the Income Summary account and allocate the earnings.		

In a legal sense, a partner does not work for a salary, nor does he invest in a partnership to earn interest; he invests and works for earnings. Consequently, when a partnership agreement provides for salaries and interest, the partners should understand that the salaries and interest are not really salaries and interest but are only a means of sharing losses and gains.

In the illustration just completed the $17,700 net income exceeded the salary and interest allowances of the partners; but Hill and Dale would use the same method to share a net income smaller than their salary and interest allowances, or to share a loss. For example, assume that Hill and Dale earned only $6,600 in a year. A $6,600 net income would be shared by the partners as in Illustration 15–2.

	Share to Hill	Share to Dale	Income Allocated
Total net income...			$ 6,600
Allocated as interest:			
Hill (8% on $15,000)...................................	$1,200		
Dale (8% on $5,000)....................................		$ 400	
Total allocated as interest........................			1,600
Balance of income after interest allowances...........			$ 5,000
Allocated as salary allowances:			
Hill..	9,000		
Dale		6,000	
Total allocated as salary allowances			15,000
Balance of income after interest and salary allowances (a negative amount)			($10,000)
Balance allocated equally:			
Hill..	(5,000)		
Dale		(5,000)	
Total allocated equally			(10,000)
Balance of income...............................			-0-
Shares of the Partners......................................	$5,200	$1,400	

Illustration 15–2

The Illustration 15–2 items enclosed in parentheses are negative items. It will be recalled that it is common practice in accounting to show negative items in red or to show them enclosed in parentheses.

A net loss would be shared by Hill and Dale in the same manner as the foregoing $6,600 net income; the only difference being that the loss-and-gain-sharing procedure would begin with a negative amount of income, in other words a net loss, and the amount allocated equally would be a larger negative amount.

Partnership financial statements

■ In most respects partnership financial statements are like those of a single proprietorship. However, one common difference is that the net income allocation is often shown on the income statement, at the end of the statement following the reported net income. For example, an income statement prepared for Hill and Dale might show in its last portion the allocation of the $6,600 net income of Illustration 15–2 as in Illustration 15–3.

Hill and Dale
Income Statement for Year Ended December 31, 19—

Sales		$123,400
~~		
Net Income..		$ 6,600
Allocation of net income to the partners:		
Robert Hill:		
Interest at 8% on investment............................	$ 1,200	
Salary allowance...	9,000	
Total...	$10,200	
Less one half the remaining deficit	(5,000)	
Share of the net income		$ 5,200
William Dale:		
Interest at 8% on investment............................	$ 400	
Salary allowance...	6,000	
Total...	$ 6,400	
Less one half the remaining deficit	(5,000)	
Share of the net income		1,400
Net Income Allocated		$ 6,600

Illustration 15–3

Ending a partnership

■ Often a partnership is terminated by the retirement of a partner. When a partner retires, he may sell his partnership interest to an outsider or to one or more of his partners, or he may withdraw his equity in the form of cash or other assets.

Sale of a partnership interest

Assume that Abbott, Burns, and Camp are equal partners in a $15,000 partnership that has no liabilities and the following assets and equities:

ASSETS		EQUITIES	
Cash	$ 3,000	Abbott, capital	$ 5,000
Merchandise	8,000	Burns, capital	5,000
Store equipment	4,000	Camp, capital	5,000
Total Assets	$15,000	Total Equities	$15,000

Camp's equity in this partnership is $5,000. If Camp sells this equity to Davis for $7,000, he is selling his $5,000 interest in the partnership assets. The entry on the partnership books to transfer the equity is:

Feb.	4	Camp, Capital	5,000.00	
		Davis, Capital		5,000.00
		To transfer Camp's equity in the partnership assets to Davis.		

After this entry is posted, the accounting equation that shows the assets and equities of the new partnership is:

ASSETS		EQUITIES	
Cash	$ 3,000	Abbott, capital	$ 5,000
Merchandise	8,000	Burns, capital	5,000
Store equipment	4,000	Davis, capital	5,000
Total Assets	$15,000	Total Equities	$15,000

Two points should be noted in regard to this transaction. First, the $7,000 Davis paid Camp is not recorded in the partnership books. Camp sold and transferred his $5,000 equity in the partnership assets to Davis. The entry that records the transfer is a debit to Camp, Capital and a credit to Davis, Capital for $5,000. Furthermore, the entry is the same whether Davis pays Camp $7,000 or $70,000. The amount is paid directly to Camp. It is a side transaction between Camp and Davis and does not affect partnership assets.

The second point to be noted is that Abbott and Burns must agree to the sale and transfer if Davis is to become a partner. Abbott and Burns cannot prevent Camp from selling his interest to Davis. On the other hand, Camp cannot force Abbott and Burns to accept Davis as a partner. If Abbott and Burns agree to accept Davis, a new partnership is formed and a new contract with a new loss-and-gain-sharing ratio must be drawn. If Camp sells to Davis and either Abbott or Burns refuses to accept Davis as a partner, under the common law the old partnership must be liquidated and Davis receives only the liquidation rights of Camp. However, under the Uniform Partnership Act this situation is treated differently, but a discussion of this is left to a more advanced text.

Withdrawal of a partner

The best practice in regard to withdrawals is for partners to provide in advance, in their partnership contract, the procedure to be followed when a partner withdraws from the partnership. When such a procedure is agreed on in advance, it commonly provides for an audit of the accounting records and a revaluation of the partnership assets. The revaluation just prior to a retirement is very desirable because it places all assets on the books at current values and causes the retiring partner's Capital account to reflect the current value of his equity. Often, if a partnership agreement provides for an audit and asset revaluation when a partner retires, it also provides that the retiring partner is to withdraw assets equal to the book amount of his revalued equity.

For example, assume that Blue is retiring from the partnership of Smith, Blue, and Short. The partners have always shared losses and gains in the ratio of Smith, one half; Blue, one fourth; and Short, one fourth. Their partnership agreement provides for an audit and asset revaluation upon the retirement of a partner. Their balance sheet just prior to the audit and revaluation is shown in Illustration 15–4.

Smith, Blue, and Short
Balance Sheet, October 31, 19—

ASSETS			EQUITIES	
Cash..........................		$11,000	Smith, capital........................	$22,000
Merchandise inventory		16,000	Blue, capital.........................	10,000
Building.................... $20,000			Short, capital	10,000
Less accum. depr.... 5,000		15,000		
Total Assets.........		$42,000	Total Equities..................	$42,000

Illustration
15–4

The audit and appraisal indicate the merchandise inventory is overvalued by $4,000 and that due to market changes the partnership building should be valued at $25,000 with accumulated depreciation of $8,000. The entries to record these revaluations are:

Oct.	31	Smith, Capital...	2,000.00	
		Blue, Capital..	1,000.00	
		Short, Capital	1,000.00	
		Merchandise Inventory............................		4,000.00
		To revalue the inventory.		
	31	Building	5,000.00	
		Accumulated Depreciation, Building		3,000.00
		Smith, Capital..		1,000.00
		Blue, Capital...		500.00
		Short, Capital		500.00
		To revalue the building.		

Losses and gains from asset revaluations are always shared by the partners in their loss-and-gain-sharing ratio. The fairness of this is easy to see when it is remembered that if the partnership did not terminate, such losses and gains would sooner or later be reflected on the income statement.

In the case of Smith, Blue, and Short, after the entries revaluing the partnership assets are recorded, a balance sheet showing the new asset values and the new equities appears as in Illustration 15–5.

Smith, Blue, and Short
Balance Sheet, October 31, 19 —

ASSETS			EQUITIES	
Cash.........................		$11,000	Smith, capital.........................	$21,000
Merchandise inventory		12,000	Blue, capital.........................	9,500
Building	$25,000		Short, capital	9,500
Less accum. depr....	8,000	17,000		
Total Assets.........		$40,000	Total Equities..................	$40,000

Illustration
15–5

After the revaluation, if Blue withdraws from the partnership and takes assets equal to his equity, the entry to record his withdrawal is:

Oct.	31	Blue, Capital	9,500.00	
		Cash..		9,500.00
		To record the withdrawal of Blue.		

In withdrawing, Blue does not have to take cash in settlement of his equity. He may take any combination of assets to which the partners agree, or he may take the new partnership's promissory note.

Needless to say, the withdrawal of Blue creates a new partnership; and consequently, a new agreement and a new loss-and-gain-sharing ratio is required.

Partner withdraws taking assets of less value than his book equity

Sometimes when a partner retires, the remaining partners may not wish to have the assets revalued and the new values recorded. In such cases the partners may agree, for example, that the assets are overvalued; and due to the overvalued assets, the retiring partner should in settlement of his equity take assets of less value than the book value of his equity. Sometimes, too, when assets are not overvalued, the retiring partner may be so anxious to retire that he is willing to take less than the current value of his equity just to get out of the partnership or out of the business.

When a partner retires taking assets of less value than his equity, he is in effect leaving a portion of his book equity in the business. In such cases, the remaining partners divide the unwithdrawn equity portion in their loss-and-gain-sharing ratio. For example, assume that Black, Brown, and Green are partners sharing gains and losses in a 2:2:1 ratio. Their assets and equities are:

ASSETS		EQUITIES	
Cash	$ 5,000	Black, capital	$ 6,000
Merchandise	9,000	Brown, capital	6,000
Store equipment	4,000	Green, capital	6,000
Total Assets	$18,000	Total Equities	$18,000

Brown is so anxious to withdraw from the partnership that he is willing to retire if permitted to take $4,500 in cash in settlement for his equity. Black and Green agree to the $4,500 withdrawal, and Brown retires. The entry to record the retirement is:

Mar.	4	Brown, Capital	6,000.00	
		Cash		4,500.00
		Black, Capital		1,000.00
		Green, Capital		500.00
		To record the withdrawal of Brown.		

In retiring, Brown did not withdraw $1,500 of his equity. This is divided between Black and Green in their loss-and-gain-sharing ratio. The loss-and-gain-sharing ratio of the original partnership was Black, 2; Brown, 2; and Green, 1. Therefore in the original partnership, Black and Green shared in a 2 to 1 ratio; and the unwithdrawn book equity of Brown is shared by Black and Green in this ratio.

Partner withdraws taking assets of greater value than his book equity

There are two common reasons for a partner receiving upon retirement assets of greater value than his book equity. First, certain of the partnership assets may be undervalued; and second, the partners continuing the business may be so anxious for the retiring partner to withdraw that they are willing for him to take assets of greater value than his book equity.

When assets are undervalued or unrecorded and the partners do not wish to change the recorded values, the partners may agree to permit a retiring member to withdraw assets of greater value than his book equity. In such cases the retiring partner is, in effect, withdrawing his own book equity and a portion of his partners' equities. For example, assume that Jones, Thomas, and Finch are partners sharing gains and losses in a 3:2:1 ratio. Their assets and equities are:

ASSETS		EQUITIES	
Cash	$ 5,000	Jones, capital	$ 9,000
Merchandise	10,000	Thomas, capital	6,000
Equipment	3,000	Finch, capital	3,000
Total Assets	$18,000	Total Equities	$18,000

Finch wishes to withdraw from the partnership; Jones and Thomas plan to continue the business. The partners agree that certain of their assets are undervalued, but they do not wish to increase the recorded values. They further agree that if current values were recorded, the asset total would be increased $6,000 and the equity of Finch would be increased $1,000. Therefore, the partners agree that $4,000 is the proper value for Finch's equity and that he may withdraw this amount in cash. The entry to record the withdrawal is:

May	7	Finch, Capital	3,000.00	
		Jones, Capital...	600.00	
		Thomas, Capital...	400.00	
		Cash...		4,000.00
		To record the withdrawal of Finch.		

Death of a partner

■ A partner's death automatically dissolves and ends a partnership, and his estate is entitled to receive the amount of his equity. The partnership contract should contain provisions for settlement in case a partner dies, and one provision should provide a method for ascertaining the current value of the deceased partner's equity. This requires at least: (a) an immediate closing of the books to determine earnings since the end of the previous accounting period and (b) a method for determining and recording current values for the assets. Upon a partner's death and after the current value of the deceased partner's equity is determined, the remaining partners and the deceased partner's estate must agree to a disposition of the equity. They may agree to its sale to the remaining partners or to an outsider, or they may agree to the withdrawal of assets in settlement. Entries for both of these procedures have already been discussed.

Liquidations

■ When a partnership is liquidated, its business is ended, the assets are converted into cash, the creditors are paid, the remaining cash is distributed to the partners, and the partnership is dissolved. Although many combinations of circumstances occur in liquidations, only three are discussed here.

All assets realized before a distribution, assets are sold at a profit

A partnership liquidation under this assumption may be illustrated with the following example. Ottis, Skinner, and Parr have operated a partnership for a number of years, sharing losses and gains in a 3:2:1 ratio. Due to several unsatisfactory conditions, the partners decide to liquidate as of December 31. On that date the books are closed, the income from operations is transferred to the partners' Capital accounts, and the condensed balance sheet shown in Illustration 15–6 is prepared.

Illustration
15–6

In any liquidation the business always ends and the assets are sold. Normally, either a gain or a loss results from the sale of each group of assets. These losses and gains are called "losses and gains from realization" and are shared by the partners in their loss-and-gain-sharing ratio. If Ottis, Skinner, and Parr sell their merchandise inventory for $12,000 and their other assets for $34,000, the sales and the gain allocation are recorded as follows:

Jan.	12	Cash	12,000.00	
		Loss or Gain from Realization	3,000.00	
		Merchandise Inventory		15,000.00
		Sold the inventory at a loss.		
	15	Cash	34,000.00	
		Other Assets		25,000.00
		Loss or Gain from Realization		9,000.00
		Sold the other assets at a profit.		
	15	Loss or Gain from Realization	6,000.00	
		Ottis, Capital		3,000.00
		Skinner, Capital		2,000.00
		Parr, Capital		1,000.00
		To allocate the net gain from realization to the partners in their 3:2:1 loss-and-gain-sharing ratio.		

Careful notice should be taken of the last journal entry just shown. In a partnership termination when assets are sold at a loss or gain, the loss or gain is allocated to the partners in their loss-and-gain-sharing ratio. Often students, in solving liquidation problems, attempt to allocate the assets to the partners in their loss-and-gain-sharing ratio. Obviously this is not correct; it is not assets but losses and gains that are shared in the loss-and-gain-sharing ratio.

After partnership assets are sold and the gain or loss allocated, the partnership cash exactly equals the combined equities of the partners and creditors. This point is illustrated for Ottis, Skinner, and Parr in the balance sheet of Illustration 15-7.

Ottis, Skinner, and Parr
Balance Sheet, January 15, 19—

ASSETS		EQUITIES	
Cash	$56,000	Accounts payable	$ 5,000
		Ottis, capital	18,000
		Skinner, capital	17,000
		Parr, capital	16,000
Total Assets	$56,000	Total Equities	$56,000

Illustration
15-7

After partnership assets are realized and the gain or loss shared, entries are made to distribute the realized cash to the proper parties. Since creditors have first claim, they are paid first. After the creditors are paid, the remaining cash is divided among the partners. Each partner has the right to cash equal to his equity or, in other words, cash equal to the balance of his Capital account. The entries to distribute the cash of Ottis, Skinner, and Parr are:

Jan.	15	Accounts Payable	5,000.00	
		Cash		5,000.00
		To pay the claims of the creditors.		
	15	Ottis, Capital	18,000.00	
		Skinner, Capital	17,000.00	
		Parr, Capital	16,000.00	
		Cash		51,000.00
		To distribute the remaining cash to the partners according to their Capital account balances.		

Notice that after losses and gains are shared and the creditors are paid, each partner receives liquidation cash equal to the balance remaining in his Capital account, because a partner's Capital account balance shows his equity in the partnership assets.

All assets realized before a distribution, assets sold at a loss, each partner's Capital account is sufficient to absorb his share of the loss

In a partnership liquidation, the assets are sometimes sold at a net loss. For example, if contrary to the assumptions of the previous illustration, the merchandise inventory of Ottis, Skinner, and Parr is sold for $9,000 and the other assets for $13,000, the entries to record the sales and loss allocation are:

Jan.	12	Cash...	9,000.00	
		Loss or Gain from Realization	6,000.00	
		Merchandise Inventory.............................		15,000.00
		Sold the inventory at a loss.		
	15	Cash...	13,000.00	
		Loss or Gain from Realization	12,000.00	
		Other Assets..		25,000.00
		Sold the other assets at a loss.		
	15	Ottis, Capital...	9,000.00	
		Skinner, Capital	6,000.00	
		Parr, Capital	3,000.00	
		Loss or Gain from Realization		18,000.00
		To allocate the loss from realization to the partners in their loss-and-gain-sharing ratio.		

After the entries for the sales and the loss allocation are recorded, a partnership balance sheet appears as in Illustration 15–8. The balance

Ottis, Skinner, and Parr
Balance Sheet, January 15, 19—

ASSETS		EQUITIES	
Cash $32,000		Accounts payable.................. $ 5,000	
		Ottis, capital 6,000	
		Skinner, capital 9,000	
		Parr, capital 12,000	
Total Assets $32,000		Total Equities.................. $32,000	

Illustration
15–8

sheet shows the equities of the creditors and partners in the partnership cash. The following entries are required to distribute the cash to the proper parties:

Jan.	15	Accounts Payable..	5,000.00	
		Cash...		5,000.00
		To pay the partnership creditors.		
	15	Ottis, Capital...	6,000.00	
		Skinner, Capital	9,000.00	
		Parr, Capital	12,000.00	
		Cash...		27,000.00
		To distribute the remaining cash to the partners according to the balances of their Capital accounts.		

Notice again that after realization losses are shared and creditors are paid, each partner receives cash equal to his Capital account balance.

All assets realized before a distribution, assets sold at a loss, a partner's Capital account is not sufficient to cover his share of the loss

Sometimes a partner's share of realization losses is greater than the balance of his Capital account. In such cases the partner whose share of losses is greater than his capital balance must, if he can, cover the deficit by paying cash into the partnership. For example, assume contrary to the previous two illustrations that Ottis, Skinner, and Parr sell their merchandise for $3,000 and the other assets for $4,000. The entries to record the sales and the loss allocation are:

Jan.	12	Cash...	3,000.00	
		Loss or Gain from Realization	12,000.00	
		Merchandise Inventory.............................		15,000.00
		Sold the inventory at a loss.		
	15	Cash...	4,000.00	
		Loss or Gain from Realization	21,000.00	
		Other Assets...		25,000.00
		Sold the other assets at a loss.		
	15	Ottis, Capital...	16,500.00	
		Skinner, Capital	11,000.00	
		Parr, Capital	5,500.00	
		Loss or Gain from Realization		33,000.00
		To record the allocation of the loss from realization to the partners in their loss-and-gain-sharing ratio.		

After the entry allocating the realization loss is posted, the Capital account of Ottis has a $1,500 debit balance and appears as follows:

Ottis, Capital

Date		Explanation	F	Debit	Credit	Balance
Dec.	31	Balance				15,000.00
Jan.	15	Share of loss from realization		16,500.00		(1,500.00)

Since the partnership agreement provides that Ottis is to take one half the losses or gains, and since his Capital account balance is not large enough to absorb his loss share in this case, he must, if he can, pay $1,500 into the partnership to cover his full share of the losses. If he is able to pay, the following entry is made:

Jan.	15	Cash..	1,500.00	
		Ottis, Capital...		1,500.00
		To record the additional investment of Ottis to cover his share of realization losses.		

After the $1,500 is received from Ottis, the partnership has $18,500 in cash; and the following entries are made to distribute it to the proper parties:

Jan.	15	Accounts Payable......................................	5,000.00	
		Cash...		5,000.00
		To pay the partnership creditors.		
	15	Skinner, Capital	4,000.00	
		Parr, Capital	9,500.00	
		Cash...		13,500.00
		To distribute the remaining cash to the partners according to the balances of their Capital accounts.		

Often when a partner's share of partnership losses exceeds his Capital account balance, he is unable to make up the deficit. In such cases, since each partner has unlimited liability, the deficit must be borne by the remaining partner or partners. For example, assume that contrary to the previous illustration, Ottis is unable to pay in the $1,500 necessary to cover the deficit in his Capital account. If Ottis is unable to pay, the deficit that he is unable to make good must be shared by Skinner and Parr in their loss-and-gain-sharing ratio. In the original loss-and-gain-sharing agreement, the partners shared losses and gains in the ratio of Ottis, 3; Skinner, 2; and Parr, 1. Therefore, Skinner and Parr shared in a 2 to 1 ratio; and the $1,500 that Ottis's share of the losses exceeded his Capital account balance is apportioned between them in this ratio. Normally the defaulting partner's deficit is transferred to the Capital accounts of the remaining partners. This is accomplished for Ottis, Skinner, and Parr with the following entry:

Jan.	15	Skinner, Capital	1,000.00	
		Parr, Capital	500.00	
		Ottis, Capital...		1,500.00
		To transfer the deficit of Ottis to the Capital accounts of Skinner and Parr.		

After the deficit is transferred, the Capital accounts of the partners appear as in Illustration 15–9.

Ottis, Capital

Date		Explanation	F	Debit	Credit	Balance
Dec.	31	Balance				15,000.00
Jan.	15	Share of loss from realization		16,500.00		(1,500.00)
	15	Deficit to Skinner and Parr			1,500.00	-0-

Skinner, Capital

Date		Explanation	F	Debit	Credit	Balance
Dec.	31	Balance				15,000.00
Jan.	15	Share of loss from realization		11,000.00		4,000.00
	15	Share of Ottis's deficit		1,000.00		3,000.00

Parr, Capital

Date		Explanation	F	Debit	Credit	Balance
Dec.	31	Balance				15,000.00
Jan.	15	Share of loss from realization		5,500.00		9,500.00
	15	Share of Ottis's deficit		500.00		9,000.00

Illustration
15–9

After the deficit is transferred, the $17,000 of liquidation cash is distributed with the following entries:

Jan.	15	Accounts Payable...	5,000.00	
		Cash...		5,000.00
		To pay the partnership creditors.		
	15	Skinner, Capital	3,000.00	
		Parr, Capital	9,000.00	
		Cash...		12,000.00
		To distribute the remaining cash to the partners according to their Capital account balances.		

It should be understood that the inability of Ottis to meet his loss share at this time does not relieve him of liability. If at any time in the future he becomes able to pay, Skinner and Parr may collect from him the full $1,500. Skinner may collect $1,000 and Parr, $500.

Questions for class discussion

1. Hill and Dale are partners. Hill dies and his son claims the right to take his father's place in the partnership. Does he have this right? Why?
2. Albert Gully cannot legally enter into a contract. Can he become a partner?

3. If a partnership contract does not state the period of time the partnership is to exist, when does the partnership end?

4. What is the meaning of the term "mutual agency" as applied to a partnership?

5. Jack and Jill are partners in the operation of a store. Jack without consulting Jill enters into a contract for the purchase of merchandise for resale by the store. Jill contends that he did not authorize the order and refuses to take delivery. The vendor sues the partners for the contract price of the merchandise. Will the firm have to pay? Why?

6. Would your answer to Question 5 differ if Jack and Jill were partners in a public accounting firm?

7. May partners limit the right of a member of their firm to bind their partnership to contracts? Is such an agreement binding (a) on the partners and (b) on outsiders?

8. What is the meaning of the term "unlimited liability" when it is applied to members of a partnership?

9. Kennedy, Porter, and Foulke have been partners for three years. The partnership is dissolving, Kennedy is leaving the firm, and Porter and Foulke plan to carry on the business. In the final settlement Kennedy places an $18,000 salary claim against the partnership. His contention is that since he devoted all of his time for three years to the affairs of the partnership, he has a claim for a salary of $6,000 for each year. Is his claim valid? Why?

10. The partnership agreement of Martin and Tritt provides for a two-thirds, one-third sharing of income but says nothing of losses. The operations for a year result in a loss. Martin claims the loss should be shared equally since the partnership agreement said nothing of sharing losses. Do you agree?

11. A, B, and C are partners with Capital account balances of $6,000 each. D gives A $7,500 for his one-third interest in the partnership. The bookkeeper debits A, Capital and credits D, Capital for $6,000. D objects. He wants his Capital account to show a $7,500 balance, the amount he paid for his interest. Explain why D's Capital account is credited for $6,000.

12. After all partnership assets are converted to cash and all creditor claims paid, the remaining cash should equal the sum of the balances of the partners' Capital accounts. Why?

13. J, K, and L are partners. In a liquidation J's share of partnership losses exceeds his Capital account balance. He is unable to meet the deficit from his personal assets, and the excess losses are shared by his partners. Does this relieve J of liability?

Class exercises

Exercise 15–1

Larr and More began a partnership by investing $6,000 and $8,000, respectively; and during its first year the partnership earned $21,000.

Required:

1. Prepare a schedule with the following columnar headings:

Ways of Sharing	Larr's Share	More's Share

2. Then complete the tabulation by listing the following ways of sharing by letter in the first column and then opposite each letter showing the share of each partner in the $21,000 net income.
   a) The partners failed to agree on a method of sharing income.
   b) The partners had agreed to share income in their investment ratio.
   c) The partners had agreed to share by allowing a $9,000 per year salary allowance to Larr, a $7,000 per year salary allowance to More, plus 10% interest on investments, and the balance equally.

Exercise 15–2

Marsh, Nalley, and Owen have equities of $7,500 each in a partnership. With the consent of Nalley and Owen, Marsh is selling his equity to Parr for $1 in cash and a bag of peanuts. Give the entry to record the sale.

Exercise 15–3

White is retiring from the partnership of Red, White, and Blue. The partners have always shared losses and gains in a 2:2:1 ratio; and on White's retirement date they have equities in the partnership as follows: Walter White, $9,000; James Red, $9,000; and Jerry Blue, $6,000.

Required:
1. Under the current date give in general journal form the entries for the retirement of White under each of the following unrelated assumptions:
   a) White retires, taking $9,000 of partnership cash for his equity.
   b) White retires, taking $10,500 of partnership cash for his equity.
   c) White retires, taking $8,100 of partnership cash for his equity.

Exercise 15–4

Abbott, Birch, and Collins formed a partnership with Abbott investing $9,000, Birch, $6,000, and Collins, $3,000. They agreed to share losses and gains equally. Their business lost heavily, and at the end of the year they decided to liquidate. After converting all partnership assets to cash and paying all creditor claims, $6,000 of partnership cash remained.

Required:
Prepare a general journal entry to record the distribution of the correct shares of cash to the partners in final liquidation of their business.

Exercise 15–5

The partnership agreement of Ross and Sears provides that income be shared by allowing salary allowances of $8,000 per year to Ross and $6,000 per year to Sears and then sharing any remaining balance equally. At the end of their first year in business, when a work sheet was prepared, it was discovered the partnership had earned just $5 during the year. Sears suggested that the $5 be given to the office boy as a bonus, thereby increasing the expenses of the year and causing the partnership to exactly break even. He further suggested that the partnership could then forget the sharing of gains and losses for the first year, since there would be none. If his suggestions are followed, who gains most and how much does he gain?

Problems **Problem 15–1**

The partnership of Abel, Brock, and Cody earned $24,300 during its first year in business.

Required:
1. Prepare entries to close the firm's Income Summary account and to allocate the net income to the partners under each of the following assumptions:
   a) The partners had not agreed on a method of sharing earnings.
   b) The partners shared earnings in the ratio of their beginning investments which were Abel, $16,000; Brock, $12,000; and Cody, $8,000.
   c) The partners shared earnings by allowing salary allowances of $500 per month to Abel, $600 per month to Brock, and $800 per month to Cody, plus interest at 10% annually on beginning investments, and the balance of income or loss equally.
2. Prepare the income statement section showing the allocation of the year's income to the partners under assumption (c) above.

Problem 15–2

Robert Kemp and Walter Lott are forming a partnership to which Kemp is to devote one half of his time and Lott is to devote full time. They have discussed the following plans for sharing gains and losses:
a) In the ratio of their investments which are to be $12,000 for Kemp and $8,000 for Lott.
b) In proportion to the time devoted to the business.
c) A salary allowance of $500 per month to Lott and the balance in the investment ratio.
d) A salary allowance of $500 per month to Lott, 8% interest annually on their investments, and the balance equally.

Required:
1. Prepare a schedule with columnar headings as follows:

Income-Sharing Plan	$30,000 Net Income		$15,000 Net Income		$9,000 Net Loss	
	Kemp	Lott	Kemp	Lott	Kemp	Lott

2. List the plans for sharing gains and losses by letter in the first column. Then opposite each plan show the partners' shares in a $30,000 annual net income, a $15,000 net income, and a $9,000 net loss.

Problem 15–3

Paul Drake is retiring from the partnership of Drake, Ellis, and Folk. The partners have always shared losses and gains in a 2:3:1 ratio; and on Drake's retirement date they have Capital account balances as follows: Paul Drake, $12,000; Eugene Ellis, $15,000; and Robert Folk, $10,000. Ellis and Folk plan to continue the business and its records under a new partnership contract.

Required:

Using the current date, give in general journal form the entries for the retirement of Drake under each of the following unrelated assumptions:

a) Drake retires and withdraws from the business, taking $2,000 in partnership cash and the note of the new partnership of Ellis and Folk for $10,000.

b) Drake withdraws, taking $13,600 of partnership cash in full settlement for his equity.

c) Drake retires, taking $8,000 in partnership cash and delivery equipment carried on the partnership books at its $4,000 cost, less $1,000 of accumulated depreciation.

d) Drake sells his partnership interest to Glenn Geer, with the consent of Ellis and Folk, taking from Geer $5,000 in cash and Geer's personal $10,000 note payable.

e) Drake sells and transfers his interest to Ellis and Folk, taking from Ellis a $10,000 personal note payable for two thirds of his interest and taking $5,000 in cash from Folk for one third of his interest.

Problem 15–4

Hart, Ivor, and Jaco plan to liquidate their partnership. They have always shared losses and gains in a 5:3:2 ratio, and just prior to the liquidation their balance sheet appeared as follows:

HART, IVOR, AND JACO
Balance Sheet, March 31, 19 –

Cash	$ 3,500	Accounts payable	$13,500
Other assets	45,000	Allen Hart, capital	10,000
		Floyd Ivor, capital	20,000
		Alvin Jaco, capital	5,000
Total Assets	$48,500	Total Equities	$48,500

Required:

Prepare general journal entries to record the sale of the other assets and the distribution of the cash to the proper parties under each of the following unrelated assumptions:

a) The other assets are sold for $50,500.

b) The other assets are sold for $30,000.

c) The other assets are sold for $22,000, and the partner with the deficit can and does pay in the amount of his deficit.

d) The other assets are sold for $20,000, and the partners have no assets other than those invested in the business.

Problem 15–5

Until March 2 of the current year Knox, Lacy, and Mann were partners sharing losses and gains in their capital ratio. On that date Knox suffered a heart attack and died. Lacy and Mann immediately ended the business operations and prepared the following adjusted trial balance:

KNOX, LACY, AND MANN
Adjusted Trial Balance, March 2, 19—

Cash	$ 4,500	
Accounts receivable	10,500	
Allowance for doubtful accounts		$ 500
Merchandise inventory	23,000	
Store equipment	13,500	
Accumulated depreciation, store equipment		3,500
Land	4,500	
Building	50,000	
Accumulated depreciation, building		9,500
Accounts payable		3,000
Mortgage payable		10,000
John Knox, capital		30,000
Robert Lacy, capital		30,000
George Mann, capital		15,000
John Knox, withdrawals	1,000	
Robert Lacy, withdrawals	1,000	
George Mann, withdrawals	1,000	
Revenues		39,000
Expenses	31,500	
Totals	$140,500	$140,500

Required:
1. Prepare entries to close the revenue, expense, income summary, and withdrawals accounts of the partnership.
2. Assume the estate of Knox agreed to accept the land and building and assume the mortgage thereon in settlement of its claim against the partnership assets, and that Lacy and Mann planned to continue the business and rent the building from the estate. Give the entry to transfer the land, building, and mortgage and to settle with the estate.
3. Assume that in the place of the foregoing the estate of Knox demanded a cash settlement and the business had to be sold to a competitor who gave $68,000 for the noncash assets and assumed the mortgage but not the accounts payable. Give the entry to transfer the noncash assets and mortgage to the competitor, and give the entries to allocate the loss to the partners and to distribute the partnership cash to the proper parties.

Alternate problems

Problem 15–1A

Robert Orr, Thomas Parks, and James Quinn invested $15,000, $12,000, and $9,000, respectively, in a partnership. During its first year the firm earned $31,200.

Required:
1. Prepare entries to close the firm's Income Summary account and to allocate the net income to the partners under each of these assumptions:
   a) The partners failed to agree as to the method of sharing earnings.
   b) The partners had agreed to share earnings in the ratio of their beginning investments.
   c) The partners had agreed to share income by allowing annual salary allowances of $8,000 to Orr, $10,000 to Parks, and $6,000 to Quinn; allowing a share of the income equal to 10% interest on partners' investments; and sharing the remaining income or loss equally.
2. Prepare the section of the partners' first-year income statement showing the allocation of the income to the partners under the foregoing assumption (c).

Problem 15–2A

Robert Owen and Delbert Price are in the process of forming a partnership to which Owen will devote one third of his time and Price will devote full time. They have under discussion the following plans for sharing gains and losses:
a) In the ratio of their investments which they have agreed to maintain at $6,000 for Owen and $9,000 for Price.
b) In proportion to the time devoted to the business.
c) A salary allowance of $500 per month to Price and the balance in their investment ratio.
d) A salary allowance of $500 per month to Price, 8% interest on their investments, and the balance equally.

Required:
1. Prepare a schedule with columnar headings as follows:

Income-Sharing Plan	$24,000 Net Income		$12,000 Net Income		$8,000 Net Loss	
	Owen	Price	Owen	Price	Owen	Price

2. List the plans by letter in the first column and show opposite each plan the shares of the partners in (a) a year's net income of $24,000, (b) a year's net income of $12,000, and (c) a year's net loss of $8,000.

Problem 15–3A

Kirby, Lang, and Mohr are partners sharing losses and gains in a 2:2:1 ratio. Kirby plans to withdraw from the partnership, and on the date of his withdrawal the partners' equities in the partnership are Kirby, $10,000; Lang, $12,000; and Mohr, $8,000. Lang and Mohr plan to continue the business and its records under a new partnership contract.

Required:
Give in general journal form the entries for the withdrawal of Kirby under each of the following unrelated assumptions:
a) Kirby, with the consent of Lang and Mohr, sells his interest to Nash, taking

from Nash $2,000 in cash and Nash's personal $10,000 note payable.
b) Kirby withdraws, taking $10,000 of partnership cash for his interest.
c) Kirby withdraws, taking $10,750 of partnership cash.
d) Kirby withdraws, taking $6,000 in cash and delivery equipment carried on the partnership books at $4,000, less $1,500 accumulated depreciation.
e) Kirby withdraws, taking $1,500 in cash and a $10,000 note payable of the new partnership.
f) Kirby transfers his interest to Lang and Mohr, taking Lang's $7,200 personal note for three fifths of his interest and Mohr's $4,800 personal note for two fifths of his interest.

Problem 15–4A

Ashby, Burns, and Coope, who have always shared losses and gains in a 2:2:1 ratio, plan to liquidate their partnership. Just prior to the liquidation their balance sheet appeared as follows:

ASHBY, BURNS, AND COOPE
Balance Sheet, April 15, 19—

Cash	$ 2,500	Accounts payable	$10,500
Other assets	44,000	Walter Ashby, capital	8,000
		George Burns, capital	20,000
		Vernon Coope, capital	8,000
Total Assets	$46,500	Total Equities	$46,500

Required:

Under the assumption the other assets are sold and the cash is distributed to the proper parties on April 20, give the entries for the sales, the loss or gain allocations, and the distributions if—
a) The other assets are sold for $50,000.
b) The other assets are sold for $31,500.
c) The other assets are sold for $21,500, and the partner with a deficit can and does pay in the amount of his deficit.
d) The other assets are sold for $20,250, and the partners have no assets other than those invested in the business.

Problem 15–5A

Mills, Nagel, and Olson are partners. Mills devotes full time to partnership affairs; Nagel and Olson devote very little time; and as a result, they share gains and losses in a 3:1:1 ratio. Of late the business has not been too profitable, and the partners have decided to liquidate. Just prior to the first realization sale, a partnership balance sheet appeared as follows:

MILLS, NAGEL, AND OLSON
Balance Sheet, October 31, 19—

Cash		$ 2,500	Accounts payable	$ 7,000
Accounts receivable		9,500	Albert Mills, capital	6,000
Merchandise inventory		16,000	Robert Nagel, capital	12,000
Equipment	$12,000		Donald Olson, capital	12,000
Less accumulated depr	3,000	9,000		
Total Assets		$37,000	Total Equities	$37,000

The assets were sold, the creditors were paid, and the remaining cash was distributed to the partners on the following dates:

Nov. 4 The accounts receivable were sold for $6,500.
    8 The merchandise inventory was sold for $11,000.
    11 The equipment was sold for $5,000.
    12 The creditors were paid.
    12 The remaining cash was distributed to the partners.

Required:

1. Prepare general journal entries to record the asset sales, the allocation of the realization loss, and the payment of the creditors.
2. Under the assumption that the partner with a deficit can and does pay in the amount of his deficit on November 12, give the entry to record the receipt of his cash and the distribution of partnership cash to the remaining partners.
3. Under the assumption that the partner with a deficit cannot pay, give the entry to allocate his deficit to his partners. Then give the entry to distribute the partnership cash to the remaining partners.

Decision problem 15–1, Sports Center

Paul Lee and Roy May operate Sports Center, a sporting goods store, as a partnership enterprise. Lee has a $45,000 equity in the business and May has a $27,000 equity. They share profits by allowing annual salary allowances of $12,000 to Lee and $10,000 to May, with any remaining profit or loss being shared 60% to Lee and 40% to May.

Ted Lee, Mr. Lee's only son, has been working for the firm on a salary basis. He was an outstanding high school and college athlete and has maintained his contacts with coaches and athletes since graduating from college, and thus attracts a great deal of business to the firm. Actually, 30% of the past three years' sales can be traced directly to Ted's association with the business, and it is reasonable to assume he was instrumental in attracting some of the balance.

Ted is paid $700 per month, but he feels this is not sufficient to induce him to remain with the firm as an employee. However, he likes his work and would like to remain in the sporting goods business. What he really wants is to become a partner in the business.

His father is anxious for him to remain in the business and proposes the following:

a) That Ted be admitted to the partnership with a 20% equity in the partnership assets.

b) That he, Paul Lee, transfer from his Capital account to that of Ted's one half of the 20% interest; that Ted contribute to the firm's assets a 6% note for the other half; and that he, Paul Lee, will guarantee payment of the note and its interest.

c) That losses and gains be shared by continuing the $12,000 and $10,000 salary allowances of the original partners and that Ted be given an $8,400 annual salary allowance, after which any remaining loss or gain would be shared 40% to Paul Lee, 40% to Roy May, and 20% to Ted Lee.

Prepare a report to Mr. May on the advisability of accepting Mr. Lee's proposal. Under the assumption that net incomes for the past three years have been $32,000, $36,000, and $38,000, respectively, prepare schedules showing *(a)* how net income was allocated during the past three years and (*b*) how it would have been allocated had the new agreement been in effect. Also, (*c*) prepare a schedule showing the partners' capital interests immediately after the admission of Ted.

Decision problem 15–2, Allen and Burns

Allen and Burns are partners sharing losses and gains as follows:

a) Annual salary allowances of $15,000 to Allen and $18,000 to Burns are allowed.

b) Interest at 6% on the excess of his Capital account balance over that of his partner is allowed the partner having the larger Capital account balance as of the beginning of the year.

c) The remaining net income is divided three fourths to Allen and one fourth to Burns.

The partnership earned $45,000 during the past year, and the partners began the year with Capital account balances of $70,000 for Allen and $60,000 for Burns.

Although the partners consider the year just ended a successful one, Burns is unhappy with his share of the net income. He feels he should have a much larger share, since he spends twice as much time on partnership affairs as Allen. Allen agrees that Burns spends double the time he spends on partnership business and also that Burns is primarily responsible for the 10% compound annual increase in partnership profits each year for the past several years. Consequently, he suggests that the partners change their loss-and-gain-sharing plan. He knows that Burns has $40,000 in two savings accounts on which he is earning interest at 5% annually, so he suggests the following:

a) Burns is to invest an additional $40,000 in the business.

b) Interest at 8% is to be paid the partners on the full amounts of their investments, which are to be Allen, $70,000; and Burns, $100,000.

c) Each partner is to get a $5,000 increase in his salary allowance, with the allowances becoming: Allen, $20,000; and Burns, $23,000.

d) Any balance remaining after salary and interest allowances is to be given in full to Burns.

Burns is interested in earning 8% on the $40,000 he now has in the bank, is pleased with the $5,000 increase in his salary allowance, and is impressed with Allen's generosity in giving him any balance over and above the partners' salary and interest allowances. However, before accepting the offer, he has come to you for advice. Advise Burns, backing your advice with profit-sharing schedules where desirable.

Chapter 16

Corporations: organization and operation

■ The three common types of business organizations are single proprietorships, partnerships, and corporations. Of the three, corporations are fewer in number; yet in dollar volume, they transact more business than do the other two combined. Thus, because of their business volume and also because almost every person reading this paragraph will at some time either work for or own an interest in a corporation, an understanding of corporations and their accounting is important. And, a start on this understanding may well be made by examining some of the advantages and disadvantages of the corporate form of business organization.

Advantages of the corporate form

■ Separate legal entity

From Chief Justice John Marshall's long ago (1818) definition and description of a corporation as "an artificial being, invisible, intangible, and existing only in the contemplation of the law" has grown the doctrine that a corporation is a legal entity, separate and distinct from the persons who own it. The owners are called *stockholders or shareholders;* they own the corporation, but they are not the corporation. The corporation in a legal sense is an artificial person, separate and distinct from its owners.

439

Separate legal entity is the most important characteristic of a corporation, since it gives a corporation all the rights and responsibilities of a person except those only a natural person may exercise, such as the right to vote or marry. Because of its separate legal entity, a corporation may buy, own, and sell property in its own name. It may sue and be sued in its own name. It may enter into contracts with both outsiders and its own shareholders. In short, through its agents, a corporation may conduct its affairs as a legal person with the rights, duties, and responsibilities of a person.

Lack of stockholders' liability

As a separate legal entity a corporation is responsible for its own acts and its own debts, and its shareholders have no liability for either. From the viewpoint of an investor, this is perhaps the most important advantage of the corporate form.

Ease of transferring ownership rights

Ownership rights in a corporation are represented by shares of stock. And all that is necessary to convey these rights is a transfer of ownership of the shares. Furthermore, since a corporation is a legal entity, the transfer has no effect on the corporation, and a stockholder may transfer and dispose of his stock at will.

Continuity of life

The death, incapacity, or withdrawal of a stockholder does not affect the life of a corporation. A corporation's life depends on its charter, and may continue for the time stated in the charter. Furthermore, this period may be of any length permitted by the laws of the state in which the corporation is organized; and at the expiration of the stated time, the charter may normally be renewed and the period extended. Thus, a perpetual life is possible for a successful corporation.

No mutual agency

Mutual agency does not exist in a corporation. A corporation stockholder, acting as a stockholder, has no power to bind the corporation to contracts. His participation in the affairs of the corporation is limited to the right to vote in the stockholders' meetings. Consequently, stockholders need not exercise the care of partners in selecting people with whom they associate themselves in the ownership of a corporation.

Ease of capital assembly

Lack of stockholders' liability, lack of mutual agency, and the ease with which an interest may be transferred make it easy for a corporation to assemble large amounts of capital from the combined investments of many stockholders. Actually, a corporation's capital-raising ability is as a rule limited only by the profitableness with which it can employ the funds of its stockholders. This is very different from a partnership. In a partnership, capital-raising ability is always limited by the number of partners and their individual wealth; and the number of partners is in turn usually limited by mutual agency and unlimited liability.

Disadvantages of the corporate form

■ Governmental control and supervision

Corporations are created by fulfilling the requirements of a state's corporation laws. Because of this, corporations are said to be "creatures of the state," and as such are subject to much closer state control and supervision than are single proprietorships and partnerships.

In addition, the rights, powers, and duties of corporations, their stockholders, and officials are derived from corporation laws. There would be no objection to this if the laws were simple and easy to understand; but unfortunately, they are notoriously diverse, complicated, and in some cases vague; and as a result the exact rights, duties, and responsibilities of corporations, their directors, and shareholders vary from state to state and are often difficult to define precisely.

Taxation

The greatest disadvantage of the corporate form is usually considered its extra burden of taxes. Corporations as business units are subject to all the taxes of single proprietorships and partnerships; and in addition, they are subject to several not levied on either of the other two. The most important of these are state and federal income taxes which together commonly exceed 50% of a corporation's income. However, insofar as the owners of a corporation are concerned, the burden does not end here. The income of a corporation is taxed twice: first as corporation income and again as personal income when distributed to the stockholders as dividends. This differs from single proprietorships and partnerships, which as business units are not subject to income taxes, and whose income is taxed only as the personal income of their owners.

Lack of stockholders' liability

A page back, lack of stockholders' liability was listed as an advantage of the corporate form. In a small corporation, when an attempt is made to borrow money or secure credit, it may also be a disadvantage since lack of stockholders' liability reduces a corporation's credit. Credit is reduced because when stockholders have no liability, a creditor may look only to the assets of the corporation for satisfaction of its claims. Consequently, credit is normally limited to an amount for which the corporation assets furnish adequate security. This differs from a partnership. If a partnership becomes bankrupt and its assets are not sufficient to meet creditor claims, the creditors may look to the partners' personal assets for satisfaction. Consequently, other things being equal, a partnership with, say, $50,000 in capital can often borrow more money than can a corporation with equal capital.

The effect on a small corporation's credit of no stockholders' liability can be and often is overcome by having a stockholder of means endorse the corporation's notes or agree to make good its obligations. But the stockholder must be willing to back the corporation, since the effect of his endorsement or agreement is to remove the limitation on his liability.

Management of a corporation

■ Although ultimate control of a corporation rests with its stockholders, this control is exercised indirectly through the election of the board of directors. The individual stockholder as a stockholder does not actively participate in management. His right as a stockholder to participate begins and ends with his vote in the stockholders' meeting, where he has one vote for each share of stock owned.

Normally a corporation's stockholders meet once each year to elect directors and transact such other business as is provided in the corporation's bylaws. Theoretically, stockholders owning or controlling the votes of 50% plus one share of a corporation's stock can elect the board and control the corporation. Actually, because many stockholders do not attend the annual meeting, a much smaller percentage is frequently sufficient for control. Commonly, stockholders who do not attend the annual meeting delegate to an agent their voting rights. This is done by signing a legal document called a *proxy*, which gives the agent the right to vote the stock.

A corporation's board of directors is responsible and has final authority for the direction of corporation affairs; but it may act only as a collective body—an individual director, as a director, has no power to transact corporation business. And, as a rule, although it has final authority, a board will limit itself to establishing policy, delegating the day-by-day direction of corporation business to the corporation's administrative officers whom it selects and elects.

A corporation's administrative officers are commonly headed by a president who is normally the chief executive officer and is directly responsible to the board for managing, controlling, and supervising the corporation's business. To aid the president, many corporations have one or more vice presidents who are vested with specific managerial powers and duties by the president and the directors. In addition, the corporation secretary keeps the minutes of the meetings of the stockholders and directors, and in a small corporation may also be responsible for keeping a record of the stockholders and the changing amounts of their stock interests. The treasurer is custodian of corporation funds.

Illustration 16–1 shows the organizational chart of a corporation. Note its lines of authority extending from the stockholders through the board and on to the administrative officers.

Organizing a corporation

■ A corporation is created by securing a charter from one of the 50 states or the federal government. Federal charters are limited to national banks, savings and loan associations, and quasi-government corporations, such as the Federal Deposit Insurance Corporation. Consequently, the majority of corporations are chartered by the states.

At one time corporation charters were granted by special acts of

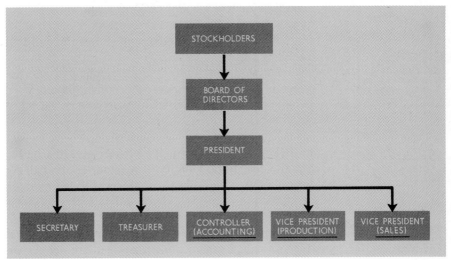

state legislatures. Today, in the various states this power has been delegated to the secretary of state or another state official; and in delegating the power, the various state legislatures have passed laws stating the requirements to be met by persons seeking such a charter. These requirements vary with the states, but in general call for filing several copies of a charter application. Normally, the application must be signed by three or more subscribers to the prospective corporation's stock who are called "incorporators." The application usually must include:

1. The name of the corporation and its legal address within the state.
2. The purpose for which the corporation is organized.
3. The amount of stock authorized and its par value, if any.
4. If there is to be more than one kind of stock, the amount of each.
5. If the stock is to be divided into different kinds or classes, a statement must be made as to the preferences, qualifications, limitations, restrictions, and rights of each class.
6. The names and addresses of the subscribers and the amount of stock subscribed by each.

Normally the secretary of state or other designated state officer is required to see that the application complies with the law. If it does and all fees, taxes, and charges have been paid, the charter is issued. In many states a copy of the application is approved and returned as the corporation charter. In any case, the corporation comes into existence with the issuance of its charter.

After the corporation comes into existence, usually at the first meeting of its stockholders, bylaws to govern the conduct of its affairs are adopted. Bylaws normally include among other things:

1. The time, place, manner of calling, and rules for conducting meetings of the stockholders and directors.
2. The number, qualifications, duties, powers, and length of office of the directors.
3. The appointment, duties, powers, compensations, and length of office of corporation officers other than directors.
4. Any proper rules and regulations to govern the acts of the directors and officers.

The bylaws together with the charter give the basic rules for conducting the corporation affairs. It is important that all acts of the stockholders, directors, and officers conform with the regulations in both.

Organization costs ■ The costs of organizing a corporation, such as costs of printing stock, legal fees, promoters' fees, and amounts paid the state to secure a charter, are called organization costs and are debited on incurrence to an account called Organization Costs. Theoretically, the sum of these costs represents an intangible asset from which the corporation will benefit throughout its life; and theoretically these costs should be written off like a prepaid expense over the corporation's life. However, since the number of years a corporation will remain in existence cannot be foretold, many accountants favor writing off such costs during a corporation's early years. Also, there is a tax advantage to this. Consequently, organization costs are commonly written off as a tax-deductible expense over, for example, the first five years of a corporation's life.

When a balance sheet is prepared for a corporation having organization costs, the amount of this asset appears thereon as an intangible asset in the intangible asset section of the statement. The intangible asset section follows immediately after the plant and equipment section.

Stock certificates and the transfer of stock ■ When a person invests in a corporation by buying its stock, he receives a stock certificate as evidence of the shares purchased. Usually in a small corporation only one certificate is issued for each block of stock purchased, the one certificate may be for any number of shares. For example, the certificate of Illustration 16–2 is for 50 shares. Large corporations commonly use preprinted 100-share denomination certificates in addition to blank certificates that may be made out for any number of shares.

Observe that the certificate of Illustration 16–2 is for *50 shares of $100 par value common stock*. When a corporation issues only one kind of stock, it is called common stock. (A corporation may issue more than one kind or class of stock, as will be explained later.) If Robert Wetzel of Illustration 16–2 invested $5,000 in Westfield Publishing Company by paying the corporation $100 per share for 50 shares of its common stock ($100 × 50 = $5,000), the investment increased the corporation's assets by $5,000 and it increased owner equity or stockholders' equity in the corporation by the same amount.

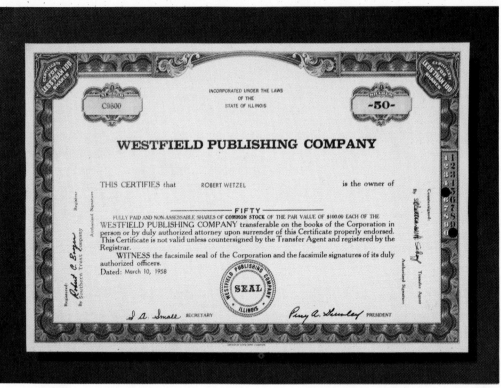

An owner of stock may transfer at will either part or all the shares represented by a stock certificate. To do so he completes the endorsement on the reverse side of the certificate and sends the certificate to the corporation secretary in a small corporation or to the corporation's transfer agent in a large one. For example, assume that Robert Wetzel, the owner of the certificate for 50 shares shown in Illustration 16–2 sells 10 of the shares to William Morris. To transfer the stock Wetzel completes the endorsement on the back of the certificate, as shown in Illustration 16–3, signs his name, and sends it to the corporation secretary or transfer agent. The old certificate is canceled and retained, and two new certificates are issued in its place. One for 10 shares is sent to Morris, and the other for 40 shares is sent to Wetzel.

Stock certificate book

When it is organized, a corporation must have a supply of stock certificates printed. In a small corporation the certificates often have stubs attached, and the certificates and stubs are bound in a Stock Certificate Book in the manner of a checkbook. As each stock certificate is issued, the name of its owner, the number of shares, and the date of issuance are entered on a blank certificate, and the certificate is signed by the proper corporation officials. At the same time, the name and address of the stock owner, the number of shares, and the date are entered on

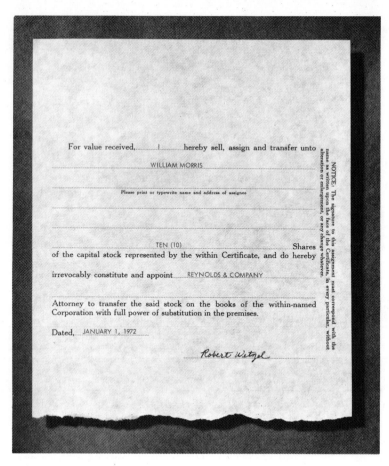

For value received,_____I_____ hereby sell, assign and transfer unto

WILLIAM MORRIS

Please print or typewrite name and address of assignee

_____TEN (10)_____ Shares
of the capital stock represented by the within Certificate, and do hereby

irrevocably constitute and appoint___REYNOLDS & COMPANY

Attorney to transfer the said stock on the books of the within-named
Corporation with full power of substitution in the premises.

Dated,___JANUARY 1, 1972

Robert Wetzel

NOTICE: The signature to this assignment must correspond, with the name as written upon the face of the Certificate, in every particular, without alteration or enlargement, or any change whatever.

Illustration
16–3
**Stock Certificate
(Reverse Side)
Showing
Endorsement for
Transferred
Stock**

the certificate stub. The certificate is then removed and delivered to its owner.

When the stock is returned for transfer, the old certificate is marked canceled, attached to its stub in the Stock Certificate Book, and one or more new certificates are issued in its place. Consequently, as a result of these procedures, the Stock Certificate Book of a small corporation contains a current record of the shares owned by each stockholder.

If a small corporation issues more than one kind or class of stock, it uses separate stock certificate books as well as separate stock accounts for each.

Transfer agent and registrar

A large corporation, one whose stock is listed on a major stock exchange, must have a registrar and a transfer agent who are assigned the responsibilities of transferring the corporation's stock, keeping its stockholder records, and preparing the official lists of stockholders for stockholders' meetings and for payment of dividends.

Assigning the duties of transferring stock and keeping stockholder records to a transfer agent and a registrar helps ensure that only the proper amount of stock is issued and that the stock records are honestly and accurately kept. Usually registrars and transfer agents are large banks or trust companies.

When the owner of stock in a corporation having a registrar and a transfer agent wishes to transfer his stock to a new owner, he completes the endorsement on the back of his certificate and, usually through a stockbroker, sends the certificate to the transfer agent. The transfer agent cancels the old certificate and issues one or more new certificates which he sends to the registrar. The registrar enters the transfer in the stockholder records and sends the new certificate or certificates to the proper owners.

Banks and trust companies acting as registrars and transfer agents commonly so act for a number of corporations; and consequently are in a position to make use of punched card and electronic equipment in keeping stockholder records for each.

Corporation accounting

■ A corporation's accounting records are as a rule like those of an equal-size single proprietorship or partnership, and generally its accounting differs only for transactions directly affecting the stockholder equity accounts. Here a difference results because a distinction is always made in corporation accounting between invested capital and capital from earnings retained in the business.

No such distinction is made in a single proprietorship or partnership where an owner's investment and changes in his equity resulting from gains and losses are recorded in the same account, the owner's Capital account. However, in a corporation the distinction is made and two kinds of owner equity accounts, (1) *contributed capital accounts* and (2) *retained earnings accounts*, are used in preserving the distinction. The contributed capital accounts, such as the Common Stock account, show amounts invested in or contributed to the corporation by stockholders or others. The retained earnings accounts show earnings retained in the business.

The distinction between contributed capital and retained earnings is necessary because in most states a corporation cannot pay a legal dividend except from retained earnings.

Corporation owner equity accounts illustrated

■ To demonstrate the use of separate accounts for contributed capital and retained earnings as found in corporation accounting and to contrast their use with the single capital account in a sole proprietorship, assume that on January 5, 1972, a single proprietorship and a corporation having five stockholders were formed. Assume further that $25,000 was invested in each. In the sole proprietorship the owner, John Ohm, invested the entire amount; and in the corporation five stockholders each bought 500 shares of its $10 par value common stock at $10 per share.

Without dates and explanations, the entries to record the investments are:

Single Proprietorship		Corporation	
Cash 25,000		Cash 25,000	
John Ohm, Capital...	25,000	Common Stock.......	25,000

And after the entries were posted, the owner equity accounts of the two concerns appeared as follows:

Single Proprietorship John Ohm, Capital				Corporation Common Stock			
Date	Dr.	Cr.	Bal.	Date	Dr.	Cr.	Bal.
Jan. 5, '72		25,000	25,000	Jan. 5, '72		25,000	25,000

To continue the illustration, it will be recalled that in a single proprietorship when the Income Summary account is closed, the amount of net income or loss is transferred from the Income Summary account to the owner's Capital account. In a corporation this differs; in a corporation the net income or loss is carried to the Retained Earnings account. For example, if in the two concerns under discussion, each earned $8,000 during the first year and retained the earnings for use in carrying on their operations, after the Income Summary accounts were closed, the owner equity of each appeared in its accounts as follows:

Single Proprietorship John Ohm, Capital				Corporation Common Stock			
Date	Dr.	Cr.	Bal.	Date	Dr.	Cr.	Bal.
Jan. 5, '72		25,000	25,000	Jan. 5, '72		25,000	25,000
Dec. 31, '72		8,000	33,000				

				Retained Earnings			
				Date	Dr.	Cr.	Bal.
				Dec. 31, '72		8,000	8,000

And the owner equity of each appeared on its balance sheet as follows:

Single Proprietorship	Corporation
OWNER EQUITY	STOCKHOLDERS' EQUITY
John Ohm, capital, January 1, 1972................................. $25,000	Common stock, $10 par value, authorized and issued 2,500 shares $25,000
Add net income...................... 8,000	Retained earnings 8,000
John Ohm, capital, December 31, 1972............................ $33,000	Stockholders' equity.............. $33,000

To continue the illustration, assume that the two concerns each lost $11,000 during their second year. If there were no withdrawals in the single proprietorship or additional investments in either concern, the owner equity accounts of each appeared at the end of the second year as follows:

Single Proprietorship

John Ohm, Capital

Date	Dr.	Cr.	Bal.
Jan. 5, '72		25,000	25,000
Dec. 31, '72		8,000	33,000
Dec. 31, '73	11,000		22,000

Corporation

Common Stock

Date	Dr.	Cr.	Bal.
Jan. 5, '72		25,000	25,000

Retained Earnings

Date	Dr.	Cr.	Bal.
Dec. 31, '72		8,000	8,000
Dec. 31, '73	11,000		(3,000)

Observe that the Retained Earnings account of the corporation has a $3,000 debit balance. A corporation is said to have a *deficit* when it has a debit balance in its Retained Earnings account, as in this illustration. A deficit is in effect a negative amount of retained earnings, and in most states a corporation with a deficit cannot pay a legal dividend.

At the end of the second year the owner equity sections on the balance sheets of the two concerns appeared as follows:

Single Proprietorship	Corporation
OWNER EQUITY	STOCKHOLDERS' EQUITY
John Ohm, capital, January 1, 1973 .... $33,000	Common stock, $10 par value, 2,500 shares authorized and issued........ $25,000
Deduct: Net loss................... (11,000)	Deduct: Deficit..................... (3,000)
John Ohm, capital, December 31, 1973 .... $22,000	Stockholders' equity $22,000

During their second year both the corporation and the proprietorship suffered losses, which in each case reduced the equities of their owners to $22,000. Notice in the illustration just given how the $22,000 equity in the corporation is shown by listing the amount of stock and deducting therefrom the $3,000 deficit.

Authorization of stock

■ When a corporation is organized, it is authorized in its charter to issue a certain amount of stock. The stock may be of one kind, common stock, or both common and preferred stock may be authorized. (Preferred stock is described and discussed later in this chapter.) However, regardless of whether one or two kinds of stock are authorized, the corporation may issue no more than the amount of each authorized by its charter.

Often a corporation will secure an authorization to issue more stock than it plans to sell at the time of its organization. This enables the corporation to expand at any time in its future through the sale of the additional stock, and without the need of applying to the state for the right to issue more. For example, a corporation needing $300,000 to begin its operations may secure the right to issue $500,000 of stock, but then issue only $300,000, keeping the remainder until a future date when it may wish to sell the stock and expand without applying to the state for the right to issue more stock.

At the time a corporation receives its charter, it is common practice to write or type across the top of each stock account the amount of stock authorized. For example, if 5,000 shares of $100 par value common stock are authorized, the memorandum written across the top of the Common Stock account might read: "Authorized on June 1, 19—, to issue 5,000 shares of $100 par value common stock." If preferred stock is also authorized, a similar memorandum telling the number of preferred shares authorized would be written across the top of the Preferred Stock account.

Selling stock for cash

■ When stock is sold for cash and immediately issued, an entry in general journal form like the following is commonly used to record the sale and issuance:

June	5	Cash...	300,000.00	
		Common Stock..................................		300,000.00
		Sold and issued 3,000 shares of $100 par value common stock.		

After authorized stock has been sold and issued, it is a common practice to show on the balance sheet both the amount of stock authorized and the amount issued, as on page 453.

Exchanging stock for assets other than cash

■ Corporations often accept assets other than cash in exchange for their stock. When they do so, the transaction is recorded in somewhat the following manner:

Apr.	3	Machinery..	10,000.00	
		Buildings	25,000.00	
		Land...	5,000.00	
		Common Stock....................................		40,000.00
		Exchanged 400 shares of common stock for machinery, buildings, and land.		

Or another example: A corporation may give shares of its stock to its promoters in exchange for their services in getting the corporation organized. In such a case the corporation receives the intangible asset of being organized in exchange for its stock, and the transaction is recorded as follows:

Apr.	5	Organization Costs..	5.000.00	
		Common Stock..		5,000.00
		Gave the promoters shares of common stock in exchange for their services in getting the corporation organized.		

When a corporation accepts assets other than cash for its stock, it is the duty of the board of directors to place a fair value on the accepted assets; and if the assets are fairly valued, such transactions are perfectly proper.

Stock subscriptions

■ Often corporations sell their stock for cash and immediately issue the stock. Often, too, when stock is first sold, especially in organizing a new corporation, it is sold by means of *subscriptions*. When stock is sold by means of subscriptions, a person wishing to become a stockholder signs a subscription blank or a subscription list on which he subscribes to a certain number of shares and agrees to pay for the stock either in one amount or in installments. When the subscription is accepted by the corporation, it becomes a contract.

When a prospective stockholder signs a corporation's subscription list or one of its subscription blanks and the corporation accepts the subscription, the corporation acquires an asset, the right to receive payment from the subscriber; and at the same time, its stockholder equity is increased by the amount the subscriber agrees to pay. The increase in assets is recorded in an account for common stock, called *Subscriptions Receivable, Common Stock;* and the increase in stockholder equity is recorded in an account for common stock, called *Common Stock Subscribed.* Both accounts are of a temporary nature. The subscriptions receivable will be turned into cash or other assets when the subscriber pays for his stock. Likewise, when payment is completed, the stock subscribed will be issued and will become outstanding stock. Normally subscribed stock is not issued until paid for.

If a corporation receives subscriptions to both common and preferred stock, separate subscriptions receivable and stock subscribed accounts must be kept for each. If the number of subscribers becomes large, the subscriptions receivable accounts often become controlling accounts that control subsidiary Subscribers' Ledgers having an account with each subscriber. The controlling account for each class of subscriptions receivable and its Subscribers' Ledger operate in the same manner as, for example, the Accounts Receivable controlling account and the Accounts Receivable Ledger discussed in a previous chapter.

When unpaid subscriptions exist on the balance sheet date, the intention is normally to collect the amounts within a relatively short period. Therefore, unpaid subscriptions normally appear on the balance sheet as current assets under the title "Subscriptions Receivable, Common Stock" or "Subscriptions Receivable, Preferred Stock."

Sale of stock through subscriptions, with collections in installments

■ Corporations selling stock through subscriptions may collect the subscriptions in one amount or in installments. To illustrate the sale of stock through subscriptions collected in installments, assume that on June 7, 19—, Northgate Corporation received a charter authorizing the issuance of 10,000 shares of $10 par value common stock. On the same day it accepted subscriptions to 5,000 of the shares at par, under subscription contracts calling for a 10% down payment to accompany the subscriptions and the balance in two equal installments due in 30 and 60 days. The subscriptions were recorded with the following entry:

June	7	Subscriptions Receivable, Common Stock........	50,000.00	
		Common Stock Subscribed......................		50,000.00
		Accepted subscriptions to 5,000 shares of common stock at par.		

Receipt of the down payments and the two installment payments were recorded with these entries:

June	7	Cash..	5,000.00	
		Subscriptions Receivable, Common Stock...		5,000.00
		Collected the down payments on the common stock subscribed.		
July	6	Cash..	22,500.00	
		Subscriptions Receivable, Common Stock...		22,500.00
		Collected the first installment payments on the common stock subscribed.		

Aug.	5	Cash...	22,500.00	
		Subscriptions Receivable, Common Stock..		22,500.00
		Collected the second installment payments		
		on the common stock subscribed.		

When stock is sold through subscriptions, the stock is paid for as soon as the subscriptions are paid in full; and as soon as the subscriptions are paid, the stock is issued. The entry to record the issuance of the Northgate common stock appeared as follows:

Aug.	5	Common Stock Subscribed............................	50,000.00	
		Common Stock..		50,000.00
		Issued 5,000 shares of common stock sold		
		through subscriptions.		

Most subscriptions are collected in full, although not always. Sometimes a subscriber fails to pay; and when this happens, the subscription contract must be canceled. In such a case, if the subscriber has made a partial payment on his contract, the amount paid may be returned. Or, a smaller amount of stock than that subscribed, an amount equal to the partial payment, may be issued. Or, in some states the subscriber's partial payment may be kept by the corporation to compensate for any damages suffered.

Subscribed stock on the balance sheet

■ In many states a subscriber to stock is granted all the rights of a stockholder upon acceptance of his signed subscription contract by the corporation to whose stock he is subscribing. Also, acceptance of such a contract increases a corporation's assets and the equity of the subscribers in the corporation. Consequently, if a corporation prepares a balance sheet after accepting subscriptions to its stock but before the stock is issued, it shows both its issued stock and its subscribed stock as follows:

STOCKHOLDERS' EQUITY

Common stock, $10 par value, 25,000 shares authorized, 15,000 shares issued.......... $150,000
Common stock subscribed, 5,000 shares... 50,000
Total common stock issued and subscribed $200,000

Cash dividends and retained earnings

■ A dividend is a distribution made to its stockholders by a corporation. Dividends are declared or voted by the board of directors, and courts have generally held that the board is final judge of when if at all a dividend should be paid. Dividends may be distributed in cash, other assets, or in a corporation's own stock. Cash dividends are the most common, and are normally stated in terms of so many dollars or cents per share of stock. For example, a corporation may declare a dividend of one dollar per share on its outstanding common stock. If it does so, an owner of 100 shares will receive $100.

Since a corporation's stockholders change, a dividend is normally declared on one date to be paid on a future date to the *stockholders of record* (stockholders according to the corporation's records) of a specified third date. For example, a board of directors may declare a dividend on December 28, to be paid on January 25 to the stockholders of record of January 20. Of the three dates involved here, December 28 is called the *date of declaration,* January 20 is the *date of record,* and January 25 is the *date of payment.* Declaring a dividend on one date to be paid on a future date gives new purchasers of the stock an opportunity to have their ownership recorded in time to receive the dividend.

A stockholder has no right to a dividend until it is declared by the board of directors. However, as soon as a cash dividend is declared, it becomes a liability of the corporation, normally a current liability, and must be paid. Furthermore, the stockholders have the right to sue and force payment of a cash dividend once it is declared. Since dividends are normally declared on one date to be paid on a future date, two entries are used to record the declaration and payment of each dividend. The first entry, which is made at the time of the declaration, reduces the stockholders' equity and records the liability for the dividend; and the second records its payment. The two entries commonly appear as follows:

Dec.	28	Retained Earnings..	25,000.00	
		Common Dividend Payable		25,000.00
		To record the declaration of a $1 per share dividend on the 25,000 shares of outstanding common stock.		
Jan.	25	Common Dividend Payable	25,000.00	
		Cash...		25,000.00
		To record payment of the dividend declared on December 28.		

Dividend policy ■ Since a corporation is a legal entity, the profits it earns belong to the corporation. The stockholders own the corporation; but they have no legal right to its profits until the board declares a dividend; and the board is the final judge of when such a dividend should be declared. In deciding upon a dividend, the board normally considers both its legality and the wisdom of its declaration.

Although the answer varies somewhat from state to state, generally, a dividend is legal when it does not reduce the stockholders' equity below the amount paid to the corporation for its stock. When state laws establish rules like the foregoing to govern the payment of dividends, the laws also normally make directors personally liable for repayment to the corporation of a dividend declared and paid in violation of the rules. A director who votes against such a dividend is not held liable; consequently, directors are usually careful not to vote for an illegal dividend.

As to the wisdom of a dividend, the directors must decide whether the corporation can spare the cash needed for its payment, or when cash is available, if the cash cannot be used to better advantage in expanding the corporation's operations for greater profits in the future. Many large corporations follow the policy of paying out in dividends around 60% of earnings and retaining the balance to finance expansion and growth.

Rights of stock-holders

■ If a corporation issues only one kind of stock, the stock is known as *common stock*. When individuals buy such stock, they acquire all the specific rights granted by the corporation's charter to its common stockholders; and they also acquire the general rights granted stockholders by the laws of the state in which the corporation is organized. The laws vary, but in general all common stockholders have the following rights:

1. The right to vote in the stockholders' meetings.
2. The right to sell or otherwise dispose of their stock.
3. The right of first opportunity to purchase any additional shares of common stock issued by the corporation. (This is called the common stockholders' *preemptive right*. It gives a common stockholder the opportunity to protect his interest in the corporation. For example, if a stockholder owns one fourth of a corporation's common stock, he has first opportunity to buy one fourth of any new common stock issued. This enables him to maintain his one-fourth interest.)
4. The right to share pro rata with other common stockholders in any dividends declared.
5. The right to share in any assets remaining after creditors are paid if the corporation is liquidated.

Preferred stock

■ A corporation may issue more than one kind or class of stock. If two classes are issued, one is generally known as common stock and the other as *preferred stock*. Preferred stock is so called because of the preferences granted its owners. These commonly include a preference as to payment of dividends, and may include a preference as to the return of the stock's par value in a liquidation.

A preference as to dividends does not give an absolute right to dividends. Rather if dividends are declared, it gives the preferred stockholders the right to receive their preferred dividend before the common stockholders are paid a dividend. In other words, if dividends are declared, a dividend must be paid the preferred stockholders before a dividend may be paid to the common stockholders. However, if the directors are of the opinion that no dividends should be paid, then neither the preferred nor the common stockholders receive a dividend.

Dividends on the majority of preferred stocks are limited to a fixed maximum amount. For example, a share of $100 par value, 6%, nonparticipating preferred stock has a preference each year to a dividend equal to 6% of its par value, or $6; but the dividend is limited to that amount.

Although dividends on the majority of preferred stocks are limited in amount, dividends on a corporation's common stock are unlimited, except by the earning power of the corporation and the judgment of its board of directors.

While dividends on most preferred stocks are limited to a fixed basic percentage or amount, some preferred stocks have the right under certain circumstances to dividends in excess of a fixed basic percentage or amount. Such preferred stocks are called *participating preferred stocks*. Participating preferred stocks may be fully participating, or their participation may be limited to a fixed amount, depending in each case on the exact terms set forth in the corporation's charter. For example, if a corporation issues fully participating, 6%, $100 par value, preferred stock and $50 par value common stock, the owners of the preferred stock have a preference to a 6% or $6 per share dividend each year. Then, each year, after the common stockholders have received a 6% or $3 per share dividend, the preferred stockholders have a right to participate with the common stockholders in any additional dividends declared. The participation is usually on the basis of the same additional percent-on-par-value-per-share dividend to each kind of stock. For instance, if in this case the common stockholders are paid an additional 2% or $1 per share dividend, the preferred stockholders should receive an additional 2% or $2 per share dividend.

Often when preferred stock is participating, participation is limited. For example, a $100 par value, 5%, preferred stock may be issued with the right to participate in dividends to 10% of its par value. Such a stock has a preference to dividends of 5% each year. It also has a right after the common stockholders receive a 5% dividend to participate in additional dividends until it has received 10 percent, or $10, per share. Its participation rights end at this point.

In addition to being participating or nonparticipating, preferred stocks are either *cumulative* or *noncumulative*. A cumulative preferred stock is one on which any undeclared dividends accumulate each year until paid. A noncumulative preferred stock is one on which the right to receive dividends is forfeited in any year in which dividends are not declared.

The accumulation of dividends on cumulative preferred stocks does not guarantee their payment. Dividends cannot be guaranteed because earnings from which they are paid cannot be guaranteed. However, when a corporation issues cumulative preferred stock, it does agree to pay its cumulative preferred stockholders both their current dividends and any unpaid back dividends, called *dividends in arrears,* before it pays a dividend to its common stockholders.

In addition to the preferences it receives, preferred stock carries with it all the rights of common stock, unless such rights are specifically denied in the corporation charter. Commonly, preferred stock is denied the right to vote in the stockholders' meetings, as in the example in a following section that tells why preferred stock is issued.

Preferred dividends in arrears on the balance sheet date

A liability for a dividend does not come into existence until the dividend is declared by the board of directors; and unlike interest, dividends do not accrue. Consequently, if on the dividend date a corporation's board fails to declare a dividend on its cumulative preferred stock, the dividend in arrears is not a liability and does not appear on the balance sheet as such. However, if there are preferred dividends in arrears, this information should appear on the balance sheet, and normally such information is given in a balance sheet footnote. For example, if three years' dividends have been missed, such a footnote might read, "Dividends for the current and two past years are in arrears on the preferred stock." When a balance sheet does not carry such a footnote, a balance sheet reader has the right to assume that all current and back dividends on the preferred stock have been paid.

Why preferred stock is issued ■ Two common reasons why preferred stock is issued can best be shown by means of an example. Suppose that three men with a total of $100,000 to invest wish to organize a corporation requiring $200,000 capital. If they sell and issue $200,000 of common stock, they will have to share control with other stockholders. However, if they sell and issue $100,000 of common stock to themselves and sell to outsiders $100,000 of 6%, cumulative preferred stock having no voting rights, they can retain control of the corporation for themselves.

Also, suppose the three promoters expect their new corporation to earn an annual after-tax return of $20,000. If they sell and issue $200,000 of common stock, this will mean a 10% return; but if they sell and issue $100,000 of each kind of stock, retaining the common for themselves, they can increase their own return to 14%, as follows:

Net after-tax income	$20,000
Preferred dividends at 6%	6,000
Balance to common stockholders (equal to 14% on their $100,000 investment)	$14,000

This is an example of what is known as securing a *leverage* on an investment. The common stockholders secure a leverage, or greater return, on their investment because the dividends on the preferred stock are less than the amount that can be earned through the use of the preferred stockholders' money.

In the example the preferred stock carries a cumulative preference as to dividends. The exact preferences granted in this and every other case always depend on what must be granted to sell the stock. As a rule, nothing is granted beyond what is necessary.

Stock values ■ Several values apply to stock. For instance, a stock may have a par value, a book value, a market value, and a redemption value.

Par value

Par value is the arbitrary value established for a share of stock in the charter of its issuing corporation and is printed on the face of each stock certificate. Par value does not establish worth, and its main significance is a legal one that is discussed in more detail in the next chapter.

Book value

The book value of a share of stock measures the equity of one share of the stock in the assets of its issuing corporation. If a corporation issues only one kind of stock, common stock, the book value or equity of all the outstanding common shares is equal to the sum of the corporation's contributed and retained capital; and consequently, the book value of one share is equal to the sum of the contributed and retained capital divided by the number of shares outstanding. For example, consider a corporation that has the following contributed and retained capital:

Common stock, $25 par value, 1,000 shares authorized and issued	$25,000
Retained earnings	6,100
Total Stockholders' Equity	$31,100

The book value of one share of the corporation's common stock is $31,100 divided by 1,000 shares, or $31.10 per share.

When a corporation issues both common and preferred stock and the book value of each is to be determined, it is first necessary to allocate total stockholders' equity between the two classes of stock. Then the equity allocated to the preferred stock is divided by the preferred shares outstanding and the equity allocated to the common stock is divided by the common shares outstanding to determine the book value of each.

The allocation of total stockholders' equity between the two classes of stock may be simple or complex, depending upon the liquidation rights granted the preferred stockholders. Preferred stockholders are commonly given a preference in a liquidation to the return of the par value of their shares plus any dividends in arrears. For example, assume a corporation has the following capitalization:

Preferred stock, $100 par value, 7% cumulative and nonparticipating, 1,000 shares authorized and outstanding	$100,000
Common stock, $10 par value, 20,000 shares authorized and outstanding	200,000
Retained earnings	40,000
Total Stockholders' Equity	$340,000

If in this case the preferred stockholders are granted a preference in a liquidation to the par value of their shares plus dividends in arrears and there are no dividends in arrears, the total stockholders' equity is divided as follows:

Total stockholders' equity $340,000
Less equity allocated to preferred stockholders:
  Par value of outstanding preferred shares 100,000
Equity of common stockholders $240,000

And the book value of each is:

Preferred stock: $100,000 ÷ 1,000 shares = $100 per share
Common stock: $240,000 ÷ 20,000 shares = $12 per share

When there is a deficit or dividends in arrears, the allocation procedure is the same but the results differ. For example, assume there are two years' dividends in arrears on the preferred stock of a corporation having the following stockholders' equity:

Preferred stock, $100 par value, 7½% cumulative and nonparticipating, 1,000
  shares authorized and outstanding $100,000
Common stock, $10 par value, 50,000 shares authorized and outstanding 500,000
Deficit .... (25,000)
  Total Stockholders' Equity $575,000

If in this case the preferred stockholders have a preference in a liquidation to the par value of their shares plus dividends in arrears, total stockholders' equity is allocated as follows:

Total stockholders' equity $575,000
Less equity allocated to preferred stockholders:
  Par value of outstanding preferred shares $100,000
  Dividends in arrears   15,000   115,000
Equity of common stockholders $460,000

And the book value per share is:

Preferred stock: $115,000 ÷ 1,000 shares = $115 per share
Common stock: $460,000 ÷ 50,000 shares = $9.20 per share

Corporations in their annual reports to their shareholders often point out the increase that has occurred in the book value of the corporation's shares during a year or other period of time. Book value is also of significance in many contracts. For example, a stockholder may enter into a contract to sell his shares at their book value at some future date. However, book value should not be confused with *liquidation value,* because if a corporation is liquidated, its assets will probably sell at prices quite different from the amounts at which they are carried on the books. Also, book value is only one of several factors that affect the market value of stock; and dividends, earning capacity, and future prospects are usually of much more importance. For instance a common stock having a $11 book value may sell for $25 per share if its earnings, dividends, and prospects are good; but it may sell for $5 per share if these factors are unfavorable.

Market value

The market value of a share of stock is the price at which a share can be bought or sold. Market values are influenced by earnings, dividends, future prospects, book value, and general market conditions.

Redemption value

Redemption values apply to preferred stocks. Often corporations issuing preferred stock reserve the right to redeem the stock by paying the preferred stockholders the par value of their stock plus a premium. The amount a corporation agrees to pay to redeem a share of its preferred stock is called the "redemption value" of the stock. Normally, a corporation reserves the right to either redeem or permit the stock to remain outstanding, as it chooses.

Questions for class discussion

1. List (*a*) the advantages and (*b*) disadvantages of the corporation form of business organization.
2. A corporation is said to be a separate legal entity. What is meant by this?
3. What effect does a separate legal existence have upon the ability of a corporation to enter into contracts with its stockholders? What effect does a corporation's separate legal existence have on the liability of its stockholders for the corporation's debts?
4. How may lack of stockholder liability be both an advantage and a disadvantage to a small corporation?
5. Before it will loan money to a small corporation, a bank insists that a large stockholder of the corporation, S. T. Larr, personally endorse the corporation's note. Why does the bank ask for the endorsement of Larr? Would the bank demand this endorsement if the business were organized as a partnership and Larr were a partner?
6. What is a proxy?
7. What are organization costs? List several.
8. What are the duties and responsibilities of a corporation's registrar and transfer agent?
9. Why is a corporation whose stock is sold on a stock exchange required to have a registrar and transfer agent? Why is such a corporation required to have both a registrar and a transfer agent?
10. List the rights of common stockholders.
11. What is the preemptive right of common stockholders?
12. What are the balance sheet classifications of the accounts: (*a*) Subscriptions Receivable, Common Stock and (*b*) Common Stock Subscribed?
13. What two kinds of proprietary accounts are used in corporation accounting? Why are the two kinds used?
14. In corporation accounting, what is a deficit?
15. What are the meanings of the following when applied to preferred stock: (*a*) preferred, (*b*) participating, (*c*) nonparticipating, (*d*) cumulative, and (*e*) noncumulative?
16. What are the meanings of the following terms when applied to stock: (*a*) par value, (*b*) book value, (*c*) market value, and (*d*) redemption value?

Exercise 16-1

A corporation has outstanding 10,000 shares of $25 par value common stock, and last year it earned $28,500, after taxes. On January 8 of this year the corporation's board of directors voted a $1.50 per share dividend on the stock, payable on February 15 to the January 20 stockholders of record. Give the entries to (a) close the corporation's Income Summary account at the end of last year and to record (b) the dividend declaration and (c) its payment. Also (d) name and give the three dates involved in the dividend declaration and payment.

Exercise 16-2

A corporation has outstanding 1,000 shares of $100 par value, 7% cumulative and nonparticipating preferred stock and 10,000 shares of $10 par value common stock; and during the first four years of its life it paid out the following amounts in dividends: first year, nothing; second year, $12,000; third year, $29,000; and fourth year, $37,000. Determine the total dividends paid to each class of stockholders each year.

Exercise 16-3

Determine the total dividends paid each class of stockholders of the previous exercise under the assumption that rather than being cumulative and nonparticipating, the preferred stock is noncumulative and nonparticipating.

Exercise 16-4

A corporation that has regularly paid all dividends on its preferred stock has outstanding 1,000 shares of $100 par value, 7% cumulative and fully participating preferred stock and 400,000 shares of $1 par value common stock. This year the corporation's board of directors voted to pay out a total of $45,000 in dividends to the two classes of stockholders. Determine the percent on par to be paid each class of stockholders and the dividend per share to be paid each class.

Exercise 16-5

The shareholders' equity section of a corporation's balance sheet appeared as follows:

SHAREHOLDERS' EQUITY

Preferred shares, 8% cumulative and nonparticipating, $100 par value, 1,500 shares issued and outstanding	$150,000
Common shares, $25 par value, 10,000 shares issued and outstanding	250,000
Retained earnings	96,000
Total Shareholders' Equity	$496,000

Required:

1. Determine the book value per share of each class of stock under the assumption that the preferred stockholders have a preference in a liquidation to the par value of their shares plus dividends in arrears and there are no dividends in arrears.

2. Determine the book value per share of each class of stock under the assumption that the current and two prior years' dividends are in arrears on the preferred shares.

Exercise 16–6

Information as to the assets, liabilities, and stockholders' equity in each of Corporations A, B, and C follow:

	Corporation A	Corporation B	Corporation C
Assets.....................................	$232,000	$287,000	$?
Liabilities.................................	41,000	?	71,000
Common stock	100,000	200,000	50,000
Retained earnings or deficit.............	?	?	?

Required:
Under the assumptions that (1) the corporations each have the same number of shares of stock outstanding and (2) the book value of Corporation A's shares is the same as the book value of Corporation B's shares and also the same as Corporation C's shares, determine the missing amounts indicated by the question marks.

Problems   **Problem 16–1**

Hilltop Corporation's charter granted it the right to issue 1,500 shares of $100 par value, 8% cumulative and nonparticipating preferred stock and 25,000 shares of $10 par value common stock. During the month following receipt of the charter the corporation completed these transactions:

Feb. 2 Sold and issued 10,000 shares of common stock at par for cash.

    5 Accepted subscriptions to 10,000 shares of common stock at par value. The subscription contracts were accompanied by 25% down payments.

    10 Exchanged 1,000 shares of preferred stock for land having a $20,000 fair market value and a building having an $80,000 fair value.

    14 Issued 500 shares of common stock to the corporation's promoters for their services in getting the corporation organized. The services were valued at $5,000 by the board of directors.

    20 Collected the balance due on the February 5 subscriptions and issued the stock.

    25 Accepted subscriptions to the remaining unissued common stock at par. Twenty-five percent down payments accompanied the subscription contracts.

Required:
Prepare general journal entries to record the foregoing transactions and prepare a February 25 classified balance sheet for the corporation.

Problem 16–2

A corporation received a charter granting it the right to issue 25,000 shares of $10 par value common stock. It then completed these transactions:

1971

Jan. 15 Sold and issued 10,000 shares of common stock at par for cash.

Feb. 10 Exchanged 10,000 shares of common stock for the following assets at their fair market values: land, $18,000; building, $42,000; and machinery, $40,000.

Dec. 10 Accepted subscriptions to the remaining unissued common stock at par. Twenty percent down payments accompanied the subscription contracts.

Dec. 31 Closed the Income Summary account. There was an $8,500 net loss.

1972

Jan. 9 Collected the balance due on the December 10 subscriptions and issued the stock.

Dec. 31 Closed the Income Summary account. There was a $29,900 net income.

1973

Jan. 6 The board of directors declared a $0.50 per share dividend on the outstanding common stock, payable on February 15 to the January 15 stockholders of record.

Feb. 15 Paid the dividend previously declared.

Required:

1. Prepare general journal entries to record the foregoing transactions.
2. Prepare the stockholders' equity section of the corporation's December 31, 1971, balance sheet.
3. Prepare a second stockholders' equity section as of the close of business on February 15, 1973.

Problem 16–3

PART 1. Kite Corporation's common stock is selling on a stock exchange today at $7.25 per share, and a just-published balance sheet shows the stockholders' equity in the corporation as follows:

SHAREHOLDERS' EQUITY

Preferred stock, 7% cumulative and nonparticipating, $10 par value, 10,000 shares authorized and outstanding	$100,000
Common stock, $5 par value, 50,000 shares authorized and outstanding	250,000
Retained earnings	84,000
Total Shareholders' Equity	$434,000

Required:

Answer these questions: (1) What is the market value of the corporation's common stock? (2) What are the par values of its (*a*) preferred stock and (*b*) common stock? (3) If there are no dividends in arrears, what are the book values of the (*a*) preferred stock and (*b*) common stock? (4) If two years' dividends are in arrears on the preferred stock, what are the book values of the (*a*) preferred stock and (*b*) common stock? (Assume the preferred stock carries the right to the return of par value plus dividends in arrears in a liquidation.)

PART 2. The stockholders' equity sections from three corporation balance sheets follow:

1. Stockholders' Equity:

Cumulative and nonparticipating, $100 par value, 6% preferred stock, authorized and issued 1,000 shares... $ 100,000
Common stock, $25 par value, 10,000 shares authorized and issued......... 250,000
Retained earnings... 64,000

Total Stockholders' Equity .... $ 414,000

2. Stockholders' Interest:

Preferred stock, $100 par value, 7% cumulative and nonparticipating, 500 shares authorized and issued .... $ 50,000*
Common stock, $100 par value, 500 shares authorized and issued 50,000
Retained earnings.. 6,000

Total Stockholders' Interest.. $ 106,000

*The current year's dividend is unpaid on the preferred stock.

3. Stockholders' Equity:

Cumulative and nonparticipating, $10 par value, 7% preferred stock, 100,000 shares authorized and issued... $1,000,000*
Common stock, $25 par value, 100,000 shares authorized and issued 2,500,000

Total contributed capital $3,500,000
Deficit .... (540,000)

Total Stockholders' Equity $2,960,000

*Three years' dividends are in arrears on the preferred stock.

Required:

Prepare a schedule showing the book value per share of the preferred and common stock of each corporation under the assumption the preferred stock carries the right to the return of par value plus dividends in arrears in a liquidation.

Problem 16–4

A corporation has outstanding 1,000 shares of $100 par value, 6% cumulative and nonparticipating preferred stock and 20,000 shares of $10 par value common stock. During a seven-year period it paid out these amounts in dividends:

1966.. $18,000
1967.. -0-
1968.. -0-
1969.. 16,000
1970.. 14,000
1971.. 24,000
1972.. 30,000

Required:

1. *a)* Prepare a form with columnar headings as follows:

Year	Total Paid to Preferred	Balance Due Preferred	Total Paid to Common	Dividend per Share Preferred	Dividend per Share Common	Percent on Par Preferred	Percent on Par Common

b) In the first column enter the years 1966 through 1972. Then determine and fill in the information opposite each year in the remaining columns. (In the last two columns indicate the percent on par paid in dividends on each class of stock. Assume there were no dividends in arrears in 1966 and in any year in which the corporation paid a dividend, it always paid the full amount of current and back dividends due the preferred stockholders before paying anything to the common stockholders.)

2. Prepare and complete a second form according to the foregoing directions under the assumption that rather than being cumulative and nonparticipating, the preferred stock of the corporation is noncumulative and nonparticipating.

3. Prepare and complete a third form according to the foregoing directions under the assumption the preferred stock of the corporation is cumulative and fully participating.

Problem 16–5

A corporation has outstanding 10,000 shares of $10 par value common stock, all owned by four men who are also the corporation's board of directors. The company needs additional capital for expansion purposes which its owners are unable to supply. Consequently, they are planning to issue at par 1,500 shares of $100 par value, 7% cumulative and nonparticipating, preferred stock to outsiders to gain the needed capital; and they have asked you to prepare a report showing the return to the two classes of stockholders from the following amounts of annual before-tax earnings:

a) $15,000 or a 6% before-tax return on the $250,000 invested.
b) $30,000 or a 12% before-tax return on the $250,000 invested.
c) $40,000 or a 16% before-tax return on the $250,000 invested.
d) $50,000 or a 20% before-tax return on the $250,000 invested.
e) $60,000 or a 24% before-tax return on the $250,000 invested.

Required:
1. Prepare a form with columnar headings as follows:

Before-Tax Earnings	Federal Income Taxes	After-Tax Earnings		Preferred Dividends		Common Dividends	
		Amount	Percent Return on Investment	Total Paid to Preferred	Percent Return on Investment	Total Paid to Common	Percent Return on Investment

2. Enter the amounts of before-tax profit in the first column.
3. Calculate the federal income tax applicable to each level of earnings and enter in the second column. (Corporations are required at this writing to pay

a 22% federal income tax on the first $25,000 of their earnings and 48% on any earnings over $25,000. Thus, the federal income tax on $50,000 of earnings is 22% of the first $25,000 plus 48% on the second $25,000, or a total of $17,500.)

4. Complete the information of the form under the assumption that all after-tax earnings are paid out in dividends.

5. Explain why in this problem at the pretax levels of $30,000 and above, the after-tax rate of return to the common stockholders is greater than the after-tax rate earned by the corporation as a whole.

6. Prepare a calculation to account for the difference between the rate of return to the corporation as a whole at the $60,000 level and the return to the common stockholders at this level.

Alternate problems

Problem 16–1A

High Surf Corporation received a charter granting it the right to issue 2,000 shares of $50 par value, 7½% cumulative and nonparticipating preferred stock and 50,000 shares of $5 par value common stock. It then completed these transactions:

Feb. 4 Sold and issued 10,000 shares of common stock at par for cash.

8 Accepted subscriptions to 20,000 shares of common stock at par. The subscription contracts were accompanied by 20% down payments.

11 Gave the corporation's attorneys 500 shares of common stock and its promoters 1,500 shares of common stock for their services in getting the corporation organized and securing its charter. The directors valued these services at $10,000.

12 Exchanged the 2,000 shares of preferred stock for the following assets at their fair market values: land, $15,000; and buildings, $85,000.

20 Accepted subscriptions to an additional 10,000 shares of common stock at par. The subscription contracts were accompanied by 20% down payments.

28 Received the balance due on the February 8 subscriptions and issued the stock.

Required:

Prepare general journal entries to record the foregoing transactions and prepare a classified balance sheet for the corporation as of February 28.

Problem 16–2A

Stetson Corporation received a charter granting it the right to issue 50,000 shares of $5 par value common stock. It then completed these transactions:

1971

Mar. 12 Sold and issued 15,000 shares of common stock at par for cash.

18 Exchanged 25,000 shares of common stock for the following assets at their fair market values: land, $25,000; building, $50,000; and machinery, $50,000.

Dec. 15 Accepted subscriptions to 5,000 shares of common stock at par. Twenty percent down payments accompanied the subscription contracts.

Dec. 31 Closed the Income Summary account. A $9,500 loss was incurred.
1972
Jan. 14 Received payment of the balance due on the subscriptions of December 15 and issued the stock.
Dec. 31 Closed the Income Summary account. A $30,300 net income was earned.

1973
Jan. 10 The board of directors declared a $0.25 per share dividend on the outstanding common stock, payable on February 20 to the January 20 stockholders of record.
Feb. 20 Paid the dividend declared on January 10.

Required:
1. Prepare general journal entries to record the foregoing transactions.
2. Prepare the stockholders' equity section of the corporation's December 31, 1971 balance sheet.
3. Prepare a second stockholders' equity section as of the close of business on February 20, 1973.

Problem 16–3A

A corporation has had outstanding since it was organized 100,000 shares of $5 par value common stock and 1,000 shares of $100 par value, 7% preferred stock. The current year's and two prior years' dividends have not been paid on the preferred stock. However, the company has recently prospered, and its board of directors wants to know how much cash will be required for dividends if a $0.50 per share dividend is paid on the common stock.

Required:
Prepare a schedule for the board of directors showing the amounts of cash required for dividends to each class of stockholders under each of the following assumptions:
a) The preferred stock is noncumulative and nonparticipating.
b) The preferred stock is cumulative and nonparticipating.
c) The preferred stock is cumulative and fully participating.
d) The preferred stock is cumulative and participating to 9%.

Problem 16–4A

Mesa Corporation has outstanding 2,000 shares of $100 par value, 6% preferred stock and 12,000 shares of $25 par value common stock. The preferred stock is cumulative and nonparticipating. During a seven-year period the corporation paid out the following amounts in dividends:

1966	$30,000
1967	-0-
1968	-0-
1969	30,000
1970	36,000
1971	48,000
1972	42,000

Required:
1. *a)* Prepare a form with columnar headings as follows:

Year	Total Paid to Preferred	Balance Due Preferred	Total Paid to Common	Dividend per Share Preferred	Dividend per Share Common	Percent on Par Preferred	Percent on Par Common

b) In the first column enter the years 1966 through 1972. Then determine and fill in the information opposite each year in the remaining columns. (In the last two columns indicate the percent on par paid in dividends on each class of stock. Assume no dividends were in arrears in 1966 and in any year in which the corporation paid a dividend, it always paid the full amount of current and back dividends due the preferred stockholders before paying anything to the common stockholders.)

2. Prepare and complete a second form according to the foregoing directions under the assumption that rather than being cumulative and nonparticipating, the preferred stock of the corporation is noncumulative and nonparticipating.

3. Prepare and complete a third form according to the foregoing directions under the assumption the preferred stock of the corporation is cumulative and fully participating.

Problem 16–5A

A corporation has outstanding 8,000 shares of $25 par value common stock, all owned by four men who are also the corporation's directors. The company needs $300,000 additional capital for expansion purposes, which its owners are unable to supply. Consequently, they are considering the issuance of 3,000 shares of $100 par value, 7% cumulative and nonparticipating, preferred stock to gain the additional capital, and they have asked you to prepare a report showing the return to the two classes of stockholders from the following amounts of annual before-tax earnings:

a) $30,000 or a 6% before-tax return on the $500,000 invested.
b) $60,000 or a 12% before-tax return on the $500,000 invested.
c) $80,000 or a 16% before-tax return on the $500,000 invested.
d) $100,000 or a 20% before-tax return on the $500,000 invested.
e) $120,000 or a 24% before-tax return on the $500,000 invested.

Required:
1. Prepare a form with columnar headings as follows:

Before-Tax Earnings	Federal Income Taxes	After-Tax Earnings		Preferred Dividends		Common Dividends	
		Amount	Percent Return on Investment	Total Paid to Preferred	Percent Return on Investment	Total Paid to Common	Percent Return on Investment

2. Enter the amounts of before-tax profit in the first column.
3. Calculate the federal income tax applicable to each level of earnings and enter in the second column. (Corporations are required to pay at this writing a 22% federal income tax on the first $25,000 of their earnings and 48%

on any earnings over $25,000. Thus, the federal income tax on $37,500 of earnings is 22% of the first $25,000 plus 48% on the next $12,500, or a total of $11,500.)

4. Complete the information of the form under the assumption that all after-tax earnings are paid out in dividends.

5. Explain why in this problem at the $60,000 and above pretax levels, the after-tax rate of return to the common stockholders is greater than the after-tax rate earned by the corporation as a whole.

6. Prepare a calculation to account for the difference between the rate of return to the corporation as a whole at the $100,000 level and the return to the common stockholders at this level.

Decision problem 16–1, Bill and Bob

Eight years ago Bill Dent went to work for a construction firm specializing in low-cost homes, and after five years he quit the company to enter the construction business on his own. Now after three years on his own, although he has little else, he has managed to build a small debt-free single proprietorship organization in which he has a $12,000 equity.

Recently he worked out some rather revolutionary construction ideas that he believes will enable him to build and market houses for 10% less than comparable houses are being built and sold by competitors. However, to carry out his ideas he needs $10,000 additional capital, which he does not have; and he has approached Bob Quinn, an old friend who recently inherited several hundred thousand dollars from his father, for a loan. After listening to his friend's ideas, Bob pointed out that to really exploit the new ideas, much more than $10,000 would be needed.

After discussing construction and marketing needs for some time, Bob suggested that instead of a loan he should go into business with Bill. After more discussion, Bill accepted his friend's offer, and it was agreed that although Bob could devote little or no time to the business, he would furnish all its needed capital. It was further agreed that Bill would devote full time to managing the business; but no agreement was reached as to whether the venture would be organized as a partnership or a corporation.

Write a report to Bill and Bob discussing the factors they should consider in choosing between a partnership form of organization for their business or a corporate form.

Decision problem 16–2, Kent Dyer

Kent Dyer recently sold his home and moved into a rental apartment. He had a $15,000 equity in the home; and as a result, he has $15,000 to invest. He is looking at two different stocks: the common stock of Whitecap Company and the preferred stock of Gale Industries. The companies have much in common, both manufacture and sell the same types of products and both have been in business about the same length of time—four years in the case of Whitecap Company and five years for Gale Industries. Also, the two companies have about the same amounts of stockholder equity, as the following equity sections from their latest balance sheets show:

WHITECAP COMPANY

Common stock, $5 par value, 200,000 shares authorized, 100,000 shares issued	$500,000
Retained earnings	100,000
Total Stockholders' Equity	$600,000

GALE INDUSTRIES

Preferred stock, $100 par value, 7% cumulative and nonparticipating, 1,000 shares authorized and issued	$100,000*
Common stock, $10 par value, 50,000 shares authorized and issued	500,000
Retained earnings	15,000
Total Stockholders' Equity	$615,000

*The current and two prior years' dividends are in arrears on the preferred stock.

Whitecap Company did not pay a dividend on its common stock during its first year's operations; however, since then, for the past three years, it has paid a $0.25 per share annual dividend on the stock. The stock is currently selling for $7.80 per share. The preferred stock of Gale Industries, on the other hand, is selling for $91 per share. However, Mr. Dyer favors this stock as an investment. He feels the stock is a real bargain since it is not only selling below its par value but also $30 below book value, and as he says, "Since it is a preferred stock, the dividends are guaranteed." Too, he feels the common stock of Whitecap Company, selling at 30% above book value and 56% above par value while paying only a $0.25 per share dividend, is overpriced.

a) Is the preferred stock of Gale Industries selling at a price $30 below its book value, and is the common stock of Whitecap Company selling at a price 30% above book value and 56% above par value?

b) From an analysis of the stockholder equity sections, express your opinion of the two stocks as investments and give the reasons for your opinion.

Chapter 17

Corporations: additional stock transactions

■ The organization of a corporation and a number of transactions involving the issuance of stock by a corporation were discussed in the previous chapter. In this chapter additional transactions involving stock are introduced, but first an understanding of the concept of minimum legal capital and the nature of stock premiums and discounts is required.

Par value and minimum legal capital

■ As previously stated, par value is an arbitrary value a corporation places on a share of its stock at the time it seeks authorization of the stock. Normally a corporation may choose a par value of any amount for its stock; but par values of $100, $50, $25, $10, $5, and $1 are common. Early corporation laws required all stocks to have a par value; but today, all states permit the issuance of stock having no par value.

When a corporation issues par value stock, the par value is printed on each certificate and is used in accounting for the stock. Also, in many states when a corporation issues par value stock, it establishes for itself a *minimum legal capital* equal to the par value of the issued stock. For example, if a corporation issues 1,000 shares of $100 par value stock, it establishes for itself a minimum legal capital of $100,000.

Laws establishing minimum legal capital normally require stockholders to invest in a corporation, assets equal in value to minimum legal capital or be liable to the corporation's creditors for the deficiency.

In other words, these laws require stockholders to give a corporation par value for its stock or be liable for the deficiency. In addition, when corporation laws set minimum legal capital requirements, they normally also make illegal any payments to stockholders for dividends or their equivalent when these payments reduce stockholder equity below minimum legal capital.

Corporation laws governing minimum legal capital were written in an effort to protect corporation creditors. The authors of these laws reasoned somewhat as follows: A corporation's creditors may look only to the assets of the corporation for satisfaction of their claims. Consequently, when a corporation is organized, its stockholders should provide it with a fund of assets equal to its minimum legal capital. Thereafter, this fund of assets should remain with the corporation and should not be returned to the stockholders in any form until all creditor claims are paid.

Although par value helps establish minimum legal capital and is used in accounting for par value stock, it does not establish a stock's worth nor the price at which a corporation must issue the stock. If purchasers are willing to pay more than par, a corporation may sell and issue its stock at a price above par. Likewise, in some states, if purchasers will not pay par, a corporation may issue its stock at a price below par. Normally a corporation's potential earning power and the supply of investment funds determine whether purchasers will pay par, less than par, or more than par.

Stock premiums and discounts

■ Premiums

When a corporation sells and issues stock at a price above its par value, the stock is said to be issued at a *premium*. A premium is an amount in excess of par paid by the purchasers of newly issued stock. For example, if a corporation sells and issues its $100 par value stock for $109 per share, the $9 in excess of par is called a "premium." And, although a premium is an amount in excess of par paid by purchasers of newly issued stock, it is not considered a profit to the issuing corporation. Rather a premium is part of the investment of the stockholders who pay more than par for their stock. When stock is issued at a premium, stockholders invest more than the legal minimum of capital; consequently since premiums are amounts in excess of minimum legal capital, they should be accounted for separately from the par value of the stock to which they apply.

Some states permit the payment of a "dividend" from amounts received as stock premiums, but others do not. Nevertheless, and regardless of legality, accountants are opposed to calling such a distribution a "dividend." Their opposition stems from the fact that such a distribution is obviously a return of invested capital and should be labeled clearly as such. Calling it a "dividend" might lead an uninformed person to believe the payment was from earnings.

Discounts

In many states it is illegal for a corporation to sell and issue stock for less than par. However, in some states, stock may be sold for less than par. When a corporation sells and issues its stock at a price below par, the stock is said to be issued at a *discount*. For example, a corporation that sells and issues its $100 par value stock at $89 per share is said to issue the stock at a discount of $11 per share. A discount is the difference between par and the price paid when the price is less than par. When stock is sold at a discount, the discount is not considered a loss to the issuing corporation, rather the corporation's stockholders are investing less than minimum legal capital. In such cases, in most states, the stockholders are contingently liable for the investment deficiency. This contingent liability is called a *discount liability*.

Careful notice should be taken that stockholders owing stock issued at a discount are not contingently liable to the issuing corporation; they are contingently liable to the corporation's creditors. Insofar as the issuing corporation is concerned, stock issued at a discount is paid for in full. However, if at any time after stock is issued at a discount the issuing corporation becomes bankrupt, its creditors may in many states force the current owners to pay to the corporation the amount of the discount if the current owners knew at the time they purchased the stock that it was originally issued at a discount. The money paid is then used for the satisfaction of the creditor claims. It should be noted from the foregoing that if the ownership of specific shares originally issued at a discount can be traced from one owner to the next and the owners knew of the discount, then the discount liability follows the stock from owner to owner.

Since a stock discount represents an investment deficiency, it should be accounted for separately from the par value of the stock to which it applies.

Entries for stock sold at a premium ■ When, for example, common stock is sold at a premium and the stock is immediately issued, the transaction may be recorded as follows:

Dec.	1	Cash..	110,000.00	
		Common Stock.................................		100,000.00
		Premium on Common Stock..................		10,000.00
		To record the sale of 1,000 shares of $100 par value common stock at $110 per share.		

If subscriptions are taken for stock at a premium, the subscriptions collected, and the stock issued, the following entries are used:

Dec.	2	Subscriptions Receivable, Common Stock	10,250.00	
		Common Stock Subscribed		10,000.00
		Premium on Common Stock		250.00
		Accepted subscriptions to 100 shares of $100 par value common stock at $102.50 per share.		
Jan.	2	Cash	10,250.00	
		Subscriptions Receivable, Common Stock		10,250.00
		Collected subscriptions in full.		
	2	Common Stock Subscribed	10,000.00	
		Common Stock		10,000.00
		Issued stock to fully paid subscribers.		

Notice that the subscriptions receivable account is debited at the time the subscription is accepted for the sum of the stock's par value and premium; this is the amount the subscribers agree to pay. Notice, too, that the stock subscribed account is credited for par value and that the premium is credited to a premium account at the time the subscriptions are accepted.

Entries for stock sold at a discount
■ Since in many states it is illegal to sell and issue stock at a discount and in those states in which it may be sold and issued at a discount a discount liability attaches to such stock, corporations seldom sell and issue stock at a discount. However, if stock is sold for cash at a discount and immediately issued, the transcation may be recorded with an entry similar to the following:

Mar.	5	Cash	8,900.00	
		Discount on Common Stock	1,100.00	
		Common Stock		10,000.00
		Sold and issued 100 shares of $100 par value common stock at $89 per share.		

If stock is subscribed at a discount and later paid for and issued, the following series of entries may be used to record the transactions:

Mar.	10	Subscriptions Receivable, Common Stock	950.00	
		Discount on Common Stock	50.00	
		Common Stock Subscribed		1,000.00
		Accepted subscriptions to 10 shares of $100 par value common stock at $95 per share.		
Apr.	10	Cash	950.00	
		Subscriptions Receivable, Common Stock		950.00
		Collected subscriptions in full.		

Apr.	10	Common Stock Subscribed	1,000.00	
		Common Stock...		1,000.00
		Issued stock to fully paid subscribers.		

Premiums, discounts, and stock subscribed on the balance sheet

■ Stock premiums and discounts help measure the capital contributions of stockholders, and on the balance sheet they are commonly added to or are deducted from the par value of the stock to which they relate in order to show the capital contribution of each class of stockholders, as in Illustration 17–1 below.

SHAREHOLDERS' EQUITY

Preferred stock, $100 par value, 6% cumulative and nonparticipating,		
2,500 shares authorized, 1,500 shares issued	$150,000	
Add premium on preferred stock	7,500	
Amount paid in...		$157,500
Common stock, $10 par value, 25,000 shares authorized, 20,000		
shares issued	$200,000	
Unissued common stock subscribed, 5,000 shares	50,000	
Total common stock issued and subscribed	$250,000	
Add premium on common stock..	20,000	
Deduct discount on common stock...	(2,500)	
Amount paid in and subscribed...		267,500
Total contributed capital...		$425,000
Retained earnings...		123,000
Total Shareholders' Equity...		$548,000

Illustration
17–1

No-par stock

■ At one time all stocks were required to have a par value; but today all jurisdictions permit the issuance of so-called no-par stocks or stocks without par value. The primary advantages claimed for no-par stock are:

1. Since no-par stock does not have a par value, it may be issued at any price without a discount liability attaching.
2. Printing a par value, say $100, on a stock certificate may cause a person lacking in knowledge to believe a share of the stock to be worth $100, when it actually may be worthless. Therefore, eliminating the par value figure helps force such a person to examine the factors that give a stock value, which are earnings, dividends, and future prospects.
3. The use of no-par shares results in more realistic values being placed on noncash assets acquired in exchange for stock. When par value stock is issued, the law in many instances says the stock may not be issued for less than par value. However, the law can easily be circumvented by issuing the stock in exchange for property other than cash and placing an inflated value on the property, a value equal to the par value of the stock. The use of no-par stock makes such a

subterfuge unnecessary and results in more realistic values being placed on assets taken in exchange for stock.

When no-par-value stock is issued, the issuance may be recorded in one of two ways. The choice depends upon the laws of the state of incorporation and the wishes of the board of directors. Some state laws require that a corporation must credit the entire proceeds from the sale of no-par stock to a no-par stock account. In other states, when no-par stock is issued, the board may choose to place a *stated value* on the stock. When a stated value is placed on no-par stock and the stock is sold for more than stated value, the no-par stock account is credited for stated value and the remainder is credited to a contributed capital account called, for instance, "Contributed Capital in Excess of Stated Value of No-Par Stock." To illustrate the two methods of recording no-par stock, assume that a corporation sells and issues 1,000 shares of its authorized no-par common stock at $42 per share.

If the corporation is organized in a state in which the entire amount received from the sale of no-par stock must be credited to a no-par stock account, it will record the sale as follows:

Sept.	20	Cash..	42,000.00	
		No-Par Common Stock............................		42,000.00
		Sold and issued 1,000 shares of no-par common stock at $42 per share.		

If the corporation is organized in a state in which the directors may place a stated value on no-par stock, accounting for its sale is similar to accounting for par value stock. For example, if the directors place a stated value of $25 per share on the foregoing stock, its sale and issuance are recorded as follows:

Sept.	20	Cash..	42,000.00	
		No-Par Common Stock............................		25,000.00
		Contributed Capital in Excess of Stated Value, No-Par Common Stock................		17,000.00
		Sold at $42 per share 1,000 shares of no-par stock having a $25 per share stated value.		

From the foregoing it is obvious that when a stated value is placed on no-par stock, the accounting treatment for such stock is similar to that for par value stock. However, a sharp distinction should be made between a par value and a stated value; they are not synonymous. A par value is more formal than a stated value. A par value is established by a corporation at the time of its organization. It appears in the corporation's charter and normally can be changed only by a vote of the stockholders and approval of the state. A stated value is more flexible. The directors of a corporation establish a stock's stated value by resolution. Normally, at any time, they may also change it by passing an additional resolution.

No-par stock and legal capital

■ State laws permitting the issuance of no-par stock vary as to minimum legal capital requirements for corporations issuing such stock. Most states require the entire amount received by a corporation from the sale of its no-par stock be considered minimum legal capital and as such be made unavailable for dividend payments. A few states permit a corporation issuing no-par stock to establish its minimum legal capital at the stock's stated value and to pay out as "dividends" any amount above stated value received from the sale of such stock.

Treasury stock

■ Corporations often reacquire shares of their own stock. Sometimes a corporation will purchase its own stock on the open market to be given to employees as a bonus. Sometimes shares are bought in order to maintain a favorable market for the stock. Occasionally a corporation in a poor financial position will receive shares of its own stock as a gift from its stockholders. Regardless, if a corporation reacquires shares of its own stock, such stock is known as *treasury stock*. Treasury stock is a corporation's own stock that has been issued and then reacquired either by purchase or gift. Notice that the stock must be the corporation's own stock; the acquisition of stock of another corporation does not create treasury stock. Furthermore, the stock must have been once issued and then reacquired; only stock issued and reacquired qualifies as treasury stock. The last point distinguishes treasury stock from unissued stock, and the distinction is important because stock once issued at par and then reacquired as treasury stock may be legally reissued at a discount without discount liability.

As just pointed out, treasury stock differs from unissued stock in that it may be sold at a discount without discount liability. However, in other respects it has the same status as unissued stock. Both are equity items rather than assets. Both are subtracted from authorized stock to determine outstanding stock when such things as book values are calculated. Neither receives dividends nor has a vote in the stockholders' meetings.

Purchase of treasury stock[1]

■ When a corporation purchases its own stock, it reduces in equal amounts both its assets and its stockholders' equity. To illustrate this, assume that on May 1 of the current year the condensed balance sheet of Curry Corporation appears as in Illustration 17–2.

---
[1] There are several ways of accounting for treasury stock transactions. This text will discuss the so-called cost basis, which seems to be the most widely used, and it will leave a discussion of other methods to a more advanced text.

Curry Corporation
Balance Sheet, May 1, 19—

ASSETS		CAPITAL	
Cash................................. $ 30,000		Common stock, $100 par	
Other assets........................ 95,000		value, authorized and	
		issued 1,000 shares........... $100,000	
		Retained earnings................ 25,000	
Total Assets $125,000		Total Capital.................. $125,000	

Illustration
17–2

If on May 1 Curry Corporation purchases 100 shares of its outstanding stock at $115 per share, the transaction is recorded as follows:

May	1	Treasury Stock, Common..............................	11,500.00	
		Cash..		11,500.00
		Purchased 100 shares of treasury stock at $115 per share.		

The debit in the foregoing entry records a reduction in the equity of the stockholders; and the credit to Cash records a reduction in assets. Both are equal to the cost of the treasury stock; and after the entry is posted, a new balance sheet will show the reductions as in Illustration 17–3.

Notice in the second balance sheet that the cost of the treasury stock appears in the stockholders' equity section as a deduction from common stock and retained earnings. In comparing the two balance sheets, notice that the treasury stock purchase reduces both assets and stockholders' equity by the $11,500 cost of the stock.

Curry Corporation
Balance Sheet, May 1, 19—

ASSETS		CAPITAL	
Cash... $ 18,500		Common stock, $100 par value,	
Other assets 95,000		authorized and issued 1,000	
		shares of which 100 are in	
		the treasury $100,000	
		Retained earnings of which $11,500	
		is restricted by the purchase of	
		treasury stock 25,000	
		Total $125,000	
		Less cost of treasury stock.............. 11,500	
Total Assets........................... $113,500		Total Capital $113,500	

Illustration
17–3

Notice also on the second balance sheet that the dollar amount of issued stock remains at $100,000 and is unchanged from the first balance sheet. The amount of *issued stock* is not changed by the purchase of treasury stock. However, the purchase of treasury stock does reduce *outstanding stock*. In Curry Corporation, the purchase reduced the outstanding stock from 1,000 to 900 shares.

There is a distinction between issued stock and outstanding stock. Issued stock is stock that has been issued; it may or may not be outstanding. Outstanding stock is stock that has been issued and is outstanding. Only outstanding stock is effective stock, receives dividends, is given a vote in the meetings of stockholders, and enters into such things as the calculation of book values.

Restricting retained earnings by the purchase of treasury stock

When a corporation purchases treasury stock, the effect on its assets and total stockholders' equity is the same as a cash dividend. When a corporation purchases treasury stock or declares a cash dividend, it transfers corporation assets to its stockholders and thereby reduces both its assets and its stockholders' equity. Consequently, since the effect is the same, most states place limitations upon treasury stock purchases just as they place limitations on dividends. These limitations usually provide that a corporation may purchase treasury stock only to the extent of retained earnings available for dividend charges, after which the retained earnings become restricted and legally unavailable for dividends. This means that (1) only a corporation with retained earnings available for dividends may purchase treasury stock; and (2) it may either purchase treasury stock to the extent of such earnings or it may use the earnings as a basis for dividends, but it may not do both. In other words, a corporation may not purchase treasury stock to the extent of its retained earnings available for dividend charges and then use the same retained earnings again as a basis for the declaration of dividends. Or again, it may not by the purchase of treasury stock transfer corporation assets to its stockholders to the extent of retained earnings available for dividends and then transfer more assets by means of cash dividends.

Notice in Illustration 17–3 how the restriction of retained earnings is shown on the balance sheet. It may also be shown by means of a balance sheet footnote.

In addition to showing such a restriction on the balance sheet, some corporations also show the restriction in the accounts. This is not required because if retained earnings are legally restricted, the earnings are restricted whether the accounts show the restriction or not. Nevertheless, to show such a restriction in the accounts, an entry is made transferring the restricted portion of retained earnings from the Retained Earnings account to an account called, for instance, Retained Earnings

Restricted by the Purchase of Treasury Stock. If such an entry is made by Curry Corporation, it appears as follows:

May	1	Retained Earnings..	11,500.00	
		Retained Earnings Restricted by the		
		Purchase of Treasury Stock		11,500.00
		To record the restriction of retained		
		earnings.		

When treasury stock is sold and retained earnings are no longer restricted because of its purchase, the restricted portion of retained earnings is returned to the Retained Earnings account.

Reissuance of treasury stock ■ When treasury stock is reissued, it may be reissued at cost, above cost, or below cost.

Reissuance at cost

When treasury stock is reissued at cost, the entry to record the transaction is the reverse of the one used to record its purchase. For example, assume that Curry Corporation sells at cost 10 of the 100 treasury shares, the purchase of which at $115 per share was previously illustrated. The entry to record the sale is:

May	27	Cash..	1,150.00	
		Treasury Stock, Common.........................		1,150.00
		Reissued 10 shares of treasury stock at its		
		$115 per share cost price.		

Notice that the sale of the 10 shares at cost restores to the corporation the same amount of assets and stockholder equity taken away when these shares were purchased.

Reissuance at a price above cost

Although treasury stock may be sold at cost, it is commonly sold at a price either above or below cost. When sold above cost, the amount received in excess of cost is commonly credited to a contributed capital account called "Contributed Capital, Treasury Stock Transactions." For example, assume that Curry Corporation sells for $120 per share an additional 10 shares of the treasury stock purchased at $115. The entry to record the transaction appears as follows:

June	3	Cash..	1,200.00	
		Treasury Stock, Common.........................		1,150.00
		Contributed Capital, Treasury Stock		
		Transactions......................................		50.00
		Sold at $120 per share treasury stock that		
		cost $115 per share.		

Reissuance at a price below cost

When treasury stock is reissued at a price below cost, the entry to record the sale normally depends upon whether there is contributed capital from previous transactions in treasury stock. If a corporation has such contributed capital, a "loss" on the sale of treasury stock may be debited to the account of this capital. For example, assume that after having sold 10 of its 100 treasury shares at $115 and 10 at $120, Curry Corporation sells 10 shares at $110. The entry to record the transaction is:

July	7	Cash...	1,100.00	
		Contributed Capital, Treasury Stock		
		Transaction	50.00	
		Treasury Stock, Common.........................		. 1,150.00
		Sold at $110 per share 10 shares of		
		treasury stock purchased at $115.		

If a corporation selling treasury stock below cost does not have contributed capital from previous treasury stock transactions, the "loss" on the sale is normally debited to Retained Earnings. For example, if Curry Corporation sells its remaining 70 shares of treasury stock at $110 per share, the following entry is made to record the transaction:

July	10	Cash...	7,700.00	
		Retained Earnings...	350.00	
		Treasury Stock, Common.........................		8,050.00
		Sold treasury stock purchased at $115 per		
		share for $110 per share.		

Retirement of stock

■ A corporation may purchase shares of its own stock which are not to be held as treasury stock but for immediate retirement, with the shares being permanently canceled upon receipt. Such action is permissible if the interests of creditors and other stockholders are not jeopardized.

When stock is purchased for retirement, all capital items related to the shares being retired are removed from the accounts; and if there is a "gain" on the transaction, it should be credited to contributed capital. On the other hand, if there is a "loss," it should be debited to Retained Earnings under the assumption that it is a sharing of retained earnings or a form of dividends.

For example, assume a corporation originally issued its $10 par value common stock at $12 per share, with the premium being credited to an account called Premium on Common Stock. If the corporation later purchased for retirement 1,000 shares of this stock at the price for which it was issued, the entry to record the retirement is:

Apr.	12	Common Stock...	10,000.00	
		Premium on Common Stock	2,000.00	
		Cash...		12,000.00
		Purchased and retired 1,000 shares of common stock at $12 per share.		

If on the other hand the corporation paid $11 per share instead of $12, the entry for the retirement at a "gain" is:

Apr.	12	Common Stock...	10,000.00	
		Premium on Common Stock	2,000.00	
		Cash...		11,000.00
		Contributed Capital from the Retirement of Common Stock		1,000.00
		Purchased and retired 1,000 shares of common stock at $11 per share.		

Or if the corporation paid $15 per share, the entry for the purchase and retirement is:

Apr.	12	Common Stock...	10,000.00	
		Premium on Common Stock	2,000.00	
		Retained Earnings..	3,000.00	
		Cash...		15,000.00
		Purchased and retired 1,000 shares of common stock at $15 per share.		

Stockholder assessments and donations ■ Sometimes when a corporation is in financial difficulty, its stockholders will vote to assess themselves a certain number of dollars per share of stock owned, with the amounts so assessed being given to the corporation. When this happens, the corporation's assets and its contributed capital are increased by the sum of the assessments and the transaction is recorded as follows:

Oct.	5	Cash..	10,000.00	
		Contributed Capital, Stockholder Assessments......................................		10,000.00
		Received stockholder assessments equal to 10% of the par value of the outstanding common shares.		

At other times stockholders will vote to return to a corporation as a gift a portion of their shares, with the donated stock to be resold to provide the corporation with additional assets.

When its stockholders donate to a corporation a portion of their shares, the stock is secured without cost. Consequently, since the acquisition does not decrease the corporation's assets nor increase its liabilities, it has no affect on stockholders' equity. On the other hand, although the acquisition of donated treasury stock has no affect on assets and equities, its sale increases both. These points may be demonstrated with Bell Corporation.

On June 1 Bell Corporation, having experienced a series of losses, finds itself in the need of additional assets to carry on its operations. In order to secure the assets the company's stockholders decide to donate to the corporation a portion of their stockholdings which are to be sold to outsiders for cash. The corporation's balance sheet before the donation appears as in Illustration 17–4.

Bell Corporation
Balance Sheet, June 1, 19—

ASSETS		CAPITAL	
Cash	$ 1,000	Common stock, $10 par	
Other assets	103,000	value, authorized and	
		issued 10,000 shares	$100,000
		Retained earnings	4,000
Total Assets	$104,000	Total Capital	$104,000

Illustration
17–4

If Bell Corporation stockholders donate pro rata one thousand shares of their stock, the donation may be recorded with a memorandum entry in the General Journal somewhat as follows:

June	1	Received on this date from the stockholders as a donation 1,000 shares of $10 par value common stock.		

Such an entry cannot be posted in the sense that dollar amounts are entered in the accounts. However, when treasury stock is received as a donation, a treasury stock account is opened in the ledger and the number of shares received is shown in the account by means of a memorandum. This memorandum is in effect a posting of the journal memorandum recording the receipt of the stock.

After Bell Corporation receives the foregoing shares from its stockholders, a new balance sheet showing its financial position appears as in Illustration 17–5.

A comparison of the balance sheets prepared before and after the donation shows that the donation did not affect either total assets nor the amount of stockholders' equity.

Although the receipt of donated treasury stock does not increase nor decrease assets and stockholders' equity, its sale increases both. For example, if Bell Corporation sells its thousand shares of donated treasury

```
                          Bell Corporation
                     Balance Sheet, June 1, 19—
           ASSETS                              CAPITAL
Cash.................................. $  1,000   Common stock, $10 par
Other assets......................    103,000      value, authorized and
                                                   issued 10,000 shares of
                                                   which 1,000 are in the
                                                   treasury .......................... $100,000
                                                 Retained earnings...............    4,000
          Total Assets ................ $104,000        Total Capital................. $104,000
```

Illustration
17–5

stock for $9.20 per share, both assets and the stockholders' equity are increased $9,200, and the transaction is recorded:

```
June   7  Cash.........................................................   9,200.00
              Contributed Capital, Sale of Donated
                 Treasury Stock.....................................               9,200.00
              Sold 1,000 shares of donated treasury
              stock at $9.20 per share.
```

After the treasury stock is sold and the transaction recorded, a balance sheet showing the new financial position of Bell Corporation appears as in Illustration 17–6.

```
                          Bell Corporation
                     Balance Sheet, June 7, 19—
           ASSETS                              CAPITAL
Cash.................................. $ 10,200   Common stock, $10 par
Other assets......................    103,000      value authorized and
                                                   issued 10,000 shares.......... $100,000
                                                 Contributed capital, sale of
                                                   donated stock ..................    9,200
                                                 Retained earnings...............    4,000
          Total Assets ................ $113,200        Total Capital................. $113,200
```

Illustration
17–6

Observe in the balance sheet prepared after the sale that both assets and stockholders' equity are increased $9,200 by the sale. The increase in assets is in cash; the increase in stockholder equity appears as contributed capital from the sale of donated stock.

Donations of capital by outsiders ■ Sometimes a corporation will receive a gift or a donation from some person or persons other than its stockholders. For example, as an inducement to locate a plant in a particular city, a corporation may receive a plant site as a gift. Such a donation increases both assets and stockholders' equity by the fair market value of the contributed asset. The increase in stockholders' equity is contributed capital, capital contributed by others than the stockholders.

For example, assume that as an inducement to locate a plant in Circle City, the Circle City Chamber of Commerce donated a plant site to a corporation. The corporation recorded the donation as follows:

Apr.	17	Land..	22,000.00	
		Contributed Capital from Donated Plant Site		22,000.00
		To record the donation of land by Circle City		
		Chamber of Commerce.		

Contributed capital in the accounts and on the statements

■ From the foregoing pages it is obvious that numerous accounts are required in recording contributed capital transactions. Actually a separate account is needed for each kind or source of contributed capital. Furthermore, in addition to separate accounts, each kind of contributed capital may be shown on the balance sheet as in Illustration 18–2 on page 507.

Contributed capital and dividends

■ Under the laws of some states, contributed capital may not be returned to stockholders as dividends. However, one reason for separate contributed capital accounts is that under the laws of some states, dividends may be debited or charged to certain contributed capital accounts. Seldom may dividends be charged against the par or stated value of the outstanding stock; however, the exact contributed capital accounts to which a corporation may charge dividends depend upon the laws of the state of its incorporation. For this reason it is usually wise for a board of directors to secure competent legal advice before voting to charge dividends to any contributed capital account.

Stock dividends

■ A stock dividend is a distribution by a corporation of shares of its own common stock to its common stockholders without any consideration being given in return therefor. Usually the distribution is prompted by a desire to give the stockholders some evidence of their interest in retained earnings without distributing cash or other corporation assets which the board of directors thinks it wise to retain in the business. A clear distinction should be made between a cash dividend and a stock dividend. Cash is distributed in a cash dividend; and as was pointed out in a previous section, such a dividend reduces both assets and stockholders' equity. A stock dividend differs in that shares of the corporation's own stock rather than cash are distributed; and such a dividend has no effect on assets, total capital, or the amount of any stockholders' equity.

A stock dividend has no effect on corporation assets, total capital, and the amount of any stockholders' equity because such a dividend involves nothing more than a transfer of retained earnings to contributed capital. To illustrate this assume that Northwest Corporation has the following capital stock and retained earnings:

CAPITAL STOCK AND RETAINED INCOME

Common stock, $100 par value, authorized 1,500 shares, issued and
  outstanding 1,000 shares... $100,000
Capital contributed by stockholders in excess of the par value of their shares...........   8,000
    Total contributed capital $108,000
Retained earnings...   35,000
    Total contributed capital and retained earnings... $143,000

Assume further that on December 28 the directors of Northwest Corporation declared a 10% or 100-share stock dividend distributable on January 20 to the January 15 stockholders of record.

If the fair market value of Northwest Corporation's stock on December 28 is $150 per share, the following entries may be made to record the dividend declaration and distribution:

Dec.	28	Retained Earnings..	15,000.00	
		Common Stock Dividend Distributable........		10,000.00
		Premium on Common Stock		5,000.00
		To record the declaration of a 100-share common stock dividend.		
Jan.	20	Common Stock Dividend Distributable..............	10,000.00	
		Common Stock.......................................		10,000.00
		To record the distribution of a 100-share common stock dividend.		

Note that the foregoing entries change $15,000 of stockholders' equity from retained earnings to contributed capital, or as it is commonly said, $15,000 of retained earnings are capitalized. Note also that the retained earnings capitalized are equal to the fair market value of the 100 shares issued ($150 × 100 shares = $15,000).

As previously pointed out, a stock dividend does not distribute funds from retained earnings to the stockholders, nor does it affect in any way the corporation assets. Likewise, it has no effect on total capital and on the individual equities of the stockholders. To illustrate these last points, assume that Johnson owned 10 shares of Northwest Corporation's stock prior to the dividend. The corporation's total contributed and retained capital before the dividend and the book value of Johnson's 10 shares were as follows:

Common stock (1,000 shares).................................... $100,000
Premium on common stock.......................................   8,000
Retained earnings   35,000
    Total contributed and retained capital $143,000

$143,000 ÷ 1,000 Shares Outstanding = $143 per Share Book Value
  $143 × 10 = $1,430 for the Book Value of Johnson's 10 Shares

A 10% stock dividend gives a stockholder one new share for each

10 shares previously held. Consequently, Johnson received one new share; and after the dividend, the contributed and retained capital of the corporation and the book value of Johnson's holdings are as follows:

Common stock (1,100 shares)..................................... $110,000
Premium on common stock....................................... 13,000
Retained earnings... 20,000
     Total contributed and retained capital.................... $143,000

$143,000 ÷ 1,100 Shares Outstanding = $130 per Share Book Value
  $130 × 11 = $1,430 for the Book Value of Johnson's 11 Shares

Before the stock dividend, Johnson owned 10/1,000 or 1/100 of the Northwest Corporation stock and his holdings had a $1,430 book value. After the dividend, he owned 11/1,100 or 1/100 of the corporation and his holdings still had a $1,430 book value. In other words, there was no effect on his equity other than that it was repackaged from 10 units into 11. Likewise, the only effect on corporation capital was a permanent transfer to contributed capital of $15,000 in retained earnings. Consequently, insofar as both the corporation and Johnson are concerned, there was no shift in equities or corporation assets.

Why stock dividends are distributed

If a stock dividend has no effect on corporation assets and stockholders' equities other than to repackage the equities into more units, why are such dividends declared and distributed?

Insofar as a corporation is concerned, a stock dividend enables it to give its shareholders some evidence of their interest in retained earnings without the necessity of distributing corporation cash or other assets to them. Consequently, stock dividends are often declared by corporations that have used the funds from earnings in expanding and, as a result, do not feel they have sufficient cash with which to pay a cash dividend.

Stockholders also commonly benefit from a small stock dividend, although they own no greater share in the issuing corporation after the dividend than before. They benefit because as a rule a small stock dividend has little or no effect on the market price per share of the issuing corporation's stock. Therefore, since each stockholder has more shares after the dividend, if the price per share is unchanged, the total market value of his holdings is increased.

Amount of retained earnings capitalized

In the entry on page 486 retained earnings equal to the fair market value of the dividend stock were capitalized in recording the stock dividend. The reason for this is best explained by quoting the American Institute's Committee on Accounting Procedure, as follows:

". . . a stock dividend does not, in fact, give rise to any change whatsoever in either the corporation's assets or its respective shareholders' proportionate interests therein. However, it cannot fail to be recognized that, merely as a consequence of the expressed purpose of the transaction and its characterization as a *dividend* in related notices to shareholders and the public at large, many recipients of stock dividends look upon them as distributions of corporate earnings and usually in an amount equivalent to the fair value of the additional shares received. Furthermore, it is to be presumed that such views of recipients are materially strengthened in those instances, which are by far the most numerous, where the issuances are so small in comparison with the shares previously outstanding that they do not have any apparent effect upon the share market price and, consequently, the market value of the shares previously held remains substantially unchanged. The committee therefore believes that where these circumstances exist the corporation should in the public interest account for the transaction by transferring from . . ." retained earnings to contributed capital "an amount equal to the fair value of the additional shares issued. Unless this is done, the amount of earnings which the shareholder may believe to have been distributed to him will be left, except to the extent otherwise dictated by legal requirements, in . . ." retained earnings and "subject to possible further similar stock issuances or cash distributions." [2]

The Committee on Accounting Procedure described a small stock dividend as being one of not more than "say, 20% to 25% of the previously outstanding shares." [3]

Large stock dividend

Although a small stock dividend may have little or no effect on the market price of a company's shares, a large dividend normally does. Consequently, the Committee on Accounting Procedure has said in regard to a large stock dividend:

"Where the number of additional shares issued as a stock dividend is so great that it has, or may reasonably be expected to have, the effect of materially reducing the share market value, the committee believes that the implications and possible constructions discussed in the preceding paragraph are not likely to exist and that the transaction clearly partakes of the nature of a stock split-up. . . ." "Consequently, the committee considers that under such circumstances there is no need to capitalize . . ." retained earnings, "other than to the extent occasioned by legal requirements." [4]

Capitalizing retained earnings to the extent of legal requirements means in most states that a corporation may record a large dividend (over 25%) by debiting Retained Earnings and crediting the stock account for the par value of the shares issued.

Stock dividends on the balance sheet

Since a stock dividend is "payable" in stock rather than in assets, it is not a liability to its issuing corporation. Therefore, if a balance sheet

---

[2] *Accounting Research and Terminology Bulletins, Final Edition* (New York: American Institute of Certified Public Accountants, 1961), pp. 51 and 52.

[3] *Ibid.*, 52.

[4] *Ibid.*, 52.

is prepared between the declaration and distribution dates of a stock dividend, the amount of the dividend distributable should appear thereon in the contributed capital section. (See Illustration 18–2 on page 507.)

Stock splits

■ Sometimes, when a corporation's stock is selling at a high price, the corporation will call it in and issue two, three, four, five, or more new shares in the place of each old share previously outstanding. For example, a corporation having outstanding $100 par value stock selling for $375 a share may call in the old shares and issue to the stockholders 2 shares of $50 par, or 4 shares of $25 par, or 10 shares of $10 par, or any number of shares of no-par stock in exchange for each $100 share formerly held. This is known as a *stock split* or a *stock split-up,* and its usual purpose is to affect a reduction in the market price of the stock and, consequently, to facilitate trading in the stock.

A stock split has no effect on total stockholders' equity, the equities of the individual stockholders, or on the balances of any of the contributed or retained capital accounts. Consequently, all that is required in recording a stock split is a memorandum entry in the stock account reciting the facts of the split. For example, such a memorandum might read, "Called in the outstanding $100 par value common stock and issued 10 shares of $10 par value common stock for each old share previously outstanding."

Accounting treatment for corporation income taxes

■ As previously stated, of the three common types of business organizations, the corporation alone as a business unit is subject to federal income taxes. Single proprietorships and partnerships as business units are not required to pay federal income taxes and normally are not required to pay state income taxes. Insofar as federal tax laws are concerned and most states laws, the income of single proprietorships and partnerships is taxed as the personal income of the single proprietor or the partners.

Federal and, where applicable, state income taxes are an expense of doing business as a corporation. However, as a rule, no attempt is made to classify the expense on the income statement; rather it is commonly listed at the end of the statement as in Illustration 17–7.

On the work sheet prepared for a corporation, state and federal income taxes are commonly treated in the nature of an adjustment in the

The Excel Manufacturing Company
Income Statement for Year Ended December 31, 19—

Revenue from sales:
Sales.. $310,000

Income before state and federal income taxes............ $ 78,700
Less state and federal income taxes....................... 32,600
Net Income .... $ 46,100

Illustration
17–7

Adjustments columns as on the work sheet on pages 628 and 629; and after the work sheet is completed an adjusting entry like the following is used to record the taxes:

Dec.	31	State and Federal Income Taxes Expense.........	32,600.00	
		State and Federal Income Taxes		
		Payable...		32,600.00
		To record the liability for income taxes.		

Questions for class discussion

1. Laws place no limit on the amounts partners may withdraw from a partnership. On the other hand, laws regulating corporations place definite limits on the amounts corporation owners may withdraw from a corporation in dividends. Why is there a difference?
2. What is a stock premium? What is a stock discount?
3. Differentiate between discount on stock and discount on a note given to a bank in order to borrow money.
4. Does a corporation earn a profit by selling its stock at a premium? Does it incur a loss by selling its stock at a discount?
5. Why do corporation laws make purchasers of stock at a discount contingently liable for the discount? To whom are such purchasers contingently liable?
6. What is the advantage of no-par stock?
7. What is treasury stock? How is it like unissued stock? How does it differ from unissued stock? What is the legal significance of this difference?
8. General Plastics Corporation bought 1,000 shares of Capital Steel Corporation stock and turned it over to its treasurer for safekeeping. Is this treasury stock? Why or why not?
9. What is the effect of a treasury stock purchase in terms of assets and stockholders' equity? What is the effect on a corporation's assets and stockholders' equity of a treasury stock donation?
10. Distinguish between issued stock and outstanding stock.
11. Why do state laws place limitations on the purchase of treasury stock?
12. What are the effects in terms of assets and stockholders' equity of the declaration and distribution of (a) a cash dividend and (b) a stock dividend?
13. What is the difference between a stock dividend and a stock split?
14. Courts have held that a dividend in the stock of the distributing corporation is not taxable income to its recipients. Why?
15. If a balance sheet is prepared between the date of declaration and the date of distribution of a dividend, how should the dividend be shown if it is to be distributed in (a) cash and (b) stock?

Class exercises

Exercise 17–1

On February 15 a corporation accepted subscriptions to 100,000 shares of its $1 par value common stock at $1.10 per share. The subscription contracts called for one fifth of the subscription price to accompany each contract as a down payment and the balance to be paid on March 15. Give the entries to record (a) the subscriptions, (b) the down payments, (c) receipt of the remaining amounts due on the subscriptions, and (d) issuance of the stock.

Exercise 17–2

On January 28 a corporation accepted subscriptions to 1,000 shares of its $100 par value preferred stock at $97 per share. The subscription contracts required that 10% of the subscription price accompany the contracts as a down payment and the balance be paid in 30 days. Give the entries to record (a) the subscriptions, (b) the down payments, (c) receipt of the remaining amounts due on the subscriptions, and (d) issuance of the stock.

Exercise 17–3

A corporation sold and issued 1,000 shares of its no-par common stock for $31,500 on February 14. (a) Give the entry to record the sale under the assumption the board of directors did not place a stated value on the stock. (b) Give the entry to record the sale under the assumption the board placed a $25 per share stated value on the stock.

Exercise 17–4

On January 31 the stockholders' equity section of a corporation's balance sheet appeared as follows:

STOCKHOLDERS' EQUITY

Common stock, $25 par value, 10,000 shares authorized and issued	$250,000
Retained earnings	85,000
Total Stockholders' Equity	$335,000

On the date of the equity section the corporation purchased 1,000 shares of treasury stock at $35 per share. Give the entry to record the purchase and prepare a stockholders' equity section as it would appear immediately after the purchase.

Exercise 17–5

On February 15 the corporation of Exercise 17–4 sold at $37 per share 500 of the treasury shares purchased on January 31, and on March 1 it sold the remaining treasury shares at $32 per share. Give the entries to record the sales.

Exercise 17–6

Stockholders' equity in a corporation appeared as follows on March 5:

Common stock, $10 par value, 100,000 shares authorized, 80,000 shares issued	$800,000
Premium on common stock	64,000
Total contributed capital	$864,000
Retained earnings	110,400
Total Stockholders' Equity	$974,400

On that date, when the stock was selling at $12.50 per share, the corporation's directors voted a 5% stock dividend distributable on April 1 to the March 15 stockholders of record. The dividend's declaration had no apparent effect on the market price of the shares, since they were still selling at $12.50 per share at the close of business on April 1.

Required:
1. Give the entries to record the declaration and distribution of the dividend.
2. Under the assumption that Jerry Jacks owned 100 of the shares on March 5 and received his dividend shares on April 1, prepare a schedule showing the numbers of shares he held on March 5 and April 1, with their total book values and total market values.

Problems   Problem 17–1

Plains Corporation was organized to buy and expand an existing manufacturing company. It received a charter giving it the right to issue 2,500 shares of $100 par value, 7% cumulative and nonparticipating preferred stock and 250,000 shares of $5 par value common stock. It then completed these transactions:

Feb. 7   Accepted subscriptions to 100,000 shares of common stock at $5.50 per share. The subscription contracts were accompanied by 20% down payments.

10   Exchanged 50,000 shares of common stock for land valued at $75,000 and a factory building valued at $200,000.

12   Accepted subscription contracts and $15,750 in down payments on 1,500 shares of preferred stock at $105 per share.

12   Gave the corporation's attorneys $1,250 in cash and 500 shares of common stock for their services in securing the corporation's charter. The directors placed a $5.50 per share value on the stock.

Mar. 9   Collected the balance due on the February 7 common stock subscriptions and issued the stock.

14   Collected the balance due on the preferred stock subscriptions and issued the stock.

31   Accepted subscription contracts accompanied by 20% down payments to 20,000 shares of common stock at $4.75 per share.

Required:
1. Prepare general journal entries to record the foregoing transactions.
2. Prepare the stockholders' equity section of the corporation's balance sheet as of the close of business on March 31.

Problem 17–2

Steel Products Company completed the following transactions:
a) Received a charter which granted it the right to issue 25,000 shares of $10 par value common stock.
b) Accepted subscriptions to 20,000 shares of stock at $11.25 per share.
c) Received a plant site valued at $10,000 as a donation from the city of Tempe in return for locating its plant in the donor city.
d) Collected the subscriptions of Transaction (b) and issued the stock.
e) Gave a contractor 1,000 shares of stock and $50,250 in cash for the erection of a factory building. The contractor had previously agreed to erect

the building for $62,000, but accepted the stock and cash in full payment on the building's completion.

f) Paid $125,000 for factory machinery.

g) During the first year's operation sold $585,400 of products for cash and paid $510,200 in operating expenses.

h) Made an adjusting entry to record depreciation of machinery, $12,100, and depreciation of factory building, $1,100. (Debit Operating Expenses Controlling.)

i) Made an adjusting entry to record state and federal income taxes payable, $30,000.

j) Closed the Sales, Operating Expenses Controlling, and State and Federal Income Taxes Expense accounts to Income Summary; and then closed the Income Summary account.

k) Declared a $0.10 per share quarterly cash dividend.

l) Declared a stock dividend of one share for each 20 previously held. The stock was selling at $12 per share on the day of the declaration.

m) Paid the cash dividend.

n) Distributed the stock dividend.

o) Purchased 1,000 shares of treasury stock at $12 per share.

p) Sold 500 shares of treasury stock at $12.50 per share.

q) Paid the state and federal income taxes payable.

r) Declared a quarterly cash dividend of $0.10 per share.

Required:

1. Open the following T-accounts: Cash; Subscriptions Receivable, Common Stock; Machinery and Equipment; Accumulated Depreciation, Machinery and Equipment; Buildings; Accumulated Depreciation, Buildings; Land; State and Federal Income Taxes Payable; Cash Dividend Payable; Common Stock; Premium on Common Stock; Common Stock Subscribed; Contributed Capital from Treasury Stock Transactions; Contributed Capital from Plant Site Donation; Retained Earnings; Stock Dividend Distributable; Treasury Stock; Income Summary; Sales; Operating Expenses Controlling; and State and Federal Income Taxes Expense.

2. Enter the transactions directly in the T-accounts using the transaction letters to identify the amounts in the accounts.

3. Prepare the stockholders' equity section of the concern's balance sheet reflecting the foregoing transactions. (See Illustration 18-2.)

Problem 17-3

The equity sections from the 1971 and 1972 balance sheets of Ogden Corporation appeared as follows:

CONTRIBUTED CAPITAL AND RETAINED EARNINGS
(as of December 31, 1971)

Common stock, $5 par value, 250,000 shares authorized, 200,000 shares issued	$1,000,000
Premium on common stock	200,000
Total contributed capital	$1,200,000
Retained earnings	975,800
Total contributed capital and retained earnings	$2,175,800

CONTRIBUTED CAPITAL AND RETAINED EARNINGS
(as of December 31, 1972)

Common stock, $5 par value, 250,000 shares authorized, 219,800 shares issued of which 2,000 are in the treasury $1,099,000
Premium on common stock 338,600

Total contributed capital $1,437,600
Retained earnings 785,300

Total $2,222,900
Less: Cost of treasury stock 21,000

Total contributed capital and retained earnings $2,201,900

On February 15, May 17, August 14, and again on November 15, 1972, the board of directors declared $0.15 per share dividends on the outstanding stock. The treasury stock was purchased on July 23. On August 14, while the stock was selling for $12 per share, the corporation declared a 10% stock dividend. The new shares were issued on September 15.

Required:

Under the assumption that there were no transactions affecting retained earnings other than the ones given, determine the 1972 net income of Ogden Corporation. Present calculations to prove your net income figure.

Problem 17–4

On December 31 of last year the stockholders' equity section from Phoenix Corporation's balance sheet appeared as follows:

STOCKHOLDERS' EQUITY

Preferred stock, $100 par value, 6% cumulative and nonparticipating, 2,500 shares authorized, 1,000 shares issued $100,000
Common stock, $10 par value, 100,000 shares authorized, 50,000 shares issued... $500,000
Add: Premium on common stock.. 75,000

Amount paid in 575,000

Total contributed capital $675,000
Retained earnings 225,000

Total Stockholders' Equity $900,000

During the current year the corporation completed the following stock-related transactions:

Mar. 25 Declared the regular semiannual $3 per share dividend on the preferred stock and a $0.50 per share dividend on the common stock.

Apr. 20 Paid to the April 15 stockholders of record the dividends declared on March 25.

30 Accepted subscriptions to 10,000 shares of common stock at $17.50 per share. Ten percent down payments accompanied the subscription contracts.

May 30 Received balance due on April 30 subscriptions and issued the stock.

Sept. 24 Declared the regular semiannual $3 per share dividend on the preferred stock and a $0.50 per share dividend on the common stock.

Oct. 20 Paid to the October 15 stockholders of record the dividends declared on September 24.

Dec. 20 Declared a 10% common stock dividend distributable on January 20 to the January 15 common stockholders of record. The December 20 stock market quotation for Phoenix Corporation's common stock was $18 per share, and the board of directors voted to use this quotation in recording the dividend.

Dec. 31 Closed the Income Summary account for the year. The year's after-tax net income was $109,000.

Required:
1. Prepare general journal entries to record the foregoing transactions.
2. Under the assumption that Jerry Payne owns 100 shares of Phoenix Corporation common stock which he plans to hold until after the distribution of the stock dividend declared on December 20, (*a*) prepare a calculation of the book value of his 100 shares as of December 31, and (*b*) another calculation of the book value of his total shares after the dividend distribution.

Problem 17-5

Last October 31 a corporation's Retained Earnings account showed a $211,800 credit balance. On that date the corporation had issued at $12 per share and had outstanding 60,000 of the 100,000 $10 par value common shares it was authorized to issue, and beginning on November 1 it completed these transactions:

Nov. 1 The board of directors declared a 20 cents per share dividend on the common stock, payable on December 1 to the November 25 stockholders of record.

Dec. 1 Paid the dividend declared on November 1.

      2 The board declared a 5% stock dividend, distributable on December 30 to the December 22 stockholders of record. The stock was selling at $18 per share, and the directors voted to use this amount in recording the dividend.

     30 Distributed the foregoing stock dividend.

     31 The corporation earned $94,500 during the year.

Jan. 2 The board of directors voted to split the corporation's stock 2 for 1 by calling in the old stock and issuing two $5 par value shares for each old $10 share held. The stockholders voted approval of the split and authorization of 200,000 new $5 par value shares to replace the $10 shares; all legal requirements were met; and the split was completed on February 1.

Required:
1. Prepare general journal entries to record the foregoing transactions and to close the Income Summary account at the year-end. (No entry is required for the split; however, a memorandum reciting the facts would be entered in the Common Stock account.)
2. Under the assumption Jerry Blue owned 500 of the $10 par value shares on October 31 and neither bought nor sold any shares during the period of the transactions, prepare a schedule showing in one column the book value per share of the corporation's stock and in the second column the book value of Blue's shares at the close of business on each of October 31, November 1, December 1, December 30, December 31, and February 1.

3. Prepare three stockholders' equity sections for the corporation, the first showing the stockholders' equity on October 31, the second on December 31, and the third on February 1.

Problem 17-6

Northern Corporation received a charter granting it the right to issue 50,000 shares of $10 par value common stock and 2,000 shares of $7\frac{1}{2}\%$ cumulative and nonparticipating, $100 par value, preferred stock on which a $3.75 dividend is payable semiannually. On June 30 of the year in which the charter was granted, 40,000 shares of the common stock were subscribed at $12.50 per share. One fifth of the subscription price accompanied the subscriptions, and all subscribers paid their remaining balances 30 days thereafter, on which date the stock was issued. The preferred stock was issued at par for cash on the same day. The company prospered from the beginning and paid all dividends on its preferred stock plus dividends on the common.

On August 10 of its fifth year when the corporation had a $128,000 balance in its Retained Earnings account and its common stock was selling at $17.50 per share, the board of directors voted a 10% common stock dividend which was distributed on September 20 to the September 15 stockholders of record.

One year later, on October 3, when the corporation had a $93,000 balance in its Retained Earnings account, the common stock was split two for one by calling in the old $10 par value shares and issuing two $5 par value shares for each old share held.

Near the end of the sixth year, on December 22, the corporation declared the regular $3.75 per share semiannual dividend on its preferred stock and a 10 cents per share dividend on its common stock, payable on January 31 to the January 20 stockholders of record.

Required:
1. Prepare general journal entries to record —
   a) The sale and issuance of the original common stock through subscriptions.
   b) The sale and issuance of the preferred stock.
   c) The declaration and distribution of the common stock dividend.
   d) The declaration and distribution of the sixth-year cash dividends.
2. Carl Hess owned 100 shares of the corporation's common stock on the record date of the fifth-year common stock dividend. Under the assumption that the market value of the stock was not affected by the stock dividend, it was still selling at $17.50 per share on the day the dividend was distributed, and that Hess neither bought nor sold any shares during the year, prepare a schedule showing the shares held by Hess, their total book value, and their total market value on the day the dividend was declared and on the day it was distributed. (Remember preferred dividends do not accrue.)
3. Prepare the stockholders' equity section of the corporation's balance sheet as of the close of business on the day the $5 par value shares were distributed. (Assume that 100,000 of these shares were authorized.)

Alternate problems

Problem 17-1A

A corporation organized to construct a shopping center received a charter granting it the right to issue 2,000 shares of $100 par value, $7\frac{1}{2}\%$ cumulative and nonparticipating, preferred stock and 100,000 shares of $10 par value common stock. It then completed these transactions:

Feb. 3   Accepted subscriptions to 60,000 shares of common stock at $11 per share. One-third down payments accompanied the subscriptions.

      6   Gave 1,000 shares of common stock to the corporation's promoters for their services in organizing the company. The board of directors placed an $11 per share value on the stock.

     10   Exchanged 1,000 shares of preferred stock for land valued at $105,000.

     15   Accepted subscriptions to 500 shares of preferred stock at $105 per share. The subscriptions were accompanied by 20% down payments.

Mar. 5   Collected the balance due on the common stock subscriptions and issued the stock.

     17   Collected the balance due on the preferred stock subscriptions and issued the stock.

     20   Accepted subscriptions to 500 shares of preferred stock at $106 per share. The subscription contracts were accompanied by 20% down payments.

Required:
1. Prepare general journal entries to record the foregoing transactions.
2. Prepare the stockholders' equity section of the corporation's balance sheet as of March 20.

Problem 17–2A

Pinion Corporation received a charter granting the right to issue 50,000 shares of $5 par value common stock. It then completed these transactions:

a)   Accepted subscriptions to 15,000 shares of common stock at $5.50 per share.

b)   Gave Corona Corporation 25,000 shares of stock for the following assets: machinery, $35,000; factory building, $85,000; and land, $17,500.

c)   Collected the subscriptions of Transaction (a) and issued the stock.

d)   Purchased additional machinery for cash, $65,000.

e)   During its first year sold $628,500 of products for cash and paid $550,300 of operating expenses.

f)   Made an adjusting entry to record depreciation on machinery, $10,700, and depreciation on factory building, $2,500. (Debit Operating Expenses Controlling.)

g)   Made an adjusting entry to record state and federal income taxes payable, $25,000.

h)   Closed the Sales, Operating Expenses Controlling, State and Federal Income Taxes Expense, and Income Summary accounts.

i)   Declared a $0.10 per share quarterly dividend.

j)   Paid the dividend previously declared.

k)   Paid the state and federal income taxes payable.

l)   Purchased 1,000 shares of treasury stock at $5.75 per share.

m)   Sold 500 of the treasury shares at $6 per share.

n)   Declared a 10% stock dividend. The stock was selling for $6 per share on the day of the declaration.

o)   Distributed the stock dividend.

p)   Declared a $0.10 per share quarterly cash dividend.

q)   The local chamber of commerce purchased and gave to the corporation a plot of land immediately to the west of the present factory building. The land had a fair market value of $15,000 and was to be used in expanding the factory and its payroll.

Required:

1. Open the following T-accounts: Cash; Subscriptions Receivable Common Stock; Machinery and Equipment; Accumulated Depreciation, Machinery and Equipment; Buildings; Accumulated Depreciation, Buildings; Land; State and Federal Income Taxes Payable; Cash Dividend Payable; Common Stock; Premium on Common Stock; Common Stock Subscribed; Contributed Capital from Treasury Stock Transactions; Contributed Capital from Plant Site Donation; Retained Earnings; Stock Dividend Distributable; Treasury Stock; Income Summary; Sales; Operating Expenses Controlling; and State and Federal Income Taxes Expense.
2. Enter the transactions directly in the accounts, using the transaction letters to identify the amounts.
3. Prepare the stockholders' equity section of a balance sheet reflecting the foregoing transactions. (See Illustration 18–2.)

Problem 17–4A

On June 27, 1972, and again on December 28 Mesa Corporation declared the regular $3 per share semiannual dividend on its preferred stock and a $0.60 per share dividend on its common stock. These were the only dividends declared by the corporation during the year. The December 28 dividends were unpaid on December 31 when the stockholders' equity in the corporation appeared as follows:

STOCKHOLDERS' EQUITY

Preferred stock, $100 par value, 6% cumulative and nonparticipating,		
5,000 shares authorized, 2,500 shares issued	$250,000	
Add: Premium on preferred stock	12,500	
Amount paid in		$ 262,500
Common stock, $10 par value, 100,000 shares		
authorized, 60,000 shares issued	$600,000	
Add: Premium on common stock	120,000	
Amount paid in		720,000
Total contributed capital		$ 982,500
Retained earnings		223,000
Total Stockholders' Equity		$1,205,500

During 1973 the corporation completed the following stock-related transactions:

Jan. 20 Paid to the January 15 stockholders of record the dividends declared on December 28 of the previous year.

Mar. 15 Accepted subscriptions to 10,000 shares of common stock at $16 per share. Twenty-five percent down payments accompanied the subscription contracts.

Apr. 14 Received the balance due on the common stock subscriptions of March 15 and issued the stock.

June 26 Declared the regular $3 per share semiannual dividend on the preferred stock and a $0.60 per share dividend on the common stock.

July 20 Paid to the July 15 stockholders of record the dividends declared on June 26.

Oct. 24 Declared a 10% common stock dividend distributable on November 20 to the November 15 stockholders of record. The October 24 stock market quotation for Mesa Corporation common stock was $16.50 per share, and the board of directors voted to use this quotation in recording the dividend.

Nov. 20 Distributed the stock dividend declared on October 24.

Dec. 29 Declared the regular $3 per share semiannual dividend on the preferred stock and a $0.55 per share dividend on the common stock.

Required:

1. Prepare general journal entries to record the foregoing transactions.

2. Gary Sears purchased 100 shares of Mesa Corporation common stock on June 12, 1972, becoming a stockholder of record on June 23. Since becoming a stockholder, he has sold none of his Mesa Corporation stock. If he continues to hold this stock until after the December 29, 1973, dividend is paid, will his cash from dividends declared by the corporation during 1973 exceed the cash he received from dividends declared by the corporation during 1972? Present figures to prove your answer.

Problem 17-5A

The stockholders' equity section of a corporation's September 30 balance sheet carried the following items:

STOCKHOLDERS' EQUITY

Common stock, $25 par value, 10,000 shares authorized, 8,000 shares issued $200,000
Premium on common stock 40,000

Total contributed capital $240,000
Retained earnings 141,600

Total Stockholders' Equity $381,600

On October 2 the board of directors declared a 40 cents per share cash dividend payable on October 31 to the October 20 stockholders of record. On November 28 the board declared a 10% stock dividend distributable on December 30 to the December 20 stockholders of record. The stock was selling for $50 per share on the day of the declaration, and the board voted to use this price in recording the dividend. The corporation earned $35,200, after taxes, during the year of the foregoing transactions, and on January 8 of the following year the board voted to split the corporation's stock 2½ for 1 by calling in the old stock and issuing 25 shares of $10 par value common stock for each 10 shares of the old $25 par value stock held. The stockholders voted approval of the split and authorization of 25,000 shares of new $10 par value stock to replace the old stock; all legal requirements were met; and the split was completed on February 15.

Required:

1. Prepare general journal entries to record the transactions and to close the Income Summary account. (No entry is needed for the split; however, a memorandum reciting the facts would be entered in the Common Stock account.)

2. Under the assumption that Dale Hall owned 200 of the $25 par value shares on September 30 and neither bought nor sold any shares during the foregoing period, prepare a schedule showing the book value per share of the corporation's stock in one column and the book value of Hall's total shares in a second column at the close of business on the following dates: September 30, October 2, October 31, December 30, December 31, and February 15.

3. Prepare the stockholders' equity section of the corporation's balance sheet as of the close of business on December 31, and prepare another equity section as of the close of business on February 15.

Decision problem 17–1, Apex Corporation

Ned Hall purchased 100 shares of Apex Corporation stock at $15 per share on January 1, 197A, when the corporation had the following stockholders' equity:

Common stock, $10 par value, 250,000 shares authorized,
200,000 shares issued and outstanding.................................. $2,000,000
Capital contributed by stockholders in excess of the par
value of their shares 250,000
Retained earnings... 560,000
Total Stockholders' Equity $2,810,000

Since purchasing the 100 shares, Mr. Hall has neither purchased nor sold any additional shares of the company's stock; and on December 31 of each year he has received dividends on the shares held as follows: 197A, $66; 197B, $82.50; and 197C, $110.

On June 30, 197A, at a time when its stock was selling for $17.50 per share, Apex Corporation declared a 10% stock dividend which was distributed one month later. On August 15, 197B, the corporation doubled the number of its authorized shares and split its stock 2 for 1; and on March 27, 197C, it purchased 10,000 shares of treasury stock at $9 per share. The shares were still in its treasury at year-end.

Required:
Under the assumption that Apex Corporation's stock had a book value of $13.50 per share on December 31, 197A, a book value of $7.20 per share on December 31, 197B, and a book value of $7.70 on December 31, 197C, do the following:
1. Prepare statements showing the nature of the stockholders' equity in the corporation at the ends of 197A, 197B, and 197C.
2. Prepare a schedule showing the amounts of the corporation's net income for each of 197A, 197B, and 197C under the assumption that the changes in the company's retained earnings during the three-year period resulted solely from earnings and dividends.

Decision problem 17–2, Blue Lake Corporation

On November 3 stockholders' equity in Blue Lake Corporation consisted of the following:

Common stock, $10 par value, 150,000 shares authorized,
100,000 shares issued and outstanding.................................. $1,000,000
Capital contributed by the common stockholders in excess of
the par value of their shares... 150,000
Retained earnings... 650,000
Total Stockholders' Equity $1,800,000

On the date of the equity section, when the stock was selling at $20 per share, the corporation's directors voted a 20% stock dividend, distributable on December 1 to the November 25 stockholders of record. The directors also voted an $0.85 per share annual cash dividend, payable on December 20 to the December 15 stockholders of record. The amount of the latter dividend was a disappointment to some stockholders, since the company had for a number of years paid a $1 per share annual cash dividend.

George Hale owned 1,000 shares of Blue Lake Corporation stock on November 25, which he had purchased a number of years ago, and as a result he received his dividend shares. He continued to hold all of his shares until after he received the December 20 cash dividend. However, he did note that his stock had a $20 per share market value on November 3, a market value it held until the close of business on November 25, when the market value declined to $17.50 per share.

Give the entries to record the declaration and payment of the dividends involved here, and answer these questions:

a) What was the book value of Hale's total shares on November 3, and what was the book value on December 1, after he received his dividend shares?
b) What fraction of the corporation did Hale own on November 3, and what fraction did he own on December 1?
c) What was the market value of Hale's total shares on November 3, and what was the market value at the close of business on November 25?
d) What did Hale gain from the stock dividend?

Chapter 18

Corporations: retained earnings and consolidations

■ Retained earnings, as the name implies, is stockholders' equity that has arisen from retaining assets from earnings in the business. The retained income includes earnings from normal operations as well as gains from such transactions as the sale of plant assets or investments.

Retained earnings may be free and unappropriated, or they may be "earmarked" or appropriated for some special purpose. Generally, only the amount of free or unappropriated retained earnings is considered immediately available for dividends. Of course, what is meant by the phrase "available for dividends" is that a credit balance exists in the Retained Earnings account and dividends may be debited thereto.

It should be remembered that dividends are normally paid in cash, and their payment reduces in like amounts both cash and stockholders' equity. The existence of accumulated earnings, as evidenced by a credit balance in the Retained Earnings account, makes the payment of dividends legally possible. However, whether dividends are paid also depends upon the availability of cash with which to pay them. If cash or assets that will shortly become cash are not available, a board may think it wise to forgo the declaration of dividends, even though retained earnings exist. Often the directors of a corporation having a large balance in its Retained Earnings account will not declare a dividend because all current assets are needed in the operation of the business.

Appropria-
tions of
retained
earnings

■ Although the entire balance of a corporation's Retained Earnings account is usually available to absorb debits from dividend declarations, it is normally not wise to exhaust the balance for this purpose. Earnings are a source of assets. Some assets from earnings should be paid out in dividends; but some should be retained for emergencies, for distribution as dividends in years in which earnings are not sufficient to pay normal dividends, and for use in expanding operations. The last reason is an important one. If a corporation is to expand and grow, it may sell additional stock to secure the assets needed in expansion; however, it may also expand by using assets acquired through earnings. Ford Motor Company is a good example of a company that has made use of the latter method. Less than $100,000 was originally invested in Ford Motor Company, and the company has grown to its present size primarily from retaining in the business assets from earnings.

When a corporation expands by retaining assets from earnings, the earnings are invested in plant, equipment, merchandise, et cetera, and are not available for dividends. Many stockholders do not understand this; and upon seeing a large amount of retained earnings reported on the balance sheet, agitate for dividends that cannot be paid because the assets from earnings are invested in the business.

Although the practice is not now as common as it once was, some corporations earmark or appropriate retained earnings as a means of informing their stockholders that assets from earnings equal to the appropriations are unavailable for dividends. Retained earnings are appropriated by a resolution passed by the board of directors; and the appropriations are recorded in the accounts and may be reported on the balance sheet as in Illustration 18–1.

STOCKHOLDERS' EQUITY			
Common stock, $1 par value, 5,000,000 shares authorized and issued			$5,000,000
Retained earnings:			
Appropriated retained earnings:			
Appropriated for plant expansion..................	$200,000		
Appropriated for working capital	250,000		
Appropriated for bonded indebtedness...........	75,000		
Total appropriated retained earnings...........		$525,000	
Unappropriated retained earnings...................		350,000	
Total retained earnings.............................			875,000
Total contributed and retained capital......			$5,875,000

Illustration
18–1

Appropriations of retained earnings are often called "reserves of retained earnings" and may appear on the balance sheet under captions such as "Reserve for plant expansion," "Reserve for working capital," and "Reserve for bonded indebtedness." Such terminology, since it seems to imply that something is held in reserve, should not be used.

Voluntary and contractual appropriations

Appropriations of retained earnings may be voluntarily made or they may be required by contract. Retained earnings appropriated for plant expansion or for working capital are examples of voluntary appropriations. The first is made to show that assets from earnings are being kept in the business for use in expanding the plant, and the second to show that the company is supplying a portion of its working capital needs from earnings. (Working capital is the excess of current assets over current liabilities.)

The two foregoing appropriations are known as discretionary appropriations. Both are made at the discretion of the board of directors; and since they are voluntary and discretionary, the board may at any time reverse its judgment and return these appropriations or any like appropriations to unappropriated retained earnings.

Illustration of a retained earnings appropriation

To illustrate an appropriation of retained earnings, assume the directors of Deeplake Corporation recognize that in five years their plant will need to be expanded by the construction of a $1,000,000 addition. To finance the expansion, the board discusses the possibility of waiting until the addition is needed and then securing the required funds through the sale of additional stock. They also discuss the possibility of financing the expansion through the annual retention for each of the next five years of $200,000 of assets from earnings. Income in excess of this amount is expected to be earned each year, and the directors decide this is the better plan.

In order each year to retain in the business $200,000 of assets from earnings, the directors recognize it is only necessary to refrain from paying out earnings equal to this amount in dividends. However, the board also recognizes that if earnings are retained, the Retained Earnings account and the amount reported on the balance sheet under the caption "Retained earnings" will grow each year and will create a demand by some stockholders for more dividends. Consequently, the board decides that in addition to retaining the assets from earnings, it will at the end of each of the succeeding five years vote an appropriation and transfer of $200,000 of retained earnings from the Retained Earnings account to the Retained Earnings Appropriated for Plant Expansion account. Also, it will show the appropriations on the balance sheet.

If the board follows through on this plan and votes the yearly appropriations, the entry to record each appropriation is:

Dec.	28	Retained Earnings	200,000.00	
		Retained Earnings Appropriated for		
		Plant Expansion		200,000.00
		To record the appropriation of retained		
		earnings.		

When a retained earnings appropriation is recorded, a portion of the balance of the Retained Earnings account is transferred to the proper appropriated retained earnings account, as in the foregoing entry. This reduces the balance of the Retained Earnings account but does not reduce total retained earnings. It merely changes a portion from free, unappropriated retained earnings to appropriated retained earnings.

Before going on, it should be observed in the foregoing situation that the transfer of $200,000 each year from the Retained Earnings account to the Retained Earnings Appropriated for Plant Expansion account does not provide funds for the expansion. Earnings provided the funds; the appropriations do nothing more than inform the stockholders of the board's intention to retain in the business assets from earnings equal to the amount appropriated.

Disposing of an appropriation of retained earnings

The purpose for which an appropriation of retained earnings was made is at times accomplished or passes, and there is no longer a need for the appropriation. When this occurs, the appropriated retained earnings should be returned to the (unappropriated) Retained Earnings account. For example, when bonds mature and are paid and there is no longer a need for an appropriation of retained earnings for bonded indebtedness, the balance of the Retained Earnings Appropriated for Bonded Indebtedness account should be returned to the Retained Earnings account.

Comprehensive treatment of equity items
■ In this and previous chapters there have been a number of illustrations showing the balance sheet treatment of stockholder equity items. Rarely, if ever, will all the illustrated items appear on a single balance sheet. However, Illustration 18–2 shows a rather comprehensive stockholder equity section as an aid to the student in dealing with whatever equity items he is called upon to handle.

In Illustration 18–2 the second item is "Capital contributed by preferred stockholders in excess of the par value of their shares, $4,000." This item resulted from preferred stock premiums. At the time the amounts originated they were probably credited to an account called "Premium on Preferred Stock." However, as in Illustration 18–2, it is common practice to show an item such as this on the balance sheet under a more descriptive caption than the name of the account in which it is recorded.

Surplus
■ The terms "contributed capital" and "retained earnings" have been in common use for a little over 15 years. Prior to the early nineteen-sixties stockholders' equity was commonly shown on published balance sheets under two main headings: (1) "Capital stock" and (2) "Surplus." Under "Capital stock" was shown the portion of stockholders' equity represented by the par or stated value of the corporation's outstanding stock, and under "Surplus" was shown the remainder of the equity.

STOCKHOLDERS' EQUITY

Preferred stock, $100 par value 7% cumulative and nonparticipating, 2,000 shares authorized, 1,000 shares issued and outstanding	$100,000	
Capital contributed by preferred stockholders in excess of the par value of their shares	4,000	
Total contributed by preferred stockholders		$104,000
Common stock, $10 par value, 50,000 shares authorized, 20,000 shares issued of which 1,000 are in the treasury	$200,000	
Common stock subscribed, 5,000 shares	50,000	
Common stock dividend distributable, 1,900 shares	19,000	
Total common stock issued and to be issued	$269,000	
Capital contributed by common stockholders in excess of the par value of their shares	52,000	
Less discount on common stock issued	(6,000)	
Total contributed and subscribed by common stockholders		315,000
Total capital contributed for shares		$419,000
Other contributed capital:		
Contributed capital from plant site donation	$ 40,000	
Contributed capital from treasury stock transactions	2,000	42,000
Total contributed capital		$461,000
Retained earnings:		
Appropriated for plant expansion	$175,000	
Restricted by the purchase of treasury stock	15,000	
Free and unappropriated	115,000	
Total retained earnings		305,000
Total contributed capital and retained earnings		$766,000
Less cost of treasury stock		(15,000)
Total Stockholders' Equity		$751,000

Illustration
18–2

"Surplus," as the word was used on these balance sheets, was defined as "that part of the stockholders' equity not represented by the par or stated value of the corporation's outstanding stock." Furthermore, "surplus" was divided into "earned surplus," which was defined as earnings retained in the business, and "capital surplus," which was surplus from all sources other than earnings. And each of these was in turn divided and subdivided to show the capital surplus sources and intended uses and earned surplus. These divisions, as they were commonly given, are shown in the lower half of Illustration 18–3 where the sources of stockholders' equity are presented in outline form, first using present-day divisions and terminology and then repeated with old divisions and terminology.

The student should examine carefully the outlines of Illustration 18–3, and should add an understanding of the terms "surplus," "capital surplus," "paid-in surplus," and "earned surplus" to his fund of accounting knowledge. An understanding of these terms is important because although their use is being discontinued on current financial statements, they are still found in the literature of accounting and on an occasional published report.

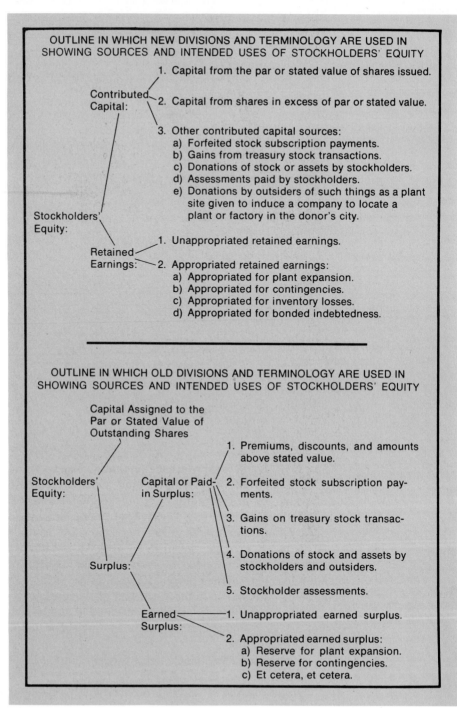

OUTLINE IN WHICH NEW DIVISIONS AND TERMINOLOGY ARE USED IN
SHOWING SOURCES AND INTENDED USES OF STOCKHOLDERS' EQUITY

Stockholders' Equity:

Contributed Capital:

1. Capital from the par or stated value of shares issued.

2. Capital from shares in excess of par or stated value.

3. Other contributed capital sources:
   a) Forfeited stock subscription payments.
   b) Gains from treasury stock transactions.
   c) Donations of stock or assets by stockholders.
   d) Assessments paid by stockholders.
   e) Donations by outsiders of such things as a plant site given to induce a company to locate a plant or factory in the donor's city.

Retained Earnings:

1. Unappropriated retained earnings.

2. Appropriated retained earnings:
   a) Appropriated for plant expansion.
   b) Appropriated for contingencies.
   c) Appropriated for inventory losses.
   d) Appropriated for bonded indebtedness.

OUTLINE IN WHICH OLD DIVISIONS AND TERMINOLOGY ARE USED IN
SHOWING SOURCES AND INTENDED USES OF STOCKHOLDERS' EQUITY

Stockholders' Equity:

Capital Assigned to the Par or Stated Value of Outstanding Shares

Capital or Paid-in Surplus:

1. Premiums, discounts, and amounts above stated value.

2. Forfeited stock subscription payments.

3. Gains on treasury stock transactions.

4. Donations of stock and assets by stockholders and outsiders.

5. Stockholder assessments.

Surplus:

Earned Surplus:

1. Unappropriated earned surplus.

2. Appropriated earned surplus:
   a) Reserve for plant expansion.
   b) Reserve for contingencies.
   c) Et cetera, et cetera.

Illustration
18–3

It is well that the use of the word "surplus" is being abandoned. Actually the term has a general connotation of an "excess" of something; however, this was not and is not its meaning in accounting. Certainly in accounting the term "surplus" was and is not meant to convey the idea there was or is an excess of corporate capital, cash, or assets of any kind. The term, properly qualified with descriptive adjectives, did and does purport to show the source or sources of some of the corporate assets.

In addition to the foregoing, it might also be wise at this time for the student to add to his fund of knowledge an understanding of the phrase "undivided profits," which still occasionally appears on the balance sheets of banks and like institutions. "Undivided profits" are nothing more than retained earnings; and since in most banks the assets from earnings are invested in the business, there is usually little likelihood the undivided profits will be divided or paid out in dividends.

Both the word "surplus" and the phrase "undivided profits" are misleading; consequently, it is good that new and more meaningful terminology has developed and that such words and phrases are less and less commonly used in published statements.

Retained earnings statement ■ At the end of each accounting period, in addition to a balance sheet and an income statement, it is customary to prepare for a corporation a retained earnings statement, or if old terminology is used, an earned surplus statement. A retained earnings statement sets out the changes that have occurred in retained earnings during an accounting period. Illustration 18–4 shows such a statement and was prepared from the information in the following two Westwood Corporation accounts:

Retained Earnings

Date		Explanations	Debit	Credit	Balance
Jan.	1, '72	Balance			180,250
Mar.	24, '72	Quarterly dividend	3,000		177,250
June	21, '72	Quarterly dividend	3,000		174,250
Sept.	27, '72	Quarterly dividend	3,000		171,250
Dec.	20, '72	Quarterly dividend	3,000		168,250
Dec.	20, '72	Stock dividend	20,000		148,250
Dec.	20, '72	Appropriation for plant expansion	25,000		123,250
Dec.	31, '72	Net income after taxes		53,400	176,650

Retained Earnings Appropriated for Plant Expansion

Date		Explanations	Debit	Credit	Balance
Dec.	22, '71			25,000	25,000
Dec.	20, '72			25,000	50,000

When the retained earnings statement of Illustration 18–4 is compared with the information shown in the corporation's Retained Earnings and Retained Earnings Appropriated for Plant Expansion accounts,

Westwood Corporation
Statement of Retained Earnings
For Year Ended December 31, 1972

Unappropriated retained earnings:		
Unappropriated retained earnings, January 1, 1972..............		$180,250
Additions:		
Net income..		53,400
Total...		$233,650
Deductions and appropriations:		
Quarterly cash dividends..	$12,000	
Dividend in common stock..	20,000	
Retained earnings appropriated for plant expansion.........	25,000	
Total deductions and appropriations.......................		57,000
Unappropriated retained earnings, December 31, 1972...........		$176,650
Appropriated retained earnings:		
Appropriated for plant expansion, balance, January 1, 1972.....	$25,000	
Appropriated during 1972	25,000	
Appropriated for plant expansion, December 31, 1972		50,000
Total Retained Earnings as of December 31, 1972		$226,650

Illustration
18–4

it is apparent the statement is nothing more than a report of the changes recorded in the accounts.

Extraordinary gains and losses

■ Extraordinary gains and losses are material gains and losses which (1) do not typically result from a company's normal business activities, (2) are not expected to occur regularly over a period of years, and (3) are not recurring factors in any evaluation of the ordinary operations of the business. Such gains and losses include gains and losses from:

a) The sale or abandonment of a plant or a significant segment of the business;
b) The sale of investments not acquired for resale;
c) The expropriation of properties;
d) A material revaluation of a foreign currency; and
e) The write-off of goodwill due to unusual events or developments within the period.

Prior to 1967 there was a lack of uniformity in our country in the treatment of extraordinary gains and losses. In the annual reports of some companies such items were placed on the income statement and entered into the determination of the net income figure for the year in which they occurred. In other companies the income statement was by-passed and such items were reported on the retained earnings statement. Obviously this resulted in the reporting of significantly different net income figures for companies that had experienced the same gains and losses.

For example, assume that in 1966 each of two companies earned

$1,000,000 from normal business activities. However, each also had a plant expropriated by an emerging nation with a resulting $1,500,000 extraordinary loss. Assume further that one company reported its extraordinary loss on its 1966 income statement, while the other bypassed its income statement and reported the loss as a deduction on its retained earnings statement. Under these assumptions the company reporting the extraordinary loss on its income statement showed a $500,000 net loss for 1966, while the company that bypassed its income statement in reporting the extraordinary loss showed a $1,000,000 net income.

As a result of this lack of uniformity, the Accounting Principles Board of the American Institute of Certified Public Accountants concluded in 1967 that an income statement said to present fairly the results of operations for a period should reflect all gains and losses recognized during the period, whether ordinary or extraordinary in nature.[1] It also concluded that extraordinary items should be disclosed separately on an income statement, with their related income tax effects, so that a user of the statement could determine the extent to which the ordinary income of the business was affected by extraordinary items. Illustration 18–5 shows such a statement.

Dale Corporation
Income Statement for Years Ended December 31, 1972 and 1973

	1973	1972
Net sales	$8,500,000	$7,600,000
Other revenue	8,000	9,000
Total revenue	$8,508,000	$7,609,000
Cost and expenses:		
Cost of goods sold	$6,000,000	$5,400,000
Selling, general and administrative expenses	500,000	450,000
Interest expense	10,000	10,000
Other deductions	8,000	7,000
Income tax	940,000	842,000
Total cost and expenses	$7,458,000	$6,709,000
Income before extraordinary gains and losses	$1,050,000	$ 900,000
Extraordinary gains and losses:		
Gain on sale of investments not held for resale		50,000
Loss from abandonment of plant assets	(25,000)	
Net Income	$1,025,000	$ 950,000

Illustration
18–5

Observe in Illustration 18–5 that income before extraordinary gains and losses is set out as a separate amount each year. These are the amounts of income earned by Dale Corporation from ordinary operation, and from these amounts are deducted the extraordinary items to arrive at each year's net income.

---

[1] "Reporting the Results of Operations," *Opinions of the Accounting Principles Board, No. 9* (New York: American Institute of Certified Public Accountants, 1967), pp. 112–13.

■ In concluding that extraordinary items should be set out separately on the income statement, as in Illustration 18–5, the Accounting Principles Board also concluded that certain items, even though material in amount and caused by unusual circumstances, are not extraordinary items, as defined above, "since they are of a character typical of the customary activities of the enterprise." These items are called normal corrections and adjustments and include:

a) Adjustments arising from changes in the estimated useful lives of plant assets;
b) Unusual bad debt losses;
c) Unusual inventory losses; and
d) Write-off of development costs.

As a result such items should be deducted on the income statement in arriving at "Income before extraordinary gains and losses." For example, if a company experiences an unusual bad debt loss due to the bankruptcy of an important customer, the amount of such loss should be added to the normal losses from bad debts and deducted as a general and administrative expense. Likewise, if a company suffers an unusual inventory loss, it should be deducted in arriving at "gross profit from sales." However, in both cases and in all such cases, if the amount of the unusual loss is material, it may be set out separately or it may be explained by means of a footnote.

■ In establishing the treatment for extraordinary items and for normal corrections and adjustments, the Accounting Principles Board recognized that certain items, which it called "prior period adjustments," are neither extraordinary items nor normal corrections and adjustments. The Board concluded that these prior period adjustments are limited to material adjustments which have all four of these characteristics:[2]

a) Are specifically identified with and directly related to the business activities of a particular prior period;
b) Are not attributable to economic events, including obsolescence, occurring subsequent to the date of the financial statements for such prior period;
c) Depend primarily on decisions or determinations by persons other than management or owners; and
d) Could not reasonably be estimated prior to such decisions or determinations.

Examples of prior period adjustments (provided they have all four characteristics) might be:

a) Nonrecurring adjustments or settlements of income taxes; and
b) Settlements of claims resulting from litigation.

[2]*Ibid.*, pp. 115–16.

And the Board concluded that such prior period adjustments with any related income tax effect should be shown on the retained earnings statement (see Illustration 18–6) as an adjustment of the opening balance of retained earnings.

Smythe Company, Inc.
Statement of Retained Earnings
For Year Ended December 31, 1973

Retained earnings, January 1, 1973	$89,000
Adjustments of prior years' income:	
Settlement of lawsuit arising from a 1969 accident	(32,000)
Retained earnings as restated	$57,000
Net income for the year	26,000
Total	$83,000
Dividends declared in 1973	(10,000)
Retained Earnings, December 31, 1973	$73,000

Illustration
18–6

Comparative single-step income statement

■ Return again to the income statement of Illustration 18–5 and note that this is a *comparative single-step income statement*. It is a comparative statement because it shows the operating results of two periods in columns side by side. This is a desirable feature that makes it easy for a statement reader to compare the results of the two periods. It is also a single-step income statement because all normal costs and expenses are deducted on it in one step. The income statements illustrated in previous chapters have been multiple-step statements on which cost of goods sold was deducted in a first step, then operating expenses in a second step, and then income taxes. This treatment for costs and expenses is satisfactory, but the multiple deductions do imply a preferential order for their recovery, when actually there is no preferential order. Consequently, to avoid the implication of a preferential order for the recovery of costs and expenses, the single-step income statement is being used more and more in published reports. Such statements may show considerable detail, but generally when published for the use of stockholders and the public, they are condensed as in Illustration 18–5.

Parent and subsidiary corporations

■ Corporations commonly own and control other corporations. For example, if Corporation A owns more than 50% of the voting stock of Corporation B, Corporation A can elect Corporation B's board of directors and thus control its activities and resources. In such a situation the controlling corporation, Corporation A, is known as the *parent company* and Corporation B is called a *subsidiary*.

When a corporation owns all the outstanding stock of a subsidiary, it can take over the subsidiary's assets, cancel its stock, and fuse the subsidiary into the parent company. However, there are often financial, legal, and tax advantages in operating a large business as a parent company controlling one or more subsidiaries rather than as a single corporation. Actually, most large American companies are parent corporations owning one or more subsidiaries.

When a business is operated as a parent company with subsidiaries, separate accounting records are kept for each corporation. Also, from a legal viewpoint the parent and each subsidiary is a separate entity with all the rights, duties, and responsibilities of a separate corporation. Nevertheless, if a parent and its subsidiaries are engaged in the same business under a unified management, the corporations are for all practical purposes a single enterprise. Therefore, it is often desirable to develop for a parent and its subsidiaries a set of *consolidated statements* in which the assets and liabilities of all the affiliated companies are combined on a single balance sheet and their revenues and expenses are combined on a single income statement, as though the business were in fact a single company.

Consolidated balance sheets

■ Principles of consolidation

When parent and subsidiary balance sheets are consolidated, duplications in items are eliminated so that the combined figures do not show more assets and equities than actually exist. For example, a parent's investment in a subsidiary is evidenced by shares of stock, the cost of which is carried in the parent company's investment account; but this stock really represents an equity in the subsidiary's assets. Consequently, if the parent's investment in a subsidiary and the subsidiary's assets are both shown on the consolidated balance sheet, the same resources are counted twice. To prevent this, the parent's investment and the subsidiary's capital accounts are offset and eliminated in preparing a consolidated balance sheet.

Likewise, a single enterprise cannot owe a debt to itself. This would be analogous to a student borrowing $20 for a date from funds he has saved for next semester's expenses and then preparing a balance sheet showing the $20 as both receivable from himself and payable to himself. To prevent such a double showing, intercompany debts and receivables are also eliminated in preparing a consolidated balance sheet.

Balance sheets consolidated at time of acquisition

When a parent and subsidiary assets and equities are combined in the preparation of a consolidated balance sheet, a work sheet is normally used to effect the consolidation. Illustration 18–7 shows such a work sheet. It was prepared to consolidate the accounts of Parent Company and its subsidiary, called Subsidiary Company, on the day Parent Company acquired control of Subsidiary Company through the purchase of 80 percent of its stock. Discussions of the work sheet's two eliminating entries follow:

ENTRY (*a*). On the same day it bought a controlling interest in Subsidiary Company, Parent Company loaned Subsidiary Company

$15,000 for use in expanding the subsidiary's operations. Since this intercompany debt resulted only in a transfer of funds within the organization and did not increase the organization's net assets, it is eliminated by means of Entry (*a*).

Parent Company and Subsidiary Company
Work Sheet for Consolidated Balance Sheet
As of Date of Consolidation

	Parent Company	Subsidiary Company	Eliminations		Consolidated Amounts
			Debit	Credit	
ASSETS					
Cash	6,000	17,000			23,000
Subsidiary's note receivable	15,000			(a) 15,000	
Accounts receivable, net	20,000	12,000			32,000
Inventories	45,000	23,000			68,000
Investment in Subsidiary Co.	100,000			(b) 100,000	
Land	25,000	9,000			34,000
Buildings and equipment, net	106,000	72,000			178,000
Excess of cost over book value			(b) 12,000		12,000
	317,000	133,000			347,000
EQUITIES					
Accounts payable	17,000	8,000			25,000
Subsidiary's note payable		15,000	(a) 15,000		
Common stock, Parent Co.	250,000				250,000
Retained earnings, Parent Co.	50,000				50,000
Common stock, Subsidiary Co.		100,000	(b) 100,000		
Retained earnings, Subsidiary Co.		10,000	(b) 10,000		
Minority interest				(b) 22,000	22,000
	317,000	133,000	137,000	137,000	347,000

Illustration
18–7

ENTRY (*b*).   When a work sheet for consolidating parent and subsidiary balance sheets is prepared, the amount of the parent's investment in a subsidiary and the balances of the subsidiary's stockholders' equity accounts are eliminated, since both represent the same thing, equities in the subsidiary's assets. Furthermore, in those cases where the parent company has purchased all of a subsidiary's stock at its book value, the entry for this elimination is very simple. In such situations the amount of the parent's investment in the subsidiary is exactly equal to the sum of the subsidiary's stockholders' equity accounts, and the investment is offset against these accounts to effect the elimination.

However, in the illustration presented here the parent company *did not pay book value for its stock* and it *did not buy all of the subsidiary's stock.* Consequently, the entry eliminating the parent company's investment and the subsidiary's capital accounts is not so simple. It is not simple (1) because of the excess over book value paid by the parent company for the subsidiary's stock and (2) because of the minority interest in the subsidiary.

Excess of investment cost over book value. At the time Parent Company purchased 80% of Subsidiary Company's stock, the subsidiary had outstanding 10,000 shares of $10 par value common stock with a book value of $11 per share. Parent Company paid $12.50 per share for the 8,000 shares it purchased; consequently, the cost of these shares exceeded their book value by $12,000, calculated as follows:

Cost of stock (8,000 shares at $12.50 per share) $100,000
Book value (8,000 shares at $11 per share) 88,000
    Excess of cost over book value........................... $ 12,000

Observe how this excess of cost over book value is set out on the work sheet in eliminating the parent's investment in the subsidiary. Then observe in Illustration 18–8 how it is shown on the consolidated

Parent Company and Subsidiary
Consolidated Balance Sheet
As of Date of Acquisition
ASSETS

Current Assets:
Cash	$ 23,000	
Accounts receivable	32,000	
Inventories	68,000	
Total Current Assets		$123,000
Plant Assets:		
Land	$ 34,000	
Buildings and equipment, net	178,000	
Total Plant Assets		212,000
Excess cost of investment in subsidiary over book value		12,000
Total Assets		$347,000

LIABILITIES AND STOCKHOLDERS' EQUITY

Liabilities:		
Accounts payable		$ 25,000
Stockholders' Equity:		
Common stock	$250,000	
Retained earnings	50,000	
Minority interest	22,000	
Total Stockholders' Equity		322,000
Total Liabilities and Stockholders' Equity		$347,000

Illustration
18–8

balance sheet. Parent Company's management either believed the market value of the subsidiary's assets was greater than their book value or it believed that Subsidiary Company's prospects were sufficiently good as to justify paying $100,000 for an 80% equity in the corporation. If the purchase was an arm's-length market transaction, either assumption justifies showing the excess cost over book value as an asset on the consolidated balance sheet.

The excess of a parent company's investment cost over the book value of its interest in a subsidiary often appears on a consolidated balance sheet as "Goodwill from consolidation." However, this is not considered good terminology.

Occasionally a parent company pays less than book value for its interest in a subsidiary. In such a situation the work sheet entry to eliminate the parent's investment sets out the amount of this excess of book value over cost as a credit. The credit then appears on the consolidated balance sheet as either a subtraction from certain of the subsidiary's assets or it might appear at the end of the consolidated assets as a subtraction headed "Allowance for overvaluation of subsidiary assets" or simply as "Excess of book value of subsidiary interest over its cost."

Minority interest. When a parent company owns a controlling interest in a subsidiary, the parent company is the subsidiary's majority stockholder. However, when the parent owns less than 100% of the subsidiary's stock, the subsidiary has other stockholders who own a minority interest in its assets and share its earnings. Consequently, when there is a minority interest and the stockholder equity accounts of the subsidiary are eliminated on a consolidated work sheet, the interest of the minority stockholders must be set out as in Illustration 18–7. In this case the minority stockholders have a 20% interest in the subsidiary; consequently, 20% of the balances of the subsidiary's common stock and retained earnings accounts is set out on the work sheet as the minority interest. This item then appears on the consolidated balance sheet in the stockholders' equity section, as in Illustration 18–8.

After a consolidated work sheet like that of Illustration 18–7 is completed, the amounts in its last column are used in preparing a consolidated balance sheet like that of Illustration 18–8.

Balance sheets consolidated at a date after acquisition

In the years after a subsidiary is acquired by a parent company, if the subsidiary's operations are profitable, it normally pays out a portion of its after-acquisition earnings in dividends and retains a portion for use in expanding its operations. If a subsidiary pays dividends, the parent company commonly records receipt of its share by debiting Cash and crediting a revenue account, such as Subsidiary's Dividends Earned. This revenue account is then closed at the end of each accounting period to the parent company's Income Summary account and on to its Retained Earnings account. Thus, earnings of a subsidiary paid out in dividends increase the assets and retained earnings of the parent company and are available for distribution as dividends to the parent company's stockholders.

When in addition to paying dividends a subsidiary retains a portion of its after-acquisition earnings for use in expanding its operations, the retention increases the subsidiary's net assets and the balance of its Retained Earnings account. The net assets and retained earnings of the affiliated companies are also increased and so is the book value of the parent company's investment and the minority interest. Furthermore, an understanding of consolidated balance sheets requires an understanding of these increases.

Consider first the increase in net assets. If a subsidiary's net assets are increased by profitable operations, there are more assets to add to those of the parent company and the other affiliated companies, if any. Consequently, an increase in a subsidiary's net assets increases the sum of the net assets of the affiliated companies.

As for the other increases, assume that Subsidiary Company earned $15,000 during the first year after Parent Company purchased control, paying out $10,000 in dividends and retaining $5,000 in its operations. The $5,000 increase in the subsidiary's retained earnings increased the book value of its stock $0.50 per share and it also increased the book value of Parent Company's investment in the subsidiary. However, in this case, as is common, the parent company carries its investment in the subsidiary at cost. Consequently, at the end of the first year after Parent Company gained control, the following entry is made on the consolidated work sheet to eliminate the subsidiary's stockholder equity accounts and the parent's investment:

| | Eliminations | |
	Debit	Credit
Investment in subsidiary		(b) 100,000
Excess of cost over book value	(b) 12,000	
Retained earnings, Parent Co.		(b) 4,000
Common stock, Subsidiary Co.	(b) 100,000	
Retained earnings, Subsidiary Co.	(b) 15,000	
Minority interest..		(b) 23,000

A comparison of the foregoing work sheet entry with Entry (*b*) on the work sheet of Illustration 18–7 will reveal:

The amounts of the subsidiary's stock and the parent's investment eliminated are the same in both entries. Likewise, the excess cost of the parent's investment over the investment's date-of-acquisition book value is unchanged. The parent company carries its investment in the subsidiary at cost, as is normal; consequently, none of these items were changed by a year's operations.

However, the eliminated amount of the subsidiary's retained earnings is $5,000 greater in the second entry, since the subsidiary increased its retained earnings by this amount during the year. Furthermore, the $5,000 increase in the subsidiary's retained earnings caused a $1,000 (20% of $5,000) increase in the equity of the minority stockholders.

Thus, the amount of the minority interest set out in the second entry is $1,000 greater. And, finally, the $5,000 after-acquisition increase in the subsidiary's retained earnings increased the total retained earnings of the affiliated companies by the amount of the parent company's equity in these earnings, which is $4,000, or 80% of the $5,000. Consequently, this amount is added to the retained earnings of the parent company.

Other con- ■ Consolidated income statements and consolidated retained earnings
solidated statements are also prepared for affiliated companies. However, prep-
statements aration of these require procedures that are beyond an elementary text. Nevertheless, a knowledge of the procedures is not necessary to an understanding of such statements. A reader needs only to recognize that all duplications in items and all profit arising from intercompany transactions are eliminated in their preparation.

Who uses ■ Consolidated statements are of no interest to minority stockholders.
con- Their interests normally go no further than the statements of the sub-
solidated sidiary in which they own stock. Likewise, creditors of a subsidiary and
statements people looking to their legal rights find little of interest in consolidated statements.

On the other hand, the stockholders of the parent company, its management, and its board of directors have a very real interest in consolidated statements. The parent company's stockholders benefit from earnings, an increase in assets, and financial strength anywhere in the organization. They likewise suffer from a loss or any weakness. And, the managers and directors of the parent company are responsible for all the resources under their control.

Questions 1. While examining a corporation balance sheet, a businessman observed
for class that the various items in the stockholders' equity section really showed
discussion sources of assets. Was this observation correct?

2. Explain how earnings increase a corporation's assets and stockholders' equity.

3. Give the accounting meanings of the terms: (a) surplus, (b) earned surplus, (c) capital surplus, and (d) paid-in surplus.

4. Why do accountants feel that the word "surplus" should not be used in published balance sheets as a term to describe a portion of the stockholders' equity?

5. Under what descriptive headings is the equity of the stockholders in a corporation shown on most present-day balance sheets?

6. Why are retained earnings sometimes appropriated?

7. Does the appropriation and transfer of retained earnings to retained earnings appropriated for plant expansion provide funds for the expansion?

How do such appropriations aid in accumulating funds for a plant expansion?

8. How does a corporation dispose of a retained earnings appropriation such as retained earnings appropriated for plant expansion?

9. What are (*a*) a parent company, (*b*) a subsidiary, and (*c*) a consolidated balance sheet?

10. When a work sheet for consolidating the balance sheets of a parent company and its subsidiaries is prepared, intercompany debts are eliminated on the work sheet. Why?

11. A consolidated balance sheet shows as an asset the item "Consolidated goodwill." What does this item represent?

12. A consolidated balance sheet shows in its stockholder equity section the item "Minority interest." What does this item represent?

Class exercises

Exercise 18–1

South Mountain Corporation received a charter and during a short period completed these transactions:

a) Began business by selling and issuing $12,000 of common stock at par for cash.

b) Purchased $10,000 of equipment for cash.

c) Sold and delivered $30,000 of services on credit.

d) Collected $27,000 of accounts receivable.

e) Paid $25,000 of operating expenses.

f) Purchased $7,000 of additional equipment, giving $4,000 in cash and a $3,000 promissory note payable.

g) Closed the Revenue from Services, Operating Expenses, and Income Summary accounts.

Required:

1. Open the following T-accounts on a sheet of ordinary notebook paper: Cash, Accounts Receivable, Equipment, Notes Payable, Common Stock, Retained Earnings, Income Summary, Revenue from Services, and Operating Expenses.

2. Record the transactions directly in the T-accounts.

3. Answer these questions:

   a) Does the corporation have retained earnings?

   b) Does it have any cash?

   c) If the company has retained earnings, why does it not also have cash?

   d) Can the corporation declare a legal cash dividend?

   e) Can it pay the dividend?

   f) In terms of assets, what does the balance of the Notes Payable account represent?

   g) In terms of assets, what does the balance of the Common Stock account represent?

   h) In terms of assets, what does the balance of the Retained Earnings account represent?

Exercise 18-2

On January 4 the directors of a corporation voted to appropriate and transfer $50,000 of the balance of the corporation's unappropriated Retained Earnings account to its Retained Earnings Appropriated for Plant Expansion account. This was the fifth of such appropriations and brought the balance of the Retained Earnings Appropriated for Plant Expansion account up to $250,000. On the same day the board also entered into a contract for construction of the plant addition for which the earnings were appropriated; and on December 3, upon completion of the addition, the contractor was paid $247,500, the contract price. Give the January 4 entry to record the appropriation and the December 3 entry to pay the contractor.

Exercise 18-3

At the end of last year the Retained Earnings account of North Lake Corporation appeared as follows:

Retained Earnings

June 27	Cash dividend	6,000	Jan.	1	Balance	103,000
Dec. 29	Cash dividend	6,000	Dec. 31		Net income	31,800
29	Stock dividend	17,500				

From the information in the account, prepare a retained earnings statement for the company.

Exercise 18-4

On June 30 Company Y had the following stockholders' equity:

Common stock, $10 par value, 10,000 shares issued and outstanding	$100,000
Retained earnings	25,000
Total Stockholders' Equity	$125,000

On the date of the equity section Company X purchased 8,000 of Company Y's outstanding shares, paying $15 per share, and a work sheet to consolidate the balance sheets of the two companies was prepared. Give the entry made on this work sheet to eliminate Company X's investment and Company Y's stockholder equity account balances.

Exercise 18-5

During the six months following its acquisition by Company X (see Exercise 18-4), Company Y earned $5,000, paid out $3,000 in dividends, and retained the balance for use in its operations. Give the entry under these assumptions to eliminate Company X's investment and Company Y's stockholders' equity account balances as of the end of the six-month period.

Exercise 18-6

Using more modern terminology, rearrange and restate the following stockholders' equity section from a corporation's balance sheet. The donated surplus arose from the donation of a plant site.

CAPITAL STOCK AND SURPLUS

Common stock, $5 par value, 100,000 shares authorized,
   80,000 shares issued $400,000
Capital surplus:
  Premium on common stock.. $ 40,000
  Treasury stock surplus   5,000
  Donated surplus...   25,000
     Total capital surplus .... $ 70,000
Earned surplus:
  Appropriated earned surplus:
    Reserve for plant expansion.. $100,000
  Unappropriated earned surplus 150,000
     Total earned surplus   250,000
      Total surplus   320,000
        Total Capital Stock and Surplus $720,000

Problems   Problem 18–1

At the end of last year a corporation's balance sheet showed the following stockholders' equity:

Common stock, $5 par value, 500,000 shares
    authorized, 400,000 shares issued...................... $2,000,000
Retained earnings:
  Appropriated for plant expansion $200,000
  Free and unappropriated....~............................... 185,000   385,000
      Total Stockholders' Equity............................. $2,385,000

During the current year the corporation completed the following transactions:

Jan.   5   The directors voted to appropriate and transfer an additional $50,000 from unappropriated retained earnings to retained earnings appropriated for plant expansion.

Nov. 2   Upon completion of the addition to the plant for which the retained earnings were appropriated, the corporation paid the contractor $237,500, the contracted price of the addition.

     15   The directors voted to return the balance of the Retained Earnings Appropriated for Plant Expansion account to (unappropriated) Retained Earnings. They also voted a stock dividend requiring the capitalization at $6.25 per share (the market price of the stock) of an amount of retained earnings equal to that returned to unappropriated retained earnings through the elimination of the plant expansion appropriation.

Dec. 28   Distributed the shares of the stock dividend declared on November 15.

Required:
1. Prepare general journal entries to record the foregoing transactions.
2. Prepare the stockholders' equity section of the corporation's balance sheet as it would appear after the distribution of the stock dividend.

Problem 18-2

The stockholders' equity in Hall Corporation consisted of the following at the beginning of the current year:

Common stock, $5 par value, 100,000 shares authorized, 50,000 shares issued and outstanding	$250,000
Premium on common stock	25,000
Retained earnings	70,000
Total Stockholders' Equity	$345,000

During the year the company completed these transactions affecting its stockholders' equity:

Apr. 14 Purchased 5,000 shares of treasury stock at $7.50 per share.

May 10 Received as a gift from the city of Butte a plot of land adjacent to the company's plant. The land had a $12,500 fair market value and was to be used to expand the company's plant and payroll.

June 23 The directors voted a 10 cents per share cash dividend payable on July 20 to the July 15 stockholders of record.

July 20 Paid the previously declared cash dividend.

Aug. 18 Sold 3,000 of the treasury shares at $8 per share.

Nov. 12 Sold the remaining treasury shares at $7.25 per share.

Dec. 18 The directors voted a 4% stock dividend distributable on January 20 to the January 15 stockholders of record. The stock was selling at $7.50 per share.

Dec. 31 Closed the Income Summary account and carried the company's $28,000 net income to Retained Earnings.

Required:
1. Prepare general journal entries to record the transactions.
2. Prepare a retained earnings statement for the year and the stockholders' equity section of the company's year-end balance sheet.

Problem 18-3

The following stockholder equity items appeared on Valley Corporation's year-end balance sheet last December 31:

Common stock, $10 par value, 50,000 shares authorized, 45,000 shares issued on which 3,000 are in the treasury	$450,000
Premium on common stock	22,500
Retained earnings of which $40,500 is restricted by the purchase of treasury stock	164,000
Cost of treasury stock	(40,500)
Total Stockholders' Equity	$596,000

The treasury stock was sold at $15 per share on August 10 of this year. Quarterly cash dividends of 20 cents per share were declared and paid in March,

June, and September; and on December 23 the directors voted a 20 cents per share cash dividend and a 2% stock dividend, both payable next January 25 to the January 15 stockholders of record. The stock was selling at $15 per share on December 23.

At the end of the year, after the cash and stock dividends were declared but before they were paid, the company treasurer prepared the following income statement for his own use:

VALLEY CORPORATION

Income Statement for Year Ended December 31, 19—

Sales	$750,000	
Gain on sale of land	5,000	
Gain on sale of treasury stock	4,500	$759,500
Less:		
Cost of goods sold	$457,000	
Selling and administrative expenses	160,000	
Interest expense	8,000	
Loss from wind storm	10,000	
Dividends declared	48,300	
Income taxes expense	55,000	738,300
Net Income		$ 21,200

Required:

Prepare for Valley Corporation (*a*) a single-step income statement for the year just ended; (*b*) a retained earnings statement; and (*c*) the stockholders' equity section of its year-end balance sheet.

Problem 18–4

Zoom Corporation's December 31, 197A, balance sheet carried the following stockholders' equity section:

Common stock, $5 par value, 100,000 shares authorized 80,000 shares issued of which 5,000 are in the treasury	$400,000	
Premium on common stock	40,000	
Total capital contributed for shares		$440,000
Retained earnings:		
Appropriated for plant expansion	$ 25,000	
Appropriated and restricted by the purchase of treasury stock	31,250	
Free and unappropriated	115,300	171,550
Total contributed capital and retained earnings		$611,550
Less cost of treasury stock		(31,250)
Total Stockholders' Equity		$580,300

At the end of 197B the corporation's unappropriated Retained Earnings account showed these amounts:

Retained Earnings

Date		Explanation	Debit	Credit	Balance
197B					
Jan.	1	Balance			115,300
May	12	Treasury stock appropriation		31,250	146,550
June	10	Cash dividend (payable July 23)	8,000		138,550
Dec.	15	Cash dividend (payable January 23)	8,000		130,550
	15	Stock dividend (distributable January 23)	28,000		102,550
	15	Plant expansion appropriation	25,000		77,550
	31	Net income		73,400	150,950

The treasury stock was sold on May 12, 197B, at $7 per share, and the June 10 cash dividend was paid on July 23. One new share will be distributed in the stock dividend for each 20 shares held on the record date.

Required:

1. Prepare entries to record the transactions reflected in the Retained Earnings account, and also entries to record the sale of the treasury stock and the payment of the June 10 cash dividend.
2. Prepare a 197B retained earnings statement for the company and also the owner equity section of its December 31, 197B balance sheet.

Problem 18-5

The following items appeared in the first two columns of a work sheet prepared to consolidate the balance sheets of Company A and Company B on the day Company A gained control of Company B by purchasing 17,000 shares of · its $5 par value common stock at $6.50 per share.

ASSETS

	Company A	Company B
Cash	$ 7,500	$ 11,000
Note receivable, Company B	10,000	
Accounts receivable, net	28,000	24,000
Inventories	42,000	35,000
Investment in Company B	110,500	
Equipment, net	80,000	70,000
Buildings, net	85,000	
Land	20,000	
Total Assets	$383,000	$140,000

EQUITIES

	Company A	Company B
Accounts payable	$ 21,000	$ 10,000
Note payable, Company A		10,000
Common stock	250,000	100,000
Retained earnings	112,000	20,000
Total Equities	$383,000	$140,000

At the time Company A acquired control of Company B it took Company B's note in exchange for $10,000 in cash and it sold and delivered $2,000 of equipment at cost to Company B on open account (account receivable). Both transactions are reflected in the foregoing accounts.

Required:

1. Prepare a work sheet to consolidate the balance sheets of the two companies and prepare a consolidated balance sheet.
2. Under the assumption that Company B earned $10,000 during the first year after it was acquired by Company A, paid out $6,000 in dividends, and retained the balance of the earnings in its operations, give the entry to eliminate Company A's investment in the subsidiary and Company B's stockholders' equity accounts at the year's end.

Alternate problems

Problem 18–1A

On January 12 of the current year the directors of a corporation voted to appropriate $40,000 of retained earnings and to retain in the business assets equal to the appropriation for use in expanding the corporation's plant. This was the fifth of such appropriations, and after it was recorded the corporation had the following contributed and retained capital:

Common stock, $10 par value, 200,000 shares authorized,	
150,000 shares issued	$1,500,000
Premium on common stock	37,500
Retained earnings appropriated for plant expansion	200,000
Unappropriated retained earnings	60,000
Total Stockholders' Equity	$1,797,500

On the following February 15 the corporation entered into a contract for the construction of the plant addition for which the retained earnings were appropriated; and on October 21, upon completion of the addition, the contractor was paid $193,500, the contract price.

At their November 10 meeting the directors voted to return the balance of the Retained Earnings Appropriated for Plant Expansion account to unappropriated retained earnings. They also voted a stock dividend requiring the capitalization at $12.50 per share (the market price of the stock) of an amount of retained earnings equal to that returned to unappropriated retained earnings through the elimination of the plant expansion appropriation.

Required:

1. Prepare entries to record (1) the January 12 appropriation, (2) the payment of the contractor, (3) the return of the appropriated retained earnings to unappropriated retained earnings, (4) the declaration of the stock dividend, and (5) the distribution of the stock dividend on December 20.
2. Prepare the stockholders' equity section of the corporation's balance sheet as of the close of business on December 20.

Problem 18–2A

At the beginning of the current year stockholders' equity in Butte Corporation consisted of the following:

Common stock, $25 par value, 15,000 shares authorized, 12,000 shares issued	$300,000
Premium on common stock	45,000
Retained earnings	115,000
Total Stockholders' Equity	$460,000

During the year the company completed these transactions:

May 10   Accepted as a gift from the city of Hillsdale a plot of land adjacent to the company's plant. The land had a $15,000 fair market value and was to be used in expanding the plant and the company's payroll.

June 15   Purchased 1,000 shares of treasury stock at $40 per share.

23   The directors voted a $0.50 per share cash dividend payable on July 25 to the July 20 stockholders of record.

July 25   Paid the dividend declared on June 23.

Aug. 3   Sold 500 of the treasury shares at $45 per share.

Oct. 12   Sold 500 of the treasury shares at $38 per share.

Dec. 15   The directors voted a $0.50 per share cash dividend payable on January 20 to the January 15 stockholders of record, and they voted a 2% stock dividend distributable on January 30 to the January 20 stockholders of record. The market value of the stock was $40 per share.

31   Closed the Income Summary account and carried the company's $31,000 net income to Retained Earnings.

Required:
1. Prepare general journal entries to record the transactions.
2. Prepare a retained earnings statement for the year and the stockholders' equity section of the company's year-end balance sheet.

Problem 18–3A

Last December 31, Hilltop Corporation's year-end balance sheet carried these stockholders' equity items:

Common stock, $25 par value, 25,000 shares authorized, 20,000 issued of which 1,000 are in the treasury	$500,000
Premium on common stock	40,000
Retained earnings of which $31,500 is restricted by the purchase of treasury stock	135,000
Cost of treasury stock	(31,500)
Total Stockholders' Equity	$643,500

The treasury stock was sold at $35 per share in August of this year, and quarterly cash dividends of $0.25 per share were declared and paid in April, July, and October. On December 21 of this year the directors declared a $0.25 per share cash dividend plus a 5% stock dividend, both payable during January of next year. The stock was selling at $35 per share on December 21.

On December 31, at the end of this year, the company treasurer prepared the following income statement for his own use:

HILLTOP CORPORATION
Income Statement for Year Ended December 31, 19—

Sales...	$650,000	
Gain on sale of unused factory land	15,000	
Gain on sale of treasury stock..................................	3,500	$668,500
Less:		
Cost of goods sold	$410,000	
Selling and administrative expenses.........................	125,000	
Interest expense	8,500	
Loss from fire..	10,000	
Dividends declared..	54,500	
Income taxes expense..	48,700	656,700
Net Income		$ 11,800

Required:
Prepare for Hilltop Corporation (*a*) a single-step income statement for the
year just ended; (*b*) a retained earnings statement; and (*c*) the stockholders'
equity section of its year-end balance sheet.

Problem 18–5A

The following assets and equities appeared on the balance sheets of Company
X and Company Y on the day Company X gained control of Company Y by
purchasing 3,600 shares of its $25 par value common stock at $35 per share.

ASSETS

	Company X	Company Y
Cash...	$ 8,000	$ 12,000
Note receivable, Company Y...............................	5,000	
Accounts receivable, net......................................	37,000	22,000
Inventories..	35,000	32,000
Investment in Company Y...................................	126,000	
Equipment, net...	75,000	70,000
Buildings, net...	100,000	
Land	25,000	
Total Assets	$411,000	$136,000

EQUITIES

Note payable, Company X....................................	$	$ 5,000
Accounts payable	24,000	11,000
Common stock..	300,000	100,000
Premium on common stock	30,000	5,000
Retained earnings	57,000	15,000
Total Equities	$411,000	$136,000

At the time Company X gained control of Company Y it took Company Y's
note in exchange for equipment that cost Company X $5,000 and it also sold
and delivered $2,000 of inventory at cost to Company Y on open account (ac-
count receivable). Both transactions are reflected in the foregoing accounts.

Required:

1. Prepare a work sheet to consolidate the balance sheets of the two companies and prepare a consolidated balance sheet.
2. Under the assumption Company Y earned $9,600 during the year after it was acquired by Company X, paid out $5,600 in dividends, and retained the balance in its operations, give the entry to eliminate Company X's investment in the subsidiary and Company Y's stockholders' equity accounts at the year's end.

Decision problem 18–1, terminology

PART 1, PACIFIC COMPANY. Each year for a number of past years the directors of Pacific Company have appropriated and placed in retained earnings appropriated for plant expansion an amount of retained earnings equal to half the year's net income, and the total of these appropriations has grown to $2,000,000. During these years the actual process of expanding and modernizing the plant has been going on; and expenditures for this purpose, financed in part by borrowing, have totaled $3,500,000. However, over the years no entries have been made in the Retained Earnings Appropriated for Plant Expansion account other than to record the appropriations. Consequently, at the last board meeting, following a statement by the company treasurer regarding the need to borrow $1,000,000 to finance a proposed new expansion, one of the company's directors stated that he could not understand why the company needed to borrow funds for expansion purposes when its latest balance sheet showed it had $2,000,000 of retained earnings appropriated for that purpose. The company treasurer blinked twice, swallowed hard, and said he would prepare a written statement explaining the nature of the retained earnings appropriated for plant expansion and why the company needed to borrow money. He then returned to his office and assigned the job of preparing the statement to you. Prepare it.

PART 2, LAKE TRUST COMPANY. Jane Roberts owns 100 shares of Lake Trust Company's common stock which her father gave her several years ago. The stock pays a $0.50 per share quarterly dividend, which has not been increased in a number of years; and while the dividend is not large, it is sufficient to give Miss Roberts a 5% return on the stock's present market value. Nevertheless, she is not happy with the dividend and confides that she has held the stock because she thought the dividend would soon be increased. She based her thinking on the company's balance sheet, which showed a large paid-in surplus, a large reserve for contingencies, and a very large balance of undivided profits. Consequently, she reasoned that with its contingencies taken care of and more cash than it needed from its paid-in surplus, Lake Trust Company would soon divide some of its undivided profits.

Lake Trust Company is a bank, and obviously Miss Roberts has been misled by some old-fashioned terminology on the bank's balance sheet. Therefore, in simple, nontechnical language explain the nature of the items Miss Roberts found misleading and supply a more meaningful name for each. Also, suggest probable reasons why in spite of its large balance of undivided profits, the bank has not increased its dividends.

Decision problem 18–2, Eastern Company

On October 3 of the current year Eastern Company gained control of Western Company through the purchase of 80% of Western Company's outstanding stock. At that time Western Company owed Eastern Company $2,000 for merchandise purchased on credit and $10,000 it had borrowed by giving a promissory note. The condensed October 3 balance sheets of the two companies follow:

EASTERN AND WESTERN COMPANIES
Balance Sheets, October 3, 19—

ASSETS

	Eastern Company	Western Company
Cash..	$ 5,000	$ 13,000
Notes receivable...	10,000	
Accounts receivable, net...	32,000	29,000
Inventories...	42,000	30,000
Investment in Western Company.............................	96,000	
Equipment, net...	75,000	60,000
Buildings, net...	80,000	
Land	20,000	
	$360,000	$132,000

EQUITIES

Accounts payable	$ 30,000	$ 7,000
Notes payable..		10,000
Common stock...	250,000	100,000
Retained earnings	80,000	15,000
	$360,000	$132,000

Prepare a consolidated balance sheet for Eastern Company and its subsidiary. Then write short explanations of why consolidated statements are prepared and the principles of consolidation.

Chapter 19

Long-term liabilities

■ When a business borrows money that is not to be repaid for a relatively long period of time, it may borrow by means of a mortgage, by means of bonds, or by issuing long-term notes.

Borrowing money with a mortgage

■ A business may borrow by placing a mortgage on some or all of its plant assets. A mortgage actually involves two legal documents. The first is a kind of promissory note called a *mortgage note,* which is secured by a second legal document called a *mortgage* or a *mortgage contract.* In the mortgage note the mortgagor, the one who mortgages property, promises to repay the money borrowed. The mortgage or mortgage contract requires a number of things of the mortgagor. Normally, among other things, the mortgagor must keep the property in a good state of repair, carry adequate insurance, pay the interest on the mortgage note, and, often, make payments to reduce the mortgage liability. These duties and responsibilities are always set forth in the mortgage contract, which also grants the mortgage holder certain rights. Among these is the right to foreclose in case the mortgagor fails in any of the pledged duties, such as paying interest, keeping the property in repair, or carrying adequate insurance. In a foreclosure a court takes possession of the mortgaged property for the mortgage holder and may order its sale. If the property is sold, the proceeds go first to pay court costs and the claims of the mortgage holder, after which any money remaining is paid to the former owner of the property.

When a business borrows by means of a mortgage, the transaction commonly involves the business and one bank or one insurance company. Since banks and insurance companies are normally restricted in the size of loans they may extend to a single borrower, there is always a limitation on the size of a mortgage loan. Consequently, large concerns often cannot find a single lender who wishes to and may legally lend to one company the amount the company wishes to borrow. In such cases, in the place of a mortgage loan, bonds are often issued. Bonds make possible the division of a large loan into portions that may be sold to many small investors.

Borrowing money by issuing bonds
■ Borrowing money by issuing bonds is similar to borrowing by giving a mortgage. Actually in many cases the only real difference is that a number of bonds, often in denominations of $1,000, are issued in the place of a single mortgage note. For all practical purposes each bond is a promissory note, promising to pay a definite sum of money to its holder, or owner of record, at a fixed future date. Like promissory notes, bonds bear interest; and like a mortgage note, they are often secured by a mortgage. However, since bonds may be owned and transferred during their lives by a number of people, they differ from promissory notes in that they do not name the lender.

When a company issues bonds secured by a mortgage, it normally sells the bonds to an investment firm, known as the *underwriter,* which in turn resells the bonds to the public. In addition to the underwriter, the company issuing bonds selects a trustee to represent the bondholders. In most cases the trustee is a large bank or trust company to whom the company issuing the bonds executes and delivers the mortgage which acts as security for the bonds. It is the duty of the trustee to see that the company fulfills all the pledged responsibilities of the mortgage contract, or as it is often called the *deed of trust.* It is also the duty of the trustee to foreclose if any pledges are not fulfilled.

Who may issue bonds
■ Most large companies are organized as corporations, and corporations have made extensive use of bonds as a means of financing. However, the sale of bonds is not a privilege limited to corporations. The federal government issues bonds, and most state and local governmental units make wide use of bonds in financing projects. However, this text, as most accounting texts, limits its consideration of bonds to corporate bonds.

Classification of bonds
■ Over the years corporation lawyers and financiers have created a wide variety of bonds, each with slightly different combinations of characteristics. As a result, a single method of classifying bonds is impossible, and bonds are classified in a number of ways. Two common ways

are, (1) as to the method of paying principal and interest and (2) as to type of security.

Bonds classified as to payment of principal and interest

When bonds are classified as to method of paying the principal, they may be *serial bonds* or *sinking fund bonds*. When serial or term bonds are issued, portions of the issue become due and are paid in installments over a period of years. For example, a corporation may issue $5,000,000 of serial bonds with the provision that $500,000 of the bonds become due and are to be paid each year until all are paid. Sinking fund bonds provide in their deed of trust that a sinking fund be created to pay the bonds at maturity. Sinking funds are discussed in more detail later in this chapter.

Bonds may be issued without provision for either installment payments or a sinking fund. Such bonds are normally payable at maturity and are often to be paid with funds from the sale of a new bond issue.

When bonds are classified as to method of interest payment, they are either *registered bonds* or *coupon bonds*. Ownership of registered bonds is registered or recorded with the issuing corporation, which offers some protection from loss or theft. Title to such bonds is transferred in much the same manner as title to stock is transferred. Interest payments are usually made by checks mailed to the registered owners.

Coupon bonds secure their name from the interest coupons attached to each bond. Each coupon calls for payment on the interest payment date of the interest due on the bond to which it is attached. The coupons are detached as they become due and are deposited with a bank for collection in much the same manner as an out-of-town note is deposited for collection. Often ownership of a coupon bond is not registered. Such unregistered bonds are payable to bearer or are bearer paper, and ownership is transferred by delivery. Sometimes bonds are registered as to principal with interest payments by coupons.

Bonds classified as to security

Bonds may be secured or unsecured. Unsecured bonds are called *debentures* and depend upon the general credit standing of their issuing corporation for security. Only financially strong corporations are able to sell unsecured bonds. When bonds are secured, they are normally secured by mortgages or liens on assets. Such bonds are often classified according to the type of assets pledged for their security. Some of the more common classifications are *real estate mortgage bonds, equipment trust bonds,* and *collateral trust bonds.* An issue of real estate mortgage bonds is normally secured by a mortgage on a portion or all of the issuing corporation's plant and equipment. Equipment trust bonds are commonly issued by railroads and are secured by a mortgage on rolling stock. Collateral trust bonds are secured by stocks, bonds, and other negotiable instruments deposited with a trustee.

■ A corporation in need of long-term funds may secure these funds by issuing either additional common stock, preferred stock, or bonds. Each has its advantages and disadvantages.

Stockholders are the owners of a corporation, and bondholders are creditors. Issuing additional common stock spreads control of management over a larger number of owners and spreads earnings over more shares. As creditors, bondholders do not share in either management or earnings. Furthermore, since bonds are usually secured by a mortgage or lien and interest payments are fixed in amount, the interest rate paid on bonds is normally less than the dividend rates on either common or preferred stocks.

As owners, stockholders receive dividends only when income sufficient for their payment has been earned. Whenever sufficient income has not been earned, stockholders receive no dividends and must wait for dividends until sufficient income is earned. This is not true of bondholders. Interest payments to bondholders must be made when due whether any income is earned or not, because if such payments are not made when due, the bondholders may foreclose and take the assets pledged for their security.

In this age of high corporation income taxes, taxes are also always a factor in a decision between issuing stocks or bonds. Bond interest is a deductible expense in calculating income subject to taxes, while dividends are a sharing of income and are not a deductible expense. Because of this the federal income tax is often one of the most important factors in a decision between issuing preferred stock or bonds. The importance of this factor is demonstrated in Illustration 19–1 where the results of three methods of securing additional funds are shown.

Often the deciding factor between issuing additional stocks or issuing bonds is the estimated amount of future earnings and their probable stability. If the rate earned per dollar invested is expected to be greater than the bond interest rate or the dividend rate on preferred stock, and is also expected to be stable, it is usually to the advantage of the common stockholders to issue either bonds or preferred stock. On the other hand, if the expected earnings rate is less than the bond interest rate or the rate of dividends on preferred stock, the common stockholders receive a greater return if additional common stock rather than either bonds or preferred stock is issued.

For example, assume that the Apex Corporation which has 20,000 shares of $100 par value common stock outstanding wishes to raise an additional $2,000,000 for expansion. The results of three methods of securing the additional funds are shown in Illustration 19–1. This table shows the results first with an assumed $600,000 operating income and then with an assumed operating income of $70,000 per year. Plan No. 1 assumes Apex Corporation issues an additional $2,000,000 of common stock which brings its common stock outstanding to 40,000 shares. Plan No. 2 assumes the additional funds are raised by issuing $2,000,000 of 7%, cumulative preferred stock. Plan No. 3 assumes $2,000,000

	Operating Income of $600,000			Operating Income of $70,000		
	Plan No. 1	Plan No. 2	Plan No. 3	Plan No. 1	Plan No. 2	Plan No. 3
Common stock now outstanding (20,000 shares)	$2,000,000	$2,000,000	$2,000,000	$2,000,000	$2,000,000	$2,000,000
Additional common stock, $100 par (20,000 shares)	2,000,000			2,000,000		
Preferred stock, 7% cumulative		2,000,000			2,000,000	
6% bonds			2,000,000			2,000,000
Total capitalization	$4,000,000	$4,000,000	$4,000,000	$4,000,000	$4,000,000	$4,000,000
Operating income before federal income tax	$ 600,000	$ 600,000	$ 600,000	$ 70,000	$ 70,000	$ 70,000
Deduct: Bond interest expense			120,000			120,000
Income (or deficit*) after bond interest expense	$ 600,000	$ 600,000	$ 480,000	$ 70,000	$ 70,000	$ 50,000*
Deduct: Federal and state income taxes of 50%	300,000	300,000	240,000	35,000	35,000	
Net income (or deficit*) after federal taxes	$ 300,000	$ 300,000	$ 240,000	$ 35,000	$ 35,000	$ 50,000*
Preferred dividends		140,000			140,000	
Income (or deficit*) after taxes and preferred dividends or bond interest	$ 300,000	$ 160,000	$ 240,000	$ 35,000	$ 105,000*	$ 50,000*
Income (or deficit*) per share of common stock	$7.50	$8.00	$12.00	$0.875	$5.25*	$2.50*

Illustration
19–1

of 6% bonds are sold. Obviously, Plan No. 3 is to the advantage of the original common stockholders if earnings are sufficiently large. However, when earnings are less than the interest on the bonds, Plan No. 1 offers the best return to the original stockholders.

Notice the effect on the three financing methods of the assumed 50% combined federal and state income tax rate. Actually, since corporation rates have reached this level, a choice between issuing stock and issuing bonds is normally a choice between common stock and bonds. Preferred stock might be issued, but normally only if the issuing corporation expected that during the life of a bond issue there might be several years during which it would not have sufficient pretax earnings to pay the bond interest. In such a case, if preferred stock were issued, the dividends on the stock could be postponed during these years.

Recording bond transactions

■ A decision to issue bonds rests with the board of directors. However, many corporations provide in their charters that such a decision must be approved by the stockholders.

When bonds are to be issued, after the resolution for their issuance is passed by the board and approved by the stockholders, the bonds are printed, and the deed of trust is drawn and deposited with the trustee of the bondholders. The deed of trust always states the total amount of bonds that is secured by it and that may be issued and sold. When the deed of trust is deposited, an entry is made to record the authorization of the bond issue. The entry is usually a memorandum entry and appears somewhat as follows:

| Dec. | 21 | On this day Simplex Corporation deposited with Northern Trust Company, trustee for its bondholders, a deed of trust authorizing the issue of $1,000,000 of 6%, 10-year bonds with interest payable semi-annually on each July 1 and January 1. | | | |

In addition to the memorandum entry in the General Journal, a memorandum as to the amount of bonds authorized is also placed in the Bonds Payable account in the ledger.

Often when an issue of bonds is authorized, more bonds are authorized than are to be immediately issued. For example, if a corporation has an immediate need for only $750,000 but the property it is mortgaging is ample to secure a $1,000,000 issue, a deed of trust is drawn for the larger amount, and $1,000,000 of bonds are authorized. Then only $750,000, the amount necessary to cover immediate needs, is sold. The remaining bonds are held in reserve to be sold when additional funds are needed. In such a situation where only $750,000 is presently needed but the property being mortgaged is sufficient to secure a $1,000,000 issue, if the deed of trust were drawn for only the $750,000 immediately needed, it would be necessary to use a second mortgage as security if an additional loan of $250,000 were later needed. Issuing a second mortgage would be undesirable because the claims of the first mortgage would take priority over those of the second, causing the second mortgage to be less desirable, and normally making a higher rate of interest necessary on it.

After the deed of trust is deposited with the trustee of the bondholders, a corporation may sell its bonds. For example, if on January 1 Simplex Corporation sells $750,000 of the bonds, the authorization of which was previously illustrated, the entry to record the sale is:

Jan.	1	Cash..	750,000.00	
		Bonds Payable		750,000.00
		Sold $750,000 of 6% bonds.		

When a corporation with bonds outstanding prepares a balance sheet, it should show both the amount of bonds authorized and the amount issued and outstanding. For example, if Simplex Corporation prepares a balance sheet immediately after the bond sale just recorded, it may show the liability as follows:

Long-Term Liabilities:
  First mortgage, 6% bonds payable, due December
    31, 1982:
    Authorized $1,000,000
    Unissued... 250,000
    Issued and outstanding $750,000

When both bonds authorized and bonds issued are shown on the balance sheet, owners of the bonds are in a position to judge whether the assets pledged as security are ample to cover the entire issue.

Authorized but unissued bonds may be sold and issued whenever funds are needed. For example, if after issuing $750,000 of the foregoing bonds Simplex Corporation finds itself in need of additional funds, it may issue the remaining bonds. When it does so, it will make this entry:

July	1	Cash..	250,000.00	
		Bonds Payable		250,000.00
		Issued the remaining authorized 6% bonds.		

After the bonds of the last entry are sold, Simplex Corporation has $1,000,000 of 6% bonds outstanding. Consequently, on each July 1 and January 1 thereafter, when it pays the semiannual interest on these bonds, it will make the following entry to record the payment:

Jan.	1	Bond Interest Expense	30,000.00	
		Cash...		30,000.00
		Made the semiannual interest payment on $1,000,000 of 6% bonds.		

At the end of their life, when the bonds are paid and retired, the entry to record their retirement is:

Dec.	31	Bonds Payable	1,000,000.00	
		Cash...		1,000,000.00
		To record the retirement of $1,000,000 of 6% bonds.		

Bonds sold between interest dates ■ When bond certificates are printed, they promise to pay a designated amount of interest on each specified interest date. Sometimes bonds are sold on their interest dates; more often they are sold between interest dates. When bonds are sold between interest dates, it is customary to charge purchasers for interest accrued since the previous interest payment and to return this accrued interest to the purchasers on the next interest date. For example, assume that on March 1, a corporation sells $100,000 of 6% bonds on which interest is payable semiannually on each January 1 and July 1. The entry to record the sale between interest dates is:

Mar.	1	Cash...	101,000.00	
		Bond Interest Expense		1,000.00
		Bonds Payable		100,000.00
		To record the sale of $100,000 of bonds on which two months' interest has accrued.		

At the end of four months, on the July 1 semiannual interest payment date, the purchasers of these bonds are paid a full six months' interest. This payment includes four months' interest earned by the bondholders after March 1 and the two months' accrued interest collected from them at the time the bonds were sold. The entry to record the payment is:

July	1	Bond Interest Expense	3,000.00	
		Cash...		3,000.00
		To record payment of the semiannual interest on the bonds.		

After this entry is posted, the Bond Interest Expense account has a $2,000 debit balance and appears as follows:

Bond Interest Expense

July 1 (Payment)	3,000.00	Mar. 1 (Accrued interest)	1,000.00

The $2,000 debit balance is the interest on the $100,000 of bonds at 6% for the four months from March 1 to July 1.

Beginning students often think it strange to charge bond purchasers for accrued interest when bonds are sold between interest dates, and to return this accrued interest in the next interest payment. However, this is the custom, all bond transactions are "plus accrued interest"; and there is a good reason for the practice. For instance, if a corporation sells portions of a bond issue to different purchasers on different dates during an interest period without charging for accrued interest, it must keep records of the bondholders and the dates on which they bought bonds. Otherwise it cannot pay the correct amount of interest to each bondholder. However, if it charges each purchaser for accrued interest at the time of his purchase, it need not keep records of the purchasers and their purchase dates, since it can pay a full period's interest to all purchasers for the period in which they purchase their bonds and every purchaser receives the interest he has earned and gets back the accrued interest paid at the time of his purchase.

Bond interest rates
■ When a corporation borrows by issuing bonds, the interest rate it must pay depends upon what lenders consider their risks to be in lending to the corporation and upon the current *market rate for bond interest*. Borrowers with lower credit standings and those in high-risk industries must pay a higher rate of interest; and the market rate for bond interest is the rate borrowers are willing to pay and lenders are willing to take for the use of money at the level of risk involved. It fluctuates from day to day at any level of risk as the supply and demand for loanable funds fluctuate.

When a corporation issues bonds, it specifies in the deed of trust and on each bond the interest rate it will pay. This rate is called the *contract rate*. Normally, when a board of directors authorizes a bond issue, it estimates the interest rate the market will demand of the corporation and offers a contract rate equal to its estimate. However, a period of time always elapses between the authorization of a bond issue and its sale, and during this period bond interest rates fluctuate. Consequently, when bonds are finally sold, their contract rate seldom coincides with the market rate.

Bonds sold at a discount
■ When a corporation offers a bond issue with a contract rate of interest below the prevailing market rate for the risk involved, the bonds can be sold only at a discount. For example, assume that a corporation offers $100,000 of 6%, 10-year bonds on which interest is payable semi-annually. Assume further that on the day the bonds are offered the prevailing interest rate for like bonds is slightly in excess of 6%, and as a

result the highest bid for the bonds is $99,000. If the corporation accepts this bid and sells the bonds, the entry to record the sale is:

Jan.	1	Cash...	99,000.00	
		Discount on Bonds Payable	1,000.00	
		Bonds Payable		100,000.00
		Sold bonds at a discount.		

The corporation of this illustration receives $99,000 that it may use for 10 years. For the use of the $99,000 it agrees to repay $100,000 and to pay $6,000 interest during each of the 10 years, a total of $60,000. Or, in other words, to the corporation the cost of using the $99,000 for 10 years is the difference between the amount received and the amounts to be paid, or is:

```
Amounts to be paid:
  Face of the bonds .............................................. $100,000
  Interest (6% annually for 10 years) ........................    60,000
    Total to be paid............................................... $160,000
Amount received:
  Bid price for the bonds........................................    99,000
  Cost of the $99,000 for 10 years........................... $ 61,000
```

If the $61,000 cost is divided equally over the 10-year life of the issue, the annual cost is $6,100. Furthermore, if the $6,100 is expressed as a percentage of the $99,000, the annual interest rate is in effect 6.16+% ($6,100 ÷ $99,000 = 0.0616+). Obviously, then, a discount has the effect of adjusting and increasing an offered contract rate.

The corporation of this illustration receives $99,000 for its bonds, but in 10 years must repay $100,000. The $1,000 discount is a cost of using the $99,000 which must be paid at maturity. However, since each year in the life of the issue benefits from the use of the $99,000, it is only fair that each should bear a fair share of the $1,000 discount.

The accounting procedure for dividing a discount and charging a fair share to each accounting period in the life of the applicable bond issue is called *amortizing* a discount. There are several methods of amortizing a discount, a common one is the straight-line method. With this method, a discount is divided equally and an equal portion is charged to each accounting period in the life of the bond issue to which it applies. For example, if the $1,000 discount on the bonds of this illustration is amortized by the straight-line method, each year in the 10-year life of the issue must bear $100. Furthermore, if each year bears $100, then each semiannual interest period must bear $50. Thus, if the $1,000 discount is amortized by the straight-line method, the following entry is made on each semiannual interest payment date to record the interest payment and the discount amortization:

July	1	Bond Interest Expense.................................	3,050.00	
		Cash..		3,000.00
		Discount on Bonds Payable......................		50.00
		To record payment of six months' interest and amortization of one twentieth of the discount.		

The $50 discount amortization at the time of each interest payment increases recorded bond interest expense $50 each six months and $100 each year. Also, the $50 amortization each six months completely writes off the $1,000 discount by the end of the issue's 10-year life.

Bonds sold at a premium

■ When a corporation offers an issue with a contract rate higher than the market rate, purchasers will normally pay more than par, and the bonds will be sold at a premium. For example, assume that a corporation offers $100,000 of $6\frac{1}{2}$%, 10-year bonds on which interest is payable semiannually. Assume further that the market rate on similar bonds is below $6\frac{1}{2}$% on the day the bonds are offered and as a result they are sold at a premium, for $102,000. The entry to record the sale is:

Jan.	1	Cash..	102,000.00	
		Premium on Bonds Payable....................		2,000.00
		Bonds Payable		100,000.00
		Sold bonds at a premium.		

The corporation of this illustration received $102,000 that it may use. To this corporation, like the previous one, the cost of using the $102,000 is the difference between the amount received and the amounts to be paid, or is:

Amounts to be paid:
Face of the bonds $100,000
Interest ($6\frac{1}{2}$% annually for 10 years) 65,000
Total to be paid... $165,000
Amount received 102,000
Cost of the $102,000 for 10 years .... $ 63,000

And, if the $63,000 cost is divided equally over the 10 years of the issue, the annual cost is $6,300, or in effect 6.18−% ($6,300 ÷ $102,000 = 0.0618−) per year. Obviously, then, a premium like a discount is also an adjustment of an offered contract rate. However, a premium has the effect of decreasing an offered contract rate.

When bonds are sold at a premium, since the premium is in effect an adjustment of the contract rate, the premium should be amortized if each accounting period in the issue's life is to bear its fair share of the borrowed money's cost. If a premium is amortized on a straight-line basis, an equal amount is written off each period. For example, if the $2,000 premium of this illustration is amortized on a straight-line basis, $200 must be written off each year or $100 must be written off with each interest payment. If $100 is written off with each payment, the entry to record the payment and the premium amortization is:

July	1	Bond Interest Expense....................................	3,150.00	
		Premium on Bonds Payable...........................	100.00	
		Cash..		3,250.00
		To record payment of six months' interest and the amortization of one twentieth of the premium.		

Observe in the foregoing entry that the premium amortization has the effect of reducing the recorded interest expense from the $3,250 paid the bondholders to $3,150.

Accrued bond interest expense ■ Often when bonds are sold, the bond interest periods do not coincide with the issuing company's accounting periods. In such cases it is necessary at the end of each accounting period to make an adjustment for interest accrued. For example, on March 1, 1973, a corporation having yearly accounting periods which end on December 31, sells $100,000 of 6%, 20-year bonds for $98,800. The interest on the bonds is to be paid semiannually on each March 1 and September 1. The entry to record the September 1 semiannual interest payment is:

Sept.	1	Bond Interest Expense....................................	3,030.00	
		Discount on Bonds Payable		30.00
		Cash..		3,000.00
		To record payment of six months' interest on the bonds and amortization of the discount.		

On December 31, 1973, and on each December 31 thereafter throughout the life of this issue, there are always four months' accrued interest on these bonds. The interest will not be paid until the following March 1; therefore, at each year-end an adjusting entry like the following is required:

Dec.	31	Bond Interest Expense....................................	2,020.00	
		Discount on Bonds Payable		20.00
		Bond Interest Payable.............................		2,000.00
		To record four months' accrued interest.		

Then, when the interest is paid on the following March 1, an entry like this is required:

Mar.	1	Bond Interest Expense...................................	1,010.00	
		Bond Interest Payable..................................	2,000.00	
		Discount on Bonds Payable		10.00
		Cash..		3,000.00
		To record payment of interest on bonds, a portion of which was previously accrued.		

Premiums and discounts on bonds outstanding less than their full term ■ The bonds previously illustrated were either 10- or 20-year bonds and were assumed to be outstanding in each case a full 10 or 20 years. Often bonds are not outstanding the full term of years in their authorized lives. For example, assume that in November, 1972, a $1,000,000 20-year bond issue dated January 1, 1973, and due January 1, 1993, was authorized. Assume further that interest is payable semiannually on the issue on each January 1 and July 1 and that the issue was sold on March 1, 1973, at a $47,600 discount.

Between January 1, 1973, and January 1, 1993, is a period of 20 years, or 240 months; but between March 1, 1973, and January 1, 1993, is only 238 months. Consequently, since the bonds will be outstanding only 238 months, the discount must be amortized over this shorter period. Therefore, when interest is paid on July 1, 1973, four months' discount, or $800 ($47,600 \times \frac{4}{238} = $800), should be written off; and on January 1, 1974, and at the end of each six months thereafter, six months' discount, or $1,200 ($47,600 \times \frac{6}{238} = $1,200), should be amortized.

Costs of a bond issue ■ When bonds are issued, there are certain costs such as attorneys' fees, printing, and so on. Often their sum is material in relation to the bond issue; and theoretically these costs are prepaid expenses that should be set up in a separate account and written off over the life of the issue. However, as a practical measure such costs are commonly added to the discount if the bonds are sold at a discount, or are deducted from the premium if sold at a premium, and are then written off with the premium or discount. This treatment is not theoretically accurate; however, it is long established and has the same effect as the more accurate treatment of such costs as a separate prepaid item.

Redemption of bonds ■ Bonds are commonly issued with the provision that they may be redeemed at the issuing corporation's option, usually upon the payment of a premium. Such bonds are known as *callable bonds*. Corporations commonly insert redemption clauses in deeds of trust because if interest rates decline, it may be advantageous to call and redeem outstanding bonds and issue in their place new bonds paying a lower interest rate.

Not all bonds have a provision giving their issuing company the right to call. However, even though the right is not provided, a company may secure the same effect by purchasing its bonds on the open market. Often such action is wise when a company has funds available and its bonds are selling at a price below par plus their unamortized premium or at a price below par minus unamortized discount. For example, a company has outstanding on their interest date $1,000,000 of bonds on which there is $12,000 unamortized premium. The bonds are selling at 98½% of par value, and the company decides to buy and retire one tenth of the issue. The entry to record the purchase and retirement is:

Apr.	1	Bonds Payable	100,000.00	
		Premium on Bonds Payable..........................	1,200.00	
		Gain on the Retirement of Bonds		2,700.00
		Cash..		98,500.00
		To record the retirement of bonds.		

The retirement results in a $2,700 gain. This gain is the difference between the cash given and the retired bonds' par value plus the applicable premium.

Back a paragraph or so the statement was made that the bonds were selling at 98½% of par value. Bond quotations are commonly made in this manner. For example, a bond may be quoted for sale at 101¼. This means the bond is for sale at 101¼% of its par value, plus accrued interest, of course, if applicable.

Convertible bonds ■ To make an issue more attractive, bond owners may be given the right to exchange their bonds for a fixed number of shares of the issuing company's common stock. Such bonds are known as convertible bonds. They offer investors initial investment security and, if the issuing company prospers, an opportunity to share in the prosperity by converting their bonds to stock. Conversion is always at the bondholders' option and is not exercised except when to do so is to their advantage.

When bonds are converted into stock, the conversion changes creditor equity into ownership equity. The generally accepted rule for measuring the contribution for the issued shares is that the book value of the liability becomes the book value of the capital contributed for the new shares. For example, assume that (1) a company has outstanding $1,000,000 of bonds upon which there is $8,000 unamortized discount; (2) the bonds are convertible at the rate of a $1,000 bond for 18 shares of $50 par value common stock; and (3) $100,000 in bonds have been presented on their interest date for conversion. The entry to record the conversion is:

May	1	Bonds Payable	100,000.00		
		Discount on Bonds Payable		800.00	
		Common Stock....................................		90,000.00	
		Premium on Common Stock		9,200.00	
		To record the conversion of bonds.			

Note in the foregoing entry that the bonds' $99,200 book value sets the accounting value for the capital contributed. Usually when bonds have a conversion privilege, it is not exercised until the stock's market value and normal dividend payments are sufficiently high to make the conversion profitable to the bondholders.

Bond sinking fund

■ Although bonds may offer a smaller return than either common or preferred stocks, they appeal to a portion of the investing public. Normally the appeal results from their fixed return and greater security. Security is usually important to bond investors. A corporation issuing bonds may offer investors a measure of security by placing a mortgage on certain of its assets. Often it will give additional security by agreeing in its deed of trust to create a *bond sinking fund*. A bond sinking fund is a fund of assets which is accumulated to pay the bondholders at maturity.

When a corporation issuing bonds agrees to create a bond sinking fund, it normally agrees to create the fund by making periodic cash deposits with a sinking fund trustee. It is the duty of the trustee to safeguard the cash, to invest it in good sound securities, and to add the interest or dividends earned to the sinking fund. Generally, when the bonds become due, it is also the duty of the sinking fund trustee to sell the sinking fund securities and to use the proceeds to pay the bondholders. The sinking fund trustee may or may not be the trustee with whom the deed of trust is deposited.

When a sinking fund is created, the amount that must be deposited periodically in order to provide a sum sufficiently large to retire a bond issue at maturity will depend upon the net rate of compound interest that can be earned on the invested funds. The rate is a compound rate because earnings are continually reinvested by the sinking fund trustee to earn an additional return, and it is a net rate because the trustee commonly deducts the fee for his services from the earnings.

To illustrate the operation of a sinking fund, assume a corporation issues $1,000,000 of 10-year bonds and agrees to deposit with a sinking fund trustee at the end of each year in the issue's life sufficient cash to create a fund large enough to retire the bonds at maturity. If the trustee is able to invest the funds in such a manner as to earn a 5% net return, $79,504 must be deposited each year and the fund will grow to maturity (in rounded dollars) as shown in Illustration 19–2.

End of Year	Amount Deposited	Interest Earned on Fund Balance	Balance in Fund after Deposit and Interest
1	$79,504	-0-	$ 79,504
2	79,504	$ 3,975	162,983
3	79,504	8,149	250,636
4	79,504	12,532	342,672
5	79,504	17,134	439,310
6	79,504	21,966	540,780
7	79,504	27,039	647,323
8	79,504	32,366	759,193
9	79,504	37,960	876,657
10	79,504	43,839*	1,000,000

Illustration 19–2

*Adjusted for rounding.

Calculating the amount that must be deposited each year in order that the deposits and their interest will produce a fund of a required size is a problem reserved for a course in mathematics of finance or advanced accounting. It is deemed sufficient here that the student understand how such a fund operates.

When a sinking fund is created by periodic deposits, the entry to record the amount deposited each year appears as follows:

Dec.	31	Bond Sinking Fund	79,504.00	
		Cash..		79,504.00
		Deposited cash with sinking fund trustee.		

Each year the sinking fund trustee invests the amount deposited, and each year he collects and reports the earnings on the investments. His earnings report results in a journal entry to record the sinking fund income. For example, if $79,504 is deposited at the end of the first year in the sinking fund, the accumulation of which is shown in Illustration 19–2, and 5% is earned, the entry to record the sinking fund earnings at the end of the second year is:

Dec.	31	Bond Sinking Fund...............................	3,975.00	
		Sinking Fund Earnings.....................		3,975.00
		To record the sinking fund earnings.		

Sinking fund earnings appear on the income statement as financial revenue in the "other revenues and expenses section."

The assets resulting from sinking fund earnings, as well as sinking fund deposits and sinking fund investments, in other words, the items making up a sinking fund, are the property of the company creating the fund and should appear on its balance sheet in the long-term investments section, as in Illustration 19–3 near the end of this chapter.

When bonds payable mature, it is usually the duty of the sinking fund trustee to convert the fund's investments into cash and pay the bondholders. Normally if the sinking fund securities when sold produce the amount needed to pay the bondholders, the trustee pays them and notifies the corporation. When the corporation receives notice that its bonds have been paid, it makes the following entry:

Jan.	3	Bonds Payable	1,000,000.00	
		Bond Sinking Fund..........................		1,000,000.00
		To record the payment of our bonds		
		by the sinking fund trustee.		

Sinking fund investments normally earn slightly more or less than anticipated. Consequently, when a sinking fund is liquidated there is always either a little more or a little less cash in the fund than is needed to pay the bondholders. If there is more cash than needed after the bondholders are paid, the excess is returned to the corporation by the trustee. The entry to record receipt of returned sinking fund cash is:

Jan.	3	Cash..	3,105.00	
		Bond Sinking Fund..........................		3,105.00
		Unused sinking fund balance		
		returned by sinking fund trustee.		

If there is insufficient cash in a sinking fund with which to pay the bondholders when bonds become due, the debtor corporation must pay the shortage into the fund. The entry to record this is:

Jan.	3	Bond Sinking Fund	1,382.20	
		Cash...		1,382.20
		To record payment of cash to the sinking		
		fund trustee to cover the fund's deficit.		

Restriction on dividends due to outstanding bonds

■ If a corporation disburses in dividends all assets acquired each year through earnings and pays out still more assets in sinking fund deposits, it may find itself within a few years without sufficient assets, particularly current assets, to operate and unable either to pay dividends or make sinking fund deposits. To prevent this, a deed of trust may restrict the dividends a corporation may pay while its bonds are outstanding.

When dividends are restricted by a deed of trust, the restriction may provide that the corporation may pay dividends in any year only to the extent that the year's earnings exceed sinking fund requirements. Or the restriction may require the corporation to appropriate retained earnings each year equal to the year's sinking fund requirements. If the latter method is used, its purpose is to reduce dividend payments by reducing the balance of the Retained Earnings account available to absorb dividend charges.

To illustrate the appropriation each year of retained earnings equal to the year's sinking fund requirements, assume that the corporation whose bond fund accumulations are shown in Illustration 19–2 must make such appropriations. Assume further that the corporation is required by its deed of trust to appropriate an amount of retained earnings each year equal to the sum of its sinking fund deposit plus the year's sinking fund earnings. If the corporation makes the appropriations, it will appropriate $79,504 the first year and will record the appropriation as follows:

Dec.	31	Retained Earnings...	79,504.00	
		Retained Earnings Appropriated for		
		Bonded Indebtedness...........................		79,504.00
		To record the appropriation of retained earnings equal to the deposit in the bond sinking fund.		

Only $79,504 must be appropriated the first year because the sinking fund deposit of the year was made at the year's end and, consequently, there were no sinking fund earnings. However, if the sinking fund earns a 5% return, at the end of the second year the corporation must appropriate $83,479 of retained earnings. This is the sum of the second year's deposit and the second year's sinking fund earnings. Furthermore, if 5% is earned, the third year's appropriation will be $87,653 ($79,504 + $8,149 = $87,653) and the appropriations will continue to grow throughout the life of the bond issue.

After a bond issue has been paid, the appropriations have served their purpose and the amount appropriated during the life of the issue is returned to unappropriated retained earnings with an entry like this:

Jan.	15	Retained Earnings Appropriated for		
		Bonded Indebtedness..........................	1,000,000.00	
		Retained Earnings		1,000,000.00
		To return the retained earnings appropriated for bonded indebtedness to unappropriated retained earnings.		

Terminology

When a corporation is required by a deed of trust to appropriate retained earnings each year equal to the year's sinking fund requirements, the total of such appropriations may appear on its balance sheet in the retained earnings section as "Retained earnings appropriated for bonded

Best Corporation
Balance Sheet, December 31, 19—
ASSETS

Current Assets:

Cash		$ 15,000
Able Corporation common stock		5,000
Accounts receivable	$ 50,000	
Less allowance for doubtful accounts	1,000	49,000
Merchandise inventory		115,000
Subscriptions receivable, common stock		15,000
Prepaid expenses		1,000
Total Current Assets		$200,000

Long-Term Investments:

Bond sinking fund		$ 15,000
Toledo Corporation common stock		5,000
Total Long-Term Investments		20,000

Plant Assets:

Land		$ 28,000
Buildings	$190,000	
Less accumulated depreciation	30,000	160,000
Store equipment	$ 85,000	
Less accumulated depreciation	20,000	65,000
Total Plant Assets		253,000

Intangible Assets:

Goodwill	23,000

Deferred Charges:

Unamortized moving costs	4,000
Total Assets	$500,000

LIABILITIES

Current Liabilities:

Notes payable	$ 10,000	
Accounts payable	24,000	
State and federal income taxes payable	16,000	
Total Current Liabilities		$ 50,000

Long-Term Liabilities:

First 6% real estate mortgage bonds, due in 1982	$100,000	
Deduct: Unamortized discount	2,000	98,000
Total Liabilities		$148,000

CONTRIBUTED CAPITAL AND RETAINED EARNINGS

Contributed Capital:

Common stock, $100 par value per share, authorized 2,500 shares, issued 2,000 shares	$200,000	
Unissued common stock subscribed, 250 shares	25,000	
Capital contributed by the stockholders in excess of the par value of their shares	33,000	
Total Contributed Capital		$258,000

Retained Earnings:

Appropriated retained earnings:			
Appropriated for bonded indebtedness	$15,000		
Appropriated for plant expansion	10,000	$ 25,000	
Unappropriated retained earnings		69,000	
Total Retained Earnings		94,000	
Contributed Capital and Retained Earnings			352,000
Total Liabilities and Capital			$500,000

Illustration
19–3

indebtedness." However, if the corporation uses older terminology, such appropriations may appear under a caption such as "Reserve for bond sinking fund" or "Sinking fund reserve." The latter captions are not good, since many balance sheet readers get the mistaken idea from them that something, cash, for example, is held in reserve. Nevertheless, they are still occasionally seen on published balance sheets.

Long-term notes

■ When bond interest rates are temporarily unfavorable and funds are available from four or five large banks or insurance companies, often long-term notes maturing in two, three, or five years are issued instead of bonds. Also, in some instances, in order to avoid the costs of issuing bonds and dealing with several thousand bondholders, long-term notes maturing in 10, 20, or more years are issued instead of bonds.

Long-term notes whether maturing in 2 or 3 or in 10 or more years are often secured by mortgages. Too, those maturing in 10 or more years may provide for sinking funds. Consequently, long-term notes take on the characteristics of both mortgages and bonds. Ordinarily they differ only in that they are placed with a few lenders, usually at par. Insofar as accounting is concerned, long-term notes receive the same treatment as mortgages or bonds.

The corporation balance sheet

■ Corporation balance sheets are normally longer and more complicated than those of either single proprietorships or partnerships. In this and the three previous chapters a number of isolated corporation balance sheet sections have been illustrated. In order to bring all of these together, the balance sheet of Best Corporation is shown in Illustration 19–3.

Observe the treatment of the bond sinking fund in Illustration 19–3. A bond sinking fund belongs to the corporation creating such a fund and appears on its balance sheet as a long-term investment. Observe also the treatment of the unamortized discount on the bonds payable. When a balance sheet is prepared, discount on outstanding bonds is subtracted thereon from the par value of the bonds. Had there been a premium on these bonds, it would have been added to the par value.

Questions for class discussion

1. What two legal documents are involved when a company borrows by giving a mortgage? What is the purpose of each?
2. What is the primary difference between a share of stock and a bond?
3. What is a deed of trust? What are some of the provisions commonly contained in a deed of trust?
4. Define or describe: (a) registered bonds, (b) coupon bonds, (c) serial bonds, (d) sinking fund bonds, (e) redeemable bonds, (f) convertible bonds, and (g) debenture bonds.
5. Why does a corporation issuing bonds between interest dates charge and collect accrued interest from the purchasers of the bonds?

6. As it relates to a bond issue, what is the meaning of the phrase "contract rate of interest"? As it relates to bonds, what is the meaning of the phrase "market rate for bond interest"?
7. What determines bond interest rates?
8. Company A issued $1,000,000 of 6%, 10-year bonds and sold them at 95; Company B issued $1,000,000 of 7%, 10-year bonds and sold them at 105. Which company incurred the higher effective rate of interest for its borrowed funds?
9. Convertible bonds are very popular with investors. Why?
10. If a $1,000 bond is sold at $98\frac{1}{4}$, at what price is it sold? If a $1,000 bond is sold at $101\frac{1}{2}$, at what price is it sold?
11. If the quoted price for a bond is $97\frac{3}{4}$, does this include accrued interest?
12. What purpose is served by creating a bond sinking fund?
13. How are bond sinking funds classified for balance sheet purposes?
14. What purpose is served by requiring a corporation to appropriate retained earnings each year equal in amount to its sinking fund deposit plus the sinking fund earnings?

Class exercises

Exercise 19–1

On March 1, 197A, a corporation sold at par plus accrued interest $1,000,000 of its 6.6% bonds. The bonds were dated January 1, 197A, and paid interest on each July 1 and January 1. (a) Give the entry to record the sale. (b) Give the entry to record the first interest payment. (c) Set up a T-account for Bond Interest Expense and post the portions of the foregoing entries that affect the account. Answer these questions: (d) How many months' interest were accrued on these bonds when they were sold? (e) How many months' interest were paid on July 1? (f) What is the balance of the Bond Interest Expense account after the entry recording the first interest payment is posted? (g) How many months' interest does this balance represent? (h) How many months' interest did the bondholders earn during the first interest period?

Exercise 19–2

On March 1, 197A, a corporation sold $1,000,000 of its $6\frac{1}{2}\%$, 10-year bonds. The bonds were dated March 1, 197A, and paid interest on each September 1 and March 1. (a) Give the entries to record the sale and the first interest payment under the assumption the bonds were sold at 99. (b) Give the entries to record the sale and first interest payment under the assumption the bonds were sold at 101.

Exercise 19–3

On March 1, 197A, a corporation sold $1,000,000 of its 6%, 10-year bonds for $994,100 plus accrued interest. The bonds were dated January 1, 197A, and paid interest on each July 1 and January 1. Give the entries to record the sale, the first interest payment, and the second interest payment.

Exercise 19–4

On February 1, 197A, a corporation sold $1,000,000 of its $6\frac{1}{2}\%$, 10-year bonds at 101. The bonds were dated February 1, 197A, and paid interest on each August 1 and February 1. On February 1, five years later, after the bond interest for the period had been paid and after one half (in total) of the premium on the issue had been amortized, the corporation purchased $200,000 of the bonds on the open market at 98 and retired them. Give the entry to record the retirement.

Exercise 19–5

Assume the bonds of the previous exercise could be converted into the issuing company's $5 par value common stock at the rate of 185 shares of stock for each $1,000 bond. Also, assume that on February 1, five years after the bonds were issued and after one half of the premium had been amortized, bondholders converted $100,000 of the bonds to common stock. Give the entry to record the conversion.

Problems   **Problem 19–1**

The stockholders of Deeplake Corporation have a $925,000 equity in the corporation, as follows:

STOCKHOLDERS' EQUITY

Common stock, no-par value, 50,000 shares authorized, 25,000 shares issued	$700,000
Retained earnings	225,000
Total Stockholders' Equity..	$925,000

The corporation needs $1,000,000 to expand; and if it expands, it estimates it can earn $400,000 per year before bond interest, if any, and taxes. Its directors are considering three plans for securing the $1,000,000:

Plan 1. Issue the 25,000 shares of remaining no-par stock at $40 per share.
Plan 2. Issue 10,000 shares of $100 par value, 7% cumulative and nonparticipating preferred stock at par.
Plan 3. Sell $1,000,000 of 6%, 20-year bonds at par.

Required:
1. Prepare calculations to show the earnings per share that will accrue to the corporation's present stockholders under each plan. (Assume a 50% income tax rate.)
2. In this situation the earnings available to the common stockholders are $40,000 greater each year if bonds rather than preferred stock are issued. Explain why the common stockholders' earnings are $40,000 greater when the difference between the bond interest and the preferred dividends is only $10,000 annually.

Problem 19–2

A corporation completed the following bond transactions:
197A
Feb. 1   Sold $2,000,000 of its own 6.3%, 10-year bonds dated February 1, 197A, with interest payable on each August 1 and February 1.
Aug. 1   Paid the semiannual interest on the bonds.

Dec. 31   Made an adjusting entry to record the accrued interest on the bonds.
197B
Feb.   1   Paid the semiannual interest on the bonds.

Required:
1. Prepare general journal entries to record the transactions under the assumption the bonds were sold at 99¼.
2. Prepare a second set of entries to record the transactions under the assumption the bonds were sold at 101½.

Problem 19–3

Dale Corporation deposited a deed of trust with the trustee of its bondholders on March 20, 1969, authorizing it to issue $2,000,000 of 6%, 20-year bonds dated April 1, 1969, with interest payable on each October 1 and April 1. It then completed these transactions:
1969
June   1   Sold the entire issue for $1,976,200 plus accrued interest.
Oct.   1   Paid the semiannual interest on the bonds.
Dec. 31   Recorded the accrued interest on the bonds.
1970
Apr.   1   Paid the semiannual interest on the bonds.
1973
Oct.   1   Paid the semiannual interest on the bonds and then purchased on the open market and retired one tenth of the issue. The bonds were purchased at 98, including the commission.
Dec. 31   Recorded the accrued interest on the bonds.
1974
Apr.   1   Paid the semiannual interest on the bonds.

Required:
Prepare general journal entries to record the transactions. Assume all transactions between April 1, 1970, and October 1, 1973, were correctly recorded.

Problem 19–4

On February 14, 1969, a corporation deposited a deed of trust with the trustee of its bondholders that authorized it to issue $1,000,000 of 6.6%, 20-year convertible bonds dated March 1, 1969, with interest payable on each September 1 and March 1. The conversion clause in the deed of trust granted the bondholders the right to convert their bonds before March 1, 1974, into shares of the company's common stock at the rate of 150 shares of $5 par value stock for each $1,000 bond. The corporation then completed these transactions:
1969
Apr.   1   Sold the entire issue for $1,011,950 plus accrued interest.
Sept. 1   Paid the semiannual interest on the bonds.
Dec. 31   Recorded the accrued interest on the bonds.
1970
Mar.   1   Paid the semiannual interest on the bonds.
Sept. 1   Paid the semiannual interest on the bonds.
1972
Mar.   1   After paying the semiannual interest on the bonds, purchased on the open market and retired bonds having a $200,000 par value. The total cash outlay was $196,000.

Sept. 1   Paid the semiannual interest on the bonds.
1973
Mar. 1   After paying the semiannual interest on the bonds, converted bonds
having a $100,000 par value to common stock.

Required:
Prepare general journal entries to record the transactions.

Problem 19–5

A corporation deposited a deed of trust with the trustee of its bondholders
on December 10, 197A, which authorized it to issue $1,000,000 of 6%, four-
year bonds dated January 1, 197B. (Four years are an unrealistically small
number of years for a bond issue; however, by using such a number, all entries
for a bond sinking fund may be required without the necessity of many repetitive entries.)

In the deed of trust the corporation agreed to create a bond sinking fund by
depositing with a trustee $230,300 at the end of each year in the life of the bond
issue. It was assumed the sinking fund investments would earn $5\frac{1}{2}\%$ net and the
fund would grow to maturity as follows:

End of Year	Amount Deposited	Interest Earned on Fund Balance	Balance in Fund after Deposit and Interest
1	$230,300	-0-	$ 230,300
2	230,300	$12,700	473,300
3	230,300	26,000	729,600
4	230,300	40,100	1,000,000

In addition to the sinking fund, the corporation agreed in its deed of trust to
appropriate retained earnings each year equal to the sum of its sinking fund
deposit plus the sinking fund earnings of that year.

After depositing the deed of trust, the corporation completed these transactions:
197B
Jan. 1   Sold the entire issue at par.
Dec. 31   Made the first annual sinking fund deposit.
     31   Appropriated retained earnings as required by the deed of trust.
197C
Dec. 31   Made the second annual sinking fund deposit.
     31   Received the sinking fund trustee's report showing the sinking fund
          earned $12,700 during the year.
     31   Appropriated retained earnings as required by the deed of trust.
197D
Dec. 31   Made the third annual sinking fund deposit.
     31   Received the sinking fund trustee's report showing the sinking fund
          earned $26,250. (This is slightly more than was anticipated the fund
          would earn. However, it is not enough to warrant a change in the
          deposit required of the corporation.)
     31   Appropriated retained earnings equal to the sinking fund deposit and
          the sinking fund earnings.

197E

Dec. 31   Made the fourth annual sinking fund deposit.

31   Received the sinking fund trustee's report showing the fund earned $40,050.

31   Appropriated retained earnings equal to the sum of the sinking fund deposit plus the year's sinking fund earnings.

197F

Jan. 15   Received a report from the sinking fund trustee showing the bonds had been paid in full. Attached to the report was a check for the excess earnings in the sinking fund.

22   The board of directors voted to return the retained earnings appropriated for bonded indebtedness to unappropriated retained earnings.

Required:

Prepare general journal entries to record the foregoing transactions.

Problem 19–6

The following alphabetically arranged items appeared on the December 31, 19–, balance sheet of Easy Street Corporation:

Accounts payable	$ 90,500
Accounts receivable	115,700
Accumulated depreciation, buildings	235,000
Accumulated depreciation, equipment	140,000
Allowance for doubtful accounts	11,200
Bond sinking fund	163,500
Buildings	1,750,000
Cash	85,600
Common stock, $5 par value	1,500,000
Discount on bonds payable	11,500
Equipment	875,000
Federal income taxes payable	42,600
First, 6%, real estate mortgage bonds payable, due in 1990	1,000,000
Inventories at lower of cost or market	241,400
Land	137,500
Notes receivable	10,000
Organization costs	12,500
Patents	25,000
Payroll taxes payable	1,500
Premium on common stock	75,000
Prepaid expenses	5,000
Retained earnings appropriated for bonded indebtedness	163,500
Subscriptions receivable, common stock	165,000
Unappropriated retained earnings	213,400
Unissued common stock subscribed	125,000

Required:

Under the assumption the corporation is authorized to issue 500,000 shares of common stock and $1,000,000 of bonds, rearrange the items into a classified balance sheet that is complete and in good form.

Problem 19–1A

A corporation is presently earning a 20% before-tax return on its stockholders' equity, which is:

STOCKHOLDERS' EQUITY

Common stock, $10 par value, 200,000 shares authorized, 100,000 shares issued	$1,000,000
Premium on common stock	200,000
Retained earnings	300,000
Total Stockholders' Equity	$1,500,000

The corporation's directors are of the opinion that if an additional $2,000,000 were invested in the business, it could earn not only a 20% return on its present stockholders' equity but also a 20% return on the additional $2,000,000, before any bond interest or income taxes, of course. Furthermore, the directors are considering three plans to secure the $2,000,000. They are:

Plan 1. Issue the corporation's 100,000 shares of authorized but unissued $10 par value common stock at $20 per share.

Plan 2. Secure an authorization and issue 20,000 shares of $100 par value, $7\frac{1}{2}$% cumulative and nonparticipating, preferred stock at par.

Plan 3. Sell $2,000,000 of $6\frac{1}{2}$%, 20-year bonds at par.

Required:

1. Prepare calculations to show the earnings per share that will accrue to the corporation's present stockholders under each plan. (Assume a 50% income tax rate.)

2. In the situation described here the earnings available to the common stockholders are $85,000 greater each year if bonds rather than preferred stock are issued. Explain why the common stock earnings are $85,000 greater when the difference between the bond interest and the preferred dividends is only $20,000 annually.

Problem 19–2A

On March 17 of the current year a corporation deposited a deed of trust with the trustee of its bondholders that authorized it to issue $1,000,000 of $6\frac{1}{2}$%, 10-year bonds dated April 1 of this year and paying interest on each October 1 and April 1. It then completed these transactions:

Apr. 1   Sold the entire issue.
Oct. 1   Paid the semiannual interest on the bonds.
Dec. 31   Recorded the accrued interest on the bonds.
Apr. 1   Paid the semiannual interest on the bonds.

Required:

1. Prepare general journal entries to record the transactions under the assumption the bonds were sold at 99.

2. Prepare a second set of entries to record the transactions under the assumption the bonds were sold at $100\frac{3}{4}$.

Problem 19–3A

On April 18, 1969, a corporation deposited a deed of trust with the trustee of its bondholders that authorized it to issue $3,000,000 of 6½%, 20-year bonds dated May 1, 1969, and paying interest on each November 1 and May 1. It then completed these transactions:

1969
June   1   Sold the entire issue for $3,047,800 plus accrued interest.
Nov. 1   Paid the semiannual interest on the bonds.
Dec. 31 Recorded the accrued interest on the bonds.
1970
May   1   Paid the semiannual interest on the bonds.
1973
Nov. 1   Paid the semiannual interest on the bonds and purchased on the open market and retired one fifth of the issue. The bonds were purchased at 97½, including the commission.
Dec. 31 Recorded the accrued interest on the bonds.
1974
May   1   Paid the semiannual interest on the bonds.

Required:
Prepare general journal entries to record the transactions. Assume all transactions between May 1, 1970, and November 1, 1973, were correctly recorded.

Problem 19–4A

On April 12, 1969, a corporation deposited a deed of trust with the trustee of its bondholders that authorized it to issue $2,000,000 of 6%, 20-year, convertible bonds dated May 1, 1969, and paying interest on each November 1 and May 1. The conversion clause in the deed of trust granted the bondholders the right to convert their bonds before May 1, 1974, into shares of the company's common stock at the rate of 80 shares of $10 par value common stock for each $1,000 bond. The company then completed these transactions:

1969
Aug. 1   Sold the entire issue for $1,976,300 plus accrued interest.
Nov. 1   Paid the semiannual interest on the bonds.
Dec. 31 Recorded the accrued interest on the bonds.
1970
May   1   Paid the semiannual interest on the bonds.
Nov. 1   Paid the semiannual interest on the bonds.
1971
Nov. 1   After paying the semiannual interest on the bonds, converted one fifth of the outstanding bonds to common stock.
Dec. 31 Recorded the accrued interest on the bonds.
1972
May   1   After paying the semiannual interest on the bonds, purchased on the open market and retired bonds having a $100,000 par value. The total cash outlay was $98,000.

Required:
Prepare general journal entries to record the transactions.

Decision problem 19–1, Electrola Company

Electrola Company's latest balance sheet shows the following stockholders' equity:

Common stock, $12.50 par value, 300,000 shares authorized, 200,000 shares issued	$2,500,000
Capital contributed by stockholders in excess of the par value of their shares	500,000
Retained earnings	800,000
Total Stockholders' Equity	$3,800,000

The company plans to expand its operations by about 50%, but to do so it will need $2,000,000 of additional capital, and the directors are considering three means of securing the money:

1. Issuing the remaining authorized common stock at $20 per share.
2. Securing an authorization and issuing 20,000 shares of $100 par value, 7½% cumulative and nonparticipating preferred stock.
3. Selling at par $2,000,000 of 6½%, 10-year bonds.

The company earned $420,000 before taxes last year, and its accounting department has prepared the following estimates of income before bond interest and taxes for the next 10 years under the assumption that the expansion program will be carried out: year 1, $582,000; year 2, $648,000; year 3, $720,000; year 4, $798,000; year 5, $882,000; year 6, $972,000; year 7, $1,062,000; year 8, $1,158,000; year 9, $1,254,000; and year 10, $1,350,000.

The company's directors want to finance the expansion in the manner that will be in the best interests of present stockholders and they have asked you to determine this for them. In your report to the directors express an opinion as to the relative merits and disadvantages of each contemplated plan. Attach to your report a schedule showing annual expected earnings per share of the common stockholders under each plan. (Assume the company's income tax rate will continue at 50%.)

Decision problem 19–2, Humboldt Corporation

Humboldt Corporation is contemplating a change in its capital structure to eliminate its outstanding 8% preferred stock. The company's capital structure consists of the following:

Preferred stock, $100 par value, 8% cumulative and nonparticipating, 20,000 shares authorized and issued, callable at par plus dividends due	$2,000,000
Preferred stock, $50 par value, 7% cumulative and nonparticipating, 40,000 shares authorized and issued, callable at par plus dividends due	2,000,000
Common stock, $10 par value, 500,000 shares authorized, 200,000 shares issued	2,000,000
Retained earnings	1,000,000
Total	$7,000,000

During the past five years the company's annual income has averaged $900,000 per year before income taxes; and considering the inelasticity of its operations, it can be assumed there will be no great change.

Two alternatives have been suggested for securing the funds to call the 8% preferred stock. They are (1) issue at par $2,000,000 of 6%, 20-year bonds and (2) offer the common stockholders the right to purchase one new share of common stock at par for each share now held.

The directors have asked you to prepare a statement showing the effect of the proposed changes on earnings applicable to the company's outstanding common stock, including earnings per share. If they are satisfied that either of the proposed changes is to the advantage of the common stockholders, they will call the necessary stockholders' meetings and seek authorization to proceed with the better of the suggested changes.

Prepare the statement requested by the board of directors. Also explain why the replacement of a $160,000 annual payment to the preferred stockholders with a $120,000 annual payment to bondholders, which amounts to a $40,000 savings or $0.20 per common share, can result in a $0.50 per share increase in the earnings of the common stockholders. You may assume that the corporation's state and federal income taxes will continue to take 50% of its income.

Accounting principles: accounting for investments

■ Modern business accounting is the result of a long, gradual evolution, beginning with the invention of double-entry bookkeeping by the merchants of the Italian trading cities during the 13th and 14th centuries and continuing today. Throughout this period its purpose has been to supply users of accounting data with useful information about a business enterprise.

When business enterprises are viewed today, they range from small owner-managed concerns to large corporations, the stocks of which are owned by thousands or hundreds of thousands of stockholders and investors. Also, when users of accounting information from the records of the latter group—large corporations—are examined, they fall into two groups: (1) the corporation *insiders* or managers, who may own little or none of the corporation's stock; and (2) *outsiders,* who are the stockholders, creditors, prospective investors, organized labor, government, and the public.

It is with the outsider group that this chapter is concerned, for its members depend upon the corporation's published financial reports for information about the corporation and its activities, and unless these reports are prepared in comformity with generally accepted accounting principles their content may be misleading and subject to manipulation.

Nature and need for accounting principles

■ What are accounting principles? From where did they come? What is the basis of their authority? Do they exist in codified form? Why are they needed? Answers to these questions tell something of the nature and need for accounting principles.

What are accounting principles?

Accounting principles are broad rules adopted by the accounting profession as guides for use in recording and reporting the affairs and activities of a business to its stockholders, investors, creditors, and other outsiders.[1]

From where did they come?

Accounting principles have evolved (and are evolving today) from the combined thinking of members of the accounting profession who were (and are) in turn influenced by the needs of business managements, governmental agencies, labor unions, stockholders, investors, and the general public. The aggregate of these influences gave (and give) rise to accounting theories. Some of the theories were (and are) accepted and some rejected. The general acceptance of a theory gave (and gives) it the status of an accounting principle.

What is the basis of their authority?

The authority of any accounting principle rests solely on its acceptance by members of the accounting profession. Accounting principles are not laws in the sense of the laws of physics and chemistry, and they do not exist anywhere in codified form; rather they are man-made and are found in the current literature of accounting, for example, in the published bulletins and opinions of the American Institute of Certified Public Accountants, in pronouncements of the American Accounting Association committees, and in the writings of accounting scholars.

Why are such principles needed?

As previously stated, accounting principles are broad rules or guides for use in recording and reporting the affairs and activities of a business. As such they make financial statements more useful and dependable and make the financial information reported by various companies more comparable. Actually, without some general agreement as to the accounting treatment for assets, liabilities, and owner equity, revenues and expenses plus certain standards of disclosure, published financial reports would often be of little value to "outsiders."

Accounting concepts

■ An understanding of accounting principles begins with the recognition of four broad concepts as to the nature of the economic setting in which accounting operates. The four do not include all aspects of the setting,

[1] *Basic Concepts and Accounting Principles Underlying Financial Statements* (New York: American Institute of Certified Public Accountants, 1970), p. 54.

but they are the more significant. The four are (1) the entity concept, (2) the going-concern concept, (3) the money concept, and (4) the periodicity concept. Three have been discussed before, but further discussion is needed.

√The business entity concept

Every business unit or enterprise is treated in accounting as a separate entity, with the affairs of the business and those of the owner or owners being kept entirely separate. Each unit is viewed as owning all resources committed to its purposes and in turn owing both its creditors and owners for having supplied the resources. Thus accounting is primarily concerned with the business unit and only secondarily interested in its owner or owners.

Corporations are in fact separate legal entities, but the separate existence of a proprietorship or partnership is an arbitrary one derived solely for accounting purposes. Nevertheless, for accounting purposes, every business is treated as a separate entity, and all its records and reports are developed from this viewpoint. Furthermore, in carrying out the accounting function, the financial position and operating results of a business unit should never be distorted by including in its records and reports either the assets or transactions of another business or the personal assets and transactions of the owner or owners. For example, the personal automobile of a single proprietor or that of the president of a small family corporation should not be included among the business assets, nor should its gas, oil, and repairs be treated as a business expense, for to do so distorts the financial position and profitability reports of the business.

√The going-concern concept

For accounting purposes, unless there is strong evidence to the contrary, it is assumed that a business will continue to operate as a going concern, earning a reasonable net income for a period longer than the life expectancy of any of its assets. In other words, it is assumed that a business will remain in operation long enough to recover the cost of its assets through the sale of its products or services.

The following income statement demonstrates the idea of recovering the cost of assets through product sales:

Excel Company
Income Statement for Year Ended December 31, 19—

Revenue	$100,000
Cost of products sold, wages, supplies, and other costs (including $5,000 depreciation on equipment)	90,000
Net Income	$ 10,000

During the year of the statement, Excel Company recovered all costs of selling its products with $10,000 left over. Included within the costs is $5,000 depreciation; and since none of the revenue earned during the year flowed out for this expense, the company recovered $5,000 of the cost of its equipment through the sale of its products.

The going-concern concept provides the foundation for balance sheet preparation and periodic income measurement. For example, it provides the justification for carrying plant assets on the balance sheet at cost less accumulated depreciation, in other words at the share of their cost applicable to future periods. It is also the justification for carrying at cost such things as stationery imprinted with the company name, though salable only as scrap paper. In all such instances the intention is to use the assets in carrying on the business operations. They are not for sale, so it is pointless to place them on the balance sheet at market or realizable values, whether these values are greater or less than book values.

The going-concern concept puts emphasis on the income statement and on the proper matching of costs and revenues. Under it the balance sheet becomes secondary, as it probably should, since earning capacity is usually more important in judging the worth of a business or its debt-paying ability.

Although the going-concern concept is applicable in most accounting situations, it should be recognized that where a business is faced with liquidation, going-concern accounting is not applicable. In such a situation liquidation accounting and liquidation values apply.

√ The money concept

One of the more important concepts under which accounting operates may best be called the money concept. Briefly, under this concept it is held that the function of accounting is not to account for value; rather it is (1) to record "dollars invested" and "dollars borrowed," (2) to trace the various commitments of these "dollars of capital" as they are invested and reinvested in the business activities, and finally (3) to measure out of gross "dollars of revenue" the recapture of "dollars of capital" with any excess being designated as "dollars of income."

Under this concept it is conceded that value, like beauty, is in the eyes of the beholder, and therefore can only subjectively be measured. It is also recognized that the "value" (purchasing power) of the accountant's unit of measure, the dollar, is itself constantly changing. Therefore, it is recognized that a balance sheet prepared under this concept simply shows the number of dollars received from all sources (from owners, from creditors, and from retained earnings) and over against this shows where these dollars are committed (in receivables, inventories, prepaid expenses, plant assets, and a balance of uncommitted cash), and a reader is not warranted in interpreting the dollar amounts shown for the various assets as the values of these assets. Rather, the amounts shown are the numbers of dollars committed to the various asset purposes, with any values being dependent upon a subjective judgment of their earning power.

The periodicity concept

Taxes based on annual earnings must be paid to governmental units; stockholders must receive annual reports and often quarterly ones; and some companies consider it necessary to divide operations into monthly periods for the preparation of internal reports for management. Consequently, the environment in which accounting operates—the business community and the government—requires that the life of a business be divided into relatively short periods and that changes in its wealth be measured over these short periods.

Yet, it is generally agreed that earnings cannot be measured precisely over a short period, that it is impossible to learn the exact earnings of a business until it has completed its last transaction and converted all its assets to cash. Nevertheless, the environment in which accounting operates requires that the life of a business be divided into accounting periods of not more than a year in length and that test readings of the progress of the business be made at the end of each period. Furthermore, when acceptable accounting principles and procedures are used in assigning revenues and expenses to proper accounting periods, although judgments and opinions are involved, confidence in the short-term reports is justified.

Accounting principles   ■ A common definition of the word *principle* is: "A broad general law or rule adopted or professed as a guide to action; a settled ground or basis of conduct or practice. . . ." Consequently, accounting principles may be described as broad rules adopted by the accounting profession as guides for use in accumulating and reporting financial data.

Brief discussions of some of the more significant principles follow.

The cost principle

Perhaps the basic principle underlying accounting records and reports is the cost principle. Under this principle it is held that cost is the appropriate basis for recording the acquisition of assets, services, and other factors of production and that cost is the basis for holding assets, services, and other factors of production in the accounts until sold, consumed, or otherwise disposed of by the business.

Under the cost principle it is recognized that it is not the purpose of accounting to account for the "value" of the various factors of production committed to the business operations. Rather, it is to account for their acquisition at cost, to hold these costs in the accounts until the factors are sold, expire, or are consumed, and finally to match the costs of the sold, expired, or consumed factors and portions thereof against revenues.

Under the cost principle a balance sheet shows the "unexpired costs" of the various production factors committed to the business operations. It does not show their "value," for value like beauty can only be subjectively measured; and also the "value" (purchasing power) of the accountant's unit of measure is constantly, though gradually, changing.

In applying the cost principle, costs are measured on a cash or cash-equivalent basis. If the consideration given for a particular production factor is cash, the measure of the cost incurred is the entire cash outlay made to secure the factor and get it ready for use. If the consideration is other than cash, the measure of the consideration is the cash-equivalent value of the consideration, or the fair value (on a cash-equivalent basis) of the thing received, whichever is more clearly evident.[2]

A deviation from cost is required for assets received by donation. Donated assets are recorded at their cash-equivalent value as of the donation date. This departure from cost is considered necessary because every business resource, regardless of its origin, should be properly accounted for, and only by charging a business with the acquisition cost or fair value of all its resources can the earning power of the enterprise be determined properly.

The cost principle is applicable in measuring equities, both owner and creditor, as well as assets. All three—assets, liabilities, and owner equities—should be recorded and reported in accordance with the cost principle.

√ The matching principle

This principle holds that a major objective of accounting is the determination of periodic net income by matching appropriate costs with revenues. The principle recognizes that streams of revenues continually flow into a business, and it requires that (1) there be a precise "cut off" in these streams at the end of an accounting period, (2) the inflows of the period be measured, (3) the costs incurred in securing the inflows be determined, and (4) the sum of the costs be deducted from the sum of the inflows to determine the period's net income.

As the terms are used here, costs include goods and services sold, goods and services consumed in the business operations, expired assets, and losses such as those from fire, storm, and the sale of capital assets. Revenues are inflows of assets from the sale of products and services and also the sale of assets other than stock in trade, such as unneeded equipment and investments. Revenues arise too from the advantageous settlement of liabilities. And, a net income results when the revenue inflows exceed the cost expirations and outflows plus casualty losses and losses from capital asset sales.

REVENUE RECOGNITION. The matching principle requires that a revenue be associated with an accounting period, and this in turn re-

---

[2] *Basic Concepts and Accounting Principles Underlying Financial Statements* (New York: American Institute of Certified Public Accountants, 1970), p. 72.

quires that the point or period in time at which revenue is realized be determined. Three commonly used bases for determining this point are (1) the sales basis, (2) the cash basis, and (3) the production basis.

Sales basis. The most commonly used basis for revenue recognition is the sales basis. Under this basis revenue is considered to be earned when a sale is completed, and a sale is completed when assets such as cash or a promise to pay cash are transferred from the buyer to the seller in exchange for title to goods or services.

Theoretically, revenue is earned throughout the whole business process, but its amount is not determinable until a price is agreed upon between a buyer and a seller and a legal sale is made. For example, a manufacturer earns part of his revenue upon completing each of these necessary business steps: (1) manufacturing goods for sale, (2) securing orders from customers, and (3) delivering the goods. Yet, until all steps are completed, there is no right to collect the sales price. The sales basis recognizes this, and under it revenue is not measured and reported until a sale is completed.

Cash basis. Where there is considerable doubt as to the amount which ultimately will be collected from a sale, it may be desirable to defer reporting revenue from the sale until collected in cash. Under the cash basis the desirability of this is perceived, and under the cash basis revenue is not recognized until collected in cash.

The cash basis for revenue recognition is often used in accounting for installment sales. Here the gross profit from a sale is held in suspense until collected in cash, at which point it is taken up as revenue. As a result, revenue from installment sales is recognized in the accounting period in which installment payments are collected in cash.

The cash basis is also commonly used by doctors, dentists, and others who perform professional services. Once doctors and dentists did not collect a large portion of fees billed, and the cash basis was justified in that it simplified accounting for uncollectible accounts. Today, its employment by professional people seems justifiable only on the basis of its simplicity, its long use, and the fact that it is acceptable for income tax purposes.

Production basis. Sometimes the sales basis for taking up revenue fails even approximately to recognize revenue in the periods in which it is earned. For example, a contractor specializing in large construction jobs often finds the typical project requires two or more years for completion. If such a contractor has a three-year project and takes up revenue on a sales basis, he will recognize the revenue from this job and take up the earnings in the year of completion. Yet portions of the revenue and earnings are actually earned in each of the three years required for completion. Furthermore, if the contractor has only a few projects under construction at any one time, he may find that none or only a small portion are completed in a single year in spite of the year being one of heavy activity. In such cases a contractor may elect to take up revenue and earnings on his projects on a percentage-of-completion basis or some other such basis that allocates earnings to the several periods in which earned.

To illustrate the production basis for recognizing revenue, assume a contractor has under construction a large dam for which the total contract price is $80,000,000 and for which the estimated construction cost is $75,000,000. As construction progresses the costs incurred are charged to a controlling account called "Cost of Construction in Progress." These costs include materials, labor, supplies, depreciation on equipment, insurance, and all other expenses related to the project. If at the end of the first accounting period in which this dam is under construction the total costs charged to the dam is $15,000,000, the entry to take up the revenue on a partial performance basis and to set up the asset increment is:

Dec.	31	Unbilled Accounts Receivable..............	16,000,000.00	
		Construction Revenue...................		16,000,000.00
		To take up revenue based on partial performance.		

The $15,000,000 construction costs that have been incurred during the first year are used in determining the revenue taken up in the foregoing entry. The $15,000,000 is one fifth of the total estimated $75,000,000 cost; consequently, the foregoing entry takes up one fifth ($80,000,000 × $\frac{1}{5}$ = $16,000,000) of the total contract price as the year's revenue from this project.

At the end of the second year, the second year's costs and the same procedures are used to take up the second year's revenue; and this continues throughout the construction period until the last year, the year in which the job is completed, when any previously unrecognized revenue is taken into the accounts.

At times actual construction costs vary from estimates. When this occurs and the variation is material, an adjustment of the amount of revenue taken into the accounts may be necessary.

MEASURING AND MATCHING COSTS. The Committee on Accounting Procedure stated in *Accounting Research Bulletin No. 13* that "it is plainly desirable to provide, by charges in the current income statement, properly classified, for all foreseeable costs and losses applicable against current revenues, to the extent that they can be measured and allocated to fiscal periods with reasonable approximation." Thus in determining net income from business operations all costs which are *applicable* to the revenue of the period should be charged against that revenue. Costs are "applicable" if it is reasonably apparent that they represent an investment in resources and services consumed in the process of realizing that particular revenue.

Costs are applicable to the revenue of the period under each of the following circumstances:

1. If there is "a direct identification or association with the revenue of the period." Illustrations of costs directly associated with a period's revenue are cost of merchandise delivered to customers, sales commissions, etc.
2. If there is "an indirect association with the revenue of the period, as in the case of office salaries or rent."
3. Also, a commonly accepted accounting axiom holds that no (money) income emerges until and unless (money) capital is preserved intact. This is to say that there can be no gain on an investment where the investment is lost. For this reason, other measurable expirations of asset costs even though not associated with production of the period's revenue must be deducted from revenue before a final measurement of net income can be made. Thus losses from fire and storm, from the sale of capital assets, and from all other causes even though not related to ordinary business operations must be deducted from revenue before any beneficial net increase in business assets can be reported.

The measurement of "expired" costs (or the costs that should be deducted from a period's revenue) is in part precise and in part estimated through consistent application of definite methods. With reference to the period of expiration, expired costs are accounted for as follows:

1. *Costs of assets and services consumed in their entirety in one period* — the measure of these costs is precisely recorded in the books in accordance with the cost principle. Part of these costs (of assets and services consumed) is normally applicable to the revenue of the period and is so charged; part is also normally applicable to the future in that it is transformed into goods or services to be sold or used in the future. This latter portion is represented largely by inventories.
2. *Costs of assets and services consumed more or less gradually over two or more periods* — costs of this type are also recorded in the books in accordance with the cost principle, but it is necessary to arrive at a rational allocation of the total as between the current and future periods. This is done through the consistent application of methods found most useful in the industry, the methods being based on experience and expert opinion. In general the cost division is made by determining first the portion of cost which seems reasonably beneficial to future periods, and then subtracting these deferred costs from the total to determine the amount to be matched with current revenue.

"Applicable costs" are deducted from current revenue only when they are measurable "with reasonable approximation." It is important that all costs incurred in producing a period's revenue be matched against that revenue. However, when in the considered judgment of the accountant, material costs applicable to current revenue cannot be determined with sufficient accuracy to satisfy the accountant, he should not include these costs in the current income statement. For example, a company introduced a new machine in which it is felt that during the first year imperfections may be found by users which the company will feel obligated to remedy, perhaps at considerable cost. Yet, no experience is available by which to estimate this applicable cost "with reasonable approximation." In a case such as this the cost that cannot be measured with a reasonable approximation should be referred to by footnote or parenthetical notation on the income statement, pointing to the omission of the expected cost and thus emphasizing the provisional nature of the net income figure. Such a cost should be reported in a later statement when its amount is known. Of course, if the potential cost is so material as to make misleading any statement of net income, the revenue from the sale of the new product may have to be deferred until a more definite computation of applicable cost can be made.

The objectivity principle

This principle holds that changes in account balances should be supported to the fullest extent possible by objective evidence. Whims and fancies plus, for example, something like an opinion of management that "an asset is worth more than it cost" have no place in accounting. To be fully useful, accounting information must, as nearly as possible, be based on objective evidence.

Bargained transactions supported by verifiable business documents originating outside the business are the best objective evidence obtainable; and whenever possible, accounting data should be supported by such documents. However, at times it is necessary to rely on an opinion or an estimate, for example, in determining depreciation or bad debts; but here also objective evidence should be used to the fullest extent possible. After all, bad debt losses of previous years are a form of objective evidence.

At times a dependable estimate cannot be made for lack of objective evidence. When this happens the estimate should not be entered in the accounts; but if pertinent, it should be disclosed by means of a balance sheet or income statement footnote.

The consistency principle

In many cases two or more methods or procedures have been derived in accounting practice to accomplish a particular accounting objective. For example, there are several methods of computing depreciation, and more than one method has been found satisfactory in arriving at the cost of inventory. In each case one method may be considered more useful for one enterprise, while another may be more satisfactory for a concern operating under different circumstances. Nevertheless, while recognizing the validity of different methods under varying circumstances, it is still necessary in order to ensure a high degree of comparability in any concern's accounting data to insist on a consistent application in the company of any given accounting method, period after period. It is also necessary to insist that any departures from this doctrine of consistency be fully disclosed on the financial statements and the effects thereof on the statements fully described.

As a result of this consistency principle, in the absence of clear indications to the contrary, a reader of a company's accounting statements is able to assume that generally accepted accounting principles have been followed in a consistent manner in the preparation of the statements. Only on the basis of this assumption can meaningful comparisons of the information in a company's statement be made year after year.

The full-disclosure principle

Under this principle it is held that financial statements and their accompanying footnotes and other explanatory materials should disclose fully and completely all relevant data of a material nature relating to the financial position and operating results of the company for which they are prepared. This does not necessarily mean that the information should be detailed, for details can at times obscure. It simply means that all information necessary to an appreciation of the company's position be reported in a readily understandable manner and that nothing of a significant nature be withheld.

Full disclosure is not limited to information in the ledger accounts. For example, any of the following would be considered relevant and should be disclosed by means of footnotes or explanatory paragraphs attached to the statements:

LONG-TERM COMMITMENTS UNDER A CONTRACT. If the company has signed a long-term lease requiring a material annual payment, this should be disclosed even though the liability does not appear in the accounts. Also, if the company has pledged certain of its assets as security for a loan, this should be revealed.

CONTINGENT LIABILITIES. A company that is contingently liable due to possible additional tax assessments, note endorsements, pending lawsuits, or product guarantees should disclose this on its statements.

ACCOUNTING METHODS. Whenever there are several acceptable accounting methods that may be followed, the company should report in each case the method used, especially when the selected method materially affects reported net income. Also, if a change has been made in accounting methods, this too should be reported, along with the effects of the change on reported net income and on balance sheet items.

EVENTS SUBSEQUENT TO THE DATE OF THE STATEMENTS. An event such as a major casualty loss, settlement of a legal action, sale of a major asset, in fact any and all significant events occurring after the balance sheet date but before the statements are released should be disclosed if the events are expected to materially affect the company's future.

The principle of conservatism

Decisions based on estimates and opinions as to future events affect financial statments. Financial statements are also affected by the selection of accounting procedures. The principle of conservatism holds that the accountant should be conservative in his estimates and opinions and in his selection of procedures, choosing those that neither unduly understate nor overstate the situation.

It is generally conceded that business executives tend toward the optimistic side in their appraisal of a business situation and that they need a counterweight of caution if a proper balance in the judgment of future prospects and unresolved risks is to be attained. Under the principle of conservatism it is held that the accountant should supply this counterweight, that in all judgment situations he should take an analytical, conservative, "show me" attitude.

Something called balance sheet conservatism was once considered the "first" principle of accounting, the objective being to place every item on the balance sheet at a conservative figure. This in itself was commendable; but it commonly resulted in overconservatism, which in turn resulted in (1) an understatement of asset and equity amounts, (2) an overstatement of costs in the year the assets were first understated, and (3) an understatement of costs on each income statement thereafter throughout the lives of the understated assets. Today, accountants recognize that balance sheet conservatism is not desirable when it misrepresents true situations; and they recognize that full and fair disclosure is a more important accounting objective.

The principle of materiality

Under this principle it is held that a strict adherence to accounting principles is not required for items of little significance because accounting must be practical. Consequently, the accountant must always weigh the costs of complying with an accounting principle against the extra accuracy gained thereby; and in those situations where the cost is relatively great and the lack of compliance will have no material effect on the financial statements, compliance is not necessary. For example, if a wastepaper basket is purchased for $2.50, its cost might better be charged to an expense account in the period of purchase than be depreciated over the asset's estimated five-year life, because the extra accuracy gained from depreciating is not worth its cost.

There is no clear-cut distinction between material and immaterial items, and no item is material or immaterial by itself. Each situation must be individually judged, and an item is material or immaterial as it relates to other items. For example, a $1,000 item on an income statement showing a $1,000,000 net income might not be significant; but it would be significant if the net income were, say, $10,000. Generally, an item is considered significant if it is sufficiently large as to influence a statement reader's judgment of a situation.

■ Transactions are recorded and financial statements are usually prepared by the employees of the company issuing the statements; and as employees they must do the company's bidding, as a rule, or seek employment elsewhere. Consequently, agreements as to generally accepted accounting principles are of no value unless there is some way of assuring outsiders that the principles were faithfully followed. In other words, outsiders need an independent representative who will examine the company's records and certify that its reported income is fairly stated, that its balance sheet carries an all-inclusive list of its assets and liabilities, that owner equity is fairly stated, and that all is in accordance with generally accepted accounting principles.

The certified public accountant fills this roll; and his importance is evidenced by the fact that for a corporation to sell its stock on a major stock exchange, and in some cases over the counter, its records must be audited by an independent certified public accountant before the stock is sold and annually thereafter. Also, in securing a loan and in fulfilling the requirements of corporate bylaws, such an audit is commonly required.

An audit of a business enterprise consists of a critical review and exploration of its internal controls and accounting records made to enable the auditor to express an opinion as to the accuracy and fairness of the concern's financial statements. Upon its completion, the auditor issues a letter or certificate which the audited concern attaches to or publishes as a part of its financial statements. A typical certificate will read:

> To the Board of Directors and
> Shareholders of XYZ Corporation:
>
> In our opinion, the accompanying statements present fairly the financial position of XYZ Corporation at December 31, 19–, and the results of its operations for the year, in conformity with generally accepted accounting principles applied on a basis consistent with that of the preceding year. Our examination was made in accordance with generally accepted auditing standards, and accordingly included such tests of the accounting records and such other auditing procedures as we considered necessary in the circumstances.
>
> A & B, Certified Public Accountants

Note in the certificate that the auditors made such tests of the accounting records as they considered necessary under the circumstances. In making an audit, auditors normally examine only a portion of the audited concern's transactions, the size of the sample being dependent upon how much the auditors feel they can rely on the audited concern's internal control systems.

If the auditor takes exception to any of the audited concern's accounting or internal control practices, he must either withhold his certificate until the condition is corrected or he must place a qualification in the certificate.

STOCKS AND BONDS AS INVESTMENTS

■ In previous chapters stocks and bonds were considered from the viewpoint of their issuing corporation; in the remainder of this chapter they will be considered from the viewpoint of an investor.

When a corporation first issues its stock or bonds, the transactions involved are between the corporation and the investors or between the corporation and an underwriter who buys the stocks or bonds from the corporation and in turn sells them to the public. However, these transactions represent only a very small portion of the daily transactions in stocks and bonds. The great daily volume of security sales are transactions between investors, some investors selling and other investors buying, with the transactions taking place through brokers who charge a commission for their services.

Brokers acting as agents for their customers buy and sell stocks and bonds on stock exchanges such as the New York Stock Exchange. Twenty million or more shares of stock and several thousand bonds are bought and sold each day on the stock exchanges, and each day the sales prices are published on the financial pages of many newspapers. Stock prices are quoted on the basis of dollars and $\frac{1}{8}$ dollars per share. For example, a stock quoted at $46\frac{1}{8}$ sold for $46.125 per share, and stock quoted at $25\frac{1}{2}$ sold for $25.50 per share. Bonds are normally issued in $1,000 denominations, but their prices are quoted on a percentage basis. For example, a $1,000 bond quoted at $98\frac{1}{8}$ sold at $98\frac{1}{8}\%$ of $1,000, or $981.25, and a $1,000 bond quoted at $86\frac{1}{4}$ sold for $862.50.

Classifying investments

■ Stocks and bonds purchased as investments are classified for balance sheet purposes as either *temporary investments* or *long-term investments*. The classification depending in each case on whether the stocks or bonds are readily marketable and upon the intention of the investing company.

Temporary investments

If securities are readily marketable and the investing company intends to keep them for only a short period, say, a year or less, the investment is classified as a temporary or short-term investment, a current asset.

Temporary or short-term investments are often made by a company whose business is seasonal in nature. Normally, in such a company during the busy season, much of the current assets is invested in inventories and accounts receivable; and during the slack or off season these inventories and accounts are turned into cash through sales and collections. Often during the slack season, in order to earn additional income, this temporarily idle cash is invested in high-grade securities which at the beginning of the next busy season are converted back to cash.

In addition to the foregoing, some companies have what they term "secondary cash reserves." These are not cash but are government and corporate bonds plus high-quality stocks held for emergencies. Here the intention is not necessarily to sell within one year but to sell in case of need. Nevertheless, these too are classified as temporary investments, a current asset.

If a balance sheet is prepared while temporary investments are held, such investments should appear as a current asset immediately following cash. Also, since temporary investments are current assets, they are normally reported on the balance sheet at lower of cost or market. However, both cost and market should be shown as follows:

Current Assets:
Cash $23,000
Temporary investments, at cost (present market value, $14,700) 13,250
Notes receivable 2,500

When a group of securities is valued at the lower of cost or market, it is considered acceptable to base the valuation on the lower of cost or market for the entire group. In other words, cost or market may be applied on a group or total basis rather than security by security.

Long-term investments

Long-term investments differ from temporary in that they are normally to be kept for a longer period. Long-term investments include funds earmarked for special purposes, such as bond sinking funds and building funds, as well as real estate and other long-term assets owned but not employed in the regular business operations. Long-term investments also include shares of stock held for purposes of controlling another corporation or for maintaining good customer or supplier relations, or for any other reason that would make their sale inadvisable.

Such investments appear in a classification of their own titled "Long-term investments," which is placed on the balance sheet immediately following the current asset section. Since there is no intention to sell, almost invariably they are reported at cost, or in the case of bonds, at cost adjusted for premium or discount amortized.

Accounting for stocks as investments ■ When stocks are purchased as investments, either short or long term, their purchase is recorded at total cost, which includes the commission paid the broker. For example, 1,000 shares of American Sales Corporation common stock are purchased as an investment at $23\frac{1}{4}$ plus a $300 broker's commission. The entry to record the transaction is:

Sept.	10	American Sales Corporation Stock...................	23,550.00	
		Cash..		23,550.00
		Purchased 1,000 shares of stock for $23,250 plus a $300 broker's commission.		

Observe in the foregoing entry that nothing is said about a premium or a discount on the American Sales Corporation stock. Nothing is said because stock premiums and discounts apply only when stock is first issued. They do not apply to sales and purchases between investors.

When cash dividends are received on stocks held as either temporary or long-term investments, an entry similar to the following is made:

Oct.	5	Cash..	1,000.00	
		Dividends Earned..		1,000.00
		Received a $1 per share dividend on the American Sales Corporation stock.		

Dividends on stocks do not accrue; consequently, an end-of-the accounting-period entry to record accrued dividends is never made. However, if a balance sheet is prepared after a dividend is declared but before it is paid, an entry debiting Dividends Receivable and crediting Dividends Earned may be made. Nevertheless, since dividend earnings are often immaterial and not taxable until received in cash, most companies do not record such dividends until received, and while this is not theoretically correct, it does keep reported and taxable dividends the same.

A dividend in shares of stock is not income, and a debit and credit entry recording it should not be made. However, a memorandum entry or a notation as to the additional shares should be made in the investment account. Also, receipt of the stock does affect the per share cost basis of the old shares. For example, if a 20-share dividend is received on 100 shares originally purchased for $1,500 or $15 per share, the cost of all 120 shares is $1,500 and the cost per share is $12.50 ($1,500 ÷ 120 shares = $12.50 per share).

When an investment in stocks is sold, normally a gain or a loss is incurred. If the amount received is greater than the original cost of the investment plus the commission on the sale and other costs, there is a gain. For example, if the 1,000 shares of American Sales Corporation common stock, the purchase of which at $23,550 was recorded above, are sold at 25¾ less a commission and taxes on the sale amounting to $315, there is a $1,885 gain, and the transaction is recorded:

Jan.	7	Cash..	25,435.00	
		American Sales Corporation Stock.............		23,550.00
		Gain on the Sale of Investments		1,885.00
		Sold 1,000 shares of stock for $25,750 less a $315 commission and other costs.		

When stocks are sold at a price less than their cost plus the sale costs, a loss is incurred. For example, if the American Sales Corporation stock of the previous illustrations is sold at 22½ less a commission and taxes of $295, a $1,345 loss is incurred, and the transaction is recorded:

Jan.	7	Cash...	22,205.00	
		Loss on the Sale of Investments	1,345.00	
		American Sales Corporation Stock.............		23,550.00
		Sold 1,000 shares of stock for $22,500 less a $295 commission and other costs.		

When an income statement is prepared, bond interest and dividends earned plus any gains or losses in investment sales are listed at the end in the "other revenues and expenses section."

Accounting for bonds as investments
■ Bonds like stocks are purchased as investments, but they differ in that interest accrues on bonds and must be accounted for. In a previous chapter it was pointed out that all bond transactions are "plus accrued interest." Consequently, when a bond is quoted between interest dates at $101\frac{1}{2}$, it means the bond is for sale at $101\frac{1}{2}$ plus accrued interest. The purchaser pays accrued interest to the seller, and if he in turn sells between interest dates, he collects accrued interest from the next buyer.

Bonds as short-term investments

Bonds purchased as short-term investments are accounted for at cost, which includes any commission paid a broker. Also, generally there is accrued interest to be accounted for as a separate item. For example, if six Zoom Corporation, $1,000, $6\frac{1}{2}\%$ bonds paying interest on each January 1 and July 1 are purchased as a temporary investment on May 1 at $102\frac{1}{2}$ plus a $15 commission and accrued interest, the cost of the bonds is $6,165 [($1,025 \times 6) + $15 = $6,165]$, and the four months' accrued interest amounts to $130 ($6,000 \times .065 \times 4/12 = $130)$. Consequently the entry to record the purchase is:

May	1	Zoom Corporation Bonds...............................	6,165.00	
		Bond Interest Earned.....................................	130.00	
		Cash...		6,295.00
		Purchased six bonds at $102\frac{1}{2}$ plus accrued interest and a $15 commission.		

Observe in the foregoing entry that the premium on the bonds, which includes the commission, is not treated as a separate item but is included within the debit to the bond investment account. However, the accrued interest is accounted for as a separate item.

On July 1, if the purchaser of the previous entry still holds these bonds, he will collect six months' interest on them, of which $130 is a return of the interest paid the previous holder when the bonds were bought and $65 is interest earned since their purchase. The receipt of the six months' interest is recorded as follows:

July	1	Cash..	195.00	
		Bond Interest Earned..............................		195.00
		Received six months' interest on the Zoom Corporation bonds.		

The net effect of the foregoing two entries on the Bond Interest Earned account is a $65 credit, which is the amount of interest earned by the buyer during the two months he has held the bonds.

Observe in the foregoing entry that in accounting for the interest on the Zoom Corporation bonds the premium on their purchase is ignored. This is the common practice. When bonds are purchased as a short-term investment, since they are not to be held to maturity, an effort is seldom if ever made to amortize the discount or premium on their purchase.

If the buyer of these bonds holds them until August 1 and then sells them at $101\frac{1}{2}$, plus accrued interest and less a $15 commission, the entry for the sale is:

Aug.	1	Cash..	6,107.50	
		Loss on Sale of Investments............................	90.00	
		Bond Interest Earned..............................		32.50
		Zoom Corporation Bonds.........................		6,165.00
		Sold six bonds at $101\frac{1}{2}$ plus accrued interest and less a $15 commission.		

At $101\frac{1}{2}$, less the commission, the bonds sold for $6,090 less $15, or for $6,075, net; consequently, there was $90 loss on their sale. Also, one month's interest, $32.50, had accrued and was collected from the new purchaser.

If the net amount received for the bonds had been greater than $6,165, there would have been a gain on the transaction.

Bonds as long-term investments

Bonds may be purchased as a long-term investment; and when they are, they are accounted for in the same manner as bonds bought for a short-term investment, with one exception. The exception has to do with accounting for interest earned. Here, since the bonds may be held to maturity, a portion of the premium or discount on the bonds may be amortized at the time of each interest receipt.

For example, 10 Zest Corporation, $1,000, 6% bonds are purchased on their interest date, January 1, 15 years before maturity at $98\frac{1}{4}$ plus a $25 commission. The bonds cost $9,850 [(10 × $982.50) + $25 = $9,850]; and since they are purchased on their interest date, there is no accrued interest. Consequently, the entry to record the transaction is:

Jan.	1	Zest Corporation Bonds...............................	9,850.00	
		Cash..		9,850.00
		Purchased 10 bonds on their interest date at 98¼ plus a $25 commission.		

As previously stated, bonds differ from stocks in that sooner or later they mature and are normally redeemed at par. For example, if the Zest Corporation bonds are held to maturity and are redeemed at face value, they produce 6% interest each year plus a $150 gain at the end of 15 years. The gain is the difference between their cost and maturity value. This difference, although a combination of discount and commission, is called a discount and is treated as an adjustment of the bond interest earned; a portion is amortized on each interest payment date. For example, if a portion of the $150 is amortized each semiannual interest date, the entry to record the interest received and the discount amortized is:

July	1	Cash..	300.00	
		Zest Corporation Bonds...............................	5.00	
		Bond Interest Earned...............................		305.00
		Received the interest on the Zest Corporation bonds and amortized one thirtieth of the discount.		

In the entry just given, the $5 debit to the bond investment account increases the book value of the Zest Corporation bonds; and after the entry is posted, the bond investment account appears as follows:

Zest Corporation Bonds

Date	Explanation	Debit	Credit	Balance
Jan. 1, '70	Purchase	9,850.00		9,850.00
July 1, '70	Discount amortization	5.00		9,855.00

If these bonds are held to maturity and the account balance is increased $5 on each semiannual interest date, when the bonds mature, they will be shown in the account at their full $10,000 maturity value.

Bonds purchased as long-term investments may be sold before maturity. If the Zest Corporation bonds are held three years and then sold, the bond investment account just prior to the sale will show a $9,880 adjusted cost basis for the bonds and will appear as follows:

Zest Corporation Bonds

Date	Explanation	Debit	Credit	Balance
Jan. 1, '70	Purchase	9,850.00		9,850.00
July 1, '70	Discount amortization	5.00		9,855.00
Jan. 1, '71	Discount amortization	5.00		9,860.00
July 1, '71	Discount amortization	5.00		9,865.00
Jan. 1, '72	Discount amortization	5.00		9,870.00
July 1, '72	Discount amortization	5.00		9,875.00
Jan. 1, '73	Discount amortization	5.00		9,880.00

If the bonds are sold after three years for $9,975 less a $25 commission, the entry to record the sale is:

Jan.	1	Cash..	9,950.00	
		Zest Corporation Bonds........................		9,880.00
		Gain on Sale of Investments....................		70.00
		Sold Zest Corporation bonds for $9,975		
		less a $25 commission.		

Bonds may be purchased as a long-term investment at a cost greater than their maturity value. In such a case the bonds are recorded at cost and the difference between cost and maturity value, called a premium, may be treated as an interest rate adjustment and amortized over the remaining life of the bonds.

Not all companies amortize discounts and premiums on long-term investments in bonds. Some prefer to take up the difference between cost and maturity value as a loss or gain at maturity.

Questions for class discussion

1. Who are the insiders of a corporation? Who are its outsiders?
2. What are accounting principles? Why are they needed?
3. What is the essence of the business entity concept?
4. What is the essence of the going-concern concept?
5. Explain how a business just breaking even (no profit or loss) will recover the cost of its plant assets over a period of years through the sale of its products.
6. Do the dollar amounts shown on a balance sheet for assets represent the value of these assets?
7. What is the essence of the periodicity concept?
8. A company constructed a machine for itself after a local shop submitted a low bid of $15,000 for building it. It cost the company $10,000 to build the machine, and in recording the acquisition the company debited Machinery for $15,000 and took up a $5,000 profit on the deal. Was this a correct treatment for the transaction? What accounting principle governs in this situation?
9. An automobile dealer offers a customer $800 cash for his used car. However, if the customer will buy a new car for $4,000, he will allow the cus-

tomer a $1,000 trade-in on his old car. (*a*) If the customer accepts the offer for trading in his old car, what is the cost of the new car to the customer? (*b*) What is the dealer's revenue from the sale of the new car?

10. When is revenue recognized under the (*a*) sales basis, (*b*) cash basis, and (*c*) production basis?

11. What is the essence of the objectivity principle?

12. What is the best objective evidence upon which to base an accounting entry?

13. May a concern change its inventory costing method at will? If it does so, what accounting principle is violated?

14. If a company changed its accounting methods at will, what would be lost?

15. What is the essence of the full-disclosure principle?

16. Under what accounting principle does an accountant justify his charging the cost of a wastebasket to an expense account in the year of purchase, rather than to an asset account the balance of which will be depreciated over the wastebasket's life?

17. What determines the number of transactions an auditor will examine in making his annual audit of a company's records?

18. What is the balance sheet classification of securities purchased as (*a*) a short-term investment and (*b*) a long-term investment? (*c*) What determines the balance sheet classification of securities purchased as an investment?

Class exercises

Exercise 20–1

A mail-order company, the accounting periods of which end each October 31, sends out its general catalog at the end of August each year; and its customers order from this catalog for a year until the new catalog arrives on about September 1 of the next year. Last August it cost $1,500,000 to print and mail the catalog, and the company followed its usual practice and charged the entire cost to an expense account on the day the catalog was mailed.

Required:
Did the company violate generally accepted accounting principles? Would you suggest an alternate treatment for the printing and mailing costs? State your position and defend it.

Exercise 20–2

Prepare general journal entries to record these transactions:

Jan. 3 Purchased as a short-term investment 500 shares of Vale Company common stock at $16\frac{1}{4}$ plus a $115 commission.

Feb. 24 Received the regular $0.20 per share quarterly dividend on the Vale Company common stock.

Mar. 27 Sold the Vale Company stock at $20\frac{1}{2}$ less a $135 commission.

Exercise 20–3

Prepare general journal entries to record these transactions:

Feb. 4 Purchased as a long-term investment 800 shares of Lake Corporation, $10 par value common stock, paying $15\frac{1}{2}$ plus a $200 commission.

Apr. 15 Received a $0.25 per share dividend on the Lake Corporation stock.
July 18 Received a 100-share stock dividend on the Lake Corporation stock.
    21 Sold the 100 shares of Lake Corporation stock received as a dividend on July 18, receiving 15¼ less a $25 commission.
Oct. 17 Changed the investment policy toward the remaining Lake Corporation shares and sold them at 13½ less a $170 commission.

Exercise 20–4

Prepare general journal entries to record these transactions:
Mar. 1 Purchased as a short-term investment six $1,000, Port Corporation 6½%, 25-year bonds on which interest is payable each January 1 and July 1. The purchase price was 102½ plus two months' accrued interest and a $15 commission.
July 1 Received the semiannual interest on the Port Corporation bonds.
Nov. 1 Sold the Port Corporation bonds at 102 plus four months' accrued interest and less a $15 commission.

Exercise 20–5

Prepare general journal entries to record these transactions:
1968
Jan. 1 Purchased as a long-term investment 10 $1,000, Bluff Corporation, 6%, 20-year bonds on their interest date 10 years before maturity, paying 97¼ plus a $25 commission.
July 1 Received a check for the semiannual interest on the Bluff Corporation bonds and amortized a portion of the purchase discount.
1973
Jan. 1 After receiving the semiannual interest on the Bluff Corporation bonds and after amortizing a total of one half the purchase discount, changed the investment policy toward the bonds and sold them at 99½ less a $25 commission.

Problems **Problem 20–1**

In each of the following unrelated cases one or more accounting principles may have been ignored. In each case in which you think a principle may have been ignored, name the principle and write a sentence or so telling what should have been done. In any case in which you think generally accepted principles were followed, write a sentence or so defending the action taken.

a) Walter Kraft, his wife, and son own all the stock in Walter Kraft, Inc., a manufacturing concern. Mr. Kraft is president and manages the company; the son is in college; and Mrs. Kraft takes no part in the management or other affairs of the company. However, during the past year the company leased an Oldsmobile 98 which was turned over to Mrs. Kraft for her personal use. She was also given a credit card, issued to the company, for use in charging gas, oil, and repairs to the car.

b) Some 10 years ago a company purchased for $15,000 a tract of land adjacent to its plant. From the time of its purchase until this year the land was carried at cost in an account, Long-Term Investment in Land. In March of this year the land was appraised by an independent appraiser and assigned a

$50,000 current market value. In June it was graded and paved for an employees' parking lot at a $40,000 cost for the grading and paving, and the company recorded the transaction as follows:

June	27	Land Improvements........................	90,000.00	
		Long-Term Investment in Land...		15,000.00
		Gain on Investments.................		35,000.00
		Cash		40,000.00

c) A company received as a gift from one of its stockholders a plot of land having a $5,000 fair market value; but to secure and clear title to the land, the company had to pay $450 in delinquent taxes plus transfer and other fees totaling $50. As a result, the bookkeeper recorded the land's acquisition at cost with a $500 debit to Land and a $500 credit to Cash.

d) Zeel Company was sued for $1,000,000 in August, 197A, by a competitor who claimed patent infringements. The company took no accounting action as a result of the suit during 197A and 197B because it was not scheduled for trial until 197C, and besides the company's directors were of the opinion that the competitor had no basis for the suit and could not win.

e) To reduce accounting costs, a company follows the practice of charging directly to an expense account at the time of purchase any machine or piece of equipment having an invoice price of $100 or less.

f) The factory building of Tiptop Company, carried in its accounts at its $200,000 cost less $75,000 accumulated depreciation, was appraised for insurance purposes and found to have a $300,000 replacement cost and to be one third depreciated. Upon receipt of the appraisal, the company president ordered a clerk in the accounting department to write up the value of the building and to credit the gain to Contributed Capital from Appraisal. The clerk, meek fellow that he was, swallowed twice and complied.

Problem 20–2

Clearwater Construction Company was low bidder on an irrigation project at $4,500,000 and it received the contract for the job. The project was begun in 197A and was scheduled for completion early in 197C. The contract provided for payments of $1,500,000 to the company at the ends of each of 197A and 197B and an additional $1,500,000 on completition of the project. The company estimated it would incur $1,080,000 of costs on the job during 197A, $2,700,000 during 197B, and $270,000 in 197C.

At the end of 197A, after having incurred $1,080,000 of costs on the job and after having received the first $1,500,000 payment on the contract price, the company's accountant was asked to prepare a 197A income statement for the company plus estimated 197B and 197C income statements. He recognized that theoretically the revenue from the job could be recognized and taken up on (a) a sales basis (on completion of the job), (b) a cash basis (as payments were received), or (c) a production basis.

Required:

1. Prepare three comparative income statements for the company. In the first recognize revenue on a sales basis, in the second on a cash basis, and in the third on a production basis. In each show 197A revenue, costs, and income

or loss in the first column, with estimated figures for 197B in the second column, and estimated figures for 197C in the third column.

2. Examine your statements and state which method of revenue recognition best matches revenues and expenses in this case.

Problem 20-3

PART 1. Phoenix Sales has been in business one year selling on an installment basis for $250 a machine that costs $150. The following information about the year's operations is available:

Sales (all on an installment basis) $375,000
Installment accounts receivable... 283,000
Expenses (including sales commissions)...................................... 60,000

Required:
Prepare (*a*) a calculation showing the company's income before taxes under the assumption it recognizes revenue on a sales basis; and (*b*) prepare a second calculation showing income before taxes under the assumption it recognizes revenue on a cash basis and matches sales commissions, $25 or 10% on each machine, with revenue.

PART 2. Bi-City Contractors began three jobs in 197A. Job No. 1 was completed during 197B, and Jobs Nos. 2 and 3 were completed in 197C. Following are the contract prices, estimated costs, and yearly costs for the jobs:

Job No.	Contract Prices	Estimated Costs	197A Costs	197B Costs	197C Costs
1	$2,500,000	$2,250,000	$1,800,000	$ 504,000	
2	4,000,000	3,600,000	1,080,000	945,000	$1,610,000
3	3,000,000	2,700,000	72,000	1,440,000	1,117,000
Total	$9,500,000	$8,550,000	$2,952,000	$2,889,000	$2,727,000

Required:
Determine the revenue the company will recognize in each of the three years if (1) it recognizes revenue on a sales basis and (2) it recognizes revenue on a production basis.

Problem 20-4

Cascade Construction Company recognized revenue on a sales basis during 197A, 197B, and 197C with these results:

CASCADE CONSTRUCTION COMPANY
Condensed Comparative Income Statement for 197A-B-C

	197A	197B	197C	Combined
Construction revenue	$340,000	$465,000	$565,000	$1,370,000
Construction costs....................	433,200	426,000	374,000	1,233,200
Construction income or loss*......	$ 93,200*	$ 39,000	$191,000	$ 136,800

During the three-year period the company began and completed three jobs. Job No. 1 was begun and completed in 197A; Job No. 2 was begun in 197A and completed in 197B; and Job No. 3 was begun in 197B and completed in 197C. The following additional information about the jobs is available:

Job No.	Contract Prices	Estimated Costs	197A Costs	197B Costs	197C Costs
1	$ 340,000	$ 306,000	$307,200		
2	465,000	418,500	126,000	$291,000	
3	565,000	508,500		135,000	$374,000
Total	$1,370,000	$1,233,000	$433,200	$426,000	$374,000

Required:
Prepare a comparative income statement showing each year's and the combined revenue, costs, and net income with revenue recognized on a production basis.

Problem 20–5

Prepare general journal entries to record the following transactions:

197A

Jan. 8 Purchased as a long-term investment 1,000 shares of Silver Corporation, $10 par value, common stock, paying 24¼ plus a $280 commission.

Mar. 1 Received a $0.30 per share quarterly cash dividend on the Silver Corporation stock.

June 1 Received a 100-share stock dividend on the Silver Corporation common stock.

2 Sold the 100 shares of Silver Corporation stock received as a dividend in the previous transaction, receiving 23½ less a $25 commission.

July 1 Purchased as a temporary investment 200 shares of Gold Corporation common stock, paying 42¾ plus $80 commission.

Aug. 28 Sold the Gold Corporation common stock at 36 less a $75 commission.

Sept. 1 Purchased as a temporary investment 10 $1,000, Copper Corporation, 6%, 20-year bonds on which interest is payable semiannually on each November 1 and May 1. The purchase price was 97 plus four months' accrued interest and a $25 commission.

Nov. 1 Received a check for the semiannual interest on the Copper Corporation bonds.

197B

Jan. 1 Sold the Copper Corporation bonds at 98¼ plus two months' accrued interest and less a $25 commission.

Mar. 1 Purchased as a long-term investment 10 Iron Corporation, $1,000, 6½%, 20-year bonds on their interest date 10 years before maturity. The purchase price was 102¾ plus a $25 commission.

Sept. 1 Received a check for the semiannual interest on the Iron Corporation bonds and amortized a portion of the purchase premium.

197C

Mar. 1 Received a check for the semiannual interest on the Iron Corporation bonds and amortized a portion of the premium.

1 Changed the investment policy toward the Iron Corporation bonds and sold them at 101½ less a $25 commission.

Problem 20–1A

In each of the following unrelated cases one or more accounting principles may have been ignored. In each case in which you think a principle may have been ignored, name the principle and write a sentence or so telling what should have been done. In any case in which you think generally accepted principles were followed, write a sentence or so defending the action taken.

a) Early this year High Flyer Company acquired the plant, equipment, and other assets of a company that had experienced a number of financial and operating problems during recent years. High Flyer Company paid for the assets acquired with 100,000 shares of its own stock, and in addition it agreed to pay $250,000 of delinquent property taxes on the acquired plant and equipment. Upon completion of the purchase, the High Flyer accountant took the plant, equipment, and other assets purchased into his company's accounts at an amount equal to the book value of the 100,000 shares of stock given, which was some 20% under their market value on the day of the purchase. He also recorded the check for the delinquent property taxes with a debit to Property Taxes Expense.

b) On January 10, 197B, a company's plant was struck by a tornado that caused $500,000 of damage to the plant. The company's insurance was adequate to pay for the physical damage to the plant, but it made no provision for the loss that would result from the one-month shutdown while repairs were being made. The company had expected to show a $1 per share profit during the first three months of 197B; however, as a result of the shutdown, it could expect to no more than break even. Nevertheless, since the wind damage occurred after the close of business on December 31, 197A, and did not affect the amount of the company's assets of that date, the company mailed its 197A statements to its stockholders without further accounting action.

c) The purchase of a stapler was recorded with a debit to the Office Equipment account for its $8 cost. The stapler was expected to have a 10-year life and no salvage value. As a result, a subsidiary plant asset record card was set up and $0.80 depreciation was recorded on the stapler at the ends of each of the first four years of its life. During the fifth year it disappeared from the office and the loss was recorded with a debit to an account called Miscellaneous Expenses and Losses.

d) A company opened a new branch in a leased building. The lease contract ran for 25 years, required no payment at the time the lease was signed, but did provide for a $36,000 annual rental charge, a material amount. The rental payment was recorded each year with a debit to Rent Expense, and no further accounting action was taken.

e) A company had a bad year during 197A; as a result, its president ordered a clerk in the accounting department to keep the Sales account open during the first two weeks of 197B and to record the sales of that period as though they had occurred during the 197A period, which ended on December 31. The clerk, fearful for his job, followed the president's orders.

f) A company changed its inventory costing method from Fifo to Lifo during 197A. The change made a material difference in its reported 197A net income. However, the year-end balance sheet and the 197A income statement both referred to the change by means of a footnote which told of the change, restated the 197A income on the basis of Fifo, and restated the reported incomes of the previous five years on the basis of Lifo.

Problem 20–2A

Big Y Construction Company won a contract to build a bridge across Rapid River for $3,600,000. It estimates it will take almost two and a half years to complete the job and that it will incur the following costs by years: 197A, $1,125,000; 197B, $1,755,000; and 197C, $360,000. The contract provides for a $1,200,000 payment to the contractor at the end of 197A, another $1,200,000 at the end of 197B, and a final $1,200,000 on completion of the job in 197C. The company has no other jobs in process and does not expect to take on any until after it completes the Rapid River bridge.

As accountant for Big Y Construction Company you have been asked to prepare estimated 197A, 197B, and 197C income statements for the company. You recognize that theoretically revenue can be recognized on this job on a sales basis (on completion of the job), on a cash basis (as payments are received), and on a production basis.

Required:
1. Prepare three comparative income statements for the company. In the first recognize revenue on a sales basis, in the second on a cash basis, and in the third on a production basis. In each show 197A revenue, costs, and income or loss in the first column, 197B figures in the second column, and 197C amounts in the third.
2. Examine your statements and state which method of revenue recognition best matches revenues and expenses in this case.

Problem 20–4A

Hard Rock Construction Company recognized revenue on a sales basis during its first three years with these results:

	197A	197B	197C	Combined
Construction revenue	$260,000	$465,000	$620,000	$1,345,000
Construction costs	452,800	381,300	374,100	1,208,200
Construction income or loss*	$192,800*	$ 83,700	$245,900	$ 136,800

During this period the company began and completed three jobs. Job No. 1 was begun and completed during 197A; Job No. 2 was begun in 197A and completed in 197B; and Job No. 3 was begun in 197B and completed in 197C. The following information as to contract prices and costs is available:

Job No.	Contract Prices	Estimated Costs	197A Costs	197B Costs	197C Costs
1	$ 260,000	$ 234,000	$235,000		
2	465,000	418,500	217,800	$198,600	
3	620,000	558,000		182,700	$374,100
Total	$1,345,000	$1,210,500	$452,800	$381,300	$374,100

Required:

Prepare a comparative income statement showing each year's and the combined revenue, costs, and net income with revenue recognized on a production basis.

Problem 20–5A

Prepare general journal entries to record these transactions:

197A

Feb. 1 Purchased as a long-term investment 10 Maple Corporation, $1,000, $6\frac{1}{2}\%$, 20-year bonds on their interest date five years before maturity at $101\frac{3}{4}$ plus a $25 commission.

Mar. 12 Purchased as a temporary investment 500 shares of Ash Corporation common stock at $35\frac{1}{4}$ plus a $195 commission.

Apr. 1 Purchased as a temporary investment 10 Oak Corporation, $1,000, 6%, 20-year bonds on which interest is payable each February 1 and August 1. The purchase price was $98\frac{1}{4}$ plus a $25 commission and two months' accrued interest.

May 5 Received a $0.40 per share dividend on the Ash Corporation stock.

Aug. 1 Received a check for the semiannual interest on the Maple Corporation bonds and amortized a portion of the purchase premium.

1 Received a check for the semiannual interest on the Oak Corporation bonds.

4 Received 100 shares of Ash Corporation common stock as a dividend on the 500 shares owned.

5 Sold the 100 shares of Ash Corporation stock received as a dividend, receiving 32 less a $35 commission.

Oct. 15 Sold the remaining shares of Ash Corporation stock at 28 less a $185 commission.

17 Purchased as a long-term investment 1,000 shares of Elm Corporation common stock at 20 plus a $270 commission.

Dec. 1 Sold the Oak Corporation bonds at $99\frac{1}{2}$ plus four months' accrued interest and less a $25 commission.

197B

Feb. 1 After receiving the semiannual interest on the Maple Corporation bonds and amortizing a portion of the purchase premium, changed the investment policy toward them and sold them at 103 less a $25 commission.

Decision problem 20–1, Northwest Bank

A year ago a senior officer in the trust department of Northwest Bank announced he would retire in one year, and it was recognized that this would create openings for promotions down the line to the junior members of the department staff. It was also recognized there would be no problems in choosing the men to promote, except as between two very junior men on the staff, Dale West and Jerry Lee. Both men had been in the trust department less than a year, had the same educational background, and seemed equal in all respects. Consequently, it was decided to give each responsibility for investing $100,000 of the bank's funds and to pick for promotion the one who did the best job.

Now, one year later, the time to choose has arrived. Both men have worked hard all year and, as between themselves, seem equal. However, in comparing their investment portfolios, Jerry Lee discovered that his portfolio had paid 0.8% more interest during the year than had Dale West's. As a result, he was elated and was certain that he would receive the promotion.

The portfolios of the two men contain the bonds listed below. (All bonds were purchased one year ago, and the number of years to maturity in each case date from the time of their purchase.)

DALE WEST'S PORTFOLIO	Cost	Cash Interest Received
$20,000 par value, 5½%, Southwest Utility Company bonds, 10 years to maturity.....................................	$ 18,000	$1,100
$30,000 par value, 5%, Atlantic Telephone Company bonds, 5 years to maturity	27,800	1,500
$27,000 par value, 6%, Blue Chip Chemical Company bonds, 7 years to maturity	25,600	1,620
$30,000 par value, 6½%, Solid Steel Company bonds, 14 years to maturity	28,600	1,950
	$100,000	$6,170

Interest received on investments: $6,170 ÷ $100,000 = 6.170% return.

JERRY LEE'S PORTFOLIO	Cost	Cash Interest Received
$46,000 par value, 7½%, Quick Buck Oil Company bonds, 10 years to maturity.....................................	$ 50,000	$3,450
$44,000 par value, 8% Blue Sky Gold Mine Company bonds, 10 years to maturity.....................................	50,000	3,520
	$100,000	$6,970

Interest received on investments: $6,970 ÷ $100,000 = 6.970% return.

Based on their portfolios, which man should receive the promotion? Give reasons for your choice and support your conclusions with a schedule or schedules comparing the earnings of the portfolios.

Decision problem 20-2, Junior Accountant III

You have just been hired as a junior accountant, and as part of your training program you have been asked to write brief answers to the following problems:

PROBLEM 1. Action Bridge Company specializes in building large dams and bridges which normally require from 18 months to three years to complete. The company has been reporting revenue on a sales basis, but this is being questioned by a new board member who recently acquired a large block of the company's stock.

Discuss the company's revenue recognition problem, giving the conditions under which you would recommend that it recognize revenue on a production basis.

PROBLEM 2. Beachside Company acquired land from H. D. Fall by issuing

10,000 shares of its common stock to him in payment therefor. The stock has a $5 per share par value, and it had a $6.25 per share market value at the time the land purchase was effected. Fall had offered to sell the land to the company for $62,000 cash, and competent appraisers valued the land at $64,000. There are various opinions as to the amount at which the land purchase should be recorded by Beachside Company. They are (a) at the par value of the stock, $50,000; (b) at the $62,500 market value of the stock; (c) at the $62,000 cash offering price of the land; and (d) at the $64,000 fair appraised value of the land.

Discuss the problem, setting forth your opinion as to the proper accounting value to be placed on the land and outlining reasons therefor.

PROBLEM 3.   In late December last year Fastbuck Company purchased the entire inventory of a bankrupt competitor, paying $30,000 for goods that would have cost $50,000 if purchased through normal sources. As a result it recorded the transaction by debiting its Purchases account for $50,000, crediting Gain on the Purchase of Inventory for $20,000, and crediting Cash for the difference.

The goods were marked for sale as if they had cost $50,000; none were sold during the year of their purchase; but all were sold without markdowns during the following year, which ended on December 31.

Discuss the accounting principles violated in recording the purchase and tell how the transaction should have been recorded.

Chapter 21

Departmentalization and control

■ A business is departmentalized or divided into departments for managerial purposes, with each department commonly being placed in charge of a manager who under perfect circumstances is responsible for both the output of the department and the resources expended in attaining that output. Output may be in units of product manufactured, dollars of sales achieved, or services performed; and resources expended may be goods sold, raw materials consumed, wages paid, depreciation, heat, lights, et cetera. And, ideally the output should be obtained with the smallest expenditure of resources.

If management is to know how well each department is performing, it is necessary for the accounting system to supply information by departments as to resources expended and outputs achieved. Such an accounting system is known as a departmental system.

Departmental information for management's use only

■ Before examining the manner in which departmental accounting systems function, it should be observed that departmental operating details when gathered are generally not made public. Rather such information is for the use of management in controlling operations, appraising performances, allocating resources, and in taking remedial actions. For example, if one of several departments is particularly profitable, perhaps it should be expanded. Or if a department is showing poor results, information as to its revenues, costs, and expenses may point to a proper remedial action.

Basis for departmentalization ■ In every departmentalized business there are two basic kinds of departments, *productive departments* and *service departments*. In a factory the productive departments are those engaged directly in manufacturing operations, and in a store they are the departments making sales. In either type of business the service departments are such departments as the general office, advertising, purchasing, payroll, and personnel departments. Obviously, the service departments are so called because they assist or perform services for the productive departments.

The division of a factory into productive departments is commonly based on manufacturing processes employed or products or components manufactured. The division in a store is usually based on kinds of goods sold, with each selling or productive department being assigned the sale of one or more kinds of merchandise.

Departmental gross profits in a merchandising business ■ Departmental managers in merchandising concerns constantly make decisions that affect the gross profits of their departments, always with the intention of maximizing them. Of course, they do not ignore operating expenses, since their ultimate objective is net income; but the factors of gross profit receive a great deal of attention, probably because they are subject to considerable managerial control.

A departmental gross profit is the function of (1) the number of dollars of goods sold and (2) the markup on the goods sold. Therefore, management of departmental gross profits begins with the accumulation of information as to sales, purchases, and inventories by departments, so that departmental gross profits may be calculated. The information is gathered in several ways; and normally a store's size, the goods it sells, and the number of its departments determine the methods and procedures used.

Two common devices for gathering information needed in calculating departmental gross profits are (1) separate departmental accounts and (2) departmental analysis sheets.

Separate departmental accounts

A store having only a few departments may provide in its General Ledger a separate set of merchandise accounts for each. If it does so, it accumulates information until the end of an accounting period as to each department's sales, sales returns, purchases, and purchases returns in the department's own accounts. Then at the end of the period it takes inventories by departments; and using the information in the several separate sets of departmental accounts, it calculates cost of goods sold and gross profits by departments.

Departmental analysis sheets

Although a store having only a few departments may readily provide a separate set of merchandise accounts for each, a store with many departments may find its ledger rather large and awkward if it follows this procedure. As a result, a store with many departments, instead of opening separate accounts for each, often accumulates departmental information as to sales, sales returns, purchases, and purchases returns on departmental analysis sheets.

When a store uses departmental analysis sheets, it provides only one undepartmentalized general ledger account for all sales, another account for sales returns, another for purchases, and another for purchases returns; and it then records its transactions and posts to these accounts as though it were not departmentalized. But, in addition to this, each day it also summarizes its merchandise transactions by departments and records the summarized amounts on analysis sheets. For example, a concern using analysis sheets in addition to recording charge sales in the usual manner in a Sales Journal will sort and total each day's charge tickets by departments and enter the totals in the proper departmental columns of a sales analysis sheet like the one of Illustration 21–1. Also, it will determine daily cash sales by departments, and in addition to recording these sales in the usual manner in a Cash Receipts Journal, it will also enter the amounts on the analysis sheet. As a result, at the end of a month or other period, the column totals on the sales analysis sheet will tell sales by departments; and the grand total of all columns should equal the balance of the Sales account.

Departmental Sales Analysis Sheet

Date		Type of Sales	Men's Wear Dept.	Boys' Wear Dept.	Men's Shoe Dept.	Men's Hat Dept.	Women's Wear Dept.
May	1	Cash sales	257.00	110.00	155.00	37.00	197.00
		Charge sales	102.00	82.00	58.00	76.00	105.00
	2	Cash sales	138.00	97.00	127.00	58.00	222.00
		Charge sales	127.00	103.00	82.00	62.00	189.00
	3	Cash sales	152.00	72.00	97.00	73.00	205.00

Illustration
21–1

When a store uses departmental analysis sheets, it uses one analysis sheet for accumulating sales figures, another analysis sheet for sales returns, another for purchases, and still another for purchases returns; and at the end of a period the several analysis sheets give departmental breakdowns of the store's sales, sales returns, purchases, and purchases returns.

Recording transactions by departments

■ The use of separate accounts or the use of analysis sheets is one variation in accounting procedures found in departmentalized merchandising concerns. There are many others. For example, a concern having only a few transactions may use columnar pen-and-ink journals in recording transactions by departments, or a concern with more transactions may use electric bookkeeping machines, punched cards, or punched paper tape.

Pen-and-ink records

Pen-and-ink journals are adapted to departmental transactions by the simple procedure of increasing the columns in each journal; a separate column is added in each journal for each department. Illustration 21–2 shows a Purchases Journal for use in a departmentalized concern having

Illustration 21–2

Purchases Journal

Date		Account Credited	F	Accounts Payable Credit	Purchases Debit		
					Men's Dept.	Boys' Dept.	Shoe Dept.
Feb.	1	Acme Mfg. Co............		250.00	250.00		
	1	N. A. Green Co..........		110.00			110.00
	2	Horn Supply Co..........		275.00	200.00	75.00	

three departments. Each invoice recorded in this journal is entered on a separate line, with the invoice amount entered in the Accounts Payable credit column and distributed to the proper departmental purchases columns according to the items purchased. The credits to individual creditor accounts entered in the Accounts Payable column are posted daily, and the column totals are posted to the Accounts Payable controlling account and the proper departmental purchases accounts at the end of the month.

Obviously, this additional-columns technique is applicable to any journal or register such as, for example, a Sales Journal or Voucher Register.

Electric bookkeeping machines

Illustration 14–2 on page 396 shows a modern electric bookkeeping machine. It was explained beginning on page 396 that this machine could be used for sales accounting, purchases, cash receipts, or any other accounting application; and it was also explained how the machine could, for example, for each charge sale produce the customer's invoice, post to the customer's account, update the customer's month-end statement, and enter the sale in the Sales Journal. In addition to this, if the machine is properly set and the right keys are depressed in the sales invoice preparation procedure, the machine will accumulate information as to sales by departments and will print out departmental sales totals after the last sales invoice is prepared each day. When used for recording purchases or returns, it will also accumulate departmental totals for these transactions.

Punched cards

Illustration 21–3 shows a type of pin-punched price tag used by many large department stores. Such tags show the price of an item of merchandise and are an essential part of the inventory control system in a store using them—an inventory control system that makes it easy to accumulate information as to sales and returns by items, colors, sizes, manufacturers, et cetera, as well as in dollar amounts by departments.

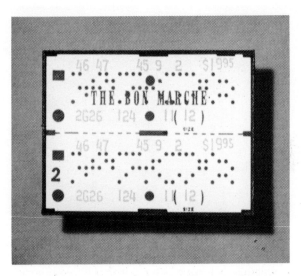

Illustration
21–3

Pin-punched price tags get their name from the pin-size holes punched in the tags. These holes carry information in the code arrangement of their punching as to an item's price, size, color, and so on. The machine used to punch the holes also prints the punched information on the tag for visual reading.

When an item of merchandise is sold, the lower half of the tag is removed by the salesclerk and placed on a spindle beside the cash register, and the upper half is left attached to the item sold. At the end of each day the spindled tag portions are taken to the accounting department and run through a tag converter, a machine that electronically repunches each tag's information into a regular full-size punched card like the ones described and illustrated in earlier chapters. After being punched, the full-size cards are automatically sorted and resorted by machine and are used to rapidly produce information as to sales by departments and other useful data.

When merchandise is returned, the customer is instructed to return with the merchandise the price tag portion left attached at the time of sale. These returned tag portions are spindled until the end of each day when they too are run through the tag converter to produce the full-size punched cards used in accounting for returns.

Punched paper tape

Some stores use punched paper tape in recording information about sales as to departments, prices, items, et cetera. The punched paper tape, which is approximately one inch in width, is produced by the cash registers on which salesclerks "ring up" sales. A sample of this tape is shown in Illustration 21–4.

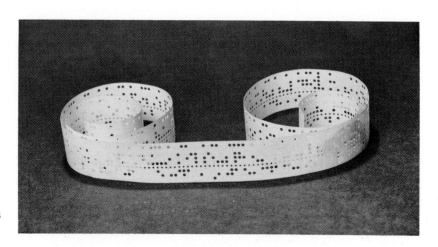

Illustration
21–4

In producing such paper tape, all that is required of the salesclerk is that he depress the proper cash register keys in "ringing up" a sale, causing the register to punch the sale information into the tape. At the end of each day the tape produced in each register is run through a tape-to-card converter which electronically converts the punched information on the tape to regular punched cards. The punched cards are then used in producing all desired summaries and reports.

Income statement showing departmental gross profits

■ Accumulating information and arriving at a gross profit figure for each selling department in a departmentalized business is not too difficult, as the foregoing pages reveal. However, to go beyond this and arrive at reliable net income figures is a little more difficult; consequently, many concerns make no effort to calculate more than gross profits by departments. Illustration 21–5 shows an income statement prepared for such a concern. The statement sets out departmental gross profits and combines these figures to arrive at a combined gross profit figure, a figure from which the unallocated operating expenses are deducted to arrive at the store's net income.

Observe in Illustration 21–5 that in addition to showing gross profits in dollar amounts, gross profits are also expressed as percentages of net sales. These percentages make departmental comparisons easier.

Valley Haberdashery
Income Statement
For Year Ended December 31, 19—

	Men's Clothing	Boys' Clothing	Shoes	Combined
Revenue from sales:				
Sales.................	$46,000	$34,000	$20,000	$100,000
Less returns......	750	425	350	1,525
Net sales	$45,250	$33,575	$19,650	$ 98,475
Cost of goods sold:				
Inventory, Jan. 1 ... $ 7,400		$ 4,200	$ 3,350	$14,950
Purchases........... 30,000		21,700	11,800	63,500
Freight-in 150		125	75	350
Goods for sale $37,550		$26,025	$15,225	$78,800
Inventory, Dec. 31.. 8,100		3,500	4,150	15,750
Cost of goods sold....	29,450	22,525	11,075	63,050
Gross profits...........	$15,800	$11,050	$ 8,575	$ 35,425
Gross profit percentages	(34.9%)	(32.9%)	(43.5%)	(36.0%)

Operating expenses:
Selling expenses:

Sales salaries	$7,000	
Sales commissions	5,000	
Advertising...	550	
Sales supplies used	200	
Depreciation of store equipment	700	
Total selling expenses.................................		$13,450

General and administrative expenses:

Office salaries	$3,800	
Office supplies used	250	
Expired insurance	300	
Bad debts..	210	
Depreciation of office equipment	150	
Depreciation of building....................................	1,200	
Property taxes..	900	
Total general and administrative expenses........................	6,810	
Total operating expenses		20,260
Net Income..		$ 15,165

Illustration
21–5

Allocating freight-in	■ Freight-in is a factor in calculating cost of goods sold. When possible, payments for freight should be analyzed and charged to individual departments so that a more accurate gross profit figure may be calculated for each. Either separate accounts or analysis sheets may be used.

In many stores the goods in a shipment are often consigned to a single department, and the freight on such a shipment may readily be charged to the responsible department. However, a shipment sometimes contains merchandise for several departments; and when this happens, it is necessary to allocate the shipment's freight charges among the departments on some fair basis, such as, for example, size and weight of the articles received.

Allocating expenses ■ If a concern goes beyond the calculation of departmental gross profits and attempts to arrive at a net income figure for each selling department, it must charge each department with its *direct expenses* and allocate to the departments any *indirect expenses*. The direct expenses of a department are those incurred for the sole benefit of that department; for example, the salary of an employee who works in only one department is a direct expense of that department. Indirect expenses are expenses incurred for the joint benefit of more than one department, for example, rent, heat, and lights. The entire amount of a direct expense may be charged directly to the department benefited by its incurrence. However, an indirect expense can only be allocated on some fair basis such as, for example, the amount of floor space occupied, as in the allocation of janitorial expenses.

When an indirect expense is allocated, portions are assigned to each department, preferably on the basis of benefits received. For example, a jewelry store purchases janitorial services from an outside firm and allocates the cost among its three departments according to the floor space occupied. If the cost of janitorial services for a period is $140 and the amounts of floor space occupied are:

Jewelry department	250 sq. ft.
Watch repair department..	125
China and silver department.....................................	<u>500</u>
Total	875 sq. ft.

The departmental shares of the janitorial expense are:

$$\text{Jewelry Department:} \quad \frac{250}{875} \times \$140 = \$40$$

$$\text{Watch Repair Department:} \quad \frac{125}{875} \times \$140 = \$20$$

$$\text{China and Silver Department:} \quad \frac{500}{875} \times \$140 = \$80$$

Bases for allocating expenses ■ In the following paragraphs, bases for allocating a representation of indirect expenses are discussed. In the discussions no hard-and-fast rules are given because several factors are often involved in an expense allocation, and the importance of the factors vary from situation to situation. Consequently, judgment rather than hard-and-fast rules is required.

Wages and salaries

An employee's wages may be either a direct or an indirect expense. If an employee spends all of his time in one department, his wages are a direct expense of the benefited department; but if an employee works in more than one department, his wages become an indirect expense that may be allocated between or among the benefited departments. Normally, working time spent in each department is a fair basis for allocating wages.

A supervisory employee at times supervises more than one department, and in such cases the time spent in each department is usually a fair basis for allocating his salary. However, since a supervisory employee is frequently on the move from department to department, the time spent in each is often difficult to measure. Consequently, some companies allocate the salary of such an employee to his departments on the basis of the number of employees in each department, while others make the allocation on the basis of the supervised departments' sales. When a supervisor's salary is allocated on the basis of employees, it is assumed that he is supervising people and the time spent in each department is related to the number of employees in each. When a supervisory employee's salary is allocated on the basis of sales, it is assumed that the time devoted to each department is related to the department's productiveness.

Rent

Rent expense is normally allocated to benefited departments on the basis of the amount and value of the floor space occupied by each.

Since all customers who enter a store must pass the departments by the entrance and only a fraction of these people go beyond the first floor, ground floor space is more valuable for retail purposes than is basement or upper floor space, and space near the entrance is more valuable than is space in an out-of-the-way corner. Yet since there is no exact measure of floor space values, all such values and the allocations of rent based on such values must depend on judgment. Nevertheless, if good judgment, statistics as to customer traffic, and the opinions of experts who are familiar with current rental values are used, fair allocations can normally be made.

Advertising

When a store advertises a department's products, if the advertising is effective, people come into the store to buy the products. However, at the same time they also often buy other unadvertised products. Consequently, advertising benefits all departments, even those the products of which are not advertised; and as a result, many stores treat advertising as an indirect expense and allocate it on the basis of sales. When advertising costs are allocated on a sales basis, a department producing one fifteenth of the total sales is charged with one fifteenth of the advertising cost and a department producing one sixth of the sales is charged with one sixth.

Although in many stores advertising costs are allocated to departments on the basis of sales, in others advertising is treated as a direct expense and charged directly to the departments. When advertising is charged directly, each advertisement is analyzed and the cost of the column inches of newspaper space or minutes of TV or radio time devoted to the products of a department is charged to the department.

Since advertising is treated by some stores as a direct expense and by others as an indirect expense, both treatments appear in the illustrations that follow.

Depreciation

Depreciation on equipment used solely in one department is a direct expense of that department; and if adequate plant asset records are kept, the depreciation applicable to each department may be learned by examining the records. Where adequate records are not maintained, depreciation must be treated as an indirect expense and allocated to the departments on the basis of the value of the equipment in each.

When the building is owned, building depreciation is normally allocated like rent.

Taxes and insurance

Taxes and insurance are indirect expenses and are allocated to departments on the basis of the insured and taxable property in each. Taxes and insurance on the building are allocated like rent.

Lights

Lighting expense is an indirect expense that is allocated on the basis of the number, size, and burning time of the lights in each department.

Heat

Heating costs are often allocated to the various floors of a building on the basis of the amount of radiation on each floor. Usually the first floor requires more radiation because of heat lost through the doors as customers enter and leave. After heating expense is allocated to the various floors, the amount allocated to each floor is assigned to the departments on the floor according to floor space occupied.

Delivery expense

The cost of delivering packages depends upon the number, size, and weight of the packages. Usually, it is impossible to consider all three factors in a single allocation basis. Consequently, the most important one is often used. Sometimes all three factors, number, size, and weight, are ignored, and delivery expenses are allocated on a sales basis. Often, too, where the number, size, and weight of packages are closely related to sales, such a basis is fair.

Mechanics of allocating expenses

■ It would be possible in most cases to analyze each indirect expense incurred and to allocate and charge portions to several departmental expense accounts at the time of incurrence or payment. However, this is seldom done because it involves too many allocations and too much work. Instead, expense amounts paid or incurred, both direct and indirect, are commonly accumulated in undepartmentalized expense

accounts until the end of a period, when a *departmental expense allocation sheet* is used to allocate and charge each expense to the benefited
departments. A departmental expense allocation sheet is shown in
Illustration 21–6 and is discussed in more detail later in this chapter.

**Allocating
service
department
expenses**

■ In order that they may sell their products, selling departments must
have the services provided by the service departments just as they must
have building space, heat, and lights. Therefore, service department
operating expenses are in effect indirect expenses of the selling departments; and if net incomes are calculated, the cost of operating each
service department should be allocated to the selling departments it
serves. The following list shows commonly used bases for these allocations:

Departments	Expense Allocation Bases
General office department	Number of employees in each department or sales.
Personnel department	Number of employees in each department.
Payroll department	Number of employees in each department.
Advertising department	Sales or amounts of advertising charged directly to each department.
Purchasing department	Dollar amounts of purchases or number of purchase invoices.
Cleaning and maintenance department	Square feet of floor space occupied.

**Depart-
mental
expense
allocation
sheet**

■ As previously stated, it would be possible to allocate and charge
most indirect expenses to departments as they are incurred or paid; but
this is seldom done. Rather, expenses are commonly accumulated in undepartmentalized expense accounts until the end of an accounting period
when a departmental expense allocation sheet is used, not only to allocate the accumulated expenses to the benefited departments but also
to allocate to the productive departments the costs of operating the
service departments. Illustration 21–6 shows such an allocation sheet.

To prepare an expense allocation sheet, the account names of the to-
be-allocated expenses are entered in the sheet's first column along with
the names of the service departments. Next, the bases of allocation are
entered in the second column, and the account balances are entered
in the third. Then, each expense account balance is allocated according
to the basis shown, and the allocated portions are entered in the departmental columns. After this the departmental columns are totaled and
the service department column totals are allocated in turn to the productive departments.

Upon completion, the amounts in the columns of an expense allocation sheet are available for preparing departmental income statements
showing net incomes by departments. Such a statement for the appliance
department of the firm of Illustration 21–6 is shown in Illustration 21–7.

Tempe Hardware Company
Departmental Expense Allocation Sheet
Year Ended December 31, 19—

Undepartmentalized Expense Accounts and Service Departments	Bases of Allocation	Expense Account Balances	Allocations of Expenses to Departments					
			General Office Dept.	Purchasing Dept.	Cleaning and Maintenance	Hardware Dept.	Housewares Dept.	Appliances Dept.
Salaries expense	Direct, payroll records	$39,050	$7,250	$6,400	$3,000	$10,200	$ 4,800	$ 7,400
Rent expense	Amount and value of space	7,200	360	360	40	3,200	814	2,426
Advertising	Sales	2,070				920	460	690
Expired insurance	Insured property	320	50	30	12	132	24	72
Depreciation of equipment	Direct, property records	1,200	200	125	50	350	175	300
Lighting expense	Wattage of lights	226	18	18	5	90	40	55
Heating expense	Floor space	960	48	48	8	424	144	288
Supplies used	Direct, requisitions	625	102	63	125	133	54	148
Total expenses by departments		$51,651	$8,028	$7,044	$3,240	$15,449	$ 6,511	$11,379
Allocation of service department expenses:								
General office	Sales		8,028			3,568	1,784	2,676
Purchasing department	Purchases			7,044		3,166	1,761	2,117
Cleaning and maintenance	Floor space				3,240	1,605	545	1,090
Total Expenses Applicable to Selling Departments		51,651				$23,788	$10,601	$17,262

Illustration
21–6

Tempe Hardware Company
Appliance Department Income Statement
For Year Ended December 31, 19—

Sales		$84,464
Cost of goods sold		59,321
Gross profit from sales		$25,143
Operating expenses:		
Sales salaries	$7,400	
Rent expense	2,426	
Advertising	690	
Expired insurance	72	
Depreciation of equipment	300	
Lighting expense	55	
Heating expense	288	
Supplies used	148	
General office expenses	2,676	
Purchasing department expenses	2,117	
Cleaning and maintenance expenses	1,090	
Total operating expenses		17,262
Appliance Department Net Income		$ 7,881

Illustration
21–7

Eliminating an unprofitable department ■ The management of a store in which departmental net incomes are calculated is often confronted with a situation in which one or more departments shows a loss. When this occurs, consideration is often given to eliminating the unprofitable department or departments; and when

Joe M. Hardt Company
Income Statement for Year Ended December 31, 19—

	Department A	Department B	Combined
Sales	$42,100	$63,150	$105,250
Cost of goods sold	31,400	37,800	69,200
Gross profit from sales	$10,700	$25,350	$ 36,050
Operating expenses:			
Selling expenses:			
Sales salaries	$ 6,000	$10,000	$16,000
Advertising	600	900	1,500
Store supplies used	150	280	430
Depreciation of store equipment	240	410	650
Rent expense	1,600	3,200	4,800
Total selling expenses	$ 8,590	$14,790	$23,380
General and administrative expenses:			
Expired insurance	$ 200	$ 350	$ 550
Bad debts expense	150	225	375
Share of general office expenses	2,580	3,870	6,450
Total general and administrative expenses	$ 2,930	$ 4,445	$ 7,375
Total operating expenses	11,520	19,235	30,755
Net Income or Loss (*)	$ 820*	$ 6,115	$ 5,295

Illustration
21–8

such consideration is given, what are known as escapable and inescapable expenses are encountered. Escapable expenses are those that would end with an unprofitable department's elimination; inescapable expenses are those that would continue even though the department were eliminated. For example, Joe M. Hardt Company is contemplating the elimination of its Department A. The company's income statement for the past year is shown in Illustration 21–8.

Joe M. Hardt Company's Department A incurred an $820 net loss for the year; however, an examination of its expenses reveals the following escapable and inescapable expenses:

	Escapable Expenses	Inescapable Expenses
Sales salaries	$6,000	
Advertising	600	
Store supplies used	150	
Depreciation of store equipment		$ 240
Rent expense		1,600
Expired insurance (merchandise and equipment)	180	20
Bad debts expense	150	
Share of the general office expenses	350	2,230
Totals	$7,430	$4,090

If Department A is discontinued, its $4,090 of inescapable expenses will have to be borne by Department B; thus, until Department A's annual loss exceeds $4,090 or until a more profitable department can be substituted, Joe M. Hardt Company is better off continuing the unprofitable department.

Aside from inescapable expenses, unprofitable departments are also often continued because they bring business to other profitable departments.

Departmental contributions to overhead

■ Many people, particularly department heads whose efficiencies are judged and whose salaries depend on the amounts of "net income" earned by their departments, are critical when such net income figures are used in making decisions as to departmental efficiencies. Their critical attitude arises from the fact that departmental net income figures are always affected by the assumptions made in the allocation of expenses.

People who are critical of departmental net income figures often suggest the substitution of *departmental contributions to overhead* when decisions are to be made. A department's contribution to overhead is the amount its revenues exceed its direct costs and expenses. In other words, a department's contribution to overhead is the amount of revenue remaining after direct items are charged but before indirect and service department expenses are allocated. Illustration 21–9 is a departmental income statement showing contributions to overhead.

Smithfield Men's Store
Departmental Income Statement for Year Ended December 31, 19—

	Men's Department	Boys' Department	Shoe Department	Combined
Revenue from sales	$100,000	$ 40,000	$ 20,000	$160,000
Cost of goods sold	65,000	24,000	12,000	101,000
Gross margin on sales	$ 35,000	$ 16,000	$ 8,000	$ 59,000
Direct expenses:				
Sales salaries	$ 18,000	$ 8,500	$ 3,500	$ 30,000
Advertising	1,000	500	300	1,800
Depreciation	700	400	300	1,400
Supplies used	300	200	100	600
Total direct expenses	$ 20,000	$ 9,600	$ 4,200	$ 33,800
Departmental contributions to overhead	$ 15,000	$ 6,400	$ 3,800	$ 25,200
Indirect expenses:				
Rent			$ 6,000	
Heating and lighting			800	
Taxes and insurance			1,200	
Total indirect expenses			$ 8,000	
Expenses of administrative departments			10,500	18,500
Net Income				$ 6,700

Illustration
21–9

Appraising departmental efficiencies
■ Net income figures are used in some stores in judging departmental efficiencies; and contributions to overhead are used for the same purpose in others. But, is either a net income figure or a contribution to overhead a good index of how well a department has performed? Some people hold that neither is. These people say that since many expenses entering into the calculation of a department's net income or into its contribution to overhead are beyond the control of the department's manager, neither net income nor contribution to overhead should be used in judging how well the department has operated.

People who oppose the use of net incomes and departmental contributions in appraising efficiencies are of the opinion that only a department's *controllable costs and expenses* should be used in judging how well the department has operated. A department's controllable costs and expenses are those over which the department's manager has some control as to the amounts expended. They are not the same as direct costs and expenses. Direct costs and expenses are those chargeable directly to a department; the amounts expended may or may not be under the control of the manager. For example, a manager often has little or no control over the amount of equipment in his department and its resulting depreciation, but he commonly has some control over the employees and the amount of work they do.

When controllable costs and expenses are used in judging a department's efficiency, statistics are prepared showing the department's output and its controllable costs and expenses. The statistics do not necessarily show either net income or contribution to overhead.

At this point a beginning student may ask, "Which best measures departmental efficiencies, net income figures, departmental contributions, or controllable costs and expenses?" The answer is that no one of the three may be applied without judgment; each is helpful, and each is used.

Joint costs ■ Joint costs which are encountered in some manufacturing concerns have much in common with indirect expenses. A joint cost is a single cost incurred to secure two or more essentially different products. For example, a meat-packer incurs a joint cost when he buys a pig from which he will get bacon, hams, shoulders, liver, heart, hide, pig feet, and a variety of other products in portions which he cannot alter. Likewise, a sawmill incurs joint costs when it buys a log and saws it into unalterable portions of Clears, Select Structurals, No. 1 Common, No. 2 Common, and other grades of lumber. In both cases, as with all joint costs, the problem is one of allocating the costs to the several joint products.

A joint cost may be, but is not commonly, allocated on some physical basis, such as the ratio of pounds, square feet, or gallons of each joint product to total pounds, square feet, or gallons of all joint products flowing from the cost. The reason this method is not commonly used is that the cost allocations resulting from its use may be completely out of keeping with the market values of the joint products, and thus may cause certain of the products to sell at a profit while other products always show a loss.

The usual method of allocating a joint cost is *in the ratio of the market values of the joint products at the point of separation.* For example, a sawmill buys for $30,000 a number of logs which when sawed produce a million board feet of lumber in the following grades and amounts:

Grade	Board Feet	Market Price per 1,000 Board Feet	Market Value of Production of Each Grade	Ratio of Market Value of Each Grade to Total
Structural	100,000	$120	$12,000	12/50
No. 1 Common	300,000	60	18,000	18/50
No. 2 Common	400,000	40	16,000	16/50
No. 3 Common	200,000	20	4,000	4/50
	1,000,000		$50,000	

If the foregoing ratios of market values by grades to the total market value of all grades is used in allocating the $30,000 joint log cost, the cost is apportioned between the grades as follows:

$$\begin{array}{lrcl}
\text{Structural:} & \$30{,}000 \times 12/50 & = & \$\ 7{,}200 \\
\text{No. 1 Common:} \ \$30{,}000 \times 18/50 & = & & 10{,}800 \\
\text{No. 2 Common:} \ \$30{,}000 \times 16/50 & = & & 9{,}600 \\
\text{No. 3 Common:} \ \$30{,}000 \times\ \ 4/50 & = & & \underline{2{,}400} \\
& & & \underline{\underline{\$30{,}000}}
\end{array}$$

Note that there are 1,000,000 board feet of lumber involved in these illustrations and the portion of No. 3 Common is $\frac{2}{10}$ of the total. If the No. 3 Common were allocated $\frac{2}{10}$ of the $30,000 log cost, it would be allocated $6,000 ($30,000 × $\frac{2}{10}$ = $6,000). This is more than the grade's $4,000 market value and would cause this grade to show a loss.

Now observe that if the No. 3 Common is allocated a share of the $30,000 joint cost based on market values by grades, it is allocated $2,400 of the $30,000. Furthermore, when the $2,400 is subtracted from the grade's $4,000 market value, $1,600 remains to cover other costs and perhaps a profit.

Questions for class discussion

1. Why is a business divided into departments?
2. Differentiate between productive departments and service departments.
3. Name several of a department store's service departments.
4. What are the productive departments of (*a*) a factory and (*b*) a store?
5. What is the purpose of a departmental sales analysis sheet? How is a sales analysis sheet used in determining sales by departments?
6. What is a pin-punched price tag? How is such a tag used in determining sales by departments?
7. How is punched paper tape used in determining sales by departments?
8. Differentiate between direct and indirect expenses.
9. Suggest a basis for allocating each of the following expenses to departments: (*a*) salary of a supervisory employee, (*b*) rent, (*c*) heat, (*d*) electricity used in lighting, (*e*) janitorial services, (*f*) advertising, (*g*) expired insurance, and (*h*) taxes.
10. How is a departmental expense allocation sheet used in allocating expenses to departments?
11. How reliable are the amounts shown as net incomes for the various departments of a store when expenses are allocated to the departments?
12. As the terms are used in departmental accounting, what are (*a*) escapable expenses and (*b*) inescapable expenses?
13. How is a department's contribution to overhead measured?
14. What are a department's controllable costs and expenses?
15. What is a joint cost? How is such a cost normally allocated?

Class exercises

Exercise 21–1

A company rents for $30,000 per year all the space in a building, which is assigned to its departments as follows:

Department A: 2,000 sq. ft. of first-floor space
Department B: 1,000 sq. ft. of first-floor space
Department C: 600 sq. ft. of second-floor space
Department D: 800 sq. ft. of second-floor space
Department E: 1,600 sq. ft. of second-floor space

The company allocates 60% of the total rent to the first floor and 40% to the second floor, and then allocates the rent of each floor to the departments on that floor on the basis of the space occupied. Determine the rent to be allocated to each department.

Exercise 21–2

A company rents for $7,200 per year all the space in a small building, and it occupies the space as follows:

Department A: 2,500 sq. ft. of first-floor space
Department B: 1,500 sq. ft. of first-floor space
Department C: 4,000 sq. ft. of second-floor space

Determine the rent expense to be allocated to each department under the assumption that first-floor space rents for twice as much as second-floor space in the city in which this company is located.

Exercise 21–3

Walter Deskin works in the men's shoe department and in the men's clothing department of Zest Department Store. His work consists of waiting on customers who enter either department and also in straightening and rearranging merchandise in either department as needed after it has been shown to customers. The store allocates his $4,000 in annual wages to the two departments in which he works. Last year the division was based on a sample of the time Deskin spent working in the two departments. To gain the sample, observations were made on several days throughout the year of the manner in which Deskin spent his time while at work. Following are the results of the observations:

Observed Manner in Which Employee Spent His Time	*Elapsed Time in Minutes*
Selling in men's shoe department	1,850
Straightening and rearranging merchandise in men's shoe department	350
Selling in men's clothing department	1,425
Straightening and rearranging merchandise in men's clothing department	375
Doing nothing while waiting for a customer to enter one of the selling departments	250

Required:
Prepare a calculation to show the shares of the employee's wages that should be allocated to the departments.

Exercise 21-4

Seal Company has two service departments, the office department and the purchasing department, and two sales departments, One and Two. During the past year the departments had the following direct expenses: general office department, $3,800; purchasing department, $2,800; Department One, $10,000; and Department Two, $7,000. The departments occupy the following amounts of floor space: office, 600; purchasing, 400; One, 1,200; and Two, 800. Department One had three times as many dollars of sales during the year as did Department Two, and during the year the purchasing department processed twice as many purchase orders for Department One as it did for Department Two.

Required:

Prepare an expense allocation sheet for Seal Company on which the direct expenses are entered by departments, the year's $6,000 of rent expense is allocated to the departments on the basis of floor space occupied, office department expenses are allocated to the sales departments on the basis of sales, and purchasing department expenses are allocated on the basis of purchase orders processed.

Exercise 21-5

Dale Realty Company has just completed a subdivision containing 15 building lots, of which 10 lots are for sale at $3,000 each and five are for sale at $4,000 each. The land for the subdivision cost $12,500, and the company spent $27,500 on street and sidewalk improvements. Assume that the land and improvement costs are to be assigned to the lots as joint costs and determine the share of the costs to assign to a lot in each price class.

Problems

Problem 21-1

Big Splash Store occupies all the space in a two-story building, and it has an account in its ledger called "Building Occupancy" to which it charged the following during the past year:

Depreciation, building	$12,000
Interest, building mortgage	17,500
Taxes, building and land	5,400
Heating expenses	1,700
Lighting expense	600
Cleaning and maintenance	12,000
Total	$49,200

The building has 6,000 square feet of floor space on each of its two floors, a total of 12,000 square feet; and the bookkeeper divided the $49,200 by 12,000 and charged the selling departments on each floor with $4.10 of occupancy cost for each square foot of floor space occupied.

Ted Smart, the manager of a second-floor department occupying 2,000 square feet of floor space, saw the $4.10 per square foot, or $8,200 of occupancy cost, charged to his department and complained. He cited a recent real estate board study which showed average rental charges for like space, including heat but not including lights, cleaning, and maintenance, as follows:

Ground-floor space .... $4.50 per sq. ft.
Second-floor space.. $3.00 per sq. ft.

Required:
Prepare a computation showing how much building occupancy cost you think should have been charged to Ted Smart's department last year.

Problem 21–2

Coast Sales carries on its operations with two service departments, the general office department and the purchasing department, and with three selling departments, A, B, and C. At the end of its annual accounting period the company's accountant prepared the following adjusted trial balance:

Coast Sales
Adjusted Trial Balance, December 31, 19—

Cash...	$ 7,875	
Merchandise inventory, Department A	9,300	
Merchandise inventory, Department B	18,200	
Merchandise inventory, Department C	14,500	
Supplies	620	
Equipment..	36,940	
Accumulated depreciation, equipment........................		$ 10,135
Jerry Collingsworth, capital		72,925
Jerry Collingsworth, withdrawals	9,000	
Sales, Department A		52,400
Sales, Department B...		104,200
Sales, Department C		68,400
Purchases, Department A..	34,400	
Purchases, Department B..	79,300	
Purchases, Department C..	41,700	
Salaries expense	36,855	
Rent expense	7,500	
Advertising expense	5,625	
Expired insurance	500	
Heating and lighting expense...................................	1,200	
Depreciation of equipment.....................................	1,820	
Supplies used	1,125	
Janitorial services..	1,600	
Totals	$308,060	$308,060

Required:
1. Prepare a departmental expense allocation sheet for Coast Sales, using the following information:

a) Coast Sales treats salaries, supplies used, and depreciation of equipment as direct departmental expenses. The payroll, requisition, and plant asset records show the following amounts of these expenses by departments:

	Salaries Expense	Supplies Used	Depr. of Equip- ment
General office	$10,295	$ 145	$ 250
Purchasing department	7,040	130	220
Department A	4,660	275	425
Department B	8,320	315	615
Department C	6,540	260	310
	$36,855	$1,125	$1,820

b) The company treats the remainder of its expenses as indirect and allocates them as follows:

   (1) Rent expense on the basis of the amount and value of floor space occupied. The general office occupies 600 square feet and the purchasing department occupies 400 square feet on a balcony at the rear of the store. This space is not as valuable as space on the main floor; therefore, the store allocates $500 of its rent to these two departments on the basis of space occupied and allocates the remainder to the selling departments on the basis of the main-floor space they occupy. The selling departments occupy main-floor space as follows: Department A, 2,000 square feet; Department B, 3,500 square feet; and Department C, 1,500 square feet.
   (2) Advertising expense on the basis of sales.
   (3) Insurance expense on the basis of the book values of the equipment in the departments, which are: general office, $2,500; purchasing, $2,000; Department A, $6,500; Department B, $9,500; and Department C, $4,500.
   (4) Heating and lighting and janitorial services on the basis of floor space occupied.

c) The company allocates general office department expenses to the selling departments on the basis of sales, and it allocates purchasing department expenses on the basis of purchases.

2. Prepare a departmental income statement for the company showing sales, cost of goods sold, expenses, and net incomes by departments and for the entire store. The year-end inventories were Department A, $11,600; Department B, $23,400; and Department C, $13,400.
3. Prepare a second income statement for the company showing departmental contributions to overhead and overall net income.

Problem 21–3

Mountain Sales Company began business last year with two selling departments and a general office department. It had the following results for the year:

MOUNTAIN SALES COMPANY
Departmental Income Statement
For Year Ended December 31, 19—

	Dept. 1	Dept. 2	Combined
Sales...	$120,000	$60,000	$180,000
Cost of goods sold	84,000	36,000	120,000
Gross profit from sales	$ 36,000	$24,000	$ 60,000
Direct expenses:			
Sales salaries.......................................	$ 12,500	$ 7,200	$ 19,700
Advertising expense	1,125	750	1,875
Store supplies used	600	300	900
Depreciation of equipment	1,025	550	1,575
Total direct expenses........................	$ 15,250	$ 8,800	$ 24,050
Allocated expenses:			
Rent expense	$ 5,400	$ 3,600	$ 9,000
Heating and lighting expense	1,080	720	1,800
Share of general office expenses	7,000	3,500	10,500
Total allocated expenses	$ 13,480	$ 7,820	$ 21,300
Total expenses	$ 28,730	$16,620	$ 45,350
Net Income	$ 7,270	$ 7,380	$ 14,650

The company plans to add a third selling department which it estimates
will produce $40,000 in sales with a 35% gross profit margin. The new depart-
ment will require the following estimated direct expenses: sales salaries, $4,500;
advertising expense, $450; store supplies, $250; and depreciation on equipment,
$525.

When the company began its operations, it was necessary to rent a store room
having selling space in excess of requirements. This extra space was assigned
to and used by Departments 1 and 2 during the year; but when Department 3
is opened, it will take over one third the space presently assigned to Department 1 and one sixth the space assigned to Department 2. The space reductions
are not expected to affect the operations or sales of the old departments.

The company allocates its general office department expenses to its selling
departments on the basis of sales. It expects the new department to cause a
$950 increase in general office department expenses.

The company expects the addition of Department 3 to bring new customers
to the store who in addition to buying Department 3 merchandise will also do
sufficient buying in the old departments to increase their sales by 5% each. It
is not expected that the increase in sales in the old departments will affect their
gross profit percentages nor any of their direct expenses other than supplies. It
is expected the supplies used will increase in proportion to sales.

Required:
Prepare a departmental income statement showing the company's expected
operating results with three departments.

Problem 21–4

Cooper Company is considering the elimination of its unprofitable Department B. The company's income statement for last year appears as follows:

Cooper Company
Income Statement for Year Ended December 31, 19—

	Dept. A	Dept. B	Combined
Sales	$76,500	$45,900	$122,400
Cost of goods sold	46,750	34,325	81,075
Gross margin on sales	$29,750	$11,575	$ 41,325

Operating expenses:
Direct expenses:

	Dept. A	Dept. B	Combined
Advertising	$ 1,175	$ 895	$ 2,070
Store supplies used	325	215	540
Depreciation of store equipment	850	475	1,325
Total direct expenses	$ 2,350	$ 1,585	$ 3,935

Allocated expenses:

	Dept. A	Dept. B	Combined
Sales salaries	$11,050	$ 6,630	$ 17,680
Rent expense	2,625	1,575	4,200
Bad debts expense	380	230	610
Office salaries	2,600	1,560	4,160
Insurance expense	200	150	350
Miscellaneous office expenses	325	200	525
Total allocated expenses	$17,180	$10,345	$ 27,525
Total expenses	$19,530	$11,930	$ 31,460
Net Income (Loss)	$10,220	$ (355)	$ 9,865

If Department B is eliminated:

1. The company has one office clerk who earns $80 per week or $4,160 per year and four salesclerks each of whom earns $85 per week or $4,420 per year. At present the salaries of two and one-half salesclerks are charged to Department A and one and one-half salesclerks to Department B. It is the opinion of management that two salesclerks may be dismissed if Department B is eliminated, leaving only two full-time clerks in Department A, and making up the difference by assigning the office clerk to part-time sales work in the department. It is felt that although the office clerk has not devoted half of her time to the office work of Department B, if she devotes the same amount of time to selling in Department A during rush hours as she has to the office work of Department B, it will be sufficient to carry the load.
2. The lease on the store building is long term and cannot be changed; therefore, the space presently occupied by Department B will have to be used by and charged to Department A. Likewise, Department A will have to make whatever use of Department B's equipment it can, since the equipment has little or no sales value.
3. The elimination of Department B will eliminate the Department B advertising expense, losses from bad debts, and store supplies used. It will also eliminate 80% of the insurance expense, the portion on merchandise, and 25% of the miscellaneous office expenses presently allocated to Department B.

Required:

1. List in separate columns the amounts of Department B's escapable and inescapable expenses.
2. Under the assumption that Department A's sales and gross profit will not be affected by the elimination of Department B, prepare an income statement showing what the company can expect to earn from the operation of Department A after Department B is eliminated.

Problem 21–5

A. Farmer produces potatoes. Last year after preparing the following income statement he remarked to his wife that they should have fed the No. 3 potatoes to the pigs and thus avoided the loss from the sale of this grade.

A. FARMER

Income from the Production and Sale of Potatoes

For Year Ended December 31, 19—

	Results by Grades			Combined
	No. 1	No. 2	No. 3	
Sales by grades:				
No. 1, 300,000 lbs. @ $0.045 per lb......	$13,500			
No. 2, 500,000 lbs. @ $0.04 per lb.......		$20,000		
No. 3, 200,000 lbs. @ $0.03 per lb.......			$6,000	
Combined...............................				$39,500
Costs:				
Land preparation, seed, planting, and cultivating @ $0.01422 per lb......	$ 4,266	$ 7,110	$2,844	$14,220
Harvesting, sorting, and grading @ $0.01185 per lb..............	3,555	5,925	2,370	11,850
Marketing @ $0.00415 per lb..............	1,245	2,075	830	4,150
Total costs......................	$ 9,066	$15,110	$6,044	$30,220
Net Income or (Loss).............	$ 4,434	$ 4,890	$ (44)	$ 9,280

On the foregoing statement A. Farmer divided his costs among the grades on a per pound basis. He did this because with the exception of marketing costs, his records did not show costs per grade. As to marketing costs, the records did show that $4,020 of the $4,150 was the cost of placing the No. 1 and No. 2 potatoes in bags and hauling them to the warehouse of the produce buyer. Bagging and hauling costs were the same for both grades. The remaining $130 of marketing costs was the cost of loading the No. 3 potatoes into trucks of a potato starch factory that bought these potatoes in bulk and picked them up at the farm.

Required:

Prepare an income statement that will show better the results of producing and marketing the potatoes.

Problem 21–1A

Zeal Department Store has in its ledger an account called "Building Occupancy Costs" to which it charged the following last year:

Building rent	$54,000
Lighting expense	2,000
Cleaning and maintenance	10,000
Total	$66,000

The store occupies all the space in a building having selling space on three levels—basement level, street level, and second-floor level. Each level has 5,000 square feet of selling space, a total of 15,000 square feet; and the bookkeeper divided the $66,000 of building occupancy cost by 15,000 and charged each selling department with $4.40 of building occupancy cost for each square foot of space occupied.

When Tom Sharp, the manager of a basement-level department having 1,500 square feet of floor space, saw the $4.40 per square foot of build occupancy cost charged to his department, he complained. In his complaint he cited a recent local real estate study which showed average charges for like space, including heat but not including lights and janitorial service, as follows:

Basement-level space	$2 per sq. ft.
Street-level space	$6 per sq. ft.
Second-floor-level space	$4 per sq. ft.

Required:
Prepare a computation showing the amount of building occupancy cost you think should be charged to Tom Sharp's department.

Problem 21–2A

Hether Sales has three selling departments, X, Y, and Z, and two service departments, general office and purchasing. At the end of an accounting period its bookkeeper brought together the following information for use in preparing the year-end statements:

SALES, PURCHASES, AND INVENTORIES:

	Dept. X	Dept. Y	Dept. Z
Sales	$95,400	$51,200	$73,400
Purchases	67,900	35,300	41,800
January 1 (beginning) inventory	12,300	8,500	10,200
December 31 (ending) inventory	14,500	9,400	7,300

DIRECT DEPARTMENTAL EXPENSES:

Hether Sales treats salaries, supplies used, and depreciation as direct departmental expenses. The payroll, requisition, and plant asset records showed the following amounts of these expenses by departments:

	Salaries Expense	Supplies Used	Depr. of Equipment
General office...	$ 9,345	$ 235	$ 625
Purchasing department..............................	6,160	195	375
Department X	10,360	385	850
Department Y	5,510	215	450
Department Z	8,140	295	500
	$39,515	$1,325	$2,800

INDIRECT EXPENSES:

The concern incurred the following amounts of indirect expenses:

Rent expense..	$6,600
Advertising expense...	5,500
Expired insurance...	750
Heating and lighting expense	1,750
Janitorial expense	2,100

Hether Sales allocates the foregoing expenses to its departments as follows:
a) Rent expense on the basis of the amount and value of floor space occupied. The general office and purchasing departments occupy space in the rear of the store which is not as valuable as space in the front; consequently, $600 of the total rent is allocated to these two departments in proportion to the space occupied by each. The remainder of the rent is divided between the selling departments in proportion to the space occupied. The five departments occupy these amounts of space: General Office, 600 square feet; Purchasing Department, 400 square feet; Department X, 3,000 square feet; Department Y, 1,500 square feet; and Department Z, 1,500 square feet.
b) Advertising expense on the basis of sales.
c) Expired insurance on the basis of equipment book values. The book values of the equipment in the departments are: General Office, $3,500; Purchasing Department, $2,000; Department X, $9,000; Department Y, $5,000; and Department Z, $5,500.
d) Heating and lighting and janitorial expenses on the basis of floor space occupied.

SERVICE DEPARTMENT EXPENSES:

Hether Sales allocates its general office department expenses to its selling departments on the basis of sales, and it allocates purchasing department expenses on the basis of purchases.

Required:
1. Prepare a departmental expense allocation sheet for the concern.
2. Prepare a departmental income statement showing sales, cost of goods sold, expenses, and net incomes by departments and for the entire store.
3. Prepare a second departmental income statement showing departmental contributions to overhead and overall net income.

Problem 21–3A

River Supply Company began its operations one year ago with two selling departments and one office department. The year's operating results are:

RIVER SUPPLY COMPANY
Departmental Income Statement
For Year Ended December 31, 19—

	Dept. A	Dept. B	Combined
Revenue from sales	$80,000	$50,000	$130,000
Cost of goods sold	52,000	30,000	82,000
Gross profit from sales	$28,000	$20,000	$ 48,000
Direct expenses:			
Sales salaries	$10,500	$ 6,000	$ 16,500
Advertising	900	675	1,575
Store supplies used	400	200	600
Depreciation of equipment	1,075	575	1,650
Total direct expenses	$12,875	$ 7,450	$ 20,325
Allocated expenses:			
Rent expense	$ 4,800	$ 2,400	$ 7,200
Heating and lighting expense	1,200	600	1,800
Share of office department expenses	4,800	3,000	7,800
Total allocated expenses	$10,800	$ 6,000	$ 16,800
Total expenses	$23,675	$13,450	$ 37,125
Net Income	$ 4,325	$ 6,550	$ 10,875

The company plans to open a third selling department which it estimates will produce $30,000 in sales with a 35% gross profit margin and requiring the following direct expenses: sales salaries, $4,500; advertising, $450; store supplies, $175; and depreciation of equipment, $350.

A year ago, when operations began, it was necessary to rent store space in excess of requirements. This extra space was assigned to and used by Departments A and B during the year; but when the new department, Department C, is opened it will take one fourth of the space presently assigned to Department A and one sixth of the space assigned to Department B.

The company allocates its general office department expenses to its selling departments on the basis of sales, and it expects the new department to cause a $525 increase in general office department expenses.

The company expects Department C to bring new customers into the store who in addition to buying goods in the new department will also buy sufficient merchandise in the two old departments to increase their sales by 5% each. And, although the old departments' sales are expected to increase, their gross profit percentages are not expected to change. Likewise, their direct expenses, other than supplies, are not expected to change. The supplies used will increase in proportion to sales.

Required:
Prepare a departmental income statement showing the company's expected operations with three selling departments.

Problem 21–5A

Ted Orchard produced and sold a half million pounds of apples last year, and he prepared the following statement to show the results:

TED ORCHARD
Income from the Sale of Apples
Year Ended December 31, 19—

	Results by Grades			Combined
	No. 1	No. 2	No. 3	
Sales by grades:				
No. 1, 200,000 lbs. @ $0.11 per lb.....	$22,000			
No. 2, 200,000 lbs. @ $0.07 per lb.....		$14,000		
No. 3, 100,000 lbs. @ $0.04 per lb.....			$ 4,000	
Combined sales				$40,000
Costs:				
Tree pruning and orchard care @ $0.021 per lb................................	$ 4,200	$ 4,200	$ 2,100	$10,500
Fruit picking, grading, and sorting @ $0.0252 per lb.........................	5,040	5,040	2,520	12,600
Marketing @ $0.0084 per lb..............	1,680	1,680	840	4,200
Total costs................................	$10,920	$10,920	$ 5,460	$27,300
Net Income or (Loss)........................	$11,080	$ 3,080	$ (1,460)	$12,700

Upon completing the statement, Mr. Orchard thought a wise course of future action might be to leave the No. 3 apples on the trees to fall off and be plowed under when he cultivated between the trees, and thus avoid the loss from their sale. However, before doing so he consulted you.

When you examined the statement, you recognized that Mr. Orchard had divided all his costs by 500,000 and allocated them on a per pound basis. You asked him about the marketing costs and learned that $3,960 of the $4,200 was incurred in placing the No. 1 and No. 2 fruit in boxes and delivering them to the warehouse of the fruit buyer. The cost for this was the same for both grades. You also learned that the remaining $240 was for loading the No. 3 fruit on the trucks of a cider manufacturer who bought this grade of fruit in bulk at the orchard for use in making apple cider.

Required:
Prepare an income statement that will reflect better the results of producing and marketing the apples.

Decision problem 21–1, Neal, Otto, and Parr   Fred Neal inherited a small plot of land; and to develop it, he entered into a partnership with John Otto, an investor, and Dale Parr, a real estate operator. Neal invested his land in the partnership at its $15,000 fair market value, Otto invested $13,000 in cash, and Parr invested $2,000; and they agreed to share losses and gains equally. The partnership installed streets and water mains costing $15,000 and divided the land into 14 building lots. They priced Lots 1, 2, 3, and 4 for sale at $3,000 each; Lots 5, 6, 7, 8, 9, 10, 11, and 12 at $3,500 each; and Lots 13 and 14 at $4,000 each. The partners agreed that Parr could take Lot 13 at cost for his personal use. The remaining lots were sold, and the partnership dissolved. Determine the amount of partnership cash each partner should receive in the dissolution.

Decision problem 21–2, Bee-Cee Company

The Bee-Cee Company bookkeeper prepared the following income statement for March of the current year:

BEE-CEE COMPANY
Income Statement for March, 19—

	Bee Department	Cee Department	Combined
Sales	$40,000	$60,000	$100,000
Cost of goods sold	28,600	42,900	71,500
Gross profit on sales	$11,400	$17,100	$ 28,500
Warehousing expenses	$ 2,950	$ 2,950	$ 5,900
Selling expenses	5,600	6,100	11,700
General and administrative expenses	1,525	1,525	3,050
Total expenses	$10,075	$10,575	$ 20,650
Net Income	$ 1,325	$ 6,525	$ 7,850

The company is a wholesaler of Bees and Cees and is organized on a departmental basis. However, the company manager does not feel that the bookkeeper's statement reflects the profit situation in the company's two selling departments and he has asked you to redraft it with any supporting schedules or comments you think desirable. Your investigation reveals the following:

1. The company sold 500 Bees and 400 Cees during March. The bookkeeper apportioned cost of goods sold between the two departments on an arbitrary basis. A Cee actually costs the company twice as much as a Bee.
2. A Bee and a Cee are of approximately the same weight and bulk. However, because there are two styles of Bees and three styles of Cees, the company must carry a 50% greater inventory of Cees than Bees.
3. The company occupies its building on the following bases:

	Area of Space	Value of Space
Warehouse	80%	60%
Bee sales office	5%	10%
Cee sales office	5%	10%
General office	10%	20%

4. Warehousing expenses for March consisted of the following:

```
Wages expense................................................ $3,000
Depreciation of building.....................................  2,000
Heating and lighting expenses...........................       500
Depreciation of warehouse equipment.................       400
        Total ................................................... $5,900
```

The bookkeeper had charged all of the building's depreciation plus all of the
heating and lighting expenses to warehousing expenses.

5. Selling expenses for March consisted of the following:

	Bee *Department*	*Cee* *Department*
Sales salaries	$4,000	$4,500
Advertising..	1,500	1,500
Depreciation of office equipment	100	100
Totals...	$5,600	$6,100

Sales salaries and depreciation were charged to the two departments on the
basis of actual amounts incurred. Advertising was apportioned by the bookkeeper. The company has an established advertising budget based on dollars
of sales which it followed rather closely in March.

6. General and administrative expenses for March consisted of the following:

```
Salaries and wages.......................................... $2,800
Depreciation of office equipment ........................   200
Miscellaneous office expenses............................    50
        Total ................................................... $3,050
```

Chapter 22

Manufacturing accounting

■ In previous chapters consideration has been given to the accounting problems of service-type and merchandising concerns. In this chapter some problems of manufacturing enterprises are examined.

Manufacturing and merchandising concerns are alike in that both depend for revenue upon the sale of one or more commodities or products. However, they differ in that a merchandising company buys the goods it sells in the finished state in which they are sold, while a manufacturing concern buys raw materials which it manufactures into the finished products it sells. For example, a shoe store buys shoes and sells them in the same form in which they are purchased; but a manufacturer of shoes buys leather, cloth, glue, nails, and dye and turns these items into salable shoes.

Basic difference in accounting ■ The basic difference in accounting for manufacturing and merchandising concerns grows from the idea in the preceding paragraph—the idea that a merchant buys the goods he sells in their finished-ready-for-sale state, while a manufacturer must create what he sells from raw materials. Because of this difference the merchant can easily determine the cost of the goods he has bought for sale by examining the debit balance of his Purchases account, but the manufacturer must combine the balances of a number of material, labor, and overhead accounts to determine the cost of the goods he has manufactured for sale.

To emphasize this difference, the cost of goods sold section from a merchandising concern's income statement is condensed and reproduced below beside that of a manufacturing company.

Merchandising Company		**Manufacturing Company**	
Cost of goods sold:		Cost of goods sold:	
Beginning merchandise inventory	$14,200.00	Beginning finished goods inventory	$ 11,200.00
Net cost of purchases	34,150.00	Cost of goods manufactured (see Manufacturing Statement)	170,500.00
Goods available for sale	$48,350.00	Goods available for sale	$181,700.00
Ending merchandise inventory	12,100.00	Ending finished goods inventory	10,300.00
Cost of goods sold	$36,250.00	Cost of goods sold	$171,400.00

Notice in the costs of goods sold section from the manufacturing company's income statement that the inventories of goods for sale are called *finished goods inventories* rather than merchandise inventories. Notice too that the "Net cost of purchases" element of the merchandising company becomes "Cost of goods manufactured (see Manufacturing Statement)" on the manufacturer's income statement. These differences result because the merchandising company buys its goods ready for sale, while the manufacturer creates its salable products from raw materials.

The words "see Manufacturing Statement" refer the income statement reader to a separate schedule called a manufacturing statement (see page 627) which shows the costs of manufacturing the products produced by a manufacturing company. The records and techniques used in accounting for these costs are the distinguishing characteristics of manufacturing accounting.

Systems of accounting in manufacturing concerns

■ The accounting system used by a manufacturing concern may be either a so-called general accounting system or a cost accounting system. A general accounting system is a noncost system. It uses periodic physical inventories of raw materials, goods in process, and finished goods; and it has as its goal the determination of the total cost of all goods manufactured during each accounting period. A cost accounting system differs in that it uses perpetual inventories and has as its goal the determination of the unit cost of manufacturing a product or performing a service. General accounting or noncost accounting systems are the subject of this chapter; cost accounting systems are discussed in the next two chapters.

Elements of manufacturing costs

■ A manufacturer takes *raw materials* and by applying *direct labor* and *factory overhead* converts these materials into finished products. Raw materials, direct labor, and factory overhead are the "elements of manufacturing costs."

Raw materials

Raw materials are the commodities that enter directly into and become a part of a finished product. Such items as leather, dye, cloth, nails, and glue are raw materials of a shoe manufacturer. Raw materials are often called *direct materials*. Direct materials are materials the costs of which are chargeable directly to the product or products manufactured, and are distinguished from *indirect materials* or factory supplies which are such items as grease and oil for machinery, cleaning fluids, etc. Indirect materials are accounted for as factory overhead.

The raw materials of a manufacturer are called "raw materials," even though they may not necessarily be in their natural raw state. For example, leather is manufactured from hides, nails from steel, and cloth from cotton. Nevertheless, leather, nails, and cloth are the raw materials of a shoe manufacturer even though they are finished goods to a previous manufacturer.

Direct labor

Direct labor is labor, the cost of which is chargeable directly to the product or products manufactured. It is often described as the labor of those people who work, either with machines or hand tools, directly on the materials converted into finished products. In manufacturing, direct labor is distinguished from *indirect labor*. Indirect labor is the labor of superintendents, foremen, millwrights, engineers, janitors, and others who do not work directly on the finished products. Indirect labor aids in production; often it makes production possible but does not enter directly into the finished product. Indirect labor is accounted for as a factory overhead cost.

In a noncost system, an account called *Direct Labor* is debited each payday for the wages of those workers who work directly on the product. Likewise, each payday, the wages of indirect workers are debited to one or more indirect labor accounts. Also, at the end of each period, the amounts of accrued direct and indirect labor are recorded in the direct and indirect labor accounts by means of adjusting entries. From this it can be seen that a manufacturing company's payroll accounting is similar to that of a merchandising concern. When a cost accounting system is not involved, no new techniques are required and only the new direct and indirect labor accounts distinguish the payroll accounting of a manufacturer from that of a merchant.

Factory overhead

Factory overhead, often called *manufacturing overhead* or *factory burden,* includes all manufacturing costs other than for direct material and direct labor. Overhead may include:

Indirect labor.	Heat, lights, and power.
Factory supplies.	Depreciation of plant and equipment.
Repairs to buildings and equipment.	Patents written off.
Insurance on plant and equipment.	Small tools written off.
Taxes on plant and equipment.	Workmen's compensation insurance.
Taxes on raw materials and work in process.	Payroll taxes on the wages of the factory workers.

Factory overhead does not include selling and administrative expenses. These are selling and administrative overhead. They are not a part of factory overhead because they are not incurred in the manufacturing operations. They are not incurred in order to produce the manufactured products.

All factory overhead costs are accumulated in overhead cost accounts which vary from company to company, with the exact accounts depending in each case upon the nature of the company and the information desired. For example, one account called "Expired Insurance on Plant Equipment" may be maintained, or an expired insurance account each for buildings and the different kinds of equipment may be used. But regardless of accounts, overhead costs are recorded with the same types of journals as are selling and administrative expenses. Some, such as indirect labor and light and power, are recorded in a Voucher Register or a Cash Disbursements Journal as they are paid and are then posted to the accounts. Others, such as depreciation and expired insurance, reach the accounts from the General Journal where they are first recorded with adjusting entries.

Accounts unique to a manufacturing company

■ Because of the nature of its operations, a manufacturing concern's ledger normally contains more accounts than that of a merchandising concern. However, some of the same accounts are found in the ledgers of both, for example, Cash, Accounts Receivable, Sales, and many selling and administrative expenses. Nevertheless, although there are accounts in common, many accounts are unique to a manufacturing company. For instance, accounts such as Machinery and Equipment, Accumulated Depreciation of Machinery and Equipment, Factory Supplies, Factory Supplies Used, Raw Materials Inventory, Raw Material Purchases, Goods in Process Inventory, Finished Goods Inventory, and Manufacturing Summary are normally found only in the ledgers of manufacturing concerns. Some of these unique accounts merit special attention.

Raw Material Purchases account

When a general accounting system is in use, the cost of all raw materials purchased is debited to an account called Raw Material Purchases. Often a special column is provided in the Voucher Register or other journal for the debits of the individual purchases, thus making it possible to periodically post these debits in one amount, the column total.

Raw Materials Inventory account

When a noncost system is in use, the raw materials on hand at the end of each accounting period are determined by a physical inventory; and through a closing entry the cost of this inventory is debited to the Raw Materials Inventory account where it becomes a record of the materials on hand at the end of one period and the beginning of the next.

Goods in Process Inventory account

All manufacturing concerns except those in which the manufacturing process is instantaneous normally have on hand at any time partially processed products called *goods in process* or *work in process*. These are products in the process of being manufactured, products that have received a portion or all of their materials and have had some labor and overhead applied but that are not completed.

In a manufacturing concern using a general accounting system the amount of goods in process at the end of each accounting period is determined by a physical inventory; and through a closing entry the cost of this inventory is debited to the Goods in Process Inventory account where it becomes a record of the goods in process at the end of one period and the beginning of the next.

Finished Goods Inventory account

The finished goods of a manufacturer are the equivalent of a store's merchandise; they are products in their completed state ready for sale. Actually, the only difference is that a manufacturing concern creates its finished goods from raw materials, while a store buys its merchandise in a finished, ready-for-sale state.

In a noncost system the amount of finished goods on hand at the end of each period is determined by a physical inventory; and through a closing entry the cost of this inventory is debited to the Finished Goods Inventory account as a record of the finished goods at the end of one period and the beginning of the next.

The three inventories — raw materials, goods in process, and finished goods — are current assets for balance sheet purposes.

Income statement of a manufacturing company

■ The income statement of a manufacturing company is similar to that of a merchandising concern. To see this, compare the income statement of Nelson Hardware Company, Illustration 5–1 on page 129, with that of Excel Manufacturing Company, Illustration 22–1 on page 626. Notice that the revenue, selling, and general and administrative expense sections are very similar. However, when the cost of goods sold sections are compared, a difference is apparent. Here the item "Cost of goods manufactured" replaces the "purchases" element, and finished goods inventories take the place of merchandise inventories.

Observe in the cost of goods sold section of Excel Manufacturing Company's income statement that only the total cost of goods manufactured is shown. It would be possible to expand this section to show the detailed costs of the materials, direct labor, and overhead entering into the cost of goods manufactured. However, if this were done, the income statement would be long and unwieldy. Consequently, the common practice is to show only the total cost of goods manufactured on the income statement and to attach a supporting schedule showing the details. This supporting schedule is called a "schedule of the cost of goods manufactured" or a "manufacturing statement."

The Excel Manufacturing Company
Income Statement for Year Ended December 31, 19—

Revenue:			
Sales			$310,000
Cost of goods sold:			
Finished goods inventory, January 1, 19—		$ 11,200	
Cost of goods manufactured (see Manufacturing Statement)		170,500	
Goods available for sale		$181,700	
Finished goods inventory, December 31, 19—		10,300	
Cost of goods sold			171,400
Gross profit			$138,600
Operating expenses:			
Selling expenses:			
Sales salaries	$18,000		
Advertising expense	5,500		
Delivery wages	12,000		
Shipping supplies used	250		
Delivery equipment insurance expired	300		
Depreciation of delivery equipment	2,100		
Total selling expenses		$ 38,150	
General and administrative expenses:			
Office salaries	$15,700		
Miscellaneous general expense	200		
Bad debts expense	1,550		
Office supplies used	100		
Depreciation of office equipment	200		
Total general and administrative expenses		17,750	
Total operating expenses			55,900
Operating income			$ 82,700
Financial expense:			
Bond interest expense			4,000
Net income before state and federal income taxes			$ 78,700
Less state and federal income taxes			32,600
Net Income			$ 46,100

Illustration
22–1

Manufacturing statement

■ The cost elements of manufacturing are raw materials, direct labor, and factory overhead; and a manufacturing statement is normally constructed in such a manner as to emphasize these elements. Notice in Illustration 22–2 that the first section of the statement shows the cost of raw materials used. Also observe the manner of presentation is the same as that used on the income statement of a merchandising company to show cost of goods purchased and sold.

The so-called second section shows the cost of direct labor used in production, and the third section shows factory overhead costs. If overhead accounts are not too numerous, the balance of each is often listed in this third section, as in Illustration 22–2. However, if overhead accounts are numerous, only the total of all may be shown; and in such cases the total is supported by a separate attached schedule showing each cost.

In the last section the calculation of cost of goods manufactured is

Excel Manufacturing Company
Manufacturing Statement for Year Ended December 31, 19—

Raw materials:			
Raw materials inventory, January 1, 19—		$ 8,000	
Raw materials purchased $85,000			
Freight on raw materials purchased 1,500			
Delivered cost of raw materials purchased............		86,500	
Raw materials available for use...........................		$94,500	
Raw materials inventory, December 31, 19—		9,000	
Raw materials used			$ 85,500
Direct labor			60,000
Factory overhead costs:			
Indirect labor		$ 9,000	
Supervision		6,000	
Power..		2,600	
Repairs and maintenance..................................		2,500	
Factory taxes...		1,900	
Factory supplies used......................................		500	
Factory insurance expired.................................		1,200	
Small tools written off......................................		200	
Depreciation of machinery and equipment............		3,500	
Depreciation of building....................................		1,800	
Patents written off		800	
Total factory overhead costs.............................			30,000
Total manufacturing costs.................................			$175,500
Add: Goods in process inventory, January 1, 19—...			2,500
Total goods in process during the year............			$178,000
Deduct: Goods in process inventory, December 31, 19—			7,500
Cost of Goods Manufactured.................................			$170,500

Illustration
22–2

completed. Here the beginning goods in process inventory is added to the sum of the manufacturing costs to show the cost of all goods in process during the period. Then, from the cost of all goods in process, the cost of the goods still in process at the end is subtracted to show cost of the goods manufactured.

The manufacturing statement is prepared from the Manufacturing Statement columns of a work sheet. The items that appear on the statement are summarized in these columns, and all that is required in constructing the statement is a rearrangement of the items into the proper statement order. Illustration 22–3 shows the manufacturing work sheet.

Work sheet for a manufacturing company

■ In examining Illustration 22–3, note first that there are no Adjusted Trial Balance columns. These columns are omitted because the experienced accountant commonly omits such columns from his work sheet to save time and effort. How a work sheet without Adjusted Trial Balance columns is prepared and how this saves time and effort were explained in Chapter 5.

To understand the work sheet of Illustration 22–3, recall that a work sheet is a tool of the accountant on which he—

The Excel Manufacturing Company
Manufacturing Work Sheet for Year Ended December 31, 19—

Account Titles	Trial Balance Dr.	Trial Balance Cr.	Adjustments Dr.	Adjustments Cr.	Mfg. Statement Dr.	Mfg. Statement Cr.	Income Statement Dr.	Income Statement Cr.	Balance Sheet Dr.	Balance Sheet Cr.
Cash	11,000								11,000	
Accounts receivable	32,000								32,000	
Allowance for doubtful accounts		300		(a) 1,550						1,850
Raw materials inventory	8,000				8,000				9,000	
Goods in process inventory	2,500				2,500				7,500	
Finished goods inventory	11,200						11,200	10,300	10,300	
Office supplies	150			(b) 100					50	
Shipping supplies	300			(c) 250					50	
Factory supplies	750			(d) 500					250	
Prepaid insurance	1,800			(e) 1,500					300	
Small tools	1,300			(f) 200					1,100	
Delivery equipment	9,000								9,000	
Accumulated depreciation of delivery equipment		2,400		(g) 2,100						4,500
Office equipment	1,700								1,700	
Accumulated depreciation of office equipment		1,200		(h) 200						1,400
Machinery and equipment	132,000								132,000	
Accumulated depr. of machinery and equipment		15,000		(i) 3,500						18,500
Factory building	190,000								190,000	
Accumulated depreciation of factory building		18,000		(j) 1,800						19,800
Land	9,500								9,500	
Patents	12,000			(k) 800					11,200	
Accounts payable		14,000								14,000
First mortgage bonds payable		100,000								100,000
Common stock		150,000								150,000
Retained earnings		33,660								33,660
Sales		310,000						310,000		
Raw material purchases	85,000				85,000					
Freight on raw materials	1,500				1,500					

Worksheet (partial)

Account	Col. 1	Adjustments (ref)	Adjustments	Col. A	Col. B	Col. C	Col. D
Power expense	2,600			2,600			
Repairs and maintenance	2,500			2,500			
Factory taxes	1,900			1,900			18,000
Sales salaries	18,000				18,000		5,500
Advertising expense	5,500				5,500		
Delivery wages	11,920	(l)	80		12,000		12,000
Office salaries	15,700				15,700		15,700
Miscellaneous general expense	200				200		200
Bond interest expense	2,000	(m)	2,000		4,000		4,000
	644,560						
	644,560						
Bad debts expense		(a)	1,550		1,550		1,550
Office supplies used		(b)	100		100		100
Shipping supplies used		(c)	250		250		250
Factory supplies used		(d)	500	500			
Factory insurance expired		(e)	1,200	1,200			
Delivery equipment insurance expired			300		300		300
Small tools written off		(f)	200	200			
Depreciation of delivery equipment		(g)	2,100		2,100		2,100
Depreciation of office equipment		(h)	200		200		200
Depreciation of machinery and equipment		(i)	3,500	3,500			
Depreciation of building		(j)	1,800	1,800			
Patents written off		(k)	800	800			
Accrued wages payable		(l)	540				540
Bond interest payable		(m)	2,000				2,000
State and federal income taxes expense		(n)	32,600	32,600		32,600	32,600
State and federal income taxes payable		(n)	32,600				
		47,640	47,640				
Cost of goods manufactured to Income Statement columns				187,000	16,500	170,500	
					170,500		
				187,000	187,000	274,200	378,850
Net Income						46,100	46,100
						320,300	424,950
					320,300	320,300	424,950

Illustration
22–3

1. Achieves the effect of adjusting the accounts before entering the adjustments in the accounts.
2. Sorts the adjusted account balances into columns according to the financial statement upon which they appear.
3. Calculates and proves the mathematical accuracy of the net income.

With the foregoing in mind, the primary difference between the work sheet of a manufacturing company and that of a merchandising company is an additional set of columns. Insofar as the adjustments are concerned, they are made in the same way on both kinds of work sheets. Also, the mathematical accuracy of the net income is proved in the same way. However, since an additional accounting statement, the manufacturing statement, is prepared for a manufacturing company, the work sheet of such a company has an additional set of columns, the Manufacturing Statement columns, into which are sorted the items appearing on the manufacturing statement.

Preparing a manufacturing company's work sheet ■ A manufacturing company's work sheet is prepared in the same manner as that of a merchandising concern. First a trial balance of the ledger is entered in the Trial Balance columns in the usual manner. Next, information for the adjustments is assembled, and the adjustments are entered in the Adjustments columns just as for a merchandising company. The adjustments information for the work sheet shown in Illustration 22–3 is as follows:

a) Estimated bad debt losses $\frac{1}{2}$% of sales, or $1,550.
b) Office supplies used, $100.
c) Shipping supplies used, $250.
d) Factory supplies used, $500.
e) Expired insurance on factory, $1,200; and expired insurance on the delivery equipment, $300.
f) The small tools inventory shows $1,100 of usable small tools on hand.
g) Depreciation of delivery equipment, $2,100.
h) Depreciation of office equipment, $200.
i) Depreciation of factory machinery and equipment, $3,500.
j) Depreciation of factory building, $1,800.
k) Yearly write-off of one seventeenth of the cost of patents, $800.
l) Accrued wages: direct labor, $400; indirect labor, $60; delivery wages, $80. All other employees paid monthly on the last day of each month.
m) One-half year's interest accrued on the bonds, $2,000.
n) State and federal income taxes expense, $32,600.

After the adjustments are completed, the amounts in the Trial Balance columns are combined with the amounts in the Adjustments columns and are sorted to the proper Manufacturing Statement, Income Statement, or Balance Sheet columns, according to the statement on which they appear.

No new techniques are required in the sorting, just two decisions for each item: First, does the item have a debit balance or a credit balance; and second, on which statement does it appear? The first decision is necessary because a debit item must be sorted to a Debit column and a credit item to a Credit column. As for the second, a work sheet is a tool for sorting items according to their statement appearance; and to properly sort the items it is only necessary to know that asset, liability, and owner equity items appear on the balance sheet and are sorted to the Balance Sheet columns. The finished goods inventory plus the revenue, selling, general and administrative, and financial expense items go on the income statement and are sorted to the Income Statement columns. And finally, the raw material, goods in process, direct labor, and factory overhead items appear on the manufacturing statement and are sorted to the Manufacturing Statement columns.

After the trial balance items with their adjustments are sorted to the proper statement columns, the ending inventory amounts are entered on the work sheet. The raw materials and goods in process inventories appear on the manufacturing statement. Therefore, the ending raw materials and goods in process inventory amounts are entered in the Manufacturing Statement credit and Balance Sheet debit columns. They must be entered in the Manufacturing Statement credit column in order to make the difference between the two columns equal cost of goods manufactured. Likewise, since these inventory amounts represent end-of-the-period assets, they must be entered in the Balance Sheet debit column with the other assets.

The ending finished goods inventory is the equivalent of an ending merchandise inventory and receives the same work sheet treatment. It is entered in the Income Statement credit column and the Balance Sheet debit column. It is entered in the Income Statement credit column so that the net income may be determined; and since it is a current asset, it must also be entered in the Balance Sheet debit column.

After the ending inventories are entered on the work sheet, the Manufacturing Statement columns are added and their difference determined. This difference is cost of the goods manufactured; and after it is determined, it is entered in the Manufacturing Statement credit column to make the two columns equal. Also, it is entered in the Income Statement debit column, the same column in which the balance of the Purchases account of a merchant is entered. After this the work sheet is completed in the usual manner.

Preparing statements

■ After completion, the manufacturing work sheet is used in preparing the statements and in making adjusting and closing entries. The manufacturing statement is prepared from the information in the work sheet's Manufacturing Statement columns, the income statement from the information in the Income Statement columns, and the balance sheet from information in the Balance Sheet columns. After this the adjusting and closing entries are prepared and posted.

■ The adjusting entries of a manufacturing company are prepared in the same way as those of a merchandising concern. An adjusting entry is entered in the General Journal for each adjustment appearing in the work sheet Adjustments columns. No new techniques are required here.

■ The account balances that enter into the calculation of cost of goods manufactured show manufacturing costs for a particular accounting period and must be closed and cleared at the end of each period. Normally they are closed and cleared through a Manufacturing Summary account, which is in turn closed and cleared through the Income Summary account.

The entries to close and clear the manufacturing accounts of Excel Manufacturing Company are as follows:

Dec.	31	Manufacturing Summary	187,000.00	
		Raw Materials Inventory		8,000.00
		Goods in Process Inventory		2,500.00
		Raw Material Purchases		85,000.00
		Freight on Raw Materials........................		1,500.00
		Direct Labor.....................................		60,000.00
		Indirect Labor....................................		9,000.00
		Supervision.......................................		6,000.00
		Power Expense...................................		2,600.00
		Repairs and Maintenance		2,500.00
		Factory Taxes....................................		1,900.00
		Factory Supplies Used..........................		500.00
		Factory Insurance Expired		1,200.00
		Small Tools Written Off		200.00
		Depr. of Machinery and Equipment.........		3,500.00
		Depreciation of Building........................		1,800.00
		Patents Written Off...............................		800.00
		To close those manufacturing accounts having debit balances.		
	31	Raw Materials Inventory	9,000.00	
		Goods in Process Inventory	7,500.00	
		Manufacturing Summary		16,500.00
		To set up the ending raw materials and goods in process inventories and to remove their balances from the Manufacturing Summary account.		

The foregoing entries are taken from the information in the Manufacturing Statement columns of the Illustration 22–3 work sheet. Compare the first entry with the information shown in the Manufacturing Statement debit column. Note how the debit to the Manufacturing Summary account is taken from the column total, and how each account having a balance in the column is credited to close and clear it. Also observe that the second entry has the effect of subtracting the ending raw materials and goods in process inventories from the manufacturing costs shown in the debit column.

The effect of the foregoing entries is to cause the Manufacturing Summary account to have a debit balance equal to the $170,500 cost of goods manufactured. This $170,500 balance is closed to the Income Summary account along with the other cost and expense accounts having balances in the Income Statement debit column. Observe the following entry which is used to close the accounts having balances in the Income Statement debit column of the Illustration 22–3 work sheet.

Dec.	31	Income Summary...	274,200.00	
		Finished Goods Inventory		11,200.00
		Sales Salaries..		18,000.00
		Advertising Expense..............................		5,500.00
		Delivery Wages......................................		12,000.00
		Office Salaries		15,700.00
		Miscellaneous General Expense		200.00
		Bond Interest Expense		4,000.00
		Bad Debts Expense................................		1,550.00
		Office Supplies Used.............................		100.00
		Shipping Supplies Used		250.00
		Delivery Equipment Insurance Expired.....		300.00
		Depreciation of Delivery Equipment........		2,100.00
		Depreciation of Office Equipment...........		200.00
		State and Federal Income		
		Taxes Expense		32,600.00
		Manufacturing Summary		170,500.00
		To close the income statement accounts having debit balances.		

After the foregoing entry, the remainder of the income statement accounts of Illustration 22–3 are closed as follows:

Dec.	31	Finished Goods Inventory	10,300.00	
		Sales	310,000.00	
		Income Summary................................		320,300.00
		To close the Sales account and to bring the ending finished goods inventory on the books.		
	31	Income Summary.......................................	46,100.00	
		Retained Earnings		46,100.00
		To close the Income Summary account.		

Inventory valuation problems of a manufacturer

■ In a manufacturing company using a noncost system, at the end of each period, a valuation must be placed on the inventories of raw materials, goods in process, and finished goods. No particular problems are encountered in valuing raw materials because the items are in the same form in which they were purchased and a cost or market price may be applied. However, placing a valuation on goods in process and finished goods is generally not so easy. This is because items of goods in process and finished goods consist of raw materials to which certain amounts of labor and overhead have been added. They are not items in the same form in which they were purchased. Consequently, a price paid a previous producer cannot be used to measure their inventory value. Instead, their inventory value must be built up by adding together estimates of the raw materials, direct labor, and overhead costs applicable to each item.

Estimating raw material costs applicable to a goods in process or finished goods item is usually not too difficult. Likewise, from its percentage of completion, a responsible plant official can normally make a reasonably accurate estimate of the direct labor applicable to an item. However, estimating factory overhead costs presents more of a problem, which is often solved by assuming that factory overhead costs are closely related to direct labor costs, and this is often a fair assumption. Frequently there is a close relation between direct labor costs and such things as supervision, power, repairs, etc. Furthermore, when this relation is used to apply overhead costs, it is assumed that the relation of overhead costs to the direct labor costs in each goods in process and finished goods item is the same as the relation between total factory overhead costs and total direct labor costs.

For example, an examination of the manufacturing statement in Illustration 22–2 will show that Excel Manufacturing Company's total direct labor costs were $60,000 and its overhead costs were $30,000. Or, an examination will show that during the year the company incurred in the production of all its products $2 of direct labor for each $1 of factory overhead costs. Or, during the year the company's overhead costs were 50% of direct labor cost.

Overhead Costs, $30,000 ÷ Direct Labor, $60,000 = 50%

Consequently, in estimating the overhead applicable to a goods in process or finished goods item, Excel Manufacturing Company may assume that this 50% overhead rate is applicable. It may assume that if in all its production the overhead costs were 50% of the direct labor costs, then in each goods in process and finished goods item this relationship also exists.

If Excel Manufacturing Company makes this assumption and its goods in process inventory consists of 1,000 units of Item X with each unit containing $3.75 of raw material and having $2.50 of applicable direct labor, then the goods in process inventory is valued as shown in Illustration 22–4.

Product	Raw Materials Cost	Direct Labor Applicable	Overhead (50% of Direct Labor)	Estimated Total Unit Cost	No. of Units	Total Inventory Valuation
Item X	$3.75	$2.50	$1.25	$7.50	1,000	$7,500.00

Illustration 22–4

Excel Manufacturing Company may use the same procedure in placing an accounting value on the items of its finished goods inventory.

1. How does the income statement of a manufacturing company differ from the income statement of a merchandising company?
2. What are the three elements of manufacturing costs?
3. What are (a) direct labor, (b) indirect labor, (c) direct material, (d) indirect material, and (e) factory overhead costs?
4. Name several items that are accounted for as factory overhead costs.
5. Name several accounts that are often found in the ledgers of both manufacturing and merchandising companies. Name several accounts that are found only in the ledgers of manufacturing companies.
6. What three new inventory accounts appear in the ledger of a manufacturing company?
7. How are the raw material inventories handled on the work sheet of a manufacturing company? How are the goods in process inventories handled? How are the finished goods inventories handled?
8. Which inventories of a manufacturing company receive the same work sheet treatment as the merchandise inventories of a merchandising company?
9. Which inventories of a manufacturing company appear on its manufacturing statement? Which appear on the income statement?
10. What accounts are summarized in the Manufacturing Summary account? What accounts are summarized in the Income Summary account?
11. What are the three manufacturing cost elements emphasized on the manufacturing statement?
12. What account balances are carried into the Manufacturing Statement columns of the manufacturing work sheet? What account balances are carried into the Income Statement columns? What account balances are carried into the Balance Sheet columns?
13. Why is the cost of goods manufactured entered in the Manufacturing Statement credit column of a work sheet and again in the Income Statement debit columns?
14. May prices paid a previous manufacturer for items of raw materials determine the balance sheet value of the items of the raw materials inventory? Why? May such prices also determine the balance sheet values of the goods in process and finished goods inventories? Why?
15. Standard Company used an overhead rate of 70% of direct labor cost to apply overhead to the items of its goods in process inventory. If the manufacturing statement of the company showed total overhead costs of $84,700, how much direct labor did it show?

Class exercises

The following items appeared in the Manufacturing Statement and Income Statement columns of Hite Manufacturing Company's year-end work sheet:

	Manufacturing Statement		Income Statement	
	Debit	Credit	Debit	Credit
Raw materials inventory......................	13,000	14,000	....	....
Goods in process inventory.................	15,000	12,000	....	....
Finished goods inventory.....................	....	....	16,000	17,000
Sales..	....	....	....	210,000
Raw material purchases......................	44,000	....	....	....
Direct labor......................................	52,000	....	....	....
Indirect labor...................................	12,000	....	....	....
Power	5,000	....	....	....
Machinery repairs	2,000	....	....	....
Rent expense, factory building..............	6,000	....	....	....
Selling expenses controlling.................	....	....	38,000	....
Administrative expenses controlling......	....	....	22,000	....
	149,000	26,000	....	....
Cost of goods manufactured................		123,000	123,000	
	149,000	149,000	199,000	227,000
Net Income......................................			28,000	
			227,000	227,000

Exercise 22–1

From the information just given, prepare a manufacturing statement for Hite Manufacturing Company.

Exercise 22–2

Prepare an income statement for Hite Manufacturing Company.

Exercise 22–3

Prepare compound closing entries for Hite Manufacturing Company, a corporation.

Exercise 22–4

A company that uses the relation between overhead and direct labor costs to apply overhead to its goods in process and finished goods inventories incurred the following costs during a year: materials, $95,000; direct labor, $80,000; and factory overhead costs, $160,000. (a) Determine the company's overhead rate. (b) Under the assumption the company's $12,500 goods in process inventory had $3,000 of direct labor costs, determine the inventory's material costs. (c) Under the assumption the company's $17,000 finished goods inventory had $5,000 of material costs, determine the inventory's labor cost and overhead costs.

Exercise 22-5

An end-of-the-accounting-period trial balance of a manufacturing company follows. To simplify the problem and to save time the trial balance is in numbers of not more than two integers.

Required:
1. Prepare a manufacturing work sheet form on ordinary notebook paper.
2. Copy the trial balance on the work sheet form and complete the work sheet using the following information:
   a) Ending inventories:
       Raw materials, $3.
       Goods in process, $5.
       Finished goods, $2.
       Factory supplies, $1.
   b) Allowance for doubtful accounts an additional $2.
   c) Expired factory insurance, $1.
   d) Depreciation of factory machinery, $3.
   e) Accrued payroll:
       Direct labor, $4.
       Indirect labor, $2.
       Office salaries, $1. (Debit Administrative Expenses controlling account.)

EASTERN MANUFACTURING COMPANY
Trial Balance, December 31, 19—

Cash	$ 4	
Accounts receivable	5	
Allowance for doubtful accounts		$ 1
Raw materials inventory	2	
Goods in process inventory	4	
Finished goods inventory	3	
Factory supplies	3	
Prepaid factory insurance	4	
Factory machinery	23	
Accumulated depreciation, factory machinery		2
Common stock		20
Retained earnings		5
Sales		81
Raw material purchases	15	
Freight on raw materials	1	
Direct labor	12	
Indirect labor	3	
Power	5	
Machinery repairs	2	
Rent expense, factory	8	
Selling expenses controlling	9	
Administrative expenses controlling	6	
	$109	$109

Problems   Problem 22-1

The following items appeared in the Manufacturing Statement and Income Statement columns of a work sheet prepared for Hilltop Manufacturing Company, Inc., on December 31, 19—, at the end of an annual accounting period:

	Manufacturing Statement		Income Statement	
	Debit	Credit	Debit	Credit
Raw materials inventory..........................	12,600	12,100	....	....
Goods in process inventory	14,800	12,900	....	....
Finished goods inventory.........................	....	....	16,100	18,800
Sales...	....	....	....	361,500
Raw material purchases...........................	59,000	....	....	....
Discounts on raw material purchases.........	....	800	....	....
Direct labor	90,000	....	....	....
Indirect labor	13,800	....	....	....
Factory supervision...............................	12,000	....	....	....
Heat, lights, and power	18,400	....	....	....
Machinery repairs	4,500	....	....	....
Rent expense, factory	7,200	....	....	....
Property taxes, machinery	1,700	....	....	....
Selling expenses controlling	....	....	30,800	....
Administrative expenses controlling	....	....	28,900	....
Expired factory insurance.......................	2,400	....	....	....
Factory supplies used	6,100	....	....	....
Depreciation expense, factory machinery ...	10,500	....	....	....
Small tools written off............................	400	....	....	....
Patents written off.................................	2,500	....	....	....
State and federal income taxes expense......	....	....	29,500	....
	255,900	25,800	....	....
Cost of goods manufactured.....................	....	230,100	230,100	....
	255,900	255,900	335,400	380,300
Net Income...			44,900	....
			380,300	380,300

Required:
1. From the information given prepare an income statement and a manufacturing statement for the company.
2. Prepare compound closing entries for the company.

Problem 22-2

Following are the items from the Manufacturing Statement columns of Cacto Manufacturing Company's work sheet prepared at the end of last year.

The illustrated columns show the items as they appeared after all adjustments were completed but before the ending work in process inventory was calculated and entered and before the cost of goods manufactured was calculated.

Cacto Manufacturing Company makes a single product called Cacto. On December 31, at the end of last year, the goods in process inventory consisted of 5,000 units of Cacto with each unit containing an estimated $0.80 of raw materials and having had an estimated $2 of direct labor applied:

	Manufacturing Statement	
	Debit	Credit
Raw materials inventory	21,200	19,300
Goods in process inventory	17,800	?
Raw materials purchased	81,400	
Direct labor...	100,000	
Indirect labor..	16,900	
Factory supervision	12,000	
Heat, light, and power..............................	8,600	
Machinery repairs....................................	6,300	
Rent expense, factory...............................	7,200	
Property taxes, machinery.........................	1,900	
Factory insurance expired.........................	3,300	
Factory supplies used...............................	7,400	
Depreciation expense, factory machinery......	16,900	
Small tools written off	500	
	301,400	?
Cost of goods manufactured		?
	301,400	301,400

Required:
1. Calculate the relation between direct labor and factory overhead costs and use this relation to determine the value of the ending goods in process inventory.
2. After placing a value on the ending goods in process inventory, determine the cost of goods manufactured.
3. Prepare a manufacturing statement for Cacto Manufacturing Company.
4. Prepare entries to close the manufacturing accounts and to summarize their balances in the Manufacturing Summary account.
5. Prepare an entry to close the Manufacturing Summary account.

Problem 22–3

The December 31, 19—, trial balance of Sun Valley Manufacturing Company's ledger carried the following items:

SUN VALLEY MANUFACTURING COMPANY
Trial Balance, December 31, 19—

Cash	$ 32,300	
Accounts receivable	36,200	
Allowance for doubtful accounts		$ 200
Raw materials inventory	37,100	
Goods in process inventory	34,400	
Finished goods inventory	48,700	
Prepaid factory insurance	4,100	
Factory supplies	13,100	
Machinery	227,500	
Accumulated depreciation, machinery		78,400
Accounts payable		25,300
Common stock		100,000
Retained earnings		94,900
Sales		692,500
Raw materials purchased	185,100	
Direct labor	159,500	
Indirect labor	36,600	
Heat, lights, and power	13,600	
Machinery repairs	9,400	
Selling expenses controlling	81,200	
Administrative expenses controlling	72,500	
Totals	$991,300	$991,300

The following adjustments and inventory information was available at the year-end:

a) Allowance for doubtful accounts to be increased to $1,700. (Debit Administrative Expenses controlling account.)

b) An examination of policies showed $3,100 of factory insurance expired.

c) An inventory of factory supplies showed $9,700 of factory supplies used.

d) Estimated depreciation of factory machinery, $31,300.

e) Accrued direct labor, $500; and accrued indirect labor, $300.

f) Estimated state and federal income taxes payable, $37,500.

g) Year-end inventories:

   (1) Raw materials, $36,700.

   (2) Goods in process consisted of 3,200 units of product with each unit containing an estimated $3.65 of materials and having had an estimated $4 of direct labor applied.

   (3) Finished goods inventory consisted of 3,000 units of product with each unit containing an estimated $7.50 of materials and having had an estimated $6 of direct labor applied.

Required:

1. Enter the trial balance on a work sheet form and make the adjustments from the information given. Then sort the items to the proper Manufacturing Statement, Income Statement, and Balance Sheet columns.

2. After the Direct Labor and factory overhead accounts have been adjusted and carried into the Manufacturing Statement columns, determine the relation between direct labor and overhead costs and use this relation to deter-

mine the overhead applicable to each unit of goods in process and finished goods. Next, calculate the balance sheet values for these inventories, enter the inventory amounts on the work sheet, and complete the work sheet.

3. From the work sheet prepare a manufacturing statement and an income statement.
4. Prepare compound closing entries.

Problem 22–4

A trial balance of Surfside Manufacturing Company's ledger on December 31, 19–, the end of an annual accounting period, appeared as follows:

SURFSIDE MANUFACTURING COMPANY
Trial Balance, December 31, 19–

Cash	$ 14,800	
Raw materials inventory	13,700	
Goods in process inventory	12,500	
Finished goods inventory	15,100	
Prepaid factory insurance	3,600	
Factory supplies	6,800	
Factory machinery	168,200	
Accumulated depreciation, factory machinery		$ 31,300
Small tools	4,100	
Patents	6,700	
Common stock		100,000
Retained earnings		16,700
Sales		370,000
Raw material purchases	62,000	
Discounts on raw material purchases		1,200
Direct labor	98,400	
Indirect labor	12,100	
Factory supervision	11,700	
Heat, light, and power	17,900	
Machinery repairs	4,200	
Rent expense, factory	6,000	
Property taxes, machinery	1,700	
Selling expenses controlling	31,400	
Administrative expenses controlling	28,300	
Totals	$519,200	$519,200

Additional Information:
1. Expired factory insurance, $2,400.
2. Factory supplies used, $5,900.
3. Depreciation of factory machinery, $10,200.
4. Small tools written off, $500.
5. Patents written off, $1,400.
6. Accrued wages payable:
   a) Direct labor, $1,600.
   b) Indirect labor, $700.
   c) Factory supervision, $300.

7. Ending inventories:
   a) Raw materials, $13,200.
   b) Goods in process consisted of 2,500 units of product with each unit containing an estimated $1.10 of raw materials and having had an estimated $2 of direct labor applied.
   c) Finished goods consisted of 2,000 units of product with each unit containing an estimated $2.60 of raw materials and having had an estimated $3.60 of direct labor applied.
8. Estimated state and federal income taxes payable, $30,000.

Required:
1. Enter the trial balance on a work sheet form. Make the adjustments from the information given. Sort the items to the proper Manufacturing Statement, Income Statement, and Balance Sheet columns.
2. After the Direct Labor account and the factory overhead cost accounts have been adjusted and carried into the Manufacturing Statement columns, determine the relation between overhead costs and direct labor cost and use the relation to determine the amount of overhead applicable to each unit of goods in process and finished goods. After overhead applicable to each unit of goods in process and finished goods is determined, calculate the inventory values of the goods in process and finished goods inventories. Enter these inventory amounts on the work sheet and complete the work sheet.
3. From the work sheet prepare a manufacturing statement and an income statement.
4. Prepare closing entries.

Problem 22–5

Maple Products began this year with the following inventories: raw materials, $9,200; goods in process, $10,300; and finished goods, $12,500. The company uses the relation between its overhead and direct labor costs to apply overhead to its inventories of goods in process and finished goods; and at the end of this year its inventories were assigned these costs:

	Raw Materials	Goods in Process	Finished Goods
Material costs	$8,600	$2,800	$ 4,500
Direct labor costs	-0-	3,600	5,600
Overhead costs	-0-	?	7,000
Totals	$8,600	?	$17,100

And this additional information was available from the company's records:

Total factory overhead costs incurred during the year.................... $ 82,500
Cost of all goods manufactured during the year 198,400

Required:
On the basis of the information given plus any data you can derive from it, prepare a manufacturing statement for Maple Products.

Problem 22–1A

The following alphabetically arranged items were taken from the Manufacturing Statement and Income Statement columns of Lake Manufacturing Company's year-end work sheet:

Advertising....................................	$ 1,200	Goods in process, December 31...	$ 7,500
Depreciation, machinery..................	2,100	Finished goods, January 1	10,500
Depreciation, office equipment..........	500	Finished goods, December 31	8,400
Depreciation, selling equipment.........	600	Miscellaneous factory expenses.......	500
Direct labor.................................	38,800	Office salaries.............................	4,200
Factory supplies used.....................	1,100	Raw material purchases	51,500
Federal income taxes expense..........	8,100	Rent expense, factory building	4,800
Freight on raw materials.................	1,500	Rent expense, office space.............	1,400
Heat and power, factory	2,000	Rent expense, selling space............	1,600
Indirect labor..............................	3,500	Repairs to machinery....................	1,800
Inventories:		Sales..	180,100
Raw materials, January 1	9,800	Sales discounts	3,400
Raw materials, December 31	10,100	Sales salaries..............................	17,500
Goods in process, January 1..........	8,200	Superintendence, factory	7,200

Required:

Prepare an income statement and a manufacturing statement for the company.

Problem 22–2A

A work sheet prepared by Valley Manufacturing Company at the end of last year had the following items in its Manufacturing Statement columns:

	Manufacturing Statement	
	Debit	Credit
Raw materials inventory..................................	12,300	13,500
Goods in process inventory	14,700	?
Raw material purchases	54,300	
Direct labor	90,000	
Indirect labor	35,600	
Heat, lights, and power	16,900	
Machinery repairs	5,200	
Rent expense, factory	12,000	
Property taxes, machinery	3,200	
Expired factory insurance.................................	2,600	
Factory supplies used	6,100	
Depreciation expense, machinery........................	15,300	
Patents written off...	2,100	
	270,300	?
Cost of goods manufactured.............................		?
	270,300	270,300

Valley Manufacturing Company's work sheet does not show the amount of the ending goods in process inventory and cost of goods manufactured. However, the company makes a single product; and on December 31, at the end of last year, there were 3,000 units of goods in process with each unit containing an estimated $1.05 of materials and having had an estimated $1.50 of direct labor applied.

Required:
1. Calculate the relation between direct labor and factory overhead costs and use this relation to place an accounting value on the ending goods in process inventory.
2. After placing a value on the ending goods in process inventory, prepare a manufacturing statement for the company.
3. Prepare entries to close the manufacturing accounts and to summarize their balances in the Manufacturing Summary account.
4. Prepare an entry to close the Manufacturing Summary account.

Problem 22–4A

Tops Manufacturing Company prepared the following trial balance at the end of its annual accounting period:

TOPS MANUFACTURING COMPANY
Trial Balance, December 31, 19—

Cash	$ 17,500	
Raw materials inventory	13,300	
Goods in process inventory	15,300	
Finished goods inventory	16,600	
Prepaid factory insurance	4,200	
Factory supplies	6,400	
Factory machinery	175,500	
Accumulated depreciation, factory machinery		$ 28,800
Small tools	3,700	
Patents	4,500	
Common stock		100,000
Retained earnings		34,400
Sales		359,700
Raw material purchases	61,800	
Discounts on raw material purchases		1,000
Direct labor	89,100	
Indirect labor	13,300	
Factory supervision	11,800	
Heat, lights, and power	17,900	
Machinery repairs	4,400	
Rent expense, factory	7,200	
Property taxes, machinery	800	
Selling expenses controlling	31,400	
Administrative expenses controlling	29,200	
Totals	$523,900	$523,900

Additional Information:
1. Expired factory insurance, $2,200.

2. Factory supplies used, $6,300.
3. Depreciation of factory machinery, $9,900.
4. Small tools written off, $700.
5. Patents written off, $1,300.
6. Accrued wages payable: (*a*) direct labor, $900; (*b*) indirect labor, $500; and (*c*) factory supervision, $200.
7. Ending inventories: (*a*) raw materials, $12,800; (*b*) goods in process consisted of 4,000 units of product with each unit containing an estimated $1.40 of materials and having had an estimated $1 of direct labor applied; and (*c*) finished goods consisted of 3,000 units of product with each unit containing an estimated $1.96 of raw materials and having an estimated $2.40 of direct labor applied.
8. Estimated state and federal income taxes expense, $29,000.

Required:
1. Enter the trial balance on a work sheet form and make the adjustments from the information given. Then sort the items to the proper Manufacturing Statement, Income Statement, and Balance Sheet columns.
2. After the Direct Labor and factory overhead cost accounts have been adjusted and carried into the Manufacturing Statement columns, determine the relation between direct labor and overhead costs and use this relation to determine the overhead applicable to each unit of goods in process and finished goods. After the amounts of overhead applicable to the units of goods in process and finished goods are determined, calculate the balance sheet values of these inventories, enter these inventory amounts on the work sheet, and complete the work sheet.
3. From the work sheet prepare a manufacturing statement and an income statement.
4. Prepare compound closing entries.

Problem 22–5A

Oak Products Company incurred a total of $217,200 of material, labor, and factory overhead costs in manufacturing its product last year; and of this amount, $93,600 represented factory overhead costs. The company began last year with the following inventories: raw materials, $8,400; goods in process, $14,500; and finished goods, $17,500. It applies overhead to its goods in process and finished goods inventories on the basis of the relation of overhead to direct labor costs; and at the end of last year it assigned the following costs to its inventories:

	Raw Materials	Goods in Process	Finished Goods
Material costs	$9,200	$4,700	$ 5,750
Direct labor costs	-0-	4,800	5,800
Overhead costs	-0-	?	8,700
Totals	$9,200	$?	$20,250

Required:
On the basis of the information given plus any information you can derive from it, prepare a manufacturing statement for Oak Products Company.

Decision
problem
22–1,
Coast Manu-
facturing
Company

Coast Manufacturing Company has been in operation for three years, manufacturing and selling a single product. Sales have increased during each of the three years, but profits have not, and the company president, Gerry Roberts, has asked you to analyze the situation and tell him why. Mr. Roberts is primarily a production man and knows nothing about accounting. The company bookkeeper knows a debit from a credit, is an excellent clerk, but has little accounting training.

The company's condensed income statements for the past three years show:

	1st Year	2nd Year	3rd Year
Sales	$250,000	$350,000	$400,000
Cost of goods sold:			
Finished goods inventory, January 1	$ 0	$ 15,000	$ 45,000
Cost of goods manufactured	165,000	256,000	280,500
Goods for sale	$165,000	$271,000	$325,500
Finished goods inventory, December 31	15,000	45,000	60,000
Cost of goods sold	$150,000	$226,000	$265,500
Gross profit from sales	$100,000	$124,000	$134,500
Selling and administrative expenses	75,000	98,000	108,000
Net Income	$ 25,000	$ 26,000	$ 26,500

Investigation disclosed the following additional information:

a) The company sold 5,000 units of its product during the first year in business, 7,000 during the second year, and 8,000 during the third. All sales were at $50 per unit, and no discounts were granted.

b) There were 500 units in the finished goods inventory at the end of the first year, 1,500 at the end of the second, and 2,000 at the end of the third.

c) The units in the finished goods inventory were priced each year at 60% of their selling price, or at $30 per unit.

Prepare a report to Mr. Roberts which shows (1) the number of units of product manufactured each year, (2) the cost each year to manufacture a unit of product, and (3) the selling and administrative expenses per unit of product sold each year. Also, (4) prepare an income statement showing the correct net income each year, using a first-in, first-out basis for pricing the finished goods inventory. And finally, (5) express an opinion as to why net income has not kept pace with the rising sales volume.

Several years ago Tommy Thompkins took over the operation of his family's cabinet shop from his father. Once the shop specialized in manufacturing cabinets for homes, but of late years it has turned more and more to building boats to the specifications of its customers. However, this business is seasonal in nature, since few people order boats in October, November, December, and January. As a result, things are rather slow around the shop during these months. Tommy has tried to increase business during the slow months. However, most prospective customers who come into the shop during these months are shoppers; and when Tommy quotes a price for a new boat, they commonly decide the price is too high and walk out. Tommy thinks the trouble arises from his application of a rule established by his father when he ran the shop. The rule is that in pricing a job to a customer, "always set the price so as to make a 10% profit over and above all costs, and be sure that all costs are included."

Tommy says that in pricing a job, the material and labor costs are easy to figure, but that overhead is another thing. His overhead consists of depreciation of building and machinery, heat, lights, power, taxes, and so on, which in total run to $600 per month whether he builds any boats or not. Furthermore, when he follows his father's rule, he has to charge more for a boat built during the slow months because the overhead is spread over fewer jobs. He readily admits that this seems to drive away business during the months he needs business most, but he finds it difficult to break his father's rule, for as he says, "Dad did alright in this business for many years."

Explain with assumed figures to illustrate your point why Tommy charges more for a boat made in December than for one built in May, a very busy month. Suggest how Tommy might solve his pricing problem and still follow his father's rule.

Cost accounting, job order and process

■ In a general accounting system for a manufacturer, such as that described in the previous chapter, physical inventories are required at the end of each accounting period in order to determine cost of goods manufactured. Furthermore, cost of goods manufactured as determined under such a system is the cost of all goods that were manufactured during the period, and commonly no effort is made to determine unit costs. A cost accounting system differs in that it is based on perpetual inventories and its emphasis is on unit costs and the control of costs.

There are two common types of cost accounting systems: (1) job order cost systems and (2) process cost systems. However, of the two there are an infinite number of variations and combinations. A job order system is described first.

JOB ORDER COST ACCOUNTING

■ In cost accounting a *job* is a turbine, machine, or other product manufactured especially for and to the specifications of a customer. A job may also be a single construction project of a contractor. A *job lot* is a quantity of identical items, such as 500 typewriters, manufactured in one lot as a job or single order; and a *job order cost system* is one in which costs are assembled in terms of jobs or job lots of product.

As previously stated, a job cost system differs from a general accounting system in that its primary objective is the determination of the cost of each job or job lot of product as it is finished. A job cost system also differs in that all inventory accounts used in such a system are perpetual inventory accounts controlling subsidiary ledgers. For example, in a job cost system the purchase and use of all materials are recorded in a perpetual inventory account called Materials which controls a subsidiary ledger having a separate ledger card (Illustration 23–1) for each different kind of material used. Likewise, in a job cost system the Goods in Process and Finished Goods accounts are also perpetual inventory accounts controlling subsidiary ledgers.

MATERIALS LEDGER CARD

Item *whatsit clip*   Stock No. *C-347*   Location in Storeroom *Bin 137*

Maximum *400*   Minimum *150*   Number to Reorder *200*

Date	Receiving Report No.	Units	Unit Price	Total Price	Requisition No.	Units	Unit Price	Total Price	Units	Unit Price	Total Price
		Received				Issued				Balance	
3/1									180	1.00	180.00
3/5					4345	20	1.00	20.00	160	1.00	160.00
3/11					4416	10	1.00	10.00	150	1.00	150.00
3/12	C-114	200	1.00	200.00					350	1.00	350.00
3/25					4713	21	1.00	21.00	329	1.00	329.00

Illustration 23–1

In addition to perpetual inventory controlling accounts, job cost accounting is also distinguished by the flow of manufacturing costs from the Materials, Factory Payroll, and Overhead Costs accounts into and through the Goods in Process and Finished Goods accounts and on to the Cost of Goods Sold account. The flow is diagrammed in Illustration 23–2 on the next page. An examination of the diagram and a moment's thought will show that costs flow through the accounts in the same way materials, labor, and overhead are placed in production in the factory, move on to become finished goods, and finally are sold.

Job cost sheets

■ The heart of a job cost system is a subsidiary ledger of *job cost sheets* called a *Job Cost Ledger*. The cost sheets are used to accumulate costs by jobs. A separate cost sheet is used for each job.

Observe in Illustration 23–3 how a job cost sheet is designed to accumulate costs. Although this accumulation is discussed in more detail

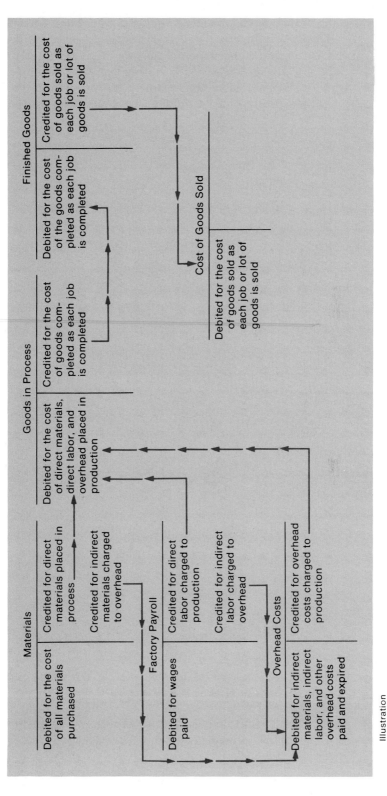

Illustration
23–2
**Diagram
Showing the
Flow of Costs
in a Job Cost
System**

later, it may be summarized as follows. When a job is begun, information as to the customer, job number, and job description is filled in on a blank cost sheet and the cost sheet is placed in the Job Cost Ledger. The job number identifies the job and simplifies the process of charging it with materials, labor, and overhead. As materials are required for the job, they are transferred from the materials storeroom and are used to

JOB COST SHEET

Customer's Name   *Cone Lumber Company*   Job No. _7452_
Address   *Eugene, Oregon*
Job Description   *10 H.P. electric motor to customer's specifications*

Date Promised   *4/1*   Date Started   *3/23*   Date Completed   *3/29*

Date	Materials		Labor		Overhead Costs Applied		
	Requisition No.	Amount	Time Ticket No.	Amount	Date	Rate	Amount
19-- Mar. 23	4698	53.00	C-3422	6.00	3/29	150 per-cent of the direct labor	$123.00
24			C-3478 C-3479	16.00 6.00			
25	4713	21.00	C-4002	16.00			
26			C-4015	16.00		Summary of Costs	
27			C-4032	12.00		Materials	$ 74.00
28			C-4044	10.00		Labor	82.00
						Overhead	123.00
						Total Cost of the job	279.00
	Total	74.00	Total	82.00	Remarks: Completed and shipped 3/29		

Illustration 23–3

complete the job. At the same time their cost is charged to the job in the Materials column of the job's cost sheet. Labor used on the job is likewise charged to the job in the Labor column; and when the job is finished, the amount of overhead applicable is entered in the Overhead Costs Applied column. After this, the cost totals are summarized to determine the job's total cost.

The Goods in Process account

■ The job cost sheets in the Job Cost Ledger are controlled by the Goods in Process account, which is kept in the General Ledger. And, the Goods in Process account and its subsidiary ledger of cost sheets operate in the usual manner of controlling accounts and subsidiary ledgers. The material, labor, and overhead costs debited to each individual job on its cost sheet must be debited to the Goods in Process account either as individual amounts or in totals. Likewise all credits to jobs on their cost sheets must be credited individually or in totals to the Goods in Process account.

In addition to being a controlling account, the Goods in Process account is a perpetual inventory account operating somewhat as follows: At the beginning of a cost period the cost of any unfinished jobs in process is shown by its debit balance. Throughout the cost period materials, labor, and overhead are placed in production in the factory; and periodically their costs are debited to the account (note the last three debits in the Goods in Process account that follows). Also, throughout the period the cost of each job completed (the sum of the job's material, labor, and overhead costs) is credited to the account as each job is finished. As a result, the account is a perpetual inventory account the debit balance of which shows after all posting is completed; and without a physical inventory, the cost of the unfinished jobs still in process. For example, the following Goods in Process account shows a $12,785 March 31 ending inventory of unfinished jobs in process.

Goods in Process

Date		Explanation	Debit	Credit	Balance
Mar.	1	Balance, beginning inventory			2,850
	10	Job 7449 completed		7,920	(5,070)
	18	Job 7448 completed		9,655	(14,725)
	24	Job 7450 completed		8,316	(23,041)
	29	Job 7452 completed		279	(23,320)
	29	Job 7451 completed		6,295	(29,615)
	31	Materials used	17,150		(12,465)
	31	Labor applied	10,100		(2,365)
	31	Overhead applied	15,150		12,785

Accounting for materials under a job cost system

■ Under a job cost system all materials purchased are placed in a materials storeroom under the care of a storeroom keeper, and are issued to the factory only in exchange for properly prepared material requisitions (Illustration 23–4). The storeroom provides physical control over materials. The requisitions enhance the control and also provide a means of charging material costs to jobs or, in the case of indirect materials, to factory overhead costs. The requisitions are used as described in the next paragraphs.

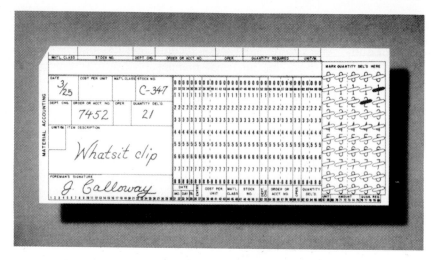

Illustration
23–4

When a material is needed in the factory, a material requisition is prepared and signed by a foreman, superintendent, or other responsible person. The requisition identifies the material and shows the number of the job or overhead account to which it is to be charged, and is given to the storeroom keeper in exchange for the material. The storeroom keeper forwards the requisition to the accounting department. Normally, requisitions are forwarded in batches, with an entire day's requisitions being a common batch.

Issuing units of material to the factory reduces the amount of that particular material in the storeroom. Consequently, when a material requisition reaches the accounting department, it is first recorded in the Issued column of the materials ledger card of the material issued. This reduces the number of units of that material shown to be on hand. Note the last entry in Illustration 23–1, which records the requisition of Illustration 23–4.

Materials issued to the factory may be used on jobs or for some overhead task, such as machinery repairs. Consequently, after being entered in the Issued columns of the proper materials ledger cards, a batch of requisitions is sorted by jobs and overhead accounts and charged to the proper jobs and overhead accounts. Materials used on jobs are charged to the jobs in the Materials columns of the job cost sheets. (Note the last entry in the Materials column on the cost sheet of Illustration 23–3 where the requisition of Illustration 23–4 is recorded.) Materials used for overhead tasks are charged to the proper overhead accounts in the Overhead Costs Ledger. A company using a job cost system commonly has an Overhead Costs controlling account in its General Ledger which controls a subsidiary Overhead Costs Ledger having an account for each overhead cost, such as Heating and Lighting or Machinery Repairs. Consequently, a requisition for light bulbs, for example, is charged to the Heating and Lighting account in the subsidiary Overhead Costs Ledger.

Material ledger cards, job cost sheets, and overhead cost accounts are all subsidiary ledger accounts controlled by accounts in the General Ledger. Consequently, in addition to the entries described in the foregoing paragraphs, entries must also be made in the controlling accounts. To make these entries, the requisitions charged to jobs and the requisitions charged to overhead accounts are accumulated until the end of a month or other cost period when they are separately totaled; and if, for example, the requisitions charged to jobs during the month total $17,150 and those charged to overhead accounts total $320, an entry like the following is made:

Mar.	31	Goods in Process..	17,150.00	
		Overhead Costs	320.00	
		Materials...		17,470.00
		To record the materials used during March.		

The debit to Goods in Process in the foregoing entry is equal to the sum of the requisitions charged to jobs on the job cost sheets during March. The debit to Overhead Costs is equal to the sum of the requisitions charged to overhead accounts, and the credit to Materials is equal to the sum of all requisitions entered in the Issued columns of the material ledger cards during the month.

Accounting for labor in a job cost system ■ Time clocks, clock cards, and a Payroll Register similar to those described in an earlier chapter are commonly used in a factory to record the hours and cost of the work of each direct and indirect labor employee. Furthermore, without the complications of payroll taxes, income taxes, and other deductions, the entry to pay the employees is as follows:

Mar.	7	Factory Payroll..	2,900.00	
		Cash...		2,900.00
		To record the factory payroll and pay the employees.		

The entry just given is repeated at the end of each pay period; consequently, at the end of a month or other cost period the Factory Payroll account has a series of debits (see Illustration 23–6) like the debit of the foregoing entry, and the sum of these debits is the total amount paid the direct and indirect labor employees during the month.

The clock cards just mentioned are a record of hours worked each day by each employee, but they do not show how the employees spent their time or the specific jobs and overhead tasks on which they worked. Consequently, if the hours worked by each employee are to be charged to specific jobs and overhead accounts, another record called a *labor time ticket* must be prepared. Labor time tickets like the one shown in Illustration 23–5 tell how an employee spent his time while at work.

The time ticket of Illustration 23–5 is a "pen-and-ink" ticket and is suitable for use in a plant in which only a small number of such tickets are prepared and recorded each day. In a plant in which many tickets are prepared, a time ticket that can be made into a punched card similar to Illustration 23–4 would be more suitable.

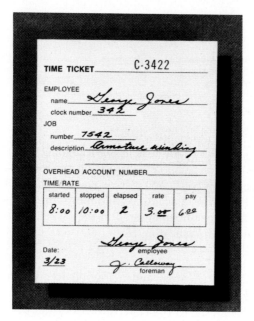

Labor time tickets serve as a basis for charging jobs and overhead accounts for an employee's wages. Throughout each day a labor time ticket is prepared each time an employee is changed from one job or overhead task to another. The tickets may be prepared by the worker, his foreman, or a clerk called a timekeeper. If the employee works on only one job all day, only one ticket is prepared. If he works on more than one job, a separate ticket is made for each. At the end of the day all the tickets of that day are sent to the accounting department.

In the accounting department the direct labor time tickets are charged to jobs on the job cost sheets (see the first entry in the Labor column of Illustration 23–3 where the ticket of Illustration 23–5 is recorded); and the indirect labor tickets are charged to overhead accounts in the Overhead Costs Ledger. The tickets are then accumulated until the end of the cost period when they are separately totaled; and if, for example, the direct labor tickets total $10,100 and the indirect labor tickets total $2,500, the following entry is made:

Mar.	31	Goods in Process...	10,100.00	
		Overhead Costs	2,500.00	
		Factory Payroll...		12,600.00
		To record the March time tickets.		

The first debit in the foregoing entry is the sum of all direct labor time tickets charged to jobs on the job cost sheets, and the second debit is the sum of all tickets charged to overhead accounts. The credit is the total of the month's labor time tickets, both direct and indirect. Notice in Illustration 23–6 that after the credit of the foregoing entry is posted, the Factory Payroll account has a $605 credit balance. This $605 is the accrued factory payroll payable at the month's end, and it is also the dollar amount of time tickets prepared and recorded during the days following the end of the March 28 pay period.

Factory Payroll				
Date	Explanation	Debit	Credit	Balance
Mar. 7	Weekly payroll payment	2,900		2,900
14	Weekly payroll payment	2,950		5,850
21	Weekly payroll payment	3,105		8,955
28	Weekly payroll payment	3,040		11,995
31	Labor cost summary		12,600	(605)

Illustration
23–6

Accounting for overhead in a job cost system

■ In a job cost system, if the cost of each job is to be determined at the time it is finished, it is necessary to associate with each job the costs of its materials, labor, and overhead. Requisitions and time tickets make possible a direct association of material and labor costs with jobs. However, overhead costs are incurred for the benefit of all jobs and cannot be related directly to any one. Consequently, to associate overhead with jobs it is necessary to relate overhead to, for example, direct labor costs and to apply overhead to jobs by means of a *predetermined overhead application rate*.

A predetermined overhead application rate based on direct labor cost is established by (1) estimating before a cost period begins the total overhead that will be incurred during the period; (2) estimating the cost of the direct labor that will be incurred in production during the period; then (3) calculating the ratio, expressed as a percentage, of the estimated overhead to the estimated direct labor cost. For example, if a cost accountant estimates that a factory will incur $180,000 of overhead during the year about to begin and that $120,000 of direct labor will be used in the factory during the period, and these estimates are used to establish an overhead application rate, the rate is 150% and is calculated as follows:

$$\frac{\text{Next Year's Estimated Overhead Costs, \$180,000}}{\text{Next Year's Estimated Direct Labor Costs, \$120,000}} = 150\%$$

After a predetermined overhead application rate is established, it is used throughout the year to apply overhead to jobs as they are finished. Overhead is assigned to each job, and its cost is calculated as follows: (1) As each job is completed the cost of its materials is determined by adding the amounts in the Materials column of its cost sheet. Then (2) the cost of its labor is determined by adding the amounts in the Labor column. Next (3) the applicable overhead is calculated by multiplying the job's total labor cost by the predetermined overhead application rate and is entered in the Overhead Costs Applied column. Finally (4) the job's material, labor, and overhead costs are entered in the summary section of the cost sheet and totaled to determine the cost of the job.

The predetermined overhead application rate is also used to assign overhead to any jobs still in process at the cost period end. Then, the total overhead assigned to all jobs during the period is recorded in the accounts with an entry like this:

Mar.	31	Goods in Process...	15,150.00	
		Overhead Costs		15,150.00
		To record the overhead applied to jobs during March.		

The foregoing entry assumes that the overhead applied to all jobs during March totaled $15,150, and after it is posted the Overhead Costs account appears as in Illustration 23–7.

Overhead Costs

Date		Explanation	F	Debit	Credit	Balance
Mar.	31	Indirect materials	G24	320		320
	31	Indirect labor	G24	2,500		2,820
	31	Miscellaneous payments	D89	3,306		6,126
	31	Accrued and prepaid items	G24	9,056		15,182
	31	Applied			15,150	32

Illustration
23–7

In the Overhead Costs account of Illustration 23–7 the actual overhead costs incurred during March are represented by four debits. The first two need no explanation; the third represents the many payments for such things as water, telephone, and so on; while the fourth represents such things as depreciation, expired insurance, taxes, and et cetera.

When overhead is applied to jobs on the basis of a predetermined overhead rate based upon direct labor costs as in the foregoing discussion, it is assumed that the overhead applicable to a particular job bears the same relation to the job's direct labor cost as the total estimated overhead of the factory bears to the total estimated direct labor costs. This assumption may not be proper in every case. However, when the ratio of overhead to direct labor cost is approximately the same for all jobs, an overhead rate based upon direct labor cost offers an easily calculated and fair basis for assigning overhead to jobs. In those cases in which the ratio of overhead to direct labor cost does not remain the same for all jobs, some other relationship must be used. Often overhead rates based upon the ratio of overhead to direct labor hours or overhead to machine-hours are used. However, a discussion of these is reserved for a course in cost accounting.

Overapplied and under-applied overhead

■ When overhead is applied to jobs by means of an overhead application rate based on estimates, the Overhead Costs account seldom, if ever, has a zero balance. At times actual overhead incurred exceeds overhead applied, and at other times overhead applied exceeds actual overhead incurred. When the account has a debit balance (overhead incurred in excess of overhead applied), the balance is known as *underapplied overhead;* and when it has a credit balance (overhead applied in excess of overhead incurred), the balance is called *overapplied overhead.* Usually the balance is small and fluctuates from debit to credit throughout a year. However, any balance in the account must be disposed of at the end of each year before a new accounting period begins.

If the year-end balance of the Overhead Costs account is material in amount, it is reasonable that it be disposed of by apportioning it among the goods still in process, the finished goods inventory, and cost of goods sold. This has the effect of restating the inventories and goods sold at "actual" cost. For example, assume that at the end of an accounting period, (1) a company's Overhead Costs account has a $1,000 debit balance (underapplied overhead), and (2) the company had charged the following amounts of overhead to jobs during the period: jobs still in process, $10,000; jobs finished but unsold, $20,000; and jobs finished and sold, $70,000. In such a situation the following entry apportions fairly the underapplied overhead among the jobs worked on during the period:

Dec.	31	Goods in Process	100.00	
		Finished Goods..	200.00	
		Cost of Goods Sold..	700.00	
		Overhead Costs.......................................		1,000.00
		To clear the Overhead Costs account and charge the underapplied overhead to the work of the accounting period.		

Besides the foregoing entry, a portion of the additional overhead charged to Goods in Process is charged to each job still in production by an entry on the job's cost sheet.

Sometimes when the amount of over- or underapplied overhead is immaterial, all of it is closed to Cost of Goods Sold under the assumption that the major share would be charged there anyway and any extra exactness gained from prorating would not be worth the extra record keeping involved.

Recording the completion of a job ■ When a job is completed, its cost is transferred from the Goods in Process account to the Finished Goods account with an entry like the following which transfers the cost of the job the cost sheet of which appears on page 652:

Mar.	29	Finished Goods..	279.00	
		Goods in Process...................................		279.00
		To transfer the cost of Job No. 7452 to		
		Finished Goods.		

In addition to the foregoing entry, and at the same time it is made, the completed job's cost sheet is removed from the Job Cost Ledger, marked "completed," and filed away. This is in effect the equivalent of posting a credit to the Job Cost Ledger equal to the credit to the Goods in Process controlling account.

Recording cost of goods sold ■ When a cost system is in use, the cost to manufacture a job or job lot of product is known as soon as the goods are finished. Consequently, when goods are sold, since their cost is known, the cost can be recorded at the time of sale. For example, if goods costing $279 are sold for $450, the cost of the goods sold may be recorded with the sale as follows:

Mar.	29	Accounts Receivable—Cone Lumber Co...........	450.00	
		Cost of Goods Sold......................................	279.00	
		Sales		450.00
		Finished Goods.......................................		279.00
		Sold for $450 goods costing $279.		

When cost of goods sold is recorded at the time of each sale as in the foregoing entry, the balance of the Cost of Goods Sold account shows at the end of an accounting period the cost of goods sold during the period.

PROCESS COST ACCOUNTING

■ A *process* is a step in manufacturing a product, and a *process cost system* is one in which costs are assembled in terms of processes or manufacturing steps.

Process cost systems are found in companies producing cement, flour, or other products the production of which is characterized by a large volume of standardized units manufactured on a more or less continuous basis. In such companies responsibility for completing each step in the production of a product is assigned to a department. Costs are then assembled by departments, and the efficiency of each department is measured by the processing costs incurred in processing the units of product that flow through the department.

Assembling costs by departments

■ When costs are assembled by departments in a process cost system, a separate goods in process account is used for the costs of each department. For example, assume a company makes a product from metal that is cut to size in a cutting department, sent to a bending department to be bent into shape, and then on to a painting department to be painted. Such a concern would collect costs in three goods in process accounts, one for each department, and costs would flow through the accounts as in Illustration 23–8.

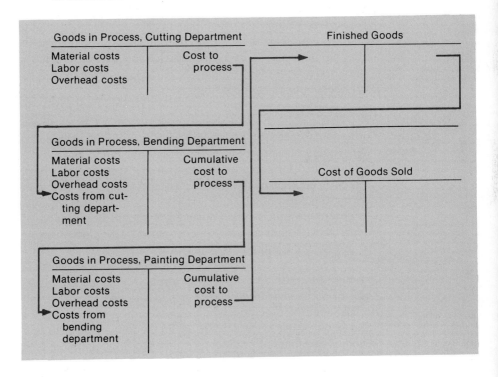

Illustration 23–8

Observe in Illustration 23–8 that each department's material, labor, and overhead costs are charged to the department's goods in process account. (It is assumed there were indirect materials charged to the bending department.) Observe too how costs are transferred from department to department, just as the product is transferred in the manufacturing procedure. The cost to cut the product in the cutting department is transferred to the bending department; and the sum of the costs in the first two departments is transferred to the third department; and finally the sum of the processing costs in all three departments, which is the cost to make the product, is transferred to finished goods.

Charging costs to departments

■ Since there are no jobs in a process cost system, accounting for material and labor costs in such a system is much simplified. Material requisitions may be used. However, a consumption report kept by the storeroom keeper and showing the materials issued to each department during a cost period is often substituted. Likewise, labor time tickets may be used; but since most employees spend all their working time in the same department, an end-of-the-period summary of the payroll records is usually all that is required in charging labor to the departments. And since there are no jobs, there is no need to distinguish between direct and indirect materials and direct and indirect labor. All that is required is that material and labor costs, both direct and indirect, be charged to the proper departments.

The lack of jobs also simplifies accounting for overhead in a process cost system. Since there are no jobs to charge with overhead on completion, predetermined overhead application rates are not required and actual overhead incurred may be charged directly to the goods in process accounts of the departments.

Equivalent finished units

■ A basic objective of a process cost system is the determination of unit processing costs for material, labor, and overhead in each processing department. This requires that (1) material, labor, and overhead costs be accumulated for each department for a cost period of, say, a month; (2) a record be kept of the number of units processed in each department during the period; and then (3) that costs be divided by units processed to determine unit costs. However, it should be observed that when a department begins and ends a cost period with partially processed units of product, the units completed in the department are not an accurate measure of the department's production. Rather, in such instances production must be measured in terms of *equivalent finished units* and unit costs become *equivalent finished unit costs.*

The idea of an equivalent finished unit is based on the assumption that it takes the same amount of labor, for instance, to one-half finish each of two units of product as it takes to fully complete one, or it takes the same amount of labor to one-third finish each of three units as to complete one. Equivalent finished units are discussed further in the Delta Processing Company illustration that follows.

Process cost accounting illustrated

■ The process cost system of Delta Processing Company, a company manufacturing a patented home remedy called Noxall, is used to illustrate process cost accounting.

The procedure for manufacturing Noxall is as follows: Material A is finely ground in Delta Processing Company's grinding department, after which it is transferred to the mixing department where Material B is added, and the resulting mixture is thoroughly mixed. The mixing process results in finished product, Noxall, which is transferred on completion to finished goods. All Material A placed in process in the grinding department is placed in process when the grinding process is first begun; but the Material B added in the mixing department is added evenly throughout its process. In other words, a product one-third mixed in the latter department has received one third of its Material B and a product three-fourths mixed has received three fourths. Labor and overhead are applied evenly throughout each department's process.

At the end of the April cost period, after entries recording materials, labor, and overhead were posted, the company's two goods in process accounts appeared as follows:

Goods in Process, Grinding Department

Date		Explanation	Debit	Credit	Balance
Apr.	1	Beginning inventory			4,250
	30	Materials	9,900		14,150
	30	Labor	5,700		19,850
	30	Overhead	4,275		24,125

Goods in Process, Mixing Department

Date		Explanation	Debit	Credit	Balance
Apr.	1	Beginning inventory			3,785
	30	Materials	2,040		5,825
	30	Labor	3,570		9,395
	30	Overhead	1,020		10,415

The production reports prepared by the company's two department foremen give the following information about inventories and goods started and finished in each department during the month:

	Grinding Department	Mixing Department
Units in the beginning inventories of goods in process	30,000	16,000
April 1 stage of completion of the beginning inventories of goods in process	1/3	1/4
Units started in process and finished during period	70,000	85,000
Total units finished and transferred to next department or to finished goods	100,000	101,000
Units in the ending inventories of goods in process......................	20,000	15,000
Stage of completion of ending inventories of goods in process......	1/4	1/3

After receiving the production reports, the company's cost accountant prepared a process cost summary, Illustration 23–9, for the grinding department. A process cost summary is a report peculiar to a processing company; a separate one is prepared for each processing department and shows: (1) the costs charged to the department, (2) the department's

Delta Processing Company
Process Cost Summary, Grinding Department
For Month Ended April 30, 19—

COSTS CHARGED TO THE DEPARTMENT:

Material requisitioned..	$ 9,900
Labor charged...	5,700
Overhead costs incurred..	4,275
	$19,875
Goods in process at the beginning of the month..	4,250
Total Costs to Be Accounted for..	$24,125

EQUIVALENT UNIT PROCESSING COSTS:

Material:	Units Involved	Fraction of a Unit Added	Equivalent Units Added
Beginning inventory..	30,000	-0-	-0-
Units started and finished...	70,000	one	70,000
Ending inventory	20,000	one	20,000
			90,000

Equivalent unit processing cost for material: $9,900 ÷ 90,000 = $0.11

Labor and overhead:	Units Involved	Fraction of a Unit Added	Equivalent Units Added
Beginning inventory	30,000	2/3	20,000
Units started and finished	70,000	one	70,000
Ending inventory..	20,000	1/4	5,000
			95,000

Equivalent unit processing cost for labor: $5,700 ÷ 95,000 = $0.06
Equivalent unit processing cost for overhead: $4,275 ÷ 95,000 = $0.045

COSTS APPLICABLE TO THE WORK OF THE DEPARTMENT:

Goods in process, one-third processed at the beginning of April:

Costs charged to the beginning inventory of goods in process during previous month...	$4,250	
Material added (all added during March)	-0-	
Labor applied (20,000 × $0.06)...	1,200	
Overhead applied (20,000 × $0.045)...	900	
Cost to process..		$ 6,350

Goods started and finished in the department during April:

Material added (70,000 × $0.11)...	$7,700	
Labor applied (70,000 × $0.06)...	4,200	
Overhead applied (70,000 × $0.045)...	3,150	
Cost to process..		15,050
Total cost of the goods processed in the department and transferred to the mixing department (100,000 units at $0.214 each)		$21,400

Goods in process, one-fourth processed at the end of April:

Material added (20,000 × $0.11)..	$2,200	
Labor applied (5,000 × $0.06)	300	
Overhead applied (5,000 × $0.045)	225	
Cost to one-fourth process		2,725
Total Costs Accounted for...		$24,125

Illustration
23–9

equivalent unit processing costs, and (3) the costs applicable to the department's goods in process inventories and its goods started and finished.

Observe in Illustration 23–9 that a process cost summary has three sections. In the first, headed Costs Charged to the Department, are summarized the costs charged to the department. Information for this section comes from the department's goods in process account. Compare the first section of Illustration 23–9 with the goods in process account of the grinding department as shown on page 663.

The second section of a process cost summary shows the calculation of equivalent unit costs. The information for this section as to units involved and fractional units applicable to the inventories comes from the production report of the department foreman. Information as to material, labor, and overhead costs comes from the first section of the summary.

Notice in the second section of Illustration 23–9 that there are two separate equivalent unit calculations. Two calculations are required because material added to the product and labor and overhead added are not added in the same proportions and at the same stages in the processing procedure of this department. As previously stated, all material is added at the beginning of this department's process, and labor and overhead are added evenly throughout the process. Consequently, the number of equivalent units of material added is not the same as the number of equivalent units of labor and overhead added.

Observe in the calculation of equivalent finished units for materials that the beginning-of-the-month inventory is assigned no material. In the grinding department all material placed in process is placed there at the beginning of the process. The 30,000 beginning inventory units were begun during March and were one-third completed at the beginning of April. Consequently, these units received all their material during March when their processing was first begun.

Note also how the $9,900 cost of the material charged to the department in April is divided by 90,000 equivalent units of material to arrive at an $0.11 per equivalent unit cost for material consumed in this department.

Now move on to the calculation of equivalent finished units for labor and overhead and note that the beginning inventory units were each assigned two thirds of a unit of labor and overhead. If these units were one-third completed on April 1, then two thirds of the work done on these units was done in April. Beginning students often have difficulty at this point. In a situation such as this they are apt to assign only an additional one-third unit of labor and overhead when two thirds is required.

Before going further observe that the essence of the equivalent unit calculation for labor and overhead is that to do two thirds of the work on 30,000 units, all the work on 70,000 units, and one fourth the work on 20,000 units is the equivalent of doing all the work on 95,000 units. Then observe how the $5,700 of labor cost and $4,275 of overhead cost charged to the department are each divided by 95,000 to determine equivalent unit costs for labor and overhead.

When a department begins and ends a cost period with partially processed units of product, it is necessary to apportion the department's costs between the units that were in process in the department at the beginning of the period, the units started and finished during the period, and the ending inventory units. This division is necessary to determine the cost of the units completed in the department during the period; and the division and assignment of costs are shown in the third section of the process cost summary.

Notice in the third section of Illustration 23–9 how costs are assigned to the beginning inventory. The first amount assigned is the $4,250 beginning inventory costs. This amount represents the material, labor, and overhead costs used to one-third complete the inventory during March, the previous cost period. Normally, the second charge to a beginning inventory is for additional material assigned to it. However, in the grinding department no additional material costs are assigned the beginning inventory because these units received all of their material when their processing was first begun during the previous month. The second charge to the beginning inventory is for labor. The $1,200 portion of applicable labor costs is calculated by multiplying the number of equivalent finished units of labor used in completing the beginning inventory by the cost of an equivalent finished unit of labor (20,000 equivalent finished units at $0.06 each). The third charge to the beginning inventory is for overhead. The applicable $900 portion is determined by multiplying the equivalent finished units of overhead used in completing the beginning inventory by the cost of an equivalent finished unit of overhead (20,000 × $.045).

After costs are assigned to the beginning inventory, the procedures used in their assignment are repeated for the units started and finished. Then the cost of the units completed and transferred to finished goods, in this case the cost of the 30,000 beginning inventory units plus the cost of the 70,000 units started and finished, is determined by adding the costs assigned to the two groups. In this situation the total is $21,400 or $0.214 per unit ($21,400 ÷ 100,000 units = $0.214 per unit).

Before going further, notice in the second section of the grinding department's process cost summary that the equivalent finished unit cost for materials is $0.11, for labor is $0.06, and for overhead is $0.045, a total of $0.215. Notice, however, in the third section of the summary that the unit cost of the 100,000 units finished and transferred is $0.214, which is less than $0.215. It is less because costs were less in the department during the previous month and the 30,000 beginning units were one-third processed at these lower costs.

The grinding department's process cost summary is completed by assigning costs to the ending inventory, and after it was completed the accountant prepared the following entry to transfer from the grinding department to the mixing department the cost of the 100,000 units processed in the department and transferred during April. Information for the entry as to the cost of the units transferred was taken from the third section of Illustration 23–9.

Apr.	30	Goods in Process, Mixing Department	21,400.00	
		Goods in Process, Grinding Department......		21,400.00
		To transfer the cost of the 100,000 units of product transferred to the mixing department.		

Posting the foregoing entry had the effect on the accounts shown in Illustration 23–10. Observe that the effect is one of transferring and

Goods in Process, Grinding Department

Date		Explanation	Debit	Credit	Balance
Apr.	1	Beginning inventory			4,250
	30	Materials	9,900		14,150
	30	Labor	5,700		19,850
	30	Overhead	4,275		24,125
	30	Units to mixing department		21,400	2,725

Goods in Process, Mixing Department

Date		Explanation	Debit	Credit	Balance
Apr.	1	Beginning inventory			3,785
	30	Materials	2,040		5,825
	30	Labor	3,570		9,395
	30	Overhead	1,020		10,415
	30	Units from grinding department	21,400		31,815

Illustration 23–10

advancing costs from one department to the next just as the product is transferred and advanced in the manufacturing procedure.

After posting the entry transferring to the mixing department the grinding department costs of the units transferred, the cost accountant prepared a process cost summary for the mixing department. Information required in its preparation was taken from the mixing department's goods in process account and production report. The summary appeared as in Illustration 23–11.

Delta Processing Company
Process Cost Summary, Mixing Department
For Month Ended April 30, 19—

COSTS CHARGED TO THE DEPARTMENT:

Materials requisitioned	$ 2,040
Labor charged	3,570
Overhead costs incurred	1,020
Total processing costs	$ 6,630
Goods in process at the beginning of the month	3,785
Costs transferred from the grinding department (100.000 units at $0.214 each)	21,400
Total Costs to Be Accounted for	$31,815

EQUIVALENT UNIT PROCESSING COSTS:

Materials, labor, and overhead:	Units Involved	Fraction of a Unit Added	Equivalent Units Added
Beginning inventory	16,000	¾	12,000
Units started and finished	85,000	one	85,000
Ending inventory	15,000	⅓	5,000
Total equivalent units			102,000

Equivalent unit processing cost for materials: $2,040 ÷ 102,000 = $0.02
Equivalent unit processing cost for labor: $3,570 ÷ 102,000 = $0.035
Equivalent unit processing cost for overhead: $1,020 ÷ 102,000 = $0.01

COSTS APPLICABLE TO THE WORK OF THE DEPARTMENT:

Goods in process, one-fourth completed at the beginning of April:

Costs charged to the beginning inventory of goods in process during previous month	$ 3,785	
Materials added (12,000 × $0.02)	240	
Labor applied (12,000 × $0.035)	420	
Overhead applied (12,000 × $0.01)	120	
Cost to process		$ 4,565

Goods started and finished in the department during April:

Costs in the grinding department (85,000 × $0.214)	$18,190	
Materials added (85,000 × $0.02)	1,700	
Labor applied (85,000 × $0.035)	2,975	
Overhead applied (85,000 × $0.01)	850	
Cost to process		23,715
Total accumulated cost of goods transferred to finished goods (101,000 units at $0.28)		$28,280

Goods in process, one-third processed at the end of April:

Costs in the grinding department (15,000 × $0.214)	$ 3,210	
Materials added (5,000 × $0.02)	100	
Labor applied (5,000 × $0.035)	175	
Overhead applied (5,000 × $0.01)	50	
Cost to one-third process		3,535
Total Costs Accounted for		$31,815

Illustration
23–11

Two points in Illustration 23–11 require special attention. The first is the calculation of equivalent finished units. Since the materials, labor, and overhead added in the mixing department are all added evenly throughout the process of this department, only a single equivalent unit calculation is required. This differs from the grinding department, the previous department, where it will be recalled that two equivalent unit calculations were required. Two were required because material placed in process and the labor and overhead placed in process were not placed in process at the same stages in the processing procedure.

The second point needing special attention in the mixing department cost summary is the method of handling the grinding department costs transferred to this department. During April, 100,000 units of product with accumulated grinding department costs of $21,400 were transferred to the mixing department. Of these 100,000 units, 85,000 were started in process in the department, finished, and transferred to finished goods. The remaining 15,000 were still in process in the department at the end of the cost period.

Notice in the first section of Illustration 23–11 how the $21,400 of grinding department costs transferred to the mixing department are added to the other costs charged to the department. Compare the information in this first section with the mixing department's goods in process account as it is shown on page 663 and again in Illustration 23–10.

Notice again in the third section of the mixing department's process cost summary how the $21,400 of grinding department costs are apportioned between the 85,000 units started and finished and the 15,000 units still in process in the department. The 16,000 beginning goods in process units received none of this $21,400 charge because they were transferred from the grinding department during the previous month. Their grinding department costs are included in the $3,785 beginning inventory costs.

The third section of the mixing department's process cost summary shows that 101,000 units of product with accumulated costs of $28,280 were completed in the department during April and transferred to finished goods. The cost accountant used the following entry to transfer the accumulated cost of these 101,000 units from the mixing department's goods in process account to the Finished Goods account.

Apr.	30	Finished Goods...	28,280.00	
		Goods in Process, Mixing Department........		28,280.00
		To transfer the accumulated grinding department and mixing department costs of the 101,000 units transferred to Finished Goods.		

Posting the foregoing entry had the effect shown in Illustration 23–12.

Goods in Process, Mixing Department

Date		Explanation	Debit	Credit	Balance
Apr.	1	Beginning inventory			3,785
	30	Materials	2,040		5,825
	30	Labor	3,570		9,395
	30	Overhead	1,020		10,415
	30	Units from grinding department	21,400		31,815
	30	Units to finished goods		28,280	3,535

Finished Goods

Date		Explanation	Debit	Credit	Balance
Apr.	30	Units from mixing department	28,280		28,280

Illustration
23–12

Questions
for class
discussion

1. What are the main two types of cost accounting systems? Which system generally fits best the needs of a manufacturer who (*a*) manufactures machinery to its customers' specifications, (*b*) manufactures adding machines in lots of 500, and (*c*) manufactures paint?

2. Give the cost accounting meaning of the following:
   a) Job order cost system. *e*) Job cost sheet.
   b) Process cost system. *f*) Labor time ticket.
   c) Job. *g*) Materials requisition.
   d) Job lot. *h*) Process cost summary.

3. What subsidiary ledger is controlled by (*a*) the Materials account and (*b*) the Goods in Process account?

4. How is the inventory of goods in process determined in a general accounting system like that described in Chapter 22? How may this inventory be determined in a job cost system?

5. What is the purpose of a job cost sheet? What is the name of the ledger containing the job cost sheets of the unfinished jobs in process? What account controls this ledger?

6. What business papers are the bases for the job cost sheet entries for (*a*) materials and (*b*) for labor?

7. Refer to the job cost sheet of Illustration 23–3. How was the amount of overhead costs charged to this job determined?

8. How is a predetermined overhead application rate established? Why is such a predetermined rate used to charge overhead to jobs?

9. Why does a company using a job cost system normally have either overapplied or underapplied overhead at the end of each accounting period?

10. At the end of a cost period the Overhead Costs controlling account has a debit balance. Does this represent overapplied or underapplied overhead?

11. What are the basic differences in the products and in the manufacturing procedures of a company to which a job cost system is applicable as opposed to a company to which a process cost system is applicable?

12. What is an equivalent finished unit of labor? Of materials?
13. What is the assumption on which the idea of an equivalent finished unit of, for instance, labor is based?
14. What is the production of a department measured in equivalent finished units if it began an accounting period with 8,000 units of product that were one-fourth completed at the beginning of the period, started and finished 50,000 units during the period, and ended the period with 6,000 units that were one-third processed at the period end?
15. The process cost summary of a department commonly has three sections. What is shown in each section?

Class exercises

Exercise 23–1

PART 1. During December, 197A, a cost accountant established his company's 197B overhead application rate based on direct labor cost. In setting the rate, he estimated the company would incur $200,000 of overhead costs during 197B and it would apply $160,000 of direct labor to the products that would be manufactured during 197B. Determine the rate.

PART 2. During February, 197B, the company of Part 1 began and completed Job No. 874. Determine the job's cost under the assumption that on its completion the job's cost sheet showed the following materials and labor charged to it:

JOB COST SHEET							
Customer's Name Hiltop Mine					Job No. 874		
Job Description 5 H.P. Solidifier							
	Materials		Labor		Overhead Costs Applied		
Date	Requisition Number	Amount	Time Ticket Number	Amount	Date	Rate	Amount
Feb. 2	1524	68.00	2116	16.00			
3	1527	47.00	2117	20.00			
4	1531	10.00	2122	16.00			

Exercise 23–2

In December, 197A, a cost accountant established the following overhead application rate for applying overhead to the jobs that would be completed by his company during 197B:

$$\frac{\text{Estimated Overhead Costs, \$147,000}}{\text{Estimated Direct Labor Costs, \$98,000}} = 150\%$$

At the end of 197B the company's accounting records showed that $149,000 of overhead costs had actually been incurred during 197B and $100,000 of direct labor, distributed as follows, had been applied to jobs during the year.

Direct labor on jobs completed and sold... $ 85,000
Direct labor on jobs completed and in the finished goods inventory...... 10,000
Direct labor on jobs still in process 5,000
$100,000

Required:
1. Set up an Overhead Costs T-account and enter on the proper sides the amounts of overhead costs incurred and applied. State whether overhead was overapplied or underapplied during the year.
2. Give the entry to close the Overhead Costs account and allocate its balance between jobs sold, jobs finished but unsold, and jobs in process.

Exercise 23–3

Dell Company uses a job cost system in which overhead is charged to jobs on the basis of direct labor cost, and at the end of a year the company's Goods in Process account showed the following:

Goods in Process

Materials	85,000	To finished goods	205,500
Labor	60,000		
Overhead	75,000		

Required:
1. Determine the overhead application rate used by the company under the assumption that the labor and overhead costs actually incurred were the same as the amounts estimated.
2. Determine the cost of the labor and the cost of the overhead charged to the one job in process at the year-end under the assumption it had $5,500 of materials charged to it.

Exercise 23–4

During a cost period a department finished and transferred 56,000 units of product to finished goods, of which 16,000 were in process in the department at the beginning of the cost period and 40,000 were begun and completed during the period. The 16,000 beginning inventory units were three-fourths completed when the period began. In addition to the 56,000 units completed, 12,000 more units were in process in the department, one-half completed when the period ended.

Required:
Calculate the equivalent units of product completed in the department during the cost period.

Exercise 23–5

Assume the department of Exercise 23–4 had $25,000 of labor charged to it during the cost period of the exercise and that labor is applied in the process of the department evenly throughout the process.

Required:
Calculate the cost of an equivalent unit of labor in the department and the

shares of the $25,000 of labor charged to the department that should be assigned to each of its inventories and to the units started and finished.

Exercise 23–6

Forty-eight thousand units of product were completed in a department and transferred to finished goods during a cost period. Of these 48,000 units, 12,000 were in process and were one-third completed at the beginning of the period and 36,000 units were begun and completed during the period. In addition to the 48,000 units completed, 10,000 more units were in process in the department three-fifths processed at the period end.

Required:
Calculate the equivalent units of material added to the product processed in the department during the period under each of the following unrelated assumptions: (*a*) All material added to the product of the department is added when the department's process is first begun. (*b*) The material added to the product of the department is added evenly throughout the department's process. (*c*) One half the material added in the department is added when the department's process is first begun and the other half is added when the process is three-fourths completed.

Problems

Problem 23–1

Late in 197A a cost accountant established his company's 197B overhead application rate by estimating his company would assign 10 men to direct labor tasks during 197B and that each man would work 2,000 hours at $3 per hour during the year. At the same time he estimated his company would incur the following amounts of overhead costs during 197B:

Indirect labor	$20,000
Factory building rent	12,000
Depreciation expense, machinery	15,000
Machinery repairs expense	3,000
Heat, lights, and power	6,000
Factory supplies expense	1,000
Total	$57,000

At the end of 197B the accounting records showed the company had actually incurred $58,560 of overhead costs during the year while completing four jobs and beginning the fifth. The completed jobs were assigned overhead on completion, and the in-process job was assigned overhead at the year-end. The jobs had the following direct labor costs:

Job No. 1 (sold and delivered)	$12,800
Job No. 2 (sold and delivered)	13,000
Job No. 3 (sold and delivered)	14,200
Job No. 4 (in finished goods inventory)	14,000
Job No. 5 (in process, unfinished)	7,000
Total	$61,000

Required:

1. Determine the overhead application rate established by the cost accountant under the assumption it was based on direct labor cost.
2. Determine the total overhead applied to jobs during the year and the amount of over- or underapplied overhead at the year-end.
3. Give the entry to dispose of the over- or underapplied overhead by prorating it between goods in process, the finished goods inventory, and cost of goods sold.

Problem 23–2

During its first cost period a company completed the following internal and external transactions:

a) Purchased materials on account, $22,000.
b) Paid factory wages, $18,800.
c) Paid miscellaneous factory overhead costs, $3,000.
d) Material requisitions were used during the cost period to charge materials to jobs. The requisitions were then accumulated until the end of the cost period when they were totaled and recorded with a general journal entry. (Instructions for the entry are given in Item *j.*) An abstract of the requisitions showed the following materials charged to jobs. (Charge the materials to the jobs by making entries directly in the job T-accounts in the subsidiary Job Cost Ledger.)

Job No. 1	$ 4,000
Job No. 2	2,100
Job No. 3	3,900
Job No. 4	4,300
Job No. 5	800
Total	$15,100

e) Labor time tickets were used to charge jobs with direct labor. The tickets were then accumulated until the end of the cost period when they were totaled and recorded with a general journal entry. (Instructions for the entry are given as Item *k.*) An abstract of the tickets showed the following labor charged to jobs. (Charge the labor to the jobs by making entries directly in the job T-accounts in the Job Cost Ledger.)

Job No. 1	$ 3,800
Job No. 2	2,200
Job No. 3	4,000
Job No. 4	3,600
Job No. 5	400
Total	$14,000

f) Job Nos. 1, 3, and 4 were completed and transferred to finished goods. A predetermined overhead application rate, 200% of direct labor cost, was used to apply overhead to each job upon its completion. (Enter the overhead in the job T-accounts; mark the jobs "completed"; and make a general journal entry to transfer their costs to the Finished Goods account.)
g) Job Nos. 1 and 4 were sold on account for a total of $40,000.

h) At the end of the cost period, charged overhead to the jobs in process, using the 200% of direct labor cost application rate. (Enter the overhead in the job T-accounts.)

i) Made a general journal entry at the end of the cost period to record depreciation on the factory building, $6,000; machinery depreciation, $6,700; expired factory insurance, $1,200; and accrued factory taxes payable, $2,000.

j) Separated the material requisitions into direct material requisitions and indirect material requisitions, totaled each kind, and made a general journal entry to record them. The requisition totals were:

Direct materials	$15,100
Indirect materials	4,000
Total	$19,100

k) Separated the labor time tickets into direct labor time tickets and indirect labor time tickets, totaled each kind, and made a general journal entry to record them. The time ticket totals were:

Direct labor	$14,000
Indirect labor	5,000
Total	$19,000

l) Determined the total overhead assigned to all jobs and made a general journal entry to record it.

Required:

1. Open the following general ledger T-accounts: Materials, Goods in Process, Finished Goods, Factory Payroll, Overhead Costs, and Cost of Goods Sold.
2. Open an additional T-account for each of the five jobs. Assume that each job's T-account is a job cost sheet in a subsidiary Job Cost Ledger.
3. Prepare general journal entries to record the applicable information of Items *a, b, c, f, g, i, j, k,* and *l.* Post the entry portions that affect the general ledger accounts opened.
4. Enter the applicable information of Items *d, e, f,* and *h* directly in the T-accounts that represent job cost sheets.
5. Present statistics to prove the balances of the Goods in Process and Finished Goods accounts.
6. List the general ledger accounts and tell what is represented by the balance of each.

Problem 23-3

If the working papers that accompany this text are not being used, omit this problem.

Rock Shop manufactures to the special order of its customers a machine called a rocksquare. On January 1 the company had a $2,230 materials inventory but no inventories of goods in process and finished goods. However, on that date it began Job No. 1, a rocksquare for High Company, and Job No. 2, a rocksquare for Low Company; and during the January cost period it completed the following summarized internal and external transactions:

1. Recorded invoices for the purchase of materials on credit. The invoices and receiving reports carried this information:

   Receiving report No. 1, Material A, 200 units at $11 each.

   Receiving report No. 2, Material B, 300 units at $5 each.

   (Record the invoices with a single general journal entry and post to the general ledger T-accounts, using the transaction number to identify the amounts in the accounts. Enter the receiving report information on the proper materials ledger cards.)

2. Materials were requisitioned as follows:

   Requisition No. 1, for Job No. 1, 100 units of Material A.

   Requisition No. 2, for Job No. 1, 120 units of Material B.

   Requisition No. 3, for Job No. 2, 80 units of Material A.

   Requisition No. 4, for Job No. 2, 100 units of Material B.

   Requisition No. 5, for 10 units of machinery lubricant.

   (Enter the requisition amounts for direct materials on the materials ledger cards and on the job cost sheets. Enter the indirect material amount on the proper materials ledger card and debit it to the Indirect Materials account in the subsidiary Overhead Costs Ledger. Assume the requisitions are accumulated until the end of the month and will be recorded with a general journal entry. Instructions for this entry follow in the problem.)

3. Received the following labor time tickets from the timekeeping department:

   Time tickets Nos. 1 through 60 for direct labor on Job No. 1, $1,000.

   Time tickets Nos. 61 through 100 for direct labor on Job No. 2, $800.

   Time tickets Nos. 101 through 120 for machinery repairs, $375.

   (Charge the direct labor time tickets to the proper jobs and charge the indirect labor time tickets to the Indirect Labor account in the subsidiary Overhead Costs Ledger. Assume the time tickets are accumulated until the end of the month for recording with a general journal entry.)

4. Made the following cash disbursements during the month:

   Paid the month's factory payroll, $2,100.

   Paid for miscellaneous overhead items totaling $1,000.

   (Record the payments with general journal entries and post the general ledger accounts. Enter the charge for miscellaneous overhead items in the subsidiary Overhead Costs Ledger.)

5. Finished Job No. 1 and transferred it to the finished goods warehouse. *(The company charges overhead to each job by means of a predetermined overhead application rate based on direct labor costs. The rate is 80%. (1) Enter the overhead charge on the cost sheet of Job No. 1. (2) Complete the cost summary section of the cost sheet. (3) Mark "Finished" on the cost sheet. (4) Prepare and post a general journal entry to record the job's completion and transfer to finished goods.)*

6. Prepared and posted a general journal entry to record both the cost of goods sold and the sale of Job No. 1 to High Company, sale price $5,000.

7. At the end of the cost period, charged overhead to Job No. 2 based on the amount of direct labor applied to the job thus far. *(Enter the applicable amount of overhead on the job's cost sheet.)*

8. Totaled the requisitions for direct materials, totaled the requisitions for indirect materials, and made and posted a general journal entry to record them.

9. Totaled the direct labor time tickets, totaled the indirect labor time tickets, and made and posted a general journal entry to record them.
10. Determined the amount of overhead applied to jobs and made and posted a general journal entry to record it.

Required:
1. Record the transactions as instructed in the narrative.
2. Complete the statements in the book of working papers by filling in the blanks.

Problem 23-4

In the sanding department of a processing concern labor is added to the department's product evenly throughout its processing. During a cost period 50,000 units of product were finished in this department and transferred to finished goods. Of these 50,000 units, 15,000 were in process at the beginning of the period and 35,000 were begun and completed during the period. The 15,000 beginning goods in process units were one-fifth completed when the period began. In addition to the foregoing units, 9,000 additional units were in process and were one-third completed at the period end.

Required:
Under the assumption that $13,800 of labor was charged to the sanding department during the period, determine (1) the equivalent units of labor applied to the department's product, (2) the cost of an equivalent unit of labor, and (3) the shares of the $13,800 that should be charged to the beginning inventory, the units started and finished, and the ending inventory.

Problem 23-5

Two operations, mixing and finishing, and two departments are used in the manufacturing procedure of Valley Processing Company. The procedure is begun in the mixing department and completed in the finishing department.

At the beginning of the May cost period there were 5,000 units of product in the mixing department which were three-fifths processed. These units were completed during the period and transferred to the finishing department. Also, the processing of 31,000 additional units were begun in the mixing department during the period. Of these 31,000 units, 23,000 were finished and transferred to the finishing department. The remaining 8,000 units were in the department in a one-half processed state at the end of the period.

It is assumed that the material, labor, and overhead applied in the mixing department are applied evenly throughout the process of the department.

At the end of the cost period, after entries recording materials, labor, and overhead were posted, the company's Goods in Process, Mixing Department account appeared as follows:

Goods in Process, Mixing Department

May 1	Balance	2,901	
31	Materials	9,280	
31	Labor	12,209	
31	Overhead	6,090	
		30,480	

Required:

1. Prepare a process cost summary for the mixing department.
2. Prepare the journal entry to transfer to the finishing department the cost of the goods completed in the mixing department and transferred.

Problem 23–6

Dale Processing Company makes a product that is processed in two departments. All the materials in the product are added in the first department, Department One, and labor and overhead are applied. The product is then complete insofar as Department One is concerned and it is transferred to Department Two. In Department Two more labor and overhead are applied and the product is completed and transferred to Finished Goods.

At the end of a cost period after entries charging Department Two with its labor and overhead costs and the cost of the units transferred to it from Department One were posted, the goods in process account of the department appeared as follows:

Goods in Process, Department Two

Date		Explanations	Debit	Credit	Balance
Apr.	1	Balance (1,200 units ⅔ processed)			2,640
	30	Labor	3,500		6,140
	30	Overhead	5,400		11,540
	30	12,000 units transferred from			
		Department One	19,200		30,740
	30	10,200 units transferred to			
		Finished Goods		?	?

Required:

1. Under the assumptions (*a*) there were no units lost or spoiled in Department Two during the period, (*b*) the units in the department's ending inventory were one-fifth processed at the period end, and (*c*) labor and overhead added to the product in the department are added evenly throughout the department's process, prepare a process cost summary for Department Two.
2. After preparing the process cost summary, prepare the entry to transfer to Finished Goods the cost of the units finished in the department and transferred.

Alternate problems

Problem 23–1A

A cost accountant estimated before a year began that his small company would incur during the year the direct labor cost of 20 men working 2,000 hours each at an average rate of $3 per hour. He also estimated the concern would incur the following overhead costs during the year:

Indirect labor..	$15,750
Superintendence..	12,000
Rent of factory building..	7,200
Heat, lights, and power	4,800
Insurance expense...	3,400
Depreciation of machinery	24,200
Machinery repairs	3,000
Supplies expense...	1,500
Miscellaneous factory expenses	1,350
Total..	$73,200

At the end of the year for which the estimates were made the cost records showed the company had actually incurred $73,350 of overhead costs and had completed and sold five jobs which had direct labor costs as follows: Job No. 603, $25,400; Job No. 604, $23,200; Job No. 605, $21,700; Job No. 606, $22,800; and Job No. 607, $24,900. In addition Job No. 608 was in process at the period end and had had $2,500 of direct labor and its share of overhead costs charged.

Required:
Under the assumption the concern used a predetermined overhead application rate based on the foregoing overhead and direct labor estimates, determine: (1) the predetermined application rate used, (2) the total overhead applied to jobs during the year, and (3) the over- or underapplied overhead at the year-end. (4) Under the further assumption that the company considered the amount of its over- or underapplied overhead to be immaterial, give the entry to close the Overhead Costs account.

Problem 23-2A

A company completed the following internal and external transactions, among others, during a cost period:
a) Purchased materials on account, $13,000.
b) Paid factory wages, $12,400.
c) Paid miscellaneous factory overhead costs, $800.
d) Material requisitions were used during the cost period to charge materials to jobs. The requisitions were then accumulated until the end of the cost period when they were totaled and recorded with a general journal entry. (Instructions for this entry are given in Item *j*.) An abstract of the requisitions showed the following materials charged to jobs. (Charge the materials to the jobs by making entries directly in the job T-accounts in the subsidiary Job Cost Ledger.)

Job No. 1...	$ 2,600
Job No. 2...	1,300
Job No. 3...	2,800
Job No. 4...	3,000
Job No. 5...	600
Total..	$10,300

e) Labor time tickets were used to charge jobs with direct labor. The tickets were then accumulated until the end of the cost period when they were totaled and recorded with a general journal entry. (Instructions for the entry are given as Item *k*.) An abstract of the tickets showed the following labor charged to jobs. (Charge the labor to the jobs by making entries directly in the job T-accounts in the Job Cost Ledger.)

Job No. 1	$2,400
Job No. 2	1,400
Job No. 3	2,600
Job No. 4	2,800
Job No. 5	400
Total	$9,600

f) Job Nos. 1, 3, and 4 were completed and transferred to finished goods. A predetermined overhead application rate, 150% of direct labor cost, was used to apply overhead to each job upon its completion. (Enter the overhead in the job T-accounts; mark the jobs "completed"; and make a general journal entry to transfer their costs to the Finished Goods account.)

g) Job Nos. 1 and 3 were sold on account for a total of $24,000.

h) At the end of the cost period, charged overhead to the jobs in process at the rate of 150% of direct labor cost. (Enter the overhead in the job T-accounts.)

i) At the end of the cost period made a general journal entry to record: depreciation, factory building, $2,300; depreciation, machinery, $4,100; expired factory insurance, $600; and accrued factory taxes payable, $1,200.

j) Separated the material requisitions into direct material requisitions and indirect material requisitions, totaled each kind, and made a general journal entry to record them. The requisition totals were:

Direct materials	$10,300
Indirect materials	2,000
Total	$12,300

k) Separated the labor time tickets into direct labor time tickets and indirect labor time tickets, totaled each kind, and made a general journal entry to record them. The time ticket totals were:

Direct labor	$ 9,600
Indirect labor	3,100
Total	$12,700

l) Determined the total overhead assigned to all jobs and made a general journal entry to record it.

Required:

1. Open the following general ledger T-accounts: Materials, Goods in Process, Finished Goods, Factory Payroll, Overhead Costs, and Cost of Goods Sold.

2. Open an additional T-account for each of the five jobs. Assume that each job's T-account is a job cost sheet in a subsidiary Job Cost Ledger.

3. Prepare general journal entries to record the applicable information of Items *a, b, c, f, g, i, j, k,* and *l.* Post the entry portions that affect the general ledger accounts opened.
4. Enter the applicable information of Items *d, e, f,* and *h* directly in the T-accounts that represent job cost sheets.
5. Present statistics to prove the balances of the Goods in Process and Finished Goods accounts.
6. List the general ledger accounts and tell what is represented by the balance of each.

Problem 23–5A

The product of Sage Processing Company is produced on a continuous basis in a single processing department in which material, labor, and overhead are added to the product evenly throughout the manufacturing process.

At the end of the current May cost period, after the material, labor, and overhead costs were charged to the Goods in Process account of the single processing department, the account appeared as follows:

Goods in Process

May 1	Balance	1,362
31	Materials	5,325
31	Labor	10,863
31	Overhead	15,194
		32,744

During the cost period the company finished and transferred to finished goods 72,000 units of the product, of which 9,000 were in process at the beginning of the period and 63,000 were begun and finished during the period. The 9,000 that were in process were one-third processed when the period began. In addition to the foregoing units, 8,000 additional units were in process and were one-fourth completed at the end of the cost period.

Required:
1. Prepare a process cost summary for the department.
2. Draft the general journal entry to transfer to Finished Goods the cost of the product finished in the department during the month.

Problem 23–6A

Hardrock Processing Company manufactures a simple product on a continuous basis in one department. All materials are added in the manufacturing process of this product when the process is first begun. Labor and overhead are added evenly throughout the process.

During the current April cost period the company completed and transferred to finished goods 43,000 units of the product. These consisted of 5,000 units that were in process at the beginning of the period and 38,000 units begun and finished during the period. The 5,000 beginning goods in process units were complete as to materials and four-fifths complete as to labor and overhead when the period began. In addition to the foregoing units, 6,000 additional units were in process at the end of the period, complete as to materials and one-half complete as to labor and overhead.

Since the company has only one processing department, it has only one Goods in Process account. At the end of the period, after entries recording material, labor, and overhead had been posted, the account appeared as follows:

Goods in Process

Apr. 1	Balance	5,333	
30	Materials	27,060	
30	Labor	9,744	
30	Overhead	14,868	
		57,005	

Required:
Prepare a process cost summary and the entry to transfer to Finished Goods the cost of the product completed in the department during April.

Decision problem 23–1, Handy Tool Company

Handy Tool Company manufactures a single product, a tool that it sells to distributors who in turn sell to hardware stores. The company uses a job cost system to accumulate costs on job lots of tools. During the past several years it has sold an average of 30,000 of the tools annually at $20 each, using about 80% of its production capacity. Next year's estimated costs for manufacturing the tool, assuming 30,000 units are produced, are $14 per unit and consist of the following:

Materials	$ 4.00
Direct labor	4.00
Manufacturing overhead (150% of direct labor cost)	6.00
Estimated cost per unit	$14.00

The company's overhead application rate was established at 150% two years ago by the accountant who set up its cost system. The same rate was used again last year and proved satisfactory, since sales volume and costs did not materially vary from the previous year. The company had planned to use the 150% rate again next year and it had estimated next year's overhead costs at $180,000 and direct labor costs for 30,000 units at $120,000. However, although the company's volume and costs have been stable in the recent past, this morning it received an offer from a mail-order company to purchase 6,000 units of its tool at $12.50 each with the mail-order company's name attached. No changes in the tool are required to fit it to the mail-order company's specifications other than affixing the company's name, which will cost 25 cents per unit for additional materials.

The company president can see no point in accepting the order, for, as he says, "Why manufacture and sell something, when you lose money on every unit sold." The sales manager is not sure the new business should be rejected, and he has asked that a further study of costs be made before a final decision is reached.

You have been asked to make the cost study. In your investigation you find that next year's estimated manufacturing overhead consists of $150,000 of what is known as fixed overhead costs plus variable overhead costs of $1 per unit for 30,000 units, which together total $180,000. (Fixed overhead costs are such costs as depreciation of factory building, taxes, insurance, and the like. They receive their name from the fact that their total amounts do not change with a change in the number of units produced but remain fixed. Variable overhead costs are costs that vary with the number of units produced and are for such things as power and indirect materials.)

You also find that selling and administrative expenses consist of $100,000 of fixed expenses plus 50 cents per unit of variable selling and administrative expenses. Acceptance of the mail-order business will not affect fixed costs nor change present variable costs per unit, including material and direct labor costs per unit.

Attach to your report a condensed columnar income statement that shows the revenue, costs, and before-tax income from present business in its first two columns; the revenue, costs, and before-tax income from the new business in the second columns; and the combined results of present and the new business in the third set of columns. In preparing the statement, show as separate amounts the material, direct labor, fixed overhead, variable overhead, fixed selling and administrative, and variable selling and administrative costs for present business, for the new business, and combined.

Decision problem 23–2, Hamond Manufacturing Company

Hamond Manufacturing Company uses a job order cost system in accounting for manufacturing costs, and following are a number of its general ledger accounts with the January 1 balances and some January postings shown. The postings are incomplete. Commonly only the debit or credit of a journal entry appears in the accounts, with the offsetting debits and credits being omitted. Also, the amounts shown represent total postings for the month and no date appears. However, this additional information is available: (1) The company charges jobs with overhead on the basis of direct labor cost, using a 150% overhead application rate. (2) The $17,000 debit in the Overhead Costs account represents the sum of all overhead costs for January other than indirect materials and indirect labor. (3) The accrued factory payroll on January 31 was $3,000.

Materials			Factory Payroll		
Jan. 1 Bal.	11,000	12,000		19,000	Jan. 1 Bal. 2,000
	15,000				

Goods in Process			Cost of Goods Sold		
Jan. 1 Bal.	6,000	48,000			
Materials	10,000				
Labor	16,000				

Finished Goods			Factory Overhead Costs		
Jan. 1 Bal.	12,000	50,000		17,000	

Copy the accounts on a sheet of paper, supply the missing debits and credits, and tie together the debits and credits of an entry with key letters. Answer these questions: (1) What was the January 31 balance of the Finished Goods account? (2) How many dollars of factory payroll were paid during January? (3) What was the cost of the goods sold during January? (4) How much overhead was actually incurred during the month? (5) How much overhead was charged to jobs during the month? (6) Was overhead overapplied or underapplied during the month?

Budgeting; standard costs

■ A *budget* is a plan of future action expressed in monetary terms; and *budgeting* is the process of planning future action.

The primary reason for preparing a budget is to maximize profits; but the benefits of budgeting go beyond this as outlined in the following section.

Other benefits from budgeting

■ Investigation, study, and research

A budget is a plan of future action, and when a concern plans, it may be assumed that its actions are based upon thorough investigations, study, and research. Not only should this result in the best conceivable plans but it should also instill in executives the habit of basing decisions upon investigations and study.

Control

A budget aids in controlling business operations. It does this by influencing the actions of people. For example, when a department manager knows that his department's expenses will be compared with the planned expenses of a budget, he is influenced toward keeping the expenses at the planned level.

Coordination

Coordination requires that a business be operated as a whole rather than as a group of separate departments. When a budget plan is prepared, each department's objectives are determined in advance, and these objectives are coordinated; for example, the production department is scheduled to produce approximately the number of units the selling department can sell.

Communication

When a budget is prepared, the budget becomes a means of informing the organization not only of plans that have been approved by management but also of budgeted actions management wishes the organization to take during the budget period.

Motivation

When obtainable budgeted objectives are set, all persons responsible can normally be depended upon to make every effort to attain or exceed the objectives for which they are personally responsible.

The budget period ■ Budget periods normally coincide with accounting periods. This means that in most companies the budget period is one year in length. However, in addition to their annual budgets, many companies prepare long-range budgets setting forth major objectives for from 3 to 5 or 10 years in advance. Such long-range budgets are often used as the framework into which each annual budget is fitted.

Although most budgets are prepared for a year, yearly budgets are commonly broken down into quarterly or monthly budgets. Short-term budgets of a quarter or a month are useful yardsticks for measuring the degree of accomplishment toward the total results desired.

When an annual budget is broken down into monthly budgets, monthly reports like that of Illustration 24–1 are prepared to compare actual achievements with the budgeted plan.

The budget committee ■ The task of preparing a budget should not be made the responsibility of any one department; and the budget definitely should not be handed down from above as the "final word." Rather budget figures and budget estimates should be developed from the bottom up. For example, the sales department should have a hand in preparing sales estimates and the production department should be responsible for preparing its own expense budget. Otherwise production and salespeople may say the budget figures are meaningless, inasmuch as they were prepared by front office personnel who know nothing of sales and production problems.

Nevertheless, the preparation of a budget needs central guidance, and this is commonly supplied by a budget committee of department heads or other high-level executives who are responsible for seeing that budget figures are realistically established and coordinated. If a depart-

Illustration
24-1

Consolidated Stores, Inc.
Income Statement with Variations from Budget
For Month Ended April 30, 19—

	Actual	Budget	Variations
Sales	$63,500	$60,000	$+ 3,500
Less: Sales returns and allowances	1,800	1,700	+ 100
Sales discounts	1,200	1,150	+ 50
Net sales	$60,500	$57,150	$+ 3,350
Cost of goods sold:			
Merchandise inventory, April 1, 19—	$42,000	$44,000	$− 2,000
Purchases, net	39,100	38,000	+ 1,100
Freight-in	1,250	1,200	+ 50
Goods for sale	$82,350	$83,200	$− 850
Merchandise inventory, April 30, 19—	41,000	44,100	− 3,100
Cost of goods sold	$41,350	$39,100	$+ 2,250
Gross profit	$19,150	$18,050	$+ 1,100
Operating expenses:			
Selling expenses:			
Sales salaries	$ 6,250	$ 6,000	$+ 250
Advertising expense	900	800	+ 100
Store supplies used	550	500	+ 50
Depreciation of store equipment	1,600	1,600	
Total selling expenses	$ 9,300	$ 8,900	$+ 400
General and administrative expenses:			
Office salaries	$ 2,000	$ 2,000	
Office supplies used	165	150	$+ 15
Rent	1,100	1,100	
Expired insurance	200	200	
Depreciation of office equipment	100	100	
Total general and administrative expenses	$ 3,565	$ 3,550	$+ 15
Total operating expenses	$12,865	$12,450	$+ 415
Income from Operations	$ 6,285	$ 5,600	$+ 685

ment submits budget figures that do not reflect proper performance, the figures should be returned to the department with the budget committee's comments. The originating department then either adjusts the figures or defends them. It should not change the figures just to please the committee, since it is important that all parties agree that the figures are reasonable and attainable.

Preparing the budget

■ A company's budget, often called the *master budget*, normally consists of a number of budgets; for example, it may be composed of a sales budget, a production budget, numerous departmental expense budgets, a plant and equipment or capital budget, and a cash budget.

Sales budget

The sales budget, an estimate of goods to be sold and revenue to be derived from sales, is the usual starting point in the budgeting procedure, since the plans of all departments are related to sales and expected revenue.

The sales budget commonly grows from a reconciliation of forecasted business conditions, plant capacity, proposed selling expenses, such as advertising, and estimates of sales. As to sales estimates, since people normally feel a greater responsibility for reaching goals they have had a hand in setting, traveling salesmen of a concern having such salesmen and department managers in a department store are asked to submit through their sales manager estimates of sales for their territories and departments. The final sales budget is then based on these estimates as reconciled for forecasted business conditions, selling expenses, and et cetera.

Merchandising, production, and material purchases budgets

In a store, merchandise must be purchased before it is sold, and in a factory it must be produced. As a result, once sales estimates are completed it is necessary to plan merchandise purchases or product production.

MERCHANDISING BUDGET. Monthly departmental sales forecasts are the usual starting point in building a store's merchandising budget. Illustration 24–2 shows such a budget for Department A of Consolidated Stores. The sales figure in Illustration 24–2 is the budgeted

---

Consolidated Stores, Inc.
Merchandising Budget for Department A, Month of February, 19—

Sales at planned selling prices (see sales budget).....................................	$ 6,800
Budgeted purchases for February:	
Cost of goods to be sold during February (60% of $6,800)......................	$ 4,080
Planned February 28th inventory...	8,000
Total merchandise required	$12,080
Inventory on February 1	7,600
Budgeted Purchases for February	$ 4,480

Illustration
24–2

February sales from the concern's previously prepared sales budget. Then since the markup in this department is 40% (based on sales), cost of goods sold is 60% of budgeted sales; and if planned inventories for the department are known, budgeted departmental purchases can be determined as in the illustration.

To produce a storewide merchandising budget, a budget similar to Illustration 24–2 is prepared for each department. Then all the departmental budgets are combined for a monthly merchandising budget for the entire store and the monthly budgets are combined again for the year's budget.

PRODUCTION AND MATERIAL PURCHASES BUDGETS. The production budget for a manufacturing concern is prepared in much the same way as a store's merchandising budget. To begin, an estimate of the units of each product to be manufactured is made, often as in Illustration 24–3.

The Marine Production Company
Production Budget
Planned Quantity of Goods to Be Manufactured
For the Year Ending December 31, 197A

Units of product required to meet sales estimates	62,300
Planned inventory, December 31, 197A	8,600
Total units required	70,900
Units in inventory, January 1, 197A	8,100
Number of Units to Be Manufactured	62,800

Illustration
24–3

After the production budget and the number of units of each product to be manufactured are determined, the next step is to set up the material purchases budget. To do this a materials specification sheet showing kinds and quantities of materials needed for proposed production is prepared. From this an estimate of materials to be purchased can be made as in Illustration 24–4 (assume in this illustration for sake of brevity that only one kind of material is needed and that two units of it are used to make each unit of finished goods).

The Marine Production Company
Material Purchases Budget
Planned Quantity and Cost of Raw Material to Be Purchased
For the Year Ending December 31, 197A

Required units of material for goods to be manufactured (62,800 × 2)	125,600
Planned inventory, December 31, 197A	21,200
Total units of material required	146,800
Units in January 1, 197A, material inventory	18,600
Units to be purchased	128,200
Estimated unit cost	× $2
Estimated Cost of Material to Be Purchased	$256,400

Illustration
24–4

After the material purchases budget is completed, labor costs and factory overhead are estimated. Then all estimates are assembled in a statement of budgeted cost of goods to be manufactured.

Expense budgets

As soon as a tentative sales estimate is made, it is communicated to department heads such as the sales manager and office manager who are asked to make expense estimates for their departments. The department heads normally base their estimates on the previous year's expenses, adjusted for increases or decreases in service expected of them, changes in wage scales, changes in supply costs, and other pertinent data. Their estimates must meet the approval of the budget committee or be increased or decreased; however, asking for estimates from department heads helps secure their cooperation in carrying out the final budget.

Plant and equipment budget

The plant and equipment or capital budget lists equipment to be scrapped and additional equipment to be purchased if the proposed production program is carried out. The purchase of additional equipment requires funds; and anticipating equipment additions in advance normally makes it easier to provide the funds.

At times estimated production may exceed plant capacity. Budgeting makes it possible to anticipate this and either revise the production schedule or increase plant capacity.

Planning plant and equipment purchases is called capital budgeting, and this is discussed in more detail in the next chapter.

Cash budget

After tentative sales, expenses, production, and equipment budgets have been set, the cash budget is prepared. This budget is important. A company should have at all times enough cash to meet needs but not too much. Too much cash is undesirable because it often cannot be profitably invested.

A cash budget requires management to forecast cash receipts and disbursements, and usually results in better cash management. Also, it enables management to arrange well in advance for loans to cover any anticipated inadequacies.

In preparing the cash budget, anticipated receipts are added to the beginning cash balance, and anticipated expenditures are deducted. Annual cash budgets are usually broken down into monthly budgets as in Illustration 24–5.

Consolidated Stores, Inc.		
Cash Budget for January, 19–		
Cash balance, January 1, 19–		$32,500
Add estimated cash receipts:		
Cash sales..	$43,200	
Collections of accounts receivable................	18,650	
Interest on investments...............................	750	
Property rentals	1,800	64,400
Available cash		$96,900
Deduct estimated disbursements:		
Accounts payable..	$41,300	
State and federal taxes................................	2,750	
Payrolls..	8,250	
Building repairs	15,300	
Dividends...	4,000	
Miscellaneous items....................................	1,200	72,800
Estimated Cash Balance, January 31, 19–		$24,100

Illustration
24–5

Master budget

After the sales, expense, production, equipment, and cash budgets are coordinated and completed, they are combined into a master budget. The master budget is then approved and transmitted to the organization as the approved objectives for the budget period.

Accounting and budgeting

■ Preparing and carrying out a budget involves all departments; consequently, it is not primarily an accounting function. However, the task of assembling data and translating it into financial terms often falls to the accounting department. Furthermore, since the accounting department is in charge of accounting records and is constantly dealing with actual transactions, it is well qualified to deal with budget data.

One budget task the accounting department is commonly called upon to perform is to prepare from the budget an estimated income statement for the budget year and an estimated balance sheet as it will appear at the end of the budget year if budget plans are carried out. This task is, in a sense, actually one of accounting for events before they happen.

Preparing estimated statements

■ Normally, when the accounting department is called on to prepare an estimated balance sheet and an estimated income statement as they will appear at the end of the budget period, it is called upon to do so a month or more before the budget period begins. For example, the accounting department may be given a copy of the budget during the last week of November and be requested to prepare estimated statements for the year beginning the following January 1.

During the last week in November, the accounting department does not know what the following December 31 post-closing or January 1 opening account balances will be. Consequently, its first task is to project the company's account balances ahead and arrive at the December 31 estimated post-closing trial balance for the current year.

After arriving at this estimated post-closing trial balance, it is commonly entered in the first two money columns of a work sheet. Next the budgeted transactions and adjustments are entered in the second pair of work sheet columns in the same manner as adjustments are entered on an ordinary work sheet. For example, if the budget calls for sales on account of $250,000, the name of the Sales account is entered on the work sheet in the Account Titles column below the names of the estimated trial balance accounts; and then Sales is credited and Accounts Receivable is debited for $250,000 in the second pair of money columns.

After all budgeted transactions and adjustments are entered on the work sheet, the estimated trial balance amounts in the first pair of money columns are combined with the budget amounts in the second pair of columns and are sorted to the proper Income Statement and Balance Sheet columns of the work sheet. After this, the estimated income statement and estimated balance sheet are prepared from the information in the Income Statement and Balance Sheet columns in the same manner as an ordinary income statement or balance sheet.

Fixed and variable budgets

■ Some concerns prepare what are known as "fixed" budgets; others prepare so-called "variable" or "flexible" budgets.

The budgets discussed thus far have been of the fixed variety. When a fixed budget is prepared, the best information available is used to arrive at an estimate of the operating level expected during the budget year. All plans are then based on this one expected or "fixed" level of activity. A fixed budget, in other words, assumes a single level of activity, and cost and expense estimates are made for this one level only.

The weakness of a fixed budget is that it makes no provision for an operating level different from that planned; and there are often years in which for unforeseen reasons the actual operating level varies substantially from the budget plan. Furthermore, when this occurs, good management requires that costs and expenses be adjusted to fit the new unplanned activity level; and under a fixed budget, for lack of planning, these adjustments have to be made on a "best-guess" basis. True, these best guesses may prove satisfactory; but planning in advance for several activity levels should produce both better cost control and more precise guidance for management.

A variable budget differs from a fixed budget in that it provides cost and expense estimates for varying rates of operating activity. For example, a concern preparing a variable budget may estimate it will sell during the coming budget year, depending upon economic conditions, from 100,000 to 160,000 units of product. It then provides in its flexible budget, for instance, a set of cost and expense estimates for the 100,000-unit level, another set for the 110,000-unit level, another for 120,000 units, still another for 130,000, and so on up to 160,000 units. In other words, when a flexible budget is prepared, cost and expense estimates are made for each of the several production levels that may be experienced. Then, as the year progresses and the actual operating level becomes known, the budget costs and expenses for that level are compared with the actual costs and expenses. Any variations provide cost control data for managerial action.

STANDARD COSTS

■ In the previous chapter it was said that there are two basic types of cost systems, job order and process, but an infinite number of variations of the two. A *standard cost system,* one based on *standard* or *budgeted costs,* is such a variation.

The costs of a job or a process as discussed in the previous chapter were historical costs, historical in the sense that they had been incurred and were history by the time they were recorded. Such costs are useful and must be recorded; but to judge whether or not they are reasonable or what they should be, management needs a basis of comparison. Standard costs offer such a basis.

Standard costs are the costs that should be incurred under normal conditions in producing a given product or part or in performing a particular service. They are established by means of engineering and accounting studies made before the product is manufactured or the service performed; and once established, they are used to judge the reasonableness of the actual costs incurred when the product or service is produced. Standard costs are also used to place responsibilities when actual costs vary from standard.

Accountants speak of *standard material cost, standard labor cost,* and *standard overhead cost;* and this terminology is used in this chapter; however, it should be observed that standard material, labor, and overhead costs are really budgeted material, labor, and overhead costs.

Establishing standard costs   ■ Great care and the combined efforts of people in accounting, engineering, personnel administration, and other management areas are required in establishing standard costs. Time and motion studies are made of each labor operation in a product's production or in performing a service to learn both the best way to perform the operation and the standard labor time required under normal conditions for performance. Exhaustive investigations are also made of the quantity, grade, and cost of each material required; and machines and other productive equipment are subject to detailed studies in an effort to achieve maximum efficiencies and to learn what costs should be.

However, regardless of care exercised in establishing standard costs and in revising them as conditions change, actual costs incurred in producing a given product or service are apt to vary from standard costs. When this occurs, the difference in total cost is likely to be a composite of several cost differences. For example, the quantity, or the price, or both the quantity and price of the material used may have varied from standard; and the labor time, or the labor price, or both the time and price of labor may have varied. Likewise, overhead costs may have varied.

Variances   ■ When actual costs vary from standard costs, the differences are called *variances*. Variances may be favorable or unfavorable. A favorable variance is one in which actual cost is below standard cost, and an unfavorable variance is one in which actual cost is above standard.

When variances occur, they are isolated and studied for possible remedial action and to place responsibilities. For example, if the standard material cost for producing 2,000 units of Product A is $800 but material costing $840 was used in producing the units, the $40 variance may have resulted from paying a price higher than standard for the material, a greater quantity of material than standard may have been used, or there may have been some combination of these causes. The price paid for a material is a purchasing department responsibility; consequently, if the variance was caused by a price greater than standard, responsibility rests with the purchasing department. On the other hand, since the production department is usually responsible for the amount of material used, if a quantity greater than standard was used, responsibility normally rests with the production department. However, if more than a standard amount of material was used because the material was of a grade below standard, causing more than normal waste, responsibility is back on the purchasing department for buying a substandard grade.

Isolating
material
and labor
variances

■ As previously stated, when variances occur, they are isolated and studied for possible remedial action and to place responsibilities. For example, assume that XL Company has established the following standard costs per unit for its Product Z:

Material (1 pound per unit at $1 per pound) $1.00
Direct labor (1 hour per unit at $3 per hour) 3.00
Overhead ($2 per standard direct labor hour) 2.00
    Total standard cost per unit $6.00

Material variances

Assume further that during May, XL Company completed 3,500 units of Product Z, using 3,600 pounds of material costing $1.05 per pound, or $3,780. Under these assumptions the actual and standard material costs for the 3,500 units are:

Actual cost: 3,600 pounds @ $1.05 per pound $3,780
Standard cost: 3,500 pounds @ $1.00 per pound 3,500
    Excess of actual over standard cost .... $ 280

Observe that the actual material cost for these units is $280 above their standard cost. This excess cost may be isolated as to causes in the following manner:

QUANTITY VARIANCE
Actual units at the standard price .... 3,600 lbs. @ $1.00 = $3,600
Standard units at the standard price .... 3,500 lbs. @ $1.00 =   3,500
    Variance (unfavorable) .... 100 lbs. @ $1.00 = $100

PRICE VARIANCE
Actual units at the actual price .... 3,600 lbs. @ $1.05 = $3,780
Actual units at the standard price .... 3,600 lbs. @ $1.00 =   3,600
    Variance (unfavorable) .... 3,600 lbs. @ $0.05 =   180
    Excess material cost $280

The foregoing analysis shows that $100 of the excess material cost resulted from using 100 more pounds than standard, and $180 resulted from a unit price $0.05 above standard. With this information management can go to the responsible individuals for explanations.

Labor variances

Labor cost in manufacturing a given part or in performing a service depends on a composite of the number of hours worked (quantity) and the wage rate paid (price). Therefore, when the labor cost for a task varies from standard, it too may be analyzed into a quantity variance and a price variance.

For example, the direct labor standard for the foregoing 3,500 units of Product Z is one hour per unit, or 3,500 hours at $3 per hour. If 3,400 hours costing $3.10 per hour were used in completing the units, the actual and standard labor costs for these units are:

```
Actual cost      3,400 hours @ $3.10 per hour.............. $10,540
Standard cost: 3,500 hours @ $3.00 per hour.............. 10,500
        Excess of actual over standard cost .................... $    40
```

In this case actual cost is only $40 over standard, but isolating the variances involved reveals the following:

```
QUANTITY VARIANCE
    Standard hours at standard price ............ 3,500 hrs. @ $3.00  =  $10,500
    Actual hours at standard price ................ 3,400 hrs. @ $3.00  =   10,200
        Variance (favorable).......................... 100 hrs. @ $3.00  =              $300

PRICE VARIANCE
    Actual hours at actual price.................... 3,400 hrs. @ $3.10  =  $10,540
    Actual hours at standard price ............... 3,400 hrs. @ $3.00  =   10,200
        Variance (unfavorable) ....................... 3,400 hrs. @ $0.10  =               340
        Excess labor cost ...........................                                          $  40
```

The foregoing analysis shows a favorable quantity variance of $300, which resulted from using 100 fewer direct labor hours than standard for the units produced. However, this favorable variance was more than offset by a wage rate $0.10 above standard.

When a factory or department has workers of various skill levels, it is the responsibility of the foreman or other supervisor to assign to each task a workman or workmen of no higher skill level than is required to accomplish the task. In this case an investigation could reveal that workers of a higher skill level were used in producing the 3,500 units of Product Z; hence, fewer labor hours were required for the work. However, because the workers were of higher grade, the wage rate paid them was higher than standard.

Charging overhead to production

■ When standard costs are used, factory overhead is charged to production by means of a predetermined standard overhead rate. The rate may be based on the relation of overhead to standard labor cost, standard labor hours, standard machine-hours, or some other measure of production. For example, XL Company charges its Product Z with $2 of overhead per standard direct labor hour; and since the direct labor standard for Product Z is one hour per unit, the 3,500 units manufactured in May were charged with $7,000 of overhead.

Before going on, recall that only 3,400 actual direct labor hours were used in producing these units. Then note again that overhead is charged to the units, not on the basis of actual labor hours but on the basis of standard labor hours. Standard labor hours are used because the amount of overhead charged to these units should not be less than standard simply because less than the standard (normal) amount of labor was used in their production. In other words, overhead should not vary from normal simply because labor varied from normal.

Establishing overhead standards

■ A variable flexible factory overhead budget is the starting point in establishing reasonable standards for overhead costs. A flexible budget is necessary because the actual production level may vary from the expected level; and when this happens, certain costs vary with production, but others remain fixed. This may be seen by examining XL Company's flexible budget shown in Illustration 24–6.

In examining Illustration 24–6, consider the first fixed cost, building rent. Unless there is some sort of escalator clause in the rent contract, rent expense is always a *fixed cost* or a cost that remains the same whether the factory is temporarily closed or is running on a one-, two-, or even a three-shift basis. On the other hand, power to run the machines is a *variable cost*, since it varies with the production level. Likewise, the remaining costs of XL Company's flexible budget are either fixed or variable as shown by their classification.

XL Company
Flexible Overhead Costs Budget
For Month Ended May 31, 19—

	Production Levels				
	60%	70%	80%	90%	100%
Production in units............................	3,000	3,500	4,000	4,500	5,000
Standard direct labor hours................	3,000	3,500	4,000	4,500	5,000
Budgeted factory overhead:					
Fixed costs:					
Building rent................................	$1,000	$1,000	$1,000	$1,000	$1,000
Depreciation, machinery...............	1,200	1,200	1,200	1,200	1,200
Supervisory salaries.....................	1,800	1,800	1,800	1,800	1,800
Totals.....................................	$4,000	$4,000	$4,000	$4,000	$4,000
Variable costs:					
Indirect labor..............................	$1,200	$1,400	$1,600	$1,800	$2,000
Indirect materials.........................	900	1,050	1,200	1,350	1,500
Power and lights..........................	600	700	800	900	1,000
Maintenance...............................	300	350	400	450	500
Totals.....................................	$3,000	$3,500	$4,000	$4,500	$5,000
Total Factory Overhead....................	$7,000	$7,500	$8,000	$8,500	$9,000

Illustration
24–6

Observe in Illustration 24–6 that XL Company has established standard costs for five production levels, ranging from 60% to 100% of capacity. Such a range is established because when actual costs are known, they should be compared with the standards for the level actually achieved and not with the standards at some other level. For example, if the plant actually operated at 70% capacity during May, actual costs incurred at this 70% level should be compared with standard costs at this level and not with costs established for the 80% or 90% levels.

In setting overhead standards, after the flexible overhead budget is prepared, management must determine the expected operating level for the plant. This can be 100% of capacity; but it seldom is since errors in scheduling work, breakdowns, and, perhaps, the inability of the sales force to sell all the product produced commonly reduced the operating level to some point below full capacity.

After the flexible budget is set up and the expected operating level is determined, overhead costs at the expected level are related to, for example, labor hours at this level to establish the standard overhead rate. The rate thus established is then used to charge overhead to production. For example, assume XL Company decided that 80% of capacity is the expected operating level for its plant. The company then arrived at its $2 per direct labor hour overhead rate by dividing the budgeted $8,000 of overhead costs at the 80% level by the 4,000 standard direct labor hours required to produce the product manufactured at this level.

Overhead variances

■ As previously stated, when standard costs are used, overhead is applied to production on the basis of a predetermined overhead rate. Then at the end of a cost period the difference between overhead applied and overhead actually incurred is analyzed and variances are calculated to set out responsibilities for the difference.

Overhead variances are computed in several ways. A common way divides the difference between overhead applied and overhead incurred into (1) the *volume variance* and (2) the *controllable variance*.

Volume variance

The volume variance is the difference between (1) *the amount of overhead budgeted at the actual operating level achieved during the period* and (2) *the standard amount of overhead charged to production during the period*. For example, assume that during May XL Company actually operated at 70% of capacity, producing 3,500 units of Product Z, which were charged with overhead at the standard rate. Under this assumption the company's volume variance for May is:

VOLUME VARIANCE
Budgeted overhead at 70% of capacity....................	$7,500
Standard overhead charged to production (3,500 standard labor hours at the $2 per hour)............	7,000
Variance (unfavorable)..	$ 500

To understand why this volume variance occurred, reexamine the flexible budget of Illustration 24–6 and observe that at the 80% level the $2 per hour overhead rate may be subdivided into $1 per hour for fixed overhead and $1 per hour for variable overhead. Furthermore, at the 80% (normal) level, the $1 for fixed overhead exactly covers the fixed overhead. However, when this $2 rate is used for the 70% level, and again subdivided, the $1 for fixed overhead will not cover all the fixed overhead because $4,000 is required for fixed overhead and 3,500 hours at $1 per hour equals only $3,500. In other words, at this 70% level the $2 per hour standard overhead rate did not absorb all the overhead incurred; it lacked $500, the amount of the volume variance. Or again, the volume variance resulted simply because the plant did not reach the expected operating level.

An unfavorable volume variance tells management that the plant did not reach its normal operating level; and when such a variance is large, management should investigate the cause or causes. Machine breakdowns, failure to schedule an even flow of work, and a lack of sales orders are common causes. The first two may be corrected in the factory, but the third requires either more orders from the sales force or a downward adjustment of the operating level considered to be normal.

Controllable variance

The controllable variance is the difference between (1) *overhead actually incurred and* (2) *the overhead budgeted at the operating level achieved.* For example, assume that XL Company incurred $7,650 of

---

XL Company
Factory Overhead Variance Report
For Month Ended May 31, 19—

VOLUME VARIANCE:

Normal production level	80%	of capacity.
Production level achieved	70%	of capacity.
Volume variance	$ 500 (unfavorable)	

CONTROLLABLE VARIANCE

	Budget	Actual	Favorable	Unfavorable
Fixed overhead costs:				
Building rent	$1,000	$1,000		
Depreciation, machinery	1,200	1,200		
Supervisory salaries	1,800	1,800		
Total fixed	$4,000	$4,000		
Variable overhead costs:				
Indirect labor	$1,400	$1,525		$125
Indirect materials	1,050	1,025	$ 25	
Power and lights	700	750		50
Maintenance	350	350		
Total variable	$3,500	$3,650		
Total controllable variances			$ 25	$175
Net Controllable Variance (Unfavorable)			150	
			$175	$175

Illustration
24–7

overhead during May; and since its plant operated at 70% of capacity during the month, its controllable overhead variance for May is:

CONTROLLABLE VARIANCE
```
Actual overhead incurred ...................................... $7,650
Overhead budgeted at operating level achieved ........  7,500
    Variance (unfavorable) ...................................... $   150
```

The controllable overhead variance measures management's efficiency in adjusting controllable overhead costs (normally variable overhead) to the operating level achieved. In this case management failed by $150 to get overhead down to the amount budgeted for the 70% level.

Although the controllable overhead variance measures management's efficiency in adjusting overhead costs to the operating level achieved, an overhead variance report is a more effective means for showing just where management achieved or failed to achieve the budgeted expectations. Such a report for XL Company appears in Illustration 24–7.

Combining the volume and controllable variances

The volume and controllable variances may be combined to account for the difference between overhead actually incurred and overhead charged to production. For example, XL Company incurred $7,650 of overhead during May and charged $7,000 to production, and its overhead variances may be combined as follows to account for the difference:

VOLUME VARIANCE
```
Budgeted overhead at production level achieved ......................... $7,500
Standard overhead charged to production (3,500 standard
    hours at $2 per hour) ......................................................  7,000
        Variance (unfavorable) .....................................................        $500

CONTROLLABLE VARIANCE
Actual overhead incurred ...................................................... $7,650
Overhead budgeted at operating level achieved ..........................  7,500
        Variance (unfavorable) .......................................................         150
    Excess of overhead incurred over overhead charged to
        production ...................................................................        $650
```

Controlling a business through standard costs ■ Business operations are carried on by people, and control of a business is gained by controlling the actions of the people responsible for its revenues, costs, and expenses. When a budget is prepared and standard costs established, control is maintained by taking appropriate action when actual costs vary from standard or from the budget.

Reports like the ones shown in this chapter are a means of calling management's attention to these variations, and a review of the reports is essential to the successful operation of a budget program. However, in making the review, management should practice the control technique known as *management by exception*. Under this technique management gives its attention only to the variances in which actual costs are significantly different from standard and it ignores the cost situations in which performance is satisfactory. In other words, management concentrates its attention on the exceptional or irregular situations and pays little or no attention to the normal.

Standard costs in the accounts

■ Standard costs can be used solely in the preparation of management reports and need not be taken into the accounts. However, in most standard cost systems such costs are taken into the accounts to facilitate both the record keeping and the preparation of reports.

No effort will be made here to go into the bookkeeping details of a standard cost system. This is reserved for a course in cost accounting. Nevertheless, when standard costs are taken into the accounts, entries like the following (the data for which are taken from the discussion of material variances on page 694) may be used to take the standard costs into the Goods in Process account and to set out in variance accounts any variances:

May	31	Goods in Process...	3,500.00	
		Material Quantity Variance.............................	100.00	
		Material Price Variance..................................	180.00	
		Materials...		3,780.00
		To charge production with 3,600 pounds of material @ $1.05 per pound.		

Variances taken into the accounts, as in the foregoing entry, are allowed to accumulate in the variance accounts until the end of an accounting period. If at that time the variance amounts are immaterial, they are closed to Cost of Goods Sold as an adjustment of the cost of goods sold. However, if the amounts are large, they may be prorated between Goods in Process, Finished Goods, and Cost of Goods Sold.

Questions for class discussion

1. What is a budget? What benefits result from preparing a budget?
2. What is the normal length of a budget period?
3. Why should each department be asked to prepare its own budget estimates?
4. What are the duties of the budget committee?
5. What is a sales budget? A departmental expense budget? A production budget? A capital budget? A cash budget? A master budget?
6. A manufacturing concern plans to begin a budget year with 1,700 units of its product on hand; it plans to sell 48,000 units during the year and to end the year with a 2,000-unit inventory. If production is to be at a uniform rate throughout the year, how many units should the concern plan to produce each month?
7. Differentiate between a fixed budget and a flexible or variable budget.
8. What is a standard cost? For what are standard costs used?
9. In standard cost accounting, what is a variance?
10. Why is a material variance isolated into a price variance and a quantity variance? Who is normally responsible for the price paid for a material?

Who is normally responsible for the amount of material used in production?

11. What is a flexible overhead costs budget? Why is such a budget used in a standard cost system?

12. What is a fixed cost? What is a variable cost? When production volume in a factory increases, do fixed costs per unit increase, decrease, or remain unchanged? Why?

13. What may cause a plant to operate below capacity?

14. What is a volume variance? What is a controllable overhead variance?

15. What does an unfavorable volume variance indicate? What does a favorable controllable variance indicate?

Class exercises

Exercise 24–1

The sales budget of Coast Department Store's Department B calls for $8,400 of sales during March. The department expects to begin March with a $6,700 inventory and end the month with a $5,500 inventory. Its cost of goods sold averages 65% of sales.

Required:
Prepare a merchandising budget for Department B showing the amount of goods to be purchased during March.

Exercise 24–2

Driftwood Company manufactures Product Z. The company's management estimates there will be 3,800 units of Product Z in the March 31 finished goods inventory and that 12,500 units will be sold during the year's second quarter. Management also believes the concern should begin the third quarter with 4,000 units of the product in its inventory.

Required:
Prepare a production budget showing the units of Product Z to be manufactured during the year's second quarter.

Exercise 24–3

PikNik Furniture Company has just completed 300 units of its deluxe picnic table using 14,500 board feet of lumber costing $3,045. The company's material standards for one unit of this table are 50 board feet of lumber at $0.20 per board foot.

Required:
Isolate the material variances incurred in manufacturing these tables.

Exercise 24–4

PikNik Furniture Company takes its standard costs into its cost records. As a result, in charging material costs to Goods in Process, it also takes any variances into its accounts.

Required:
1. Under the assumption that the materials used to manufacture the tables of Exercise 24–3 were charged to Goods in Process on March 5, give the entry to charge the materials and to take the variances into the accounts.

2. Under the further assumption that the material variances of Exercise 24–3 were the only variances of the year and were considered immaterial, give the year-end entry to close the variance accounts.

Exercise 24–5

A company has established the following standard costs for one unit of its product:

Material (1 unit @ $5 per unit) .... $ 5
Direct labor (1 hr. @ $3 per hr.)   3
Factory overhead (1 hr. @ $4 per hr.)................   4
    Standard cost... $12

The $4 per direct labor hour overhead rate is based on a normal 80% of capacity operating level and the following monthly flexible budget information:

	Operating Levels		
	75%	80%	85%
Budgeted production in units....................	7,500	8,000	8,500
Budgeted overhead:			
Fixed overhead................................	$16,000	$16,000	$16,000
Variable overhead	15,000	16,000	17,000

During the past month the company operated at 75% of capacity, producing 7,500 units of product with the following overhead costs:

Fixed overhead costs $16,000
Variable overhead costs...................................... 15,250
    Total overhead costs................................. $31,250

Required:
Isolate the overhead variances into a volume variance and a controllable variance.

Problems   **Problem 24–1**

Sandy Manufacturing Company manufactures a steel product called a "sand tap." Each "sand tap" requires 80 pounds of steel and is produced in a single operation by a stamping process. The concern's management estimates there will be 1,500 units of the product and 50 tons of steel on hand on March 31 of the current year, and that 12,000 units of the product will be sold during the year's second quarter. Management also believes that due to the possibility of a strike in the steel industry, the concern should begin the third quarter with a 150-ton steel inventory and 2,000 finished "sand taps."

Required:
Prepare a second-quarter production budget and a second-quarter steel pur-

chases budget for the company. The production budget should be in units of product and the steel purchases budget should be in tons of steel.

Problem 24–2

Tidewater Sales expects to have a $5,800 cash balance on December 31 of the current year. It also expects to have a $35,200 balance of accounts receivable and $20,900 of accounts payable. Its budgeted sales, purchases, and cash expenditures for the following three months are:

	January	February	March
Sales..	$24,000	$18,000	$27,000
Purchases...	14,000	17,300	18,000
Payroll...	2,400	2,400	2,800
Rent...	1,000	1,000	1,000
Other cash expenses.................................	1,200	1,600	1,400
Purchase of store equipment......................	...	5,000	...
Payment of quarterly dividend	...	...	4,000

All sales are on account; and past experience indicates that 85% is collected in the month following the sale, 10% in the next month, and 4% in the third month. Application of the experience to the December 31 accounts receivable balance indicates that $28,000 of the $35,200 will be collected in January, $5,200 in February, and $1,600 in March.

Purchases of merchandise on account are paid in the month following each purchase; likewise, the store equipment will be paid for in the month following its purchase.

Required:
Prepare cash budgets for the months of January, February, and March.

Problem 24–3

A company has established the following standard costs for one unit of its product:

Material (3 lbs. @ $5 per lb.).............................	$15.00
Direct labor (3 hrs. @ $3.50 per hr.).....................	10.50
Overhead (3 hrs. @ $3 per hr.)	9.00
Total standard cost	$34.50

The $3 per direct labor hour overhead rate is based on a normal, 90% of capacity, operating level for the company's plant and the following flexible budget information for March:

	Operating Levels		
	80%	90%	100%
Production in units	800	900	1,000
Direct labor hours.......................................	2,400	2,700	3,000
Fixed factory overhead	$4,500	$4,500	$4,500
Variable factory overhead............................	$3,200	$3,600	$4,000

During March the company operated at 80% of capacity, producing 800 units of product having the following actual costs:

Material (2,350 lbs. @ $5.10 per lb.)..................... $11,985
Direct labor (2,500 hrs. @ $3.40 per hr.)..............   8,500
Fixed factory overhead costs............................   4,500
Variable factory overhead costs   3,325

Required:
Isolate the material and labor variances into price and quantity variances and isolate the overhead variance into the volume variance and the controllable variance.

Problem 24-4

Sunshine Company has established the following standard costs per unit for the product it manufactures:

Material (4 lbs. @ $0.75 per lb.)......................... $ 3.00
Direct labor (2 hrs. @ $3.50 per hr.)....................   7.00
Overhead (2 hrs. @ $2.50 per hr.) 5.00
Total standard cost $15.00

The $2.50 per direct labor hour overhead rate is based on a normal, 80% of capacity, operating level and the following flexible budget information for one month's operations.

	Operating Levels		
	75%	80%	85%
Production in units	1,500	1,600	1,700
Standard direct labor hours..........................	3,000	3,200	3,400
Budgeted factory overhead:			
Fixed costs:			
Depreciation, building.............................	$1,200	$1,200	$1,200
Depreciation, machinery..........................	1,700	1,700	1,700
Taxes and insurance	300	300	300
Supervisory salaries................................	1,600	1,600	1,600
Total fixed costs	$4,800	$4,800	$4,800
Variable costs:			
Indirect materials	$ 750	$ 800	$ 850
Indirect labor	1,500	1,600	1,700
Power...	375	400	425
Maintenance..	375	400	425
Total variable costs	$3,000	$3,200	$3,400
Total Factory Overhead............................	$7,800	$8,000	$8,200

During March the company operated at 75% of capacity, produced 1,500 units of product, and incurred the following actual costs:

Material (5,900 lbs. @ $0.78 per lb.).....................		$ 4,602
Direct labor (3,060 hrs. @ $3.45 per hr.)..............		10,557
Overhead costs:		
Depreciation expense, building.........................	$1,200	
Depreciation expense, machinery	1,700	
Taxes and insurance.......................................	300	
Supervisory salaries	1,600	
Indirect materials..	735	
Indirect labor...	1,560	
Power...	385	
Maintenance	340	7,820
Total		$22,979

Required:

1. Isolate the material and labor variances into price and quantity variances and isolate the overhead variance into the volume variance and the controllable variance.
2. Prepare a factory overhead variance report showing the volume and controllable variances.

Problem 24–5

Seal Company has established the following standard costs for one unit of its product:

Material (3 lbs. @ $1.25 per lb.)..........................	$3.75
Direct labor (½ hr. @ $3 per hr.).........................	1.50
Overhead (½ hr. @ $2.60 per hr.)........................	1.30
Total standard cost	$6.55

The $2.60 per direct labor hour overhead rate is based on a normal, 80% of capacity operating level, and at this level the company's monthly output is 4,000 units. However, production does vary slightly, and each 1% variation results in a 50-unit increase or decrease in the production level. Following are the company's budgeted overhead costs at the 80% level for one month:

SEAL COMPANY
Budgeted Monthly Factory Overhead at 80% Level

Fixed costs:		
Depreciation expense, building.........................	$1,000	
Depreciation expense, machinery	800	
Taxes and insurance.......................................	200	
Supervision..	1,200	
Total fixed costs.......................................		$3,200
Variable costs:		
Indirect materials...	$ 800	
Indirect labor..	480	
Power..	320	
Repairs and maintenance	400	
Total variable costs....................................		2,000
Total Overhead Costs		$5,200

During March of the current year the company operated at 70% of capacity and incurred the following actual costs:

Material (10,620 lbs.)	$12,744
Direct labor (1,700 hrs.)	5,185
Depreciation expense, building	1,000
Depreciation expense, machinery	800
Taxes and insurance	200
Supervision	1,200
Indirect materials	725
Indirect labor	400
Power	295
Repairs and maintenance	360
Total costs	$22,909

Required:

1. Prepare a flexible overhead budget for the company showing the amount of each fixed and variable cost at the 70%, 80%, and 90% levels.
2. Isolate the material and labor variances into quantity and price variances and isolate the overhead variance into the volume variance and the controllable variance.
3. Prepare a factory overhead variance report showing the volume and controllable variances.

Alternate problems

Problem 24–1A

Tri-Products sells three products that it purchases in their finished ready-for-sale state. The products' March 1 inventories are Product X, 3,900 units; Product Y, 3,750 units; and Product Z, 6,300 units. The company's manager is disturbed because each product's March 1 inventory is excessive in relation to immediately expected sales. Consequently, he has set as a goal a month-end inventory for each product that is equal to one half the following month's expected sales. Expected sales in units for March, April, May, and June are as follows:

	Expected Sales in Units			
	March	April	May	June
Product X	5,000	4,600	5,000	3,800
Product Y	2,800	2,800	3,400	3,600
Product Z	6,000	5,400	5,200	5,800

Required:

Prepare purchases budgets in units for the three products for each of March, April, and May.

Problem 24–2A

During the latter part of February, Terry Hale, owner of Pinetop Sales approached his bank for a $10,000 loan to be made on April 1 and repaid 60 days thereafter with interest at 6%. He planned to increase his store's inventory by $10,000 during March and needed the loan to pay for the merchandise during April. The bank's loan officer was interested in Mr. Hale's ability to repay the loan and asked him to forecast his store's May 31 cash position.

On March 1 Pinetop Sales expected to have a $4,100 cash balance, $28,000 of accounts receivable, and $14,600 of accounts payable. Its budgeted sales, purchases, and cash expenditures for the following three months are as follows:

	March	April	May
Sales	$24,000	$25,000	$23,000
Merchandise purchases	25,500	15,000	14,000
Payroll	2,400	2,400	2,400
Rent	1,000	1,000	1,000
Other cash expenses	1,200	1,100	1,300
Repayment of bank loan			10,100

The budgeted March purchases include the inventory increase. All sales are on account; and past experience indicates 80% is collected in the month following the sale, 15% in the next month, 4% in the next, and the remainder is not collected. Application of this experience to the March 1 accounts receivable balance indicates $22,500 of the $28,000 will be collected during March, $4,000 during April, and $1,000 during May. All merchandise is paid for in the month following its purchase.

Required:
Prepare cash budgets for March, April, and May for Pinetop Sales under the assumption the bank loan will be paid on May 31.

Problem 24–3A

Gull Manufacturing Company makes a single product for which it has established the following standard costs per unit:

Material (5 lbs. @ $0.50 per lb.)	$2.50
Direct labor (1 hr. @ $3 per hr.)	3.00
Factory overhead (1 hr. @ $3.25 per hr.)	3.25
Total Standard Cost	$8.75

The $3.25 per direct labor hour overhead rate is based on a normal, 90% of capacity, operating level and the following flexible budget information:

	Operating Levels		
	80%	90%	100%
Production in units	1,600	1,800	2,000
Standard direct labor hours	1,600	1,800	2,000
Fixed factory overhead	$3,600	$3,600	$3,600
Variable factory overhead	$2,000	$2,250	$2,500

During June the company operated at 80% of capacity, producing 1,600 units of product which were charged with the following standard costs:

Material (8,000 lbs. @ $0.50 per lb.)........................ $ 4,000
Direct labor (1,600 hrs. @ $3 per hr.)...................... 4,800
Factory overhead costs (1,600 hrs. @ $3.25 per hr.)..... 5,200
    Total standard cost $14,000

Actual costs incurred during June were:

Material (8,100 lbs)... $ 3,969
Direct labor (1,550 hrs.) 4,805
Fixed factory overhead costs............................. 3,600
Variable factory overhead costs 2,115
    Total actual costs $14,489

Required:
Isolate the material and labor variances into price and quantity variances and isolate the overhead variance into the volume variance and the controllable variance.

Problem 24–4A

Green Hill Company has established the following standard costs per unit for the product it manufactures:

Material (4 lbs. @ $1.50 per lb.)........................ $ 6.00
Direct labor (3 hrs. @ $3 per hr.)...................... 9.00
Overhead (3 hrs. @ $1.50 per hr.)...................... 4.50
    Total standard cost $19.50

The $1.50 per direct labor hour overhead rate is based on a normal, 85% of capacity, operating level and the following flexible budget information for one month's operations.

	Operating Levels		
	80%	85%	90%
Production in units	1,600	1,700	1,800
Standard direct labor hours..........................	4,800	5,100	5,400
Budgeted factory overhead:			
Fixed costs:			
Rent of factory building.........................	$1,800	$1,800	$1,800
Depreciation expense, machinery.............	1,600	1,600	1,600
Taxes and insurance	200	200	200
Supervisory salaries.............................	1,500	1,500	1,500
Total fixed costs	$5,100	$5,100	$5,100
Variable costs:			
Indirect materials	$ 640	$ 680	$ 720
Indirect labor	1,200	1,275	1,350
Power	320	340	360
Maintenance.......................................	240	255	270
Total variable costs	$2,400	$2,550	$2,700
Total Factory Overhead Costs	$7,500	$7,650	$7,800

During April the company operated at 90% of capacity, produced 1,800 units of product, and incurred the following actual costs:

Material (7,250 lbs. @ $1.48 per lb.)...................		$10,730
Direct labor (5,300 hrs. @ $3.10 per hr.).............		16,430
Overhead costs:		
Rent of factory building.................................	$1,800	
Depreciation expense, machinery	1,600	
Taxes and insurance......................................	200	
Supervisory salaries	1,500	
Indirect materials...	700	
Indirect labor..	1,310	
Power...	355	
Maintenance	300	7,765
Total costs		$34,925

Required:

1. Isolate the material and labor variances into quantity and price variances and isolate the overhead variance into the volume variance and the controllable variance.
2. Prepare a factory overhead variance report showing the volume and controllable variances.

Decision problem 24–1, Salish Company

Salish Company manufactures Product M for which the demand is seasonal and which cannot be stored for long periods; consequently, the number of units manufactured varies with the season. In accounting for costs, the company charges actual costs incurred to a goods in process account maintained for the product, which it closes at the end of each quarter to Finished Goods. At the end of last year, which was an average year, the following cost report was prepared for the company manager:

SALISH COMPANY
Quarterly Report of Costs for Product M
Year Ended December 31, 19—

	1st Quarter	2d Quarter	3rd Quarter	4th Quarter
Materials...	$ 31,200	$ 38,900	$ 15,700	$ 7,900
Direct labor......................................	93,400	116,000	47,000	23,600
Fixed overhead costs	42,000	42,000	42,000	42,000
Variable overhead costs.......................	51,200	63,900	25,900	13,000
Total manufacturing costs	$217,800	$260,800	$130,600	$ 86,500
Production in units	40,000	50,000	20,000	10,000
Cost per unit	$5.445	$5.216	$6.530	$8.650

The manager has asked you to explain why unit costs for the product varied from a low of $5.216 in the second quarter to a high of $8.65 in the last quarter, and he has asked you to suggest a better way to accumulate or allocate costs.

He feels he must have quarterly reports for purposes of control, so attach to your explanation a schedule showing what last year's material, labor, and overhead costs per unit would have been had your suggestion or suggestions been followed for the year.

Decision problem 24–2, Shopcraft Company

Ted Hall has been an employee of Shopcraft Company for nine years, the last seven of which he has worked in the casting department. Eight months ago he was made foreman of the department, and since then has been able to end a long period of internal dissention, high employee turnover, and inefficient operation in the department. Under Ted's supervision the department's production has increased, employee morale has improved, absenteeism has dropped, and for the past two months the department has regularly been beating its standard for the first time in years.

However, a few days ago Joe Weeks, an employee in the department, suggested to Ted that the company install a new kind of controls on the department's furnace similar to those developed by a competitor. The controls would cost $15,000 installed and would have a 10-year life and no salvage value. They should increase production 10%, reduce maintenance costs $500 per year, and do away with the labor of one man.

Ted's answer to Joe was, "Forget it. We are doing OK now; we don't need the extra production; and besides, jobs are hard to find and if we have to let someone go, who'll it be?"

Do you think standard costs had anything to do with Ted's answer to Joe? Explain. Do you agree with Ted's answer? Should Ted be the person to make a decision such as this? How can a company be sure that suggestions such as Joe's are not lost in the chain of command?

Chapter 25

Managerial decisions

■ A business decision involves choosing between two or more courses of action, with the best choice normally being the one offering the highest return on the investment or the greatest cost savings. Business managers at times make such decisions intuitively and without trying to measure systematically the advantages and disadvantages of each possible choice. Often they make intuitive decisions because they are unaware of any other way to choose; but sometimes the available information is so sketchy or unreliable that systematic measurement is useless. Also, intangible factors such as convenience, prestige, and public opinion are at times more important than the factors that can be reduced to a quantitative basis. Nevertheless, in many situations it is possible to reduce the anticipated consequences of alternative choices to a quantitative basis and measure them systematically. This chapter will examine several.

Capital budgeting

■ Planning plant asset investments is called *capital budgeting*. The plans may involve new buildings, new machinery, or whole new projects; but in every case the objective is to earn a satisfactory return on the invested funds; and to accomplish this often requires some of the most crucial and difficult decisions faced by management. The decisions are difficult because they are commonly based on estimates projected well into a future that is at best uncertain; and they are crucial because (1) large sums of money are often involved; (2) funds are committed for long periods of time; and (3) once a decision is made and a project is begun, it may be difficult or impossible to reverse the effects of a poor decision.

Capital budgeting involves the preparation of cost and revenue estimates for all proposed projects, an examination of the merits of each, and a choice of those worthy of investment. It is a broad field, and this text must limit its discussion to three ways of comparing investment opportunities. They are the *payback period,* the *return on average investment,* and *discounted cash flows.*

Payback period

A successful investment in a machine or other plant asset will produce a *net cash flow,* and the payback period for the investment is the time required to recover the investment through this net cash flow. For example, assume that Murray Company is considering several capital investments, among which is the purchase of a machine to be used in manufacturing a new product. The machine will cost $16,000, have an eight-year service life, and no salvage value. The company estimates that 10,000 units of the machine's product will be sold each year, and the sales will result in $1,500 of after-tax net income, as shown in Illustration 25–1.

Annual sales of new product...		$30,000
Deduct:		
Cost of materials, labor, and overhead other than		
depreciation on the new machine......................................	$15,500	
Depreciation on the new machine	2,000	
Additional selling and administrative expenses	9,500	27,000
Annual before-tax net income...		$ 3,000
Income tax (assumed rate, 50%)..		1,500
Annual after-tax net income from new product sales.................		$ 1,500

Illustration
25–1

Through annual sales of 10,000 units of the new product, Murray Company expects to gain $30,000 of revenue and $1,500 of net income. The net income will be available to pay back the new machine's cost; but in addition, since none of the funds that flow in from sales will flow out for depreciation, so will the amount of the annual depreciation charge. The $1,500 of net income and the $2,000 depreciation charge total $3,500, and together they are the *annual net cash flow* expected from the investment. Furthermore, this annual net cash flow will pay back the $16,000 investment in the new machine in 4.6 years, calculated as follows:

$$\frac{\text{Cost of New Machine, \$16,000}}{\text{Annual Net Cash Flow, \$3,500}} = 4.6 \text{ Years to Recover Investment}$$

The answer given in the foregoing calculation is 4.6 years. Actually, when $16,000 is divided by $3,500, the result is just a little over 4.57; but 4.6 years is close enough for a decision. Remember that the calculation is based on an estimated net income and estimated depreciation; consequently, it is pointless to carry the calculation to several decimal places.

In choosing investment opportunities, a short payback period is a desirable factor because (1) the sooner an investment is recovered the sooner the funds may be reinvested in another project and (2) a short payback period also means a short "bail-out period" if conditions should change. However, the payback period should never be the only factor considered, because it ignores the length of time revenue will continue to be earned after the end of the payback period. For example, one investment may pay back its cost in three years and cease to produce revenue at that point, while a second investment may require five years to pay back its cost but will continue to produce income for another 15 years.

Rate of return on average investment

The rate of return on the average investment in a machine is calculated by dividing the after-tax net income from the sale of the machine's product by the average investment in the machine. For example, Murray Company estimates it will earn $1,500 after-tax net income from selling the product of the $16,000 machine it proposes to buy. As to average investment, each year depreciation will reduce the book value of the machine $2,000; consequently, the company may assume it will have $16,000 invested in the machine during its first year, $14,000 during the second, $12,000 during the third, and so on for the machine's eight-year life. Or, in other words, the company may assume it will have an amount equal to the machine's book value invested each year. If it makes this assumption, then the average amount it will have invested during the eight-year life is the average of the machine's book values. This is $9,000 and may be calculated as follows:

Year	Book Value		
1	$16,000		
2	14,000		
3	12,000		
4	10,000	$\frac{\$72,000}{8} =$	$9,000 Average Book Value
5	8,000		and Average Investment
6	6,000		
7	4,000		
8	2,000		
Total	$72,000		

In the foregoing calculation the eight yearly book values were averaged to determine average investment. A shorter way to the same answer is to average the book values of the machine's first and last years in this manner:

$$\frac{\$16,000 + \$2,000}{2} = \$9,000$$

And since the answer is the same either way the calculation is made, the shorter calculation is preferable.

After average investment is determined, the rate of return on average investment is calculated, as previously stated, by dividing the estimated annual after-tax profit from the sale of the machine's product by average investment, as follows:

$$\$1,500 \div \$9,000 = 16\tfrac{2}{3}\% \text{ Return on Average Investment}$$

At this point students commonly want to know if $16\tfrac{2}{3}\%$ is a good investment return. The answer is that it is better than, say, 12%, but not as good as 18%; or in other words, a return is good or bad only when related to other returns. Also, factors other than return, such as risk, are always involved in investment decisions. However, when average investment returns are used in comparing and deciding between capital investments, the one having the least risk, the shortest payback period, and the highest return for the longest time is usually the best.

Rate of return on average investment is a measure of investment profitability. It is easy to calculate and understand; and as a result it has long been used in comparing investment opportunities. Furthermore, when the investment opportunities produce uniform cash flows, it offers a fair means of comparison. However, when cash flows are not uniform from year to year, a more precise tool, such as *discounted cash flows,* offers a better means of comparison.

Discounted cash flows

When a business invests in a new plant asset, it expects to secure from the investment a stream of future cash flows, and normally it will not invest unless the flows are sufficient to return the amount of the investment plus a satisfactory net income. Furthermore, when choosing among investment opportunities of equal size and risk, the best is normally the one producing the cash flow with the largest *positive net present value.* A positive net present value is a present value in excess of the amount of the investment.

The concept of present value

As a rule a business will not invest $1 today unless it expects to get back somewhat more than $1 later on, with the "somewhat more" being earnings or interest on the investment. Likewise, if an investment today will return $1 a year from now, the investment's *present value* is somewhat less than $1. How much less depends upon how much the business expects to earn. If it expects to earn, say, 10% on the investment, the expectation of receiving $1 a year from now has a present value of $0.909. This can be verified thus: $0.909 invested today at 10% will earn $0.0909 in one year, and the $0.909 invested plus the $0.0909 earned will equal $0.9999, which rounds to the $1 expected.

Likewise, the present value of $1 to be received two years hence is $0.826 if 10% compound interest is expected. This also can be verified as follows: $0.826 invested at 10% will earn $0.0826 during the first year it is invested, and the $0.826 invested plus $0.0826 earned equals $0.9086 at the end of the first year. Then, during the second year the $0.9086 will earn $0.09086, and $0.9086 plus $0.09086 equals $0.99946, which rounds to the $1 expected.

Present value tables

The present value of $1 to be received any number of years in the future can be found by using the formula, $\$1/(\$1 + i)^n$, with i being the interest rate and n the number of years to the expected payment. However, the formula need not be used, since tables showing present values computed with the formula are readily available. Illustration 25–2 shows a portion of such a table, with the amounts rounded to three decimal places. (Three decimal places would not be sufficiently accurate for some uses, but it will suffice here.)

Present Value of $1 at Compound Interest

Years Hence	6%	8%	10%	12%	14%	15%
1	0.943	0.926	0.909	0.893	0.877	0.870
2	0.890	0.857	0.826	0.797	0.769	0.756
3	0.840	0.794	0.751	0.712	0.675	0.658
4	0.792	0.735	0.683	0.636	0.592	0.572
5	0.747	0.681	0.621	0.567	0.519	0.497
6	0.705	0.630	0.564	0.507	0.456	0.432
7	0.665	0.583	0.513	0.452	0.400	0.376
8	0.627	0.540	0.467	0.404	0.351	0.327
9	0.592	0.500	0.424	0.361	0.308	0.284
10	0.558	0.463	0.386	0.322	0.270	0.247

Illustration 25–2

Observe in Illustration 25–2 that the first figure in the 10% column is the 0.909 used in the previous section to introduce the concept of present value. The 0.909 in the 10% column means that the expectation of receiving $1 a year from today has a present value of $0.909 when discounted at 10%. Then note that the second figure in the 10% column is the 0.826 previously used, which means that the expectation of receiving $1 two years hence, discounted at 10%, has a present value of $0.826.

Using a present value table

A present value table like Illustration 25–2 shows present values of $1 discounted at several different rates and is easy to use. For example, what is the present value of $1,000 discounted at 8% for five years? To determine the answer, go down the 8% column to the amount opposite five years. It is 0.681; and $0.681 is the present value of $1 to be received five years hence when the discount rate is 8%. Therefore, the present value of $1,000 discounted five years at 8% is 1,000 times this amount or is $681.

Using present values in investment decisions

When a business uses the concept of present value in weighing an investment opportunity, it compares the present value of the investment's expected cash flows with the amount that must be invested to secure these flows. For example, if Murray Company expects a 10% compound return on its capital investments, it will weigh the opportunity to invest in the machine described in the payback calculation on page 712 as in Illustration 25–3.

Analysis of Proposed Investment in Machine

Years Hence	Present Value of $1 at 10%	Net Cash Flows	Present Value of Net Cash Flows
1	0.909	$3,500	$ 3,181.50
2	0.826	3,500	2,891.00
3	0.751	3,500	2,628.50
4	0.683	3,500	2,390.50
5	0.621	3,500	2,173.50
6	0.564	3,500	1,974.00
7	0.513	3,500	1,795.50
8	0.467	3,500	1,634.50
Total present value............................			$18,669.00
Amount to be invested........................			16,000.00
Positive Net Present Value..................			$ 2,669.00

Illustration
25–3

To secure the machine of Illustration 25–3, Murray Company must invest $16,000. However, from the sale of the machine's product the company will recapture $2,000 of its investment each year in the form of depreciation; and in addition, it will earn a $1,500 annual profit. Or in other words, the company will receive from the investment a $3,500 annual net cash flow for eight years. Now observe in Illustration 25–3 that the present value of these cash flows is $2,669 more than the required $16,000 investment. Consequently, if Murray Company considers a 10% compound return satisfactory, then this machine is a good investment, since through the sale of the machine's product the company will recover its investment, plus a 10% compound return, and $2,669 in addition.

Generally, when the cash flows from an investment, discounted at a satisfactory rate, have a present value in excess of the investment, the investment is a good one and should be accepted. Also, when several investment opportunities of the same size and risk are being compared, the one having the highest positive net present value is the best.

Cash flows not uniform

Present value analysis has its greatest usefulness when cash flows are not uniform. For example, assume a company can choose one capital investment from among Projects A, B, and C. Each requires a $12,000 investment and will produce cash flows as follows:

Years Hence	Annual Cash Flows		
	Project A	Project B	Project C
1	$ 5,000	$ 8,000	$ 1,000
2	5,000	5,000	5,000
3	5,000	2,000	9,000
	$15,000	$15,000	$15,000

Note that all three projects produce the same total cash flow. However, the flows of Project A are uniform, those of Project B are greater in the earlier years, while those of Project C are greater in the later years. Consequently, when present values of the cash flows, discounted at 10%, are compared with the required investments, the statistics of Illustration 25–4 result.

	Years Hence	Present Values of Cash Flows Discounted at 10%		
		Project A	Project B	Project C
	1	$ 4,545	$ 7,272	$ 909
	2	4,130	4,130	4,130
	3	3,755	1,502	6,759
Total present values............		$12,430	$12,904	$11,798
Required investments.........		12,000	12,000	12,000
Net Present Values		+$ 430	+$ 904	−$ 202

Illustration
25–4

Note that an investment in Project A has a $430 positive net present value, an investment in Project B a $904 positive net present value, and an investment in Project C a $202 negative net present value. Therefore, if a 10% return is required, an investment in Project C should be rejected, since the investment's net present value indicates it will not earn such a return. Furthermore, as between Projects A and B, other things being equal, Project B is the better investment, since its cash flows have the higher net present value.

Selecting the earnings rate

The selection of a satisfactory earnings rate for capital investments is always a matter for top-management decision. Formulas have been devised to aid management; but in many companies the choice of a satisfactory or required rate of return is largely subjective. Management simply decides that enough investment opportunities can be found that will earn, say, a 10% compound return, and this becomes the minimum below which the company refuses to make an investment of average risk.

Whatever the required rate, it is always higher than the rate at which money can be borrowed, since the return on a capital investment must include not only interest but also an additional allowance for risks involved. Therefore, when the rate at which money can be borrowed is around 6%, a required after-tax return of 10% compounded may be acceptable in industrial companies, with a lower rate for public utilities and a higher rate for companies in which investment opportunities are unusually good or the risks are high.

Replacing plant assets

In our dynamic economy, new and better machines are constantly coming on the market. As a result the decision to replace an existing machine with a new and better machine is common. Often the existing machine is in good condition and will produce the required product; but the new machine will do the job with a large savings in operating costs. In such a situation management must decide whether the after-tax savings in operating costs justifies the investment.

The amount of after-tax savings from the replacement of an existing machine with a new machine is complicated by the fact that depreciation on the new machine is a tax-deductible expense. There can be other complications too; consequently, a discussion of the replacement of plant assets is deferred to a more advanced course.

Accepting additional business ▪ Costs obtained from a cost accounting system are average costs and also historical costs. They are useful in product pricing and in controlling operations, but in a decision to accept an additional volume of business they are not necessarily the relevant costs. In such a decision the relevant costs are the additional costs, commonly called the *incremental* or *differential costs*.

For example, a concern operating at its normal capacity, which is 80% of full capacity, has annually produced and sold approximately 100,000 units of product with the following results:

Sales (100,000 units @ $10)		$1,000,000
Materials (100,000 units @ $3.50)	$350,000	
Labor (100,000 units @ $2.20)	220,000	
Overhead (100,000 units @ $1.10)	110,000	
Selling expenses (100,000 units @ $1.40)	140,000	
Administrative expenses (100,000 units @ $0.80)	80,000	900,000
Operating Income		$ 100,000

The concern's sales department reports it has an exporter who has offered to buy 10,000 units of product at $8.50 per unit. The sale to the exporter is several times larger than any previous sale made by the company; and since the units are being exported, the new business will have no effect on present business. In order to determine whether the order should be accepted or rejected, management of the company ask that statistics be prepared to show the estimated net income or loss that would result from accepting the offer. It received the following figures based on the average costs previously given:

Sales (10,000 units @ $8.50)		$85,000
Materials (10,000 units @ $3.50)	$35,000	
Labor (10,000 units @ $2.20)	22,000	
Overhead (10,000 units @ $1.10)	11,000	
Selling expenses (10,000 units @ $1.40)	14,000	
Administrative expenses (10,000 units @ $0.80)	8,000	90,000
Operating Loss		$ (5,000)

If a decision were based solely on the foregoing estimates, the new business would likely be rejected. However, before rejecting the order, the costs of the new business were examined more closely and the following additional information obtained: (1) Manufacturing 10,000 additional units of product would require materials and labor at $3.50 and $2.20 per unit just as with normal production. (2) However, the 10,000 units could be manufactured with overhead costs in addition to those already incurred of only $5,000 for power, packing, and handling labor. (3) Commissions and other selling expenses resulting from the sale would amount to $2,000 in addition to the selling expenses already incurred. And (4) $1,000 additional administrative expenses in the form of clerical work would be required if the order were accepted. Based on this added information, the statement of Illustration 25–5 showing the

	Present Business	Additional Business	Present Plus the Additional Business
Sales	$1,000,000	$85,000	$1,085,000
Materials	$350,000	$35,000	$385,000
Labor	220,000	22,000	242,000
Overhead	110,000	5,000	115,000
Selling expenses	140,000	2,000	142,000
Administrative expense	80,000	1,000	81,000
Total	900,000	65,000	965,000
Operating Income	$ 100,000	$20,000	$ 120,000

Illustration
25–5

effect of the additional business on the company's normal business was prepared.

It is obvious from Illustration 25–5 that when present business is charged with all present costs and the additional business is charged only with its incremental or differential costs, accepting the additional business at $8.50 per unit will apparently result in $20,000 additional profit.

Incremental or differential costs always apply to a particular situation at a particular time. For example, adding units to a given production volume might or might not increase depreciation expense. If the additional units require the purchase of more machines, depreciation expense is increased. Likewise, if present machines are used but the additional units shorten their life, more depreciation expense results. However, if present machines are used and their depreciation depends more on the passage of time or obsolescence rather than on use, additional depreciation expense might not result from the added units of product.

Buy or make ■ Incremental or differential costs are often a factor in a decision as to whether a given part or product should be bought or made. For example, a manufacturer has idle machines upon which he can make Part 417 of his product. This part is presently purchased at a $1.20 delivered cost per unit. The manufacturer estimates that to make Part 417 would cost $0.45 for materials, $0.50 for labor, and an amount of overhead. At this point a question arises as to how much overhead should be charged. If the normal overhead rate of the department in which the part would be manufactured is 100% of direct labor cost, and this amount is charged against Part 417, then the unit costs of making Part 417 would be $0.45 for materials, $0.50 for labor, and $0.50 for overhead, a total of $1.45. At this cost, the manufacturer would be better off to buy the part at $1.20 each.

However, on a short-run basis the manufacturer might be justified in ignoring the normal overhead rate and in charging Part 417 for only the added overhead costs resulting from its manufacture. Among these added overhead costs might be, for example, power to operate the machines that would otherwise be idle, depreciation on the machines if the part's manufacture resulted in additional depreciation, and any other overhead that would be added to that already incurred. Furthermore, if these added overhead items total less than $0.25 per unit, the manufacturer might be justified on a short-run basis in manufacturing the part. However, on a long-term basis, Part 417 should be charged a full share of all overhead.

Any amount of overhead less than $0.25 per unit results in a total cost for Part 417 that is less than the $1.20 per unit purchase price. Nevertheless, in making a final decision as to whether the part should be bought or made, the manufacturer should consider in addition to costs such things as quality, the reactions of customers and suppliers, and other intangible factors. When these additional factors are considered, small cost differences may become a minor factor.

Other costs ■ *Sunk costs, out-of-pocket costs,* and *opportunity costs* are additional costs encountered in managerial decisions.

A sunk cost is a cost resulting from a past irrevocable decision, and is sunk in the sense that it cannot be avoided. As a result, sunk costs are irrelevant in decisions affecting the future.

An out-of-pocket cost is a cost requiring a current outlay of funds. Material costs, wages, supplies, heat, and power are examples. Generally, out-of-pocket costs can be avoided; consequently, they are relevant in decisions affecting the future.

Costs as discussed thus far have been outlays or expenditures made to obtain some benefit, usually goods or services. However, the concept of costs can be expanded to include *sacrifices made to gain some benefit*. For example, if a job that will pay $1,200 for working during the summer must be rejected in order to attend summer school, the $1,200 is an opportunity cost of attending summer school.

Obviously, opportunity costs are not costs in the accounting sense of the term and they are not entered in the accounting records; but they may be relevant in a decision involving rejected opportunities, such as in a decision to scrap or rebuild defective units of product, where both sunk and opportunity costs are commonly encountered.

Scrap or rebuild defective units ■ Any costs incurred in manufacturing units of product that do not pass inspection are sunk costs and as such should not enter into a decision as to whether the units should be sold for scrap or be rebuilt to pass inspection. For example, a concern has 10,000 defective units of product that cost $1 per unit to manufacture. The units can be sold as they are for $0.40 each, or they can be rebuilt for $0.80 per unit, after which they can be sold for their full price of $1.50 per unit. Should the company rebuild the units or should it sell them as they are? Obviously, the original manufacturing costs of $1 per unit are sunk costs and are irrelevant in the decision; so based on the information given, the comparative returns from scrapping or rebuilding are:

	As Scrap	Rebuilt
Sale of defective units	$4,000	$15,000
Less cost to rebuild		(8,000)
Net Return	$4,000	$ 7,000

From the information given, it appears that rebuilding is the better decision, and this is true if the rebuilding does not interfere with normal operations. However, suppose that to rebuild the defective units the company must forgo manufacturing 10,000 new units that will cost $1 per unit to manufacture and can be sold for $1.50 per unit. In this situation the comparative returns may be analyzed as follows:

	As Scrap	Rebuilt
Sale of defective units	$ 4,000	$15,000
Less cost to rebuild		(8,000)
Sale of new units	15,000	
Less cost to manufacture new units	(10,000)	
Net Return	$ 9,000	$ 7,000

If the defective units are sold without rebuilding, then the new units can also be manufactured and sold, with a $9,000 return from the sale of both the new and old units, as shown in the first column of the analysis. Obviously this is better than forgoing the manufacture of the new units and rebuilding the defective units for a $7,000 net return.

The foregoing situation may be analyzed also on an opportunity cost basis as follows: If to rebuild the defective units the company must forgo manufacturing the new units, then the return on the sale of the new units is an opportunity cost of rebuilding the defective units. This opportunity cost is measured at $5,000 (revenue from sale of new units, $15,000, less their manufacturing costs, $10,000, equals the $5,000 benefit that will be sacrificed if the old units are rebuilt); and an opportunity cost analysis of the situation is as follows:

	As Scrap	Rebuilt
Sale of defective units	$4,000	$15,000
Less cost to rebuild		(8,000)
Less opportunity cost (return sacrificed by not manufacturing the new units)		(5,000)
Net Return	$4,000	$ 2,000

Observe that it does not matter whether this or the previous analysis is made, since either way there is a $2,000 difference in favor of scrapping the defective units.

Product pricing ■ Many companies have control over the price at which they sell a product. Such companies in pricing a product can and do add a fair profit to the cost of the product's materials, labor, and overhead, and then, because of a monopoly or through aggressive advertising and selling, they can get the price asked.

In setting a product's price, numerous factors are often involved. Two common factors are (1) if demand for a product is elastic, the number of units sold will vary with the price; and (2) when production volume varies, some costs vary with volume and some remain fixed.

The first of the above factors can be stated in another way: When demand for a product is elastic and its price is lowered, at each successive lower price more units will be sold; and if the price is increased, at each successive higher price fewer units will be sold.

The second factor was encountered in the previous chapter; but for a better understanding, consider the following expenses incurred in driving an automobile 8,000 miles per year:

Expenses That Vary with Mileage		Annual Fixed Expenses	
Gasoline and oil	$210	Depreciation	$400
Tires	28	Insurance	72
Lubrication	16	License fee	10
Repairs	20		$482
	$274		

The lists show the expenses incurred in driving a car 8,000 miles per year. If the car were driven 12,000 miles in a year rather than 8,000, the expenses incurred for gasoline, oil, tires, lubrication, and repairs would increase in proportion to the increase in mileage. However, the annual fixed expenses would remain more or less fixed and unchanged.

Just as there are expenses that remain fixed and expenses that vary with the miles a car is driven, there are also costs and expenses that remain fixed and costs and expenses that vary with the number of units of product manufactured in a factory. And as will be shown, these fixed and variable costs and expenses are often a factor in setting product prices.

In setting a product's price, management normally tries to set the price at an amount that will result in the greatest reasonable profit. The profit must be within reason or new competition, and sometimes government intervention, is invited. Normally, the greatest profit results from the price that produces the greatest *contribution margin*. Contribution margin may be defined as revenue from sales less variable costs or costs that vary with sales. For example, in setting the price for a new product on which the variable costs are $10 per unit, management of Electronics, Inc., prepared the estimates of Illustration 25–6.

Obviously, from Illustration 25–6, the price that will produce the greatest contribution margin is $17.50. At this price 30,000 units can be sold and $225,000 in contribution margin earned. The $17.50 price pays all variable costs of its volume and leaves $225,000 in contribution margin to cover the fixed costs and provide a profit.

Suggested Sales Price per Set	Units That Can Be Sold	Sales Revenue	Variable Costs	Contribution Margin
$20.00	10,000	$200,000	$100,000	$100,000
17.50	30,000	525,000	300,000	225,000
15.00	36,000	540,000	360,000	180,000
12.00	48,000	576,000	480,000	96,000
11.00	60,000	660,000	600,000	60,000

Illustration
25–6

If a company manufactures more than one product, its pricing problems become more complicated and are often affected by capacity to produce. For example, Taplett Company manufactures two products,

Product M having variable costs of $12 per unit and Product S having variable costs of $16 per unit. The products are similar but noncompetitive; and although the materials from which they are manufactured differ, the machines and methods used in their manufacture are almost identical. Taplett Company has the capacity to produce either 10,000 Product M units, or 10,000 Product S units, or a number of Product M units plus a number of Product S units, the sum of which is 10,000. In setting prices, Taplett Company prepared the Illustration 25–7 estimates.

An examination of Illustration 25–7 shows that Taplett Company can gain the greatest contribution margin from each product at prices of $20 for Product M and $23 for Product S. However, these prices require production of 5,000 Product M units and 7,000 Product S units, a total of 12,000 units. Since Taplett Company can produce only 10,000 units, the greatest contribution margin within its capacity to produce will be gained at prices of $25 for Product M and $23 for Product S.

Suggested Sales Price per Unit	Units That Can Be Sold	Sales Revenue	Variable Costs	Contribution Margin
Product M				
$25.00	3,000	$ 75,000	$ 36,000	$39,000
20.00	5,000	100,000	60,000	40,000
18.00	6,000	108,000	72,000	36,000
16.00	8,000	128,000	96,000	32,000
15.00	10,000	150,000	120,000	30,000
Product S				
$30.00	2,000	$ 60,000	$ 32,000	$28,000
25.00	5,000	125,000	80,000	45,000
23.00	7,000	161,000	112,000	49,000
22.00	8,000	176,000	128,000	48,000
21.00	9,500	199,500	152,000	47,500

Illustration 25–7

Obviously pricing problems are usually more complicated than the ones in the foregoing simplified situations. For example, in the foregoing situations the fact that some costs are neither fixed nor variable is ignored. Nevertheless, and regardless, factors of demand and fixed and variable costs are present in almost all manufacturing and marketing situations; and if management is to maximize profits, it must know as much as possible about the fixed, the semifixed, and the variable costs of manufacturing and marketing each of its products.

Volume-profit analysis ■ An analysis of the effects of changes in sales volume on profits can be useful in decisions involving the introduction of a new product, an increase or decrease in production level, and so on. Such an analysis is often called a *break-even analysis,* since the determination of the *break-even point* or the point of zero profit is often involved. However, management is normally interested in more than breaking even; therefore, the analysis usually involves probable profits at various levels of activity.

Break-even point

A company sells for $100 per unit a single product having $70 of variable costs per unit sold. If the fixed costs involved in selling the product are $24,000, the company breaks even on the product as soon as it sells 800 units or as soon as its sales volume reaches $80,000. This break-even point may be determined as follows:

1. Each unit sold at $100 pays its $70 variable costs and contributes $30 toward the fixed costs.
2. The fixed costs are $24,000; consequently, 800 units ($24,000 ÷ $30 = 800) must be sold to pay the fixed costs.
3. And 800 units at $100 each produce an $80,000 sales volume.

The $30 amount that the sales price of this product exceeds variable costs per unit is its *contribution margin per unit.* In other words, the contribution margin per unit is the amount that the sale of one unit contributes toward payment of the fixed costs and a profit.

Also, the contribution margin of a product expressed as a percentage of its sales price is its *contribution rate.* For instance, the contribution rate of the $100 product of this illustration is 30% ($30 ÷ $100 = 30%).

And with contribution margin and contribution rate defined, it is possible to set up the following formulas for calculating a break-even point in units and in dollars:

$$\text{Break-Even Point in Units} = \frac{\text{Fixed Costs}}{\text{Contribution Margin}}$$

$$\text{Break-Even Point in Dollars} = \frac{\text{Fixed Costs}}{\text{Contribution Rate}}$$

Application of the second formula to figures for the product of this illustration gives this result:

$$\text{Break-Even Point in Dollars} = \frac{\$24,000}{30\%} = \frac{\$24,000}{0.30} = \$80,000$$

Break-even chart

A break-even point may be charted as in Illustration 25–8. Such a chart makes it easier to visualize the relation of sales, fixed and variable costs, and the break-even point. Note in Illustration 25–8 how the line representing sales begins at zero and moves upward. Note also how the line representing fixed and variable costs begins at the $24,000 fixed cost level and intersects the sales line at $80,000. This intersection point is the break-even point. When sales go above $80,000, increasing profits

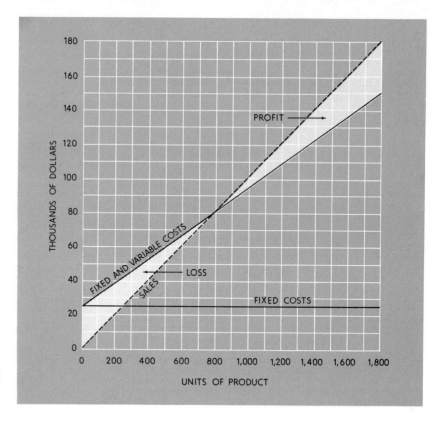

Illustration 25-8

Graph axes: THOUSANDS OF DOLLARS (vertical, 0 to 180) vs UNITS OF PRODUCT (horizontal, 0 to 1,800). Labels: PROFIT, FIXED AND VARIABLE COSTS, SALES, LOSS, FIXED COSTS.

are earned as is shown by the increasing spread between the lines; and when sales fall below this point, a loss in incurred.

In preparing a break-even chart like Illustration 25-8, it is desirable to have the break-even point fall near the center of the graph. To achieve this the break-even point is calculated first and then a total sales volume of approximately twice this amount is used in preparing the graph. In Illustration 25-8 the 800-unit break-even point is a little less than half the 1,800-unit total sales volume, but close enough.

Sales required for a desired net income

A slight extension of the concept behind the break-even calculation will produce a formula that may be used in determining the sales level necessary to produce a desired net income. The formula is:

$$\text{Sales at Desired Income Level} = \frac{\substack{\text{Fixed} \\ \text{Costs}} + \substack{\text{Net} \\ \text{Income}} + \substack{\text{Income} \\ \text{Taxes}}}{\text{Contribution Rate}}$$

To illustrate the formula's use, assume the company of the previous section, the company having $24,000 of fixed costs and a 30% contribution rate has set a $20,000 after-tax income goal for itself. Assume further that in order to have a $20,000 net income, the company must earn $28,500 and pay $8,500 in taxes. Under these assumptions, $175,000 of sales are necessary to produce a $20,000 net income. This is calculated as follows:

$$\text{Sales at Desired Income Level} = \frac{\text{Fixed Costs} + \text{Net Income} + \text{Income Taxes}}{\text{Contribution Rate}}$$

$$\text{Sales at Desired Income Level} = \frac{\$24,000 + \$20,000 + \$8,500}{30\%}$$

$$\text{Sales at Desired Income Level} = \frac{\$52,500}{30\%} = \$175,000$$

Margin of safety

The difference between a company's current sales and sales at its break-even point is known as its margin of safety. The margin of safety is the amount sales may decrease before a loss is incurred. It may be expressed in units of product, dollars, or as a percentage of sales. For example, if current sales are $100,000 and the break-even point is $85,000, the margin of safety is $15,000 or 15% of sales, calculated as follows:

$$\frac{\text{Sales} - \text{Break-Even Sales}}{\text{Sales}} = \text{Margin of Safety}$$

or

$$\frac{\$100,000 - \$85,000}{\$100,000} = 15\% \text{ Margin of Safety}$$

The volume-profit situations just described represent an oversimplification of the normal. The company of the break-even illustration was assumed to have only one product, while most companies have many products, the sales of which result in different amounts of fixed and variable costs. Also in the illustrated situations it is assumed that costs are either fixed or variable. Some costs are fixed, some vary directly with sales, and some vary with sales but not in the same proportion as sales. Nevertheless, the illustrated situations serve to introduce volume-profit analysis and complicated situations may be left to an advanced course.

Questions for class discussion

1. What is capital budgeting? Why are capital budgeting decisions crucial to the business concern making the decisions?
2. If depreciation is an expense, explain why, when a machine's product is sold at a profit, the portion of the machine's cost recovered each year through the sale of the product includes both the profit from the product's sale and the year's depreciation charge.
3. What is the average amount invested in a machine during its life if the machine cost $28,000, has an estimated five-year life, and an estimated $3,000 salvage value?

4. Why is the present value, today's value, of the expectation of receiving $100 a year hence less than $100? What is the present value of the expectation of receiving $100 one year hence, discounted at 8%?

5. What is indicated when the present value of the net cash flows from an investment in a machine, discounted at 12%, exceeds the amount of the investment? What is indicated when the present value of the net cash flows, discounted at 12%, is less than the amount of the investment?

6. A company manufactures and sells 250,000 units of product in this country at $5 per unit. The product costs $3 per unit to manufacture. Can you describe a situation under which the company may be willing to sell an additional 25,000 units abroad at $2.75 per unit?

7. What is a sunk cost? An out-of-pocket cost? An opportunity cost? Is an opportunity cost a cost in the accounting sense of the term?

8. What is a fixed cost? A semifixed cost? A variable cost?

9. When there are fixed costs in the production of a product and the number of units manufactured is increased, do the fixed costs per unit increase or decrease? Why?

10. What is the break-even point in the production and sale of a product?

11. A company sells a product for $80 per unit. The variable costs of producing and selling the product are $56 per unit. What is the product's contribution margin per unit? What is its contribution rate?

Class exercises

Exercise 25–1

Machine A cost $8,000 and has an estimated four-year life and no salvage value. Machine B cost $12,000 and has an estimated five-year life and a $2,000 salvage value. Under the assumption that the average investment in each machine is the average of its yearly book values, calculate the average investment in each machine.

Exercise 25–2

A company is planning to purchase a machine and add a new product to its line. The machine will cost $20,000, have a four-year life, no salvage value, and will be depreciated on a straight-line basis. The company expects to sell 10,000 units of the machine's product each year with these results:

Sales		$50,000
Costs:		
Materials, labor, and overhead excluding depreciation on the new machine	$26,000	
Depreciation on new machine	5,000	
Selling and administrative expenses	15,000	46,000
Operating income		$ 4,000
Income taxes		2,000
Net Income		$ 2,000

Required:
Calculate (1) the payback period and (2) the return on the average investment in this machine.

Exercise 25–3

Under the assumption the company of Exercise 25–2 demands a 12% compound return from capital investments, determine the total present value and net present value of the net cash flows from the machine it is planning to buy. Use the table of Illustration 25–2.

Exercise 25–4

A company manufactures a number of products, one of which sells for $80 per unit. The fixed costs of manufacturing this product are $25,000, and the variable costs are $60 per unit.

Required:
1. Determine the product's break-even point in units.
2. Determine the product's break-even point in dollars.
3. Determine the sales volume in dollars that the company must achieve if it is to earn a $10,000 after-tax (50% rate) profit from the sale of the product.

Exercise 25–5

Product Z is sold for $25 per unit. The fixed costs of selling the product are $60,000, and the variable costs are $15 per unit. Calculate the break-even point for the product and prepare an income statement showing sales, fixed costs, and variable costs at the break-even point.

Problems   **Problem 25–1**

A company is planning to add a new product to its line, the production of which will require new machinery costing $45,000 and having a five-year life and no salvage value. This additional information is available:

Estimated annual sales of new product............................ $150,000	
Estimated costs:	
Materials	30,000
Labor..	40,000
Overhead excluding depreciation on new machinery......	38,000
Selling and administrative expenses............................	25,000
State and federal income taxes	50%

Required:
Using straight-line depreciation, calculate (1) the payback period on the investment in new machinery, (2) the rate of return on the average investment, and (3) the net present value of the net cash flows discounted at 12%.

Problem 25–2

A company has an opportunity to invest in either of two projects. Project A requires an investment of $40,000 for new machinery having a five-year life and no salvage value. Project B requires an investment of $35,000 for new machinery having a seven-year life and no salvage value. The products of the projects differ; however, each will produce an estimated $3,000 after-tax profit for the life of the project.

Required:

Calculate the payback period, the return on average investment, and the net present value of the net cash flows from each project discounted at 10%. Use the table of Illustration 25–2. State which project you think is the better investment and why.

Problem 25–3

Handy Tool Company manufactures a small tool that it sells to wholesalers at $3 each. The company manufactures and sells approximately 100,000 of the tools each year, and a normal year's costs for the production and sale of this number of tools are as follows:

Materials	$ 60,000
Direct labor	50,000
Manufacturing overhead	75,000
Selling expenses	30,000
Administrative expenses	25,000
	$240,000

A mail-order concern has offered to buy 10,000 of the tools at $2.25 each to be marketed under the mail-order concern's trade name. If accepted, the order is not expected to affect sales through present channels.

A study of normal costs and their relation to the new business reveals the following: (*a*) Material costs are 100% variable. (*b*) The per unit direct labor costs for the additional units will be 50% greater than normal since their production will require overtime at time and one half. (*c*) Of a normal year's manufacturing overhead costs, two thirds will remain fixed at any production level from zero to 150,000 units and one third will vary with volume. (*d*) There will be no additional selling costs if the new business is accepted. (*e*) Acceptance of the new business will increase administrative costs $1,500.

Required:

Prepare a comparative income statement that shows (1) in one set of columns the operating results and operating income of a normal year, (2) in the second set of columns the operating results and income that may be expected from the new business, and (3) in the third set of columns the combined results from normal and the expected new business.

Problem 25–4

Zeppo Company lost $1,000 last year in selling 2,000 units of its Product X, as the following income statement shows:

ZEPPO COMPANY
Last Year's Sales of Product X

Sales		$100,000
Costs:		
Fixed	$26,000	
Variable	75,000	101,000
Net Loss from Sales of Product X		$ (1,000)

The company has discovered that if it will install a new machine, it can save enough piece-rate labor and spoiled materials to reduce the variable costs of manufacturing Product X by 20%. However, the new machine will increase fixed costs $2,400 annually.

Required:
1. Calculate last year's dollar break-even point for Product X.
2. Calculate the dollar break-even point under the assumption the new machine is installed.
3. Prepare a break-even chart under the assumption the new machine is installed. Use 3,000 as the maximum number of units on your chart.
4. Prepare an income statement showing expected annual results with the new machine installed, no change in Product X's price, and sales at last year's level. Assume a 50% income tax rate.
5. Calculate the sales level required to earn a $10,000 per year after-tax income with the new machine installed and no change in the selling price of Product X. Prepare an income statement showing the results at this sales level.

Problem 25–5

Last year Sandhill Company sold 20,000 units of its product at $20 per unit. To manufacture and sell the product required $100,000 of fixed manufacturing costs and $20,000 of fixed selling and administrative expenses. Last year's variable costs and expenses per unit were:

Material	$8.00
Direct labor (paid on a piece-rate basis)	3.00
Variable manufacturing overhead costs	.60
Variable selling and administrative expenses	.40

A new material has just come on the market that will cut the material cost of producing the product in half if substituted for the material presently being used. The substitution will have no effect on the product's quality; but it will give the company a choice in pricing the product. (1) The company can maintain the present per unit price, sell the same number of units, and make an extra $4 per unit profit as a result of the substitution. Or (2) it can reduce the product's price $4 per unit to an amount equal to the material savings, and because of the reduction, increase the number of units sold by 60%. If the latter choice is made, the fixed manufacturing overhead and fixed selling and administrative expenses will not change and the remaining variable costs and expenses will vary with volume.

Required:
1. Calculate the break-even point in dollars for each alternative.
2. Prepare a break-even chart for each. The company's capacity is 40,000 units, and this should be used as the upper limit of your charts.
3. Prepare a comparative income statement showing sales, total fixed costs, and total variable costs and expenses, operating income, income taxes (50% rate), and net income for each alternative.

Problem 25–1A

A company is considering adding a new product to its line, of which it estimates it can sell 20,000 units annually at $10 per unit. To manufacture the product will require new machinery having an estimated five-year life, no salvage value, and costing $60,000. The new product will have a $4 per unit direct material cost and a $2 per unit direct labor cost. Manufacturing overhead chargeable to the new product, other than for depreciation on the new machinery, will be $33,000 annually. Also, $25,000 of additional selling and administrative expenses will be incurred annually in producing and selling the product, and state and federal income taxes will take 50% of the before-taxes profit.

Required:
Using straight-line depreciation, calculate (1) the payback period on the investment in new machinery, (2) the rate of return on the average investment, and (3) the net present value of the net cash flows discounted at 12%.

Problem 25–2A

A company has the opportunity to invest in either of two projects. Project X requires an investment of $56,000 for new machinery having a seven-year life and no salvage value. Project Y requires an investment of $60,000 for new machinery having a five-year life and no salvage value. Sales of the two projects will produce the following estimated annual results:

		Project X		*Project Y*
Sales...		$130,000		$150,000
Costs:				
Materials	$30,000		$36,000	
Labor.....................................	27,000		35,000	
Manufacturing overhead including depreciation on new machinery	38,000		44,000	
Selling and administrative expenses.............................	25,000	120,000	25,000	140,000
Operating income		$ 10,000		$ 10,000
State and federal income taxes........		5,000		5,000
Net Income..............................		$ 5,000		$ 5,000

Required:
Calculate the payback period, the return on average investment, and the net present value of the net cash flows from each project discounted at 12%. State which project you think the better investment and why.

Problem 25–3A

Roxbury Company annually sells at $10 per unit 100,000 units of its product. At the 100,000-unit production level the product costs $9 a unit to manufacture and sell, and at this level the company has the following costs and expenses:

Fixed manufacturing overhead costs	$100,000	
Fixed selling expenses......................................	50,000	
Fixed administrative expenses	60,000	
Variable costs and expenses:		
Materials ($2 per unit)....................................	200,000	
Labor ($2.50 per unit)	250,000	
Manufacturing overhead ($1.50 per unit)	150,000	
Selling expenses ($0.50 per unit)	50,000	
Administrative expenses ($0.40 per unit)	40,000	

All the units the company presently sells are sold in this country. However, recently an exporter has offered to buy 10,000 units of the product for sale abroad; but he will pay only $8.90 per unit, which is below the company's present $9 per unit manufacturing and selling costs.

Required:
Prepare an income statement that shows (1) in one set of columns the revenue, costs, expenses, and income from selling 100,000 units of the product in this country; (2) in a second set of columns the additional revenue, costs, expenses, and income from selling 10,000 units to the exporter; and (3) in a third set of columns the combined results from both sources. (Assume that acceptance of the new business will not increase any of the company's fixed costs and expenses nor change any of the variable per unit costs and expenses.)

Problem 25–4A

Surfside Company incurred a $4,000 loss last year in selling 4,000 units of its Product A, as the following income statement shows:

SURFSIDE COMPANY
Last Year's Income Statement for Product A

Sales		$100,000
Costs:		
Fixed..	$24,000	
Variable..	80,000	104,000
Net Loss from Sale of Product A.......................		$ (4,000)

The production manager has pointed out that the variable costs of Product A can be reduced 25% by installing a machine to do a labor operation presently done by hand. However, the new machine will increase fixed costs by $6,400 annually.

Required:
1. Calculate last year's dollar break-even point for Product A.
2. Calculate the dollar break-even point for Product A under the assumption the new machine is installed.
3. Prepare a break-even chart under the assumption the new machine is installed. Use 6,000 as the maximum number of units on your chart.
4. Prepare an income statement showing expected annual results with the new machine installed, no change in the selling price of Product A, and no change in the number of units sold. Assume a 50% income tax rate.
5. Calculate the sales level required to earn a $12,000 per year after-tax in-

come with the new machine installed and no change in the selling price of Product A. Prepare an income statement showing the results at this sales level.

Problem 25–5A

Last year Drift Company earned an unsatisfactory 2.5% after-tax return from the sale of 50,000 packages of its Product M at $1 each. The company buys Product M in bulk and packages it for resale. Following are last year's costs for the product:

Costs of bulk Product M (sufficient for 50,000 packages)...... $25,000
Packaging materials and other variable packaging costs........ 5,000
Fixed costs............. 17,500
Income tax rate 50%

It has been suggested that if the selling price of the product is reduced 10% and a slight change made in its packaging, the number of units sold can be doubled. The packaging change will increase packaging costs 10% per unit, but doubling the sales volume will gain a 5% reduction in the product's bulk purchase price. The packaging and volume changes will not affect fixed costs.

Required:
1. Calculate the dollar break-even points for Product M at the $1 per unit sales price and at $0.90 per unit.
2. Prepare a break-even chart for the sale of the product at each price. Use 100,000 units as the upper limit of your charts.
3. Prepare a condensed comparative income statement showing the results of selling the product at $1 per unit and the estimated results of selling it at $0.90 per unit.

Decision problem 25–1, Aluminum Company

Aluminum Company operates 10 aluminum plants, one of which is located at Reedsport. The Reedsport plant no longer produces a satisfactory profit due to its distance from raw material sources, relatively high electric power costs, and lack of modern machinery. Consequently, construction of a new plant to replace the Reedsport plant is under consideration.

The new plant would be located close to a raw material source and near low-cost hydroelectric power; but its construction would necessitate abandonment of the Reedsport plant. The company president favors the move; but several members of the board are not convinced the Reedsport plant should be abandoned in view of the great loss that would result.

You have been asked to make recommendations concerning the proposed abandonment and construction of the new plant. Data developed during the course of your analysis include the following:

LOSS FROM ABANDONING THE REEDSPORT PLANT. The land, buildings, and machinery of the Reedsport plant have a $3,800,000 book value. Very little of the machinery can be moved to the new plant. Most will have to be scrapped. Therefore, if the plant is abandoned, it is estimated that only $800,000 of the remaining investment in the plant can be recovered through the sale of its land

and buildings, the sale of scrap, and by moving some of its machinery to the new plant. The remaining $3,000,000 will be lost.

INVESTMENT IN THE NEW PLANT. The new plant will cost $12,000,000, including the book value of any machinery moved from Reedsport, and will have a 20-year life. It will also have double the 25,000-ton capacity of the Reedsport plant, and it is estimated the 50,000 tons of aluminum produced annually can be sold without a price reduction.

COMPARATIVE PRODUCTION COSTS. A comparison of the production costs per ton at the old plant with the estimated costs at the new plant shows the following:

	Old Plant	New Plant
Raw material, labor, and plant costs (other than depreciation)	$325	$275
Depreciation	18	12
Total costs per ton	$343	$287

The higher per ton depreciation charge of the old plant results primarily from depreciation being allocated to fewer units of product.

Prepare a report analyzing the advantages and disadvantages of the move, including your recommendation. You may assume that the Reedsport plant can continue to operate long enough to recover the remaining investment in the plant; however, due to the plant's high costs, operation will be at the break-even point. Present any pertinent analyses based on the data given.

Decision problem 25–2, Bay City Chemical Company

Bay City Chemical Company produces a high-protein content cattle feed additive at its Waldport plant. The plant produced at near capacity last year with the results shown in the following condensed income statement:

Sales (300,000 lbs.)	$600,000
Cost of goods manufactured and sold (fixed, $100,000; variable, $240,000)	340,000
Gross margin	$260,000
Selling and administrative expenses (fixed, $80,000; variable, $60,000)	140,000
Income before Taxes	$120,000

Export Company has offered a five-year contract to buy 200,000 pounds of the additive annually at $1.60 per pound for export sales. Delivery on the contract would require a plant addition that would double fixed manufacturing costs. The contract would not affect present fixed and variable selling and administrative expenses. Variable manufacturing costs would vary with volume.

Management is not certain it should enter into the contract, and it has asked for your opinion, including the following:

1. An estimated income statement for the first year following the plant addition, assuming no change in domestic sales.

2. A comparison of break-even sales levels before the plant addition and after the contract expiration. Assume after-contract sales and expense levels, other than fixed manufacturing costs, will be at the same levels as last year.
3. A statement showing net income after the contract expiration but at sales and expense levels of last year, other than fixed manufacturing costs.

Chapter 26

Analyzing
and
interpreting
financial statements

■ According to the dictionary, to analyze is to separate the parts of a whole so as to see their relation to the whole and to each other. Also, according to the dictionary, to interpret something is to explain it or to tell its meaning. Consequently, to analyze and interpret financial statements is to separate the statements into parts so as to see the relation of the parts to the whole and to each other, and to tell the meaning of what is seen.

Why financial statements are analyzed ■ Management, owners, investors, creditors, and others analyze the statements of a business to determine its overall position and also to find out about certain aspects of that position in which they are particularly interested. For example, owners and prospective investors are always concerned with the overall position of a business in which they own stock or in which they are about to invest; but they are also especially interested in its earnings and its earnings prospects, because both dividends and an increase in the market value of the company's shares are closely related to earnings and the likelihood of their increasing. Likewise, creditors are interested in the total picture, although they are primarily interested in debt-paying ability. However, debt-paying ability cannot be separated from the total picture, nor can it be separated from earnings, since the payment of a debt, particularly a long-term debt, often depends on earnings.

**Compara-
tive
statements**

■ Numerous books have been written on the analysis and interpretation of financial statements. Obviously, we can examine only some of the more fundamental techniques; and a good place to begin is with comparative statements.

A commonly used analyzing and interpreting technique is the preparation of comparative statements. To see the value of a comparative statement, recognize that a single balance sheet, for example, shows assets, liabilities, and owner equity as of a specific date; but a company's comparative balance sheet shows these items for two or more dates and, consequently, shows changes that have taken place. The changes probably resulted from past operating policies, and their interpretation offers a guide to the future.

In its most simple form a comparative balance sheet consists of the item amounts from two of a company's successive balance sheets arranged side by side in a single statement, so that changes in item amounts may be seen. However, in examining such a statement the average person has difficulty grasping significant changes. Consequently, a comparative balance sheet showing only dollar amounts may be improved by also showing in both dollar amounts and in percentages the changes that have occurred. To accomplish this, two additional columns are added to a simple comparative balance sheet. In the first is shown in dollars the increase or decrease for each item, and in the second is shown the percentage increase or decrease. (See Illustration 26–1.)

When changes in items are shown in both dollars and percentages, items showing either a large dollar change or a large percentage change stand out and are readily seen by the person examining the statement. For example, in the comparative balance sheet of Illustration 26–1, the item "Cash" shows a large dollar change and the item "Notes receivable" shows a large percentage change. The large dollar change in "Cash" stands out in the column showing increases and decreases in dollar amounts. Likewise, although the dollar amount is small, the large percentage change in "Notes receivable" stands out in the column showing percentage changes.

A comparative income statement is prepared in the same manner as a comparative balance sheet. Normally, a company's income statement amounts for two or more successive periods are placed side by side, with dollar and percentage changes in additional columns. Such a statement is shown in Illustration 26–2.

Analyzing and interpreting comparative statements

In analyzing and interpreting comparative data, it is necessary for the analyst to select for study any items showing significant dollar or percentage changes. The analyst normally considers the changes individually

Anchor Supply Company
Comparative Balance Sheet
December 31, 1972, and December 31, 1973

	Years Ended December 31		Amount of Increase or Decrease* during 1973	Percentage of Increase or Decrease* during 1973
	1973	1972		
ASSETS				
Current Assets:				
Cash.........	$ 14,000	$ 89,000	$ 75,000*	84.3*
Notes receivable	4,000	1,500	2,500	166.7
Accounts receivable, net.........	68,000	64,000	4,000	6.3
Merchandise inventory	190,000	184,000	6,000	3.3
Prepaid expenses	5,800	6,000	200*	3.3*
Total Current Assets.........	$281,800	$344,500	$ 62,700*	18.2*
Investments:				
Real estate.........	-0-	$ 30,000	$ 30,000*	100.0*
Apex Company 6% bonds.........	-0-	50,000	50,000*	100.0*
Total Investments.........	-0-	$ 80,000	$ 80,000*	100.0*
Plant Assets:				
Office equipment	$ 5,000	$ 5,000		
Less accumulated depreciation	1,500	1,200		
	$ 3,500	$ 3,800	$ 300*	7.9*
Store equipment.........	$ 24,000	$ 11,000		
Less accumulated depreciation.........	6,200	4,300		
	$ 17,800	$ 6,700	11,100	165.7
Buildings.........	$210,000	$ 60,000		
Less accumulated depreciation.........	33,200	32,000		
	$176,800	$ 28,000	148,800	531.4
Land.........	$ 50,000	$ 20,000	30,000	150.0
Total Plant Assets.........	$248,100	$ 58,500	$189,600	324.1
Total Assets	$529,900	$483,000	$ 46,900	9.7
LIABILITIES				
Current Liabilities:				
Notes payable.........	-0-	$ 10,000	$ 10,000*	100.0*
Accounts payable	$ 53,400	60,000	6,600*	11.0*
Wages payable	800	1,200	400*	33.3*
Total Current Liabilities.........	$ 54,200	$ 71,200	$ 17,000*	23.9*
Long-Term Liabilities:				
Mortgage payable.........	$ 60,000	$ 10,000	$ 50,000	500.0
Total Liabilities.........	$114,200	$ 81,200	$ 33,000	40.6
CAPITAL				
Common stock, $10 par value.........	$250,000	$250,000		
Retained earnings.........	165,700	151,800	$ 13,900	9.2
Total Capital.........	$415,700	$401,800	$ 13,900	3.5
Total Liabilities and Capital.........	$529,900	$483,000	$ 46,900	9.7

Illustration
26–1

	Years Ended December 31		Amount of Increase or Decrease* during 1973	Percentage of Increase or Decrease* during 1973
	1973	1972		
Gross sales	$973,500	$853,000	$120,500	14.1
Sales returns	13,500	10,200	3,300	32.4
Net sales	$960,000	$842,800	$117,200	13.9
Cost of goods sold	715,000	622,500	92,500	14.9
Gross profit from sales	$245,000	$220,300	$ 24,700	11.2
Operating expenses:				
Selling expenses:				
Advertising	$ 10,000	$ 5,000	$ 5,000	100.0
Sales salaries	113,500	98,000	15,500	15.8
Store supplies used	3,200	2,800	400	14.3
Depreciation of store equipment	1,900	1,700	200	11.8
Delivery expense	12,800	14,000	1,200*	8.6*
Total selling expenses	$141,400	$121,500	$ 19,900	16.4
General and administrative expenses:				
Office salaries	$ 32,500	$ 31,000	$ 1,500	4.8
Officers' salaries	24,000	24,000		
Office supplies used	1,300	1,250	50	4.0
Expired insurance	1,600	1,200	400	33.3
Depreciation of office equipment	300	300		
Depreciation of buildings	1,200	950	250	26.3
Bad debts	2,400	2,200	200	9.1
Total general and admin. expenses	$ 63,300	$ 60,900	$ 2,400	3.9
Total operating expenses	$204,700	$182,400	$ 22,300	12.2
Operating income	$ 40,300	$ 37,900	$ 2,400	6.3
Financial revenue and expense:				
Interest earned	1,300	2,050	750*	36.6*
	$ 41,600	$ 39,950		
Interest expense	2,300	1,100	$ 1,200	109.1
Income before taxes	$ 39,300	$ 38,850	$ 450	1.2
Income taxes	12,300	12,150	150	1.2
Net Income	$ 27,000	$ 26,700	$ 300	1.1

Illustration
26–2

and jointly to determine the reasons for each and to determine if possible whether they are favorable or unfavorable. For example, in the comparative balance sheet of Anchor Supply Company, Illustration 26–1, the first item showing a significant change is "Cash." It shows a large decrease, and at first glance this appears unfavorable. However, when the decrease in "Cash" is considered with the decrease in "Investments" and the increase in "Store equipment," "Buildings," and "Land," plus the increase in "Mortgage payable," it becomes apparent the company has materially increased its plant assets between the two balance sheet dates. Further study reveals the company has apparently constructed a new building on land it has held as an investment until needed in this expansion. Also, it seems the company has paid for its new plant assets by reducing cash, selling its Apex Company bonds, and issuing a $50,000 mortgage.

The second item showing a significant change on the comparative balance sheet is "Notes receivable," which shows a large percentage increase. From the balance sheet itself there is no ready explanation for this increase. However, it warrants further investigation by the analyst, even though the dollar amount is comparatively small.

As a management tool for controlling operations, a comparative income statement is usually more valuable than a comparative balance sheet. For example, on the comparative income statement shown in Illustration 26–2, "Gross sales" increased 14.1% and "Net sales" increased 13.9%. At the same time, "Sales returns" increased 32.4%, or at a rate more than twice that of gross sales. Returned sales represent wasted sales effort and indicate dissatisfied customers; consequently, such an increase in returns should be investigated, and the reason therefor determined if at all possible.

On the income statement of Anchor Supply Company, in addition to the large increase in the "Sales returns," it is significant that the rate of increase in "Cost of goods sold" is greater than that of "Net sales." This is an unfavorable trend and should be remedied if at all possible.

In attempting to account for Anchor Supply Company's increase in sales, the increase in advertising and the large increase in plant assets merit attention. It is reasonable to expect a large expenditure for advertising to increase sales. It is also reasonable to expect an increase in plant assets to result in a sales increase in a merchandising company or a decrease in cost of goods sold in a manufacturing company.

Calculating percentage increases and decreases

When percentage increases and decreases are calculated for comparative statements, the increase or decrease in an item is divided by the amount shown for the item in the base year. No problems arise in these calculations when positive amounts are shown in the base year. For example, in Illustration 26–3 all items show positive amounts in the 1972 base year. However, when no amount is shown for an item in

	1973	(Base Year) 1972	Amount of Increase or Decrease*	Percent of Increase or Decrease*
Item one	$15,000	$10,000	$ 5,000	50
Item two	5,000	10,000	5,000*	50*
Item three	-0-	10,000	10,000*	100*
Item four (a negative* amount in the second year)	5,000*	10,000	15,000*	150*

Illustration
26–3

the base year or a negative amount is shown, an increase or decrease percentage is not calculated. For example, in Illustration 26–4 the items have no amounts or negative amounts in the 1972 base year, and percentages are not calculated.

	1973	(Base Year) 1972	Amount of Increase or Decrease*	Percent of Increase or Decrease*
Item one	$1,200	-0-	$1,200	
Item two (negative* amount in 1972)	3,500	$500*	4,000	
Item three (negative* amounts in both years)	500*	250*	250*	
Item four (negative* amounts in both years)..................	100*	400*	300	

Illustration
26–4

Trend percentages

Trend percentages or index numbers are useful in comparing data from a company's financial statements covering a number of years, since trend percentages emphasize changes that have occurred during the period. They are calculated as follows:

1. A base year is selected; it should be a representative year for all items.
2. Each item amount on the base year statement is assigned a weight of 100%.
3. Then each item from the statements for the years after the base year is expressed as a percentage of its base year amount. To find these percentages, the item amounts in the years after the base year are divided by the amount of the item in the base year.

For example, if 1968 is made the base year for the data of Illustration 26–5, the trend percentages for "Sales" are calculated by dividing by

	1968	1969	1970	1971	1972	1973
Sales	$210,000	$204,000	$292,000	$284,000	$310,000	$324,000
Cost of goods sold.......................	145,000	139,000	204,000	198,000	218,000	229,000
Gross profit...............................	$ 65,000	$ 65,000	$ 88,000	$ 86,000	$ 92,000	$ 95,000

Illustration
26–5

$210,000 the amount shown for "Sales" in each year after the first. The trend percentages for "Cost of goods sold" are found by dividing by $145,000 the amount shown for "Cost of goods sold" in each year after the first. And, the trend percentages for "Gross profit" are found by dividing the amounts shown for "Gross profit" by $65,000. When these divisions are made, the trends appear as in Illustration 26–6.

	1968	1969	1970	1971	1972	1973
Sales	100	97	139	135	148	154
Cost of goods sold	100	96	141	137	150	158
Gross profit	100	100	135	132	142	146

Illustration
26–6

It is interesting to note in the Illustration 26–6 trends that while after the second year the sales trend is upward, the cost of goods sold trend is upward at a slightly more rapid rate. This indicates a contracting gross profit rate and should receive attention.

It should be pointed out in a discussion of trends that the trend for a single balance sheet or income statement item is seldom too informative. However, a comparison of trends for related items often tells the analyst a great deal. For example, a downward sales trend with an upward trend for merchandise inventory, accounts receivable, and loss on bad debts would generally indicate an unfavorable situation. Likewise, a downward sales trend accompanied by an upward trend for cost of goods sold and selling expenses would also appear unfavorable. Also, an upward sales trend with a higher upward trend for accounts receivable, merchandise inventory, bad debts, and selling expense might indicate that sales are being achieved at too great a cost. On the other hand, an upward sales trend with a downward trend or a slower upward trend for accounts receivable, merchandise inventory, and selling expenses would indicate an increase in operating efficiency.

Common-size comparative statements

The comparative statements illustrated thus far do not show proportional changes in items except in a general way. Changes in proportions are often shown and emphasized by means of *common-size comparative statements.*

A common-size statement is so called because of the manner in which it presents items. For example, on a common-size balance sheet (1) the asset total is assigned a value of 100%; (2) the total of the liabilities and owner equity is also assigned a value of 100%; and then (3) each individual asset, liability, and owner equity item is shown as a fraction of one of the 100% totals. When several balance sheets are presented in this manner as a means of analysis, the items of each are expressed in common-size figures, fractions of 100%. A common-size comparative balance sheet for Anchor Supply Company is shown in Illustration 26–7.

A common-size income statement is constructed in much the same manner as a common-size balance sheet. Net sales are assigned a 100% value, and then each statement item is shown as a percentage of net sales.

Common-size income statements are very informative and are a useful

Anchor Supply Company
Common-Size Comparative Balance Sheet
December 31, 1972, and December 31, 1973

	Years Ended December 31		Common-Size Percentages	
	1973	1972	1973	1972
ASSETS				
Current Assets:				
Cash	$ 14,000	$ 89,000	2.64	18.43
Notes receivable	4,000	1,500	0.76	0.31
Accounts receivable, net	68,000	64,000	12.83	13.25
Merchandise inventory	190,000	184,000	35.86	38.10
Prepaid expenses	5,800	6,000	1.09	1.24
Total Current Assets	$281,800	$344,500	53.18	71.33
Investments:				
Real estate	-0-	$ 30,000	-0-	6.21
Apex Company 6% bonds	-0-	50,000	-0-	10.35
Total Investments	-0-	$ 80,000	-0-	16.56
Plant Assets:				
Office equipment	$ 5,000	$ 5,000		
Less accumulated depreciation	1,500	1,200		
	$ 3,500	$ 3,800	0.66	0.78
Store equipment	$ 24,000	$ 11,000		
Less accumulated depreciation	6,200	4,300		
	$ 17,800	$ 6,700	3.36	1.39
Buildings	$210,000	$ 60,000		
Less accumulated depreciation	33,200	32,000		
	$176,800	$ 28,000	33.36	5.80
Land	$ 50,000	$ 20,000	9.44	4.14
Total Plant Assets	$248,100	$ 58,500	46.82	12.11
Total Assets	$529,900	$483,000	100.00	100.00
LIABILITIES				
Current Liabilities:				
Notes payable	-0-	$ 10,000	-0-	2.07
Accounts payable	$ 53,400	60,000	10.08	12.42
Wages payable	800	1,200	0.15	0.25
Total Current Liabilities	$ 54,200	$ 71,200	10.23	14.74
Long-Term Liabilities:				
Mortgage payable	60,000	10,000	11.32	2.07
Total Liabilities	$114,200	$ 81,200	21.55	16.81
CAPITAL				
Common stock, $10 par value	$250,000	$250,000	47.18	51.76
Retained earnings	165,700	151,800	31.27	31.43
Total Capital	$415,700	$401,800	78.45	83.19
Total Liabilities and Capital	$529,900	$483,000	100.00	100.00

Illustration
26–7

management tool. This is because when the common-size 100% sales amount is assumed to represent one sales dollar, then the common-size amounts for the remaining income statement items show how each sales dollar was distributed to costs, expenses, and profit. For example, on the comparative income statement shown in Illustration 26–8, the 1972 cost of goods sold consumed 73.86 cents of each sales dollar. In 1973 cost of goods sold consumed 74.48 cents from each sales dollar. While this increase is apparently small, if in 1973 the proportion of cost of goods sold had remained at the 1972 level, more than $6,000

Anchor Supply Company
Common-Size Comparative Income Statement
Years Ended December 31, 1972, and December 31, 1973

	Years Ended December 31		Common-Size Percentages	
	1973	1972	1973	1972
Gross sales	$973,500	$853,000	101.41	101.21
Sales returns	13,500	10,200	1.41	1.21
Net sales	$960,000	$842,800	100.00	100.00
Cost of goods sold	715,000	622,500	74.48	73.86
Gross profit from sales	$245,000	$220,300	25.52	26.14
Operating expenses:				
Selling expenses:				
Advertising	$ 10,000	$ 5,000	1.04	0.59
Sales salaries	113,500	98,000	11.82	11.63
Store supplies used	3,200	2,800	0.33	0.33
Depreciation of store equipment	1,900	1,700	0.20	0.20
Delivery expense	12,800	14,000	1.33	1.66
Total selling expenses	$141,400	$121,500	14.72	14.41
General and administrative expenses:				
Office salaries	$ 32,500	$ 31,000	3.38	3.68
Officers' salaries	24,000	24,000	2.50	2.85
Office supplies used	1,300	1,250	0.14	0.15
Expired insurance	1,600	1,200	0.17	0.14
Depreciation of office equipment	300	300	0.03	0.04
Depreciation of buildings	1,200	950	0.13	0.11
Bad debts	2,400	2,200	0.25	0.26
Total general and administrative expenses	$ 63,300	$ 60,900	6.60	7.23
Total operating expenses	$204,700	$182,400	21.32	21.64
Operating income	$ 40,300	$ 37,900	4.20	4.50
Financial revenue and expense:				
Interest earned	1,300	2,050	0.14	0.24
	$ 41,600	$ 39,950		
Interest expense	2,300	1,100	0.24	0.13
Income before taxes	$ 39,300	$ 38,850	4.09	4.61
Income taxes	12,300	12,150	1.28	1.44
Net Income	$ 27,000	$ 26,700	2.81	3.17

Illustration
26–8

additional gross profit would have been earned. When this $6,000 additional gross profit is viewed with the 1973 net income in mind, it becomes important.

Common-size percentages point out efficiencies and inefficiencies that are otherwise difficult to see, and for this reason are a valuable management tool. To illustrate, sales salaries of Anchor Supply Company took a higher percentage of each sales dollar in 1973 than in 1972. On the other hand, office salaries took a smaller percentage of each 1973 sales dollar. Furthermore, although the loss from bad debts was greater in 1973 than in 1972, loss from bad debts took a smaller proportion of each sales dollar in 1973 than in 1972.

Analysis of working capital

■ The term *working capital* is used to denote the excess of a company's current assets over its current liabilities; and when balance sheets are analyzed, working capital always receives close attention. This is as it should be. Adequate working capital enables a company to carry sufficient inventories, meet current debts, take advantage of cash discounts, and extend favorable terms to customers. These are desirable. A company that is deficient in working capital and unable to do these things is in a poor competitive position. Its survival chances are normally small, unless its working capital position is improved. Inadequacy of working capital has ended the business lives of many companies whose total assets were far in excess of liabilities.

Many factors affect working capital requirements. The nature of the business in which a particular company is engaged is one factor. For example, railroads, public utilities, and other companies in which inventories consist only of supplies used in making repairs, need proportionately less working capital than do manufacturing or merchandising companies. Likewise, merchandising concerns selling on a cash basis need less working capital than concerns granting credit. Consequently, when the adequacy of working capital is studied, consideration must be given to the type of business under review.

Current ratio

A company's working capital should be sufficient to enable it to pay debts as they become due. However, working capital is not a measure of debt-paying ability. This may be demonstrated by the following example:

	Company A	Company B
Current assets	$100,000	$20,000
Current liabilities	90,000	10,000
Working capital	$ 10,000	$10,000

In the example, Company A's current assets are five times greater than Company B's, and both have the same amount of working capital. However, Company B's current assets are twice its current liabilities, while Company A's are only a little more than once its current liabilities.

Company B's current assets may shrink in half when turned into cash and still be adequate to meet current debts. On the other hand, Company A's current assets may shrink only 10% and still be adequate to meet current debts. Obviously, as the example shows, the relation of current assets to current liabilities is a more important measure of debt-paying ability than is the amount of working capital.

The relation of a company's current assets to its current liabilities is known as its *current ratio*. The current ratio of the foregoing Company B is calculated as follows:

$$\frac{\text{Current Assets, } \$20{,}000}{\text{Current Liabilities, } \$10{,}000} = 2$$

A current ratio is calculated by dividing current assets by current liabilities. After the division is made, the relation is expressed as, for example, Company B's current assets are two times its current liabilities, or Company B has $2 of current assets for each $1 of current liabilities, or simply Company B's current ratio is 2 to 1.

The current ratio is the relation of current assets and current liabilities expressed mathematically. A high current ratio indicates a large amount of current assets to current liabilities. The higher the ratio, the more liquid is a company's current position, and normally the better it can meet current obligations.

For many years bankers and other credit grantors measured a credit-seeking company's debt-paying ability by whether or not it had a 2 to 1 current ratio. Today most credit grantors realize that the 2 to 1 rule of thumb is not an adequate test of debt-paying ability. They realize that whether or not a company's current ratio is good or bad depends upon at least three factors:

1. The nature of the company's business.
2. The composition of its current assets.
3. The turnover of certain of its current assets.

The nature of a company's business has much to do with its working capital requirements. A public utility or railroad which normally has no inventories other than supplies and which grants little or no credit can often operate on a current ratio less than 1 to 1. On the other hand, because a misjudgment of style can make a finished goods inventory almost worthless, a company manufacturing articles in which style is the important sales factor may find a current ratio of more than 2 to 1 to be inadequate. Perhaps the best test of the adequacy of a company's current ratio is a comparison with the current ratios of a number of its close competitors. However, these are often unavailable.

Composition of current assets

In an analysis of debt-paying ability, the current asset composition is important. Normally, a company with a high proportion of cash to accounts receivable, merchandise inventory, and other current assets is in a better position to meet quickly its current debts than is a company with most of its current assets tied up in accounts receivable and merchandise. The company with cash may pay its current debts at once. The company with accounts receivable and merchandise normally must turn these items into cash before it can pay. In turning accounts and merchandise into cash there is always a possibility of shrinkage. However, when current assets are analyzed, the fact that merchandise is normally sold for more than its balance sheet amount and consequently produces more than its balance sheet amount of cash should not be ignored.

Current asset composition may be examined in two ways. A schedule showing the percentage of each current asset to total current assets may be constructed, and the *acid-test ratio* may be calculated. A schedule showing the current asset composition of Anchor Supply Company appears as in Illustration 26–9.

	December 31, 1973		December 31, 1972	
	Amount	Percent	Amount	Percent
Current Assets:				
Cash...	$ 14,000	4.97	$ 89,000	25.83
Notes receivable	4,000	1.42	1,500	.44
Accounts receivable, net...............	68,000	24.13	64,000	18.58
Merchandise inventory...................	190,000	67.42	184,000	53.41
Prepaid expenses........................	5,800	2.06	6,000	1.74
Totals	$281,800	100.00	$344,500	100.00

Illustration 26–9

The acid-test ratio offers an easily calculated quick check on current asset composition. The acid-test ratio is often called the *quick ratio* because it is the ratio of "quick assets" to current liabilities. "Quick assets" are cash, notes receivable, accounts receivable, and marketable securities. They are the current assets that can quickly be turned into cash. An acid-test ratio of 1 to 1 is normally considered satisfactory. However, this is a rule of thumb and should be applied with care. The acid-test ratio of Anchor Supply Company on December 31, 1973, is calculated as follows:

Quick Assets:		Current Liabilities:	
Cash	$14,000	Accounts payable	$53,400
Notes receivable.................	4,000	Wages payable...................	800
Accounts receivable............	68,000	Total	$54,200
Total	$86,000		

Acid-Test Ratio = $86,000 ÷ $54,200 = 1.59, or Acid-Test Ratio = 1.59 to 1

Turnover of accounts receivable

Certain current asset turnovers affect working capital requirements. For example, Companies A and B sell the same amounts of merchandise on credit each month. However, Company A grants 30-day terms to its customers, while Company B grants 60 days. Both collect their accounts at the end of the credit periods granted. But as a result of the difference in terms, Company A turns over or collects its accounts twice as rapidly as does Company B. Also, as a result of the more rapid turnover, Company A requires only one half the investment in accounts receivable that is required of Company B.

Accounts receivable turnover is calculated by dividing net sales for a particular year by end-of-the-year accounts receivable. Illustration 26–10 shows the calculation of Anchor Supply Company's accounts receivable turnover. The turnover of 14.12 times in 1973 in comparison with 13.16 times in 1972 indicates the company's accounts receivable were collected more rapidly in 1973.

	1973	1972
Net sales for year	$960,000	$842,800
Year-end accounts receivable	68,000	64,000
Time accounts receivable were turned over (net sales ÷ accounts receivable)	14.12	13.16

Illustration 26–10

Theoretically, only charge sales rather than the sum of charge and cash sales should be used in calculating this turnover. Likewise, accounts receivable before subtracting allowance for bad debts should be used. However, information as to charge sales is seldom available in a published balance sheet, and many published balance sheets report accounts receivable at their net amount. Consequently, total charge and cash sales and net accounts receivable must often be used in the calculation.

Likewise, as in calculating merchandise turnover, which is discussed later, if year-end accounts receivable are not representative, an average of the year's accounts receivable by months may be used in calculating accounts receivable turnover.

Days' sales uncollected

Accounts receivable turnover is one indication of the speed with which a company collects its accounts. *Days' sales uncollected* is another indication of the same thing. To illustrate the calculation of days' sales uncollected, assume a company had charge sales during a year of $250,000, and that it has $25,000 of accounts receivable at the year-end. In other words, one tenth of its charge sales, or the charge sales made during one tenth of a year, or the charge sales of 36.5 days ($\frac{1}{10} \times 365$ days in a year = 36.5 days) are uncollected. This calculation of days' sales uncollected in equation form appears as follows:

$$\frac{\text{Accounts Receivable, \$25,000}}{\text{Charge Sales, \$250,000}} \times 365 = 36.5 \text{ Days' Sales Uncollected}$$

Days' sales uncollected takes on more meaning when credit terms are known. According to a rule of thumb, a company's accounts receivable should not exceed one and one-third times the days in its credit period when it does not offer discounts and one and one-third times the days in its discount period when it does. If the company, whose days' sales uncollected is calculated in the illustration just given, offers 30-day terms, then 36.5 days is within the rule-of-thumb amount. However, if its terms are 2/10, n/30, 36.5 days' sales uncollected would seem excessive.

Days' sales uncollected is sometimes used as a test of a company's accounts receivable. If days' sales uncollected are excessive, it is assumed that some accounts are probably old and uncollectible.

Turnover of merchandise inventory

A company's merchandise turnover is the number of times its average inventory is sold during an accounting period. Merchandise turnover is a test of merchandising efficiency. A high turnover is considered a mark of good merchandising. Also, from a working capital point of view, a company with a high turnover requires a smaller investment in inventory than one producing the same sales with a low turnover. Merchandise turnover is calculated by dividing cost of goods sold by average inventory. Cost of goods sold is the amount of merchandise at its cost price that was sold during an accounting period; average inventory is the average amount of merchandise, at its cost price, on hand during the period. The 1973 merchandise turnover of Anchor Supply Company is calculated as follows:

$$\frac{\text{Cost of Goods Sold, \$715,000}}{\text{Average Merchandise Inventory, \$187,000}} = \text{Merchandise Turnover of 3.82 Times}$$

The cost of goods sold is taken from the company's 1973 income statement. The average inventory is found by dividing by two the sum of the $184,000, January 1, 1973, inventory and the $190,000, December 31, 1973, inventory. In a company in which beginning and ending inventories are not representative of the inventory normally on hand, a more accurate turnover may be secured by using the average of all the 12 month-end inventories rather than just the beginning- and end-of-the-year inventories.

Standards of comparison ■ When financial statements are analyzed by computing ratios and turnovers, the analyst must determine whether the ratios and turnovers obtained are good, bad, or just average. In a decision as to whether ratios are good, bad, or average, the analyst must have some basis for comparison. The following are available:

1. A trained analyst may compare the ratios and turnovers of the company under review with his own mental standards built up from past experiences.
2. An analyst may calculate for purposes of comparison the ratios and turnovers of a selected group of competitive companies in the same industry as the one whose statements are under review.
3. Published ratios and turnovers such as those put out by Dun & Bradstreet may be secured for comparison.
4. Some local and national trade associations gather data from their members and publish standard or average ratios for their trade or industry. These offer the analyst a very good basis of comparison when available.
5. Rule-of-thumb standards may be used as a basis for comparison.

Of the five foregoing standards, the ratios and turnovers of a selected group of competitive companies normally offer the best basis for comparison. Rule-of-thumb standards should be applied with care if erroneous conclusions are to be avoided.

Other balance sheet and income statement relations

■ Several balance sheet and income statement relations in addition to those having to do with working capital are important to the analyst. Some of the more important are discussed in the following pages.

Capital contributions of owners and creditors

The share of a company's assets contributed by its owners and the share contributed by creditors are always of interest to the analyst. The owner and creditor contributions of Anchor Supply Company are shown in Illustration 26–11.

Creditors like to see a high proportion of owner equity because owner equity acts as a cushion in absorbing losses. The greater the equity of

	1973	1972
Total liabilities	$114,200	$ 81,200
Total owner equity	415,700	401,800
Total liabilities and owner equity	$529,900	$483,000
Creditors' equity (line 1 divided by line 3)	21.55%	16.81%
Owner equity (line 2 divided by line 3)	78.45%	83.19%

Illustration
26–11

the owners in relation to that of the creditors, the greater the losses that can be absorbed by the owners before the creditors begin to lose.

From the creditors' standpoint a high percentage of owner equity is desirable. However, if an enterprise can earn a return on borrowed capital in excess of the capital's cost, then an increase in creditor equity is often desirable from the owners' viewpoint. When a company operates on borrowed capital, it trades or operates on capital supplied by its creditors. For this reason, when a company operates on borrowed capital, it is said to be *trading on the equity*. It is trading on the equity of its creditors. When returns are in excess of the cost of borrowed capital, trading on the equity is often desirable from the viewpoint of the business owners. However, if earnings are unstable, it may be dangerous.

Pledged plant assets to long-term liabilities

Companies commonly borrow by issuing a note or bonds secured by a mortgage on certain of their plant assets. The ratio of pledged plant assets to long-term debt is often calculated to measure the security granted to mortgage or bondholders by the pledged assets. This ratio is calculated by dividing the pledged assets' book value by the liabilities for which the assets are pledged. It is calculated for Anchor Supply Company in 1972 and 1973 as in Illustration 26–12.

	1973	1972
Buildings	$210,000	$60,000
Less accumulated depreciation	33,200	32,000
Buildings, net	$176,800	$28,000
Land	50,000	20,000
Book value of pledged plant assets	$226,800	$48,000
Mortgage payable	$ 60,000	$10,000
Ratio of pledged assets to secured liabilities	3.78 to 1	4.8 to 1

Illustration
26–12

The usual rule-of-thumb minimum for this ratio is 2 to 1. However, the ratio needs careful interpretation because it shows relation between the *book value* of pledged plant assets and long-term liabilities. Even when depreciation is accurately estimated and recorded, book values do not measure the amount that would be secured in a foreclosure or a liquidation. Estimated liquidation values or foreclosure values are a better measure of the protection offered bond or mortgage holders by pledged assets. Often, in situations in which assets are pledged, the long-term earning ability of the company whose assets are pledged is more important to long-term creditors than the pledged assets' book value.

Times fixed interest charges are earned

The number of times fixed interest charges are earned is often calculated to measure the security of the return offered to bondholders or a mortgage holder. The number of times fixed interest charges are earned is determined by dividing income (before deducting income taxes and fixed interest charges) by the amount of the fixed interest charges. Since fixed interest charges are an expense that is deducted before the calculation of income taxes, income before deducting fixed interest charges and income taxes is used in the calculation. Likewise, since the calculation is the number of times fixed interest charges are earned, fixed interest charges are not deducted in arriving at the income used in the calculation. Often the return to a company's long-term creditors is considered secure if the company consistently earns its fixed interest charges two or more times each year.

Rate of return on total assets employed

The return earned on total assets employed is a measure of management's performance. Assets are used to earn a profit, and management is responsible for the way in which they are used; consequently, the return on assets employed is a measure of management's performance.

The return figure used in this calculation should be after-tax income plus interest expense, since interest paid creditors is a return for assets they have supplied. Likewise, if the amount of assets has fluctuated during the year, an average of the assets employed should be used.

The calculation of the rates of return earned by Anchor Supply Company on assets employed during 1972 and 1973 is shown in Illustration 26–13.

	1973	1972
Net income after taxes	$ 27,000	$ 26,700
Add interest expense	2,300	1,100
Net income before interest expense	$ 29,300	$ 27,800
Total assets at beginning of the year	$483,000	$475,000
Total assets at end of the year	529,900	483,000
Average assets employed	$506,450	$479,000
Rate of return on total assets employed (line 3 divided by line 6)	5.79%	5.80%

Illustration 26–13

In the case of Anchor Supply Company the two-year change in the rates is insignificant, and it is impossible to tell whether the returns are good or bad without some basis of comparison. The best comparison would be the returns earned by similar-size companies engaged in the same kind of business, or a comparison could be made with the returns earned by this company in previous years. Neither of these is available in this case.

Rate of return on common stockholders' equity

A primary reason for the operation of a corporation is to earn a net income for its common stockholders; and the rate of return on the common stockholders' equity is a measure of the success achieved in this area.

For Anchor Supply Company the 1972 and 1973 rates of return on its common stockholders' equity are computed in Illustration 26–14.

	1973	1972
Net income after taxes	$ 27,000	$ 26,700
Common stockholders' equity, beginning of year	$401,800	$390,200
Common stockholders' equity, end of year	415,700	401,800
Average common stockholders' equity	$408,750	$396,000
Rate of return on common stockholders' equity (line 1 divided by line 4)	6.61%	6.74%

Illustration
26–14

Compare the returns on stockholders' equity as shown in Illustration 26–14 with the returns on total assets shown in Illustration 26–13 and note that the return on the common stockholders' equity is greater in both years. The greater return results from trading on the equity or from leverage gained by using borrowed money.

Trading on the equity can be either favorable or unfavorable to the common stockholders. When the average rate of interest paid for borrowed capital is less than the return on total assets employed, the common stockholders gain from trading on the equity; but when the average rate paid for borrowed capital is greater than the return on total assets, common stockholders lose.

When there is preferred stock outstanding, the preferred dividend requirements must be subtracted from net income to arrive at the common stockholders' share of income to be used in calculating the rate of return on common stockholders' equity.

Earnings per share of common stock

Earnings per share is one of the most commonly quoted figures on the financial pages of daily newspapers. When a company has no preferred stock outstanding, earnings per share is computed by dividing net income after taxes by the outstanding shares of common stock. When there is preferred stock, any preferred dividend requirements have to be deducted from net income to determine income available to the common stockholders.

Anchor Supply Company has 25,000 common shares, but no preferred stock outstanding; consequently, the 1972 earnings per share on its common stock was $1.07 ($26,700 ÷ 25,000 = $1.068) and the 1973 earnings per share was $1.08, a very small increase for 1973.

In quoting earnings per share, any significant change in the number of shares outstanding during the year should be disclosed, particularly if there has been a large stock dividend or a stock split. Also, if the effects of any significant extraordinary gains and losses are included in the earnings figure, they should be disclosed.

Price-earnings ratio

Price-earnings ratios are commonly used in comparing investment opportunities. A price-earnings ratio is calculated by dividing market price per share by earnings per share. For example, if Anchor Supply Company's common stock sold at $15 per share at the end of 1972, the stock's end-of-the-year price-earnings ratio is calculated:

$$\frac{\$15 \text{ Market Price per Share}}{\$1.07 \text{ Earnings per Share}} = 14.02$$

After the calculation is made, it may be said that the stock had a 14.02 to 1 price-earnings ratio at the end of 1972, or it may be said that $14.02 was required at that time to buy $1 of this company's 1972 earnings.

In comparing price-earnings ratios it must be remembered that such ratios vary from industry to industry. For example, in the steel industry a 10 or 12 to 1 price-earnings ratio is normal, while in growth industries, such as the chemical or drug industries, 20 or 30 to 1 ratios are not uncommon.

The effect of price level changes ■ When financial statements for a period of several years are analyzed, the analyst must keep in mind the effect on the statements of *price level changes*. Price level changes are changes in the purchasing power of money. Often, if price level changes are ignored, incorrect conclusions may be drawn. For example, during the 1945 through 1959 period many companies showed a large dollar increase in sales when their physical volume of sales actually remained unchanged or increased only a small amount. In these companies the increase in dollar sales volume was caused by the decrease in the purchasing power of the dollar. During these years, 1945–59, a dollar purchased a smaller amount of goods each year; or, in other words, during each of these years it required an increasing number of dollars to buy the same amount of goods.

Price level changes affect income statement items, but their effect is not limited to such items. They also affect the balance sheet. For example, many companies are operating today with plant assets, the replacement costs of which are several times their reported balance sheet amounts. This is particularly true of buildings purchased or constructed some years ago.

No effort will be made here to enter into an exhaustive discussion of the effect of price level changes on financial statements. Such a discussion is reserved for a more advanced course. However, the student should be aware of this phenomenon.

Other
analytical
devices

■ Many analytical devices are available to aid the analyst in separating financial statement parts so as to see the relation of the parts to the whole and to each other. Several kinds of comparative statements, ratios, and turnovers have been discussed in this chapter; break-even analysis was discussed in a previous chapter; and the funds flow statement is the subject of the next chapter. All are valuable tools of the analyst. However, they do not replace his good judgment. They are only tools that aid in bringing the data under review into a sharper focus.

Questions
for class
discussion

1. Why does a comparative balance sheet often have columns showing increases and decreases in both dollar amounts and percentages?
2. When trends are calculated and compared, what item trends should be compared with the trend of sales?
3. Why are common-size statements so called?
4. What items are assigned a value of 100% (*a*) on a common-size balance sheet and (*b*) on a common-size income statement?
5. Define the term working capital.
6. For the following transactions tell which increase working capital, which decrease working capital, and which have no effect on working capital:
   a) Collected accounts receivable.
   b) Borrowed money from the bank by giving an interest-bearing note.
   c) Declared a cash dividend.
   d) Paid a cash dividend previously declared.
   e) Sold plant assets at their book value.
   f) Sold merchandise at a profit.
7. Why is adequate working capital of importance to a business?
8. List several factors that have an effect on working capital requirements.
9. A company has a 2 to 1 current ratio. List several reasons why this ratio may not be adequate.
10. Tell the significance of each of the following ratios and turnovers and tell how each is calculated:
    a) Current ratio.
    b) Acid-test ratio.
    c) Turnover of accounts receivable.
    d) Turnover of merchandise inventory.
    e) Rate of return on common stockholders' equity.
    f) Ratio of pledged plant assets to long-term liabilities.
11. How are days' sales uncollected calculated? What is the significance of the number of days' sales uncollected?
12. Why do creditors like to see a high proportion of owner equity?
13. What is the ratio of pledged plant assets to long-term liabilities supposed to measure? Why must this ratio be interpreted with care?
14. What does the rate of return on assets employed tell about management?
15. What is meant by the phrase "trading on the equity"?
16. What are price level changes? Why must the effect of price level changes be considered when statements covering a period of years are analyzed?

Exercise 26-1

Where possible calculate percentages of increase and decrease for the following unrelated items. The parentheses indicate deficit items.

	1973	1972
Equipment, net	$80,000	$60,000
Notes receivable	-0-	3,000
Notes payable	10,000	-0-
Retained earnings	(2,400)	12,000
Cash	10,000	(1,000)

Exercise 26-2

Calculate trend percentages for the following items and tell whether the situation shown by the trends is favorable or unfavorable:

	1969	1970	1971	1972	1973
Sales	$200,000	$226,000	$238,000	$248,000	$260,000
Cost of goods sold	120,000	144,000	162,000	168,000	180,000
Accounts receivable	20,000	25,000	27,000	28,000	31,000

Exercise 26-3

Express the following income statement information in common-size percentages and tell whether the situation shown is favorable or unfavorable.

GREENHILL SALES COMPANY
Comparative Income Statement
Years Ended December 31, 1972, and 1973

	1973	1972
Sales	$100,000	$90,000
Cost of goods sold	66,800	59,850
Gross profit from sales	$ 33,200	$30,150
Operating expenses	25,100	22,320
Net Income	$ 8,100	$ 7,830

Exercise 26-4

The year-end statements of Blue Lake Sales Company follow:

BLUE LAKE SALES COMPANY
Balance Sheet, December 31, 19—

ASSETS		EQUITIES	
Cash	$ 6,000	Accounts payable	$ 20,000
Accounts receivable, net	24,000	Mortgage payable, secured by	
Merchandise inventory, net	28,500	a lien on the plant assets	35,000
Prepaid expenses	1,500	Common stock, $10 par value	100,000
Plant assets, net	140,000	Retained earnings	45,000
Total Assets	$200,000	Total Equities	$200,000

BLUE LAKE SALES COMPANY
Income Statement for Year Ended December 31, 19—

Sales..		$365,000
Cost of goods sold:		
Merchandise inventory, January 1, 19—	$ 31,500	
Purchases..	267,000	
Goods available for sale.......................................	$298,500	
Merchandise inventory, December 31, 19—	28,500	
Cost of goods sold		270,000
Gross profit on sales...		$ 95,000
Operating expenses		74,000
Operating income...		$ 21,000
Mortgage interest expense		2,100
Income before taxes		$ 18,900
Income taxes..		4,900
Net Income		$ 14,000

Required:
Calculate the following: (*a*) current ratio, (*b*) acid-test ratio, (*c*) days' sales uncollected, (*d*) merchandise turnover, (*e*) capital contribution of owners expressed as a percent, (*f*) ratio of pledged plant assets to long-term debt, (*g*) times fixed interest charges earned, (*h*) return on stockholders' equity, and (*i*) earnings per share. (Assume all sales were on credit and the stockholders' equity was $135,000 on January 1.)

Exercise 26–5

Common-size and trend percentages for a company's sales, cost of goods sold and expenses follow:

COMMON-SIZE PERCENTAGES				TREND PERCENTAGES			
	1971	*1972*	*1973*		*1971*	*1972*	*1973*
Sales.........................	100.0	100.0	100.0	Sales.........................	100.0	95.0	90.0
Cost of goods sold......	64.0	63.0	63.0	Cost of goods sold	100.0	93.5	88.6
Expenses	28.0	28.0	27.0	Expenses....................	100.0	95.0	86.8

Required:
Present statistics to prove whether the company's net income increased, decreased, or remained unchanged during the three-year period represented above.

Problems   Problem 26-1

The year-end statements of Tiptop Sales Company follow:

TIPTOP SALES COMPANY
Balance Sheet, December 31, 19—

Cash	$ 12,000	Accounts payable	$ 19,800
Temporary investments	8,000	Accrued wages payable	550
Notes receivable	2,500	Income taxes payable	4,650
Accounts receivable, net	23,000	Mortgage payable, secured by	
Merchandise inventory	36,300	a lien on the plant assets	70,000
Prepaid expenses	1,200	Common stock, $10 par value	100,000
Plant assets, net	168,000	Retained earnings	56,000
Total Assets	$251,000	Total Equities	$251,000

TIPTOP SALES COMPANY
Income Statement for Year Ended December 31, 19—

Sales		$460,000
Cost of goods sold:		
Merchandise inventory, January 1, 19—	$ 33,700	
Purchases	300,100	
Goods available for sale	$333,800	
Merchandise inventory, December 31, 19—	36,300	
Cost of goods sold		297,500
Gross profit from sales		$162,500
Operating expenses		136,850
Operating income		$ 25,650
Mortgage interest expense		4,500
Income before taxes		$ 21,150
Income taxes		4,650
Net Income		$ 16,500

Required:
Calculate the following: (*a*) current ratio, (*b*) acid-test ratio, (*c*) days' sales uncollected, (*d*) merchandise turnover, (*e*) ratio of pledged plant assets to long-term debt, (*f*) times fixed interest charges earned, (*g*) return on total assets employed, (*h*) return on stockholders' equity, and (*i*) earnings per share. Assume all sales were on credit, assets employed at the beginning of the year totaled $249,000, and stockholders' equity at the beginning of the year was $144,000.

Problem 26–2

The condensed statements of Century Supply Company follow:

CENTURY SUPPLY COMPANY
Comparative Income Statements
Years Ended December 31, 1970, 1971, and 1972
(In Thousands of Dollars)

	1970	1971	1972
Sales	$8,000	$9,000	$10,000
Cost of goods sold	5,688	6,480	7,150
Gross profit from sales	$2,312	$2,520	$ 2,850
Selling expenses	$1,216	$1,359	$ 1,500
Administrative expenses	784	855	940
Total expenses	$2,000	$2,214	$ 2,440
Income before taxes	$ 312	$ 306	$ 410
State and federal income taxes	152	149	196
Net Income	$ 160	$ 157	$ 214

CENTURY SUPPLY COMPANY
Comparative Balance Sheets
December 31, 1970, 1971, and 1972
(In Thousands of Dollars)

ASSETS

	1970	1971	1972
Current assets	$ 750	$ 615	$ 696
Long-term investments	50	5	
Plant and equipment	2,400	2,676	2,664
Total Assets	$3,200	$3,296	$3,360

LIABILITIES AND CAPITAL

	1970	1971	1972
Current liabilities	$ 250	$ 280	$ 290
Common stock	2,000	2,100	2,100
Other contributed capital	50	61	61
Retained earnings	900	855	909
Total Liabilities and Capital	$3,200	$3,296	$3,360

Required:
1. Calculate each year's current ratio.
2. Express the income statement data in common-size percentages.
3. Express the balance sheet data in trend percentages.
4. Comment on any significant relationships revealed by the ratios and percentages.

Problem 26–3

Following are data from the statements of two companies selling similar products:

	Company X	Company Y
Cash	$ 8,500	$ 12,500
Notes receivable	3,500	2,000
Accounts receivable	30,000	40,000
Merchandise inventory	44,000	54,800
Prepaid expenses	1,200	1,200
Plant and equipment, net	165,800	172,500
Total Assets	$253,000	$283,000
Current liabilities	$ 40,000	$ 50,000
Mortgage payable	50,000	50,000
Common stock, $10 par value	100,000	100,000
Retained earnings	63,000	83,000
Total Liabilities and Capital	$253,000	$283,000

Data from the Current Year's Income Statements

Sales	$480,000	$550,000
Cost of goods sold	377,200	437,400
Interest expense	3,000	3,500
Net income	16,695	18,060

Beginning-of-the-Year Data

Merchandise inventory	$ 38,000	$ 53,200
Total assets	247,000	277,000
Stockholders' equity	155,000	178,200

Required:
1. Calculate current ratios, acid-test ratios, merchandise turnovers, and days' sales uncollected for the two companies. Then state which company you think is the better short-term credit risk and why.
2. Calculate earnings per share, rate of return on total assets employed, and rate of return on stockholders' equity. Then under the assumption that each company's stock can be purchased at book value, state which company's stock you think is the better investment and why.

Problem 26-4

The condensed comparative statements of Reynard Sales Company follow:

Reynard Sales Company
Comparative Income Statements
For Years Ended December 31, 19AA-AG
(In Thousands of Dollars)

	19AA	19AB	19AC	19AD	19AE	19AF	19AG
Sales	$400	$500	$572	$680	$760	$840	$872
Cost of goods sold	250	310	360	430	515	585	604
Gross profit from sales	$150	$190	$212	$250	$245	$255	$268
Operating expenses	100	110	118	138	197	220	238
Income before Taxes	$ 50	$ 80	$ 94	$112	$ 48	$ 35	$ 30

REYNARD SALES COMPANY
Comparative Balance Sheets
December 31, 19AA–AG
(In Thousands of Dollars)

ASSETS

	19AA	19AB	19AC	19AD	19AE	19AF	19AG
Cash...	$ 20	$ 14	$ 17	$ 15	$ 12	$ 10	$ 4
Accounts receivable, net.......................	40	52	54	62	88	90	92
Merchandise inventory	100	118	141	165	204	218	226
Other current assets............................	2	4	4	6	2	4	2
Long-term investments	38	38	38	38			
Plant and equipment, net......................	200	198	204	202	446	450	440
Total Assets	$400	$424	$458	$488	$752	$772	$764

LIABILITIES AND CAPITAL

	19AA	19AB	19AC	19AD	19AE	19AF	19AG
Current liabilities.................................	$ 50	$ 64	$ 82	$ 90	$140	$156	$159
Long-term liabilities	40	38	36	34	182	180	178
Common stock.....................................	200	200	200	200	250	250	250
Premium on common stock	50	50	50	50	60	60	60
Retained earnings	60	72	90	114	120	126	117
Total Liabilities and Capital	$400	$424	$458	$488	$752	$772	$764

Required:
1. Calculate trend percentages for the items of the statements.
2. Analyze and comment on any situations shown in the statements.

Problem 26–5

A company began the month of May with $200,000 of current assets, a $2\frac{1}{2}$ to 1 current ratio, and a $1\frac{1}{4}$ to 1 acid-test ratio. During the month it completed the following transactions:

May 1 Bought $20,000 of merchandise on account. (The company uses a perpetual inventory system.)

5 Sold for $10,000 merchandise that cost $5,000.

7 Collected a $2,500 account receivable.

11 Paid a $10,000 account payable.

15 Wrote off a $1,500 bad debt against the allowance for doubtful accounts.

18 Declared a $1 per share cash dividend on the 10,000 shares of outstanding common stock.

28 Paid the dividend declared on May 18.

29 Borrowed $10,000 by giving the bank a 60-day, 6% note.

30 Borrowed $25,000 by placing a 10-year mortgage on the plant.

31 Used the $25,000 proceeds of the mortgage to buy additional machinery.

Required:
Prepare a schedule showing the company's current ratio, acid-test ratio, and working capital after each of the foregoing transactions. Carry decimals three places.

Problem 26–1A

The year-end statements of Clock Sales Company follow:

CLOCK SALES COMPANY
Income Statement for Year Ended December 31, 19–

Sales...		$510,000
Cost of goods sold:		
Merchandise inventory, January 1, 19–	$ 37,800	
Purchases..	320,400	
Goods available for sale......................................	$358,200	
Merchandise inventory, December 31, 19–	34,200	
Cost of goods sold		324,000
Gross profit from sales...		$186,000
Operating expenses		158,700
Operating income...		$ 27,300
Mortgage interest expense		4,200
Income before taxes		$ 23,100
Income taxes..		5,100
Net Income		$ 18,000

CLOCK SALES COMPANY
Balance Sheet, December 31, 19–

Cash	$ 8,600	Accounts payable	$ 23,800
Temporary investments	10,000	Accrued wages payable	1,100
Notes receivable	3,000	Income taxes payable.............	5,100
Accounts receivable, net.........	25,500	Mortgage payable, secured by	
Merchandise inventory	34,200	a lien on the plant assets......	68,000
Prepaid expenses...................	1,200	Common stock, $5 par value ...	100,000
Plant assets, net	170,000	Retained earnings..................	54,500
Total Assets	$252,500	Total Equities................	$252,500

Required:
Calculate the following: (*a*) current ratio, (*b*) acid-test ratio, (*c*) days' sales uncollected, (*d*) merchandise turnover, (*e*) ratio of pledged plant assets to long-term debt, (*f*) times fixed interest charges earned, (*g*) return on total assets employed, (*h*) return on stockholders' equity, and (*i*) earnings per share. Assume all sales were on credit, the assets totaled $247,500 on January 1, and the stockholders' equity at the beginning of the year was $145,500.

Problem 26–2A

The condensed statements of Fannin Sales Company follow:

FANNIN SALES COMPANY
Comparative Income Statements
Years Ended December 31, 1970, 1971, and 1972
(In Thousands of Dollars)

	1970	1971	1972
Sales	$5,000	$6,000	$6,500
Cost of goods sold	3,600	4,398	4,745
Gross margin on sales	$1,400	$1,602	$1,755
Selling expenses	$ 700	$ 810	$ 884
Administrative expenses	500	$ 588	637
Total expenses	$1,200	$1,398	$1,521
Income before taxes	$ 200	$ 204	$ 234
State and federal income taxes	90	92	105
Net Income	$ 110	$ 112	$ 129

FANNIN SALES COMPANY
Comparative Balance Sheets
December 31, 1970, 1971, and 1972
(In Thousands of Dollars)

ASSETS

	1970	1971	1972
Current assets	$ 400	$ 256	$ 240
Plant and equipment	1,200	1,380	1,440
Total Assets	$1,600	$1,636	$1,680

LIABILITIES AND CAPITAL

	1970	1971	1972
Current liabilities	$ 125	$ 131	$ 127
Common stock, $10 par value	1,000	1,000	1,000
Other contributed capital	175	175	175
Retained earnings	300	330	378
Total Liabilities and Capital	$1,600	$1,636	$1,680

Required:
1. Calculate each year's current ratio.
2. Express the income statement data in common-size percentages.
3. Express the balance sheet data in trend percentages.
4. Comment on any significant relationships revealed by the ratios and percentages.

Problem 26–3A

Following are the condensed 1972 and 1973 statements of Corona Sales:

CORONA SALES
Comparative Income Statements
Years Ended December 31, 1972–73

	1973	1972
Sales (all on credit)..	$476,000	$451,000
Cost of goods sold:		
Merchandise inventory, January 1........................	$ 43,000	$ 41,000
Purchases	305,600	273,800
Goods for sale..	$348,600	$314,800
Merchandise inventory, December 31	56,000	43,000
Cost of goods sold	$292,600	$271,800
Gross profit from sales...	$183,400	$179,200
Operating expenses	163,400	156,600
Income before Taxes..	$ 20,000	$ 22,600

CORONA SALES
Comparative Balance Sheets
December 31, 1972–73

ASSETS

	1973	1972
Cash...	$ 14,000	$ 12,000
Accounts receivable	38,000	44,000
Merchandise inventory...	56,000	43,000
Plant assets, net...	104,000	102,000
Total Assets...	$212,000	$201,000

LIABILITIES AND STOCKHOLDERS' EQUITY

	1973	1972
Accounts payable...	$ 26,000	$ 28,000
Notes payable	10,000	6,000
Mortgage payable (due in 1980)..............................	40,000	40,000
Common stock	100,000	100,000
Retained earnings...	36,000	27,000
Total Liabilities and Stockholders' Equity	$212,000	$201,000

Required:
1. Calculate common-size percentages for sales, cost of goods sold, gross profit from sales, operating expenses, and income before taxes; and calculate the current ratio, acid-test ratio, merchandise turnover, and days' sales uncollected for each of the two years.
2. Comment on the situation shown by your calculations.

Problem 26–5A

A company had $180,000 of current assets, a 3 to 1 current ratio, and a 1½ to 1 quick ratio. It then completed the following transactions:

a) Collected a $2,500 account receivable.

b) Wrote off a $1,000 bad debt against the allowance for doubtful accounts.

c) Borrowed $20,000 by giving its bank a 60-day, 6% note.

d) Bought $10,000 of merchandise on credit. The company uses a perpetual inventory system.

e) Declared a $0.50 per share cash dividend on its 20,000 shares of outstanding common stock.

f) Paid the dividend declared in (e) above.

g) Declared a 1,000-share stock dividend. The stock was selling at $15 per share on the day of the declaration.

h) Distributed the dividend stock of (g) above.

i) Sold for $10,000 merchandise that cost $5,000.

Required:
Prepare a schedule showing the company's current ratio, its acid-test ratio, and the amount of its working capital after each of the foregoing transactions. Carry decimals three places.

Decision problem 26–1, Boyson's Department Store

As controller of Boyson's Department Store you have calculated the following ratios, turnovers, and percentages to enable you to answer questions the directors will ask at their next meeting.

	1973	1972	1971
Current ratio	2.91/1	2.47/1	2.09/1
Acid-test ratio	0.88/1	1.07/1	1.48/1
Merchandise turnover	9.5 times	10.1 times	10.5 times
Accounts receivable turnover	6.9 times	7.4 times	8.2 times
Return on stockholders' equity	6.11%	6.51%	6.89%
Return on total assets	6.20%	6.29%	6.52%
Sales to plant assets	4.70/1	4.50/1	4.20/1
Sales trend	124.00	114.00	100.00
Selling expenses to net sales	14.65%	14.85%	15.21%

Using the statistics given, answer each of the following questions and explain how you arrived at your answer.

a) Is it becoming easier for the company to meet its current debts on time and to take advantage of cash discounts?

b) Is the company collecting its accounts receivable more rapidly?

c) Is the company's investment in accounts receivable decreasing?

d) Are dollars invested in inventory increasing?

e) Is the company's investment in plant assets increasing?

f) Is the stockholders' investment becoming more profitable?

g) Is the company using debt leverage to the advantage of its stockholders?

h) Did the dollar amount of selling expenses decrease during the three-year period?

Decision problem 26–2, Able and Best Companies

Able and Best Companies are competitors; both were organized about 10 years ago; and both have seen their sales increase tenfold during the 10-year period. However, the tenfold increase is not as good as it sounds, because the costs and selling prices of the items the companies sell have doubled during the same period. Nevertheless, the sales of the companies have and are increasing. Both offer the same credit terms; age their accounts receivable to allow for bad debts; and collect their accounts in about the same length of time. Actually about the only real difference in the accounting procedures of the two companies is that Able Company has since its organization used Lifo in costing its goods sold and Best Company has used Fifo.

The current ratios of the two companies for the past four years were as follows:

CURRENT RATIOS

	Able Company	Best Company
December 31, 197A	3.1 to 1	5.4 to 1
December 31, 197B	3.4 to 1	5.8 to 1
December 31, 197C	2.8 to 1	6.0 to 1
December 31, 197D	2.6 to 1	6.1 to 1

You are the loan officer of a bank and both companies have come to your bank for 90-day loans. In addition to the current ratios, you note that Able Company turned its inventory twice as fast as Best Company in each of 197A and 197B and three times as fast in each of the last two years. You also discover that for each $10,000 of current liabilities the companies have the following amounts of inventory:

	Able Company	Best Company
December 31, 197A	$19,000	$44,000
December 31, 197B	23,000	49,000
December 31, 197C	16,000	52,000
December 31, 197D	14,000	54,000

Which company do you think is the better short-term credit risk? Back your opinion with computations showing why. Are the inventory turnovers of the two companies comparable? Explain. Which company seems to have the better inventory turnover?

Chapter 27

Flow of funds;
flow of cash

■ Occasionally in a successful corporation, upon examination of their company's income statement, management personnel will make the following observation and ask the following question: "Our income statement shows ample net income, yet we seem to be having more and more trouble finding funds to meet our current obligations. Has our reported net income actually been earned; and if so, what has happened to the money?" In such a situation an analysis of the flow of funds in the operation of the business will reveal what happened to earnings; it will also show what happened to funds from other sources.

Nature of funds

■ When the word "funds" is used in the phrase "flow of funds," the term has reference to more than the "cash" of a business. Actually, it means working capital or, in other words, current assets minus current liabilities.

When the term "funds" is used in this broad sense, it is easy to see why current assets are considered "funds." The more important current assets are cash, accounts receivable, and inventory, and are often called "circulating assets." They are so called because in a sense they circulate: the cash is used to buy merchandise, which is sold and turned into accounts receivable, which are collected and turned back into cash, which is used to buy more merchandise, and so on. Actually, the accounts receivable are only one step away from cash and the merchandise is only two.

Although it is easy to see where cash, accounts receivable, and inventory fit into the picture of a concern's funds, it is sometimes a little difficult to see the place of the current liabilities. However, when it is remembered that in addition to having sufficient cash and an adequate supply of merchandise, a company must also pay its debts when due, the place of the current liabilities becomes clear—current liabilities must be paid from current assets. Or in other words, current liabilities are negative working capital items that must be deducted from current assets in arriving at total "free funds" available for use in operating the business.

Flow of funds ■ Funds flow into a business and they flow out. Consequently, in analyzing a concern's flow of funds one must examine both sources and uses of funds.

Sources of funds

Transactions that increase working capital are sources of funds. Some of the more common sources are:

CURRENT OPERATIONS. Funds in the form of cash and accounts receivable flow into a business from sales; and funds flow out for expenses and goods sold. Consequently, funds are increased as a result of normal operations if the inflow from sales exceeds the outflow for expenses and goods sold.

In an analysis of a concern's funds the income statement is examined to determine the amount of funds from operations. However, although reported net income is the amount revenues exceeded expenses, reported net income does not generally represent the amount of funds from this source. This is because on an income statement expenses such as depreciation, depletion, and bond discount did not cause a funds outflow in the period of the statement.

For example, Rexel Sales Company, Illustration 27–1, experienced a $50,000 funds inflow from sales during the year. It also experienced

Rexel Sales Company
Income Statement for Year Ended December 31, 19—

Sales		$50,000
Cost of goods sold		30,000
Gross profit from sales		$20,000
Operating expenses:		
Sales salaries	$8,000	
Rent expense	1,200	
Depreciation of equipment	1,000	10,200
Net Income		$ 9,800

Illustration
27–1

outflows of $30,000 for goods sold, $8,000 for salaries, and $1,200 for rent; but there was no funds outflow for depreciation of equipment. Consequently, during this period Rexel Sales Company gained funds equal to the sum of its reported net income plus recorded depreciation, or it gained $9,800 plus $1,000 or a $10,800 total of funds from operations.

LONG-TERM LIABILITIES. Transactions that increase long-term liabilities increase working capital and, therefore, are sources of funds regardless of whether long-term notes, mortgages, or bonds are involved. On the other hand, short-term credit, whether obtained from banks or other creditors, is not a source of funds because short-term credit does not increase working capital. For example, if $10,000 is borrowed for a short period, say six months, both current assets and current liabilities are increased; but since both are increased the same amount, total working capital is unchanged.

SALE OF NONCURRENT ASSETS. When a plant asset, long-term investment, or other noncurrent asset is sold for cash or receivables, working capital is increased by the amount of the sale; therefore, such sales are sources of funds.

SALE OF CAPITAL STOCK. The issuance of stock for cash or current receivables increases current assets; as a result, such sales are sources of funds. Likewise, an additional investment of current assets by a single proprietor or partner is also a source of funds.

Uses of funds

When funds flow out for purposes other than current asset acquisitions or the payment of current liabilities, the outflows are called uses or applications of funds. A list of uses or applications includes:

PURCHASE OF NONCURRENT ASSETS. When noncurrent assets such as plant and equipment or long-term investments are purchased, working capital is reduced; consequently, such purchases are uses of funds.

PAYMENT OF NONCURRENT LIABILITIES. Payment of a long-term debt such as a mortgage, bonds, or a long-term note reduces working capital and is a use of funds. Likewise, a contribution to a debt retirement fund, bond sinking fund, preferred stock retirement fund, or other special noncurrent fund is also an application of funds.

DECLARATION OF A DIVIDEND. The declaration of a dividend which is to be paid in cash or other current assets reduces working capital and is a use of funds. Note that it is the declaration that is the use. The declaration creates a current liability, dividends payable, and therefore is an application or use as soon as voted by the board of directors. The final payment of a dividend previously declared does not affect total working capital because it reduces current assets and current liabilities in equal amounts.

Funds statement ■ When a funds flow analysis is made, a report of the analysis called a "funds statement," a "funds flow statement," a "statement of sources and uses of funds," or a "statement of sources and application of funds" is prepared. Observe in Illustration 27–2 that such a statement, like an income statement, covers a period of time. Its purpose is to report increases and decreases in each working capital item and to present an analysis of the changes in working capital.

Note how the change in each individual working capital item and the change in total working capital are shown in the first part or section, headed "Working Capital Changes."

Moss Corporation
Funds Statement for Year Ended December 31, 1973

WORKING CAPITAL CHANGES	Dec. 31, 1972	Dec. 31, 1973	Working Capital Increases	Working Capital Decreases
Current Assets:				
Cash	$ 8,000	$ 5,000		$ 3,000
Notes receivable	500	1,200	$ 700	
Accounts receivable, net	12,000	18,000	6,000	
Merchandise inventory	16,000	21,000	5,000	
Prepaid expenses	1,000	800		200
Total Current Assets	$37,500	$46,000		
Current Liabilities:				
Accounts payable	$ 9,000	$12,500		3,500
Dividends payable	700	1,000		300
Total Current Liabilities	$ 9,700	$13,500		
Working Capital	$27,800	$32,500		
			$11,700	$ 7,000
Net Increase in Working Capital (see analysis below)				4,700
			$11,700	$11,700

FLOW OF FUNDS

Sources of new working capital:
Current operations:
Net income per income statement $11,600
Add: Depreciation of equipment 800
Depreciation of building 900 $13,300

Other sources:
Issuance of stock 16,500
     Total new working capital $29,800

Uses of working capital:
Addition to building $14,000
Purchase of land 3,000
Payment of mortgage 5,000
Declaration of dividends 3,100
     Total working capital used 25,100
Net Increase in Working Capital .... $ 4,700

Illustration
27–2

Observe in the second part or section, headed "Flow of Funds," how the change in total working capital is analyzed and accounted for by showing sources of new working capital and uses made of working capital. Note that the corporation of Illustration 27–2 experienced a $29,800 inflow of new working capital from operations and the sale of stock, and $25,100 of working capital was applied to other than working capital purposes; consequently, working capital increased $4,700 during the period. If the reverse had been true and more working capital had been used than was received, working capital would have decreased.

The funds statement of Illustration 27–2 has two sections, and funds statements are often prepared in this way. However, some accountants prefer to prepare the two sections as two separate statements. In such cases the first section becomes the first statement and is called a statement of working capital changes; and the second section becomes the second statement and is called a funds flow statement, a statement of the flow of working capital, or a statement of sources and uses of funds. Also, if a comparative balance sheet is prepared (see page 739), some accountants do not prepare the first section or statement showing working capital changes. They omit this section or statement because the information shown therein as to increases and decreases in working capital items is also shown on the comparative balance sheet.

Preparing funds statement

■ **Changes in working capital section**

A comparative balance sheet or, if this is not available, balance sheets for the beginning and end of the period under review are the information source for the first section of a funds statement.

In preparing this first section the current asset and current liability amounts at the beginning of the period are entered in the first money column and the amounts at the end are put in the second. Next in each column the current assets are totaled, the current liabilities are totaled, and the difference, the amount of working capital, is shown. After this the increase or decrease in each working capital item is entered, the increases in the third column and the decreases in the fourth. Then the increases are added, the decreases are added, and the difference, the net increase or decrease, along with the final column totals are entered.

Flow of funds section

To prepare the second half of a funds statement, the accounting entries in each noncurrent balance sheet account in the ledger are examined for sources and uses of funds. Normally, the preparation of a working paper (see Illustrations 27–3 and 27–4) is a convenient way to bring together the results of these examinations. After the working paper is completed (see Illustration 27–4), the flow of funds section of the formal funds statement is prepared from the information accumulated on the bottom portion of the working paper.

Moss Corporation
Funds Statement Working Paper
For Year Ended December 31, 1973

	1 Account Balances Dec. 31, 1972	2 Analyses Debit	3 Analyses Credit	4 Account Balances Dec. 31, 1973
Debits				
Working capital	27800—			32500—
Noncurrent accounts:				
Equipment	8000—			7500—
Building	31000—			45000—
Land	8000—			11000—
Totals	74800—			96000—
Credits				
Accumulated depr., equipment	2100—			2400—
Accumulated depr., building	8800—			9700—
Mortgage payable	5000—			
Common stock	35000—			50000—
Premium on common stock				1500—
Retained earnings	15900—			20400—
Reserve for plant expansion	8000—			12000—
Totals	74800—			96000—
Funds provided by:				
Operations:				
Other sources:				
Funds used for:				

Illustration
27–3

Funds statement working paper

■ A funds statement working paper is prepared for the sole purpose of bringing together in an orderly manner information as to a concern's sources and uses of funds. In preparing the working paper the changes in each noncurrent balance sheet account balance between the beginning and end of the period under review are analyzed and one or more analyzing entries is entered in the Analyses columns of the work sheet. Noncurrent balance sheet accounts are balance sheet accounts other than current asset and current liability accounts. The changes in these accounts are analyzed because each change resulted from a transaction that either (1) increased funds (a source), (2) decreased funds (a use),

Moss Corporation
Funds Statement Working Paper
For Year Ended December 31, 1973

	1 Account Balances Dec. 31, 1972	2 Analyses Debit	3 Analyses Credit	4 Account Balances Dec. 31, 1973
Debits				
Working capital	27800 —	(k) 4700 —		32500 —
Noncurrent accounts:				
Equipment	8000 —		(a) 500 —	7500 —
Building	31000 —	(b) 14000 —		45000 —
Land	8000 —	(c) 3000 —		11000 —
Totals	74800 —			96000 —
Credits				
Accumulated depr., equipment	2100 —	(a) 500 —	(d) 800 —	2400 —
Accumulated depr., building	8800 —		(e) 900 —	9700 —
Mortgage payable	5000 —	(f) 5000 —		
Common stock	35000 —		(g) 15000 —	50000 —
Premium on common stock			(g) 1500 —	1500 —
Retained earnings	15900 —	(i) 3100 —	(h) 11600 —	20400 —
		(j) 4000 —		
Reserve for plant expansion	8000 —		(j) 4000 —	12000 —
Totals	74800 —			96000 —
Funds provided by:				
Operations:				
Net income		(h) 11600 —		
Depreciation of equipment		(d) 800 —		
Depreciation of building		(e) 900 —		
Other sources:				
Sale of stock		(g) 16500 —		
Funds used for:				
Building addition			(b) 14000 —	
Purchase of land			(c) 3000 —	
Payment of mortgage			(f) 5000 —	
Dividends to stockholders			(i) 3100 —	
Change in working capital:				
Increases in working capital			(k) 4700 —	
Totals		64100 —	64100 —	

Illustration
27–4

or (3) did not involve funds; and most resulted from transactions that either increased or decreased funds. Observe in Illustration 27–4 that the analyzing entry or entries on each line exactly account for the amount of change in the item on that line. Note too that each entry also sets out a source or use of funds or accounts for the effects of a book-keeping entry which did not involve funds.

A funds statement working paper is prepared as follows:

1. First, the amount of working capital at the beginning of the period under review is determined and entered on the first line in the first money column; then the amount of working capital at the end is determined and entered in the last column. Amounts of working capital at the beginning and end are determined by subtracting current liabilities from current assets.

2. After determining and entering the working capital amounts, the next step is to list the noncurrent balance sheet accounts with their amounts. The balance sheet amounts as of the beginning of the period are entered in the first column and those of the end are put in the last. Observe that debit balance items are listed first and are followed by credit balance items. This is a convenience that places depreciation items with the liability and capital items.

3. After the noncurrent account balances are entered, the working capital amount and the debit items in each column are added, after which the credit items are added. Observe that debits must equal credits. Note also that at this stage in its preparation the working paper appears as in Illustration 27–3.

4. Next the noncurrent accounts in the ledger are examined and analyzing entries are entered in the Analyses columns. These entries are discussed in more detail in the next section of this chapter.

5. After the last analyzing entry is entered, the working paper is completed by adding the columns.

After the working paper is completed (see Illustration 27–4), the information at the bottom of the paper as to sources and uses of funds is employed in preparing the "Flow of Funds" section of the formal funds statement.

In passing it should be observed that since a funds statement working paper is prepared solely for the purpose of bringing together information as to sources and uses of funds, the analyzing entries on the paper are placed only on the working paper and are never entered in the accounts.

Analyzing entries
■ Analyzing entries on a funds statement working paper do two things: (1) they account for or explain the amount of change in each noncurrent account and (2) they set out sources and uses of funds.

To understand why the change in each noncurrent account is accounted for or explained with one or more analyzing entries, remember that during a period every transaction that caused an increase or decrease in working capital also increased or decreased the balance of a noncurrent account. Consequently, when all increases and decreases in noncurrent accounts are explained by means of analyzing entries, all sources and uses of funds are set out on the working paper.

Sources of information for analyzing entries

Although the information needed in completing the analyzing entries on a funds statement working paper can normally be taken from a company's balance sheet, income statement, and statement of retained earnings, it is often easier to determine what caused various changes in noncurrent account balances if the accounts can be examined.

When the accounts are available, the accountant will examine them before beginning his working paper, making notes on any unusual transactions. He will then use his notes in making the analyzing entries to set out the effects of these transactions.

In cases where the accounts are unavailable, each change in a noncurrent account is assumed to have been caused by the most common type of transaction that would cause such a change. For example, on the Moss Company working paper the balance of the Land account increased $3,000 between the beginning and end of the period covered. If the Moss Company accounts were unavailable, it would be assumed that this change was caused by the most logical transaction, and in this case the actual transaction, the purchase of land for cash.

Order in which analyzing entries are made

Analyzing entries on a funds statement working paper need not be made in any particular order; however, many accountants simply begin with the first noncurrent account showing a change and make one or more entries to account for the change. They then turn to the next account, and so on down the working paper. An examination of the key letters on the working paper of Illustration 27–4 will show that this was the procedure followed in its preparation.

Analyzing entries illustrated

Analyzing entries are of three kinds: (1) those that set out sources of funds, (2) those that set out uses of funds, and (3) those that account for the effects of entries that did not involve funds. As a group, analyzing entries that set out uses are easiest to explain; consequently, this group will be discussed first.

ANALYZING ENTRIES THAT SET OUT USES OF FUNDS. Analyzing entries b, c, f, and i set forth uses of funds on the working paper of Illustration 27–4. An explanation of each follows:

b) The debit balance of Moss Company's Building account increased from $31,000 to $45,000 during the period of the working paper. An examination of the accounts revealed that the increase was caused by the payment of $14,000 for an addition to the building. This was a use of funds, and the following analyzing entry was made on the working paper to account for the change and to set out the use:

| | Analyses | |
	Debit	Credit
Building..	(b) 14,000	
Funds used for:		
Building addition..		(b) 14,000

c) On April 23 Moss Company purchased a tract of land paying $3,000 cash. When the transaction was recorded, it caused the debit balance of the Land account to increase from $8,000 to $11,000. The analyzing entry on the working paper that accounts for the change in the Land account and sets out this use is:

| | Analyses | |
	Debit	Credit
Land	(c) 3,000	
Funds used for:		
Purchase of land		(c) 3,000

f) On November 15 Moss Corporation paid the remaining $5,000 due on a mortgage on its plant and equipment, reducing the credit balance of its Mortgage Payable account to zero. The analyzing entry to account for this change and to set out the funds use is:

| | Analyses | |
	Debit	Credit
Mortgage payable...	(f) 5,000	
Funds used for:		
Payment of mortgage...		(f) 5,000

i) During 1973, at the end of each of the first three quarters in the year, the board of directors declared a $700 quarterly cash dividend; and on December 22, 1973, they declared a fourth $1,000 dividend payable on January 15, 1974. This fourth dividend brought the total dividends declared during the year to $3,100. Each declaration was recorded with an entry debiting Retained Earnings and crediting Dividends Payable. On the working paper the four declarations were treated as one and the following single analyzing entry was made to account for $3,100 of the $4,500 total change in the balance of the Retained Earnings account and to set out the funds use:

| | Analyses | |
	Debit	Credit
Retained earnings...	(i) 3,100	
Funds used for:		
Dividends to stockholders		(i) 3,100

Observe the foregoing analyzing entries as they appear above and on the working paper of Illustration 27–4. Note in each case that the debit of the analyzing entry accounts for a change in a noncurrent account and the credit is to the phrase "Funds used for:" and an explanation of the use. Now recall the bookkeeping entries that were used during the year in recording the transactions of these analyzing entries. The recording entries in general journal form appeared as follows:

May	12	Building	14,000.00	
		Cash..		14,000.00
		Paid for addition to building.		
Apr.	23	Land...	3,000.00	
		Cash...		3,000.00
		Purchased land.		
Nov.	15	Mortgage Payable	5,000.00	
		Cash..		5,000.00
		Paid mortgage.		
......	...	Retained Earnings.....................................	3,100.00	
		Dividends Payable...................................		3,100.00
		Declared dividends. (Actually there were four separate entries that totaled this amount.)		

Note that each transaction was originally recorded with a credit to a working capital account. In each case these credits recorded reductions in working capital. Now observe that each analyzing entry is like its original recording entry except that the phrase "Funds used for:" and an explanation of the use are substituted for the original credit to Cash or Dividends Payable. This is common of all analyzing entries that set out uses of funds. Always in such analyzing entries the phrase "Funds used for:" and an explanation of the use are substituted for the original credit to a working capital account.

ANALYZING ENTRIES THAT SET OUT SOURCES OF FUNDS. Four analyzing entries, g, h, d, and e, are required on the working paper of Illustration 27–4 to set out Moss Company's 1973 sources of new working capital. Each is alike in that the phrase "Funds provided by:" and an explanation of the source is debited; each differs as to the account credited. Explanations of the entries follow:

g) On November 3 Moss Company sold for cash and immediately issued 1,500 shares of its $10 par value common stock at $11 per share. This transaction was a source of funds, and the entry in general journal form to record it appeared as follows:

Nov.	3	Cash..	16,500.00	
		Common Stock		15,000.00
		Premium on Common Stock......................		1,500.00
		Sold and issued common stock.		

On the working paper of Illustration 27–4 the following analyzing entry was made to set out this source of funds:

	Analyses	
	Debit	Credit
Funds provided by:		
Sale of stock..	(g) 16,500	
Common stock...		(g) 15,000
Premium on common stock..		(g) 1,500

Note that Cash is debited in the November 3 recording entry shown first above. The debit to Cash recorded an increase in working capital. Observe that the analyzing entry is like the recording entry except that the phrase "Funds provided by:" and an explanation is substituted for the original debit to Cash.

h) The 1973 income statement of Moss Company showed a $11,600 net income. In the 1973 closing entries the amount of this net income was carried to the Retained Earnings account and was partially responsible for the $4,500 change in the balance of this account. However, the $11,600 of earnings was a source of funds; consequently, the following analyzing entry was made on the working paper to set out the source:

	Analyses	
	Debit	Credit
Funds provided by:		
Operations:		
Net income	(h) 11,600	
Retained earnings...		(h) 11,600

d) and (e) Moss Company deducted as expenses on its 1973 income statement $800 depreciation on its equipment and $900 depreciation on its building. As previously explained, although depreciation expense is a rightful deduction from revenues in arriving at net income, the amount of depreciation so deducted must be added to net income in arriving at funds from current operations. Consequently, the following analyzing entries were made on the working paper to account for the changes in the accumulated depreciation accounts and to set out the depreciation amounts with reported net income under "funds provided by operations."

	Analyses	
	Debit	Credit
Funds provided by:		
Operations:		
Depreciation of equipment	(d) 800	
Depreciation of building	(e) 900	
Accumulated depreciation, equipment		(d) 800
Accumulated depreciation, building		(e) 900

ACCOUNTING ENTRIES THAT DID NOT INVOLVE FUNDS. As previously stated, analyzing entries on a funds statement working paper are of three kinds: (1) those that set out sources of funds, (2) those that set out uses of funds, and (3) those that account for the effects of accounting entries that did not involve funds. The following two entries are of the last kind:

a) During 1973 Moss Company retired and scrapped fully depreciated equipment carried on the books at $500. The entry to record the retirement was:

Aug.	27	Accumulated Depreciation, Equipment	500.00	
		Equipment		500.00
		Retired fully depreciated equipment.		

Since funds were not affected by this retirement, the following analyzing entry was made on the working paper to account for the changes in the accounts involved:

	Analyses	
	Debit	Credit
Accumulated depreciation, equipment	(a) 500	
Equipment		(a) 500

Observe that the accounts debited and credited in both entries are the same. In the analyzing entry the debit to Accumulated Depreciation, Equipment helps to account for the change in the balance of this account and the credit to Equipment does account for the change in the Equipment account.

j) At its December meeting the Moss Company board of directors appropriated $4,000 of the balance of its Retained Earnings account as a "reserve for plant expansion" (retained earnings appropriated for plant expansion). Since this transaction did not involve funds, the following analyzing entry was made on the working paper to account for the changes in the accounts involved:

	Analyses	
	Debit	Credit
Retained earnings..	(j) 4,000	
Reserve for plant expansion		(j) 4,000

Notice that the debit of the foregoing entry along with the debit of analyzing entry (*i*) and the credit of entry (*h*) exactly account for the change in the balance of the Retained Earnings account. Also observe that the credit of the foregoing entry accounts for the change in the balance of the Reserve for Plant Expansion account.

Completing the working paper

The foregoing analyzing entries account for all the changes in noncurrent accounts on the working paper of Illustration 27–4. However, in completing the paper a final entry is made to account for the change in the amount of working capital as it appears on the first line of the paper. The entry is:

	Analyses	
	Debit	Credit
Working capital	(k) 4,700	
Increase in working capital		(k) 4,700

Had there been a decrease in working capital instead of an increase, this entry would have a debit to "Decrease in working capital" and a credit to working capital.

After the entry accounting for the change in working capital is made, the working paper is completed by adding the Analyses columns. Then the information on the bottom portion of the paper, the information as to funds sources and uses, is employed to complete the funds flow section of the formal funds statement.

Usefulness of a funds statement ■ In addition to telling from where funds came and where they were used, a funds statement also provides information as to the effectiveness with which management has handled working capital during the period of the statement, shows the adequacy of present funds, and tells a stockholder or investor something of management's plans for the future.

For example, how effective was the Moss Company management in handling working capital during 1973? An examination of the concern's funds statement, Illustration 27–2, shows that in spite of a $4,700 increase in working capital, cash decreased a little over one third, from $8,000 to $5,000, and accounts payable increased in approximately the same proportion, from $9,000 to $12,500. Further examination shows increases of $6,000 in accounts receivable and the $5,000 in inventory, increases that approximately equal and account for the total change in cash, accounts payable, and total working capital. Is this good?

Probably not. For instance, was the increase in inventory an intentional increase that will result in greater sales, or was it a result of poor merchandising? And, unless sales on credit increased materially during the final weeks of 1973, the increase in accounts receivable can only be blamed on slower collections.

As to revealing management's plans, sources and uses of funds are objective evidence of management decisions to dilute ownership rights by issuing more stock, trade on the equity by increasing long-term debt, expand or modernize the plant, or accumulate funds for better investment opportunities expected in the future.

Cash flow

■ Cash flow distinguished from funds flow

Since the word "funds" in the phrase "funds flow" does not mean "cash," it follows that "funds flow" and "cash flow" are different. While funds flow refers to the flow of working capital, cash flow relates to the inflow and outflow of cash only.

Planning and controlling cash flow, or "managing money," is an important phase of management's work. However, cash flow is also important to creditors, stockholders, and investors because cash flow affects ability to meet liabilities, pay dividends, replace plant assets, and to expand or grow.

A complete discussion of cash flow is not attempted in this text.[1] Rather, a simple analysis based on the difference between the accrual basis and the cash basis of accounting is used to introduce the subject and show the nature of a cash flow statement.

Cash flow statement

Illustration 27–5 shows a cash flow statement. Note how such a statement covers a period of time and accounts for the increase or decrease in cash by showing sources and uses of cash.

A work sheet similar to the funds statement working paper is ordinarily used to analyze changes in noncash accounts and to bring together the data for a cash flow statement. However, a discussion of this work sheet is deferred to a more advanced text and the cash flow statement of Illustration 27–5 is based on information in Illustrations 27–6 and 27–7.

An examination of Illustration 27–5 will show that Royal Hardware Company's cash increased during the period of the statement. It was increased $7,000 by "cash from current operations" and $4,500 by cash from the sale of investments; and it was decreased $1,000 by dividends and $6,500 by the purchase of plant assets. Or there was a $4,000 net increase. The cash inflow from the sale of investments and the outflows for dividends and plant assets need no explanation, but the inflow of cash from operations does.

---

[1] See G. A. Welsch, C. T. Zlatkovich, and J. A. White, *Intermediate Accounting* (Homewood, Ill.: Richard D. Irwin, Inc., 1968).

Royal Hardware Company
Cash Flow Statement for Year Ended December 31, 19—

Beginning cash balance			$2,200
Cash was provided by:			
Operations:			
Reported net income (accrual basis)		$ 1,500	
Adjustments to convert income from accrual to cash basis:			
Excess of accrual basis sales over cash basis sales	$ (500)		
Excess of accrual basis cost of sales over cash basis cost	2,000		
Depreciation expense	3,500		
Bad debts expense	200		
Excess of accrual basis salaries and wages over cash basis	400		
Excess of other expenses on a cash basis over an accrual basis	(100)		
Net adjustment		5,500	
Cash from operations		$ 7,000	
Other sources of cash:			
Sale of investments		4,500	
Total cash provided during period		$11,500	
Cash was used to:			
Pay dividends	$1,000		
Purchase new plant assets	6,500		
Total uses of cash during period		7,500	
Net increase in cash			4,000
Ending Cash Balance			$6,200

Illustration
27–5

Royal Hardware Company
Income Statement for Year Ended December 31, 19—

Sales, net			$50,000
Cost of goods sold:			
Inventory, January 1, 19—	$10,000		
Purchases, net	32,000		
Goods for sale	$42,000		
Inventory, December 31, 19—	11,000		
Cost of goods sold		31,000	
Gross profit from sales		$19,000	
Operating expenses:			
Depreciation expense	$ 3,500		
Bad debts expense	200		
Salaries and wages	10,000		
Other expenses	3,800		
Total operating expenses		17,500	
Net Income		$ 1,500	

Illustration
27–6

Condensation of Royal Hardware Company's Cash Account	
(Debits)	**(Credits)**
Balance, January 1 2,200	Cash merchandise purchases 1,000
Cash sales 20,000	Payments to creditors for
Accounts receivable collections 29,500	merchandise purchased 28,000
Sale of investment securities 4,500	Salary and wage payments 9,600
	Payments for other expenses 3,900
	Plant asset purchases 6,500
	Dividend payments 1,000
56,200	50,000

Illustration
27–7

Cash from current operations

If a company uses a cash basis of accounting (see explanation in following section), its net income figure shows the amount of cash it gained from operations. However, since most companies use an accrual basis, for most companies it is necessary to convert their net income from an accrual basis to a cash basis to determine "cash from operations." Note that this is done on a cash flow statement, and understanding the conversion requires a little thought along these lines:

a) Cash flowed into Royal Hardware Company from sales; but the amount did not equal the $50,000 sales figure. (See Illustration 27–6.) Rather, cash from goods sold consisted of cash sales, $20,000, plus collections from customers, $29,500, or to $49,500. (See Illustration 27–7.) Consequently, since cash from goods sold was $500 less than the income statement sales figure, $500 is subtracted in changing income from an accrual basis to a cash basis in Illustration 27–5. (Remember that placing an item in parentheses means it is a subtraction.)

b) Likewise, $31,000 did not flow out to pay for goods sold (Illustration 27–6). Rather the actual cash outflow for merchandise amounted to $29,000, $1,000 for cash purchases plus $28,000 paid to creditors for merchandise (see Illustration 27–7). Therefore, since the cash outflow was $2,000 less than cost of goods sold, $2,000 is added in converting income from an accrual to a cash basis.

c) Since depreciation and bad debts expense did not take cash, the amounts of these income statement items are added back in the conversion.

d) And since cash paid for wages and salaries was $400 less than the income statement amount for this expense and cash paid out for "other expenses" was $100 more than the income statement amount, $400 is added and $100 is subtracted in the conversion.

Cash and accrual bases of accounting

■ There are two bases of accounting in common use: (1) the cash basis and (2) the accrual basis. Under the cash basis of accounting, revenues are considered earned at the time they are received in cash, and expenses are considered to be incurred at the time cash is disbursed in their payment. Consequently, under this system the gain or loss of an accounting period is the difference between revenue receipts and expense disbursements. On the other hand, under the accrual basis of accounting, revenues are credited to the period in which they are earned regardless of when payments are received and expenses are charged to the period in which they are incurred regardless of when cash is disbursed. As a result, under the accrual basis the gain or loss of an accounting period is the difference between revenues earned and expenses incurred. Most enterprises of any size use the accrual basis.

Questions for class discussion

1. What is a funds statement designed to show?
2. When the word "funds" is used in connection with a funds statement, what are "funds"?
3. What are circulating assets and why are they so called?
4. List several sources of funds. Where may a company apply funds?
5. On December 12 a company borrowed $10,000 by giving its bank a 60-day, interest-bearing note. Will this transaction appear on the year-end funds statement as a source of funds?
6. A company that began an accounting period with $45,000 of merchandise inventory, ended the period with $40,000 of inventory. Was this decrease in inventory a source of funds?
7. A company wrote off a fully depreciated plant asset. What account balances appearing on the company's funds statement working paper were affected by the write-off? How was the write-off treated on the funds statement working paper? Why was it treated in this manner?
8. Explain why such expenses as depreciation, amortization of patents, and of bond discount are added to the net income in order to determine funds provided by business operations.
9. What are the three kinds of analyzing entries on a funds statement working paper?
10. When a funds statement working paper is prepared, all changes in noncurrent balance sheet account balances between the beginning and end of the period covered by the statement are accounted for on the working paper. Why?
11. What is the primary difference between a "cash flow" statement and a "funds" statement?
12. Do short-term bank loans appear on a funds statement as a source of funds? Why or why not? Do they appear on a cash flow statement as a source of cash?

Exercise 27–1

Prepare from the following condensed income statement a list and the total of funds from operations:

ALBERTA CORPORATION, LTD.
Income Statement for Year Ended December 31, 19—

Sales..		$800,000
Cost of goods sold		520,000
Gross profit from sales...		$280,000
Operating expenses:		
Salaries and wages (including $1,000 accrued)	$125,000	
Depreciation expense	15,000	
Rent expense	36,000	
Patents written off...	3,000	
Bad debts expense (allowance method)....................	4,000	183,000
Operating income..		$ 97,000
Bond interest expense (including $6,000 accrued and		
$500 of bond discount amortized).......................		12,500
Net Income		$ 84,500

Exercise 27–2

The 1972 and 1973 trial balances of Ontario Company follow. From the information prepare the working capital changes section of the company's 1973 funds statement:

	1972		1973	
Cash..	$ 12,000		$ 10,000	
Notes receivable...	3,000		5,000	
Accounts receivable, net	30,000		25,000	
Merchandise inventory	50,000		55,000	
Prepaid expenses.......................................	1,000		2,000	
Equipment..	100,000		109,000	
Accumulated depreciation, equipment		$ 20,000		$ 25,000
Notes payable...		8,000		10,000
Accounts payable		20,000		18,000
Taxes payable...		5,000		4,000
Wages payable		1,000		2,000
Mortgage payable (due 1990).........................		25,000		25,000
Common stock		100,000		100,000
Retained earnings		17,000		22,000
Totals...	$196,000	$196,000	$206,000	$206,000

Exercise 27–3

Spring Company's 1972 and 1973 balance sheets carried the following items:

Debits	December 31 1972	1973
Cash	$ 4,000	$ 5,000
Accounts receivable, net..	9,000	8,000
Merchandise inventory	18,000	20,000
Equipment	15,000	19,000
Totals...	$46,000	$52,000

Credits		
Accumulated depreciation, equipment............................	$ 3,000	$ 4,000
Accounts payable..	5,000	7,000
Taxes payable...	2,000	1,000
Common stock, $10 par value	25,000	27,000
Premium on common stock..	5,000	6,000
Retained earnings...	6,000	7,000
Totals...	$46,000	$52,000

Required:

Prepare a funds statement working paper and a funds statement, using the following information from the company's 1973 income statement and accounts:

a) The company earned $6,000 during 1973.

b) Its equipment depreciated $1,500 in 1973.

c) Equipment costing $4,500 was purchased.

d) Fully depreciated equipment that cost $500 was discarded and its cost and accumulated depreciation were removed from the accounts.

e) Two hundred shares of stock were sold and issued at $15 per share.

f) The company declared $5,000 of dividends during the year.

Exercise 27–4

From the following income statement and analysis of the Cash account, both for the same year, prepare a cash flow statement.

HOWE COMPANY

Income Statement for Year Ended December 31, 19—

Sales, net		$ 91,000
Cost of goods sold:		
Merchandise inventory, January 1, 19—	$12,000	
Purchases..	50,000	
Goods for sale	$62,000	
Merchandise inventory, December 31, 19—	11,000	
Cost of goods sold		51,000
Gross profit from sales		$ 40,000
Operating expenses:		
Salaries and wages expense	$12,000	
Rent expense..	9,000	
Depreciation expense, equipment	4,000	
Bad debts expense	1,000	26,000
Net Income		$ 14,000

Cash Account Analysis

Cash balance, January 1, 19–		$ 8,000
Debits:		
Cash sales	$40,000	
Accounts receivable collections	52,000	
Bank loan..	5,000	97,000
Total		$105,000
Credits:		
Payments to creditors for merchandise	$51,500	
Salaries and wages paid	11,800	
Rent payments..	9,000	
Payment for new equipment purchased....................	12,200	
Dividends paid...	10,000	94,500
Cash Balance, December 31, 19–.............................		$ 10,500

Problems   **Problem 27–1**

Bragg Company's 1972 and 1973 balance sheets carried these items:

	December 31	
Debits	*1972*	*1973*
Cash	$ 4,300	$ 7,500
Accounts receivable, net...	10,000	8,000
Merchandise inventory..	32,000	31,500
Prepaid expenses...	1,200	1,000
Equipment	24,000	30,100
Totals...	$71,500	$78,100

Credits		
Accumulated depreciation, equipment............................	$ 4,800	$ 6,100
Accounts payable...	17,900	14,300
Notes payable...	1,500	2,500
Mortgage payable...	10,000	6,000
Common stock, $10 par value	25,000	30,000
Premium on common stock...		2,500
Retained earnings..	12,300	16,700
Totals...	$71,500	$78,100

Required:

Prepare a funds statement working paper and a funds statement for the company, using this additional information from its 1973 income statement and accounting records:

a) Net income for the year, $7,400.

b) The equipment depreciated $2,100 during the year.

c) Fully depreciated equipment that cost $800 was discarded, and its cost and accumulated depreciation were removed from the accounts.

d) Equipment costing $6,900 was purchased.
e) The mortgage was reduced by a $4,000 payment.
f) Five hundred shares of common stock were issued at $15 per share.
g) Dividends totaling $3,000 were declared and paid.

Problem 27–2

Coral Company's 1972 and 1973 balance sheets carried these items:

	December 31	
Debits	*1972*	*1973*
Cash...	$ 11,800	$ 12,700
Accounts receivable, net	33,400	34,900
Merchandise inventory...	86,700	85,900
Other current assets	1,800	2,000
Office equipment..	6,100	5,400
Store equipment...	27,800	31,700
Totals	$167,600	$172,600

Credits		
Accumulated depreciation, office equipment .... $	2,400	$ 2,500
Accumulated depreciation, store equipment.................	6,500	7,400
Accounts payable...	20,200	19,500
Notes payable	5,000	4,500
Federal income taxes payable	3,300	3,500
Common stock, $5 par value......................................	100,000	105,000
Premium on common stock..	5,500	8,500
Retained earnings...	24,700	21,700
Totals	$167,600	$172,600

An examination of the company's statements and accounts showed:
a) A $15,000 net income was earned in 1973.
b) Depreciation charged on office equipment, $600; and on store equipment, $1,500.
c) Office equipment that had cost $700 and had been depreciated $500 was sold for its book value.
d) Store equipment costing $4,500 was purchased.
e) Fully depreciated store equipment that cost $600 was discarded, and its cost and accumulated depreciation were removed from the accounts.
f) Cash dividends totaling $10,000 were declared during the year.
g) A 1,000-share stock dividend was declared and distributed during the year at a time the company's stock was selling at $8 per share.

Required:
Prepare a funds statement working paper and a funds statement for the company.

Problem 27–3

The 1972 and 1973 balance sheets of Hydra Sales carried the following debit and credit amounts:

| | December 31 | |
Debits	1972	1973
Cash	$ 22,300	$ 16,100
Accounts receivable, net	15,600	16,200
Merchandise inventory	51,400	50,200
Prepaid expenses	1,100	1,300
Store equipment	24,300	26,000
Office equipment	4,200	4,400
Land		20,000
Building		100,000
Totals	$118,900	$234,200

Credits		
Accumulated depreciation, store equipment	$ 3,600	$ 5,200
Accumulated depreciation, office equipment	1,300	1,400
Accumulated depreciation, building		1,200
Accounts payable	18,700	17,300
Taxes payable	4,100	4,400
Mortgage payable		80,000
Common stock, $10 par value	80,000	100,000
Premium on common stock		4,000
Retained earnings	11,200	20,700
Totals	$118,900	$234,200

An examination of the company's 1973 income statement and accounting records showed:

a) A $15,500 net income for the year.
b) Depreciation on store equipment, $2,400; on office equipment, $400; and on the building, $1,200.
c) Store equipment that cost $2,500 was purchased during the year.
d) Fully depreciated store equipment that cost $800 was discarded and its cost and accumulated depreciation were removed from the accounts.
e) Office equipment that cost $500 and had been depreciated $300 was traded in on new office equipment priced at $800. A $300 trade-in allowance was received.
f) During the year the company purchased the building it occupied and had previously rented, paying $40,000 in cash and giving a mortgage for the balance.
g) Two thousand shares of common stock were issued at $12 per share.
h) Dividends totaling $6,000 were declared during the year.

Required:
Prepare a funds statement working paper and a funds statement for the company.

Problem 27–4

The debit and credit amounts from Pacific Corporation's 1972 and 1973 balance sheets and its noncurrent accounts follow:

	December 31	
Debits	1972	1973
Cash..	$ 22,900	$ 18,700
Accounts receivable, net	32,100	30,400
Merchandise inventory..	56,400	55,100
Prepaid expenses	1,700	1,900
Store equipment...	32,800	40,400
Land..	30,000	30,000
Building..	112,500	181,000
Totals	$288,400	$357,500

Credits

Accumulated depreciation, store equipment.................	$ 13,700	$ 16,200
Accumulated depreciation, building..........................	20,200	23,600
Accounts payable...	24,600	25,700
Wages payable..	1,800	2,100
Income taxes payable	4,200	4,100
Mortgage interest payable......................................		1,000
Cash dividends payable..	7,500	5,000
Mortgage payable...		50,000
Common stock, $10 par value	150,000	150,000
Premium on common stock......................................	15,000	18,000
Stock dividend distributable...................................		7,500
Retained earnings..	51,400	54,300
Totals	$288,400	$357,500

Store Equipment

Date		Explanation	Debit	Credit	Balance
1973					
Jan.	1	Balance			32,800
Apr.	4	Purchased new equipment	8,700		41,500
	7	Discarded equipment		1,100	40,400

Accumulated Depreciation, Store Equipment

Date		Explanation	Debit	Credit	Balance
1973					
Jan.	1	Balance			13,700
Apr.	7	Discarded equipment	1,100		12,600
Dec.	31	Year's depreciation		3,600	16,200

Land

Date		Explanation	Debit	Credit	Balance
1973					
Jan.	1	Balance			30,000

Building

Date		Explanation	Debit	Credit	Balance
1973					
Jan.	1	Balance			112,500
Mar.	17	Building addition	68,500		181,000

Accumulated Depreciation, Building

Date		Explanation	Debit	Credit	Balance
1973					
Jan.	1	Balance			20,200
Dec.	31	Year's depreciation		3,400	23,600

Mortgage Payable

Date		Explanation	Debit	Credit	Balance
1973					
Mar.	15			50,000	50,000

Common Stock

Date		Explanation	Debit	Credit	Balance
1973					
Jan.	1	Balance			150,000

Premium on Common Stock

Date		Explanation	Debit	Credit	Balance
1973					
Jan.	1	Balance			15,000
Dec.	23	Stock dividend		3,000	18,000

Stock Dividend Distributable

Date		Explanation	Debit	Credit	Balance
1973					
Dec.	23	Stock dividend		7,500	7,500

Retained Earnings

Date		Explanation	Debit	Credit	Balance
1973					
Jan.	1	Balance			51,400
Dec.	23	Stock dividend	10,500		40,900
	23	Cash dividend	5,000		35,900
	31	Net income		18,400	54,300

Required:
Use the information given to prepare a funds statement working paper and a funds statement for the company.

Problem 27–5

Last year's income statement and analysis of the Cash account of Cedar Sales follow:

CEDAR SALES

Income Statement for Year Ended December 31, 19—

Sales, net		$125,400
Cost of goods sold:		
Merchandise inventory, January 1, 19—	$15,300	
Purchases, net...	76,600	
Goods for sale	$91,900	
Merchandise inventory, December 31, 19—	16,700	
Cost of goods sold		75,200
Gross profit from sales		$ 50,200
Operating expenses:		
Salaries and wages..	$26,400	
Rent expense...	7,200	
Depreciation of store equipment.............................	1,800	
Bad debts expense	500	
Store supplies used	600	
Other operating expenses......................................	1,300	
Total operating expenses......................................		37,800
Net Income		$ 12,400

Analysis of Cash Account

Cash balance, January 1, 19—		$ 3,900
Debits:		
Cash sales...	$27,600	
Accounts receivable collections..............................	98,700	
Sale of equipment	300	
Bank loan..	6,000	132,600
Total		$136,500
Credits:		
Rent payments...	$ 7,200	
Payments to creditors for merchandise purchased	75,900	
Payments to creditors for store supplies bought	700	
Salary and wage payments	26,300	
Other expense payments.......................................	1,200	
New store equipment purchased.............................	9,800	
Personal withdrawals by the proprietor.....................	9,000	130,100
Cash Balance, December 31, 19—..............................		$ 6,400

The equipment was sold at book value.

Required:

Prepare a cash flow statement for Cedar Sales.

Alternate problems

Problem 27–2A

The 1972 and 1973 balance sheets of Northwest Company carried these items:

	December 31	
Debits	*1972*	*1973*
Cash...	$ 12,600	$ 10,200
Accounts receivable, net	32,900	35,100
Merchandise inventory..	86,400	85,200
Prepaid expenses	1,800	1,500
Office equipment...	5,600	5,000
Store equipment..	28,300	29,800
Totals	$167,600	$166,800

Credits		
Accumulated depreciation, office equipment	$ 2,400	$ 2,600
Accumulated depreciation, store equipment.................	6,500	7,500
Accounts payable...	23,500	22,400
Notes payable	5,000	10,000
Common stock, $10 par value.................................	100,000	110,000
Premium on common stock......................................	5,500	6,500
Retained earnings..	24,700	7,800
Totals	$167,600	$166,800

Required:

Use the following additional information and prepare a funds statement working paper and a funds statement for the company.

a) The company suffered a $1,900 net loss during 1973.

b) Depreciation expense charged on office equipment during the year, $500; and on store equipment, $1,700.

c) Office equipment carried at its $600 cost less $300 accumulated depreciation was sold at its book value.

d) Store equipment costing $2,200 was purchased.

e) Fully depreciated store equipment that cost $700 was discarded, and its cost and accumulated depreciation were removed from the accounts.

f) Cash dividends totaling $4,000 were declared during the year.

g) A 1,000-share stock dividend was declared and distributed. On the declaration date the company's shares were selling at $11 each.

Clay Barton, as a single proprietor, operates Clay's Country Store. At the ends of 1972 and 1973 the store's balance sheets carried this information:

	December 31	
Debits	*1972*	*1973*
Cash	$ 6,400	$ 7,100
Accounts receivable, net	17,200	16,800
Merchandise inventory	33,700	36,400
Other current assets	800	500
Store equipment	8,400	13,100
Totals	$66,500	$73,900

Credits		
Accumulated depreciation, store equipment	$ 3,200	$ 1,800
Accounts payable	16,800	14,200
Clay Barton, capital	46,500	57,900
Totals	$66,500	$73,900

Clay Barton's 1973 statement showing changes in the proprietor's Capital account carried the following information:

Clay Barton, capital, January 1, 1973		$46,500
Add additional investment		5,000
Total investment		$51,500
Net income per income statement	$12,400	
Less withdrawals	6,000	
Excess of income over withdrawals		6,400
Clay Barton, Capital, December 31, 1973		$57,900

The store equipment accounts showed: (1) $1,200 depreciation expense on store equipment recorded in 1973; (2) store equipment costing $4,800 was purchased; (3) equipment carried on the books on the day of its exchange at its $2,800 cost, less $2,400 accumulated depreciation, was traded on new equipment having a $3,100 cash price, a $600 trade-in allowance was received; and (4) fully depreciated equipment that cost $200 was junked and its cost and accumulated depreciation were removed from the accounts.

Required:
Prepare a funds statement working paper and a funds statement for the store.

Problem 27–5A

Finlay Supply's income statement and analysis of its Cash account for the year of the statement follow:

Income Statement for Year Ended December 31, 19—

Sales, net..		$113,500
Cost of goods sold:		
Merchandise inventory, January 1, 19—..................	$ 21,200	
Purchases, net...	79,500	
Goods available for sale.......................................	$100,700	
Merchandise inventory, December 31, 19—.............	22,300	
Cost of goods sold		78,400
Gross profit from sales..		$ 35,100
Operating expenses:		
Rent expense	$ 6,000	
Salaries and wages	15,900	
Bad debts expense	600	
Depreciation expense, store equipment....................	1,400	
Other operating expenses	1,700	
Total operating expenses.....................................		25,600
Net Income		$ 9,500

Analysis of Cash Account

Cash balance, January 1, 19—................................		$ 4,300
Debits:		
Cash sale receipts	$ 37,200	
Accounts receivable collections.............................	75,900	
Sale of equipment	200	
Bank loan..	5,000	118,300
Total..		$122,600
Credits:		
Creditor payments for merchandise.........................	$ 78,300	
Rent payments	6,500	
Salary and wage payments....................................	15,700	
Other expense payments	1,600	
Payment for new store equipment purchased	5,800	
Personal withdrawals by proprietor.........................	8,400	116,300
Cash Balance, December 31, 19—		$ 6,300

The equipment was sold at book value.

Required:
Prepare a cash flow statement for the concern.

Decision problem 27–1, Fisherman's Paradise   Terry Davis owns Fisherman's Paradise, a sporting goods store; and during 1973 he remodeled and replaced $20,000 of the store's fully depreciated equipment with new equipment costing $25,000. However, by the year-end he was having trouble meeting the store's current expenses and had to secure a $6,000 short-term bank loan. As a result he asked his accountant to prepare some sort of a report showing what had happened to the store's funds during the year. The accountant analyzed the changes in the store's 1973 accounts and produced the following funds statement:

FISHERMAN'S PARADISE
Funds Statement, Year Ended December 31, 1973

Sources of funds:

Income from operations...............................	$17,700	
Depreciation on store equipment.................	5,000	
Additional investment of proprietor	5,000	$27,700

Uses of funds:

Purchase of new equipment:

Cost..	$25,000		
Less mortgage placed on equipment..........	12,500	$12,500	
Personal withdrawals of proprietor		12,000	24,500
Net Increase in Funds..................................			$ 3,200

On reading the report, Mr. Davis was dumbfounded by the $3,200 increase in funds in a year he knew his store's bank balance had decreased by $8,000. Also, he could not understand how depreciation was a source of funds, but the $6,000 bank loan was not. Explain these points to Mr. Davis, and attach to your explanations any additional or different statement from that prepared by the accountant that you think helps to make your explanation clear.

The following post-closing trial balances were used by the accountant in preparing the store's funds statement:

FISHERMAN'S PARADISE
1972–73 Post-Closing Trial Balances

	Dec. 31, 1972		Dec. 31, 1973	
Cash...	$10,500		$ 2,500	
Accounts receivable.........................	14,300		17,600	
Allowance for doubtful accounts		$ 300		$ 500
Merchandise inventory	17,400		29,600	
Prepaid expenses............................	500		800	
Store equipment	40,000		45,000	
Accumulated depr., store equipment ...		26,000		11,000
Notes payable................................				6,000
Accounts payable		11,500		10,000
Accrued payables		700		600
Mortgage payable (due 1975–80)........				12,500
Terry Davis, capital........................		44,200		54,900
Totals......................................	$82,700	$82,700	$95,500	$95,500

Decision problem 27-2, Western Store

At the end of 1973 the accountant of Western Store prepared the following funds statement and the income statement at the top of the next page for the store's owner, Ted West.

WESTERN STORE
Funds Statement for Year Ended December 31, 1973

FUNDS CHANGES	Dec. 31, 1972	Dec. 31, 1973	Funds Increases	Decreases
Current assets:				
Cash	$15,500	$ 3,000		$12,500
Accounts receivable	32,000	38,000	$ 6,000	
Merchandise inventory	25,000	35,000	10,000	
Prepaid expenses	500	1,000	500	
Total current assets	$73,000	$77,000		
Current liabilities:				
Notes payable		$ 5,000		5,000
Accounts payable	$25,000	21,000	4,000	
Salaries and wages payable	2,000	1,000	1,000	
Total current liabilities	$27,000	$27,000		
Funds	$46,000	$50,000		
			$21,500	$17,500
Increase in Funds				4,000
			$21,500	$21,500

FLOW OF FUNDS

Funds were provided by:
Current operations:
Net income $30,000
Depreciation of plant assets 12,000

Total new funds $42,000
Funds were used for:
Purchases of new plant assets $20,000
Reduction of mortgage 6,000
Personal withdrawals of proprietor 12,000

Total uses of funds 38,000
Increase in Funds .... $ 4,000

When Mr. West saw the income statement, he was amazed to learn that his net income had doubled in 1973, and he could not understand how this could happen in a year in which his cash had declined to the point that he had found it necessary in late December to secure a $5,000 short-term bank loan in order

	1972		1973	
Sales......................................		$250,000		$300,000
Cost of goods sold:				
Inventory, January 1	$ 30,000		$ 25,000	
Purchases	150,000		190,000	
Goods for sale......................	$180,000		$215,000	
Inventory, December 31	25,000		35,000	
Cost of goods sold		155,000		180,000
Gross profit from sales...............		$ 95,000		$120,000
Operating expenses:				
Salaries and wages	$ 69,000		$ 76,000	
Depreciation of plant assets.....	9,500		12,000	
Insurance and supplies............	1,500		2,000	
Total operating expenses.........		80,000		90,000
Net Income		$ 15,000		$ 30,000

to meet his current expenses. His accountant pointed to the funds statement by way of explanation, but this statement only confused Mr. West further. He could not understand how depreciation could be a source of funds, while a bank loan was not, and he could not understand how his funds could increase $4,000 at a time when his cash decreased $12,500.

Explain the points Mr. West finds confusing. Attach to your explanation a statement showing the cash generated by his store's 1973 operations and a second statement showing the store's sources and uses of cash.

Chapter 28

Tax considerations in business decisions

■ Not too many years ago, when tax rates were low, management could afford to ignore or dismiss as of minor importance the tax effects of a business decision; but today, when about half the income of a business must commonly be paid out in income taxes, this is no longer wise. Today, a successful management must constantly be alert to every possible tax savings, recognizing that it is often necessary to earn two "pretax dollars" in order to keep one "after-tax dollar," or that a dollar of income tax saved is commonly worth a two-dollar reduction in any other expense.

Tax planning

■ When a taxpayer plans his affairs in such a way as to incur the smallest possible tax liability, he is engaged in tax planning. Tax planning requires the application of tax laws to the alternate ways in which every transaction may be completed, and a choice in each case of the way that will result in the smallest tax liability.

Normally tax planning requires that a tax-saving opportunity be recognized at the time it arises. This is because although it is sometimes possible to take advantage of a previously overlooked tax saving, the common result of an overlooked opportunity is a lost opportunity, since the Internal Revenue Service usually deems the original action in a tax situation the final action for tax purposes.

Since effective tax planning requires an extensive knowledge of both tax laws and business procedures, it is not the purpose of this chapter to make expert tax planners of elementary accounting students. Rather, the purpose is to make students aware of the merits of effective tax planning, recognizing that for complete and effective planning, the average student, businessman, or citizen should seek the advice of a certified public accountant, tax attorney, or other qualified person.

Tax evasion and tax avoidance

■ In any discussion of taxes a clear distinction should be drawn between tax evasion and tax avoidance. Tax evasion is illegal and may result in heavy penalties; but tax avoidance is a perfectly legal and profitable activity.

Taxes are avoided by preventing a tax liability from coming into existence. This may be accomplished by any legal means, for example, by the way in which a transaction is completed, or the manner in which a business is organized, or by a wise selection from among the options provided in the Internal Revenue Code. It makes no difference how, so long as the means is legal and it prevents a tax liability from arising.

In contrast, tax evasion involves the fraudulent denial and concealment of an existing tax liability. For example, taxes are evaded when taxable income, such as interest, dividends, tips, fees, or profits from the sale of stocks, bonds, and other assets, is unreported. Taxes are also evaded when items not legally deductible from income are deducted. For example, taxes are evaded when the costs of operating the family automobile are deducted as a business expense, or when charitable contributions not allowed or not made are deducted. Insofar as this text is concerned, tax evasion is illegal and should be scrupulously avoided.

State and municipal income taxes

■ Most states and a number of cities levy income taxes, in most cases modeling their laws after the federal laws. However, other than noting the existence of such laws and that they increase the total tax burden and make tax planning even more important, the following discussion is limited to the federal income tax.

History and objectives of the federal income tax

■ Although the federal government first used an income tax during the War between the States, the history of today's federal income tax dates from the 1913 ratification of the Sixteenth Amendment, which cleared away all questions as to the constitutionality of such a tax. Since its ratification, Congress has passed more than 40 revenue acts and other laws implementing the tax, placing the responsibility for their enforcement in the hands of the Treasury Department acting through the Internal Revenue Service.

The original purpose of the federal income tax was to raise revenue, but over the years this original goal has been expanded to include the following and other nonrevenue objectives:

1. To assist small businesses.
2. To encourage foreign trade.
3. To encourage exploration for oil and minerals.
4. To redistribute the national income.
5. To control inflation and deflation.
6. To stimulate business.
7. To attain full employment.
8. To support social objectives.

Also, just as the objectives have expanded over the years, so have the rates and the number of people required to pay taxes. In 1913 the minimum rate was 1% and the maximum for individuals was 7. This contrasts with today's minimum 14% rate for individuals and maximum of 70. Likewise, the total number of tax returns filed has grown from a few thousand in 1913 to well over 100,000,000 last year.

Synopsis of the federal income tax ■ The following brief synopsis of the federal income tax is given at this point because it is necessary to know something about the federal income tax in order to appreciate its effect on business decisions.

Classes of taxpayers

Federal income tax law recognizes four classes of taxpayers: individuals, corporations, estates, and trusts. Members of each class must file returns and pay taxes on taxable income.

A business operated as a single proprietorship or partnership is not treated as a separate taxable entity under the law. Rather, a single proprietor must report the income from his business on his individual return; and although a partnership must file an information return showing its net income and the distributive shares of the partners, each partner is required to include his share on his individual return. In other words, the income of a single proprietorship or partnership, whether withdrawn from the business or not, is taxed as the individual income of the single proprietor or partners.

The treatment given corporations under the law is different, however. A business operated as a corporation must file a return and pay taxes on its taxable income. Also, if a corporation pays out in dividends some or all of its "after-tax income," its stockholders must report these dividends as income on their individual returns. Because of this, it is commonly claimed that corporation income is taxed twice, once to the corporation and again to its stockholders.

The individual income tax

The amount of federal income tax an individual must pay each year depends upon his gross income, deductions, exemptions, and tax credits; and it is calculated as follows:

Gross income..		$x,xxx
Less: Deductions to arrive at adjusted gross income....................		x,xxx
Adjusted gross income...		$x,xxx
Less: a) Itemized deductions (or a standard deduction)	$xxx	
b) Deduction for exemptions...	xxx	
Taxable income..		$x,xxx
Taxable income (from previous calculation) multiplied by the proper tax rates equals income tax before tax credits and prepayments		$x,xxx
Less: Tax credits and prepayments...		x,xxx
Net Tax Payable (or Refund)		$ xxx

Several of the items in the calculation just outlined require additional explanation, for example:

GROSS INCOME. Income tax law defines gross income as *all income from whatever source derived, unless expressly excluded by law.* Gross income therefore includes income from operating a business, gains from property sales, dividends, interest, rents, royalties, and compensation for services, such as salaries, wages, fees, commissions, bonuses, and tips. Actually, the answers to two questions are all that is required to determine whether an item should be included or excluded. The two questions are: (1) Is the item income? (2) Is it expressly excluded by law? If an item is income and not specifically excluded, it must be included.

Certain items are recognized as not being income, for example, gifts, inheritances, scholarships, social security benefits, workmen's compensation insurance, and in most cases the proceeds of life insurance policies paid upon the death of the insured. These are not income and are excluded.

Other items, such as the first $100 of dividend income and interest on the obligations of the states and their subdivisions are specifically excluded. In the case of the first exclusion, Congress, in partial recognition of the claim that corporation income is "taxed twice," and for other reasons, has so written the law as to permit an individual owner of stock in qualifying domestic corporations to exclude from gross income the first $100 in dividends received on this stock. In case of the second, the Supreme Court has held that the power to tax the interest paid on debts of the states and their subdivisions is the power to destroy these governmental units, and consequently violates constitutional guarantees. As a result, interest on the bonds of the states and their subdivisions, with a few exceptions, is excluded from gross income.

DEDUCTIONS TO ARRIVE AT ADJUSTED GROSS INCOME. These are generally deductions of a business nature. For example, all ordinary and necessary expenses of carrying on a business, trade, or profession are deductions to arrive at adjusted gross income. To understand this, recognize that under income tax law gross profit from sales (sales less cost of goods sold) is gross income to a merchant, that gross legal fees earned are gross income to a lawyer, and gross rentals from a building are gross income to a landlord. Consequently, the merchant, the lawyer, and the landlord may each deduct all ordinary and necessary expenses of carrying on his business or profession, such as salaries, wages, rent, depreciation, supplies used, repairs, maintenance, insurance, taxes, interest, and so on.

In addition to the foregoing business expenses, from a tax management point of view, a very important deduction from gross income is the long-term capital gain deduction, which permits under certain circumstances the deduction from gross income of one half the net long-term gains from capital asset sales and exchanges. This is discussed in more detail later in this chapter.

DEDUCTIONS FROM ADJUSTED GROSS INCOME. By legislative grace an individual taxpayer is permitted certain deductions from adjusted gross income. These are of two kinds. The first consists of certain personal expenses, commonly called itemized deductions, and the second is a deduction for exemptions.

In the case of the first kind of deduction, the taxpayer has a choice. He may either deduct his allowable itemized deductions (personal interest expense, state and local taxes, charitable contributions, medical expenses, casualty losses over $100 for each loss, and so on) or he may deduct a standard deduction. The standard deduction is the larger of a $1,000 low-income allowance ($500 for a married individual filing a separate return) or a percentage standard deduction. For 1973 and after the percentage standard deduction is 15% of adjusted gross income, with a maximum of $2,000 ($1,000 each for a married couple filing separate returns).

As to the second kind of deduction, the deduction for exemptions, a taxpayer is allowed one exemption for himself and one for each dependent. Dependents commonly include each minor child or closely related person for whom the taxpayer contributes more than half toward the dependent's support. Additional exemptions are allowed if the taxpayer or his wife is over 65 or if either is blind. If a husband and wife file a joint return, each is a taxpayer and they combine their exemptions. For each exemption, the taxpayer may deduct $750 from adjusted gross income in 1973 and thereafter.

FEDERAL INCOME TAX RATES. Federal income tax rates are progressive in nature. By this is meant that each additional segment or bracket of taxable income is subject to a higher rate than the preceding segment or bracket. This may be seen by examining Illustration 28–1 which shows the rates for an unmarried person not qualifying as a head of household and for married persons filing a joint return.

To use the rate schedules of Illustration 28–1, a taxpayer reads down the columns marked "If taxable income is:" until he comes to the bracket of his taxable income. For example, if an unmarried taxpayer's taxable income is $8,400, the taxpayer reads down the proper columns to the bracket "over $8,000 but not over $10,000." The remaining columns then tell him that the tax on $8,400 is $1,590 plus 25% of the excess over $8,000, or is $1,590 + (25% × $400) or is $1,690.

Schedule X—Single Taxpayers and Married Persons Filing Separate Returns

If the amount on line 50, Form 1040 is: Enter on lines 19 and 51, Form 1040:
Not over $500....14% of the amount on line 50.

Over—	But not over—		of excess over—
$500	$1,000	$70+15%	$500
$1,000	$1,500	$145+16%	$1,000
$1,500	$2,000	$225+17%	$1,500
$2,000	$4,000	$310+19%	$2,000
$4,000	$6,000	$690+21%	$4,000
$6,000	$8,000	$1,110+24%	$6,000
$8,000	$10,000	$1,590+25%	$8,000
$10,000	$12,000	$2,090+27%	$10,000
$12,000	$14,000	$2,630+29%	$12,000
$14,000	$16,000	$3,210+31%	$14,000
$16,000	$18,000	$3,830+34%	$16,000
$18,000	$20,000	$4,510+36%	$18,000
$20,000	$22,000	$5,230+38%	$20,000
$22,000	$26,000	$5,990+40%	$22,000
$26,000	$32,000	$7,590+45%	$26,000
$32,000	$38,000	$10,290+50%	$32,000
$38,000	$44,000	$13,290+55%	$38,000
$44,000	$50,000	$16,590+60%	$44,000
$50,000	$60,000	$20,190+62%	$50,000
$60,000	$70,000	$26,390+64%	$60,000
$70,000	$80,000	$32,790+66%	$70,000
$80,000	$90,000	$39,390+68%	$80,000
$90,000	$100,000	$46,190+69%	$90,000
$100,000	...	$53,090+70%	$100,000

Schedule Y—Married Taxpayers Filing Joint Returns and Certain Widows and Widowers

If the amount on line 50, Form 1040 is: Enter on lines 19 and 51, Form 1040:
Not over $1000....14% of the amount on line 50.

Over—	But not over—		of excess over—
$1,000	$2,000	$140+15%	$1,000
$2,000	$3,000	$290+16%	$2,000
$3,000	$4,000	$450+17%	$3,000
$4,000	$8,000	$620+19%	$4,000
$8,000	$12,000	$1,380+22%	$8,000
$12,000	$16,000	$2,260+25%	$12,000
$16,000	$20,000	$3,260+28%	$16,000
$20,000	$24,000	$4,380+32%	$20,000
$24,000	$28,000	$5,660+36%	$24,000
$28,000	$32,000	$7,100+39%	$28,000
$32,000	$36,000	$8,660+42%	$32,000
$36,000	$40,000	$10,340+45%	$36,000
$40,000	$44,000	$12,140+48%	$40,000
$44,000	$52,000	$14,060+50%	$44,000
$52,000	$64,000	$18,060+53%	$52,000
$64,000	$76,000	$24,420+55%	$64,000
$76,000	$88,000	$31,020+58%	$76,000
$88,000	$100,000	$37,980+60%	$88,000
$100,000	$120,000	$45,180+62%	$100,000
$120,000	$140,000	$57,580+64%	$120,000
$140,000	$160,000	$70,380+66%	$140,000
$160,000	$180,000	$83,580+68%	$160,000
$180,000	$200,000	$97,180+69%	$180,000
$200,000	...	$110,980+70%	$200,000

Illustration
28–1

A husband and wife have a choice. They may combine their incomes and use the rate schedule shown for married individuals or they may file separate returns using the schedule for single taxpayers.

Also, a person who can qualify as a head of household may use a rate schedule (not shown) in which the rates fall between those for unmarried individuals and those for married couples filing jointly. Generally a head of household is an unmarried or legally separated person who maintains a home in which live his or her unmarried child or other qualifying dependent.

Regardless of the rate schedule used, it is generally recognized that our federal income tax rates are steeply progressive. Proponents claim that this is only fair, since the taxpayers most able to pay, those with higher incomes, are subject to higher rates. Opponents, on the other hand, claim the high rates stifle initiative. For example, a young unmarried executive earning $25,000 per year, upon being offered a new job carrying additional responsibilities and a $5,000 salary increase, might turn the new job down, feeling the after-tax increase in pay insufficient to compensate for the extra responsibilities. In this case he could keep after federal income taxes just $2,800 of the increase.

Whether or not our progressive income tax rates stifle initiative is probably open to debate. However, there is no question that the rates do cause high-income taxpayers to search for tax-saving opportunities.

TAX CREDITS AND PREPAYMENTS. Most taxpayers have income taxes withheld from salaries and wages, and many are required to make advance payments of estimated tax. Both are examples of prepayments. A taxpayer who is retired may receive a retirement income credit, and some taxpayers are eligible for a foreign tax credit. However, these need not be discussed here.

Special tax treatment of capital gains and losses

From a tax-saving point of view, one of the most important features of our federal income tax laws is the special treatment given long-term gains from capital asset sales and exchanges. The usual effect of this special treatment is a tax on net long-term capital gains that is one half, or less than one half, the tax on an equal amount of income from some other source, commonly called "ordinary income." For this reason, whenever possible, tax planners try to cause income to emerge in the form of long-term capital gains rather than as ordinary income.

The Internal Revenue Code defines a capital asset as any item of property except (a) inventories, (b) trade notes and accounts receivable, (c) real property and depreciable property used in a trade or business, (d) copyrights and similar property in the hands of the creator of the copyrighted works or his donee and certain other transferees, and (e) any government obligation due within one year and issued at a discount. Common examples of capital assets held by individuals and subject to sale or exchange are stocks, bonds, and a personal residence.

A gain on the sale of a capital asset occurs when the proceeds of the sale exceed the *basis* of the asset sold, and a loss occurs when the asset's basis exceeds the proceeds. The basis of a purchased asset is generally its cost less any depreciation previously allowed or allowable for tax purposes. Not all capital assets are acquired by purchase; but rules for determining the basis of an asset acquired other than by purchase are at times complicated and need not be discussed here.

For tax purposes, a distinction is made between short- and long-term capital gains and losses. Short-term gains and losses result when capital assets are held six months or less before being sold or exchanged, and long-term gains and losses result when such assets are held more than six months. Furthermore, under the law, net short-term gains must be reported in full and are taxed as ordinary income; but only one half the amount of any net long-term capital gains must be included in adjusted gross income, and the maximum tax is limited to 25% of the total of such net gains, if the total does not exceed $50,000 ($25,000 for a married taxpayer filing a separate return).

For example, if a taxpayer has $1,000 of long-term gains, no losses, and other income that places these gains in a 36% bracket, he is required to include only $500 of the gains in adjusted gross income and to pay only a $180 ($500 × 36% = $180) tax thereon. Consequently, his effective tax rate on the gains is 18% ($180 ÷ $1,000 = 18%), and is one half what it would be if the $1,000 were ordinary income.

Often a high-income taxpayer's capital gains fall in a tax bracket where if the tax thereon were calculated as in the preceding paragraph, the effective rate would exceed 25%, but in such cases the tax is limited to 25%, if such gains do not exceed the previously mentioned $50,000 or $25,000. For example, assume that a taxpayer has $1,000 of capital gains, no losses, and other income that causes these gains to fall in the 70% bracket. If the taxpayer calculated his tax as in the foregoing example, the indicated tax resulting from the calculation would be $350 ($500 × 70% = $350), or the effective rate would be 35% ($350 ÷ $1,000 = 35%). Consequently, since this exceeds the 25% maximum, the taxpayer is permitted by law to limit his tax to 25% of the $1,000, or to $250. Note that this is considerably less than half the $700 the tax would be if the $1,000 were ordinary income.

In the preceding paragraphs the terms "net long-term gains" and "net short-term gains" appear. When long-term gains exceed long-term losses, a net long-term gain results. Likewise, when long-term losses exceed long-term gains, a net long-term loss occurs. Short-term gains and losses are combined in a like manner to arrive at either a net short-term gain or loss.

When a taxpayer has a combination of long-term gains and losses and short-term gains and losses, it is necessary to combine these gains and losses according to certain tax rules, called "offsetting rules," in order to arrive at the amount of net long-term capital gains subject to the special tax treatment outlined above. These rules are complicated, and their discussion is deferred to an advanced course.

When an individual's net short-term capital losses exceed his net long-term capital gains, he may deduct up to $1,000 of the excess losses ($500 for a married taxpayer filing a separate return) from ordinary income in the year of the loss. However, when net long-term capital losses exceed net short-term capital gains, he may deduct from ordinary income in the year of the loss only one half of the excess losses up to $1,000 ($500 for a married taxpayer filing a separate return). A carry-over provision is available to allow deduction in subsequent years of amounts in excess of the $1,000 or $500 limitations.

One last point needs to be made in regard to real property and depreciable property used in a taxpayer's trade or business (see definition of capital assets in a previous paragraph). Such properties are not capital assets according to the law; consequently, when sold or exchanged, the excess of losses over gains is fully deductible in arriving at taxable income. However, if such properties are held over six months, the excess of gains over losses is eligible for long-term capital gain treatment, except to the extent of certain amounts of depreciation taken after 1961.

As to depreciation taken after 1961, a share of the gain equal to a portion or all of this depreciation, depending on the nature of the property and the method of depreciation, must be treated as ordinary income.

The corporation income tax

For federal tax purposes, the taxable income of a corporation organized for profit is calculated in much the same way as the taxable income of an individual. However, there are important differences, five of which follow:

a) Instead of the $100 dividend exclusion of an individual, a corporation may deduct from gross income the first 85% of dividends received from stock it owns in other domestic corporations. This in effect means that only 15% of such dividends are taxed.

b) The capital gains of a corporation are also treated differently, with the maximum tax on such gains being limited to 30% of their total.

c) A corporation may only offset capital losses against capital gains; and if in any year the offset results in a net capital loss, the loss may not be deducted from other income, but it may be carried back to the three preceding years and forward to the next five years and deducted from any capital gains of those years.

d) The standard deduction and the deduction for exemptions do not apply to a corporation, and a corporation does not have certain other deductions of an individual, such as that for personal medical expenses.

e) In addition to the foregoing, the big difference between the corporation and the individual income tax is that the corporation tax is not progressive but consists of a *normal tax* and a *surtax*. The first $25,000 of a corporation's taxable income is subject to a 22% normal tax and is exempt from the surtax; however, income in excess of $25,000 is subject to both the 22% normal tax and a 26% surtax.

Tax effects of business alternatives

■ Alternative decisions commonly have different tax effects. Following are several examples illustrating this.

Form of business organization

The difference between individual and corporation tax rates commonly affects one of the basic decisions a businessman must make, namely, that as to the legal form his business should take. Should it be a single proprietorship, partnership, or corporation? The following factors influence the decision:

a) As previously stated, a corporation is a taxable entity. Its income is taxed at corporation rates, and any portion distributed in dividends is taxed again as individual income to its stockholders. On the other hand, the income of a single proprietorship or partnership, whether withdrawn or left in the business, is taxed only once, as individual income of the proprietor or partners.

b) In addition, a corporation may pay reasonable amounts in salaries to stockholders who work for the corporation, and the sum of these salaries is a tax-deductible expense in arriving at the corporation's taxable income. In a partnership or a single proprietorship on the other hand, salaries of the partners or the proprietor are nothing more than allocations of income.

In arriving at a decision as to the legal form his business should take, a businessman, with the foregoing points in mind, must estimate how he will fare taxwise under each form, and select the best. For example, assume that a businessman is choosing between the single proprietorship and corporate forms, and that he estimates his business will have annual gross sales of $250,000, with cost of goods sold and operating expenses, other than his own salary as manager, of $218,000. Assume further that $12,000 per year is a fair salary for managing such a business and the owner plans to withdraw all profits from the business. Under these assumptions the businessman will fare taxwise as shown in Illustration 28–2.

Operating results under each form:	Proprietorship		Corporation	
Estimated sales		$250,000		$250,000
Cost of goods sold and operating expenses other than owner-manager's salary	$218,000		$218,000	
Salary of owner-manager	-0-	218,000	12,000	230,000
Before-tax income		$ 32,000		$ 20,000
Corporation income tax at 22%		-0-		4,400
Net Income		$ 32,000		$ 15,600
Owner's after-tax income under each form:				
Single proprietorship net income		$ 32,000		
Corporation salary				$ 12,000
Dividends				15,600
Total individual income		$ 32,000		$ 27,600
Individual income tax (assuming a joint return with deductions and exemptions amounting to $6,000 under both forms plus a $100 dividend exclusion under the corporation form)		6,380		4,860
Owner's After-Tax Income		$ 25,620		$ 22,740

Illustration
28–2

Under the assumptions of Illustration 28–2 the businessman will incur the smaller tax and have the larger after-tax income under the single proprietorship form. However, this may not be true in every case. For instance, if he has large amounts of income from other sources, he may find he would incur less tax if the business were organized as a corporation.

Furthermore, in the example just given it is assumed that all profits are withdrawn and none are left in the business for growth. This happens. However, growth is commonly financed through retained earnings; and when it is, the relative desirability of the two forms may change. This is because income retained in a business organized as a corporation is not taxed as individual income to its stockholders, but the income of a single proprietorship or partnership is so taxed, whether retained in the business or withdrawn.

For instance, if the business of Illustration 28–2 is organized as a single proprietorship, the tax burden of the owner remains the same whether he withdraws any of his profits or not. But, in case of the corporation, if all $15,600 of the dividends are retained in the business, the owner is required to pay individual income taxes on his $12,000 salary only. This would reduce his annual individual income tax from the $4,860 shown in Illustration 28–2 to $1,000, and would reduce the total tax burden with the corporation form to $5,400 ($4,400 + $1,000), which is $980 less than the tax burden under the single proprietorship form.

The foregoing is by no means all of the picture. Other tax factors may be involved. For example, a corporation may incur an extra tax if after it has accumulated $100,000 of retained earnings, it unreasonably accumulates additional retained earnings beyond the needs of the business. Also, under present laws a corporation may elect to be taxed somewhat like a single proprietorship, thus eliminating the corporate tax. Furthermore, in a decision as to the legal form a business should take, factors other than taxes are often important, for example, lack of stockholder liability in a corporation.

Dividends and growth

It was pointed out earlier in this chapter that it is normally to a taxpayer's advantage to have income emerge in the form of long-term capital gains rather than as ordinary income. Furthermore, earnings paid out in dividends result in ordinary income to stockholders, but earnings retained in an incorporated business commonly result in growth and an increase in stock values, which may be turned into long-term capital gains through a later sale of the stock. For this reason it is often to the advantage of the owner of an incorporated business to forego dividends and at a later date, through the sale of the business, to take the profits of his business in the form of long-term gains resulting from growth. Or he may keep the stock until his death, in which case a tax on the capital gain may be escaped entirely.

Method of financing

When a business organized as a corporation is in need of additional financing, the owners may supply the corporation whatever funds are needed by purchasing its stock. However, an overall tax advantage may often be gained if instead of purchasing stock, they supply the funds through long-term loans. Insofar as the owners are concerned, beyond the allowable dividend exclusion, it makes no difference on their individual returns whether they report interest or dividends from the funds supplied. However, whether the corporation issues stock or floats a loan usually makes a big difference on its return. Interest on borrowed funds is a tax-deductible expense, but dividends are a distribution of profits and have no effect on the corporation's taxes. Consequently, if owners lend the corporation funds rather than buy its stock, the total tax liability (their own plus their corporation's) will be reduced.

In making financial arrangements such as these, owners must be careful not to overreach themselves in attempting to maximize the interest deduction of their corporation. If they do so and thereby create what is called a "thin corporation," one in which the owners have supplied an unreasonably "thin" portion of capital, the Internal Revenue Service may disallow the interest deductions and require that they be treated as dividends. Furthermore, repayment of "principle" may also be held to be dividends.

Timing transactions

The timing of transactions can be of major importance in tax planning. For example, securities may be held a little longer in order to make the gain on their sale subject to treatment as a long-term capital gain. Or as another example, if a company has several items of real or depreciable property to be sold and some of the sales will result in losses and others in gains, the losses should be taken in one year and the gains in another. The losses and gains should be taken this way because if the losses and gains are both incurred in the same year, they must be offset. However, if the losses are taken in one year and the gains in another, the losses may be deducted in full from other ordinary income, while the gains become eligible in their year for long-term capital gain treatment, at least to the extent they exceed depreciation taken after 1961.

Forms in which related transactions are completed

The tax consequences of related transactions are often dependent upon the forms in which they are completed. For example, the sale of one property at a profit and the immediate purchase of another like property normally results in a taxable gain on the property sold, but an exchange of these properties may result in a tax-free exchange.

A tax-free exchange occurs when like kinds of property are exchanged for each other, or when one or more persons transfer property to a corporation and immediately thereafter are in control of the corporation. Control in such cases is interpreted as meaning that the transferring persons (or person) own 80% of the corporation's voting stock after the transfer.

At first glance it seems that it should be to anyone's advantage to take a tax-free exchange rather than to pay taxes, but this may not be so. For example, 10 years ago a corporation acquired, for $50,000, land then at the edge of the city. Today, due to booming growth, the land is well within the city and has a fair market value of $250,000. Aside from a fully depreciated fence, the land is without improvements, having been used over the years for storage of idle equipment and excess inventory. The corporation plans to move part of its operations to a suburb and has an opportunity to trade the city property for vacant suburban acreage on which it would build a factory. Should it make the trade? From a tax viewpoint, since the new land is not depreciable, the answer is probably, yes, the company should make the tax-free exchange.

However, if the suburban property rather than being vacant consisted of land having a fair market value of $25,000 with a suitable factory building thereon valued at $225,000, the corporation would probably be better off if it sold the city property, paid the tax on its gain, and purchased the suburban factory and its site. The corporation would probably be better off because the gain on the city land would be taxable as a long-term capital gain on which the tax would not exceed $60,000 (30% of [$250,000 − $50,000] = $60,000). However, by purchasing the new factory, the corporation gains the right to deduct the building's $225,000 cost (over its life) in the form of depreciation, an expense deductible in full in arriving at taxable income.

Accounting basis and procedures

With certain exceptions, the accounting basis and procedures used by a taxpayer in keeping his records must also be used in computing his taxable income. Generally, a taxpayer keeps his records on either a cash or accrual basis (see page 786); but regardless of which he uses, the basis and any procedures used must clearly reflect income and be consistently followed.

When inventories are a material factor in calculating income, a taxpayer is required to use the accrual basis insofar as the inventories are concerned. However, in a business or profession in which inventories are not a factor, a taxpayer may use a pure cash basis in arriving at taxable income. Furthermore, since a cash-basis taxpayer can often shift revenue receipts and expense payments from one year to another, being on a cash basis is commonly an advantage.

An accrual-basis taxpayer cannot shift income from year to year by timing receipts and payments; however, somewhat of the same thing may be accomplished through a choice of accounting procedures. For example, recognition of revenue on an installment basis (discussed in Chapter 20) commonly shifts revenue from one year to another for a merchant making installment sales. Likewise, a contractor may use the percentage-of-completion basis (Chapter 20) to shift construction revenue from one year to another and to level taxable income over a period of years.

Furthermore, any taxpayer may shift taxable income to future years through a choice of inventory and depreciation procedures. For example, during periods of rising prices the Lifo inventory method results in charging higher costs for goods sold against current revenues, and thus reduces taxable income and taxes. It may be argued that this only postpones taxes since in periods of declining prices the use of Lifo results in lower costs and higher taxes. However, the history of recent years has been one of constantly rising prices; therefore, it may also be argued that Lifo will postpone taxes indefinitely.

Depreciation methods that result in higher depreciation charges in an asset's early years and lower charges in later years, such as the sum-of-the-years'-digits or declining-balance methods, also postpone taxes. And while tax postponement is not as desirable as tax avoidance, postponement does give the taxpayer interest-free use of tax dollars until these dollars must be paid to the government.

Before turning to a new topic, it should be pointed out that the opportunities for tax planning described in these pages are only illustrative of those available. The wise businessman will seek help from his tax consultant in order to take advantage of every tax-saving opportunity.

Net income and taxable income

■ The taxable income of a business commonly differs from its reported net income. It differs because (1) net income is determined by the application of generally accepted accounting principles, (2) while tax rules are used in determining taxable income, and (3) the rules differ from the generally accepted accounting principles on some points. For example:

a) The application of accounting principles requires that the full amount of any material gains from long-term capital asset sales and exchanges be taken into reported net income, but for tax purposes only 50% of the net gains from such sales commonly enters into taxable income.

b) For accounting purposes, interest received on state and municipal bonds must be included in net income, but such interest is usually not taxable income.

c) As a rule, unearned income, such as rent collected in advance, is taxable in the year of receipt; however, under an accrual basis of accounting such items are taken into income in the year earned regardless of when received.

d) Accounting principles require an estimate of future costs, such as, for example, costs of making good on guarantees; and accounting principles require a deduction of such costs from revenue in the year the guaranteed goods are sold. However, tax rules do not permit the deduction of such costs until after the guarantor has to make good on his guarantee.

In addition to the foregoing, reported net income commonly differs from taxable income because the taxpayer is permitted by law in some cases to use one method or procedure for tax purposes and a different method or procedure in keeping his accounting records. For example, a taxpayer may elect to use declining-balance depreciation for tax purposes but to use straight-line depreciation in his accounting records.

Many accountants believe the interests of government, business, and the public would better be served if there were more uniformity between taxable income and reported net income. However, since the federal income tax is designed to serve other purposes than raising revenue, it is apt to be some time before this is achieved.

Taxes and the distortion of net income

■ When one accounting procedure is elected for tax purposes and a different procedure is used in the accounting records, a problem arises as to how much income tax expense should be deducted each year on the income statement. If the tax actually incurred in such situations is deducted, reported net income often varies from year to year due to the postponement and later payment of taxes. Consequently, in such cases, since stockholders may be misled by these variations, many accountants are of the opinion that income taxes should be allocated in such a way that any distortion resulting from postponing taxes is removed from the income statement.

To appreciate the problem involved here, assume that a corporation has installed a $100,000 machine, the product of which will produce a half million dollars of revenue in each of the succeeding four years and $80,000 of income before depreciation and taxes. Assume further that the company must pay income taxes at a 50% rate (round number assumed for easy calculation) and that it plans to use straight-line depreciation in its records but the declining-balance method for tax purposes. If the machine has a four-year life and an $8,000 salvage value, annual depreciation calculated by each method will be as follows:

Year	Straight Line	Declining Balance
1	$23,000	$50,000
2	23,000	25,000
3	23,000	12,500
4	23,000	4,500
Totals	$92,000	$92,000

And since the company has elected declining-balance depreciation for tax purposes, it will be liable for $15,000 of income tax on the first year's income, $27,500 on the second, $33,750 on the third, and $37,750 on the fourth. The calculation of these taxes is shown in Illustration 28-3.

Annual Income Taxes:	Year 1	Year 2	Year 3	Year 4	Total
Income before depreciation and income taxes	$80,000	$80,000	$80,000	$80,000	$320,000
Depreciation (declining balance)	50,000	25,000	12,500	4,500	92,000
Taxable income	$30,000	$55,000	$67,500	$75,500	$228,000
Annual Income Taxes (50% of Taxable Income)	$15,000	$27,500	$33,750	$37,750	$114,000

Illustration
28-3

Furthermore, if the company were to deduct its actual tax liability each year in arriving at income to be reported to its stockholders, it would report the amounts shown in Illustration 28–4.

Income after Deducting Actual Tax Liabilities	Year 1	Year 2	Year 3	Year 4	Total
Income before depreciation and income taxes............	$80,000	$80,000	$80,000	$80,000	$320,000
Depreciation (straight line)	23,000	23,000	23,000	23,000	92,000
Income before taxes	$57,000	$57,000	$57,000	$57,000	$228,000
Income taxes (actual liability of each year)	15,000	27,500	33,750	37,750	114,000
Remaining Income..	$42,000	$29,500	$23,250	$19,250	$114,000

Illustration
28–4

Observe in Illustrations 28–3 and 28–4 that total depreciation, $92,000, is the same whether calculated by the straight-line or the declining-balance method. Also note that the total tax liability for the four years, $114,000, is the same in each case. Then note the distortion of the final income figures in Illustration 28–4, due to the postponement of taxes.

If this company should report successive annual income figures of $42,000, $29,500, $23,250, and then $19,250, some of its stockholders might be misled as to the company's earnings trend. Consequently, in cases such as this many accountants think income taxes should be allocated so that the distortion caused by the postponement of taxes is removed from the income statement. These accountants advocate that—

When one accounting procedure is used in the accounting records and a different procedure is used for tax purposes, the tax expense deducted on the income statement should not be the actual tax liability, but the amount that would be payable if the procedure used in the records were also used in calculating the tax.

If the foregoing is applied in this case, the corporation will report to its stockholders in each of the four years the amounts of income shown in Illustration 28–5.

Net Income That Should Be Reported to Stockholders	Year 1	Year 2	Year 3	Year 4	Total
Income before depreciation and income taxes............	$80,000	$80,000	$80,000	$80,000	$320,000
Depreciation (straight line)	23,000	23,000	23,000	23,000	92,000
Income before taxes	$57,000	$57,000	$57,000	$57,000	$228,000
Income taxes (amounts based on straight-line depreciation)...	28,500	28,500	28,500	28,500	114,000
Net Income	$28,500	$28,500	$28,500	$28,500	$114,000

Illustration
28–5

In examining Illustration 28–5, recall that the company's tax liabilities are actually $15,000 in the first year, $27,500 in the second, $33,750 in the third, and $37,750 in the fourth, a total of $114,000. Then observe that when this $114,000 liability is allocated evenly over the four years, the distortion of the annual net incomes due to the postponement of taxes is removed from the published income statements.

Entries for the allocation of taxes

■ When income taxes are allocated as in Illustration 28–5, the tax liability of each year and the deferred taxes are recorded with a work sheet adjustment and an adjusting entry, after which the taxes are paid. The adjusting entries and the entries in general journal form for the payment of the taxes (without explanations) are as follows:

Year 1	Income Taxes Expense	28,500.00	
	Income Taxes Payable		15,000.00
	Deferred Income Taxes		13,500.00
Year 1	Income Taxes Payable	15,000.00	
	Cash		15,000.00
Year 2	Income Taxes Expense	28,500.00	
	Income Taxes Payable		27,500.00
	Deferred Income Taxes		1,000.00
Year 2	Income Taxes Payable	27,500.00	
	Cash		27,500.00
Year 3	Income Taxes Expense	28,500.00	
	Deferred Income Taxes	5,250.00	
	Income Taxes Payable		33,750.00
Year 3	Income Taxes Payable	33,750.00	
	Cash		33,750.00
Year 4	Income Taxes Expense	28,500.00	
	Deferred Income Taxes	9,250.00	
	Income Taxes Payable		37,750.00
Year 4	Income Taxes Payable	37,750.00	
	Cash		37,750.00

In the entries the $28,500 debited to Income Taxes Expense each year is the amount that is deducted on the income statement in reporting annual net income. Also, the amount credited to Income Taxes Payable each year is the actual tax liability of that year.

Observe in the entries that since the actual tax liability in each of the first two years is less than the amount debited to Income Taxes Expense, the difference is credited to Deferred Income Taxes. Then note that in the last two years, since the actual liability each year is greater than the debit to Income Taxes Expense, the difference is debited to Deferred Income Taxes. Now observe in the following illustration of the company's Deferred Income Taxes account that the debits and credits exactly balance each other out over the four-year period:

Deferred Income Taxes

Year	Explanation	Debit	Credit	Balance
1			13,500.00	13,500.00
2			1,000.00	14,500.00
3		5,250.00		9,250.00
4		9,250.00		-0-

Questions for class discussion

1. Jackson expects to have $500 of income in a 50% bracket; consequently, which should be more desirable to him: (a) a transaction that will reduce his income tax by $100 or (b) a transaction that will reduce an expense of his business by $150?
2. Why must a taxpayer normally take advantage of a tax-saving opportunity at the time it arises?
3. Distinguish between tax avoidance and tax evasion. Which is legal and desirable?
4. What are some of the nonrevenue objectives of the federal income tax?
5. What nonrevenue objective is gained by granting a $25,000 surtax exemption to corporations?
6. What questions must be answered in determining whether an item should be included or excluded from gross income for tax purposes?
7. Name several items that are not income for tax purposes.
8. What justification is given for permitting an individual to exclude the first $100 of dividends from domestic corporations from his gross income for tax purposes?
9. For tax purposes, define a capital asset.
10. What is a short-term capital gain? A long-term capital gain?
11. An individual has had capital asset transactions that have resulted in nothing but long-term capital gains. What special tax treatment may be given these gains?
12. For tax purposes, what is "ordinary income"?
13. Why do tax planners try to have income emerge as a long-term capital gain?
14. Differentiate between the normal tax and the surtax of a corporation.
15. It is often a wise tax decision for the owner of an incorporated business to forgo the payment of dividends from the earnings of his business. Why?
16. Why does the taxable income of a business commonly differ from its net income?

Class exercises

Exercise 28–1

List the letters of the following items and write after each either the word *included* or *excluded* to tell whether the item should be included or excluded from gross income for federal income tax purposes.

a) A portable TV set having a $100 fair market value which was received as a door prize.

b) Tips received while working as a parking lot attendant.

c) Cash inherited from a deceased aunt.

d) Scholarship received from a state university.

e) Social security benefits.

f) Workmen's compensation insurance received as the result of an accident while working on a part-time job.

g) Gain on the sale of a personal automobile bought and rebuilt.

h) First $100 of dividends from stock in domestic corporations received by an individual.

i) First $850 of $1,000 in dividends on stock in domestic corporations received by a corporation.

j) Interest on a savings account.

Exercise 28–2

During 1973 Ted Hall furnished more than half the support of his sister, a college student living in a girls' dormitory. Ted is unmarried and earned $9,200 as the employee of an electronics company. He had $1,182 of federal income tax and $468 of F.I.C.A. tax withheld from his paychecks. He also received $100 interest on a savings account and $80 in dividends from a domestic corporation in which he owned stock. During the year he paid $95 state income tax, $165 interest on the balance owed on a car he purchased, and gave his church $250. Show the calculation of Ted's taxable income in the manner outlined on page 804. Then using the rate schedule of Illustration 28–1, show the calculation of the net federal income tax payable or refund due Ted.

Exercise 28–3

A married taxpayer who files a joint return and had no other capital gains sold for $7,500 a number of shares of stock he had purchased for $5,500. Use the rate schedule of Illustration 28–1 and determine the amount of federal income tax the taxpayer will have to pay on the gain from this transaction under each of the following unrelated assumptions:

a) The taxpayer had $9,200 of taxable income from other sources and had held the shares four months.

b) The taxpayer had $9,200 of taxable income from other sources and had held the shares for eight months.

c) The taxpayer had $16,100 of taxable income from other sources and had held the shares six months.

d) The taxpayer had $16,100 of taxable income from other sources and had held the shares for six months and one day.

e) The taxpayer had $53,300 of taxable income from other sources and had held the shares for two months.

f) The taxpayer had $53,300 of taxable income from other sources and had held the shares for seven months.

Problems   **Problem 28–1**

Ted Moss has operated Mesa Sales for a number of years with the following average annual results:

MESA SALES
Income Statement for an Average Year

Sales		$280,000
Cost of goods sold	$165,000	
Operating expenses	85,000	250,000
Net Income		$ 30,000

Mr. Moss is unmarried and without dependents and has been operating Mesa Sales as a single proprietorship. He has been withdrawing $12,000 each year to pay his personal living expenses, including $2,250 of charitable contributions, state and local taxes, and other itemized deductions. He has no income other than from Mesa Sales.

Required:

1. Assume that Mr. Moss is considering the incorporation of his business beginning with the 1973 tax year and prepare a comparative income statement for the business showing its net income as a single proprietorship and as a corporation. Assume that if he incorporates, Mr. Moss will pay $12,000 per year to himself as a salary, which is a fair amount.

2. Use the rate schedule of Illustration 28–1 and determine the amount of federal income tax Mr. Moss will have to pay for himself and for his business under each of the following assumptions: (*a*) the business is not incorporated; (*b*) the business is incorporated, pays Mr. Moss a $12,000 annual salary as manager, and also pays him $12,000 per year in dividends; and (*c*) the business is incorporated, pays Mr. Moss a $12,000 salary, but does not pay any dividends.

Problem 28–2

Ted and June Pace, husband and wife who file a joint return, own all the outstanding stock of Pace Corporation. The corporation has an opportunity to expand, but to do so it will need $50,000 additional capital. The Paces have the $50,000 and can either lend this amount to the corporation at 7% interest or they can invest the $50,000 in the corporation, taking its presently unissued stock in exchange for the money.

They calculate that with the additional $50,000 the corporation will earn $30,000 annually after paying Ted $15,000 per year as president and manager but before interest on the loan, if made, and before income taxes. They require $20,000 for personal living expenses and their own income taxes. Consequently, if they invest the additional $50,000 in the corporation, they will pay $5,000 per year to themselves in dividends in addition to Ted's salary. But if they lend the corporation the $50,000, they will use the interest on the loan, plus $1,500 in dividends and Ted's salary for their personal expenses.

Required:

Determine whether the loan to the corporation or an investment in its stock is to the best interest of the Paces.

Problem 28–3

Dale Isley owns all the outstanding stock of Metal Products, Inc. The corporation is a small manufacturing concern; however, over the years it has purchased and owns stocks costing $85,000 (present market value much higher) which it holds as long-term investments. The corporation has seldom paid a dividend, but it does pay Mr. Isley a $12,000 annual salary as president and manager. Last year the corporation earned $28,000, after its president's salary but before income taxes, consisting of $20,000 in manufacturing income and $8,000 in dividends on its long-term investments.

Mr. Isley is a widower and has no dependents, but he had $2,250 of itemized deductions last year plus a single $750 exemption deduction. He had no income last year other than his corporation salary and $1,000 in interest from a real estate loan.

Required:

1. Prepare a comparative statement showing for last year the operating income, investment income, total income, share of the dividend income excluded, taxable income, and income tax of the corporation under the (*a*) and (*b*) assumptions which follow. (*a*) The corporation owns the investment stocks and had the operating income just described. (*b*) The corporation had the operating income described; but instead of owning the investment stocks, over the years it paid dividends (none last year) and Mr. Isley used them to buy the stocks in his own name rather than in the corporation name.
2. Calculate the amounts of individual income tax and corporation income tax incurred by Mr. Isley and the corporation under the (*a*) assumptions, and the amounts that would have been incurred under the (*b*) assumptions. Also calculate the amount of individual income tax Mr. Isley would have incurred with the business organized as a single proprietorship and the stocks registered in Mr. Isley's name. Under this last assumption remember that the corporation's operating income plus its president's salary equal the operating income of the single proprietorship. Use the rate schedule of Illustration 28–1 in all individual income tax calculations.

Problem 28–4

Early in January 197A, Deeplake Corporation installed a new machine in its plant that cost $300,000 and was estimated to have a four-year life and a $20,000 salvage value. The machine enabled the company to add a new product to its line that produces $200,000 of income annually before depreciation and income taxes. The company allocates income taxes in its reports to its stockholders, since it uses straight-line depreciation in its accounting records and sum-of-the-years'-digits depreciation for tax purposes.

Required:

1. Prepare a schedule showing 197A, 197B, 197C, 197D, and total net income for the four years after deducting sum-of-the-years'-digits depreciation and actual taxes. Assume a 50% income tax rate.
2. Prepare a second schedule showing each year's net income and the four-year total after deducting straight-line depreciation and actual taxes.
3. Prepare a third schedule showing income reported to stockholders with straight-line depreciation and allocated taxes.
4. Set up a T-account for Deferred Income Tax and show therein the entries that result from allocating the income taxes.

Problem 28–1A

Richard Hall is married and files a joint return with his wife. They have no income other than from Valley Sales, a profitable single proprietorship business that Mr. Hall owns and which averages $350,000 annually in sales, with a 40% gross profit and $100,000 of operating expenses. The Halls have no dependents, but each year they have $2,500 of itemized deductions and two exemptions. In the past Mr. Hall has withdrawn $12,000 annually from the business for personal living expenses plus sufficient additional cash to pay the income tax on their joint return.

Mr. Hall thinks he can save taxes by reorganizing his business into a corporation beginning with the 1973 tax year. If the corporation is organized, it will issue 1,000 shares of no-par stock, 990 to Mr. Hall and 10 to Mrs. Hall. Also, $15,000 per year is a fair salary for managing such a business, and the corporation will pay that amount to Mr. Hall as president and manager.

Required:
1. Prepare a comparative income statement for the business showing its net income as a single proprietorship and as a corporation.
2. Use the rate schedule of Illustration 28–1 and determine the amount of federal income taxes the Halls will pay for themselves on a joint return and for the business under each of the following assumptions: (*a*) the business remains a single proprietorship; (*b*) the business is incorporated, pays Mr. Hall a $15,000 salary, but pays no dividends; (*c*) the business is incorporated, pays Mr. Hall a $15,000 salary, and pays $16,000 in dividends, $15,840 to Mr. Hall and $160 to Mrs. Hall. (Each may exclude the first $100 of dividends.)

Problem 28–2A

Douglas Corporation is planning an expansion program that will cost $100,000 and will increase its earnings $20,000 annually before interest on the money used in the expansion, if borrowed, and before income taxes. All the outstanding stock of Douglas Corporation is owned by the Douglas family, and the family will supply the money to finance the expansion, either investing an additional $100,000 in the corporation by purchasing its unissued stock or lending it $100,000 at 7% interest.

The corporation presently earns in excess of $25,000 annually and pays $20,000 per year to the family in dividends. If the loan is made, the dividends will be reduced by an amount equal to the interest on the loan.

Required:
Present statistics to show whether it would be advantageous for the family to make the loan or to purchase the corporation's stock. Assume that no additional dividend exclusions will be gained by issuing the stock.

Problem 28–3A

Lee Hall, Jr., recently inherited the business of his father. The business, Hydraulics, Inc., is a small manufacturing corporation; however, a share of its assets, $75,000 at cost, consists of blue-chip investment stocks purchased over the years by the corporation from earnings. The father was the sole owner of the corporation at his death, and before his death he had paid himself a $15,000 annual salary for a number of years as president and manager. Over the years the corporation seldom paid a dividend but instead had invested any earnings not needed in the business in the blue-chip stocks previously mentioned. At the father's death the market value of these stocks far exceeded their cost.

Lee's mother is dead, and after Lee graduated from college, the father had no dependents. His tax return for the year before his death showed $16,500 of gross income, consisting of his $15,000 corporation salary plus $1,500 interest from real estate loans. It also showed $3,250 of itemized deductions plus a single $750 exemption deduction. The corporation had earned during the year before the father's death $23,000 from its manufacturing operations plus $10,000 in dividends from its investments, a total of $33,000 after the president's salary but before income taxes.

Required:

1. Prepare a comparative statement showing for the year before the father's death the corporation's operating income, dividend income, total income, share of the dividend income excluded, taxable income, and income tax under the following (*a*) and (*b*) assumptions. (*a*) The corporation owns the investment stocks and had the operating income just described. (*b*) The corporation had the operating income described; but instead of owning the investment stocks, over the years it paid dividends (none last year) and Lee Hall, Sr. used the dividends to buy the stocks in his own name rather than in the corporation name.
2. Calculate the amounts of individual income tax and corporation income tax incurred by Mr. Hall, Sr., and the corporation for the year before Mr. Hall's death under the foregoing (*a*) assumptions, and the amounts that would have been incurred under the (*b*) assumptions. Also calculate the amount of individual income tax Mr. Hall would have incurred with the business organized as a single proprietorship and the stocks registered in his own name. Under this last assumption remember that the corporation's operating income plus the salary paid its president equal the operating income of the single proprietorship. Use the rate schedule of Illustration 28–1 in the individual income tax calculations.

Problem 28–4A

At a $200,000 cost, Green Hill Corporation installed a new machine in its plant early in January, 197A, so that it could add a new product to its line. It estimated the new machine would have a four-year life, a $16,000 salvage value, and its product would produce $180,000 of income each year before depreciation and income taxes at an assumed 50% rate. The company uses declining-balance depreciation at twice the straight-line rate for tax purposes and straight-line depreciation for its accounting records. It also allocates income taxes in its reports to stockholders.

Required:

1. Prepare a schedule showing 197A, 197B, 197C, 197D and total net income for the four years from the sale of the new product after deducting declining-balance depreciation and actual income taxes.
2. Prepare a second schedule showing each year's income and total net income after deducting straight-line depreciation and actual income taxes.
3. Prepare a third schedule showing income reported to stockholders with straight-line depreciation and allocated income taxes.

4. Set up a T-account for Deferred Income Tax and show therein the entries that result from allocating the income taxes.

Decision problem 28–1, Arcadia Corporation

Ted Cole and his wife own all the outstanding stock of Arcadia Corporation, a company Ted organized several years ago and which is growing rapidly and needs additional capital.

Gary Ross, a friend of the Coles, examined the following comparative income statement, which shows the corporation's net income for the past three years and which was prepared by its bookkeeper, and expressed a tentative willingness to invest $50,000 in the corporation by purchasing a portion of its unissued stock.

ARCADIA CORPORATION
Comparative Income Statement, 197A, 197B, and 197C

	197A	197B	197C
Sales	$700,000	$750,000	$825,000
Costs and expenses other than depreciation and federal income taxes	$425,000	$450,000	$500,000
Depreciation expense	105,000	110,000	125,000
Federal income taxes	65,000	70,000	75,000
Total costs and expenses	$595,000	$630,000	$700,000
Net Income	$105,000	$120,000	$125,000

However, before making a final decision, Gary Ross asked permission for his own accountant to examine the accounting records of the corporation. Permission was granted, the examination was made, and the accountant prepared the following comparative income statement covering the past three years.

ARCADIA CORPORATION
Comparative Income Statement, 197A, 197B, and 197C

	197A	197B	197C
Sales	$700,000	$750,000	$825,000
Costs and expenses other than depreciation	$425,000	$450,000	$500,000
Depreciation expense*	105,000	110,000	125,000
Total costs and expenses	$530,000	$560,000	$625,000
Income before federal income taxes	$170,000	$190,000	$200,000
Applicable federal income taxes	85,000	95,000	100,000
Net Income	$ 85,000	$ 95,000	$100,000

*The corporation deducted $145,000 of depreciation on its 197A tax return, $160,000 on its 197B return, and $175,000 on its 197C return.

Ted was surprised at the difference in annual net incomes reported on the two statements and immediately called for an explanation from the public accountant who set up the corporation's accounting system and who prepares the annual tax returns of the corporation and the Coles.

Explain why there is a difference between the net income figures on the two income statements. Prepare a statement that will justify the amounts shown on the corporation bookkeeper's statement. Account for the difference in the reported net incomes. Assume a 50% federal income tax rate.

*This book has been set in 10 point Times
Roman. Chapter numbers and titles are in
30 point Helvetica. The size of the type page
is 32$\frac{1}{2}$ by 49$\frac{1}{2}$ picas.*